The Frege Reader

Dummett: Frege

cash
MW
11-3

explen main point
Freg on Sin / Linguistic

Meaning
(consistent
ad
own
undisling

Tyler
Burge

heise / Stead / Reg

The Frege Reader

Edited by
MICHAEL BEANEY

Blackwell
Publishing

© 1997 by Blackwell Publishing Ltd

BLACKWELL PUBLISHING
350 Main Street, Malden, MA 02148-5020, USA
9600 Garsington Road, Oxford OX4 2DQ, UK
550 Swanston Street, Carlton, Victoria 3053, Australia

First published 1997

13   2010

Library of Congress Cataloging-in-Publication Data

Frege, Gottlob, 1848–1925
[Selections. English. 1997]
The Frege reader / edited by Michael Beaney.
    p.   cm. — (Blackwell readers)
Includes bibliographical references and index.
ISBN 978-0-631-19444-6 (alk. paper) – ISBN 978-0-631-19445-3 (pbk: alk. paper)
1. Logic. 2. Logic, Symbolic and mathematical. 3. Language and languages—Philosophy. 4. Mathematics—Philosophy. 5. Philosophy.
I. Beaney, Michael. II. Title. III. Series.
B3245.F22E52   1997   96—47027
193—dc21   CIP

ISBN 978-0-631-19444-6 (alk. paper); ISBN 978-0-631-19445-3 (pbk: alk. paper)

A catalogue record for this title is available from the British Library.

Set in 10 on 12 pt Plantin by Graphicraft
Printed and bound in Singapore
by Ho Printing Singapore Pte Ltd

The publisher's policy is to use permanent paper from mills that operate a sustainable forestry policy, and which has been manufactured from pulp processed using acid-free and elementary chlorine-free practices. Furthermore, the publisher ensures that the text paper and cover board used have met acceptable environmental accreditation standards.

For further information on
Blackwell Publishing, visit our website:
http://www.blackwellpublishing.com

To Peter Geach
and to the memory
of Max Black

Contents

Preface

This *Reader* brings together, for the first time in a single volume, all of Frege's seminal papers, substantial parts of all three of his books, and additional selections from his posthumous writings and correspondence. Since its primary aim is to make these works accessible to students of logic, philosophical logic and the philosophy of language, I have also provided short introductions to each piece, summaries of sections omitted and editorial footnotes (editorial footnotes are numerically ordered, and located, where they coexist on a page, beneath Frege's own footnotes, which are alphabetically ordered). The possibility of simply letting Frege's writings speak for themselves is unrealistic in a collection intended for use as a course book: not only is Frege's work often hard to understand (for although Frege is a remarkably clear writer, the *point* of what he is doing may easily be missed), but also, as a pioneer in the field of logic, Frege's key ideas and terminology evolved during the course of his career, and he was not always explicit about the changes that occurred. But I have not sought to impose interpretations of the text: most of the editorial footnotes simply contain references to other passages in Frege's writings, comments on points of translation, or elucidations of some of the logical notation or conceptions. However, in the introduction to the volume as a whole, besides providing a sketch of Frege's life, works and achievement, I have included a brief discussion of two central issues in the interpretation of Frege's philosophy, in order to provide the interested student with some sense of current controversies and the importance of Frege to philosophy today. Perhaps one of the most difficult things facing someone new to Frege's work is his logical symbolism, which never did succeed in becoming adopted by other logicians. It is easier to master than might at first sight appear, and Frege's own explanation of it in the *Begriffsschrift* is admirably clear; but I have also provided a brief account of it and its translation into modern notation in Appendix 2.

Almost all the material from Frege's works gathered here has appeared, in some translated form, in previous English editions, most of it published by Blackwell. I have included a substantial part of Geach and Black's *Translations from the Philosophical Writings of Gottlob Frege* (*TPW*), and made further selections from Frege's *Collected Papers* (*CP*), *Posthumous Writings* (*PW*) and *Philosophical and Mathematical Correspondence* (*PMC*).

(For the abbreviations used to refer to Frege's work, see the list of Abbreviations and Bibliography.) I have, however, provided new translations of material from the *Begriffsschrift*, the *Grundlagen* and Volume I of the *Grundgesetze*, mainly to avoid inconsistencies of style and terminology through the volume. J. L. Austin's translation of the *Grundlagen* (which was first published as *The Foundations of Arithmetic* in 1950) has been praised for its readability, but in places Austin offers too free a rendering of Frege's prose and he himself admitted (in his preface to the second edition) that his version was too long. Although Frege is indeed at his most informal in this work, Austin's translation makes him sound, at times, too much like an Oxford linguistic philosopher, and it certainly sits uneasily with the translations of Frege's other works. As far as the existing translations of Volume I of the *Grundgesetze* are concerned, the translation by Jourdain and Stachelroth (in *TPW*) would have needed revision and expansion, and the translation by Furth (in *BLA*) uses different terminology and provides, I think, too literal a version. In the new translations, I hope the right balance has been struck between fluency and faithfulness, but if I have managed to improve on previous translations, then it is in large part due to my having learnt from them; and I gratefully acknowledge the help that they provided. The opportunity has also been taken to make a few minor revisions to some of the translations reprinted here, in consultation (where possible) with the original translators. As far as the rendering of Frege's key terms throughout this volume is concerned, the policy adopted in other Blackwell editions has in general been followed, the only significant change being the translation (or non-translation) of 'Bedeutung' and its cognates. Details of the renderings can be found in the Glossary; and I discuss the controversial issue of the translation of 'Bedeutung' in §4 of the Introduction.

Whilst editorial responsibility remains entirely my own, on questions of selection and translation I have benefited from the advice of a number of people, and I would like to thank, in particular, Wonbae Choi, Michael Dummett, Peter Geach, Mike Harnish, Mark Helme, Peter Long, Sharon Macdonald, Brian McGuinness, Peter Simons, Peter Sullivan and Roger White. I would also like to thank Duckworth Publishers for permission to use material from my book, *Frege: Making Sense*, and, from Blackwell Publishers, Stephan Chambers and Steve Smith for encouraging the project in the early stages, and Nathalie Manners and Robert Peberdy for steering the book through the final stages of publication. I owe a particular debt of gratitude to Stephen Ryan, whose supererogatory copy-editing of a complex typescript resulted in many improvements to both the translations and the editorial material. The volume is dedicated to Peter Geach and to the memory of Max Black, the two philosophers who did most to make Frege's writings available to the English-speaking world.

Michael Beaney

Abbreviations of Works by Frege

The following abbreviations are used for works by Frege referred to in the editorial material. Full citations are provided in the Bibliography, where a complete list of Frege's works, chronologically ordered, can be found. Where a date is set in square brackets in column two, the work concerned is listed in the Bibliography under the first date given in column three.

ACN	1882	'On the Aim of the "Conceptual Notation"'
APCN	1879	'Applications of the "Conceptual Notation"'
BLA	[1964]	*The Basic Laws of Arithmetic* (tr. of part of *GG*, 1893, 1903, by M. Furth)
BLC	1880/81	'Boole's Logical Calculus and the Concept-script'
BLF	1882	'Boole's Logical Formula-language and my Concept-script'
BS	1879	*Begriffsschrift*
BSA	1964	*Begriffsschrift und andere Aufsätze* (ed. I. Angelelli)
BSLD	1906	'A Brief Survey of my Logical Doctrines'
CES	1895	'A Critical Elucidation of Some Points in E. Schröder . . .'
CN	1972	*Conceptual Notation* (tr. of *BS* by T. W. Bynum)
CO	1892	'On Concept and Object'
CP	[1984]	*Collected Papers* (tr. by M. Black et al. of *KS*, 1967)
CSB	1892	'[Comments on *Sinn* and *Bedeutung*]'
CT	1923	'Compound Thoughts'
DPE	before 1884	'[Dialogue with Pünjer on Existence]'
EG	1899–1906?	'On Euclidean Geometry'
FA	[1950]	*The Foundations of Arithmetic* (tr. of *GL*, 1884, by J. L. Austin)
FC	1891	'Function and Concept'
FG	1971	*On the Foundations of Geometry* (ed. and tr. by E.-H. W. Kluge)

FGI	1903	'On the Foundations of Geometry: First Series'
FGII	1906	'On the Foundations of Geometry: Second Series'
FR	1997	*The Frege Reader* (ed. M. Beaney)
GG	1893/1903	*Grundgesetze der Arithmetik*, Vol. I, 1893; Vol. II, 1903
GL	1884	*Die Grundlagen der Arithmetik*
GR	1873	'On a Geometrical Representation of Imaginary Forms in the Plane'
IL	1906	'Introduction to Logic'
KS	1967	*Kleine Schriften* (tr. by M. Black et al. as *CP*)
LI	1977	*Logical Investigations* (now in *CP*)
LM	1914	'Logic in Mathematics'
MBLI	1915	'My Basic Logical Insights'
MC	1874	'Methods of Calculation . . .'
N	1918	'Negation'
NLD	1919	'[Notes for Ludwig Darmstaedter]'
NS	1969	*Nachgelassene Schriften* (tr. by P. Long and R. White as *PW*)
OCN	1891/92	'On the Concept of Number'
PCN	1897	'On Mr. Peano's Conceptual Notation and My Own'
PMC	[1980]	*Philosophical and Mathematical Correspondence* (tr. by H. Kaal of *WB*, 1976)
PW	[1979]	*Posthumous Writings* (tr. by P. Long and R. White of *NS*, 1969)
PWLB	1897	'Logic'
RH	1894	'Review of E. G. Husserl, *Philosophie der Arithmetik* I'
SB	1892	'On *Sinn* and *Bedeutung*'
SJCN	1882	'On the Scientific Justification of a Conceptual Notation'
SKM	1924/25	'Sources of Knowledge of Mathematics . . .'
T	1918	'Thought'
TPW	1952	*Translations from the Philosophical Writings of Gottlob Frege*
WB	1976	*Wissenschaftlicher Briefwechsel* (tr. by H. Kaal as *PMC*)

Glossary

The various key terms used by Frege have been translated in the present volume as follows (unless otherwise indicated in the text):

andeuten[1]	indicate
Anschauung	intuition
Anzahl[2]	Number
Art des Gegebenseins	mode of presentation
bedeuten[3]	mean, signify [in his early work]
	refer to, stand for [in his later work]
Bedeutung[3]	meaning, significance [in his early work]
	Bedeutung [left untranslated in his later work]
Begriff[4]	concept
begrifflicher Inhalt[5]	conceptual content
Begriffsschrift[6]	*Begriffsschrift* [left untranslated throughout]
Behauptungssatz	assertoric sentence
beiderseits eindeutig[7]	one-one
Bestimmungsweise	mode of determination

---

[1] This term is applied, in particular, to letters used as variables, which do not mean [*bedeuten*] anything by themselves, but merely indicate (indefinitely) [(unbestimmt) *andeuten*]. Cf. e.g. *FC*, p. 133 below; *GG*, I, §1 (p. 211 below).

[2] On the translation of 'Anzahl' by 'Number' (with a capital 'N') and 'Zahl' by 'number', see fn. 6 on p. 91 below.

[3] For discussion of the problems involved in translating 'bedeuten' and 'Bedeutung', see Introduction, §4.

[4] In Frege's later work, a concept is the *Bedeutung* of a concept word (see especially *CSB*, pp. 172–80 below), and is regarded as an 'unsaturated' entity (see especially *CO*, pp. 181–93 below).

[5] The term is used in *BS* (see especially §3; p. 53 below). It is the notion of 'conceptual content' that later bifurcates into the notions of 'Sinn' and 'Bedeutung'.

[6] Literally translated as 'concept-script' or 'conceptual notation', Frege uses the term to refer to his logical symbolism, and it also formed the title of his first book, which introduced this symbolism. It is left untranslated in the present volume; and the context makes clear when Frege is referring to his logical system and when to his first book.

[7] On Frege's use of this term, see fn. 10 on p. 198 below.

beurteilbarer Inhalt[8]	judgeable content
Beziehung	relation
eindeutig[9]	many-one
formal	formal(ist)
Gedanke	thought [understood, in his later work, as the *sense* expressed by a proposition]
Gegenstand	object
gewöhnliche (Bedeutung)[10]	customary (*Bedeutung*)
gleich[11]	equal, identical
Gleichheit[11]	equality, identity
Gleichung[11]	equation
gleichzahlig	equinumerous
Inhalt	content
Merkmal[12]	mark
objectiv[13]	objective
Satz[14]	sentence, proposition, theorem, clause
Sinn	sense
Stufe	level (of a concept or function)
Umfang eines Begriffes	extension of a concept
ungerade (Bedeutung)[15]	indirect (*Bedeutung*)
ungesättigt[16]	unsaturated
Urteil	judgement

[8] Geach, in *TPW*, translated this term (used in *BS*) as 'content of possible judgement'. The simpler and more literal 'judgeable content' is preferred here.

[9] On Frege's (logical) definition of a *many-one* relation, see p. 77 below.

[10] On Frege's distinction between 'customary' and 'indirect' *Bedeutung*, see *SB*, pp. 154, 159ff. below.

[11] On the translation of 'gleich', 'gleichheit' and 'Gleichung', see fn. 3 on p. 85 below. Frege makes it clear that he treats 'equality' ('Gleichheit') and 'identity' ('Identität') as synonymous (see e.g. fn. A on p. 151 below).

[12] On the notion of a 'mark', see *GL*, §53 (pp. 102–3 below); *CO*, pp. 189–90 below.

[13] Frege distinguishes what is *objective* (*objectiv*) from what is *actual* (*wirklich*); see *GL*, §26 (cf. p. 96 below). Numbers, for example, according to Frege, are *objective* but not *actual* objects.

[14] Some writers now distinguish between *sentence* (the linguistic expression) and *proposition* (what a sentence *expresses* – what Frege might have called its *sense* or the *thought* it expresses): on this view, two different sentences, e.g. 'Pegasus ist ein Pferd' and 'Pegasus is a horse', can express the same proposition. The distinction was not drawn by Frege, and is not observed here: 'sentence' and 'proposition' are to be understood synonymously. 'Satz' can also mean 'theorem' or just 'clause', and these have been used too, according to the context.

[15] Cf. fn. 10 above.

[16] On the 'unsaturated' nature of concepts and other functions, see especially *CO*, pp. 181–93 below. In *TPW*, the translated term is kept in quotation marks to signal that it is being used metaphorically. Frege does indeed make clear its metaphorical use, but since he does not so signal it himself, and it is fairly clear that it *is* metaphorical, the policy has not been followed here.

Verneinung	negation
Vorstellung[17]	idea, image
Wahrheitswert	truth-value [in his later work, regarded as the *Bedeutung* of a sentence]
Wertverlauf[18]	value-range (of a function)
Zahl[19]	number

---

[17] By 'Vorstellung', Frege always understands something essentially private and subjective – to be sharply distinguished from 'Begriff' ('concept') and 'Gedanke' ('thought').
[18] On the translation of this term, and Frege's understanding of it, see fn. 2 on p. 135 below.
[19] Cf. fn. 2 above.

Introduction

With the publication of his first book in 1879, Gottlob Frege revolutionized logic; and together with Russell, Moore and Wittgenstein, he is generally regarded as one of the founders of analytic philosophy, which has dominated the English-speaking world for most of this century. Yet his works remained largely unread in his lifetime, and although he influenced Husserl, Russell, Wittgenstein and Carnap, in particular, and corresponded with mathematicians such as Peano and Hilbert, his ideas were not always understood or accepted; and it is only in the last fifty years that interest in his writings and engagement with his thought have really taken off. In the first two sections of this introduction, I provide a brief account of Frege's life and works,[1] and indicate the nature and significance of his achievement. The recent blossoming of interest in Frege's work has led to a variety of 'Fregean' or 'neo-Fregean' views and approaches, and this variety, and Frege's perceived importance, has generated increasing controversy over the interpretation of his philosophy. In the third section, I identify some of the main issues in these debates, and highlight some of the differing views. One particular problem has been the understanding of Frege's notion of 'Bedeutung', reflected in the controversy over the translation of 'Bedeutung' and its cognates into English. I discuss this in some detail in the final section, and explain the policy adopted in the present volume.[2]

1. Frege's Life and Works[3]

Gottlob Frege (christened Friedrich Ludwig Gottlob Frege) was born in Wismar, on the German Baltic coast, on 8 November 1848. His father, Karl Alexander (1809–66), was the founder and principal of a private

[1] For a chronology of the main events, see Appendix 1 below; and for a complete list of Frege's works, see the Bibliography below.
[2] A list of Frege's key terms, and their translations, is provided in the Glossary above.
[3] The biographical details in the present section are taken from Bynum, 1972a. The account of Frege's works is drawn from my *Frege: Making Sense* (1996), which contains a fuller discussion of Frege's development and motivation (see especially chs. 3–4 on Frege's logicist project).

girls' school, and his mother, Auguste Bialloblotzky (who died in 1878), was a teacher and later herself principal of the school. He attended the *Gymnasium* in Wismar from 1864 to 1869, and having passed his *Abitur* in the spring of 1869, went on to the University of Jena. He spent four semesters there, taking courses in chemistry, mathematics and philosophy, before transferring to the University of Göttingen (perhaps on the advice of his mentor at Jena, Ernst Abbe), where he spent five semesters, studying physics, mathematics and philosophy of religion. He was awarded his doctorate in December 1873 for his dissertation 'On a Geometrical Representation of Imaginary Forms in the Plane' (*GR*), which, developing the work of Gauss, who had been one of those responsible for legitimating complex numbers by showing how they could be represented as points on a plane, showed how imaginary forms could be represented geometrically.

Despite being a work in pure geometry, Frege's dissertation nevertheless hints at the subsequent direction of his thought. For he is clearly concerned with how results in one area can be extended into another (cf. *GR*, p. 3). What allows this is the underlying arithmetic, which can encompass the non-intuitable as well as the intuitable; and this was something that Frege emphasized throughout his later work. Indeed, it provided the starting-point for his next piece of work, his *Habilitationsschrift*, the dissertation required to qualify as a university lecturer, submitted in early 1874 to the University of Jena as part of his application for a teaching post. Entitled 'Methods of Calculation based on an Extension of the Concept of Magnitude' (*MC*), it is in this work that Frege's foundationalist interests emerge. What underlies the concept of magnitude, and makes it independent of intuition, Frege argues, are the general properties of addition, and it is addition that is 'the subject of those fundamental propositions from which the whole of arithmetic grows as from a seed' (*MC*, p. 57). All other methods of calculation derive from addition – repeated addition, for example, yielding multiplication. What is involved here, Frege suggests, is the iterative application of an operation, which can be represented by an appropriate function, such that the value of the function for a given argument can itself become the argument of that function (*MC*, p. 58). Adding 1, for example, can be represented by the successor function, $f(x) = x + 1$, adding 2 by $ff(x)$, and so on; doubling by $g(x) = x + x$, quadrupling by $gg(x)$, and so on. Frege goes on to explore the relationships between various types of mathematical function; but the key point to note here is the central role that the notion of a function is suggested as playing in the required theory of magnitude, making possible the connection between different areas of arithmetic (ibid.). It was Frege's development of function theory that was to prove crucial in the transformation of logic that he was shortly to effect.

On the completion of his *Habilitationsschrift*, and on the necessary oral examination, public disputation and trial lecture, in May 1874 Frege was appointed to the post of *Privatdozent* (an unsalaried lectureship) at the University of Jena, where he stayed for the rest of his career. In the first few years, his teaching load was heavy, and he only published four short pieces,[4] three of them reviews, before the appearance of his first book, *Begriffsschrift*, in 1879. Although this work is now hailed as inaugurating the age of modern logic (I say more about this in the next section), it is clear from the Preface that Frege's aim in developing a more powerful logical theory was not so much to improve on traditional logic for its own sake as to provide arithmetic with the strongest possible foundations (see pp. 48–52 below). Since the firmest foundations were seen as logical ones, the task became to ascertain how much of arithmetic could be derived from logic. Having explained his logical theory in Parts I and II, in Part III Frege did indeed succeed in showing that mathematical induction could be analysed purely logically (see pp. 75–7 below), and this no doubt encouraged him in the attempt to derive the whole of arithmetic from logic. This *logicist* project, as it is now called, was to occupy him for the next quarter of a century.

But why was it felt necessary to provide arithmetic with foundations at all? The answer lies in the developments in mathematics that the nineteenth century had witnessed. In the work of Gauss, Lobatchevsky, Bolyai and Riemann, the first non-Euclidean geometries had been constructed, by replacing Euclid's notorious fifth axiom, the axiom of parallels, by an alternative axiom. Many assumed that contradictions would sooner or later emerge, but when double elliptic geometry was shown to be applicable to the surface of a sphere, 'lines' being interpreted as great circles, it became clear that non-Euclidean geometries were consistent if Euclidean geometry was consistent (since the configurations on which they could be mapped were Euclidean). As we have just seen, Frege himself had been concerned to show how imaginary forms could be represented geometrically by extending analytic geometry to incorporate complex numbers. But if non-Euclidean geometry could be modelled within Euclidean geometry, and Euclidean geometry, through analytic geometry, could be grounded in number theory (by the end of the nineteenth century, Hilbert had shown that Euclidean geometry was consistent if arithmetic was consistent), this still left the consistency of number theory unclear. This question was made more pressing by the continuing controversy over the existence of negative numbers and complex numbers. When Hamilton added to the problems by inventing *quaternions* (hypercomplex numbers), which failed to obey the law of commutativity in multiplication, and Cayley introduced *matrices* (a further type of

---

[4] See *CP*, pp. 93–100/*KS*, pp. 85–91.

hypernumber), the moral was clear: one cannot just assume that the basic properties of one number system automatically carry over to any enlargement of that system. This was something that Frege himself was to stress in his critique of formalist theories of arithmetic (see pp. 124–5 below).

But the most important motivation behind the growing concern with the foundations of arithmetic in the nineteenth century was the need to rigorize the differential and integral calculus, i.e. mathematical analysis. The key to the interpretation of the calculus was the concept of a 'limit', and it was Cauchy who made the first attempt to define this notion in terms of convergent sequences. Misleading talk of 'infinitesimals' was finally purged by Weierstrass, who recognized that if progress was to be made in areas where geometrical intuition gives out, then analysis needed to be grounded in number theory. Weierstrass, Cantor and Dedekind all provided accounts of the real numbers in terms of convergent sequences of rational numbers; and given that the rational numbers could be readily defined in terms of the natural numbers, the necessary foundations looked secure. But the natural numbers were still assumed as given, and this was something that Frege regarded as unacceptable, especially since he could find no clear account of what they were.[5] He thus took upon himself the task of completing the reductive process: defining the natural numbers in purely logical terms.

On the publication of the *Begriffsschrift*, Frege was promoted to *ausserordentlicher Professor*, which finally gave him a salary; but the book itself received discouraging reviews, his 'concept-script' being judged inferior to the Boolean logic of his leading contemporaries.[6] This induced Frege to examine carefully the work of Boole, and to write several papers demonstrating the greater power of his own theory.[7] This task occupied him in the three years that followed the publication of the *Begriffsschrift*, and the work analysing the concept of number, which had been heralded in the closing sentence of the Preface to the *Begriffsschrift*, was consequently delayed. But the criticism did, however, have one positive effect: it made Frege aware of the need to explain his ideas and sketch his proposed derivation of arithmetic from logic informally, *before* embarking on the programme of providing rigorous proofs using his 'concept-script'. He read up on the work of philosophers who had written about mathematics, and realized the importance of locating his own views against the

[5] Cf. the Introduction to *GL*, pp. 84–91 below.
[6] The reviews are reprinted in *CN*, App. I, pp. 209–35. Part of the failure to appreciate Frege's achievement was no doubt due to the two-dimensional character of his symbolism, which John Venn in his curt review (1880) dismissed as 'cumbrous and inconvenient'. The lack of any simple sign for conjunction or disjunction is also a disadvantage. Cf. Appendix 2 below.
[7] See *BLC*, *BLF* and *ACN*. I say more about this in the next section.

background of the traditional disputes. The result was *Die Grundlagen der Arithmetik* (*The Foundations of Arithmetic*), published in 1884, and recognized now, though not at the time, as a philosophical masterpiece, containing a penetrating critique of rival conceptions of arithmetic and an original account of his own.

Locating his position within a Kantian framework (albeit slightly modified by the definitions offered in §3; see pp. 92–3 below), Frege argues in Part I that arithmetic is neither a system of synthetic *a priori* truths, as Kant himself had maintained, nor a system of synthetic *a posteriori* truths, as Mill had thought, leaving only the possibility that it is a system of analytic *a priori* truths, as Leibniz had held. In Part II, Frege criticizes both empiricist and psychologistic conceptions of number – number is neither a property of external things, since what number we ascribe to things depends on the concept under which they are classified, nor is it an idea, since this would make it subjective. Numbers, according to Frege, are objective but non-actual. In §46, in Part III, he formulates his key thesis – that a statement of number (saying how many of something there are) contains an assertion about a concept. To say that there is one God, for example, is to say that the concept *God* is uniquely instantiated; and the important point here is that such construals enable number statements to be formalized purely logically (see pp. 103, 105 below). In Part IV, Frege goes on to offer definitions of the concept of number, the successor relation and the individual numbers – in terms of extensions of concepts. Since the concepts chosen can themselves be logically defined, and assuming that the notion of an extension of a concept is also unproblematically logical (I return to this shortly), then Frege's claim in the Conclusion to have made it 'probable' that arithmetic can be derived from logic looks justified.

With his informal account published, Frege then concentrated on the rigorous demonstration of the logicist thesis, building on his definitions and using his logical system (with certain revisions) to prove the laws of arithmetic. This resulted in his *magnum opus*, the *Grundgesetze der Arithmetik* (*Basic Laws of Arithmetic*), the first volume of which appeared in 1893 and the second volume in 1903.[8] However, in the nine years that passed between the publication of the *Grundlagen* and the appearance of Volume I of the *Grundgesetze*, a number of important changes in his views occurred, reflected in three papers that he published in the early 1890s – 'Function and Concept', 'On *Sinn* and *Bedeutung*' and 'On Concept and Object'. All three are now regarded as classics of analytic

---

[8] Frege had great difficulty finding a publisher for the *Grundgesetze*. In the end, Hermann Pohle of Jena (who had published his lecture 'Function and Concept') agreed to publish it in instalments, the publication of the second being conditional upon the favourable reception of the first (cf. *GG*, I. p. V). The second volume, it seems, was brought out at Frege's own expense.

philosophy; and the second, in particular, introducing his famous distinction between *Sinn* and *Bedeutung*, is probably the single most widely known and influential work in modern philosophy of language, which is not to say that the distinction is universally accepted or its interpretation uncontroversial (I say more about this below). As far as Frege's logicist project is concerned, however, the most important development was the simplifying of his ontology. Frege had emphasized the distinction between concept and object in the *Grundlagen* – a result of his use of function-argument analysis in the *Begriffsschrift*; but in the category of *object* he now made clear he included, firstly, *truth-values* (taken as the *Bedeutungen* of sentences), so that concepts could then be construed as functions that map objects onto one of the two objects, the True and the False (i.e. functions whose value is a truth-value), and secondly, *extensions of concepts*, which could then also be taken as legitimate arguments of functions. Although, as we have just noted, Frege had introduced extensions of concepts in the *Grundlagen*, he had not at the time felt committed to their use (see p. 115, fn.5, and p. 128 below); and it seems, in fact, that he went through a stage, immediately after its publication, of trying to do without them.[9] But the attempt failed, and he soon reverted to his original definitions. His three papers of the early 1890s, then, can be seen as reinforcing, and indeed as offering justification for, his appeal to extensions of concepts. Although these papers are frequently read as self-standing essays in the emerging field of philosophical logic (and can indeed be profitably read as such), their original role was to provide philosophical support to his logicist project.

After the publication of Volume I of the *Grundgesetze*, Frege was promoted to Honorary Ordinary Professor, which was unsalaried but without administrative duties. With a generous stipend that he also received from the Carl Zeiss *Stiftung*,[10] this freed him more for research; and he was certainly productive in the decade or so that followed. Not only did he make further progress on the *Grundgesetze*, but he also published a number of critical reviews of the work of others. His 1894 review of Husserl's *Philosophie der Arithmetik* was instrumental in converting Husserl away from his early psychologism (see p. 224 below). From 1894 to 1896 he was in regular correspondence with Peano, and published two pieces explaining the advantages of his own logical notation over the system that Peano was developing, which Peano did indeed modify as

---

[9] This is suggested by the brief notes that Scholz, the collector of Frege's *Nachlaß*, made on one of Frege's lost manuscripts, dating from just after *GL* (see item no. 47 in the catalogue printed in Veraart, 1976: p. 95). For details of this, see Burge, 1984: §II.

[10] This was a foundation run by Ernst Abbe with profits he received from the Zeiss lens and camera company, which he had helped to establish. The foundation gave a lot of money to the University of Jena.

a result of reading Frege's work.[11] It was Peano's notation that Russell took over, and it was through Peano that Russell came to learn of Frege's work – an event, however, that was to have disastrous consequences for Frege.

The source of Frege's problems was, after all, his appeal to extensions of concepts, and in particular, his conception of them as *objects* – when taken together with his assumption that every concept must be defined for all objects. For this latter assumption implies that every concept divides up all objects into those that do, and those that do not, fall under it (there is no third possibility);[12] with the assumption that extensions of concepts are objects, it implies that extensions themselves can be divided into those that fall under the concept whose extensions they are (e.g. the extension of '( ) is an extension'), and those that do not (e.g. the extension of '( ) is a horse'). But now consider the concept '( ) is the extension of a concept under which it does not fall'. Does the extension of *this* concept fall under the concept or not? If it does, then it does not, and if it does not, then it does.

This contradiction was discovered by Russell in 1902, and he wrote to Frege informing him of it on 16 June, as the second volume of the *Grundgesetze* was in press. Now known as Russell's paradox, Frege immediately recognized its seriousness.[13] A correspondence ensued, and Frege attempted to repair the damage in an appendix. What he held responsible for the contradiction was his fifth axiom, about which he had admitted some unease in the Preface to Volume I (see p. 195 below). Restricted to the specific case of concepts, Axiom V can be formulated as follows:

(V$_c$) Whatever falls under concept F falls under concept G, and vice versa, if and only if the concepts F and G have the same extension.[14]

According to Frege, Axiom V legitimates the appeal to extensions of concepts by laying down a criterion of identity for them (two extensions are the same if and only if their respective concepts apply to the same objects). If every concept is defined for every object, then Axiom V guarantees that every concept has an extension, and if these extensions are themselves objects, then it assures us that the extension of the concept

---

[11] For Frege's two pieces, see *PMC*, pp. 112–18 (*KS*, pp. 234–9; *WB*, pp. 181–6) and *PCN*. For Frege's correspondence with Peano, see *PMC*, pp. 108–29/*WB*, pp. 175–98.
[12] For this assumption, see especially *GG*, II, §56 (p. 259 below).
[13] See pp. 253–4 below. In its more familiar form, Russell's paradox is generated by asking whether the class of all classes that are not members of themselves is itself a member of itself or not: if it is, then it is not; and if it is not, then it is. Cf. p. 280 below.
[14] In its full generality, Axiom V may be stated thus: Two functions F and G always have the same value for the same argument if and only if the function F has the same *value-range* as the function G. Cf. pp. 213–14 below. On the notion of a 'value-range', see p. 135 below.

'( ) is the extension of a concept under which it does not fall' is an object; but it is just this that leads to contradiction.

Frege's response to the paradox was simply to outlaw the applicability of concepts to their own extensions, resulting in the following restriction of (V_c):

> (V_c') Whatever falls under concept F, except its own extension, falls under concept G, and vice versa, if and only if the concepts F and G have the same extension.[15]

Unfortunately, however, this too has been found to generate contradiction, in domains of more than one object;[16] and although it is unclear just when Frege accepted that his system had been fatally undermined, the planned third volume of the *Grundgesetze* was never completed, and by the end of his life Frege was certainly admitting that his logicist project had resulted in failure.[17]

In his last fifteen years at Jena, Frege published little, but the reason was as much personal grief as intellectual disappointment. His children by his wife, Margaret Lieseburg (born in 1856), had died young, and although they had adopted a son, Alfred, around 1900, his wife too died in 1905, leaving him to bring up the child without her. Bad health, also, was to plague him for the rest of his life. He did, however, have a significant influence on two more people, at the very start of their philosophical careers, who were to play a major role in developing and transmitting his ideas. In 1911 he was visited by Wittgenstein, then a student of aeronautics, who had read about his views in Appendix A of Russell's *Principles of Mathematics*; and it was Frege who recommended that Wittgenstein go to Cambridge to study with Russell. From 1910 to 1914 several of Frege's lecture courses were attended by Carnap, who studied at Jena; and Carnap, like Wittgenstein, was quite explicit about the influence that Frege's work had on him.[18]

---

[15] Cf. *GG*, II, App., p. 288 below; *PMC*, p. 150.

[16] See the references cited in fn. 30 on p. 288 below.

[17] See pp. 368–73 below. According to Bynum (1972a: p. 48), Frege was still defending his logicist project in 1914. Admittedly, his 1914 lecture notes, *LM* (see the next footnote), contain no rejection of logicism, but nor do they contain an endorsement. Carnap's account of Frege's lectures (1963: §1), on which Bynum's view is based, is equally inconclusive. Dummett (1991a: pp. 5–6), on the basis of remarks in *NS*, and in particular, a comment, in some jottings entitled 'What may I regard as the result of my work?', that 'the extension of a concept or class is not the primary thing for me' (*PW*, p. 184), has suggested that Frege abandoned his logicist project in 1906. But whilst revealing doubts about his appeal to extensions of concepts (which he had had, in any case, from the beginning), this does not show that Frege had altogether given up hope of deriving arithmetic from logic.

[18] Cf. Wittgenstein, *TLP*, Preface; Carnap, 1963: §§1–2. Frege's notes for one of these

Frege retired from the University of Jena in 1918, and moved to Bad Kleinen, near to his home town of Wismar. In the last years of his life, he published a series of papers entitled 'Logical Investigations', the final fruit of various attempts that he had made during his life to write a textbook on logic – explaining his views, in particular, on truth, thought, *Sinn* and *Bedeutung*, the nature of logic, negation and generality. The first of these papers, 'Der Gedanke', in arguing for the indefinability of truth and the objectivity of thought, is second only to 'Über Sinn und Bedeutung' in the influence that it has had on subsequent philosophy. But Frege was not to live to see his influence, or to enjoy the widespread recognition and acclaim that this works deserved and were eventually to receive. He died, at the age of 77, on 26 July 1925.

In a note attached to his will, bequeathing his unpublished letters and papers to his son, Alfred, Frege wrote:

> Dear Alfred,
> Do not despite the pieces I have written. Even if all is not gold, there is gold in them. I believe there are things here which will one day be prized much more highly than they are now. Take care that nothing gets lost.
> > Your loving father.
> It is a large part of myself which I bequeath to you herewith.[19]

In 1935, Alfred Frege handed over the papers – Frege's *Nachlaß* – to Heinrich Scholz of the University of Münster, who had been trying to track them down, and Scholz and his collaborators set to work to edit them for publication. During the war the originals were deposited in the University Library for safe-keeping, but were nevertheless destroyed by Allied bombing on 25 March 1945. Although typescript copies had fortunately been made of most of what had been judged as the important pieces, Scholz had to have them copied again after the war to prepare an edition. But illness prevented Scholz from completing the project before he himself died in 1956; and it was not until 1969 that the *Nachgelassene Schriften* was published, edited by a group of scholars set up by Hans Hermes, Scholz's successor at Münster, and this was followed by an

---

courses, 'Logic in Mathematics' (*LM*), were preserved and published posthumously in *NS*, pp. 219–70/*PW*, pp. 203–50 (the first nine pages of which are reprinted below, pp. 308–18). Carnap's account of Frege's lectures contains one of the few descriptions of Frege himself (around 1910): 'Frege looked old beyond his years. He was of small stature, rather shy, extremely introverted. He seldom looked at the audience. Ordinarily we saw only his back, while he drew the strange diagrams of his symbolism on the blackboard and explained them. Never did a student ask a question or make a remark, whether during the lecture or afterwards. The possibility of a discussion seemed to be out of the question.' (1963: p. 5.)

[19] *PW*, p. ix/*NS*, p. xxxiv. The information that follows about the history of Frege's *Nachlaß* is taken from *NS*, pp. xxxiv–xxxix/*PW*, pp. ix–xiii.

edition of Frege's correspondence in 1976. More than fifty years after Frege's death, then, what had survived of the gold of which Frege had spoken was finally exhibited; and Frege's prophecy that it would one day be prized much more highly than it was when he wrote has since been amply fulfilled. A selection from his *Nachlaß* is reprinted in the present volume, in addition to his more well-known works.

2. Frege's Achievement

Frege's most remarkable and indisputable achievement was the revolution that he effected in logic, which for over 2000 years, ever since its origins in Aristotle's *Prior Analytics*, had been dominated by syllogistic theory. Propositional logic had indeed emerged at the time of the Stoics, and been developed in the work of Boole and others on the 'algebra of logic' in the middle of the nineteenth century, but even then it had only been regarded as one part of Boolean algebra, dependent upon the more fundamental calculus of classes. One of Frege's achievements in the *Begriffsschrift* was to give a self-contained and rigorously axiomatized exposition of propositional logic, in effect relying on just two connectives (negation and the conditional), two rules of inference (*modus ponens* and an implicit rule of substitution), and six axioms.[20] But it was in his creation of what we now know as predicate logic, through his invention of quantifier notation, that the real logical breakthrough occurred.

Frege's crucial move lay in extending the idea of function-argument analysis from mathematics to logic. At the simplest level, 'Caesar is mortal', for example, is construed as the value of the function '( ) is mortal' for the argument 'Caesar'.[21] But what of the analysis of a proposition such as 'All humans are mortal'? Traditional logic had treated this too as of subject-predicate form, but as Frege recognized, 'All humans' does not have the same semantic role as the proper name 'Caesar'. Instead, what Frege does is treat this as a *complex* proposition involving *two* functions, '( ) is human' and '( ) is mortal', between which a certain relation is being stated to obtain, namely, that whatever satisfies the

---

[20] Frege himself speaks of the 'completeness' of his system of logic, though it was left to Łukasiewicz (1934) to *prove* the completeness of Frege's propositional calculus. Łukasiewicz also proved the redundancy of the third axiom, deriving it from the first two. The remaining five axioms are all independent of each other. It is true that Frege remarks in the Preface to *BS* that he later noticed that the last two axioms can be combined into one, but this depended on the introduction of Frege's symbol for identity of content. On the connectives, rules and axioms of Frege's system, cf. Appendix 2 below.

[21] Using inverted commas here is not meant to prejudge the question of exactly what Frege took functions and arguments to be, on which his views developed; see fn. 29 on p. 66 below.

former (i.e. results in something true) satisfies the latter.[22] Representing it as 'For all x, if x is human, then x is mortal', we can regard this as composed of two simpler propositions, 'x is human' and 'x is mortal',[23] linked by a propositional connective and bound by a quantifier. In modern notation, this would be formalized as '$(\forall x)(Hx \to Mx)$', 'Hx' symbolizing 'x is human' and 'Mx' symbolizing 'x is mortal'.[24] The analysis thus depends both on the use of function-argument notation and on propositional logic (which is presupposed in the use of the propositional connectives). Frege's creation of quantification theory resulted from amalgamating the two.

It is worth indicating the significance of this synthesis in the history of logic by briefly comparing Frege's achievement with Boole's. Boole (1847, 1854) had distinguished between 'primary propositions', the subject matter of the theory of classes (embracing syllogistic theory), and 'secondary propositions', with which propositional logic was concerned, and had shown how, under different 'interpretations', the same algebraic system could be used to represent both. But just because *different* 'interpretations' were involved, Boole – unlike Frege – had been unable to formalize inferences in which *both* primary and secondary propositions occur. Boole himself gave as an example of a primary proposition 'All inhabitants are either Europeans or Asiatics', and as an example of a secondary proposition 'Either all the inhabitants are Europeans, or they are all Asiatics' (1847: pp. 58–9). But although Boole distinguished these, he seems to have failed to recognize the logical connection between them. For the first, of course, follows from the second; yet there is no way of representing this in the Boolean system. The formalization in Frege's logic, however, is straightforward.[25] As Frege himself remarked in a critique of Boole's calculus that he wrote shortly after the publication of the *Begriffsschrift*, 'The real difference [between the two systems] is that I avoid [the Boolean] division into two parts . . . and give a homogeneous presentation of the lot. In Boole the two parts run alongside one

---

[22] Again, this way of putting things is not meant to prejudge the issue of what Frege understood the 'value' of such functions to be for a given argument. In his later work, it was explicitly stated to be a *truth-value* (see pp. 137–9 below), but in his early work, Frege seemed to slide between taking it as an *expression* whose content was what he called a 'judgeable content' and taking it as that content itself, where there was also unclarity as to exactly what 'judgeable contents' were (cf. pp. 65–8 below).

[23] Strictly speaking, these are not themselves propositions, but what Frege later called 'quasi-propositions' ('uneigentliche Sätze'; see p. 296 below) and Russell called *propositional functions*, which yield a proposition when the 'x' is replaced by a proper name.

[24] For Frege's own formalization, see p. 73 below; and for an explanation of the relationship between Frege's symbolism and modern notation, see Appendix 2 below.

[25] In modern notation, '$[(\forall x)(Ix \to Ex) \vee (\forall x)(Ix \to Ax)] \to (\forall x)[Ix \to (Ex \vee Ax)]$'. For further discussion of Frege's advance over Boole, see Dudman, 1976; Beaney, 1996: §2.2.

another, so that one is like the mirror image of the other, but for that very reason stands in no organic relation to it.' (*BLC*, p. 14.)

Besides providing a far more 'organic' theory, in which predicate logic builds on propositional logic, Frege's invention of quantifier notation also resolved one of the outstanding problems that had confronted Aristotelian logic – the analysis of statements of *multiple generality*. The ambiguity of statements such as 'Every philosopher admires some logician' is difficult to express in syllogistic theory, but in Fregean logic is readily reflected in the differing *scope* of the quantifiers. In modern notation, the two readings would be formalized as follows:

(1) $(\forall x)(Px \rightarrow (\exists y)(Ly \ \& \ Axy))$. [For all x, if x is a philosopher, then there is some y such that y is a logician and x admires y.]

(2) $(\exists y)(Ly \ \& \ (\forall x)(Px \rightarrow Axy))$. [There is some y such that y is a logician and for all x, if x is a philosopher, then x admires y.]

In (1), the universal quantifier has wider scope than the existential quantifier; in (2) the existential quantifier has wider scope than the universal quantifier. In arithmetic, statements of multiple generality, such as 'Every number has a successor' or 'Every even number is the sum of two primes', are very common; and clearly, even to attempt to show that arithmetic can be derived from logic requires some way of formalizing such statements. Although the significance of his notation for generality only dawned on Frege gradually,[26] it is this that we now recognize as Frege's greatest single logical achievement.

Without Frege's new system of logic, the project of deriving arithmetic from logic would have looked quite unrealistic; with it, Frege managed to provide logical definitions of the ancestral of a relation and of a many-one relation, and hence to give a logical analysis of mathematical induction (see pp. 75–7 below). In the *Grundlagen*, he also showed how to provide logical definitions of number statements of the form 'There are n F's'; and with the introduction of *extensions of concepts*, or *classes*, how to define the individual numbers (see pp. 105–20 below). In defining the number 0, for example, as the extension of the concept 'equinumerous to the concept *not identical with itself*', Frege in effect characterized it as the class of all classes with the same number of members as the null class.[27] Although Russell's paradox was to reveal the dangers involved in so naïvely talking of classes of classes, modern set theory still

---

[26] Surprisingly, there is no mention of it at all in his Preface to *BS*; and even in his long critique of Boolean logic, he only modestly proclaims that his 'Begriffsschrift', 'thanks to the notation for generality, commands a somewhat wider domain than Boole's formula language' (*BLC*, p. 46; cf. pp. 14–15). He did, however, provide many examples of formalized statements of multiple generality, in both *BS* and *BLC*.

[27] Such a definition is not circular, since 'equinumerosity' can itself be defined purely logically; see pp. 117–18 below.

proceeds by defining zero in terms of the null set – in fact, by *identifying* zero with the null set, and generating the natural numbers from this basis. Despite the collapse of Frege's own project, then, Frege still claims his place as one of the founders of mathematical logic and set theory. In the *Grundgesetze*, in developing a formal language adequate for the purposes of arithmetic, and in specifying rules governing the legitimate construction of complex expressions from simpler ones, Frege also laid the basis for modern semantic theory; and although there is controversy over whether Frege can be regarded as providing a semantic theory for natural language (as opposed to an ideal logical language), the connection he suggested between the sense of a proposition and its truth-conditions has been highly influential from Wittgenstein and Tarski to Davidson and Dummett.[28]

Within the philosophy of mathematics, Frege's criticisms of psychologism, empiricism, and formalism, at least in the forms in which they had been developed up to his time, are widely recognized as devastating; and although there are undoubtedly problems in trying to interpret Frege's own brand of Platonism and reconcile it with his logicism, Platonism remains a powerful force amongst mathematicians and philosophers of mathematics today; and logicism too is back on the philosophical agenda.[29] Once again, despite Russell's paradox, Frege is still regarded as one of the greatest philosophers of mathematics that there has ever been.

But it is in the areas of philosophical logic, the philosophy of language, the philosophy of mind, epistemology and metaphysics that Frege's ideas have become most widely known; and here his importance lies in his thinking through the philosophical implications of his new logic and the philosophical issues raised by his new analyses. From this derive all his characteristic philosophical conceptions and theses: the distinction between axioms, rules and definitions; the repudiation of subject-predicate analysis in favour of function-argument analysis; the dissociation of assertoric force from predication; the notion of 'content' (which later split into 'Sinn' and 'Bedeutung'); the logical priority of judgements over concepts, from which his notorious 'context principle' can be seen as a generalization; the construal of concepts and relations as functions; the distinctions between concept and object, first-level and second-level concepts, subsumption and subordination; the construal of existence in terms of a second-level concept (implying the rejection of the ontological argument for the existence of God); the requirement that concepts be sharply defined, and the associated criticism of piecemeal definition; the construal of numbers, extensions of concepts, truth-values and thoughts as objects;

[28] Cf. especially *GG*, I, §32 (pp. 221–2 below); Wittgenstein, *TLP*; Tarski, 1931; Davidson, 1967, 1970; Dummett, 1975, 1976.
[29] See esp. Wright, 1983.

the distinctions between *Sinn* and *Bedeutung*, direct and indirect *Sinn* and *Bedeutung*; the indefinability of truth; the objectivity and timelessness of thoughts. Some of these are now taken so completely for granted that expositions in elementary textbooks often fail to mention Frege's name at all; some remain fiercely contested; but all have a fundamental place in modern analytic philosophy.

The methods and lines of thought that Frege introduced, and the questions that his own work raises, are no less important than his specific doctrines and principles. His critical attitude towards ordinary language, for example, and his concern to develop a logical language that more accurately reflects 'contents' or 'thoughts', have had a profound influence on the development of analytic philosophy. In the philosophy of mathematics, and in metaphysics more generally, the question whether numbers are objects, and whether abstract entities can be regarded as legitimately introduced by 'contextual definition', has recently been the subject of intense debate. In the philosophy of language, the question whether all expressions have both a *Sinn* and a *Bedeutung*, and exactly what these are for each class of expression, is the starting-point of a great deal of work. In epistemology and the philosophy of mind, the question of the nature of thoughts, and the problems posed, in particular, by intensionality and indexicality, are of central concern. On all these issues, Frege's writings are both the source of the problems discussed and the inspiration behind the development of certain responses. I say more about some of these issues in the next section; but mere mention of them here is enough to indicate the extent of Frege's importance in modern philosophy.

3. Issues of Interpretation

In this section I briefly consider two particular issues of controversy in the interpretation of Frege's philosophy – concerning, firstly, the role of the so-called 'context principle' in Frege's work, and secondly, Frege's conception of sense, in relation to both names and indexicals. Taken together they do, I think, give a fair indication of the range of problems that are currently debated. This is not to deny that there are other fundamental disputes, but most of them do at some point connect with at least one of these controversies. I mention some of the other issues along the way, commenting, in particular, on the question of Frege's status as one of the founders of analytic philosophy. Whilst introducing many of the ideas and methods characteristic of analytic philosophy, Frege also expressed views and attitudes that are now repudiated or simply forgotten; and indeed, his own philosophy developed and changed over time. Not only must we be sensitive to the danger of reading Frege anachronistically, then, but we must also constantly bear in mind that probing particular texts may yield not a coherently worked out theory hidden below the surface but ideas and conceptions that call for refinement, revision or constructive criticism.

The context principle is generally regarded as one of Frege's most important principles, and in some form, has been endorsed by subsequent philosophers from the early Wittgenstein onwards. It is first formulated in the Introduction to the *Grundlagen*, as the second of Frege's three 'fundamental principles': 'The meaning of a word must be asked for in the context of a proposition, not in isolation' (see p. 90 below); and it plays a crucial role in the central sections of the *Grundlagen*. Yet despite its obvious importance, it is not stated again in his later work (unlike the other two principles), though nor is it explicitly repudiated. The explanation of this, and the question of just what, if anything, did survive of the principle, have been matters of considerable dispute.[30]

Perhaps the first point to note is that the principle, as formulated, tells us very little; indeed, as it stands, it hardly seems controversial at all. What is important is the *use* that Frege makes of it during the course of his argument ('The meaning of a principle must be asked for in the context of a theory, not in isolation'). In the *Grundlagen*, its role seems clear. By §60, where the principle is first put to work, Frege has criticized both empiricist and psychologistic conceptions of number. But an obvious question then arises: if numbers are not physical or mental entities, then how can they be apprehended? Frege's answer is that we apprehend them by grasping the sense of propositions in which number terms occur. Two sections later, the context principle is appealed to again in stating, more specifically, that what is needed is to define the sense of a numerical equation. The suggestion, it turns out, is to use the first of the following propositions to define the second:

(Na) The concept F is equinumerous to the concept G. (There are as many objects falling under concept F as under concept G, i.e. there are just as many F's as G's.)

(Nb) The number of F's is equal to the number of G's. (The number that belongs to the concept F is the same as the number that belongs to the concept G.)

Frege's idea here is a stroke of genius.[31] For if Frege is right that (Na) and (Nb) have the same 'content' (cf. §64), then, by the context principle, the meaning of (Na) as a whole guarantees that the constituents

[30] On the controversial issue of Frege's contextualism, see e.g. Dummett, 1981b: ch. 19; 1991a: chs. 15–18; 1995 (Dummett's views have developed over the period); Resnik, 1980: pp. 161–71; Currie, 1982: pp. 148–66; Wright, 1983: ch. 1; Baker and Hacker, 1984: ch. 8.

[31] Dummett has gone so far as to say that '§62 is arguably the most pregnant philosophical paragraph ever written . . . it is the very first example of what has become known as the "linguistic turn" in philosophy' (1991a: p. 111). It is an exaggeration worth making.

of (Nb) – in particular, the number terms, 'the number of F's' and 'the number of G's' – also have a meaning. Grasping the sense of (Na), then, is thereby to grasp the sense of 'the number of F's', i.e. to apprehend the relevant number.[32] Nothing else is required in the explanation of how it is that we apprehend numbers. Furthermore, if the question of what exactly numbers are is regarded as still undecided at this stage,[33] the answer can now be given that they are the *Bedeutungen* of number terms, whose objectivity is guaranteed by the truth of the relevant propositions, and whose logical nature is guaranteed by the logical definability of (Na), in terms of one-one correlation (see pp. 117–18 below). The epistemological and ontological issues would thus seem to be settled simultaneously.

However, Frege goes on to raise three objections to his suggested contextual definition, the first two of which he answers (§§63–5), but the third of which he sustains (§§66–7).[34] According to this third objection, such a definition, whilst enabling us to determine when two numbers are equal, when given to us *as* numbers (as the numbers that belong to a certain concept), does not tell us exactly *what* numbers are, that is, what distinguishes them from any other objects, such as Julius Caesar or England. It is as a result of this objection, which has come to be known as 'the Caesar problem' (after its initial statement in §56), that Frege goes on to offer *explicit* definitions instead, in terms of extensions of concepts. So does this then mean that Frege's contextual definition, and hence the context principle itself, is rejected during the very course of the *Grundlagen*? This would clearly conflict with Frege's description of the principle in the Introduction as a 'fundamental principle' – and the principle is in any case *reaffirmed* in the Conclusion (see p. 127 below). The answer is that the contextual definition is only criticized as *insufficient*, not as incorrect – it still lays down a *necessary* condition for the identity of numbers; and Frege's later explicit definitions do indeed satisfy the original contextual equivalence (see pp. 116–17 below).

But if the context principle is still regarded as underlying the argument of the *Grundlagen*, and Frege's appeal to extensions of concepts is retained in the *Grundgesetze*, then why is the context principle never again endorsed? The short answer is that in the form in which it appeared

[32] The terms 'content' ('Inhalt'), 'meaning' ('Bedeutung') and 'sense' ('Sinn') are all being used here interchangeably, as Frege himself used them in his argument in the *Grundlagen*.

[33] By §62, Frege takes himself to have established that numbers are objects (rather than concepts), since number terms are proper names (cf. *GL*, §§38, 51), and indeed, that they are objective, though non-actual (cf. *GL*, §§26, 61); but their precise nature remains unclear.

[34] Frege's argument actually proceeds by taking the analogous case of defining the direction of a line in terms of parallelism (see pp. 110–14 below). I transfer the argument to the case of number.

in the *Grundlagen*, it could not have been, since at that time Frege was operating with an undifferentiated notion of 'content', which is later replaced by the dual notions of 'Sinn' and 'Bedeutung'. But this only raises the question why Frege did not formulate two new context principles, one concerning sense and the other concerning *Bedeutung*, which might be stated as follows:[35]

(CPB) The *Bedeutungen* of parts of a sentence are determined by the *Bedeutung* of the whole.

(CPS) The senses of parts of a sentence are determined by the sense of the whole.

To what extent could these principles be said to underlie Frege's later philosophy? Let us first consider the case of functional expressions – in particular, concept words. Now it is certainly true that, throughout his work, Frege held what may be called the priority thesis – that judgements or thoughts are logically prior to concepts.[36] This reflects his view that concepts are arrived at by splitting up 'contents' (to use his early term) in function-argument analysis, or that concepts are 'unsaturated' (as he put it from 1882 onwards). It would then seem natural to suggest that, on Frege's later view, the sense of a concept word (by means of which the concept itself – the *Bedeutung* of the concept word – is grasped, at least in contexts where the relevant proposition is judged to have a truth-value) is determined by the sense of the proposition in which the concept word occurs, in accordance with some particular mode of analysis. At the ontological level too, given Frege's *extensional* view of concepts, concepts themselves, as the *Bedeutungen* of concept words, can be regarded as determined by the set of true propositions (i.e. those that have the True as their *Bedeutung*) in which the concept words occur. Difficulties remain here, but there is at least a *prima facie* case for saying that, for concept words, the two principles (CPB) and (CPS), suitably understood or modified, underlie Frege's later work.[37]

---

[35] Talk of 'determination' here is meant to reflect Frege's remark in *GL* that 'It is enough if the proposition as a whole has a sense; its parts thereby also obtain their content' (see p. 108 below). The issue is one of *direction of explanation*: there is nothing more to explaining the *Sinn/Bedeutung* of the parts of a proposition than explaining (defining) the *Sinn/Bedeutung* of the proposition as a whole.

[36] For an early statement, see e.g. *BS*, §9 (pp. 65–8 below); *BLC*, pp. 16–17; and for a later statement, see e.g. *NLD*, p. 362 below.

[37] For Frege's understanding of the *Sinn* and *Bedeutung* of concept words, see especially *CSB*, pp. 172–80 below. The main difficulty lies in reconciling such contextualism with the *compositionalism* that increasingly asserted itself in Frege's later work, which might be stated in a form that directly contradicts (CPB) and (CPS): 'The *Sinn/Bedeutung* of a complex expression is determined by the *Sinn/Bedeutung* of its parts'. Implicit in the semantic theory of *GG* (see esp. I, §§28–32), such compositionalism was later explicitly

The case of *proper names* is more problematic, since no corresponding thesis concerning the logical priority of judgements over objects can be ascribed to Frege at the time of the *Begriffsschrift*, and on his later view (from the 1890s), such a thesis could not have been stated in this form, since both thoughts and truth-values were themselves regarded as objects. But as far as (CPS) is concerned, it might well be maintained that, at least at the level of explaining what it is for expressions to have sense, propositions have priority over names, even if, in accounting for how I understand the senses of complex expressions, the order is reversed.[38] But with regard to (CPB), at least as far as our use of ordinary language is concerned, and given Frege's conception of the *Bedeutung* of a proposition as a truth-value, it does seem implausible to suppose that the *Bedeutung* of a name, i.e. the object it refers to, is somehow determined by the truth-value of a proposition in which it occurs.[39] Here, it seems, whether a proposition has a truth-value is dependent on whether the names it contains have referents.

However, it has been argued that it is precisely with regard to the *Bedeutung* of names that the context principle was most firmly endorsed, at least within the logical system of the *Grundgesetze*. To appreciate this, let us go back to the central argument of the *Grundlagen*. As we saw above, Frege criticized the suggested contextual definition of (Nb) in terms of (Na) on the ground that it did not sufficiently determine the relevant objects, and went on instead to offer explicit definitions in terms of extensions of concepts. But this, of course, only raises the question of how Frege thought that the appeal to extensions of concepts was justified. The answer, at the time of the *Grundlagen*, was clearly inadequate: since these are *logical* objects, we are just assumed to know what they are. By the time of the *Grundgesetze*, however, after Frege had convinced himself that there was no other way of grounding his logicist project (cf. p. 6 above), their introduction was legitimized in his famous Axiom V. Restricting its formulation once again to extensions of concepts (cf. p. 7 above), what Axiom V can be regarded as doing is asserting the equivalence between the following two propositions:[40]

---

stated by Frege (in 1914) to be required to account for our ability to use and understand new linguistic constructions (see pp. 319–20 below; cf. *LM*, p. 225; *CT*, p. 390). For an attempt at reconciling Frege's contextualism with his compositionalism, in relation to concepts, see Dummett, 1981b: ch. 15.

[38] This is Dummett's position, encapsulated in his slogan: 'in the order of *explanation* the sense of a sentence is primary, but in the order of *recognition* the sense of a word is primary' (1981a: p. 4; cf. 1981b: p. 374).

[39] I say more about Frege's conception of the *Bedeutung* of expressions in the next section.

[40] To avoid possible misunderstanding of the labelling here, it should be noted that what Frege understands by '(Va)' and '(Vb)' in his appendix to *GG*, II (see p. 283 below) is *not* the corresponding generalized versions of (Ca) and (Cb) formulated here, i.e. 'The

(Ca) The concept F applies to the same objects (yields the same truth-value for the same argument) as the concept G.

(Cb) The extension of the concept F is equal to [identical with] the extension of the concept G.

What we have here, of course, is a pair of propositions that stand in an analogous relation to that between (Na) and (Nb); and indeed, the purpose of Axiom V seems precisely to *contextually define* extensions of concepts. If so, then the context principle does, after all, remain at the very heart of Frege's logicism. For let us assume that (Ca) is indeed true (i.e. has itself a *Bedeutung*) for particular concepts F and G; and let us also assume the truth of Axiom V. Then (Cb) must itself be true (i.e. have a *Bedeutung*), and according to Frege, this is enough to guarantee that 'the extension of the concept F' has a *Bedeutung*, i.e. that there *is* such a thing as the extension of the concept F.

Now the question clearly arises of how Frege thought that the Caesar problem could be solved in the case of extensions of concepts; and the answer to this is by no means straightforward.[41] But the main point here is simply to note that there does seem to be an implicit appeal to a context principle governing the determination of the *Bedeutung* of terms for extensions of concepts. There is nothing more to the explanation of the existence of extensions of concepts, according to Frege, than the truth of certain propositions; and there is nothing more to the explanation of our apprehension of extensions of concepts than our grasp of those truths. As at the time of the *Grundlagen*, the ontological and epistemological questions are thus seen as answered simultaneously.[42] Of course, we now know that Frege's system is inconsistent, precisely due to Axiom V; and this inevitably raises questions about the legitimacy of contextual definition. But Frege's error, we might say, lay not in contextual definition as such, but in the supposition that the extensions of concepts thereby

function F has the same value for each argument as the function G' and 'The value-range of the function F is equal to the value-range of the function G', but rather the corresponding generalized versions of the *conditionals* '(Ca) → (Cb)' and '(Cb) → (Ca)', respectively.

[41] Frege is aware of the problem, and addresses it in *GG*, I, §§10, 29. 31. In essence, what Frege attempts to prove is that terms for value-ranges (which include extensions of concepts) have *Bedeutungen* so long as the values of all the primitive functions are determined for those *Bedeutungen* as arguments. Here too, then, the context principle is seen as operating: the *Bedeutung* of a value-range term is determined by determining the *Bedeutungen* of all propositions in which it appears. For discussion, see Moore and Rein, 1986; Resnik, 1986; Dummett, 1991a: chs. 16–18; 1995. It should, of course, be emphasized that whatever implicit appeal Frege may have made to the context principle in *GG*, and whatever the status of Axiom V, Frege's official position in his later work is quite clearly that contextual definitions are to be repudiated; see especially *GG*, II, §§56–67 (pp. 259–70 below).

[42] Cf. *GG*, II, §147 (pp. 278–9 below).

defined were already members of the domain over which the concepts themselves were defined. For if the extensions so defined are taken to constitute a separate, higher-level domain, then the contradiction will not arise (since the possibility of their falling under the concepts whose extensions they are is ruled out). But if extensions should be seen as a *different* kind of object from those in the initial domain, then in what sense are they 'real' or 'objective'? Frege naïvely assumed that there is such a thing as the domain of *all* objects;[43] but if we allow that there are different kinds of objects, falling in different domains, some objects dependent on others, then where exactly are we to draw the boundaries and how is any hierarchy to be structured? These are the questions that Frege's work has bequeathed.[44]

What the problems we have highlighted reveal is the tension between Frege's *realism*, which is what he took *objectivism* to demand (objectivity requiring objects of the appropriate kind), and the *contextualism* that seemed to lie at the basis of his *logicism*. For, with the benefit of hindsight, what the strategy of contextual definition suggests is the possibility of *eliminating* the need to suppose that all logically significant parts of a true (or false) proposition must have a *Bedeutung*, realistically construed, as long as there is some analysis of that proposition that reveals its 'underlying' logical form. Only at this most fundamental level need we demand that all logically significant parts have a *Bedeutung*. Such an eliminativist strategy was precisely what Russell's theory of descriptions introduced;[45] and it is important to recognize that although the materials were present in Frege's work for use in pursuing such a strategy, Frege did not himself do so. His status as one of the founders of analytic philosophy, then, should not mislead us into attributing to him every characteristic thesis and project of the modern analytic philosopher. The possibility of an objectivism without realism, buttressed by a programme

---

[43] If sets are themselves objects, then this can be shown very simply to be false. For as Cantor proved, the set of all subsets of a given set is larger than the original set, since a set of n members has 2^n subsets (taken as including both itself and the null set) and $2^n > n$, for all n, even where n is infinite. A set of two objects a and b, for example, has $2^2 = 4$ subsets: $\emptyset$, $\{a\}$, $\{b\}$, $\{a, b\}$; and a set of three objects a, b and c has $2^3 = 8$ subsets: $\emptyset$, $\{a\}$, $\{b\}$, $\{c\}$, $\{a, b\}$, $\{a, c\}$, $\{b, c\}$, $\{a, b, c\}$. But now consider the set of *all objects*. There are more subsets of this set than there are members of the set itself; so that if sets are themselves regarded as objects, then we clearly arrive at the contradiction that there are more objects (viz. subsets) than there are objects (viz. members). So there is no such thing as the set of *all* objects (abstract as well as concrete).

[44] The first attempt at an answer was Russell's theory of types, developed precisely in response to the contradiction he had discovered.

[45] As Russell himself remarked, the central point of his theory of descriptions was that 'a phrase may contribute to the meaning of a sentence without having any meaning at all in isolation' (*MPD*, p. 64).

of contextual analysis, might be a favoured option now, in certain areas of philosophy, but it is not one that Frege ever contemplated.[46]

That Frege assumed that objectivism requires realism is equally evident in his conception of sense. Indeed, the development of his thought seems to have been towards a rather extreme form of Platonism, at exhibited in his late paper 'Der Gedanke' (see pp. 325–45 below). However, to trace this development, and to appreciate some of the problems raised by his conception of sense, we need to go back to his first book. For although the distinction between *Sinn* and *Bedeutung* did not emerge until the 1890s, Frege had recognized in the *Begriffsschrift* that the same 'content' – for example, a geometrical point – can be 'determined' in more than one way, a fact that requires for its expression a special symbol, representing 'identity of content' (see pp. 64–5 below). The distinction between 'content' and 'mode of determination' clearly corresponds to the later distinction between 'Bedeutung' and 'Sinn', as applied in the case of names; yet at the beginning of 'On *Sinn* and *Bedeutung*', Frege criticizes his *Begriffsschrift* account. So what exactly was his objection? What Frege repudiates is his earlier conception of identity as a relation between *names*, not contents; for on the assumption that the name/bearer relationship is always arbitrary, this implies that identity statements 'express no proper knowledge' (see pp. 151–2 below). Now we might well reject the assumption here, arguing that there is often a good reason why a particular name is chosen to represent something. But in a way, this is just Frege's point – what is important is the *sense* we attach to

[46] Of course, it is true that Frege's realism only becomes prominent as his thought develops, which has led some, most notably Sluga (1977, 1980), to argue that Frege, at least in his early work, was a transcendental idealist rather than a realist (of the traditional kind). But the extent of Kant's influence is, I think, frequently overestimated. Frege's remarks on the self as an object of thought in 'Der Gedanke' (see pp. 339–41 below), for example, hardly indicate an appreciation of the subtle complexities of Kant's theory of the self, to which anyone who had ever read Kant properly would be sensitive. Frege does indeed make use of the Kantian analytic/synthetic, *a priori/a posteriori* framework in *GL*, but this is less a reflection of sympathy with Kantian ideas (he does, after all, criticize Kant's conception of arithmetic) than an attempt to make his ideas more accessible to a philosophical readership, before the formal work of *GG* was undertaken (cf. fn. 18 on p. 83 below). It is worth noting that after *GL*, Frege never again uses the terms 'analytic' and 'synthetic' (except where Kant's views are mentioned, as e.g. at the beginning of *SB*). Even when referring to *GL*, he talks of having 'sought to make it probable that arithmetic is a branch of logic' (see p. 208 below) rather than of having aimed to show that arithmetic is a body of 'analytic' truths (cf. fn. 60 below). His logicism aside, in his basic metaphysical outlook, Frege does not so much move forward from Kant as look backward to Plato. But the issue is admittedly controversial in the secondary literature. For discussion of Frege's realism, see Dummett, 1981a: ch. 14; 1976; 1981b: ch. 20; 1982; Sluga, 1976; 1977; 1980: chs. 3–4; 1984; Currie, 1978; 1981; 1982: pp. 176–91; Wright, 1983; Hale, 1984; Ricketts, 1986; Weiner, 1990: Part II; Burge, 1992.

that name, not the mere sign itself. The critique of the *Begriffsschrift* account, then, is not the volte-face that it might appear, since there too it was the 'mode of determination of a content' that was crucial. What was wrong was just Frege's characterization of 'identity of content' as a relation between names (which, anyway, made the term 'identity of content' inappropriate).

What led Frege to treat 'identity of content' as a relation between names was the perceived difficulty with the only envisaged alternative. For if what is symbolized is a relation between *contents*, that is, between the *objects* designated by the terms flanking the identity sign, then a true statement of the form '$a = b$' would appear to say the same as one of the form '$a = a$'; yet the former may express genuine knowledge, whilst the latter is a mere tautology. However, the distinction between 'Sinn' and 'Bedeutung' enables this difficulty to be overcome, and hence removes the motivation for the *Begriffsschrift* construal. Identity is indeed a relation between objects, or *Bedeutungen*; the informativeness of identity statements is explained by difference in *Sinn*, or 'mode of presentation' of the *Bedeutung* (see pp. 151–2 below).

The distinction between *Sinn* and *Bedeutung* seems well motivated, at least in the case of names such as 'the Morning Star' and 'the Evening Star': two such names can refer to the same object (e.g. Venus), whilst doing so in different ways, reflecting different aspects of the object referred to (Venus can be seen in the morning, or in the evening).[47] However, even here, there is an apparent inconsistency in Frege's account of the distinction that has caused a certain amount of controversy, concerning the question whether a name can properly be said to have a sense if it lacks a referent. If the sense of a name is a 'mode of presentation' of its referent, as Frege's explanation at the beginning of 'On *Sinn* and *Bedeutung*' suggests, then this implies that if there is no referent, then there can be no 'mode of presentation' of it, and hence no sense. Yet Frege frequently remarks that names can have senses without referents. He states this quite explicitly in 'On *Sinn* and *Bedeutung*' itself, citing 'the least rapidly convergent series' as an example of a name that has a sense but demonstrably no *Bedeutung* (see p. 153 below). Fictional names such as 'Odysseus', though, provide his usual examples of names with sense but no *Bedeutung*;[48] and this has led some to suggest that it is only in fictional discourse that, to use Frege's words, 'sense is

---

[47] I justify my use of the verb 'refer to' in discussing Frege's ideas here in the next section.

[48] See e.g. *SB*, p. 157 below; *PMC*, pp. 152–3 (pp. 255–7 below); *PMC*, pp. 164–5 (pp. 290–2 below); *IL*, pp. 293–4 below. To avoid empty names in the case of a logically perfect language, Frege suggests that we can simply stipulate that their referent is the number 0 (cf. *SB*, p. 163 below). In *GG*, Frege introduces a special function to effect just this; see Appendix 2 below.

independent of whether there is a *Bedeutung* (cf. p. 291 below), and that what we have here are not real thoughts but only 'mock thoughts'.[49] However, even when talking of 'mock thoughts', Frege does not deny that they *are* thoughts, but merely wishes to record that they are not to be taken 'seriously', i.e. that they are not thoughts for which it is appropriate to seek their truth-value (since they lack one). And were we to find out that a fictional name did, after all, have a *Bedeutung*, then, as Frege puts it, 'The thoughts would strictly remain the same; they would only be transposed from the realm of fiction to that of truth'.[50] Frege's appeal to fictional discourse is clearly intended to *substantiate* the independence thesis – that sense is independent of *Bedeutung* – and does not merely serve to circumscribe the area to which its applicability is restricted.

But if this is right, then how is the conflict between the conception of senses as 'modes of presentation' and the independence thesis to be resolved? What we need to do here is to reinstate Frege's earlier talk of 'modes of determination', and allow ourselves to distinguish between 'modes of determination' and 'modes of presentation'.[51] To talk of 'modes of determination' is to talk of 'routes' to referents,[52] or less metaphorically, of 'conditions' that something must meet to be the referent of a given name;[53] and it may well turn out that there is nothing at the end of the journey, i.e. that meets the condition. On Frege's view, then, it is 'modes of determination' that are the fundamental type of sense, 'modes of presentation' being 'modes of determination' plus something else – the referents of the names being appropriately present. Frege readily utilized both conceptions, but failed to distinguish them, just because of his overriding concern with the 'realm of truth', that is, with logical or scientific contexts, where the propositions involved are taken to be true (i.e. to themselves have a *Bedeutung*). It is for these contexts that his logical language was devised, and here, as Frege did indeed stress, the use of names *presupposes* that they have referents.[54] Certainly, in mathematics, and on Frege's assumption that there are mathematical

---

[49] Evans (1982: ch. 1), in particular, has argued for this view. Frege himself talks of 'mock thoughts' ('Scheingedanke') in *PWLB*, p. 130 (cited by Evans on p. 29); p. 230 below. Cf. *PMC*, p. 152 (p. 256 below); *T*, p. 330 below. For criticism of Evans' 'Russellian' interpretation of Frege, see Bell, 1990b.

[50] *IL*, p. 293 below. Cf. *SB*, p. 157 below: 'The thought remains the same whether "Odysseus" has a *Bedeutung* or not'.

[51] On the need for this distinction, cf. Beaney, 1996: §6.3; Simons, 1995.

[52] Frege himself uses the metaphor of senses as 'routes' to referents in e.g. *OCN*, p. 85, senses indicating 'different ways in which it is possible for us to arrive at the same thing'. Cf. Dummett, 1981a: p. 96.

[53] For this conception of the sense of an expression, cf. Dummett, 1976; Bell, 1984.

[54] Cf. *DPE*, p. 60: 'The rules of logic always presuppose that the words we use are not empty, that our sentences express judgements, that one is not playing a mere game with words'.

objects, the distinction seems unnecessary. Since mathematical objects are regarded as 'independent' ('selbständig'), talk of 'modes of presentation' seems appropriate; but since we do not have access to these objects independently of our powers of conceptualization (we cannot, for example, just 'see' them), 'modes of presentation' are equally 'modes of determination'.[55] Nevertheless, it must still be emphasized that, on Frege's view, expressions in the 'realm of truth', i.e. in logic or science, have a referent *not* in virtue of their having a sense, but in virtue of their being 'logical' or 'scientific'.

However, even if we restrict ourselves to the 'realm of truth', where the distinction between 'modes of presentation' and 'modes of determination' is elided, Frege's conception of the *Sinn* and *Bedeutung* of names is still open to a second objection. 'The Morning Star' and 'the Evening Star' can both refer to Venus, and '6 + 1' and '8 − 1' can both refer to the number 7, and 'the pupil of Plato and teacher of Alexander the Great' and 'the teacher of Alexander the Great who was born in Stagira' can both refer to Aristotle, whilst doing so in different ways, their senses reflecting the way in which their referents are 'presented' or 'determined'; but what is the sense of the expressions 'Venus', '7' and 'Aristotle' themselves? What Frege called 'proper names' ('Eigennamen') included what we now term 'definite descriptions', such as 'the Morning Star', as well as 'simple' or 'genuine' proper names, such as 'Aristotle'; and whilst Frege's distinction between *Sinn* and *Bedeutung* applies very well in the case of definite descriptions, it is more problematic in the case of 'simple' proper names. The dilemma that confronts Frege with regard to 'simple' names can be easily stated. Either such names have no sense at all, but purely *refer*; or else they are to be treated as *disguised* definite descriptions, i.e. as abbreviations of more complex expressions which make clearer the 'mode of presentation' or 'mode of determination' that is their sense.[56] But in the latter case, if these complex expressions are themselves made up of 'simple' expressions that in turn are disguised definite descriptions, then we are threatened with either infinite regress or circularity, and our understanding of language would appear to be totally ungrounded.[57] There is no doubt that Frege rejects the first horn:

[55] Geometrical points, for example, are 'determined' or 'presented' as intersections of lines; and numbers too can be 'presented' by 'determining' their position in the number sequence relative to another number, e.g. as its successor.

[56] Examples of such disguised definite descriptions are 'Hesperus' and 'Phosphorus', which are indeed conventionally taken as abbreviating 'the Evening Star' and 'the Morning Star', respectively.

[57] E.g. if by 'John Stuart Mill' we mean 'the son of James Mill', then either 'James Mill' is defined as 'the father of John Stuart Mill', in which case we have a circularity, or else it is defined in some other way, in which case an infinite regress threatens – which can only be halted by the emergence of a more complex circularity (involving more than two names) further down the definitional path.

since the sense of a sentence is dependent on the senses of its parts, if a sentence has a sense, then any component name, however simple, must itself have a sense. Does he, then, equate the sense of a 'simple' name with the sense of some corresponding definite description? This is certainly what is suggested by his notorious 'Aristotle' footnote at the beginning of 'On *Sinn* and *Bedeutung*' (see p. 153 below; and cf. *T*, pp. 332–3 below). But aside from being open to the logical objection just raised, such a view concerning the sense of a 'simple' name has obvious counterintuitive implications. For let us assume that someone does indeed equate the sense of 'Aristotle' with the sense, say, of 'the pupil of Plato and teacher of Alexander the Great'; then presumably, for that person, the statement 'Aristotle is the pupil of Plato and the teacher of Alexander the Great' will be *analytic*.[58] Yet this is quite implausible: at least for the vast majority of definite descriptions applicable to Aristotle, that such a description applies to Aristotle seems a *contingent* truth, and hence clearly cannot be analytic.[59]

Now it might be replied that Frege's main point in this footnote was just to highlight how far short ordinary language falls of the ideal logical language that he was primarily concerned to develop, and that any objections that might be raised to his account of sense only reveal the inadequacies of ordinary language. The fact that there might be disagreement over what statements about Aristotle count as 'analytic' shows that ordinary proper names cannot be simply incorporated into a logical system without having their sense uniquely defined. But Frege's criticism of ordinary language here does not in itself rule out interpreting him as offering a 'description theory' of proper names. As in the case of fictional names, it may be that the appeal to ordinary proper names was intended to reinforce his conception of sense, not merely to circumscribe the limits of its applicability. The point of the footnote is to make clear that, in the case of an ordinary proper name, there is typically no *unique* definite description that supplies *the* sense of the name. Only in an ideal language can the demand for uniqueness be satisfied, and here we are indeed happy with 'analytic' definitions at its core.[60] In the case of Frege's

---

[58] If any proposition of the form '*A* is *B*' is analytic, it is surely one where '*A*' and '*B*' have exactly the same sense.

[59] It is Kripke, in his seminal work *Naming and Necessity* (1980), who has most strongly pressed this objection to a 'description theory' of proper names, by considering the use of such names in modal contexts – although Kripke does think that there are some definite descriptions, concerning its causal origin, that yield necessary (though *not* analytic or *a priori*) truths about a given object.

[60] The term 'analytic' must be used here with caution. As mentioned in fn. 46 above, after *GL* Frege does not himself use the term, for one very good reason: with the *Sinn/Bedeutung* distinction in place, it is by no means clear that his logicist definitions and axioms embody the sameness of sense that would seem to be a condition of their 'analyticity'. What underlies the problem here is the so-called *paradox of analysis*, which

reconstruction of arithmetic, for example, the natural numbers are explicitly defined in terms of extensions of concepts, the number 0 being identified with the extension of the concept 'equinumerous to the concept *not identical with itself*', from which the other numbers can then be successively defined (see pp. 118–20 below). Of course, the logical objection raised above must then be faced; and Frege's answer here is that the complex expressions used in the definitions are understood in virtue of grasping the concept *not identical with itself* and other such *logical* concepts, which he assumes we know if we can think at all. Furthermore, as we have seen, our apprehension of extensions of concepts as objects is taken as guaranteed by our acceptance of Axiom V.

However, even here, as the problems with Axiom V show, Frege's conception is fundamentally flawed, and despite his assumption that the chain of definitions could be grounded on logical notions, there did indeed turn out to be a circularity at the very basis of his system.[61] The supposition that a logical system can somehow pull itself up by its own bootstraps is incoherent; any logical system must be grounded on something external to it, and this can only be mediated by the use of ordinary language. But this then means that we cannot brush aside the problems confronting a 'description theory' of proper names in ordinary language.[62] For if people typically associate *different* senses with the 'simple' names they use, then the thoughts that different people express by names of those names will also differ, threatening the objectivity of thought on which Frege laid so much stress throughout his life – at least where objectivity is taken to imply *communicability*. And the logical objection must again be faced: how is the infinite regress of definitions to be avoided without circularity?

At this point, if we wish to retain Frege's basic distinction between *Sinn* and *Bedeutung*, but still provide an account of the sense of 'simple' names that makes genuine room for the objectivity of thought, and allows it to be grounded satisfactorily, then we are going to have to modify Frege's account. One approach, which has recently been developed with some sophistication, relies upon the concept of *knowing which* – a form of knowing which involves having a *discriminating conception* of an object.

Frege did indeed recognize (see *RH*, pp. 224–6 below, and *LM*, pp. 308–18 below), but to which he failed to provide a satisfactory response. I discuss the issue in some detail in Beaney, 1996: ch. 5 and §8.5.

[61] See fn. 41 above, and the references cited there.

[62] Of course, even if there were no problems with the logical system of *GG*, the question of the applicability of Frege's ideas to ordinary language would still arise – a question that has greatly occupied Frege's successors, and which naturally arises as a result of exploring Frege's work. It is frequently remarked that Frege should not be seen as a philosopher of language, in anything like the modern sense, and whilst this is right, this is not to say that thinking through Frege's ideas does not lead us into the concerns of modern philosophy of language.

On this view, I grasp the sense of an ordinary proper name if I know *which object* is referred to, knowledge that enables me to distinguish that object from other things and that may be manifested in any number of different ways.[63] Such an approach allows us to preserve what is often regarded as one of Frege's central insights – that the referent of a name can only be apprehended through some particular means of identification. As Frege himself puts it, 'it is via a sense, and only via a sense, that a proper name is related to an object' (see p. 180 below). In the 'Aristotle' footnote, Frege suggests that different people may attach *different* senses to the name 'Aristotle', since they may have different means of identifying him; but there is no need to take this line in order to respect the insight just mentioned. So long as each person has *some* means of identification, it does not matter *which* means it is. In the case of 'simple' names there is no *one way* of identifying the referent which a person must possess in order to be attributed a grasp of the sense of the name. The point can be clarified by distinguishing the following two theses:

(MIS)   There is some particular means of identifying the referent of a name that is possessed by anyone who grasps its sense.

(SMI)   Anyone who grasps the sense of a name possesses some particular means of identifying the referent.

What is involved here is an elementary scope distinction. Although (MIS) – where the existential quantifier has wider scope than the universal quantifier – might be appropriate for definite description, (SMI) – where the universal quantifier has wider scope – is all that is required in the case of 'simple' names.[64] Grasp of the sense of 'Aristotle', in other words, can be *shown* by *saying* what its referent is in any number of different ways: which person is referred to may be indicated by stating that he is the pupil of Plato and teacher of Alexander the Great, or the teacher of Alexander the Great who was born in Stagira, or by means of any other uniquely identifying description. Expressing the matter like this at least preserves something of Frege's idea in the 'Aristotle' footnote.[65]

[63] Cf. Wiggins, 1975, 1976; McDowell, 1977, 1984; and especially Evans, 1982.

[64] Compare this with the scope distinction drawn on p. 12 above in explaining the significance of quantifier notation: we have a good example of its usefulness here. Whilst (MIS) is of $\exists\forall$ form, (SMI) is of $\forall\exists$ form. That Frege's own tools are being used to refine his own ideas is a testament to his logical achievement.

[65] Cf. Dummett, 1981a: p. 227: 'for Frege, we *say* what the referent of a word is, and thereby *show* what its sense is'. (The distinction between *saying* and *showing* is taken from Wittgenstein's *Tractatus*.) McDowell (1977) and Evans (1982: ch. 1), in particular, have developed this idea, building also on Davidson's work (see especially Davidson, 1967), in arguing that a theory of sense (theory of meaning) can be based on a theory of reference (theory of truth), so long as the axioms that assign referents to terms do so in an appropriate way, *showing* the sense of the terms. Evans (p. 16, fn. 14), albeit in a slightly different context, draws a similar distinction to that drawn here between (MIS) and (SMI); cf. Dummett, 1975: p. 130.

Nevertheless, it must be emphasized that what is being offered here amounts to a *revision* of Frege's conception of the sense of proper names. The failure to distinguish between definite description and 'simple' names is, in itself, easily rectified; and the scope distinction just drawn seems subtle enough to suggest that only a minor refinement is being made. But if we look more closely at the two theses, we can see that their implications are significantly different. For whilst (MIS) licenses *identifying* the sense of a name with a particular means of identification (a 'mode of presentation'), which – to someone with Platonist inclinations – might itself be regarded as some kind of object, (SMI) does not. But if (MIS) is rejected in the case of 'simple' names, what then *is* the sense of such a name? Frege himself was indeed led into treating senses as objects, but (SMI) seems quite incompatible with such a view. Grasp of the sense of a name, according to the conception captured in (SMI), consists not in apprehending some *object* that is the sense, but in an *ability* – the ability to distinguish the object that is its *referent*.[66] Now it might be argued that this remains consistent with Frege's fundamental assumption, mentioned above, that objectivity requires objects: all that has been abandoned is the idea that objectivity of senses requires that *senses* be objects. But this nevertheless represents a significant departure from Frege's own views; for what we have here is objectivism without the Platonism towards which Frege was pulled. Our use of language is indeed grounded, but on the referents of our 'simple' terms and on our ordinary linguistic practices, not on any mysterious abstract entities.

We can now see why, in revising Frege's conception in order to provide a more satisfactory account of the sense of 'simple' names, there is a great temptation to read him as insisting that senses *require* there to be referents, at least in the 'realm of truth'. For on this reading, the revision looks less radical and the account more 'Fregean' than is actually the case. But whilst the approach just sketched may be the right line to take, we are not aiding our understanding of Frege if we attribute to him conceptions that were only present in his thought, at best, in an embryonic form, conceptions that in fact conflict with other views of his that were more fully developed. Of course, the attraction of Frege's conception of senses as 'modes of presentation' of referents has often been felt to lie precisely in the possibility it opens up of *avoiding* positing senses as independent objects which we must somehow apprehend in addition to their referents. But that Frege did not pursue this path comes out clearly, firstly, in his account of intensional contexts in 'On *Sinn* and *Bedeutung*', where senses are regarded as the *indirect referents*

[66] That understanding the meaning of an expression should be seen as an *ability* is something that Wittgenstein came to emphasize in his later work, precisely in response to the mythology of senses that he saw as underlying both Frege's thought and his own earlier philosophy (heavily influenced by Frege).

of expressions, and secondly, in his late essay 'Der Gedanke'.[67] I shall say something about each in turn.

Frege held that the *Bedeutung* of a complex expression is determined by the *Bedeutungen* of its parts;[68] and his conception of senses as indirect referent arises as a result of defending this principle against an objection concerning its application in *intensional* contexts (i.e. contexts involving the ascription of a propositional attitude – '*X* knows that *p*', '*X* believes that *p*', etc.). Consider the following two propositions:

(GMM) Gottlob believes that the Morning Star is the Morning Star.
(GME) Gottlob believes that the Morning Star is the Evening Star.

(GMM) may clearly be true without (GME) being true, despite the fact that 'the Morning Star' and 'the Evening Star' (considered in normal contexts) refer to the same object, i.e. have the same *Bedeutung* (i.e. despite the fact that both embedded identity statements are true, i.e. have the same *Bedeutung*). But if the component parts all have the same *Bedeutung*, then (GMM) and (GME) ought also to have the same *Bedeutung*, i.e. the same truth-value, if Frege's principle holds. However, rather than repudiating the principle, or restricting its applicability to extensional contexts, Frege denies that in intensional contexts the *Bedeutung* of an expression remains the same as it is in extensional contexts; instead, its intensional or *indirect Bedeutung* becomes its *customary* sense (see *SB*, p. 154 below). In other words, in (GME), for example, the *Bedeutung* of 'the Morning Star is the Evening Star' is the sense or *thought* that this identity statement expresses in normal, extensional contexts; and this is clearly different from the thought expressed by 'the Morning Star is the Morning Star'. Frege's strategy here seems reasonable, for we surely do want to say that the truth-value of propositions such as (GMM) or (GME) depends on what *thought* is expressed (in extensional contexts) by the embedded sentence. To make this explicit, (GMM) and (GME) might be rephrased as follows:

(GMM′) Gottlob holds as true the thought expressed by 'the Morning Star is the Morning Star'.

---

[67] A third source for the conception of senses as objects might also be suggested here. For in Frege's later ontology, the only other possibility is that senses are concepts; yet talk of '*the* sense' of an expression, on Frege's view, indicates an object, not a concept. However, Frege admitted that use of terms of the form '*the* concept *F*' generated problems for this view (cf. *CO*, pp. 181–93 below); so such linguistic considerations cannot in themselves be regarded as conclusive.

[68] The principle is implicit in *SB* (see especially pp. 156–9 below), and is stated more explicitly in his later work (cf. fn. 37 above). I say more about Frege's conception of the *Bedeutung* of expressions in the next section.

(GME′)   Gottlob holds as true the thought expressed by 'the Morning
          Star is the Evening Star'.

In stating what someone believes, I refer to the *thoughts* that they hold
as true; and these thoughts just are, according to Frege, the senses of
the appropriate sentences.

Now Frege's doctrine of indirect *Bedeutung* has proved as controversial as any other aspect of his theory of *Sinn* and *Bedeutung*; and the
problem of providing a satisfactory account of intensional contexts has
generated a huge literature.[69] But here the point is only to emphasize just
how deeply integrated the conception of senses as objects was in Frege's
philosophy, and indeed, given his other views, just how well-motivated
it seems to be. For if we can *refer* to thoughts, is it not plausible to treat
them as *objects*? Can someone else's thought not be the *object* of my own
thought? And if thoughts are objective, and I can share other people's
thoughts, then must there not be *something* that we are sharing? That
the answer to these questions is positive comes out most clearly of all in
Frege's late paper 'Der Gedanke', where he does indeed feel compelled
to adopt a strong form of Platonism about senses in order to do their
objectivity justice. Since thoughts undoubtedly exist, according to Frege,
the central question is what kind of objects they are. Frege argues that
they can be neither *physical* objects, because thoughts cannot themselves
be perceived, nor *mental* objects, i.e. ideas, since thoughts must be distinguished from ideas if we are to avoid the absurdities of psychologism
(see pp. 334–6 below).[70] He was led to conclude that thoughts had to
be treated as a distinct kind of object, located in a 'third realm'. We might
call this metaphysical thesis – that thoughts inhabit a separate realm of
their own – Frege's *semainomenalism*.[71] If phenomenalism is the view that
the world of phenomena (ideas, sense impressions, sensations, etc.) is
the primary reality, and noumenalism is the view that the noumenal world

---

[69] Besides distinguishing between customary and indirect *Bedeutung*, Frege also distinguishes between customary and indirect *sense*; and this raises the possibility of an infinite
hierarchy of *Bedeutungen* and senses. Frege may well have accepted this possibility, just
as he countenanced an infinite hierarchy of functions, each with a corresponding value-
range; but many have attempted to find ways of avoiding it. Cf. especially Dummett,
1981a: ch. 9; 1981b: ch. 6; Parsons, 1980; and for further discussion of the problem of
intensionality, see especially the papers collected in Salmon and Soames, 1988.

[70] Frege was deeply hostile to psychologism throughout his life. His repudiation of it was
reflected in the first of the three 'fundamental principles' of *GL*: 'There must be a sharp
separation of the psychological from the logical, the subjective from the objective' (see
p. 90 below); and unlike the second, the context principle, this first principle was constantly reaffirmed in his later work. See especially *GG*, I, Introd., pp. 202–7 below. For
discussion of Frege's anti-psychologism in its historical context, see Kusch, 1995.

[71] Cf. Beaney, 1996: §7.5. The introduction of this term is prompted by the ancient Stoic
conception of *semainomena* – the things signified or expressed by words, of which the
most important were *lekta*, distant ancestors of Fregean *thoughts*; cf. Beaney, 1996: §1.5.

(the realm of things in themselves) is the ultimate reality, then semaino-menalism can be defined as the view that it is the world of meanings or senses that has a fundamental status. Typically, the noumenalist will believe in the existence of a world of phenomena as well, but will hold that such a world is ontologically secondary; and so too the semaino-menalist may believe in the existence of other worlds – in Frege's case, both the physical and mental worlds (the 'first' and 'second' realms) – but will still regard the semainomenal world, just as Plato conceived his Forms, as intellectually purer and more basic.[72]

The particular characteristic of the semainomenal world that grants it its privileged status is the *timelessness* of its inhabitants. What this means for Frege is that thoughts are understood as the senses of 'complete' sentences (see pp. 343–4 below) – sentences in which all indexicality, we might say, has been 'cashed out'.[73] The idea can be illustrated by considering the following sentence involving the indexical 'today':

(TS)   Today is sunny.

Uttered today, this clearly expresses a different thought from that that would be expressed if it were uttered tomorrow (one might be true and the other false). So the sentence on its own does not fully express the thought: to grasp the 'complete' thought, we also need to take into account the *context of utterance*. But if we do so, then the following might be offered as expressing the thought in a more complete form, cashing out the indexical by substituting the exact date:

(DS)   14 June 1996 is sunny.

Of course, if this is to work, then the 'is' here must be understood *time-lessly*, i.e. in the sense in which the 'is' in '3 is a prime number' is under-stood, since taken as a verb in the present tense, it must be replaced by 'was' when someone wants to express the thought on a later day and would have had to be replaced by 'will be' had someone expressed the thought on an earlier day (cf. pp. 331–2, 343–4 below).

---

[72] As these positions are envisaged here, Hume and Mach, for example, would count as phenomenalists, Berkeley, Leibniz and Kant as noumenalists, and Plato, Meinong and Frege as semainomenalists.

[73] *Indexicals*, or *demonstratives* as they are also called, are expressions such as 'I', 'you', 'here', 'there', 'now', 'then', 'this', or 'that', whose reference depends systematically on the context. 'Gottlob Frege' or 'the author of the *Begriffsschrift*' as used by me today is likely to refer to the same person as when used by you tomorrow, but the referent of 'I' depends on *who* is using the word, and the referent of 'today' depends on *when* the word is used. An understanding of the *context* of utterance is thus essential in determining the truth-value of any sentence using a demonstrative; and it is this context-dependence that constitutes the phenomenon of indexicality.

Now the first point to note here is that (DS) is still not fully 'complete', since we clearly need to say *where* it is sunny, and perhaps also be more precise as to the time:

(DSL)   At noon on 14 June 1996 it is sunny in Leeds.

But there is implicit indexicality here too, for the time has been specified relative to the Christian calendar, and 'Leeds' is being assumed to refer to the city in England. Clearly, the process of cashing out indexicality can go on indefinitely, and if every sentence contains *some* indexicality, then there can be no such thing as a 'complete' articulation of the thought involved.[74] It is hardly surprising that Frege was led to locate thoughts, as 'complete' and 'timeless' entities, in an ethereal realm: they would seem, necessarily, to transcend our human powers of articulating them.

However, even if we allow that (DS) cashes out *some* of the indexicality in (TS), do the utterances of (TS) and (DS) today really express the same thought? Surely it is perfectly possible to think that today is sunny without knowing what date it is? And if it is possible to hold one sentence as true but not the other (perhaps by being mistaken about the date), then, by Frege's own criterion for sameness of sense,[75] they cannot express the same thought. Since the same will apply to any attempt to cash out an indexical by means of some definite description, the whole idea of filling out a sentence to capture the thought expressed on a given occasion of use in a more 'complete' form breaks down.[76]

Yet Frege himself clearly does allow that the thought expressed by an utterance of (TS) today can be expressed in a different form on a

[74] This clearly holds for *contingent* truths; but it surely also holds for *necessary* truths. For does '3 is a prime number', for example, not need to be filled out as 'In the system of natural numbers, 3 is a prime number', and so on?

[75] There has been some controversy over just what Frege's criterion for sameness of sense is. Frege was uncharacteristically reluctant to specify such a criterion, and there are just two occasions on which he does so in anything like a careful form, both as it happens in the same year, 1906 (see pp. 299–300 and 305–6 below). But even then, the criteria he offers seem in conflict, one appearing to ground sameness of sense on what Frege calls 'equipollence', understood epistemically, and the other on logical equivalence. Elsewhere, more loosely, Frege talks of two propositions having *different* senses if one can be held to be true and not the other (see e.g. p. 321 below), which is consistent with the former criterion (with suitable qualifications); and it is this to which appeal is being made here. However, on none of the occasions when he formulates or alludes to a criterion does Frege take indexicality into account (do the propositions involved have to be 'complete' propositions?); so the applicability of any such criterion to the present case must remain problematic. But this only reinforces the main point here: that indexicality generates particular difficulties for Frege's conception of sense. For discussion of Frege's criteria, see the references cited in fn. 3 on p. 299 below.

[76] It is this that Perry (1979) has called *the problem of the essential indexical*.

different day. He specifically states that to express the same thought tomorrow I will have to use the following sentence (cf. p. 332 below):

(Y₁S)   Yesterday was sunny.

Just as in his early work Frege emphasized that the same 'content' can be represented by more than one sentence, so too in his later work he was insistent that the same thought can be expressed in many different ways. Clearly, in the case of thoughts expressed using an indexical, or *dynamic* thoughts as they have been called, indexical substitution is essential if there is to be any possibility of *keeping track* of such thoughts.[77] To express tomorrow the thought that today is sunny, I will have to say 'Yesterday was sunny'; the day after tomorrow, I will have to say 'The day before yesterday was sunny'; and so on. But does the 'and so on' here not hide the real problem? What am I to say in a week's time? Taking the 'and so on' literally, I might use the following:

(Y₇S)   The day before the day before the day before the day before the day before the day before yesterday was sunny.

But there is obviously a better sentence, which abbreviates this:

(LFS)   Last Friday was sunny.

However, this assumes grasp of the concept of a *day of the week*, and we seem back with our original problem. For I can surely think that today is sunny without knowing what day of the week it is, so that the use of (LFS) would seem to introduce something new into the thought. The point is quite obvious if we consider how the thought would be expressed in a few years' time: to express the thought as succinctly as possible, I am surely going to have to help myself to the concept of a *date* and use (DS) again.

There appears, then, to be no sharp dividing line between the use of 'today' and the use of dates, i.e. no obvious point at which our original thought 'becomes' a different thought as tracking it proceeds. There is thus clearly pressure to treat both (TS) and (DS) as expressing the *same* thought. But such a thought must then be conceived of as sufficiently

---

[77] The terms come from Evans (1981). Commenting on Frege's example here, Evans writes: 'Frege's idea is that being in the same epistemic state may require different things of us at different times; the changing circumstances force us to change in order to keep hold of a constant reference and a constant thought – we must run to keep still' (p. 308). Calling such a thought a *dynamic* thought, he goes on: 'the *way of thinking of an object* to which the general Fregean conception of sense directs us is, in the case of a dynamic Fregean thought, a *way of keeping track of an object*' (p. 311).

abstracted from its linguistic expression as to make the variety of its articulations possible. Yet the Platonism that this suggests conflicts with our ordinary understanding of 'thoughts', whose individuation, we suppose, depends on the concepts utilized in their articulation. Certainly, if the thought expressed by a sentence depends on the senses of its components, and senses are 'modes of presentation', then, since conceiving of today simply as today and conceiving of it as the date it is seem rather different, the two corresponding thoughts would seem to be different.

The tension revealed here is most acute of all in the case of the indexical 'I', which Frege himself admits raises particular problems (see pp. 332–3 below). According to Frege, we are each presented to ourselves in a 'special and primitive way', suggesting that thoughts expressed about ourselves by means of 'I' cannot be grasped by anyone else. This seems in clear conflict with the objectivity of thoughts upon which Frege placed so much emphasis throughout his work. Are there purely subjective thoughts after all? Yet Frege still maintains that something is communicated when I express a thought using 'I', something which someone else might express by using my name. But he nevertheless insists that the thought that someone else might so express is different from my own I-thought. So what exactly is the relationship between these two thoughts, and what precisely is it that is communicated in such cases? Frege's account of I-thoughts takes up less than two pages, and raises far more questions than it answers. But once again we can see the difficulties that indexicality poses for Frege's conception of sense.[78]

Clearly, (TS) and (DS), as uttered today, have *something* in common – they both 'refer to', as we might put it, the same event (the sun's shining on a particular day). According to Frege, however, the 'reference' or 'Bedeutung' of a sentence is its *truth-value*, and although the two sentences may indeed share this 'Bedeutung', it is something that is also shared by any other sentence with the same truth-value. (TS) and (DS) have something else in common than mere truth-value; yet the only other possibility, in Frege's ontology, is the *thought* they express. It is hardly surprising, then, if there is a temptation to treat (TS) and (DS) as expressing the *same* thought. Clearly, if we had some other notion, finer-grained than the notion of 'Bedeutung' yet coarser-grained than Frege's original notion of 'Sinn' (as introduced in 'On *Sinn* and *Bedeutung*'), we might be able to do better justice to the similarities and differences here. An obvious candidate is Frege's early notion of 'conceptual content', which, if a metaphysical gloss could be put on the notion, might be best characterized as referring to a 'state of affairs',

---

[78] For discussion of these difficulties, see Perry, 1977, 1979; Burge, 1979; Dummett, 1981b: ch. 6; Evans, 1981; Yourgrau, 1982; McGinn, 1983: ch. 5; Noonan, 1984; Forbes, 1987; Beaney, 1996: §§7.5, 8.3.

'event' or 'circumstance'.[79] We could then say that (TS) and (DS) have both the same truth-value *and* the same 'content', whilst expressing *different* 'thoughts', involving as they do different concepts in their articulation.[80] Treating the thoughts expressed as different is at least better in line with Frege's usual criterion for sameness of sense.[81] Once again, it seems, what is required here are finer distinctions than Frege himself drew. And if we do introduce a further notion to do the work that Frege's later notion of 'thought' seems intended to do, then we can reject, or at least avoid the Platonist implications of, Frege's conception of senses as objects.

Let me conclude this section by noting an important connection between the two issues that we have briefly discussed here. For let us assume that we do indeed have some way of specifying what it is for two expressions to have the same sense, and let us simply label the relationship involved here 'cognitive equivalence'. Then we can immediately offer the following 'contextual definition' of 'sense':

(Sa)   Expression 'A' is cognitively equivalent to expression 'B'.
(Sb)   The sense of 'A' is identical with the sense of 'B'.

Of course, the legitimacy of such a 'contextual definition' depends on (Sa) being definable without appeal to the concept of 'sense'; but an obvious suggestion as to how this might be done emerges from 'On *Sinn* and *Bedeutung*' itself:

(Sa')   Expression 'A' is intersubstitutable *salva veritate* in all intensional contexts with expression 'B'.[82]

The connection between Frege's use of the context principle and his conception of senses as objects is now clear, for if the analogy with

---

[79] See e.g. *BS*, §2 (p. 53 below; cf. §§3, 9), where Frege talks of 'circumstances' ('Umstände') as being judgeable contents. Cf. Dummett, 1981b: pp. 176f.; Currie, 1984: §2. Dummett comments on the debate between Grossmann (1969: ch. 1), who had criticized Frege for not including states of affairs in his ontology, and Kluge (1970), who had argued that they *were* included. The right answer seems to be that they were included at the time of *BS*, but were later regarded as *true thoughts*, inhabiting the realm of sense rather than *Bedeutung*. Reintroducing 'states of affairs' is not, of course, without its own difficulties: problems with negative, general and existential propositions are notorious. The point here is only to highlight the conceptual space between the notions of truth-value and thought.

[80] Another way of putting this point would be to say that Frege confused the *object* of a thought with its *content* (cf. Dummett, 1986), where the *object* of a thought is what is here called 'content' (the translation of Frege's early notion of 'Inhalt'), and the *content* of a thought is what is here called the 'thought' itself.

[81] Cf. fn. 75 above.

[82] I ignore here the complications that arise from admitting a hierarchy of senses (cf. fn. 69 above). To avoid circularity, of course, the notion of an 'intensional context' must itself be defined without appeal to the notion of 'sense'.

Axiom V holds, then the truth of (Sa'), on Frege's view, guarantees that the relevant terms for senses have referents. However, if, as suggested above, what the strategy of contextual definition really opens up is the possibility of *eliminating* the need to suppose that the abstract terms so defined have a reference, realistically construed, then what we actually have here is a way of avoiding treating senses as independent objects, whilst maintaining objectivity about senses – to the extent that (Sa) can be satisfactorily defined.[83] Securing objectivism without Platonism is arguably the central problem that Frege's work poses; and appreciating the interconnections between the elements of Frege's thought, as well as the difficulties that his views encounter, is the first step towards providing an answer.

4. The Translation of 'Bedeutung'

Few terms in the history of philosophy have given rise to as much controversy over their translation into English as Frege's term 'Bedeutung', as used in his work from the 1890s, in particular. Aristotle's notion of *eudaimonia* and Hegel's notion of *Geist* have been vigorously debated for a longer period of time; but even here there is not the range of cognate terms to exacerbate the problem. 'Bedeutung' has been variously translated as 'reference', 'denotation', 'meaning', 'significance', 'indication' and 'nominatum'; and 'semantic value', 'semantic role', and 'truth-value potential' have also been used in explaining what Frege had in mind in his later work. The verb 'bedeuten' has been translated as 'refer to', 'denote', 'stand for', 'mean', 'signify' and 'indicate'; and there are other terms such as 'bedeutungslos', 'bedeutungsvoll' and 'gleichbedeutend' that need to be taken into account in deciding on a policy. It is fair to say that 'reference' and 'refer to' have been the most widely endorsed; but 'meaning' and its cognates were the terms that were adopted when it was decided to standardize the translation of key terms across the various editions of Frege's works that were published by Blackwell.[84] Given the controversy that this caused, some comment on it is appropriate here.

---

[83] (Sa'), for example, might be taken to indicate that what is basic is our *use* of language – in particular, our practices of intersubstituting words – as constrained by our judgements as to the truth-value of propositions, in ascribing beliefs, etc. to people.

[84] The decision was taken at a meeting in the early 1970s attended by Michael Dummett, Peter Geach, William Kneale, Roger White and a representative from Blackwell. The translation of 'Bedeutung' by 'meaning' was unanimously agreed after lengthy discussion. (Dummett had used 'meaning' himself in his 1967 article on Frege, though he reverted to 'reference' in *Frege: Philosophy of Language*, which appeared in 1973). I am grateful to Roger White for this information.

'Meaning' and its cognates were first used in the translation of Frege's *Posthumous Writings* by Peter Long and Roger White; and the criticism it immediately prompted led to a detailed defence of the policy.[85] The defence was based on what was called the *principle of exegetical neutrality*: 'if at any point in a text there is a passage that raises for the native speaker legitimate questions of exegesis, then, if at all possible, a translator should strive to confront the reader of his version with the same questions of exegesis and not produce a version which in his mind resolves those questions'.[86] Since 'meaning' does indeed best capture how 'Bedeutung' is normally used in German, and Frege's own use of 'Bedeutung' sounds as odd in German as 'meaning' does when used in translating his work into English, 'meaning' is the term to employ in respecting this principle. The use of any other term involves an interpretation of the text, and it is not the task of the translator to prejudge issues of exegesis. Now the obvious response to this is to point out that all translation involves interpretation, since it is, after all, the *sense* of the words, and not the mere words themselves, that a translator is trying to capture. So what, more specifically, makes interpreting 'Bedeutung' as anything other than 'meaning' inappropriate exegesis? Three particular arguments were offered in support of the policy. The first concerns Frege's use of 'Bedeutung' and its cognates *prior* to 1891, which was when the distinction between *Sinn* and *Bedeutung* first appeared and 'Bedeutung' first acquired its technical sense. Given that 'meaning' often does capture Frege's *early* use of 'Bedeutung' quite naturally and unproblematically, then if 'meaning' is used in translating his early work and 'reference', say, in translating his later work, then an impression is given of a radical change in terminology which does not appear to the German reader. Retaining 'meaning' avoids this problem. The second argument concerns Frege's use of 'Bedeutung' in his later work when it is either not clear that he is using it in his technical sense (perhaps, in the case of Frege's posthumously published writings, because the dating of the text itself is uncertain) or clear that he is not using it in his technical sense (for example, when expounding the views of others). To decide when Frege is or is not using 'Bedeutung' in his technical sense is to make an exegetical decision that it is not the task of the translator to make. Once again, these problems are avoided if 'meaning' is used throughout. The third argument concerns the use of terms such as 'Bedeutung', 'meaning' and 'reference' in the philosophical literature

---

[85] For criticism, see especially Bell, 1980; and for their response, Long and White, 1980.
[86] Long and White, 1980: p. 196. Bell had interpreted exegetical neutrality to require that 'every word of the original should be translated by its exact English equivalent (if there is one)', which he rightly pointed out 'is no sooner stated than seen to be false' (1980: p. 193). But, as Long and White replied, this is certainly a caricature of exegetical neutrality, and the principle just stated was their improved formulation.

after Frege. Frege's work was the single most important influence on Wittgenstein, for example, and not only is 'meaning' the natural translation of 'Bedeutung' as used by Wittgenstein, but some of what Wittgenstein said would make no sense at all if it were not so translated. And as far as the use of 'reference' is concerned, since Strawson's essay 'On Referring', in particular, talk of 'reference' may carry implications that would be quite inappropriate in the case of Frege's views, making 'reference' a potentially misleading term to the modern reader.

Responses can be made to all three arguments. With regard to Frege's early work, it is not true that 'meaning' and 'mean' are always the best terms to use in translating 'Bedeutung' and 'bedeuten'. Frege does use 'bedeuten', in particular, in the sense of 'refer to' or 'denote';[87] and it is arguably in this sense that Frege uses it, technically, in his later work. Using 'refer to' or 'denote' at the appropriate places in his early work, as well as in his later work, then, would also indicate the continuity of terminology, whilst the use of 'mean' elsewhere in his early work and its relative absence in his later work would highlight the change in his views. Of course, such an approach would involve more 'interpretation' than some might allow; but it might well be replied that it is just the kind of 'interpretation' that a translator *should* undertake in seeking to capture the sense of a philosopher's words. A similar response can be made to the second argument. Translators of philosophical texts are always having to make decisions as to when a term is being used in a technical sense or not; and where there is a genuine possibility of dispute the honest strategy is surely to record the decision – either by placing the original term in brackets after its translation, or by explaining the translation in a footnote. Long and White talk of the using of footnotes as a 'wretched expedient', but given the importance of the issue concerning 'Bedeutung', in particular, this might seem the only sensible policy. As to the third argument, this cuts both ways. Wittgenstein's use of 'Bedeutung' may suggest that 'meaning' is the best choice; but Russell's account of Frege's views in 'On Denoting' suggests quite the opposite. For Russell uses 'meaning' to translate 'Sinn', 'denotation' being used to render 'Bedeutung'.[88] Since many lecture courses in philosophical logic or the philosophy of language begin with Frege's essay 'On *Sinn* and *Bedeutung*', and then go on to Russell's theory of descriptions, the translation of 'Bedeutung' as 'meaning' is particularly confusing.

The principle of exegetical neutrality is only one of a number of principles that might be formulated to guide the translator, and as with any

---

[87] See e.g. *BS*, §5 (pp. 55–7 below).
[88] Russell had used 'indication' to translate 'Bedeutung' in his earlier account of Frege's views in Appendix A of *POM*.

principle its application must be balanced against the application of other principles. Translators are usually in a better position than most of their readers to know when a term is being used in a technical sense, or when questions of exegesis arise, and it seems reasonable to expect them to give their readers the benefit of that knowledge. Of course, others may disagree with their interpretive decisions; but as long as the problematic terms or exegetical questions are noted, there can be no real cause for complaint. What might be offered as equally important, in other words, is the *principle of interpretive integrity*: 'if at any point in a text there is a term or passage that raises legitimate questions of exegesis, then, whilst using their interpretive skills to offer the best translation they can, a translator should, if at all possible, note the original word(s) used and justify the translation offered, to enable the reader to make up their own mind about the issues involved'. Of course, this might be criticized as a licence to print footnotes; but judgement must clearly be exercised in its application: what footnotes will be appropriate will depend on the nature of the controversies, the purpose of the translation, the intended readership, and so on.

Nevertheless, it remains the case that 'meaning' *is* the most natural translation of 'Bedeutung', and that Frege's technical use of 'Bedeutung', particularly with regard to sentences, strikes a discordant note amongst native German speakers, which should not be toned down for English speakers. Talk of 'No men are mortal' and '2 + 2 = 5', for example, as having the same *Bedeutung* sounds bizarre to the German reader; talk of them as having the same *meaning* certainly sounds no less bizarre to the English reader.[89] But it might still be suggested that the use of 'meaning' *exacerbates* the problem for English speakers. If so, is there any other single term that might do the job instead? If there is no single alternative, and a policy is adopted of using different terms depending on the context, what are the relevant considerations? To answer these

---

[89] Bell appeals to the absurdity of such remarks, as expressed in English, in *criticizing* the translation of 'Bedeutung' as 'meaning': 'what could be more unattractive or confusing to the newcomer than to discover that a philosopher revered for his incisive clarity of style and for his profound insight into how language works, seems to believe that the sentence "no men are mortal" has the same meaning as the sentence "2 + 2 = 5"; or that every sentence of fiction is quite without meaning; or that the predicate "is a round square" is perfectly meaningful [because determinate], while the predicate "is a christian" is in fact meaningless [because vague]? It was presumably to avoid just such consequences as these that every translator, up to the present time, has avoided rendering "*Bedeutung*" as "meaning". They were, I think, not wrong to do so.' (1980: p. 195.) But, as Long and White reply (1980), Frege's own use of 'Bedeutung' strikes the German reader as eccentric. So the real question, as I go on to ask, is whether the use of 'meaning' makes Frege's views seem *more* eccentric to the English reader. Of course, using 'reference' instead does not *eliminate* the eccentricity: the question here is whether it reflects the eccentricity of Frege's own use of 'Bedeutung' better than 'meaning'.

questions, and to indicate some of the complexities involved, we need to
look more closely at the various uses of such terms as 'meaning', 'mean',
'reference' and 'refer to', and draw a number of distinctions. Perhaps
the first distinction to be drawn is between meaning as a *relation* and
meaning as an *object* (i.e. as the *thing meant*).[90] Understood as a relation,
a further distinction can then be drawn between meaning as a *horizontal*
relation and meaning as a *vertical* relation – depending on whether the
relata are in the same ontological category, i.e. on the same level, or
not. The verb 'mean' can itself, then, be used in either a horizontal or
a vertical sense. I use it in its horizontal sense in saying that 'bachelor'
means 'unmarried man', or that heavy clouds mean rain, for example; I
use it in its vertical sense in saying that 'the Philosopher' means Aristotle or that a word means the idea or thing it stands for. In the case
of explaining the 'meaning' of a linguistic expression, then, I can either
give an alternative linguistic expression, 'meaning' here being understood
as a horizontal relation, or specify its extra-linguistic correlate, 'meaning' here being understood as a vertical relation. This extra-linguistic
correlate can itself come to be called the 'meaning' of the expression,
'meaning' then being understood as an object, i.e. as the thing meant.

How do these distinctions apply in the case of other terms? A verb
such as 'signify', it seems, also has both a horizontal and a vertical sense,
whereas verbs such as 'connote' or 'imply' have a predominantly horizontal sense, and verbs such as 'denote' or 'designate' have a predominantly vertical sense. The verb 'refer to' might also seem to have primarily
a vertical sense, though talk of 'cross-referencing', for example, also
indicates a horizontal sense. Like 'meaning', terms such as 'signification', 'connotation', 'denotation', 'designation' and 'reference' can be
understood as standing for either a relation or an object (i.e. the thing
signified, connoted, etc.) – although, in the case of 'reference', a distinction is often drawn between *reference* (the relation) and *referent* (the
thing referred to).[91] There are also more subtle distinctions that might

[90] The term 'object' here is being used in its widest possible sense, i.e. as including both
what Frege calls 'objects' and what he calls 'concepts'. On the relation/object distinction
here, compare Ogden and Richards at the beginning of chapter 9 of their classic work,
The Meaning of Meaning: 'We may either take Meaning as standing for the relation
between A and B, when A means B, or as standing for B. In the first case the meaning
of A will be its relation to B, in the second it will be B.' They go on to distinguish *sixteen*
conceptions of meaning, divided into three groups, with further subdistinctions, which,
whether or not one accepts everything they say, indicates very well the complexities
involved in talk of 'meaning'.

[91] After the remark quoted in the previous footnote, Ogden and Richards go on: 'This
ambiguity [between meaning as relation and meaning as object] once it is understood
gives rise to little difficulty, but the avoidance of it by the symbols "reference" and
"referent" is one of the distinct advantages of that vocabulary' (p. 185).

be drawn here. It seems to me that what verb it is appropriate to use in specifying a vertical relation, for example, may partly depend on the nature of the relata involved. I myself would tend to talk of proper names or definite descriptions as *referring to* something (e.g. of 'the pupil of Plato and teacher of Alexander the Great' as referring to Aristotle), whilst talking of schematic letters, term variables or abstract symbols as *denoting* or *standing for* something (e.g. of 'a', 'b', 'c', etc. as denoting or standing for objects in the domain of discourse).[92] Lying behind this, perhaps, is the idea of 'referring to' being something that *we do* in *using* language and 'denoting' or 'standing for' being something that a linguistic expression somehow does, or is imputed to do, by itself.[93] Of course, at this level of detail, intuitions as to the use of words may vary widely, and their philosophical significance is debatable. But they do indicate some of the complexities involved here, and how disagreements may express themselves in subtle ways.

Can similar distinctions be drawn in the case of German? The first point to note is that 'bedeuten' too can be used in both a horizontal and a vertical sense; and it is this fact that provides support to those who have suggested that 'mean' or 'signify' are the best translations. To use 'refer to' or 'denote' is indeed to make more of an interpretive decision – to interpret someone as using 'bedeuten' in its vertical sense. However, in defence of 'reference' and its allies, it might be pointed out that there is not the range of terms in German to express this vertical sense, and that 'bedeuten' is in fact the most natural choice to do so. To this extent, then, there is a *difference* between the German word 'bedeuten'

---

[92] Is it an accident, I wonder, that 'refer to' is widely used by those discussing Frege's views in the context of the philosophy of language, whilst 'denote' was used by Furth in his translation of Part I of *GG* and (where it *is* used) tends to be used more by those who see Frege primarily as a logician and philosopher of mathematics? Verbs too, it should be noted, have both a *Sinn* and a *Bedeutung*; and there is certainly much that could be said about the *Sinn* and *Bedeutung* of referring verbs.

[93] In chapter 1 of *The Meaning of Meaning*, Ogden and Richards draw a triangle with 'Thought or Reference', 'Symbol' and 'Referent' at the vertices, and use 'refers to' to relate 'Thought or Reference' to 'Referent', 'symbolises' to relate 'Symbol' to 'Thought or Reference', and 'stands for' to relate 'Symbol' to 'Referent'. They themselves speak of 'stands for' as an *imputed* relation, since, strictly speaking, it is *we*, in our use of language, who relate symbol to referent via 'thought'. As alluded to above, since Strawson (1950), in particular, 'referring' has indeed been seen as something that *we do* in *using* language: expressions by themselves may have 'meaning', but it is only when *used*, appropriately, that they also have 'reference'. 'Denoting', on the other hand, seems to be something that an expression itself somehow does, independently of the particular intentions of the person using the expression on a given occasion. Such a distinction between 'denoting' and 'referring' was drawn by Donnellan (1966) in his adjudication of the debate between Russell (in 'On Denoting') and Strawson (in 'On Referring'). There are other variants of the distinction in the subsequent literature.

and the English word 'mean': the former is more frequently employed in expressing the vertical sense, whilst in English we might well use an alternative, e.g. 'refer to', 'denote' or 'stand for'. The only everyday German word used in a predominantly vertical sense is 'bezeichnen' ('designate'); and it is notable that when Frege is explaining his notion of 'Bedeutung', he does indeed use 'bedeuten' and 'bezeichnen' interchangeably.[94] There are, then, some grounds for translating 'Bedeutung' as 'reference'; and we might also note here that talk of 'No men are mortal' and '2 + 2 = 5' as having the same *reference* still strikes the English reader as bizarre, the eccentricity of Frege's own use of 'Bedeutung' thus still being conveyed.

However, with regard to the issue of the *Bedeutung* of sentences, in particular, not everyone *has* accepted the eccentricity of Frege's terminology; and it has been suggested that Frege's views seem much less absurd if 'Bedeutung' is understood in the sense of 'significance' or 'importance', which is indeed what 'Bedeutung' can sometimes mean in German (just as in English we might talk of the 'meaning' of an event, for example).[95] According to Frege, the 'significance' or 'value' of a proposition, as far as logic and science are concerned, lies in its *truth-value*. What could be more natural, then, than to *equate* the *Bedeutung* of a sentence with its truth-value?[96] Such a conception of 'Bedeutung' as 'value' might seem to be reinforced by the argument that Frege offers in 'Function and Concept', which was where the distinction between *Sinn* and *Bedeutung* first appeared. Here the *Bedeutung* of a sentence is seen as the 'value' that a function (concept) yields when 'completed' by an object.[97] Frege focuses on identity statements to motivate his conception, where it is less easy to see how anything other than a 'truth-value' might be the 'value'; but the functional connection established

---

[94] See e.g. *SB*, p. 156 below; *CSB*, p. 173 below. We should also note here two further German phrases that are used in both a horizontal and a vertical sense – 'sich beziehen auf' and 'Bezug nehmen auf' – both of which are naturally translated as 'refer to' (or 'make reference to'). 'Reference' is uncontroversially one of the meanings of 'Bezug', and the latter is often used by German-speaking philosophers in explaining Frege's views (cf. fn. 105 below). But 'Bezug' does not have the semantic connotations of 'Bedeutung' that might have made it a more suitable choice for Frege (and it has other meanings that are quite *un*suitable).

[95] There are occasions in Frege's works when 'significance' is certainly the right term to use in translating 'Bedeutung': see e.g. *BS*, pp. 49, 53, 54 below; *GL*, p. 86 below. On the interpretation of Frege's notion of 'Bedeutung' as 'significance', see especially Tugendhat, 1970; Dummett, 1981b: ch. 7; Gabriel, 1984.

[96] Cf. *SB*, pp. 156–8 below; *PMC*, pp. 152–3 (pp. 255–7 below).

[97] See *FC*, pp. 137–9 below. On the two notions of 'value' that Frege then seems to be assimilating, one technical (as in *FC*) and the other non-technical (as in *SB*), see Gabriel, 1984. Cf. also Potts, 1982.

here between the *Bedeutung* of a whole and the *Bedeutung* of its parts is the key principle. It is this principle that Frege presupposes in what may be called the *argument from substitutivity* that he offers in 'On *Sinn* and *Bedeutung*'. In considering what the *Bedeutung* of a sentence might be, Frege asks what remains constant when proper names with the same *Bedeutung* are intersubstituted within the sentence: his answer is the truth-value of the sentence. So too he argues that what is *missing* when one of the parts of a sentence *lacks* a *Bedeutung* is also its truth-value. Given the principle that the *Bedeutung* of a whole is determined by the *Bedeutung* of its parts, it then seems natural to *identify* the *Bedeutung* of a sentence with its truth-value. Now it has to be said that all of Frege's arguments *underdetermine* this identification: there are other possibilities as to what remains constant in substitutions, for example – most notably, the 'state of affairs' represented.[98] But the point here is just to indicate the motivation behind interpreting 'Bedeutung' as 'value' or 'significance'. For if the *Bedeutung* of a sentence is conceived of as its truth-value, then given Frege's underlying principle, the *Bedeutung* of its parts can be seen as whatever it is that contributes to determining that truth-value: the 'significance' of an expression, in other words, lies in its 'truth-value potential'.[99]

This suggestion that the *Bedeutung* of an expression should be seen as its 'significance' was quite explicitly made in order to *play down* Frege's realism;[100] and it is clear that there is a close connection between the issues discussed in the last section and the controversy over the translation of 'Bedeutung'. For if, in focusing on the semantic and epistemological aspects of Frege's philosophy, the ontological issues are bracketed off, then it is natural to focus on *Bedeutung* as a horizontal rather than vertical relation. To suggest that the 'Bedeutung' of an expression consists in its 'truth-value potential' – the contribution it makes to determining the truth-value of sentences in which it appears – is indeed to stress the horizontal relation that an expression has to other expressions. But for the reasons given above, this is not (solely) how Frege himself conceived of 'Bedeutung'. To return to the first distinction drawn above in considering the uses of 'meaning', on the vast majority of occasions on which Frege uses the term 'Bedeutung', it is *Bedeutung* as an object rather

---

[98] For criticism of Frege's arguments, see Beaney, 1996: §6.2. To suggest that the 'state of affairs' represented is also a candidate for the *Bedeutung* of a sentence is not to say that there are no problems here; cf. fn. 79 above.

[99] As Tugendhat explains this latter term, 'two expressions . . . have the same truth-value potential if and only if, whenever each is completed by the same expression to form a sentence, the two sentences have the same truth-value' (1970: p. 180).

[100] Cf. Tugendhat's remark that Frege's 'so-called "realism" appears to be overemphasized in the literature' (1970: p. 185).

than a relation that he clearly has in mind.[101] It may be indeed be right to separate the question of what it is for an expression to *have Bedeutung* from the question of what kind of entity the *Bedeutung* of an expression *is*, and to reject Frege's answer to the second question, at least in the case of sentences;[102] but this should not cloud our appreciation of the ontological weight that Frege himself placed on his notion of 'Bedeutung'. Of course, to translate 'Bedeutung' as '*referent*' on the appropriate occasions would be going too far in the other direction – exaggerating the analogy between sentences referring to the True and the False and proper names referring to the objects that are their bearers. Using 'reference' does at least preserve the ambiguity of *Bedeutung* as relation and *Bedeutung* as object; though even this might be felt to undervalue the horizontal aspects of Frege's notion of 'Bedeutung' (especially if the context principle is still seen as playing an important role in Frege's later work).

In the end, then, the choice of a term to translate 'Bedeutung' cannot be dissociated from the interpretation of Frege's philosophy. So what should a sensible policy be? If forced to choose, I myself would use 'reference', since I do think that for Frege the vertical sense of 'Bedeutung' has priority over the horizontal sense. 'Meaning', it seems to me, does make Frege's views more eccentric than they are in German, whereas 'significance', whilst making some of those views less eccentric, obscures Frege's realism. 'Reference' is to be preferred to 'denotation', since it is a more everyday term, and 'denotation' is *only* used in a vertical sense.[103]

---

[101] For example, in *SB* itself, Frege uses the term 'Bedeutung' 138 times, and on well over 100 of those occasions it is quite clear that he means the *object* referred to, i.e. translating the term as 'referent' here would be perfectly appropriate. Frege talks of *the Bedeutung* of an expression, or of an expression having *a Bedeutung* rather than simply having *Bedeutung*. As he states explicitly, 'The *Bedeutung* of a proper name is the object itself which we designate by using it . . . A proper name . . . *stands for* [*bedeutet*] or *designates* [*bezeichnet*] its *Bedeutung*' (*SB*, pp. 155–6 below). On most of the other occasions, Frege's talk is of words having their customary or indirect *Bedeutung*, where it would not be wrong to use 'referent', but just more natural to say 'reference'.

[102] Cf. Gabriel, 1984: p. 191.

[103] 'Reference' is also to be preferred to 'signification', which has also been suggested as a translation, and in some ways would be a good choice. Like 'meaning', it has both a vertical and a horizontal sense, and sits nicely between 'reference' and 'significance'. Frege himself had suggested, in a letter to Peano, that 'Sinn' and 'Bedeutung' would be best translated into Italian as 'senso' and 'significazione' (*PMC*, p. 128); so it might well have had Frege's support. (We should, however, note that 'senso' and 'riferimento' are now preferred in modern Italian discussions; see e.g. Penco, 1994.) But 'signification' is perhaps just too must of a mouthful for frequent use in an English translation (and 'On Sense and Signification' sounds like a hybrid work by Austen and Austin), and with 'signify' as its corresponding verb, it has too many Saussurean and structuralist connotations (where horizontal relations predominate). In any case, as Simons (1992: p. 758) notes, 'it would be asking for trouble to suggest *yet* another translation'.

Admittedly, 'reference' does now have Strawsonian connotations, which are absent in Frege's work, but given that Frege at least *ought* to be read before Strawson, these should not be misleading (by the time one reaches Strawson, one should be in a position to recognize the differences). However, as the comments above indicate, there is room for genuine exegetical dispute here; and the obvious answer is simply to leave the term 'Bedeutung' untranslated. Many philosophers who now write about Frege do just this; and there are obvious precedents: 'eudaimonia' and 'Geist', mentioned above, are just two examples of terms that are frequently used in the philosophical literature untranslated.[104] There is clearly no better way to respect the principle of exegetical neutrality, although this would hardly be the strategy to adopt for every term about which there might be disagreement.[105] But given the controversy that surrounds Frege's conception of *Bedeutung*, in particular, and the way that this brings to a focus all of the central issues in Frege's philosophy, this does seem the only sensible course to take. Where the noun is concerned, this presents no problems at all. To talk of Frege's conception of the *Bedeutung* of a sentence as a truth-value does not sound inelegant. In the case of the verb, however, due to its inflections, leaving its occurrences untranslated is far less natural. But inelegance aside, it is actually easier and less controversial to find an appropriate translation. In most of the contexts where Frege uses 'bedeuten', it is clear that he is using it in its vertical sense: proper names refer to objects, concept words refer to concepts, and sentences refer to truth-values; and 'refer

[104] Other obvious examples are 'anomie', 'Dasein', 'noema', 'Sittlichkeit', 'Übermensch' and 'Weltanschauung', as well as technical terms that are now so thoroughly part of philosophical vocabulary that the question of their translation no longer arises – e.g. 'a priori', 'a posteriori', 'de re', 'de dicto', 'salva veritate'. In anthropology, of course, it is the rule rather than the exception to leave key or problematic terms from different conceptual schemes untranslated. The only difficulty in the case of Frege's use of 'Bedeutung' is that the term is also widely used in many everyday senses, and leaving it untranslated only works when it is clear from the context that it is Frege's views that are under discussion.

[105] It also fails to solve the problems that German-speaking philosophers encounter in seeking to explain Frege's ideas. In his book on Frege, Kutschera writes: 'We call the sense of an expression also its "Bedeutung" and what Frege calls "Bedeutung" its "Bezug" ["reference"], its "Extension" or "Denotation". To avoid misunderstanding, in what follows we will index the word "Bedeutung" with an F where it is to be understood in Frege's sense (i.e. as reference)' (1989: p. 64; my translation). 'Bedeutung$_F$' is then used in the account of Frege's views. Cf. Simons, 1992: p. 758: 'The one translation into English that every native speaker of German I have asked agrees to be unfortunate is the "obvious" translation as "meaning". Why throw away (say my informants) that lucky advantage we English speakers have of *not* being misled by the standard meaning (!) of "Bedeutung" when in German a long explanation has to be given that Frege clearly *was* deviating from standard German usage, as Husserl and others acknowledged by *not* following Frege. German discussions now often *follow* English terminology by using words like *Referenzgegenstand* or *Bezug(sgegenstand)* for Frege's *Bedeutung*.'

to' and 'stand for' are the two English expressions that have generally been used in the translations of Frege's later work that appear in the present volume ('stand for' in the translations by Geach, Black, and Long and White). The German term has, however, been placed in square brackets immediately afterwards, in accordance with the principle of interpretive integrity. In the end, what is most important is to make sure that each occurrence of 'bedeuten', however it is translated, is signalled; and this is the policy that has been followed here.[106]

---

[106] In the first two editions of *TPW*, which was the first collection of Frege's works to be published in English (though not the first book – *FA* had appeared in 1950; *TPW* in 1952), 'Bedeutung' was rendered as 'reference' and 'bedeuten' either by 'stand for' or occasionally by 'designate' (except in the translation of Part I of *BS*). In the third edition, after the meeting to standardize the translation of Frege's terms as far as possible in the various works published by Blackwell (see fn. 84 above), 'meaning' was preferred to 'reference' and 'mean' to 'stand for'. This change may not have been to everyone's liking, but more unfortunate was the unsystematic nature of the revision. Only 'stand for' was replaced by 'mean', leaving other occurrences of 'bedeuten' with a different translation, and since 'mean' had already been used in translating other expressions (e.g. 'meinen', 'das heißt'), the result was that it was not always clear when Frege himself had used 'bedeuten'. And as far as the substitution of 'reference' was concerned, not only were some occurrences of 'reference' retained by mistake (see e.g. pp. 69, 141), but 'thing meant' was quite often used instead of 'meaning' – presumably because it was felt that the latter did indeed produce absurd results on occasions (the principle of exegetical neutrality did not seem to operate here). But even the use of 'thing meant' produced errors. For example, in the second edition of *TPW*, the first sentence of the fourth paragraph of *SB* reads: 'The sense of a proper name is grasped by everybody who is sufficiently familiar with the language or totality of designations to which it belongs; but this serves to illuminate only a single aspect of the reference [*Bedeutung*], supposing it to have one.' In the third edition, the latter clause reads 'but this serves to illuminate only a single aspect of the thing meant, supposing it to have one', suggesting now that the 'one' refers back to 'a single aspect' rather than, as it should be, 'Bedeutung'. There is a lesson here: there is never any simple term that can do all the work of a term in another language; and the translation of each occurrence of a term must always be considered in the light of the context. Straightforward intersubstitution of two terms, however synonymous they might appear, never does preserve meaning in all contexts. Even in reverting to the original German term, as in the present volume, the meaning of each sentence as a whole has to be checked; and in the translations taken from *TPW* I have occasionally had to make slight changes simply to allow 'Bedeutung' to remain untranslated. Leaving it untranslated, of course, guarantees that Frege's use of the noun is then clear; but in placing the German term immediately after each translated occurrence of the verb, I have also sought to signal every use that Frege makes in his later writings of 'bedeuten'.

Begriffsschrift

a formula language
of pure thought modelled
on that of arithmetic[1]

[*Begriffsschrift* was Frege's first book, published in 1879. 'Begriffsschrift', which literally means 'concept-script' (it has also been translated as 'conceptual notation', but is here left untranslated), was the name that Frege gave to his logical symbolism, reflecting his avowed aim of providing a means of capturing the 'conceptual content' ('Begriffsinhalt') of propositions.[2] The book embodies Frege's first attempt, by extending the use of function-argument analysis in mathematics to logic (to which the subtitle alludes), to develop a logical system that was capable of representing arithmetical propositions and inferences, his ultimate goal being to demonstrate that arithmetic was *reducible* to logic.[3] Arithmetic contains many statements of *multiple generality* (e.g. 'Every number has a successor', 'Every even number is the sum of two primes'), and traditional (syllogistic) logic had had great difficulty in analysing such statements. What inaugurated modern logic was Frege's invention of quantifier notation, first explained in §11 of the *Begriffsschrift*; and it was his resulting construction of what we now know as predicate logic that made possible a satisfying treatment of multiple generality. But besides inventing predicate logic, Frege also offered an axiomatization of propositional logic;[4] and Frege's further significant advance lay in showing how the two traditional parts of logic, syllogistic theory and propositional logic, could be organically integrated into one comprehensive theory.[5]

[1] Translated by Michael Beaney. Page numbers in the margin are from the original edition.
[2] But cf. *NLD*, p. 362 below, for Frege's later suggestion that the name may have been misleading, since judgements were regarded as logically prior to concepts.
[3] For discussion of Frege's logicist project, see the Introduction, pp. 2–8, 15–20 above.
[4] For details, see Appendix 2 below.
[5] This is made clear by Frege himself in a (posthumously published) paper (*BLC*) written shortly after *BS*, comparing his own system with that of Boole; see the Introduction, pp. 11–12 above.

What follows here is the Preface, in which Frege outlines his motivation, and most of Part I, which explains his symbolism. A note on Part II and a summary of Part III are provided at the end.]

Preface

The recognition of a scientific truth generally passes through several stages of certainty. Perhaps first guessed from a limited number of particular cases, a universal proposition becomes more and more firmly established by being connected with other truths through chains of inference – whether conclusions that find confirmation in other ways are derived from it, or whether, conversely, it is recognized as following from already established propositions. It can thus be asked, on the one hand, by what path a proposition was gradually reached, and on the other hand, in what way it is now finally to be most firmly established. The former question possibly needs to be answered differently for different people; the latter is more definite, and its answer is connected with the inner nature of the proposition concerned. The firmest proof is obviously the purely logical, which, prescinding from the particularity of things, is based solely on the laws on which all knowledge rests. Accordingly, we divide all truths that require justification into two kinds, those whose proof can be given purely logically and those whose proof must be grounded on empirical facts. But there is no inconsistency in a proposition belonging to the first kind and yet being such that it can never be apprehended by a human mind without the operation of the senses.[A] Thus it is not psychological origination but the most perfect method of proof that lies at the basis of the division. Now in considering the question of to which of these two kinds arithmetical judgements belong, I first had to see how far one could get in arithmetic by inferences alone, supported only by the laws of thought that transcend all particulars. The course I took was first to seek to reduce the concept of ordering in a series to that of *logical* consequence, in order then to progress to the concept of number. So that nothing intuitive could intrude here unnoticed, everything had to depend on the chain of inference being free of gaps. In striving to fulfil this requirement in the strictest way, I found an obstacle in the inadequacy of language: however cumbersome the expressions that arose, the more complicated the relations became, the less the precision was attained that my purpose demanded. Out of this need came the idea of the present *Begriffsschrift*. It is thus intended to serve primarily to test in the most reliable way the validity of a chain of inference

[A] Since without sense perception no mental development is possible for beings known to us, the latter holds for all judgements.

and to reveal every presupposition that tends to slip in unnoticed, so that its origin can be investigated. The expression of anything that is without significance[6] for *logical inference* has therefore been eschewed.[7] I have called, in §3, that which solely mattered to me *conceptual content* [*begrifflicher Inhalt*]. This point must therefore always be kept in mind if the nature of my formula language is to be understood correctly. From this the name 'Begriffsschrift' also arose. Since I restricted myself in the first place to the expression of such relations as are independent of the particularity of things, I was also able to use the expression 'formula language of pure thought'. The modelling on the formula language of arithmetic, which I indicated in the title, refers more to the fundamental ideas than to the detailed construction. Any attempt to establish an artificial similarity by construing a concept as the sum of its marks was far from my mind.[8] My formula language comes closest to that of arithmetic in the way that letters are used.[9] |

I believe I can make the relationship of my *Begriffsschrift* to ordinary language clearest if I compare it to that of the microscope to the eye. The latter, due to the range of its applicability, due to the flexibility with which it is able to adapt to the most diverse circumstances, has a great superiority over the microscope. Considered as an optical instrument, it admittedly reveals many imperfections, which usually remain unnoticed only because of its intimate connection with mental life. But as soon as scientific purposes place great demands on sharpness of resolution, the eye turns out to be inadequate. The microscope, on the other hand, is perfectly suited for just such purposes, but precisely because of this is useless for all others.

Likewise, this *Begriffsschrift* is an aid devised for particular scientific proposes, and should therefore not be condemned because it is no good for others. If it fulfils these purposes to some extent, then the lack of new truths in my work may be overlooked. I would console myself on

[6] Throughout this translation of *BS*, unless otherwise indicated, 'Bedeutung' (or any of its cognates) has been rendered as either 'meaning' or 'significance' (or their corresponding cognate). Conversely, unless otherwise indicated, any occurrence of either 'meaning' or 'significance' (or any of their cognates) in the English version should be taken as the translation of 'Bedeutung' (or its corresponding cognate). For discussion of the problems involved in translating 'Bedeutung', see the Introduction, §4 above.

[7] Frege's idea here is that any feature of the overall meaning of an expression that makes no difference to the validity of any argument in which that expression is used is irrelevant for logical purposes; an idea that is later reflected in the distinction that Frege draws between 'sense' (corresponding, in this context, to his earlier 'conceptual content') and 'tone' or 'shading' ('Beleuchtung'); cf. especially *PWLB*, pp. 239–44 below.

[8] By 'marks' ('Merkmale') of a concept Frege means those concepts into which the concept can be analysed. The concept *mammal*, for example, is a mark of the concept *whale*. Cf. *GL*, §53 (pp. 102–3 below); *CO*, pp. 189–90 below.

[9] What Frege is referring to here is the use of *variables*, fundamental to both logic and arithmetic.

this with the knowledge that a development in method also furthers science. Bacon indeed thought it preferable to invent a means by which everything can be found easily than to discover a particular thing, and all great scientific advances in modern times have indeed had their origin in an improvement in method.

Leibniz too recognized – perhaps overestimated – the advantages of an appropriate symbolism. His conception of a universal characteristic, a *calculus philosophicus* or *ratiocinator*,[B] was too grandiose for the attempt to realize it to go further than the bare preliminaries. The enthusiasm that seized its originator in considering what an immense increase in the mental power of mankind would arise from a symbolism suited to things themselves let him underestimate the difficulties that | such an enterprise faces. But even if this great aim cannot be achieved at the first attempt, one need not despair of a slow, step by step approach. If a problem in its full generality appears insoluble, it has to be limited provisionally; it can then, perhaps, be dealt with by advancing gradually. Arithmetical, geometrical and chemical symbols can be regarded as realizations of the Leibnizian conception in particular fields. The *Begriffsschrift* offered here adds a new one to these – indeed, the one located in the middle, adjoining all the others. From here, with the greatest prospect of success, one can then proceed to fill in the gaps in the existing formula languages, connect their hitherto separate fields into the domain of a single formula language and extend it to fields that have hitherto lacked such a language.

I am convinced that my *Begriffsschrift* can be successfully applied wherever a special value has to be placed on the validity of proof, as in the case of laying the foundations of the differential and integral calculus.

It seems to me to be even easier to extend the domain of this formula language to geometry. Only a few more symbols would have to be added for the intuitive relations that occur here. In this way one would obtain a kind of *analysis situs*.

The transition to the pure theory of motion and thence to mechanics and physics might follow here. In the latter fields, where besides conceptual necessity, natural necessity prevails,[10] a further development of the symbolism with the advancement of knowledge is easiest to foresee. But that is no reason to wait until such advancement appears to have come to an end.

If it is a task of philosophy to break the power of words over the human mind, by uncovering illusions that through the use of language

---

[B] On this, see Trendelenburg, *Historische Beiträge zur Philosophie*, Vol. 3. [Frege's reference is to Trendelenburg's essay 'On Leibniz's Project of a Universal Characteristic', which seems to have been the main source of Frege's understanding of Leibniz's conception. Cf. Sluga, 1980: ch. 2, §4.]

[10] The German words here are 'Denknotwendigkeit' and 'Naturnotwendigkeit', respectively.

Use for philosophers: strip away rhetoric r language in order to examine solely the propositions themselves.

often almost unavoidably arise concerning the relations of concepts, by freeing thought from | the taint of ordinary linguistic means of expression, then my *Begriffsschrift*, further developed for these purposes, can become a useful tool for philosophers. Admittedly, as is surely inevitable in the case of external means of representation, even this cannot make thought pure again; but the deviations can, at least, be limited to the unavoidable and harmless, whilst at the same time, just because they are of a quite different kind from those typical of ordinary language, protection is provided against the one-sided influence of one of these means of expression.

The very invention of this *Begriffsschrift*, it seems to me, has advanced logic. I hope that logicians, if they are not put off by first impressions of unfamiliarity, will not repudiate the innovations to which I was driven by a necessity inherent in the subject matter itself. These deviations from what is traditional find their justification in the fact that logic hitherto has always followed ordinary language and grammar too closely. In particular, I believe that the replacement of the concepts *subject* and *predicate* by *argument* and *function* will prove itself in the long run. It is easy to see how taking a content as a function of an argument gives rise to concept formation. What also deserves notice is the demonstration of the connection between the meanings of the words: if, and, not, or, there is, some, all, etc.

Only the following remains to be mentioned in particular.

The restriction, in §6, to a single mode of inference is justified by the fact that in *laying the foundations* of such a *Begriffsschrift* the primitive elements must be as simple as possible if perspicuity and order are to be achieved. This does not rule out, *later*, transitions from several judgements to a new one, which are possible by this single mode of inference only in an indirect way, being converted into direct ones for the sake of abbreviation. In fact, this may be advisable for later applications. In this way, then, further modes of inference would arise. |

VIII   I realized later that formulae (31) and (41) can be combined into the single one

$$\vdash (\top\!\top a \equiv a)$$

which makes a few more simplifications possible.[11]

Arithmetic, as I remarked at the beginning, was the starting point of the train of thought that led me to my *Begriffsschrift*. I therefore intend to apply it to this science first, seeking to provide further analysis of its concepts and a deeper foundation for its theorems. I announce in the

[11] Formulae (31) and (41) are two of the axioms that Frege laid down for his logical system, which can be combined using his symbol for identity of content; see Appendix 2 below.

[handwritten margin note, left:] logic: reliant on language (which can be arbitrary)

[handwritten note, bottom:] perspicuity: plain to understanding due to clear presentation.

elucidate: to make lucid by explanation or analysis.

third Part some preliminary results that move in this direction. Progression along the indicated path, the elucidation of the concepts of number, magnitude, etc., will form the object of further investigations, to which I shall turn immediately after this work.[12]

Jena, 18 December 1878

I. Explanation of the Symbols

§1. The symbols used in the general theory of magnitude fall into two kinds. The first consists of the letters, each of which represents either a number left undetermined or a function left undetermined. This indeterminacy makes it possible to use letters for the expression of the general validity of propositions, as in

$$(a + b)c = ac + bc.$$

The other kind consists of such symbols as $+$, $-$, $\sqrt{}$, 0, 1, 2, each of which has its own particular meaning.

I adopt this fundamental idea of distinguishing two kinds of symbols, which unfortunately is not strictly carried through in the theory of magnitude,[c] *in order to make it generally applicable in the wider domain of pure thought.* I therefore divide all the symbols I use into *those by means of which one can represent different things* and *those that have a quite determinate sense.* The first are the *letters,* and these should serve primarily to express *generality.* For all their indeterminacy, it must be insisted that a letter *retain,* in the same context, the meaning once given to it.

Judgement

§2. A judgement will always be expressed by means of the symbol

$$\vdash$$

which stands to the left of the symbol or complex of symbols which gives the content of the judgement. If the small vertical stroke at the left
2   end of the horizontal one | is *omitted,* then the judgement will be transformed into a *mere complex of ideas,* of which the writer does not state whether he recognizes its truth or not. For example, let

---

[c] Consider 1, log, sin, Lim.

[12] The elucidation of the concept of number was finally published in the *Grundlagen* in 1884 (see pp. 84ff. below), and the formal attempt to provide a deeper foundation for the theorems of arithmetic in the *Grundgesetze,* Volume I of which appeared in 1893 (see pp. 194ff. below), and Volume II of which appeared in 1903 (see pp. 258ff. below). For details of this period, see the Introduction, pp. 4–8 above.

$$\vdash\!\!\!-\!\!\!-A$$

mean the judgement: 'Opposite magnetic poles attract one another';[D]
then

$$-\!\!\!-\!\!\!-A$$

will not express this judgement, but should merely arouse in the reader
the idea of the mutual attraction of opposite magnetic poles, in order,
say, to draw conclusions from it and by means of these to test the
correctness of the thought. In this case we *paraphrase* using the words
'*the circumstance that*' or '*the proposition that*'.

Not every content can become a judgement by placing $\vdash\!\!\!-\!\!\!-$ before
its symbol; for example, the idea 'house' cannot. We therefore distinguish between *judgeable* and *unjudgeable* contents.[E]

The horizontal stroke, from which the symbol $\vdash\!\!\!-\!\!\!-$ is formed, *binds
the symbols that follow it into a whole, and assertion, which is expressed by
means of the vertical stroke at the left end of the horizontal, relates to this
whole.* The horizontal stroke may be called the *content stroke*, the vertical
the *judgement stroke*. The content stroke serves generally to relate any
symbol to the whole formed by the symbols that follow the stroke. *What
follows the content stroke must always have a judgeable content.*

§3.   A distinction between *subject* and *predicate* finds *no place* in my
representation of a judgement. To justify this, I note that the contents of
two judgements can differ in two ways: either the conclusions that can
be drawn from one when combined with certain others | also always
follow from the second when combined with the same judgements, or
else this is not the case. The two propositions 'At Plataea the Greeks
defeated the Persians' and 'At Plataea the Persians were defeated by the
Greeks' differ in the first way. Even if a slight difference in sense can
be discerned, the agreement predominates. Now I call that part of the
content that is the *same* in both the *conceptual content*. Since *only this* has
significance for the *Begriffsschrift*, no distinction is needed between propositions that have the same conceptual content. If it is said, 'The subject is the concept with which the judgement is concerned', then this
applies also to the object. It can therefore only be said: 'The subject is

[D] I use capital Greek letters as abbreviations, to which the reader may attribute an
appropriate sense if I do not specifically explain them. [The '*A*' here is a capital alpha.]
[E] On the other hand, the circumstance that there are houses (or that there is a house)
would be a judgeable content (cf. §12). The idea 'house', however, is only a part of this.
In the proposition 'Priam's house was of wood' one cannot replace 'house' by 'circumstance that there is a house'. For a different kind of unjudgeable content, see the example
that follows formula 81. [The reference here is to §27, where Frege remarks that propositions involving vague concepts such as the concept *heap* do not have judgeable contents;
cf. fn. 54 on p. 76 below.]

the concept with which the judgement is primarily concerned'. The linguistic significance of the position of the subject in the word-order lies in its *marking* the place where what one particularly wants to draw the attention of the listener to is put. (See also §9.) This can have the purpose, for example, of indicating a relation between this judgement and others, thereby facilitating the listener's grasp of all the interconnections. Now all those features of language that result only from the interaction of speaker and listener – where the speaker, for example, takes the listener's expectations into account and seeks to put them on the right track even before a sentence is finished – have no counterpart in my formula language, since here the only thing that is relevant in a judgement is that which influences its *possible consequences*. Everything that is necessary for a valid inference is fully expressed; but what is not necessary is mostly not even indicated; *nothing is left to guessing*. In this I closely follow the example of the formula language of mathematics, in which subject and predicate can also be distinguished only by violating it. Imagine a language in which the proposition 'Archimedes was killed at the capture of Syracuse' is expressed in the following way: 'The violent death of Archimedes at the capture of Syracuse is a fact'. Even here, if one wants, subject and predicate can be distinguished, but the subject contains the

4   whole content, and the predicate serves only to present it as | a judgement. *Such a language would have only a single predicate for all judgements, namely, 'is a fact'*. It can be seen that there is no question here of subject and predicate in the usual sense. *Our Begriffsschrift is such a language and the symbol* |—— *is its common predicate for all judgements*.

In my first draft of a formula language I was misled by the example of ordinary language into constructing judgements out of subject and predicate. But I soon convinced myself that this was an obstacle to my particular goal and only led to useless prolixity.

§4.   The following remarks should suffice, for our purposes, to explain the significance of the distinctions that are made with regard to judgements.

A distinction is drawn between *universal* and *particular* judgements: this is not really a distinction between judgements, but between contents. *One ought to say: 'a judgement with a universal content', 'a judgement with a particular content'*. For these properties belong to the content even when it is *not* presented as a judgement, but as a proposition. (See §2.)

The same applies to negation. In an indirect way one says, for example: 'Suppose that the lines *AB* and *CD* were not equal'. Here the content, that the lines *AB* and *CD* are not equal, contains a negation, but this content, although capable of being judged, is nevertheless not presented as a judgement. Negation therefore attaches to the content, irrespective of whether this appears as a judgement or not. I therefore hold it more appropriate to regard negation as a mark of a *judgeable content*.

The distinction between categorical, hypothetical and disjunctive judgements seems to me to have only grammatical significance.[F]

The apodeictic judgement is distinguished from the assertoric in that it indicates the existence of universal judgements from which the proposition can be inferred, whereas in the case of an assertoric judgement such an indication is lacking. If I call a proposition necessary, I thereby give a hint as to my grounds for judgement. *But since this does not affect the conceptual content | of the judgement, the apodeictic form of a judgement has no significance for us.*

5

If a proposition is presented as possible, then either the speaker is refraining from judgement, by indicating that he knows no laws from which its negation would follow; or else he is saying that the proposition's negation in its universal form is false. In the latter case we have what is usually called a *particular affirmative judgement* (see §12). 'It is possible that the Earth will one day collide with another heavenly body' is an example of the first case, and 'A cold can result in death' an example of the second.[13]

Conditionality

§5. If A and B denote[14] judgeable contents (§2), then there are the following four possibilities:

[F] The grounds for this will emerge from my work as a whole.

[13] In this latter case, in other words, the negation of the particular affirmative proposition 'A cold can result in death' (i.e. 'Some colds can result in death') is the universal negative proposition 'No colds can result in death'. Particular affirmative and universal negative propositions were traditionally seen as contradictories, and as far as this relationship was concerned, Frege did not depart from the traditional view. Cf. §12, pp. 73–4 below.

[14] Except in the penultimate paragraph, throughout this section the verb 'bedeuten' has been translated as 'denote' and the noun 'Bedeutung' as denotation'. Other translations (e.g. Geach, Bauer-Mengelberg, Bynum) render the verb as 'stand for' and the noun as 'meaning', but this obscures the connection between Frege's use of them. Since 'stand for' does not have a corresponding noun, and 'meaning' is inappropriate in the one context in which 'Bedeutung' is used (in the third paragraph), 'denote' and 'denotation' have therefore been chosen. What we have in this section is the *vertical* use of 'bedeuten' and 'Bedeutung' – the relation involved is that between a sign and its extra-linguistic correlate – a use, arguably, that corresponds to Frege's 'official' use of these words in his work from 1891 onwards. (For the distinction between the vertical and horizontal uses of 'Bedeutung' and its cognates, see the Introduction, §4.) Certainly, neither 'mean' and 'meaning' nor 'signify' and 'significance' (or 'signification') adequately capture Frege's use of 'bedeuten' and 'Bedeutung' in the present section; though nor, it has to be said, does 'refer to' and 'reference', since what we have here are schematic letters and abstract symbols rather than ordinary linguistic expressions such as proper names or definite descriptions. The former, it seems more appropriate to say, 'denote' or 'represent' or

(1) *A* is affirmed and *B* is affirmed;
(2) *A* is affirmed and *B* is denied;
(3) *A* is denied and *B* is affirmed;
(4) *A* is denied and *B* is denied.

now denotes the judgement that *the third of these possibilities does not obtain, but one of the other three does.*[15] Accordingly, if

is denied, then this is to say that the third possibility does obtain, i.e. that *A* is denied and *B* affirmed.

Of the cases in which

is affirmed, the following deserve emphasis:

1. *A* is to be affirmed. Then the content of *B* is quite irrelevant. For example, let $\vdash\!\!\!-\!\!- A$ denote: $3 \times 7 = 21$, and *B* denote the circumstance that the Sun is shining. Here only the first two of the four cases mentioned above are possible. There need not exist a causal | connection between the two contents.

2. *B* is to be denied. Then the content of *A* is irrelevant. For example, let *B* denote the circumstance that perpetual motion is possible, and *A* the circumstance that the world is infinite. Here only the second and fourth of the four cases are possible. There need not be a causal connection between *A* and *B*.

3. One can make the judgement

without knowing whether *A* and *B* are to be affirmed or denied. For example, let *B* denote the circumstance that the Moon is in quadrature [with the Sun], and *A* the circumstance that it appears as a semicircle. In this case

'stand for' something, whilst the latter 'refer to' something (or not, as the case may be). Which verb is used may also depend on the kind of thing that is, or is taken to be, the extra-linguistic correlate, which further complicates the problems of interpretation and translation. (Cf. Introduction, pp. 40ff.)

[15] I.e. it represents the judgement that *B materially implies A* – symbolically, $B \to A$, as it would now be expressed. For further explanation of Frege's symbolism, see Appendix 2 below.

can be translated with the aid of the connective 'if': 'If the Moon is in quadrature, then it appears as a semicircle'. The causal link implicit in the word 'if', however, is not expressed by our symbols, although a judgement of this kind can be made only on the basis of such a link. For this link is something general, but an expression for generality has not yet been introduced (see §12).

Let us call the vertical stroke which joins the two horizontals the *conditional stroke*. The part of the upper horizontal stroke to the left of the conditional stroke is the content stroke for the denotation of the complex symbol

which has just been explained; to this is attached any symbol that is to be related to the content of the expression as a whole. The part of the horizontal stroke between A and the conditional stroke is the content stroke of A. The horizontal stroke to the left of B is the content stroke of B.

It is now easy to see that

7 | denies the case in which A is denied, and B and Γ are affirmed. This must be thought of as constructed from Γ and

in the same way as the latter is constructed from B and A. Thus we first have the denial of the case in which Γ is affirmed and

is denied. But the denial of the latter means[16] that A is denied and B affirmed. From this results what was given above. If a causal link exists, then one can also say: 'A is the necessary consequence of B and Γ'; or: 'If the circumstances B and Γ obtain, then A too obtains'.

[16] The word 'bedeutet', in the construction 'bedeutet, daß . . .', is here being used in its *horizontal* sense, making 'means' the more appropriate translation. Cf. fn. 14 above.

It is no less easy to see that

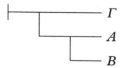

denies the case in which B is affirmed, but A and Γ are denied.[17] If a causal connection between A and B is assumed, this can be translated: 'If A is the necessary consequence of B, then it can be concluded that Γ obtains'.

§6. From the explanation given in §5 it is clear that from the two judgements

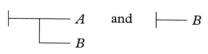

the new judgement $\vdash A$ follows. Of the four cases enumerated above, the third is excluded by

and the second and fourth by $\vdash B$, so that only the first is left. |

8   This inference could perhaps be written thus:

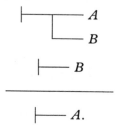

This would be tedious if long expressions stood in the places of A and B, since each of them would have to be written twice. I therefore use the following abbreviation. Each judgement that occurs in the context of a proof is given a number which is written to the right of the judgement at its first occurrence. For example, let the judgement

---

[17] This is a slip on Frege's part. The complex symbol in fact denies the case(s) in which Γ is denied and *either* A is affirmed *or* B is denied. The slip was first spotted by Schröder (1880), in his review of *BS*; and later recognized by Frege himself (see e.g. *PMC*, p. 132/ *WB*, p. 213).

– or one containing it as a special case – be called X. Then I write the inference thus:

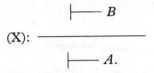

(X):

Here it is left to the reader to construct from $\vdash$ B and $\vdash$ A the judgement

and to see if it accords with the cited judgement X.[18] |

. . .

9   In logic, following Aristotle, a whole series of modes of inference are enumerated; I use just this one – at least in all cases where a new judgement is derived from more than one single judgement.[19] For the truth that lies in another mode of inference can be expressed in a judgement of the form: if M holds, and if N holds, then Λ holds too; in symbols:

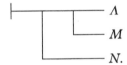

From this judgement and $\vdash$ N and $\vdash$ M, $\vdash$ Λ follows as above. Thus an inference of whatever kind can be reduced to our case. Since it is therefore possible to manage with a single mode of inference, perspicuity demands that this be done. Otherwise, there would be no reason to stop at the Aristotelian modes of inference; new ones could be added indefinitely: a special mode of inference could be made from every judgement expressed in a formula in §§13 to 22.[20] *This restriction to a single mode of inference, however, is in no way intended to express a*

[18] What Frege means here, as indicated by his use of the verb 'stimmen' (translated as 'accord'), is that the constructed judgement must be either X itself or a *substitution instance* of X. As his later practice (in Parts II and III) shows, the judgement to be constructed is almost always a substitution instance of the judgement cited, with an indication given of the substitutions to make. (Cf. Bynum in *CN*, p. 118, fn. 4.) The next two paragraphs of the text, in which Frege gives two further illustrations of his method of abbreviating inferences, are here omitted.

[19] The single mode of inference that Frege is referring to is *modus ponens*, although he seems to recognize here that other rules of inference are involved when moving from a single judgement, e.g. as in substitution.

[20] I.e. in Part II, where Frege lays down axioms for his logical system, and derives some theorems.

psychological proposition, but only to settle the question of formulation to max-
10   *imize effectiveness.* | Some of the judgements that replace Aristotelian
modes of inference will be given in §22 (formulae 59, 62, 65).[21]

Negation

§7.   If a small vertical stroke is attached to the underside of the content stroke, then this is intended to express the circumstance that *the
content does not obtain*. Thus, for example,

means '*A* does not obtain'. I call this small vertical stroke the *negation
stroke*. The part of the horizontal stroke to the right of the negation
stroke is the content stroke of *A*, the part to the left of the negation
stroke, on the other hand, is the content stroke of the negation of *A*.
Here, as elsewhere in the *Begriffsschrift*, without the judgement stroke
no judgement is made.

$$\top\!-\!A$$

merely invites the formation of the idea that *A* does not obtain, without
expressing whether this idea is true.

  We now consider some cases in which the symbols for conditionality
and negation are combined.

means: 'The case in which *B* is to be affirmed and the negation of *A*
is to be denied does not obtain'; in other words, 'The possibility of
affirming both *A* and *B* does not exist', or '*A* and *B* exclude one
another'. Thus only the following three cases remain:

  A is affirmed and *B* is denied;
  A is denied and *B* is affirmed;
  A is denied and *B* is denied.

From the foregoing, it is easy to give the meaning of each of the three
parts of the horizontal stroke in front of *A*.

---

[21] Frege offers, for example, a formalization of 'All *G*'s are *F*'s; *x* is a *G*; therefore *x* is an
F', a version of the syllogistic mode of inference traditionally called *Barbara*. For discussion
of the relationship between Aristotelian and Fregean logic, which is actually more complex
and philosophically significant than Frege realized, see Beaney, 1996: ch. 2 and app. 1.

means: 'The case in which *A* is denied and the negation of *B* is affirmed
11 | does not obtain', or 'Both *A* and *B* cannot be denied'. Only the fol-
lowing possibilities remain:

A is affirmed and *B* is affimed;
A is affirmed and *B* is denied;
A is denied and *B* is affirmed.

A and *B* between them exhaust the possibilities. Now the words 'or'
and 'either . . . or' are used in two ways. '*A* or *B*' may mean, firstly, just
the same as

i.e. that nothing other than *A* and *B* is thinkable. E.g. if a quantity of
gas is heated, then its volume or its pressure increases. Secondly, the
expression '*A* or *B*' may combine the meanings of

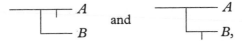

so that firstly, there is no third possibility other than *A* and *B*, and
secondly, *A* and *B* are mutually exclusive. Of the four possibilities only
the following two then remain:

A is affirmed and *B* is denied;
A is denied and *B* is affirmed.

Of the two uses of the expression '*A* or *B*', the first, which does not
exclude the coexistence of *A* and *B*, is the more important, and *we shall
use the word 'or' with this meaning*. Perhaps it is appropriate to draw a
distinction between 'or' and 'either . . . or', only the latter having the
secondary meaning of mutual exclusion.

can then be translated by '*A* or *B*'.[22] Similarly,

---

[22] Frege is clearly distinguishing here the 'inclusive' from the 'exclusive' sense of 'or'.
Modern logicians follow Frege in taking the former – symbolized as '∨' – to be the more
basic, 'either *A* or *B*' in the exclusive sense being readily definable as '*A* or *B* (in the
inclusive sense), but not both'. Frege, however, does not have a primitive symbol for 'or',
instead defining it by means of the symbols for conditionality and negation; i.e. in
modern notation, '*A* ∨ *B*' is defined as '¬*B* → *A*'. As he goes on to show, 'either *A* or
B' in the exclusive sense can then be defined as '¬[(¬*B* → *A*) → ¬(*B* → ¬*A*)]'.

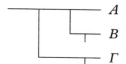

has the meaning of '*A* or *B* or *Γ*'. |

12

means

is denied', or 'The case in which *A* and *B* are both affirmed obtains'. Conversely, the three possibilities left open by

are excluded. Accordingly,

can be translated: 'Both *A* and *B* are facts'. It is also easy to see that

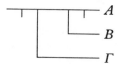

can be rendered by '*A* and *B* and *Γ*'. If 'either *A* or *B*' with the secondary meaning of mutual exclusion is to be symbolized, then

must be expressed. This gives:

Instead of expressing 'and' by means of the symbols for conditionality and negation, as is done here, conditionality could also be represented, conversely, by means of a symbol for 'and' and the symbol for negation. One might introduce, say,

$$\left\{ \begin{array}{l} \Gamma \\ \varDelta \end{array} \right.$$

as the symbol for the conjoined content of Γ and $\varDelta$, and then render |

13

I chose the other way, since inference seemed to me to be expressed more simply that way.[23] The difference between 'and' and 'but' is of a kind that has no expression in this *Begriffsschrift*. A speaker uses 'but' when he wants to hint that what follows is different from what might at first be supposed.

means: 'Of the four possibilities, the third, namely that A is denied and B is affirmed, obtains'. This can therefore be translated: 'B and (but) not A obtains'.

The complex symbol

can be translated in the same way.

means: 'The case in which A and B are both denied obtains'. This can therefore be translated: 'Neither A nor B is a fact'.

It goes without saying that the words 'or', 'and', 'neither . . . nor' are considered here only in so far as as they combine *judgeable* contents.

[23] Frege recognizes here that conjunction might have been taken instead as one of the primitive connectives, but given the fundamental role that *modus ponens* plays in his logical system, clearly feels that 'B, $B \rightarrow A$; therefore A' is more perspicuously expressed by means of the conditional.

Identity of content

§8.   Identity of content[24] differs from conditionality and negation by
relating to names, not to contents. Whilst elsewhere symbols simply
represent their contents, so that each combination into which they enter
merely expresses a relation between their contents, they at once stand
14   for themselves as soon as they | are combined by the symbol for iden-
tity of content; for this signifies [*bezeichnet*] the circumstance that two
names have the same content. Thus with the introduction of a symbol
for identity of content a bifurcation in the meaning of every symbol is
necessarily effected, the same symbols standing one moment for their
content, the next moment for themselves. This makes it appear at first
as if it were here a matter of what pertains to the *expression* alone, *not to
the thought*, and as if there were no need at all for different symbols for
the same content and hence for a symbol for identity of content either.
To show that this appearance is deceptive, I take the following example
from geometry.[25]

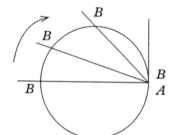

[*As the line turns in the direction
of the arrow, B moves towards A,
until they coincide.*]

On the circumference of a circle lies a fixed point *A*, around which a
straight line rotates. When the latter forms a diameter, let us call the point
at the opposite end to *A* the point *B*. Let us then call, more generally,
the point of intersection of the line and the circumference at any given
moment the point *B*, resulting from the rule that continuous changes
in position of the line always correspond to continuous changes in position of *B*. The name *B* therefore denotes[26] something indeterminate so
long as the relevant position of the line is not given. It can now be asked:
what point is yielded when the line is perpendicular to the diameter?

---

[24] The German term here is 'Inhaltsgleichheit', which has also been translated as 'equality of content'. Throughout his writings, both here and in his later work, Frege makes
clear that he understands 'Gleichheit' in the sense of 'identity'; so either rendering is
correct. Cf. *SB*, fn. A, p. 151 below.
[25] Following Geach, a diagram is added here to help the reader. Compare this with the
example Frege later gives in *SB*, p. 152 below.
[26] The verb 'bedeutet' is again being used in its *vertical* sense, making 'denotes' the more
appropriate translation; cf. fn. 14 above.

The answer will be: the point *A*. The name *B* has therefore in this case the same content as the name *A*; and yet just one name could not have been used from the beginning, since the justification for doing so is only provided by this answer. The same point is determined in two ways:

(1) immediately through intuition [*Anschauung*],
(2) as the point *B* when the line is perpendicular to the diameter.

To each of these two modes of determination there corresponds a separate name. The need for a symbol for identity of content thus rests on the following: the same content can be fully determined in different ways; but that, in a particular case, *the same content* is actually given by *two modes of determination* is the content of a *judgement*. Before this judgement can be made, two different names corresponding to the two modes of determination must be provided for that that is thereby determined. But the judgement requires for its expression a symbol for | identity of content to combine the two names. It follows from this that different names for the same content are not always merely a trivial matter of formulation, but touch the very heart of the matter if they are connected with different modes of determination.[27] In this case the judgement as to identity of content is, in the Kantian sense, synthetic. A secondary reason for introducing a symbol for identity of content is that it is occasionally useful to introduce an abbreviation in place of a lengthy expression. The abbreviation and the original expression must then be stated to have the same content.

$$\vdash\!\!\!-\!\!\!- (A \equiv B)$$

is therefore to mean: *the symbol A and the symbol B have the same conceptual content, so that A can always be replaced by B and vice versa.*

The function

§9. Let us suppose that the circumstance that hydrogen is lighter than carbon dioxide is expressed in our formula language. Then in place of the symbol for hydrogen we can insert the symbol for oxygen or that for nitrogen. This changes the sense in such a way that 'oxygen' or 'nitrogen' enters into the relations in which 'hydrogen' stood before. If an expression is thought of as variable in this way, it splits up into a constant

---

[27] It is this idea that Frege later realized required the distinguishing between *Sinn* and *Bedeutung*. Two names may have the same *Bedeutung* (the same 'content'), but different senses (if, as in the example here, they are connected with different 'modes of determination'). For Frege's later critique of his *BS* view that identity of content merely relates to names, see the opening passage of *SB*, pp. 151–2 below.

component, which represents the totality of relations, and a symbol which can be thought of as replaceable by others and which denotes[28] the object that stands in these relations. The former component I call a function, the latter its argument. This distinction has nothing to do with the conceptual content, but only with our way of grasping it. Although as viewed in the way just indicated, 'hydrogen' was the argument and 'being lighter than carbon dioxide' the function, we can also grasp the same conceptual content in such a way that 'carbon dioxide' becomes the argument and

16   'being heavier than hydrogen' the function. We | need then only think of 'carbon dioxide' as replaceable by other ideas such as 'hydrogen chloride gas' or 'ammonia'.[29]

'The circumstance that carbon dioxide is heavier than hydrogen'

and

'the circumstance that carbon dioxide is heavier than oxygen'

are the same function with different arguments if 'hydrogen' and 'oxygen' are regarded as arguments; on the other hand, they are different functions of the same argument if 'carbon dioxide' is taken as the argument.

Consider now the example: 'the circumstance that the centre of mass of the solar system has no acceleration, if only internal forces act on the solar system'. Here 'solar system' occurs in two places. We can therefore take this as a function of the argument 'solar system' in different ways, depending on whether we think of 'solar system' as replaceable at its first occurrence or at its second or at both (but in the last case by the same argument both times). These three functions are all different. The proposition that Cato killed Cato shows the same thing. Here, if we think of 'Cato' as replaceable at its first occurrence, then 'killing Cato' is the function; if we think of 'Cato' as replaceable at its second occurrence, then 'being killed by Cato' is the function; finally, if we think of 'Cato' as replaceable at both occurrences, then 'killing oneself' is the function.

---

[28] The verb 'bedeutet' is again being used here in its *vertical* sense; cf. fn. 14 above.

[29] As both this paragraph and the rest of the section reveal, there is a certain amount of unclarity as to what exactly Frege takes functions and arguments to be. They are initially, and officially (see the fourth paragraph), characterized as *expressions*. But Frege also uses inverted commas to indicate not expressions but the corresponding *ideas (Vorstellungen)* or *concepts*, which Frege himself seems to want to distinguish from the expressions (see especially the sixth paragraph). In his later work, on the other hand, after the *Sinn/Bedeutung* distinction had been drawn, functions are quite clearly regarded as the *Bedeutungen* of functional expressions – 'incomplete' or 'unsaturated' expressions that result from removing one or more proper names from a sentence – and arguments are taken as objects. See especially *CSB*, pp. 172ff. below.

We now express the matter generally:

If, in an expression (whose content need not be a judgeable content), a simple or complex symbol occurs in one or more places, and we think of it as replaceable at all or some of its occurrences by another symbol (but everywhere by the same symbol), then we call the part of the expression that on this occasion appears invariant the function, and the replaceable part its argument.

Accordingly, since something can occur as argument and at the same time at places in the function where it is not thought of as replaceable, we distinguish the argument-places from the other places in the function. |

17 A warning should be issued here against an illusion which the use of ordinary language easily generates. If the two propositions

'The number 20 is representable as the sum of four squares'

and

'Every positive whole number is representable as the sum of four squares'

are compared, it appears to be possible to take 'being representable as the sum of four squares' as the function which has as its argument 'the number 20' one time and 'every positive whole number' the other time. The error of this view can be recognized in realizing that 'the number 20' and 'every positive whole number' are not concepts of the same rank. What is asserted of the number 20 cannot be asserted in the same sense of 'every positive whole number', though it may well be asserted of every positive whole number in certain circumstances.[30] The expression 'every positive whole number', unlike 'the number 20', does not by itself alone give rise to an independent idea, but only acquires a sense in the context of a proposition.[31]

[30] Here what Frege seems to be referring to by the phrase in inverted commas, as indicated by the previous sentence, is indeed a *concept* (cf. the previous fn.); although it might more naturally have been taken to refer to the *set* of positive whole numbers, in which case the point would be that what can be asserted of each positive whole number, taken individually, cannot necessarily be asserted of all the positive whole numbers, taken collectively.
[31] This could be regarded as the first appeal in Frege's work to a context principle – here governing only subject terms involving quantifiers such as 'every positive whole number', whose semantic contribution to the meaning of sentences in which they appear does not lie in signifying a single object, as plausibly occurs in the case of genuine proper names. This is presumably what Frege means by saying that there is no 'independent idea' ('selbständige Vorstellung') involved here. Propositions of the form 'Every *A* is a *B*' are analysed not in subject-predicate terms – taking 'Every *A*' as the subject – but in function-argument terms, the proposition being construed as 'For all *x*, if *x* is an *A*, then *x* is a *B*' (cf. the next fn.). By the time of *GL*, however, the appeal to a context principle has become generalized. All words, and *in particular*, such proper names as 'the number 20', only have meaning in the context of a proposition, although numbers are nevertheless taken as 'independent' ('selbständige') objects. See especially *GL*, §60 (pp. 108–9 below); and for discussion, see the Introduction, §3 above.

For us the different ways in which the same conceptual content can be taken as a function of this or that argument has no importance so long as function and argument are fully determined. But if the argument becomes *indeterminate* as in the judgement 'You can take as argument for "being representable as the sum of four squares" whatever positive whole number you like: the proposition always remains correct', then the distinction between function and argument acquires significance with regard to *content*.[32] Conversely too, the argument can be determinate but the function indeterminate. In both cases, through the opposition between the *determinate* and the *indeterminate* or the *more* and the *less* determinate, the whole splits up into *function* and *argument* according to its content and not merely according to our way of grasping it.

If, in a function, a symbol that has up to now been viewed as not replaceable[G] is thought of as replaceable at some or all of the places at which it occurs,
18 *then, by being grasped in this way,* | *a function is obtained that has another argument besides the previous one.* In this way *functions of two or more arguments* arise. Thus, for example, 'the circumstance that hydrogen is lighter than carbon dioxide' can be taken as a function of the two arguments 'hydrogen' and 'carbon dioxide'.

The subject [of a proposition] is usually intended by the speaker to be the principal argument; the next most important often appears as the object. Through the choice of [grammatical] forms such as active and passive, and words such as 'heavier' and 'lighter', 'give' and 'receive', ordinary language has the freedom of allowing whatever part of the proposition it wishes to appear as the principal argument, a freedom, however, that is limited by the paucity of words.

§10. *In order to express an indeterminate function of the argument A, let us enclose A in brackets after a letter, as in*

$$\Phi(A).$$

Similarly,

$$\Psi(A, B)$$

signifies a function of the two arguments A and B, which is not further determined. Here the places of A and B in the brackets represent the places

---

[G] Equally, a symbol that has already been thought of as replaceable [at some places] can also be regarded as replaceable at places where it was previously seen as constant.

[32] The German phrase here is 'gewinnt . . . eine *inhaltliche* Bedeutung'. Frege's claim rests on his construal of propositions of the form 'Every *A* is a *B*' as 'For all *x*, if *x* is an *A*, then *x* is a *B*', which clearly does presuppose function-argument analysis (see §§11–12 of *BS* below), and, Frege would argue, does not just give us an alternative way of regarding the content, but represents the structure of the content itself.

that A and B occupy in the function, irrespective of whether *A* or *B* occupy one or more places. *Thus*

$$\Psi(A,\ B) \quad and \quad \Psi(B,\ A)$$

are in general different.

Indeterminate functions of several arguments are expressed in a corresponding way.

$$\vdash\!\!\!-\!-\ \Phi(A)$$

can be read: '*A* has the property *Φ*'.

$$\vdash\!\!\!-\!-\ \Psi(A, B)$$

may be translated as '*B* stands in the *Ψ*-relation to *A*' or '*B* is a result of an application of the procedure *Ψ* to the object *A*'.[33]

Since the symbol *Φ* occurs in the expression *Φ*(*A*) and | can be thought of as replaced by other symbols *Ψ*, *X*, by means of which other functions of the argument *A* are then expressed, *Φ*(*A*) *can be regarded as a function of the argument Φ*. One sees here particularly clearly that the concept of function in Analysis, which in general I have followed, is far more restricted than that developed here.[34]

Generality

§11.   In the expression of a judgement, the complex of symbols to the right of $\vdash\!\!\!-\!-$ can always be regarded as a function of one of the symbols occurring in it. *If a Gothic [old German] letter is put in place of the argument, and a concavity containing this letter inserted in the content stroke, as in*

$$\vdash\!\!\!-\!\smile\!\!\alpha\!\frown\!\!-\!-\ \Phi(\alpha),$$

then this signifies the judgement that the function is a fact whatever may be taken as its argument.[35] Since a letter used as a symbol for a function, such as *Φ* in *Φ*(*A*), can be regarded as the argument of a function, it can be replaced by a Gothic letter in the manner just specified. The meaning of a Gothic letter is subject only to the obvious restrictions that the complex of symbols following a content stroke must still remain judgeable (§2), and that, if the Gothic letter occurs as a symbol for a function,

[33] It should be noted that the relational expression '*Ψ*(*A*, *B*)' is here understood the opposite way round to how modern logicians, and indeed Frege himself in *GG* (I, §4; pp. 214–15 below), understand expressions of this form. Cf. fn. 28 on p. 214 below.
[34] For fuller discussion of Frege's development of the concept of function, see *FC*, pp. 130ff. below.
[35] In modern notation, '(∀x)*Fx*'. On the differences between Frege's symbolism and modern symbolism, see Appendix 2 below.

this circumstance must be taken into account. *All other conditions which must be imposed on what may replace a Gothic letter are to be included in the judgement.* From such a judgement, therefore, however many *judgements with less general content* we like can be derived, by replacing the Gothic letter each time by something different, the concavity in the content stroke disappearing again.[36] The horizontal stroke to the left of the concavity in

$$\vdash\!\!\!-\!\!\!-\!\!\!\cup_{\!\alpha}\!\!\!-\!\!\!-\ \Phi(\alpha)$$

is the content stroke for [the judgeable content] that $\Phi(\alpha)$ is valid whatever may be substituted for α; the horizontal stroke to the right of the concavity | is the content stroke of $\Phi(\alpha)$, where α must be thought of as substituted by something definite.

   From what was said above about the meaning of the judgement stroke, it is easy to see what an expression such as

$$-\!\!\!-\!\!\!-\!\!\!\cup_{\!\alpha}\!\!\!-\!\!\!-\ X(\alpha)$$

means. This expression can occur as part of a judgement, as in

$$\vdash\!\!\!\top\!\!\cup_{\!\alpha}\!\!\!-\ X(\alpha),\qquad \vdash\!\!\!\!\!\begin{array}{l}\rule{1.5cm}{0.4pt}\ A\\ \rule{0.8cm}{0pt}\llcorner\!\!\cup_{\!\alpha}\!\!\!-\ X(\alpha).\end{array}$$

It is clear that from these judgements, unlike from

$$\vdash\!\!\!-\!\!\!\cup_{\!\alpha}\!\!\!-\ \Phi(\alpha),$$

less general judgements cannot be derived by substituting something definite for α.

$$\vdash\!\!\!\top\!\!\cup_{\!\alpha}\!\!\!-\ X(\alpha)$$

denies that $X(\alpha)$ is always a fact whatever may be substituted for α. This in no way denies that α can be given a meaning Δ such that $X(\Delta)$ is a fact.[37]

$$\vdash\!\!\!\!\!\begin{array}{l}\rule{1.5cm}{0.4pt}\ A\\ \rule{0.8cm}{0pt}\llcorner\!\!\cup_{\!\alpha}\!\!\!-\ X(\alpha)\end{array}$$

means that the case in which

$$-\!\!\!-\!\!\!\cup_{\!\alpha}\!\!\!-\ X(\alpha)$$

is affirmed and A is denied does not obtain. But this in no way denies that the case in which $X(\Delta)$ is affirmed and A is denied obtains; since, as we have just seen, $X(\Delta)$ can be affirmed and yet

---

[36] From '$(\forall x)Fx$', in other words, we can derive Fa, Fb, Fc, etc.

[37] Here the word 'Bedeutung' might also be translated as 'value'. Cf. fn. 39 below.

$$\underline{\quad\underset{\alpha}{\frown}\quad} X(\alpha)$$

denied. Thus here also α cannot be substituted by whatever we like without threatening the truth of the judgement. This explains why the concavity with the Gothic letter inscribed is necessary: *it delimits the scope of the generality signified [bezeichnete] by the letter. Only within its scope does a Gothic letter retain its meaning*; the same Gothic letter can occur within various scopes in one judgement, without the meaning that may be ascribed to it in one scope carrying over to the others. The scope of a Gothic letter can include that of another, as the example |

21

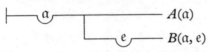

shows. In this case *different* letters must be chosen; e may not be replaced by α. It is, of course, permitted to replace a Gothic letter everywhere in its scope by another particular one, provided that there are still different letters standing where different letters stood before. This has no effect on the content. *Other substitutions are only allowed if the concavity immediately follows the judgement stroke*, so that the content of the whole judgement makes up the scope of the Gothic letter. Accordingly, since this case is particularly important, I shall introduce the following abbreviation for it. *An italic letter always has as its scope the content of the whole judgement*, without this needing to be signified [*bezeichnet*] by a concavity in the content stroke. If an italic letter occurs in an expression that is not preceded by a judgement stroke, then this expression is senseless.[38] *An italic letter may always be replaced by a Gothic letter that does not yet occur in the judgement*, the concavity being inserted immediately after the judgement stroke. E.g. instead of

$$\vdash\!\!\!-\!\!\!- X(a)$$

one can put

$$\vdash\!\!\!-\underset{\alpha}{\frown}\!\!\!- X(\alpha)$$

if *a* occurs only in the argument-places of $X(a)$.

It is also clear that from

$$\vdash\!\!\!-\!\!\begin{array}{l}\!\!-\Phi(a)\\[4pt]\!\!-A\end{array}$$

one can derive

---

[38] As Bynum remarks (*CN*, p. 132, fn. 16), Frege need only have insisted that the *content stroke* should precede every expression containing an italic letter – the content stroke, that is, that has as its scope the whole of the symbol combination in which that italic letter appears (it may appear more than once).

if A is an expression in which a does not occur, and if a stands only in the
argument-places of Φ(a). If

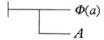

is denied, then it must be possible to provide a meaning for *a* such that
Φ(*a*) is denied.[39] Thus if

were denied and *A* affirmed, then it would have to be possible to
provide a meaning for *a* such that *A* was affirmed and Φ(*a*) denied. But
because of |

22

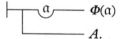

this cannot be done; since this [symbol] means that, whatever *a* may
be, the case in which Φ(*a*) is denied and *A* affirmed is excluded. Hence
one cannot deny

and affirm *A*; i.e.:

. . .

Something similar applies when more conditional strokes are
involved.[40]

§12. We now consider some combinations of symbols.

23 | means that something can be found, say *Δ*, such that *X(Δ)* is denied.
It can therefore be translated: 'There are some things that do not have
the property *X*'.[41]

---

[39] Here, and in the next sentence, the phrase 'eine Bedeutung für *a* angeben' might also
be translated 'to find a value for *a*', highlighting a use of 'Bedeutung' that is close to
Frege's later technical use of the term. Cf. the Introduction, pp. 42f. above.

[40] Immediately prior to this remark, Frege provides one further example, involving two
conditional strokes, which is omitted here.

[41] I.e. '¬(∀x)Fx', which is equivalent to '(∃x) ¬Fx', here calling the property *X* (symbolized by the Greek letter *chi*) 'F'.

The sense of

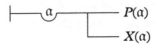

is different. This means: 'Whatever α may be, $X(α)$ is always to be denied', or: 'There is nothing that has the property X'; or, if we call something that has property X [*chi*] a X: 'There is no X'.[42]

$$\underline{\quad α \quad}\ \Lambda(α)$$

is denied by

$$\vdash\ α\ \Lambda(α).$$

It can therefore be translated: 'There are Λ's'.[H][43]

means: 'Whatever may be substituted for α, the case in which $P(α)$ would have to be denied and $X(α)$ affirmed does not obtain'. It is thus possible here that, for some meanings that could be given to α,[44]

$P(α)$ would have to be affirmed and $X(α)$ affirmed; for others,
$P(α)$ would have to be affirmed and $X(α)$ denied; for still others,
$P(α)$ would have to be denied and $X(α)$ denied.

It can therefore be translated: 'If something has the property X, then it also has the property P', or: 'Every X is a P', or: 'All X's are P's'.[45] *This is how causal connections are expressed.*

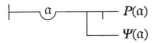

means: 'No meaning can be given to α such that $P(α)$ and $\Psi(α)$ could both be affirmed'. It can | therefore be translated: 'What has the property Ψ does not have the property P', or: 'No Ψ is a P'.[46]

24

[H] This is to be understood as including the case 'There is one Λ'. If e.g. $\Lambda(x)$ signifies the circumstance that x is a house, then

$$\vdash\ α\ \Lambda(α)$$

reads: 'There are houses or is at least one house'. Cf. §2, fn. E.

[42] I.e. '$(\forall x)\ \neg Fx$', which is equivalent to '$\neg(\exists x)Fx$'.
[43] I.e. '$\neg(\forall x)\ \neg Fx$', which is equivalent to '$(\exists x)Fx$'.
[44] I.e. 'for some values of α'. Cf. fn. 39 above.
[45] I.e. '$(\forall x)(Fx \rightarrow Px)$', again calling the property X here 'F'.
[46] I.e. '$(\forall x)(\Psi x \rightarrow \neg Px)$'.

denies

and can therefore be rendered as: 'Some Λ's are not P's'.[47]

denies that no M is a P, and therefore means: 'Some[I] M's are P's'; or: 'It is possible for a M [*mu*] to be a P'.[48]

The square of logical opposition thus results:[49]

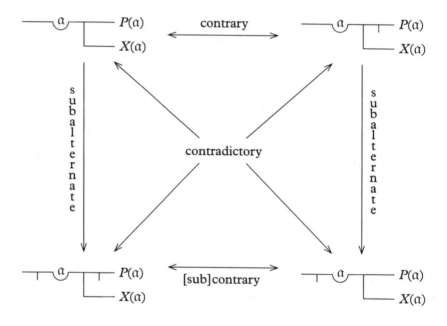

[I] The word 'some' ['*einige*'] is always to be understood here as including the case 'one'. One might expand by saying: 'some or at least one'.

[47] I.e. '$\neg(\forall x)(\Lambda x \rightarrow Px)$', which is equivalent to '$(\exists x)(\Lambda x \,\&\, \neg Px)$'.

[48] I.e. '$\neg(\forall x)(Mx \rightarrow \neg Px)$', which is equivalent to '$(\exists x)(Mx \,\&\, Px)$'.

[49] Frege's reproduction of the Aristotelian square of opposition is misleading in several respects, for Frege fails to point out that the traditional relations of contrariety, sub-contrariety (which in the text Frege did not himself distinguish from contrariety) and subalternation are all invalidated under his formalizations. See Appendix 2 below.

[This marks the end of Part I. In Part II, entitled 'Representation and Derivation of some Judgements of Pure Thought' (§§13–22), Frege lays down nine axioms,[50] and illustrates the use of his *Begriffsschrift* by showing how various propositions can be formulated and proved within it. In Part III, entitled 'Some Elements from a General Theory of Series', he then provides an analysis of mathematical induction. A summary of this follows here.

Frege starts by defining the notion of an *hereditary property*. A property F is *hereditary in the f-series* if the following condition is met (formulating it in modern notation rather than Frege's *Begriffsschrift*):[51]

(HP) $(\forall x)(Fx \rightarrow (\forall y)(f(x, y) \rightarrow Fy))$. (Cf. §24, formula 69.)

'$f(x, y)$' is understood as symbolizing that 'y is a result of an application of the procedure f to x' or, equivalently, that 'y stands in the f-relation to x'. (HP) can then be read as follows:

(HP†)   From the proposition that x has the property F, whatever x may be, it can be inferred that every result of an application of the procedure f to x has the property F. (Cf. §24.)

Frege gives the following example to illustrate the idea. Let '$f(x, y)$' mean that y is the child of x, and let F be the property of being a human being. Then the f-series is the series starting with x and continuing through the descendants of x, and it is clear that F is hereditary, since every child of a human being is in turn a human being (ibid.).

With the notion of an hereditary property, Frege proceeds to define the concept of *following in a series*, or as it would now be termed, the concept of the *proper ancestral* of a relation. Using (HP) to abbreviate the formula given above, 'b follows a in the f-series' can be defined thus:

(PA) $(\forall F)(\{(HP) \ \& \ (\forall y)(f(a, y) \rightarrow Fy)\} \rightarrow Fb)$. (Cf. §26, formula 76.)

In words, this reads:

(PA†)   From the two propositions that the property F is hereditary in the f-series and that every result of an application of the procedure f to a has the property F, whatever F may be, it can be inferred that b has the property F. (Cf. §26.)

Clearly, if b does follow a in the f-series, then any hereditary property that a has will also be possessed by b, so that (PA) holds (cf. §27, formula

---

[50] For details, see Appendix 2 below.
[51] The labelling that follows – (HP), (PA), etc. – is also not Frege's own.

77).[52] Conversely, if, whenever F is an hereditary property, and anything that is a result of an application of f to a has the property F, b also has the property F, then b must follow a in the f-series (cf. §28, formula 93).[53] For consider the property of *following a in the f-series*. This clearly satisfies (HP), and hence is hereditary (cf. §28, formula 97). Any result of applying f to a, of course, possesses this property (cf. §28, formula 91), so that both conjuncts of the antecedent of (PA) hold. If (PA) itself holds, then (by *modus ponens*) Fb can be deduced, i.e. b has the property of following a in the f-series. So 'b follows a in the f-series' and (PA) are equivalent.

It is easy to see how a characterization of mathematical induction can now be provided. For the following proposition can immediately be written down:

(MI) $(Fa$ & (HP) & (PA)$) \rightarrow Fb$. (Cf. §27, formula 81.)

From Fa and (HP), $(\forall y)(f(a, y) \rightarrow Fy)$ can be derived, from which, with (HP) again, by (PA), Fb results. Expressed in words, (MI) reads:

(MI†)   If a has a property F which is hereditary in the f-series, and if b follows a in the f-series, then b has the property F. (Cf. §27.)

This is precisely the key step in mathematical induction. For with the additional assumption that the first member of the f-series has the hereditary property F, it can clearly be shown that every member of the f-series has the property F.[54]

Frege goes on to define 'b belongs to the f-series beginning with a', that is, what would now be termed the *ancestral* of the f-relation, which can be formulated, very simply, thus:

(AR) $b = a \ \lor$ (PA). (Cf. §29, formula 99.)

---

[52] It should be noted here that (PA) involves quantification over functions, i.e. presupposes second-order predicate logic. Frege did not at the time of *BS* distinguish between first-order and higher-order quantification, and his derivation of formula 77 in fact requires amendment; cf. Bynum's footnote to this derivation in *CN*, pp. 174–5, and fn. 88 of his 'Editor's Introduction', 1972b: §8/*CN*, p. 72.

[53] On the necessary amendment to its derivation, see Bynum's footnote in *CN*, p. 183 (cf. fn. 52 above). On the informal demonstration of the validity of the converse relation in what follows, by considering the property of *following a in the f-series*, cf. Currie, 1982: p. 38.

[54] Frege gives the following example: let F be the property of being a heap of beans, and f be the procedure of removing one bean. Then the result is obtained – this is the traditional Sorites paradox – that one bean and even no beans at all is a heap of beans. The property of being a heap cannot, therefore, be hereditary in the f-series; and this is due, Frege suggests, to the vagueness of the concept *heap*, which allows some values of 'x is a heap' to be indeterminate (cf. §27).

The reading here is equally straightforward:

(AR†) b is the same as a, or b follows a in the f-series. (Cf. §29.)

In the remainder of Part III, Frege derives further properties of series, using the notions introduced, and offers one final definition, of the *many-one* relation. A procedure f is *many-one* (*eindeutig*) if the following condition obtains:

(MO) $(\forall x)(\forall y)\{f(x, y) \rightarrow (\forall z)(f(x, z) \rightarrow z = y)\}$. (Cf. §31, formula 115.)

Informally, this reads:

(MO†) From the circumstance that y is a result of an application of the procedure f to x, whatever x may be, it can be inferred that every result of an application of the procedure f to x is the same as y. (Cf. §31.)

Although Frege does not himself do so in the *Begriffsschrift*, it is also worth formulating here the condition that must be met for a relation to be *one-many*:

(OM) $(\forall x)(\forall y)\{f(x, y) \rightarrow (\forall w)(f(w, y) \rightarrow w = x)\}$.

A *one-one* relation can then be defined as a relation that is both many-one and one-many, that is, that fulfils the combined condition:[55]

(OO) $(\forall x)(\forall y)\{f(x, y) \rightarrow ((\forall z)[f(x, z) \rightarrow z = y] \ \& \ (\forall w)[f(w, y) \rightarrow w = x])\}$.

Developing Frege's earlier example, we may say that the relation of parent to eldest child is thus many-one, the relation of father to child (in cases where there is more than one child) one-many, and the relation of father to eldest child one-one.

Both the analysis of mathematical induction and the definition of a one-one relation were to play a crucial role in Frege's subsequent work; what he had shown in the *Begriffsschrift* was that they could be given in

---

[55] To say that a relation is many-one is not to say that, for any member of the f-series, there is necessarily more than one (immediate) predecessor, but merely that, for any member, there is only one result of applying f, i.e. that any member has a unique (immediate) successor. Similarly, to say that a relation is one-many is merely to say that any member has a unique (immediate) predecessor. There is nothing paradoxical, then, about a one-one relation being both many-one and one-many.

purely logical terms.[56] As he remarked in his introduction to Part III:

> one sees in this example how pure thought, regardless of any content given
> through the senses or even *a priori* through an intuition, is capable of
> bringing forth by itself, from the content which arises from its own nature,
> judgements which at first sight only seem possible on the basis of some
> intuition. This can be compared to condensation, by means of which air,
> which appears to a child's mind to be nothing, can be transformed into a
> visible fluid forming drops. The propositions about series developed [in this
> Part] far surpass in generality all similar propositions that can be derived
> from any intuition of series. (§23)

The success of his initial condensations no doubt convinced Frege of
the possibility of providing logical definitions of *all* arithmetical concepts
and forms of reasoning. The next step was to provide definitions of the
numbers themselves, and this was the task he undertook in his second
book, *The Foundations of Arithmetic*.[57]]

---

[56] As he later put it in *GL*, §80: 'Only by means of this definition of following in a series
is it possible to reduce the transition from n to $(n + 1)$, which is apparently peculiar to
mathematics, to the general laws of logic'. Cf. *GL*, §91 (p. 124 below).

[57] See pp. 84–129 below.

Letter to Marty,
29.8.1882[1]

[Anton Marty (1847–1914) was a pupil of Brentano, and was professor of philosophy at Prague University from 1890. There is some doubt[2] as to whether this letter was addressed to Marty rather than to Carl Stumpf (1848–1936), a close colleague of Marty and professor of philosophy at Prague at the time, since it is Stumpf who replies to the letter.[3] But the letter itself is important for the light it sheds on Frege's development between the publication of the *Begriffsschrift* in 1879 and the *Grundlagen* in 1884. Frege's logicist ambition, and its underlying motivation, are clearly revealed here; and he has become more aware of the significance of his invention of quantifier notation, which enables him to formalize universal and particular propositions, and exhibit the logical relations between them. The letter also marks the first appearance of Frege's doctrine of the 'unsaturated' nature of concepts.[4]]

163

Jena

29 August 1882

Dear Colleague,

Your friendly postcard gave me much pleasure, the more so as I have found only very little agreement up to now. Allow me to give you some more information about my *Begriffsschrift*, in the hope that you will perhaps have occasion to call attention to it in a journal; it would make it easier for me to publish further works. I have now nearly completed a book in which I treat the concept of Number[5] and demonstrate that the first principles of computation which up to now have generally been regarded as unprovable axioms can be proved from definitions by means of logical laws alone, so that they may have to be regarded as analytic judgements in Kant's sense. It will not surprise me and I even expect that you will

---

[1] Translated by Hans Kaal (*PMC*, pp. 99–102; from *WB*, pp.162–5; page numbers from the latter in the margin).

[2] Cf. *PMC*, p. 99/*WB*, p. 162.

[3] See *PMC*, pp. 171–2/*WB*, pp. 256–7.

[4] Cf. e.g. *FC*, p. 139 below; *CSB*, pp. 173–6 below; *GG*, I, §1 (pp. 211–12 below); *NLD*, pp. 363–4 below; and esp. *CO*, pp. 181–93 below.

[5] On the translation of 'Anzahl' as 'Number', see fn. 6 on p. 91 below.

raise some doubts about this and imagine that there is a mistake in the definitions, in that, to be possible, they presuppose judgements which I have failed to notice, or in that some other essential content from another source of knowledge has crept in unawares. My confidence that this has not happened is based on the application of my *Begriffsschrift*, which will not let through anything that was not expressly presupposed, even if it seems so obvious that in ordinary thought we do not even notice that we are relying on it for support. This seems to place the value and the power of discursive thought in the right light. For whereas Leibniz may well have overestimated it when he hoped to prove everything from concepts, Kant on the contrary seems to me to place too low an estimate on the significance [*Bedeutung*] of analytic judgements because he sticks to oversimple examples. I regard it as one of Kant's great merits to have recognized the propositions of geometry as synthetic judgements, but I cannot allow him the same in the case of arithmetic.[6] The two cases are anyway quite different. The field of geometry is the field of possible spatial intuition; arithmetic recognizes no such limitation. Everything is enumerable, not just what is juxtaposed in space, not just what is successive in time, not just external phenomena, but also inner mental processes and events and even concepts, which stand neither in temporal nor in spatial but only in logical relations to one another.[7] The only barrier to enumerability is to be found in the imperfection of concepts. Bald people for example cannot be enumerated as long as the concept of baldness is not defined so precisely that for any individual there can be no doubt whether he falls under it. Thus the area of the enumerable is as wide as that

164　of conceptual thought, and | a source of knowledge more restricted in scope, like spatial intuition or sense perception, would not suffice to guarantee the general validity of arithmetical propositions. And to enable one to rely on intuition for support, it does not help at all to let something spatial represent something non-spatial in enumeration; for one would have to justify the admissibility of such a representation. But I wanted to tell you something about my *Begriffsschrift*. You emphasize the division between the function of judgement and the matter judged. The distinction between individual and concept seems to me even more important.[8] In language the two merge into each other. The proper name 'sun' becomes a concept name when one speaks of suns, and a concept name with a demonstrative serves to designate an individual. In logic, too, this

---

[6] Cf. *GL*, §§88–9 (pp. 122–3 below).

[7] Cf. *GL*, §14 (see p. 95 below).

[8] That this distinction must be kept in mind is the third of the three 'fundamental principles' of *GL* (see p. 90 below).

distinction has not always been observed (for Boole only concepts really exist).[9] The relation of subordination of a concept under a concept is quite different from that of an individual falling under a concept.[10] It seems that logicians have clung too much to the linguistic schema of subject and predicate, which surely contains what are logically quite different relations.[11] I regard it as essential for a concept that the question whether something falls under it have a sense.[12] Thus I would call 'Christianity' a concept only in the sense in which it is used in the proposition 'This way of life is Christianity', but not in the proposition 'Christianity continues to spread'. A concept is unsaturated [*ungesättigt*] in that it requires something to fall under it; hence it cannot exist on its own. That an individual falls under it is a judgeable content, and here the concept appears as a predicate and is always predicative. In this case, where the subject is an individual, the relation of subject to predicate is not a third thing added to the two, but it belongs to the content of the predicate, which is what makes the predicate unsaturated. Now I do not believe that concept formation can precede judgement, because this would presuppose the independent existence of concepts, but I think of a concept as having arisen by decomposition from a judgeable content. I do not believe that for any judgeable content there is only one way in which it can be decomposed, or that one of these possible ways can always claim objective pre-eminence.[13] In the inequality 3 > 2 we can regard either 2 or 3 as the subject. In the former case we have the concept 'smaller than 3', in the latter, 'greater than 2'. We can also regard '3 and 2' as a complex subject. As a predicate we then have the concept of the relation of the greater to the smaller. In general I represent the falling of an individual under a concept by $F(x)$, where x is the subject (argument) and $F(\ )$ the predicate (function), and where the empty place in the parentheses after F indicates unsaturation. The subordination of a concept $\Psi(\ )$ under a concept $\Phi(\ )$ is expressed by[14] |

165

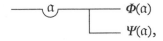

$$\Phi(\alpha)$$
$$\Psi(\alpha),$$

[9] For a detailed critique of Boolean logic, see *BLF* and especially *BLC*.

[10] On the importance of distinguishing subordination from subsumption, cf. *CSB*, p. 175 below; *CO*, pp. 189–90; below; *IL*, p. 296 below; 'Letters to Husserl, 1906', p. 303 below; *NLD*, p. 363 below.

[11] Cf. *BS*, Preface (p. 51 above).

[12] Cf. esp. *GG*, II, §56 (p. 259 below).

[13] Cf. *BS*, §9 (pp. 65–8 above); *CO*, p. 188 below.

[14] I.e. '$(\forall x)(\Psi x \rightarrow \Phi x)$', in modern notation.

which makes obvious the difference between subordination and an individual's falling under a concept. Without the strict distinction between individual and concept it is impossible to express particular and existential judgements accurately and in such a way as to make their close relationship obvious. For every particular judgement is an existential judgement.

$$\vdash \!\!-\!\!\top\!\!-\!\!\cup\!\!\alpha\!\!-\!\!\top\!\!- \; \alpha^2 = 4$$

means [*bedeutet*]: 'There is at least one square root of 4'.

$$\vdash \!\!-\!\!\top\!\!-\!\!\cup\!\!\alpha\!\!-\!\!\top\!\!\top\!\!- \; \alpha^2 = 4$$
$$\qquad\qquad\qquad\quad \vdash \alpha^3 = 8$$

means [*bedeutet*]: 'Some (at least one) cube roots of 8 are square roots of 4'. One can insert here two negation strokes that cancel each other:

$$\vdash \!\!-\!\!\top\!\!-\!\!\cup\!\!\alpha\!\!-\!\!\top\!\!\top\!\!\top\!\!- \; \alpha^2 = 4$$
$$\qquad\qquad\qquad\quad \vdash \alpha^3 = 8$$

and think of this as composed of

$$\vdash , \quad -\!\!\top\!\!-\!\!\cup\!\!\alpha\!\!-\!\!\top\!\!- , \quad \text{and} \quad \top\!\!\top\!\!- \; \alpha^2 = 4$$
$$\qquad\qquad\qquad\qquad\qquad\qquad\quad \vdash \alpha^3 = 8.$$

The latter takes the place of $\alpha^2 = 4$ in

$$\vdash \!\!-\!\!\top\!\!-\!\!\cup\!\!\alpha\!\!-\!\!\top\!\!- \; \alpha^2 = 4,$$

so that it can be translated as: 'There is at least one number which is both a cube root of 8 and a square root of 4'. Existential judgements thus take their place among other judgements.[15] I should still like to show you how Kant's refutation of the ontological argument becomes intuitively very obvious when presented in my way[16] and what the value of the concavity is, which is my sign of generality,[17] but I fear I have already overburdened you with my long letter. I find it difficult to gain entry into the philosophical journals. Please excuse this letter as springing from my unsatisfied need for communication. I find myself in a vicious circle: before people pay attention to my *Begriffsschrift*, they want to see what it can do, and I in turn cannot show this without presupposing familiarity with it. So it seems that I can hardly count on any readers for the book I mentioned at the beginning. If you would be so good as to answer

[15] Cf. *BS*, §12 (pp. 72–4 above).
[16] See *GL*, §53 (pp. 102–3 below).
[17] See *BS*, §§11–12 (pp. 69–74 above).

me, I would ask you to communicate your doubts. I should like to find out what you think of the scientific value of the demonstration I am planning, supposing it succeeds and is carried out with the most painstaking precision.[18]

Yours sincerely,
G. Frege

---

[18] In his reply (dated 9 September 1882) to what seems clear is this letter, Stumpf encourages Frege in his work, but recommends that he explain his planned demonstration in ordinary language first, before setting it out in his logical symbolism (cf. *PMC*, pp. 171–2/*WB*, pp. 256–7). Frege apparently heeded Stumpf's advice: the *Grundlagen* of 1884 did indeed provide an informal sketch of his logicist project; and the formal demonstration had to wait until the *Grundgesetze*, Volume I of which appeared in 1893.

The Foundations of Arithmetic

a logico-mathematical investigation into the concept of number[1]

[*Die Grundlagen der Arithmetik* was published in 1884. What follows here is the Introduction, §§1–4 (which further explain Frege's task), §§45–69 (which establish the philosophical foundations of Frege's logicist project), and §§87–91 and 104–9 (from the Conclusion). Summaries of the remaining sections are provided at the relevant points.]

I

Introduction

If we ask what the number one is, or what the symbol 1 means,[2] we are more often than not given the answer: a thing. And if we then point out that the proposition

'The number one is a thing'

is not a definition, since it has the definite article on one side and the indefinite on the other, and that it only says that the number one belongs to the class of things, but not which thing it is, then we may well be invited to choose whatever we like to call the number one. But if everyone was allowed to understand by this name whatever he liked, then the same proposition about the number one would mean different things to different people; such propositions would have no common content. Some may reject the question, noting that the meaning of the

---

[1] Translated by Michael Beaney. Page numbers in the margin are from the original edition.

[2] Throughout this translation of *GL*, unless otherwise indicated, 'Bedeutung' and its cognates have been translated as 'meaning' and its cognates. On the translation of 'Bedeutung', see the Introduction, §4 above.

(margin handwritten note: Problem with the standard definition.)

letter *a* in arithmetic cannot be given either; and if it were said: *a* means a number, then the same mistake would be made as in the definition: one is a thing. Now the rejection of the question in the case of *a* is quite justified: it means no particular, specifiable number, but serves instead to express the generality of propositions. If, in $a + a - a = a$, we substitute for *a* any number we like, but the same throughout, | then a true equation is always obtained.[3] It is in this sense that the letter *a* is used. But in the case of one, the matter is essentially different. Can we, in the equation $1 + 1 = 2$, substitute for 1 both times the same object, say the Moon? It seems rather that we must substitute something different for the first 1 as for the second. Why is it that we must do here precisely what would be a mistake in the other case? Arithmetic does not manage with the letter *a* alone, but must also use other letters, *b*, *c*, etc., in order to express in general form relations between different numbers. So it might be supposed that the symbol 1 cannot be sufficient either, if it served in a similar way to confer generality on propositions. But does the number one not appear as a particular object with specifiable properties, e.g. that of remaining unchanged when multiplied by itself? In this sense, there are no properties of *a* that can be specified; since whatever is asserted of *a* is a common property of numbers, whereas $1^1 = 1$ asserts nothing of the Moon, nor of the Sun, nor of the Sahara, nor of the Peak of Tenerife; for what could the sense of such an assertion be?

To such questions not even a mathematician is likely to have a satisfactory answer ready to give. Yet is it not shameful that a science should be so unclear about its most prominent object, which is apparently so simple? Small wonder than no one can say what number is. If a concept that is fundamental to a great science poses difficulties, then it is surely an imperative task to investigate it in more detail and overcome these difficulties, especially since complete clarity will hardly be achieved concerning negative, fractional and complex numbers, so long as insight into the foundation of the whole structure of arithmetic is deficient. |

III   Admittedly, many will not think this worth the trouble. This concept, they suppose, is quite adequately treated in the elementary textbooks

---

[3] 'Gleichung' has, throughout this volume, been translated as 'equation', which is what it unambiguously means. However, as noted above (p. 64, fn. 24), it is nevertheless clear that Frege understood 'Gleichheit' ('equality') in the sense of 'identity', and regarded equations as identities. (Cf. *BS*, §8 (pp. 64–5 above), where his symbol for 'Inhaltsgleichheit' was introduced; and *SB*, fn. A, p. 151 below.) It was this that led Austin to render 'Gleichung' as 'identity' in what is still the only complete translation of *GL* (see *FA*, p. II, fn.). But it is certainly more natural to call $1 + 1 = 2$, say, an *equation*, rather than an *identity*; and this has been respected here. Since Frege's primary concern in *GL* is obviously with arithmetic, 'Gleichheit' and 'gleich' too have normally been translated here as 'equality' and 'equal', although 'identity' and 'identical' have occasionally also been used (with the German term in square brackets following them) where they are clearly more appropriate.

and thereby settled once and for all. Who can then believe that he still has something to learn about so simple a matter? So free from any difficulty is the concept of positive whole number taken to be, that it is assumed that it can be explained scientifically and definitively to children, and that everyone, without further reflection or acquaintance with what others have thought, knows all about it. The first precondition for learning is thus frequently lacking: the knowledge that we do not know. The result is that we remain content with a crude conception, even though Herbart[A] has already provided a better one. It is depressing and discouraging that again and again an insight once achieved threatens to be lost in this way, and that so much work appears to be done in vain, because in our inflated conceit we do not think it necessary to appropriate its fruits. My work too, I am well aware, is exposed to such a danger. This crudity of conception surfaces when calculation is described as aggregative, mechanical thought.[B] I doubt that there is any such thought. Aggregative imagination there may well be; but that has no significance [*Bedeutung*] for calculation. Thought is essentially the same everywhere: it is not the case that there are different kinds of laws of thought depending on the object [of thought]. The differences [in thought] merely consist in the greater or lesser purity and independence from psychological influences and external aids such as ordinary language, numerals | and suchlike, and also in the degree of refinement in the structure of concepts; but it is precisely in this respect that mathematics aims not to be surpassed by any other science, not even philosophy.

It will be seen from the present work that even an inference like that from n to $n + 1$, which is apparently peculiar to mathematics, is based on general logical laws, and that there is no need of special laws for aggregative thought. Admittedly, it is possible to manipulate numerals mechanically, just as it is possible to speak like a parrot; but that can scarcely be called thinking. It only becomes possible after mathematical symbolism has been so developed, through genuine thinking, that it does the thinking for us, so to speak. This does not show that numbers are formed in a particularly mechanical way, as sand, say, is formed from grains of quartz. It is in the interest of mathematicians, I think, to counter such a view, which is characterized by a disparagement of the principal object of their science and thereby that science itself. Yet even mathematicians are prone to say such things. Sooner or later, however, the concept of number must be recognized as having a finer structure than most of the concepts of other sciences, even though it is still one of the simplest in arithmetic.

[A] *Collected Works*, ed. Hartenstein, Vol. X, Part I, 'Umriss pädagogischer Vorlesungen', §252, fn. 2: 'Two does not mean [*heisst nicht*] two things, but doubling' etc.
[B] K. Fischer, *System der Logik und Metaphysik oder Wissenschaftslehre*, 2nd edn., §94.

In order, then, to dispel this illusion that no difficulties at all are posed by the positive whole numbers, but that general agreement prevails, it seemed to me a good idea to discuss some of the views of philosophers and mathematicians on the questions raised here. It will be seen how little accord is to be found, even outright contradictions emerging. Some say, for example, 'units are identical [*gleich*] with one another'; others hold that they are different; and both sides have reasons for their claim that cannot be rejected out of hand. Here I shall try | to motivate the need for a more exact investigation. At the same time, this preliminary elucidation of the views expressed by others will clear the ground for my own conception, by convincing people beforehand that these other paths do not lead to the goal, and that my opinion is not just one of many equally justified opinions; and so I hope to settle the question definitively, at least in essentials.

Admittedly, this has led me to take a more philosophical approach than many mathematicians may deem appropriate; but a fundamental investigation of the concept of number will inevitably turn out to be somewhat philosophical. The task is shared by mathematics and philosophy.

If the co-operation between these sciences, despite many attempts from both sides, is not as productive as might be wished or is surely possible, then this seems to me to be due to the prevalence of psychological modes of investigation, which have even penetrated logic. With this trend mathematics has no points of contact at all, and this easily explains the aversion of many mathematicians to philosophical investigations. When, for example, Stricker[C] calls the ideas of number motor phenomena, dependent on muscle sensations, no mathematician can recognize his numbers in this or knows where to begin with such a proposition. An arithmetic founded on muscle sensations would certainly be sensational, but it would also turn out to be just as vague as this foundation. No, arithmetic has nothing at all to do with sensations. Just as little has it to do with mental images, compounded from the traces of earlier sense impressions. The fluctuating and indeterminate nature of these forms stands in stark contrast to the determinate and | fixed nature of mathematical concepts and objects. It may well be useful to investigate the ideas and changes of ideas that occur during mathematical thinking; but psychology should not suppose that it can contribute anything at all to the foundation of arithmetic. To the mathematician as such, these mental images, their origin and change are irrelevant. Stricker himself says that he associates nothing more than the idea of the symbol 100 with the word 'hundred'. Others may have the idea of the letter C or something else; does it not follow from this that these mental images are completely irrelevant and incidental to the essence

[C] *Studien über Association der Vorstellungen* (Vienna, 1883).

of the matter as it concerns us here, just as incidental as blackboard and chalk, and that they do not deserve to be called ideas of the number one hundred at all? The essence of the matter should not be seen to lie in such ideas! The description of the origin of an idea should not be taken for a definition, nor should the account of the mental and physical conditions for becoming aware of a proposition be taken for a proof, and nor should the discovery [*Gedachtwerden*] of a proposition be confused with its truth! We must be reminded, it seems, that a proposition just as little ceases to be true when I am no longer thinking of it as the Sun is extinguished when I close my eyes. Otherwise we would end up finding it necessary to take account of the phosphorous content of our brain in proving Pythagoras' theorem, and astronomers would shy away from extending their conclusions to the distant past, for fear of the objection: 'You reckon that $2 \times 2 = 4$ held then; but the idea of number has a development, a history! One can doubt whether it had reached that stage by then. How do you know that this proposition already existed at that point in the past? Might not the creatures living at that time have held the proposition $2 \times 2 = 5$, from which | the proposition $2 \times 2 = 4$ only evolved through natural selection in the struggle for existence; and might not this in turn, perhaps, be destined in the same way to develop further into $2 \times 2 = 3$?' *Est modus in rebus, sunt certi denique fines!*[4] The historical mode of investigation, which seeks to trace the development of things from which to understand their nature, is certainly legitimate; but it also has its limitations. If everything were in continual flux and nothing remained fixed and eternal, then knowledge of the world would cease to be possible and everything would be thrown into confusion. We imagine, it seems, that concepts originate in the individual mind like leaves on a tree, and we suppose that their nature can be understood by investigating their origin and seeking to explain them psychologically through the working of the human mind. But this conception makes everything subjective, and taken to its logical conclusion, abolishes truth. What is called the history of concepts is really a history either of our knowledge of concepts or of the meanings of words. Often it is only through enormous intellectual work, which can last for hundreds of years, that knowledge of a concept in its purity is achieved, by peeling off the alien clothing that conceals it from the mind's eye. What are we then to say when someone, instead of carrying on this work where it still seems incomplete, ignores it entirely, and enters the nursery or takes himself back to the earliest conceivable stage of human development, in order there to discover, like John Stuart Mill, some gingerbread or pebble arithmetic! It remains only to ascribe to the flavour

---

[4] 'There is moderation in all things; there are, in short, fixed limits'; a quotation from Horace, *Satires*, Book I, I, line 106.

of the cake a special meaning for the concept of number. This is surely the exact opposite of a rational procedure and in any case as unmathematical as it could possibly be. No wonder that mathematicians want nothing to do with it! Instead of finding concepts in particular purity near to their imagined source, | everything is seen blurred and undifferentiated as through a fog. It is as though someone who wanted to learn about America tried to take himself back to the position of Columbus as he caught his first dubious glimpse of his supposed India. Admittedly, such a comparison proves nothing; but it does, I hope, make my point. It may well be that the history of discoveries is useful in many cases as preparation for further research; but it should not aspire to take its place.

As far as mathematicians are concerned, combatting such views would scarcely have been necessary; but since I wanted to resolve the disputed issues, as far as possible, for philosophers as well, I was forced to involve myself a little in psychology, if only to repel its incursion into mathematics.

Besides, psychological turns of phrase occur even in mathematical textbooks. If someone feels obliged to give a definition, and yet cannot do so, then he will at least describe the way in which the object or concept concerned is arrived at. This case is easily recognized by the absence of any further mention of such an explanation. For teaching purposes, such an introduction to things is quite in order; only it should always be clearly distinguished from a definition. A delightful example of how even mathematicians can confuse the grounds of proof with the mental or physical conditions for constructing proofs is afforded by E. Schröder,[D] in offering the following, under the heading 'Special Axiom': 'The intended principle could well be called the Axiom of the Inherence of Symbols. It gives us the assurance that in all our elaborations and inferences the symbols | remain fixed in our memory – and even firmer on paper', etc.

Now just as much as mathematics must refuse any assistance from psychology, it must accept its close connection with logic. Indeed, I endorse the view of those who regard a sharp separation as impossible. It is at least granted that any investigation into the validity of a proof or the legitimacy of a definition must be logical. But such issues are not at all to be dismissed from mathematics, since it is only by resolving them that the necessary certainty is attained.

Admittedly, in this direction too I go somewhat further than is usual. Most mathematicians are content, in investigations of a similar kind, when they have satisfied their immediate needs. If a definition allows itself to be used in proofs, if contradictions are nowhere encountered,

---

[D] *Lehrbuch der Arithmetik und Algebra* [Leipzig, 1873].

if connections are revealed between apparently distant things, and if this
yields greater order and regularity, then the definition is usually regarded
as sufficiently established and few questions are asked about its logical
justification. This procedure has in any case the advantage that it is
unlikely entirely to fail in its purpose. I too think that definitions must
show their worth by their fruitfulness, by their usefulness in constructing proofs. But it is well to observe that the rigour of a proof remains
an illusion, however complete the chains of inference may be, if the
definitions are only justified retrospectively, by the non-appearance of
any contradiction. Fundamentally, then, only an empirical certainty is
ever achieved, and it must really be accepted that in the end a contradiction might still be encountered that brings the whole edifice down
in ruins. That is why I have felt obliged to go back somewhat further
into the general logical foundations than most mathematicians, perhaps,
would regard as necessary. |

X   In this investigation I have adhered to the following fundamental
principles:

> There must be a sharp separation of the psychological from the logical, the
>   subjective from the objective;
> The meaning of a word must be asked for in the context of a proposition,
>   not in isolation;
> The distinction between concept and object must be kept in mind.

To comply with the first, I have used the word 'idea' ['*Vorstellung*']
always in the psychological sense, and have distinguished ideas from
both concepts and objects. If the second principle is not observed, then
one is almost forced to take as the meaning of words mental images or
acts of an individual mind, and thereby to offend against the first as
well. As concerns the third point, it is a mere illusion to suppose that
a concept can be made into an object without altering it. From this it
follows that a widely held formalist theory of fractional, negative numbers, etc., is untenable. How I intend to improve on it can be only indicated in the present work. In all these cases, as with the positive whole
numbers, it will come down to fixing the sense of an equation.[5]

My results will, I think, at least in essentials, win the approval of
those mathematicians who take the trouble to consider my arguments.
They seem to me to be in the air, and separately they have, perhaps,
already been stated, at least in rough form; though they may well be new
in their connections with one another. I have sometimes been surprised
that accounts that come so close to my conception on one point deviate
so sharply on another.

The reception by philosophers will be varied, depending on their

[5] See §§62ff. (pp. 109ff. below).

Insuperable: incapable of being surmounted.

Induction arbitrary?

XI. standpoint; it will certainly be worst by | those empiricists who would recognize only induction as the original mode of inference, and even that not really as a mode of inference, but as habituation. One or another, perhaps, will take this opportunity to examine afresh the foundations of his theory of knowledge. To those who might want to declare my definitions unnatural, I would suggest that the question here is not whether they are natural, but whether they go to the heart of the matter and are logically unobjectionable.

I cherish the hope that even philosophers will find something useful in the present work, if they examine it without prejudice. |

* * *

1 §1.   After departing for a long time from Euclidean rigour, mathematics is now returning to it, and even striving to take it further. In arithmetic, simply as a result of the origin in India of many of its methods and concepts, reasoning has traditionally been less strict than in geometry, which had mainly been developed by the Greeks. This was only reinforced by the discovery of higher analysis; since considerable, almost insuperable difficulties stood in the way of a rigorous treatment of this subject, whilst at the same time there seemed little profit in the expenditure of effort in overcoming them. Later developments, however, have shown more and more clearly that in mathematics a mere moral conviction, based on many successful applications, is insufficient. A proof is now demanded of many things that previously counted as self-evident. It is only in this way that the limits to their validity have in many cases been determined. The concepts of function, continuity, limit and infinity have been shown to require sharper definition. Negative and irrational numbers, which have long been accepted in science, have had to submit to a more exacting test of their legitimacy.

Thus everywhere efforts are being made to provide rigorous proofs, precise determinations of the limits of validity and, as a means to this, sharp definitions of concepts. |

2 §2.   This path must eventually lead to the concept of Number[6] and the simplest propositions holding of the positive whole numbers, which

[6] I follow Austin here (cf. *FA*, p. 2, fn.) in translating 'Anzahl' by 'Number' (with a capital 'N'), leaving 'number' for the more general term 'Zahl'. The distinction plays little role in *GL* (cf. Frege's own fn. G below), but it does acquire significance in *GG*, II (anticipated at *GG*, I, §§41–2), when Frege distinguishes the real numbers ('reelen Zahlen') from the natural or cardinal numbers ('Anzahlen'), which are now to be understood as different from the positive whole numbers ('positiven ganzen Zahlen'). 'The natural numbers answer the question "How many objects of a certain kind are there?", whilst the real numbers can be regarded as measurement numbers [*Masszahlen*], which state how large a magnitude is compared with a unit magnitude' (*GG*, II, §157).

form the foundation of the whole of arithmetic. Admittedly, numerical formulae such as $5 + 7 = 12$ and laws such as that of the associativity of addition are so frequently confirmed by the countless applications that are made of them every day, that it can seem almost ludicrous to call them into question by demanding a proof. But it lies deep in the nature of mathematics always to prefer proof, wherever it is possible, to inductive confirmation. Euclid proved many things that would have been granted him anyway. And it was the dissatisfaction even with Euclidean rigour that led to the investigation of the Axiom of Parallels.[7]

Thus this movement towards ever greater rigour has already in many ways left behind the originally felt need, and the need has itself grown more and more in strength and extent.

The aim of proof is not only to place the truth of a proposition beyond all doubt, but also to afford insight into the dependence of truths on one another. After one has been convinced of the immovability of a boulder by vain attempts to shift it, the question then arises as to what secures it so firmly. The further these investigations are pursued, the fewer become the primitive truths to which everything is reduced; and this simplification is in itself a worthwhile goal. Perhaps the hope is even raised that, by bringing to light the general principles involved in what people have instinctively done in the simplest cases, general methods of concept-formation and justification may be discovered that will also be useful in more complicated cases.

§3.   Philosophical motives too have influenced my investigation. Questions as to the *a priori* or *a posteriori*, synthetic or analytic nature of arithmetical truths here await their answer. For even though these concepts themselves belong to philosophy, I still believe that no decision can be reached without help from mathematics. Admittedly, this depends on the sense that is given to the questions.

It frequently happens that we first discover the content of a proposition and then provide a rigorous proof in another, more difficult way, by means of which the conditions of its validity can often also be discerned more precisely. Thus in general the question as to how we arrive at the content of a judgement has to be distinguished from the question as to how we provide the justification for our assertion.

Now these distinctions between *a priori* and *a posteriori*, synthetic and analytic, in my opinion,[E] concern not the content of the judgement but the justification for making the judgement. Where there is no such justification, there is no possibility of drawing the distinctions either.

[E] By this I do not, of course, wish to introduce new senses, but only to capture what earlier writers, in particular *Kant*, have meant [*gemeint*]. [Cf. §§88–9, pp. 122–3 below.]

[7] For Frege's view of the Axiom of Parallels, see *EG*, pp. 251–2 below.

An *a priori* error is thus just as much an absurdity as, say, a blue concept. If a proposition is called *a posteriori* or analytic in my sense, then this is a judgement not about the psychological, physiological and physical conditions that have made it possible to form the content of the proposition in our mind, nor about how someone else, perhaps erroneously, has come to hold it to be true, but rather about the ultimate ground on which the justification for holding it to be true rests.

In this way the question is removed from the domain of psychology and assigned to that of mathematics, if it concerns a mathematical truth. It now depends on finding a proof and following it back to the primitive truths. If, on the way, only general logical laws and definitions are encountered, then the truth is analytic, assuming that propositions on which the admissibility of any definition rests are also taken into account. If it is not possible to provide a proof, however, without using truths that are not of a general logical nature, but belong instead to the domain of a particular science, then the proposition is synthetic. For a truth to be *a posteriori*, it must be impossible for its proof to avoid appeal to facts, that is, to unprovable and non-general truths that contain assertions about particular objects. If, on the other hand, it is possible to provide a proof from completely general laws, which themselves neither need nor admit of proof, then the truth is *a priori*.[F]

§4. Starting from these philosophical questions, we arrive at the same demand that had arisen independently in the domain of mathematics: that the fundamental theorems of arithmetic, wherever possible, must be proved with the greatest rigour; since only if the utmost care is taken to avoid any gaps in the chain of inference can it be said with certainty upon what primitive truths the proof is based; and only if these are known can the philosophical questions be answered.

If an attempt is now made to meet this demand, then propositions are very soon encountered that cannot be proved so long as the concepts that occur in them cannot be analysed into simpler ones or the propositions cannot be reduced to something more general. Now here it is above all Number which must be defined or recognized as indefinable. This is the task of the present work.[G] On its outcome depends the decision as to the nature of arithmetical laws.

[F] If general truths are recognized at all, then it must also be granted that there are such primitive laws, since from purely individual facts nothing follows, except on the basis of a law. Even induction rests on the general proposition that this procedure can establish the truth or at any rate the probability of a law. For those who deny this, induction is nothing more than a psychological phenomenon, a way in which people come to believe in the truth of a proposition, without this belief thereby being at all justified.

[G] In what follows, therefore, unless otherwise indicated, no other numbers than the positive whole numbers will be under discussion, the numbers which answer the question 'how many?' [Cf. fn. 6 above.]

Before tackling these questions themselves, I shall first say something to provide a hint as to their answers. For if it should turn out that there are reasons, from other points of view, why the fundamental theorems of arithmetic are analytic, then this would also speak in favour of their provability and the definability of the concept of Number. Reasons for holding that these truths are *a posteriori* would have the opposite effect. The points at issue here may therefore first be submitted to a preliminary examination.

[The next forty sections (§§5–44; *GL*, pp. 5–58) are omitted here; but the following summary is offered of the main points, under the headings that Frege provides.

I. Views of certain writers on the nature of arithmetical propositions

Are numerical formulae provable? (§§5–8)

Frege argues against Kant that the lack of self-evidence of complex numerical formulae such as '135664 + 37863 = 173527' shows not that they are synthetic but that they are provable (§5). He agrees with Leibniz that even such simple formulae as '2 + 2 = 4' are provable via axioms and definitions, though he criticizes Leibniz's own proof for missing out the associative law. Defining every number in terms of its predecessor allows us to reduce the infinite set of numbers to the number one and the successor relation. (§6.) Frege argues against Mill's view that the truth of '3 = 2 + 1' depends on the empirical possibility of separating three objects, say, $^0_0{}^0$, into two parts, thus, oo o. It is just as well, Frege remarks, that not everything in the world is nailed down, for otherwise this separation could not be achieved, and 2 + 1 would not be 3! And what would be the physical facts underlying the numbers 0 and 1, or very large numbers? In fact, we can number more than just objects that we can physically separate: we can speak of three strokes of a clock, three sensations of taste, or three methods of solving an equation. (§7.) Frege accepts that we may require experience to *learn* the truths of arithmetic, but that does not make those truths 'empirical' as that term is used in opposition to 'a priori', since (as he stated in §3) the issue here concerns *justification*. (§8.)

Are the laws of arithmetic inductive truths? (§§9–11)

Frege argues here that Mill always confuses the applications of an arithmetical proposition with the pure proposition itself. That 2 unit volumes of liquid added to 5 unit volumes of liquid make 7 unit volumes of liquid only holds if the volume does not change as a result, say, of some chemical reaction; and '+', for example, does not mean a process of heaping up, since it can be applied in quite different situations. (§9.) Induction itself, if understood as involving judgements of probability, *presupposes* arithmetic. (§10.)

Are the laws of arithmetic synthetic *a priori* or analytic? (§§12–17)

Frege's definitions in §3 rule out the possibility of there being any analytic *a posteriori* truths, so if Mill's view that arithmetical truths are synthetic *a posteriori* is rejected, the only other possibilities are that they are synthetic *a priori*, as Kant thought, or analytic *a priori*. But in criticizing Kant, Frege remarks that it is all too easy to appeal to inner intuition when other grounds cannot be found. (§12.) Arithmetic is different from geometry (§13), which indeed contains synthetic truths. The basis of arithmetic lies deeper than that of either empirical science or geometry: 'The truths of arithmetic govern the realm of the numerable. This realm is the broadest; for to it belongs not only the actual, not only the intuitable, but everything thinkable. Should not the laws of number, then, stand in the most intimate connection with those of thought?' (§14.)[8] Frege endorses Leibniz's view that arithmetical propositions are analytic, though he recognizes that there is a sense in which *all* truths are 'analytic' for Leibniz (§15); and he quotes with approval Leibniz's remark that 'the concern here is not with the history of our discoveries, which is different for different people, but with the connection and natural order of truths, which is always the same' (§17; see Leibniz, *NE*, IV, vii, 9).

II. Views of certain writers on the concept of Number

Whilst, if Part I is right, arithmetical propositions may be provable, and every individual number greater than 1 definable in terms of its predecessor, this still leaves the status of the general laws governing proof unclear, and the number one itself and the successor relation to be defined. Frege discusses the number one in Part III; here he investigates the general concept of Number, since it is from this that the general laws are to be derived. (§§18–20.)

---

[8] Cf. 'Letter to Marty, 29.8.1882', p. 80 above.

Is Number a property of external things? (§§21–25)

Frege offers two reasons for not regarding numbers as properties such as solidity or colour. Firstly, such properties belong to external things independently of any choice of ours, whereas what Number we ascribe to something depends on our way of viewing it. The *Iliad*, for example, can be thought of as one poem, or as twenty-four Books, or as some large Number of verses; and a pile of cards can be thought of as one pack or as fifty-two cards. (§22.) *One* pair of boots can be thought of as *two* boots (§25). Secondly, number is applicable over a far wider range, being applicable, in particular, to what is *non*-physical, such as ideas, concepts and syllogistic figures (§24).

Is number something subjective? (§§26–27)

But this does not mean that number is subjective. Number is no less objective than, say, the North Sea, where there is also an element of human choice in determining its boundaries. Frege distinguishes what is *objective* (*objectiv*) from what is *actual* (*wirklich*), the latter being the *handleable* (*handgreiflich*) or *spatial* (*räumlich*), such that what is actual is only part of what is objective. Both the axis of the Earth and the centre of mass of the solar system are objective, but they are not actual like the Earth itself. What is objective is what is law-governed, conceivable and judgeable – independent of sensation, intuition and imagination, but not of reason, as Frege characterizes it. (§26.) Frege also objects to treating number as an idea, because this would make arithmetic psychology. 'If the number two were an idea, then it would straightaway be mine only. Another's idea is already, as such, another idea. We would then have perhaps many millions of twos. We would have to say: my two, your two, one two, all twos.' But there may then be not only, in some cases, many more numbers than we would normally countenance, but also, in other cases, none where they would be expected. '10^{10}', for example, might turn out to be an empty symbol, since there might be no being capable of having the appropriate idea. (§27.)[9]

Numbers as sets (§28)

Frege mentions one final theory, construing Numbers either as sets of objects or as sets of units. Neither view provides an account of the numbers 0 and 1; but his objections are clarified in Part III.

---

[9] Cf. *GG*, I, Preface, pp. XIV–XIX (pp. 201–6 below), which contains a more sustained attack on psychologism than Frege provides in *GL*, though the essential points remain.

III. Views on *Einheit* and *Eins*[10]

Does the number word 'one' express a property of objects?
(§§29–33)

Further arguments are added to those offered in §§21–25 against viewing the number one, in particular, as a property of objects. Firstly, since
'oneness' would presumably be a property possessed by everything,
describing something as 'one' would say nothing at all. 'Only through
the possibility of something not being wise does the assertion that
Solon is wise gain a sense. The content of a concept diminishes as its
extension grows; if the latter becomes all-embracing, then the content
must be lost entirely.' Secondly, if 'one' were a predicate, then 'Solon
was one' would be just as legitimate as 'Solon was wise'. But 'Solon
was one' is unintelligible on its own — without, say, 'wise man' being
understood from the context. The point is even clearer in the plural
case: 'Whilst we can combine "Solon was wise" and "Thales was wise"
into "Solon and Thales were wise", we cannot say "Solon and Thales
were one". The impossibility of this would not be perceived if "one" as
well as "wise" were a property both of Solon and of Thales.' (§29.)

Are units identical with one another [*Sind die Einheiten
einander gleich*]? (§§34–39)

Frege poses a dilemma for the view that numbers are sets. Either the
things of which numbers are sets are different (as they would be if they
were different objects), or else they are identical. If they are different,
then there will be as many twos, say, as there are different pairs of objects
in the universe. If they are identical (as talk of sets of 'units' would seem
to suggest, supposedly abstracting away from all particular characteristics
of objects), then (so to speak) they merge into one, and plurality is never
attained. (§§34–39.) A distinction must be drawn between *unit* (*Einheit*)
and *one* (*Eins*). 'Unit' is a concept word, whereas '1' is a proper name,
and as such, does not admit of a plural. 'We say "the number one" and
indicate by the definite article a definite and unique object of scientific
inquiry. There are not different numbers one, but only one.' (§38.)

Attempts to overcome the difficulty (§§40–44)

Frege considers various attempts to resolve the problem of the supposed identity of 'units', by, amongst others, Jevons and Schröder, but
finds them all wanting.

[10] Whilst 'Eins' clearly means 'one', 'Einheit' causes problems of translation, since it can
mean 'unit' as well as 'unity' or 'oneness'. The ambiguity needs to be borne in mind in
understanding Frege's arguments in this Part. Cf. fn. 18 below.

The translation resumes at the point where Frege begins to develop his positive account.]

58   Solution of the difficulty

§45. Let us now review what we have so far established and the questions that still remain unanswered.

Number is not abstracted from things in the way that colour, weight and hardness are, and is not a property of things in the sense that they are. The question still remains as to what it is of which something is asserted in making a statement of number [*Zahlangabe*].[11]

Number is not anything physical, but nor is it anything subjective, an idea.

Number does not result from the adding of thing to thing. Even naming each addition does not alter the situation.

The expressions 'multitude', 'set', 'plurality', due to their vagueness, are unsuitable for use in defining number.

With regard to one [*Eins*] and unity [*Einheit*], the question remains as to how the element of choice in our conceptions, which seems to blur every distinction between one and many, is to be restricted.

Distinguishability, indivisibility, unanalysability cannot be taken as marks[12] of what we express by the word 'one'.

If the things to be numbered are called units, then the unconditional assertion that units are identical [*gleich*] is false. That they are identical in certain respects is no doubt correct but worthless. The difference between the things to be numbered is actually necessary if the number is to be greater than 1.

It thus seems that we must ascribe two contradictory properties to units: identity [*Gleichheit*] and distinguishability.

A distinction must be drawn between one [*Eins*] and unit [*Einheit*].
59 The word 'one', as the proper name of an object | of mathematical inquiry, does not admit of a plural. It therefore makes no sense to let numbers result from the combination of ones. The plus sign in $1 + 1 = 2$ cannot mean such a combination.

§46. To throw light on the matter, it will help to consider number in the context of a judgement that brings out its ordinary use. If, in looking at the same external phenomenon, I can say with equal truth 'This is a copse' and 'These are five trees', or 'Here are four companies' and 'Here are 500 men', then what changes here is neither the individual nor the whole, the aggregate, but rather my terminology. But that is

---

[11] On the translation of this term, see fn. 13 below.
[12] On Frege's use of the term 'Merkmal', see §53 (pp. 102–3 below); *CO*, pp. 189–90 below.

only a sign of the replacement of one concept by another. This suggests as the answer to the first question of the previous section that a statement of number contains an assertion about a concept.[13] This is perhaps clearest in the case of the number 0. If I say 'Venus has 0 moons', then there is no moon or aggregate of moons to assert anything of at all; but instead it is the concept 'moon of Venus' to which a property is ascribed, namely, that of including nothing under it. If I say 'The King's carriage is drawn by four horses', then I am ascribing the number four to the concept 'horse that draws the King's carriage'.[14]

It may be objected that a concept such as 'inhabitant of Germany', even though its marks remain the same, would have a property that changed from year to year, if a statement of number did assert something about it. It is fair to reply that objects too change their properties without preventing us from recognizing them as the same. But here there is a more particular explanation. For the concept 'inhabitant of Germany' contains the time as a variable component, or, to put it mathematically, | is a function of the time. Instead of 'a is an inhabitant of Germany', we can say 'a inhabits Germany', and this relates to the present point in time. Thus there is already something fluid in the concept itself. On the other hand, the same number belongs to the concept 'inhabitant of Germany at the beginning of the year 1883, Berlin time' throughout eternity.

§47. That a statement of number expresses something factual independent of our conceptions can only surprise those who regard a concept as something subjective like an idea. But this view is wrong. If, for

---

[13] The translation of this key Fregean thesis – '*die Zahlangabe enthält eine Aussage von einem Begriffe*' – has generated some controversy. For Frege, a '*Zahlangabe*' answers the question 'How many?' (cf. fn. 6 and Frege's fn. G above), and takes the form 'There are *n F*'s', and 'statement of number' (perhaps most literally, 'giving of a number') is as good a translation as any. '*Aussage*' has been more problematic, since 'assertion', which is what it usually means, is generally used to identify a certain kind of *speech act*, to be distinguished from questions, commands, etc.; whereas, it has been argued, there are clearly legitimate uses of number terms in asking, say, 'Are there five plates on the table?', or ordering, say, 'Put your two knives on the floor!' Dummett has suggested that the thesis is best rendered as 'The content of an ascription of number consists in predicating something of a concept' (1991a: p. 88); but the conciseness of Frege's own formulation is then lost. In any case, when we do make a *statement* of number (i.e. say 'There are *n F*'s'), we can indeed be seen as *asserting* something about a concept, and there is nothing in this that implies that questions, say, cannot be asked involving number terms. Frege just happens to have restricted his thesis to statements (where there is a truth-value to be ascribed); and the question as to what to say in the case of other speech acts – how to generalize the thesis – is left open. Frege's key point, then, is simply that, in answering the question 'How many?', we are saying something about a concept; and the most accurate, as well as the most concise, translation of his thesis is therefore the one adopted here – to be understood, though, in the light of what has just been said.

[14] The verb translated twice here as 'ascribe' is 'beilegen': see fn. 16 below.

example, we subordinate the concept of body to the concept of what has weight, or the concept of whale to the concept of mammal, then we are thereby asserting something objective. Now if the concepts were subjective, then the subordination of one to the other, as a relation between them, would also be subjective, just as a relation between ideas is. Admittedly, at first sight the proposition

'All whales are mammals'

appears to be about animals, not concepts; but if it is asked which animal is then being spoken of, there is no single one that can be picked out. Even assuming that a whale is present, our proposition still asserts nothing about it. We cannot infer from it that the animal present is a mammal, without the additional proposition that it is a whale, as to which our proposition says nothing. In general, it is impossible to speak of an object without in some way designating or naming it. But the word 'whale' does not name any individual creature. If it be replied that an individual, definite object is certainly not what is being spoken of, but rather an indefinite one, then I suspect that 'indefinite object' is only another expression for 'concept', and a poorer, self-contradictory
61 one at that. | Even if our proposition can only be justified by observing individual animals, this proves nothing as to its content. Whether it is true or not, or on what grounds we hold it as true, is irrelevant to the question as to what the proposition is about. If, then, a concept is something objective, then an assertion about it can also contain something factual.

§48. The false impression given by some earlier examples that different numbers may belong to the same thing is explained by the fact that objects were there taken as the bearers of number. As soon as we restore to its rightful place the true bearer, the concept, numbers reveal themselves as just as mutually exclusive in their realm as colours are in theirs.

We now also see how number can come to be thought of as arrived at by abstraction from things. What is actually obtained is a concept, in which the number is then discovered. Thus abstraction often does, in fact, precede the formation of a judgement of number. The confusion is the same as if it were said: the concept of fire risk is obtained by building a half-timbered house with wooden gables, thatched roof and draughty chimneys.

The power of collecting together that a concept has far surpasses the unifying power of synthetic apperception. By means of the latter it would not be possible to combine the inhabitants of Germany into a whole; but they can certainly be brought under the concept 'inhabitant of Germany' and counted.

The extensive applicability of number can now also be explained. It is indeed puzzling how the same can be asserted of physical and mental phenomena alike, of the spatial and temporal as well as of the non-spatial and non-temporal. But this is not at all what happens in statements of number. Only concepts, under which the physical | and mental, the spatial and temporal, the non-spatial and non-temporal are brought, are ascribed numbers.

62

§49. We find confirmation of our view in Spinoza, who says:[H] 'I answer that a thing is called one or single merely with respect to its existence, and not its essence; for we conceive of things in terms of number only after they have been brought under a common measure. For example, whoever holds in his hand a sesterce and a dollar will not think of the number two unless he can give this sesterce and this dollar one and the same name, viz. piece of silver or coin; then he can affirm that he has two pieces of silver or coins; since he designates by the name coin not only the sesterce but also the dollar.' When he goes on: 'From this it is clear that a thing is called one or single only after another thing has been conceived that (as has been said) agrees with it', and when he thinks that God cannot be called one or single in any real sense, because we can form no abstract concept of his essence, then he goes wrong in thinking that a concept can only be acquired directly by abstraction from particular objects. A concept can just as well be acquired via its marks; and then it is possible for nothing to fall under it. If this did not happen, we would never be able to deny existence, and hence the affirmation of existence would lose its content too.

§50. E. Schröder[I] emphasizes that, to be able to speak of the frequency of a thing, the name of this thing must always be a *generic term*, a general concept word (*notio communis*): 'For as soon as an object is pictured completely – with all | its properties and relations, it will stand out in the world as unique and its like will no longer be found. The name of the object then takes on the character of a *proper name (nomen proprium)* and the object cannot be thought of as one that occurs anywhere else. But this holds not only of *concrete* objects; it holds in general of anything, even where the idea of it arises through *abstractions*, provided only that this idea contains in it sufficient elements to fully determine the thing concerned . . . [Becoming an object that can be counted] is only possible for a thing in so far as one disregards or *abstracts from* some of its characteristic marks and relations, which distinguish it from

63

[H] Baumann, *Die Lehren von Zeit, Raum und Mathematik* [Berlin, 1868], Vol. I, p. 169. [Most of Frege's quotations from other writers are taken from this edited collection. The original work in this case is Spinoza's *Epistolae doctorum quorundam virorum*, No. 50.]
[I] Op. cit., p. 6.

all other things, by means of which the name of the thing then becomes a concept applicable to more things.'

§51.   The truth in this account is clothed in such distorted and misleading language that it has to be disentangled and sifted out. First of all, it will not do to call a general concept word the name of a thing. The illusion then arises that number is a property of things. A general concept word just designates a concept. Only with the definite article or a demonstrative pronoun does it function as a proper name of a thing, but it then ceases to function as a concept word. The name of a thing is a proper name. An object does not occur anywhere else, but several objects may fall under a concept. That a concept is not only obtained by abstraction from the things that fall under it has already been noted in connection with Spinoza. Here I will add that a concept does not cease to be a concept when only one single thing falls under it, which thing is therefore completely determined by it. It is just that what belongs to such a concept (e.g., satellite of the Earth) is the number one, | which is a number in the same sense as 2 and 3. With a concept the question is always whether anything, and if so what, falls under it. With a proper name such questions make no sense. One should not be deceived by the use in language of a proper name, e.g. Moon, as a concept word, and vice versa; the distinction nevertheless remains. As soon as a word is used with the indefinite article or in the plural without an article, it is a concept word.

§52.   Further confirmation of the view that number is ascribed to concepts can be found in our ordinary use of language, in saying ten man, four mark, three barrel.[15] The use of the singular here may indicate that the concept is intended, not the thing. The advantage of this form of expression is particularly evident in the case of the number 0. Elsewhere, admittedly, language ascribes number to objects, not to concepts: we say 'number of bales' just as we say 'weight of bales'. Thus we are apparently speaking of objects, whereas in truth we intend to assert something of a concept. This use of language is confusing. The expression 'four thoroughbred horses' generates the illusion that 'four' qualifies the concept 'thoroughbred horse' just as 'thoroughbred' qualifies the concept 'horse'. However, only 'thoroughbred' is such a mark; we use the word 'four' to assert something of a concept.

§53.   By properties that are asserted of a concept I do not, of course, mean [*verstehe*] the marks that make up the concept. These are properties

---

[15] This is a direct translation of the German. In English we might talk, for example, of a ten man crew, a five pound note or a three barrel consignment.

of the things that fall under the concept, not of the concept. Thus 'right-angled' is not a property of the concept 'right-angled triangle'; but the proposition that there is no right-angled, rectilinear, equilateral triangle does express a property of the concept 'right-angled, rectilinear, equilateral triangle'; it ascribes to this the number zero. |

65   In this respect existence is similar to number. Affirmation of existence is indeed nothing other than denial of the number zero. Since existence is a property of concepts, the ontological proof of the existence of God fails in its aim.[16] But oneness [*Einzigkeit*] is just as little a mark of the concept 'God' as existence. Oneness cannot be used to define this concept any more than strength, spaciousness and homeliness can be used together with stones, mortar and beams to build a house. However, it should not be concluded that a property of a concept can never be deduced from the concept, that is, from its marks. Under certain circumstances this is possible, just as we can occasionally infer the durability of a building from the type of stone. It would therefore be going too far to assert that oneness or existence can never be inferred from the marks of a concept; it is just that this can never happen as directly as the mark of a concept can be ascribed as a property to an object that falls under the concept.

It would also be wrong to deny that existence and oneness can ever be marks of concepts. They are just not marks of concepts in which language suggests they are included. If, for example, all concepts under which only one object falls, are collected under one concept, then oneness is a mark of this concept. Under it would fall, for example, the concept 'moon of the Earth', though not the heavenly body itself. Thus a concept can fall under a higher one, that is to say, a concept of second order. But this relationship is not to be confused with that of subordination.[17]

[16] We should, perhaps, note here that it is potentially misleading to say that existence is a property of concepts, just as Frege himself later warns us against calling numbers themselves properties of concepts (see §57). Rather, affirming the existence of something is to be understood as attributing to the relevant concept the property of *being instantiated* (e.g. to say that God exists is to say that the concept *God* falls under the [second-level] concept *is instantiated*), just as saying that there are *n F*'s is to be understood as attributing to the concept *F* the property of *being instantiated n-fold*. To talk, in the latter case, of 'ascribing' numbers to concepts is not to be confused with 'ascribing' properties to things. Perhaps we should distinguish the 'ascription' of numbers from the 'attribution' of properties. Unfortunately, Frege himself uses one word – 'beilegen' – for both (e.g. in §46); so it seems best just to note the potential confusions here, rather than ascribe to Frege himself a more subtle distinction.

[17] In other words, 'The concept *moon of the Earth* is a concept under which only one object falls' asserts a relationship between a first-level and a second-level concept (as Frege later calls them; see esp. *CO*, pp. 183, 189–90 below), whereas 'All whales are mammals' asserts that the concept *whale* is subordinate to the concept *mammal* (cf. §47). Cf. also *NLD*, p. 364 below.

§54. It now becomes possible to give a satisfactory account of units. E. Schröder says on p. 7 of his textbook cited above: 'This generic term or concept | will be called the denomination [*Benennung*] of the number formed in the way indicated and constitutes the essence of its unit'.

In fact, would it not be most appropriate to call a concept the unit that relates to the Number which belongs to it?[18] We can then give a sense to assertions that are made about the unit, that it is separated from its surroundings and indivisible. For the concept to which the number is ascribed does in general delimit what falls under it in a definite way. The concept 'letter in the word "Zahl"' delimits the *Z* from the *a*, the *a* from the *h*, and so on. The concept 'syllable in the word "Zahl"' picks out the word as a whole and as indivisible in the sense that the parts do not now fall under the concept. Not all concepts work this way. We can, for example, divide up what falls under the concept 'red' in a variety of ways, without the parts ceasing to fall under it. To such a concept no finite number belongs. The proposition concerning the distinguishability and indivisibility of units can therefore be stated thus:

Only a concept that delimits what falls under it in a definite way and allows no arbitrary division [of what falls under it] into parts[19] can constitute the unit that relates to a finite Number.

It will be noticed, however, that indivisibility here has a special meaning.

We can now easily answer the question as to how the identity of units

[18] 'Einheit' again causes problems of translation here. Schröder talks of the concept constituting 'das Wesen ihrer Einheit', and Frege is clearly picking up on this idea in suggesting that we call a concept 'Einheit . . . in Bezug auf die Anzahl, welche ihm zukommt', i.e. that we identify a concept with the 'unitness' that enables us to regard the objects that fall under the concept as its 'units'. The ambiguity of the word 'Einheit' is rather lost in translating it simply as 'unit'. A concept is not itself a unit but instead constitutes the condition that has to be met for an object to be its unit. But perhaps with the definite article, the term 'the unit' has a similar degree of ambiguity in English, referring either to a particular object or else to the concept by means of which objects are to be sorted ('the unit of assessment'). Compare, for example, 'The horse is a noble creature', which can be construed as being either about a particular horse ('The horse in the stable over there is a noble creature') or about the concept *horse* ('All horses are noble creatures' or 'The concept *horse* is subordinate to the concept *noble creature*'). In the latter sense we might perhaps talk of the concept being *the unit* – by means of which objects are to be sorted and hence numbered. And as Frege goes on to argue in this section, we must indeed distinguish between the unit *qua* individual object (which makes units different) and the unit *qua* instantiation of a concept (which makes units the same); though, strictly speaking, even this is not quite how Frege himself puts it, since in the latter case, we might still be taken as referring to objects, which can just be regarded in a certain way (as all falling under the same concept) – whereas what is actually identical across the cases is the concept itself.

[19] I.e. what is now called a *sortal* concept – a concept that *sorts* into particulars the objects that fall under it, which can then be counted.

is to be reconciled with their distinguishability. The word 'unit' is being used here in a double sense. Units are identical if the word has the meaning explained above. In the proposition 'Jupiter has four moons', the unit is 'moon of Jupiter'. Under this concept falls moon I as well as moon II, moon III and moon IV. Thus we can say: the unit to which I relates is identical with the unit to which II relates, and so on. Here

67 we have identity. But if it is the distinguishability | of units that is asserted, then by this is understood the distinguishability of the things numbered.

IV. The concept of Number

Every individual number is an independent object

§55. Having recognized that a statement of number contains an assertion about a concept, we can attempt to complete the Leibnizian definitions of the individual numbers by defining 0 and 1.

It is natural to say: the number 0 belongs to a concept if no object falls under it. But this appears to replace 0 by 'no', which means the same. The following formulation is therefore preferable: the number 0 belongs to a concept if, whatever a may be, the proposition holds universally that a does not fall under that concept.

In a similar way we could say: the number 1 belongs to a concept F if, whatever a may be, the proposition does not hold universally that a does not fall under F, and if from the propositions

'a falls under F' and 'b falls under F'

it follows universally that a and b are the same.

It still remains to give a general definition of the transition from one number to the next. We could try the following formulation: the number $(n + 1)$ belongs to the concept F if there is an object a falling under F such that the number n belongs to the concept 'falling under F, but not a'.[20]

---

[20] In modern notation, using the device of the *numerical quantifier*, '$\exists_n x$' being read as 'there are n x's such that', the three definitions here can be formalized thus:

(F_0)   '$(\exists_0 x)Fx$' is defined as '$(\forall x) \neg Fx$'.
(F_1)   '$(\exists_1 x)Fx$' is defined as '$\neg(\forall x) \neg Fx$ & $(\forall x)(\forall y)(Fx$ & $Fy \rightarrow x = y)$'.
(F_{n+1})   '$(\exists_{n+1} x)Fx$' is defined as '$(\exists x)[Fx$ & $(\exists_n y)(Fy$ & $x \neq y)]$'.

What this shows, of course, is that number statements of the form 'The number n belongs to a concept F' can indeed be logically defined. The objection that Frege goes on to raise is not that these definitions are wrong, but that they are, as they stand, insufficient to determine what numbers are.

§56. These definitions offer themselves so naturally after our previous results that an explanation is required as to why they cannot satisfy us.

The last definition is the most likely to raise doubts; for strictly speaking the sense of the expression | 'the number n belongs to the concept G' is just as unknown to us as that of the expression 'the number $(n + 1)$ belongs to the concept F'. We can, of course, by means of this and the second definition say what is meant by

'the number $1 + 1$ belongs to the concept F',

and then, using this, give the sense of the expression

'the number $1 + 1 + 1$ belongs to the concept F',

and so on; but we can never – to take an extreme example – decide by means of our definitions whether the number *Julius Caesar* belongs to a concept, or whether that well-known conqueror of Gaul is a number or not. Furthermore, we cannot prove with the help of our attempted definitions that if the number a belongs to the concept F and the number b belongs to the same concept, then necessarily $a = b$. The expression '*the* number that belongs to the concept F' could not therefore be justified and it would thus be quite impossible to prove a numerical equality, since we would be unable to apprehend a definite number at all. It is only an illusion that we have defined 0 and 1; in truth we have only determined the sense of the phrases

'the number 0 belongs to',
'the number 1 belongs to';

but this does not allow us to distinguish 0 and 1 here as independent, reidentifiable objects.

§57. This is the place to gain a clearer understanding of our thesis that a statement of number contains an assertion about a concept. In the proposition 'The number 0 belongs to the concept F', 0 is only a part of the predicate, if the concept F is taken as the real subject.[21] I have therefore avoided calling a number such as 0, 1 or 2 a *property* of a concept. The individual number, by forming only a part of the predicate, appears precisely as an independent object. I have already remarked above that we say 'the number 1' and use the definite article to register 1 as an object. | This independence manifests itself throughout arithmetic – as, for example, in the equation $1 + 1 = 2$. Since what

---

[21] I.e. rewriting the proposition as 'The concept F is ascribed the number 0', 'the number 0' is only a part of the predicate 'is ascribed the number 0'.

concerns us here is to define a concept of number that is useful for science, we should not be put off by the attributive form in which number also appears in our everyday use of language. This can always be avoided. For example, the proposition 'Jupiter has four moons' can be converted into 'The number of Jupiter's moons is four'. Here the 'is' should not be taken as a mere copula, as in the proposition 'The sky is blue'. This is shown by the fact that one can say: 'The number of Jupiter's moons is the number 4'. Here 'is' has the sense of 'is equal to', 'is the same as'. We thus have an equation that asserts that the expression 'the number of Jupiter's moons' designates the same object as the word 'four'. And equations are the prevalent form of proposition in arithmetic. It is no objection to this account that the word 'four' contains nothing about Jupiter or moons. There is also nothing in the name 'Columbus' about discovery or America and yet it is the same man who is called both Columbus and the discoverer of America.

§58.   It might be objected that we can form no idea[J] at all of the object that we are calling four or the number of Jupiter's moons as something independent. But it is not the independence that we have granted to number that is to blame. It is very easy to think that in the idea of four spots on a die there is something that corresponds to the word 'four'; but that is an illusion. Imagine a green meadow and test whether the idea changes when the indefinite article is replaced by the number word 'one'. Nothing happens, whereas something does correspond in the idea to the word 'green'. | If we picture the printed word 'gold', we do not at first think of any number in doing so. If we now ask ourselves how many letters it contains, then the result is the number 4; but the idea does not thereby become any more definite, but may remain quite unchanged. We only discover the number on the introduction of the concept 'letter in the word "gold"'. In the case of the four spots on a die, the matter is somewhat obscured, since the concept springs so immediately to mind, due to the similarity of the spots, that we hardly notice its intervention. The number can be pictured neither as an independent object nor as a property in an external thing, since it is neither something sensible nor a property of an external thing. The matter is certainly clearest in the case of the number 0. One will try in vain to picture 0 visible stars. One may well imagine the sky completely clouded over; but there is nothing in this that corresponds to the word 'star' or to 0. One only pictures a situation that prompts the judgement: there is now no star to be seen.

§59.   Every word, perhaps, evokes some idea in us, even such a word as 'only'; but the idea need not correspond to the content of the word;

[J] 'Idea' taken in the sense of something pictorial.

it may be quite different in different people. One may well picture here a situation which invites a proposition in which the word occurs; or the spoken word may call to mind the written word.

This does not only happen in the case of particles. There is certainly no doubt that we cannot form any idea of our distance from the Sun. For even though we know the rule concerning how many measuring rods must be laid end to end, we still fail in every attempt to sketch a picture, according to this rule, that even only faintly approximates to

71   what we want. But that is no reason to doubt the | correctness of the calculation which determined the distance, and it in no way prevents us from basing further inferences on the existence of this distance.

§60. Even so concrete a thing as the Earth cannot be pictured as we know it to be; but we content ourselves with a ball of moderate size, which serves us as a symbol for the Earth; yet we realize that this is very different from it. Now even though our idea often fails at all to capture what we want, we still make judgements about an object such as the Earth with great confidence, even where its size is at issue.

We are quite often led by our thought beyond the imaginable, without thereby losing the support for our inferences. Even if, as it seems to be, it is impossible for us as human beings to think without ideas, it may still be that their connection with thought is entirely inessential, arbitrary and conventional.

That no idea can be formed of the content of a word is therefore no reason for denying it any meaning or for excluding it from use. The appearance to the contrary doubtless arises because we consider the words in isolation and in asking for their meaning look only for an idea. A word for which we lack a corresponding mental picture thus appears to have no content. But one must always keep in mind a complete proposition. Only in a proposition do the words really have a meaning.[22] The mental pictures that may pass before us need not correspond to the logical components of the judgement. It is enough if the proposition as a whole has a sense; its parts thereby also obtain their content.

This observation, it seems to me, is likely to throw light on a good

72   many | difficult concepts, such as that of the infinitesimal,[K] and its implications are certainly not restricted to mathematics.

The independence that I am claiming for number is not to be taken

---

[K] It all depends on defining the sense of an equation of the form

$$df(x) = g(x)dx,$$

rather than showing that there is a line bounded by two distinct points whose length is dx.

[22] This marks Frege's first use of the context principle in *GL*. For discussion of the role of the context principle in Frege's philosophy, see the Introduction, pp. 15–20 above.

to mean that a number word designates something when not in the
context of a proposition, but I only intend by this to exclude the use
of a number word as a predicate or attribute, which rather changes its
meaning.

§61.   But, it may perhaps be objected, even if the Earth cannot really
be pictured, it is still an external thing, which has a definite location;
but where is the number 4? It is neither outside us nor in us. In the
spatial sense, that is certainly true. Fixing the location of the number
4 makes no sense; but it follows from this only that it is not a spatial
object, not that it is not an object at all. Not every object is somewhere.
Even our ideas[L] are in this sense not in us – under our skin. Here there
are ganglion cells, blood corpuscles and suchlike, but not ideas. Spatial
predicates are not applicable to them: one idea is neither to the right
nor to the left of another; there are no distances between ideas meas-
urable in millimetres. If we nevertheless speak of them as in us, then
we mean by this that they are subjective.

But even if [we admit that] what is subjective has no location, how
is it possible for the number 4, which is objective, not to be anywhere?
Now I maintain that there is no contradiction at all in this. The number
4 is, in fact, exactly the same for everyone who deals with it; but this
has nothing to do with being spatial. Not every objective object [*object-
ives Gegenstand*] has a location. |

73   To obtain the concept of Number, the sense of a numerical
equation must be determined

§62.   How, then, is a number to be given to us, if we cannot have any
idea or intuition of it? Only in the context of a proposition do words
mean something. It will therefore depend on defining the sense of a
proposition in which a number word occurs. As it stands, this still
leaves much undetermined. But we have already established that number
words are to be understood as standing for independent objects. This
gives us a class of propositions that must have a sense – propositions
that express recognition [of a number as the same again]. If the symbol
a is to designate an object for us, then we must have a criterion that
decides in all cases whether *b* is the same as *a*, even if it is not always
in our power to apply this criterion. In our case we must define the
sense of the proposition

'The number that belongs to the concept *F* is the same as the number that
belongs to the concept *G*';

[L] Understanding this word purely psychologically, not psychophysically.

that is, we must represent the content of this proposition in another way, without using the expression

'the Number that belongs to the concept *F* '.

In doing so, we shall be giving a general criterion for the equality of numbers. When we have thus acquired a means of grasping a definite number and recognizing it as the same again, we can give it a number word as its proper name.

§63. Hume[M] has already mentioned such a means: 'When two numbers are so combined, as that the one has always a unit answering to every unit of the other, we pronounce them equal'. The | view that equality of numbers must be defined in terms of one-one correlation[23] seems recently to have gained widespread acceptance amongst mathematicians.[N] But it initially raises logical doubts and difficulties, which we ought not to pass over without examination.

The relationship of equality [*Gleichheit*] does not hold only amongst numbers. From this it seems to follow that it ought not to be defined specially for this case. One would think that the concept of equality would already have been fixed, from which, together with the concept of Number, it must then follow when Numbers are equal to one another, without requiring any further, special definition.

Against this, it is to be noted that for us the concept of Number has not yet been fixed, but is only to be determined by means of our definition. Our aim is to form the content of a judgement that can be construed as an equation on each side of which is a number. We thus do not intend to define equality specially for this case, but by means of the concept of equality, taken as already known, to obtain that which is to be regarded as being equal. Admittedly, this seems to be a very unusual kind of definition, which has certainly not yet received sufficient attention from logicians; but that it is not unheard of may be shown by a few examples.

§64. The judgement 'Line *a* is parallel to line *b*', in symbols:

$$a \parallel b,$$

[M] Baumann, op. cit., Vol. II, p. 565 [Hume, *A Treatise of Human Nature*, Book I, Part III, §1, p. 71].

[N] Cf. E. Schröder, op. cit., pp. 7–8; E. Kossak, *Die Elemente der Arithmetik, Programm des Friedrichs-Werder'schen Gymnasiums* (Berlin, 1872), p. 16; G. Cantor, *Grundlagen einer allgemeinen Mannichfaltigkeitslehre* (Leipzig, 1883).

---

[23] Frege actually uses the phrase 'eindeutige Zuordnung', by which he means a *many-one* relation, 'beiderseits eindeutige Zuordnung' being what he calls *one-one* correlation, i.e. a relation that is both many-one and one-many (see p. 77 above). But it seems more natural to talk of the latter here.

can be construed as an equation. If we do this, we obtain the concept of direction and say: 'The direction of line a is equal to the direction of line b'. | We thus replace the symbol // by the more general =, by distributing the particular content of the former to a and b. We split up the content in a different way from the original way and thereby acquire a new concept. Admittedly, the process is often seen in reverse, and parallel lines are frequently defined as lines whose directions are equal. The proposition 'If two lines are parallel to a third, then they are parallel to one another' can then very easily be proved by appealing to the corresponding proposition concerning equality [of directions]. It is only a pity that this stands the true situation on its head! For everything geometrical must surely originate in intuition. I now ask whether anyone has had an intuition of the direction of a line. Of the line, certainly! But is the direction of a line distinguished in intuition from the line itself? Hardly! This concept [of direction] is only found through a mental act that takes off from intuition. On the other hand, one does have an idea of parallel lines. The proof just mentioned only works by covertly presupposing, in the use of the word 'direction', what is to be proved; for were the proposition 'If two lines are parallel to a third, then they are parallel to one another' false, then a // b could not be transformed into an equation.

Similarly, from the parallelism of planes, a concept can be obtained that corresponds to that of direction in the case of lines. I have seen the word 'orientation' ['*Stellung*'] used for this. From geometrical similarity there arises the concept of shape, so that, for example, instead of 'The two triangles are similar', one says: 'The two triangles have equal shapes' or 'The shape of the one triangle is equal to the shape of the other'. So too, from the collinear relationship of geometrical figures, a concept can be obtained for which a name has still to be found. |

§65. Now in order to get, for example, from parallelism[O] to the concept of direction, let us try the following definition: the proposition

'Line a is parallel to line b'

is to mean the same as

'The direction of line a is equal to the direction of line b'.

This definition is unusual inasmuch as it apparently specifies the already known relation of equality, whereas it is actually intended to

[O] To express myself more easily and to be more readily understood, I take here the case of parallelism. The essentials of the discussion can be readily carried over to the case of numerical equality.

introduce the expression 'the direction of line a', which only occurs incidentally. From this there arises a second doubt, as to whether such a definition might not involve us in conflict with the well-known laws of identity [*Gleichheit*].[24] What are these? As analytic truths, they should be derivable from the concept itself. Leibniz[P] offers the following definition:

'*Eadem sunt, quorum unum potest substitui alteri salva veritate*'.[25]

I shall adopt this definition of identity [*Gleichheit*] as my own. Whether one says 'the same' ['*dasselbe*'], like Leibniz, or 'equal' ['*gleich*'], is unimportant. 'The same' may appear to express complete agreement, 'equal' only agreement in this or that respect; but a form of words can be employed in which this distinction ceases to apply: instead of 'The lines are equal in length', for example, one can say 'The length of the lines is equal' or 'the same'; instead of 'The surfaces are identical [*gleich*] in colour', one can say 'The colour of the surfaces is identical [*gleich*]'.[26]
77 And this is the way we used the word in the examples above. | In universal substitutability, in fact, all the laws of identity [*Gleichheit*] are contained.

In order to justify our suggested definition of the direction of a line, we would thus have to show that

'the direction of a'

can be everywhere substituted by

'the direction of b',

[P] *Non inelegans specimen demonstrandi in abstractis* (Erdmann edn. [*Oper. Philos.* I], p. 94).

[24] Here is one occasion on which the translation of 'Gleichheit' as 'identity' rather than 'equality', which Frege goes on to indicate he treats as synonymous, is more appropriate.
[25] 'Those things are the same of which one can be substituted for the other without loss of truth.' What Frege understands by this (since, taken literally, it involves use/mention confusion) is what is often called *Leibniz's Law* – interpreted as comprising both the Principle of the Indiscernibility of Identicals (reading the equivalence from left to right) and the Principle of the Identity of Indiscernibles (reading the equivalence from right to left):

$$x = y \leftrightarrow (\forall F)(Fx \leftrightarrow Fy).$$

As this formulation in modern notation shows, what is provided here is a definition of identity in purely logical terms (allowing quantification over properties); and it is this that supports Frege in taking the concept of identity as already known.
[26] The impossibility of translating 'gleich' everywhere by either 'equal' or 'identical' is shown up here. It is 'equal' more than 'identical' that might be taken to express agreement only in this or that respect; yet whilst we may talk of two lines being *equal* in length, we talk of two surfaces being *identical* in colour. But since Frege wants to show that 'equal' and 'the same' (viz. 'identical') can be treated as synonymous, the alternation in the translation here only highlights Frege's point.

if line *a* is parallel to line *b*. This is made simpler by initially knowing no other assertion about the direction of a line than that it agrees with the direction of another line. We would therefore need to demonstrate only the substitutability in an equality of this kind, or in contents that contain such equalities as components.[Q] All other assertions about directions would first have to be defined, and for these definitions we could adopt the rule that the substitutability of the direction of a line by that of one parallel to it must remain valid.

§66. But yet a third doubt arises about our suggested definition. In the proposition

'The direction of *a* is equal to the direction of *b*'

the direction of *a* appears as an object[R] and we have in our definition a means of reidentifying this object should it appear in another guise, say, as the direction of *b*. But this means | does not provide for all cases. It cannot, for example, be used to decide whether England is the same as the direction of the Earth's axis. Excuse the apparently nonsensical example! Of course, no one is going to confuse England with the direction of the Earth's axis; but that is no thanks to our definition. That says nothing as to whether the proposition

'The direction of *a* is equal to *q*'

is to be affirmed or denied, unless *q* itself is given in the form 'the direction of *b*'. What we lack is the concept of direction; for if we had this, then we could stipulate that if *q* is not a direction, then our proposition is to be denied, and if *q* *is* a direction, then the original definition decides the matter. Now it is natural to offer the definition:

q is a direction, if there is a line *b* whose direction is *q*.

But it is now clear that we have come round in a circle. In order to apply this definition, we would already have to know in each case whether the proposition

---

[Q] In a hypothetical judgement, for example, an equality of directions could occur as either antecedent or consequent.

[R] The definite article indicates this. A concept is for me a possible predicate of a singular judgeable content, an object a possible subject of such a content. If in the proposition

'The direction of the axis of the telescope is equal to the direction of the Earth's axis'

we take the direction of the axis of the telescope as subject, then the predicate is 'equal to the direction of the Earth's axis'. This is a concept. But the direction of the Earth's axis is only a part of the predicate; it is an object, since it can also be made the subject.

'*q* is equal to the direction of *b*'

is to be affirmed or denied.

§67.   If one were to say: *q* is a direction if it is introduced by means of the definition offered above, then the way in which the object *q* is introduced would be treated as a property of it, which it is not. The definition of an object asserts, as such, really nothing about it, but instead stipulates the meaning [*Bedeutung*] of a symbol. After this has been done, it transforms itself into a judgement which does deal with the object, but now it no longer introduces it but stands on the same level as other assertions about it. If this way out were chosen, it would presuppose that an object can only be given in one single way; for otherwise it would not follow, from the fact that *q* was not introduced by means of our definition, | that it could not have been so introduced. All equations would then come down to this, that whatever is given to us in the same way is to be recognized as the same. But this is so self-evident and so unfruitful that it is not worth stating. Indeed, no conclusion could ever be drawn here that was different from any of the premises. The multitude of meaningful [*bedeutsame*] uses of equations depends rather on the fact that something can be reidentified even though it is given in a different way.

§68.   Since we cannot in this way obtain a sharply defined concept of direction nor, for the same reasons, such a concept of Number, let us try another way. If line *a* is parallel to line *b*, then the extension of the concept 'line parallel to line *a*' is equal to the extension of the concept 'line parallel to line *b*'; and conversely, if the extensions of these two concepts are equal, then *a* is parallel to *b*. Let us therefore suggest the definitions:

the direction of line *a* is the extension of the concept 'parallel to line *a*';
the shape of triangle *d* is the extension of the concept 'similar to triangle *d*'.

If we want to apply this to our own case, then we have to substitute for directions or triangles concepts, and for parallelism or similarity the possibility of correlating one-one the objects that fall under the one concept with those that fall under the other. If this possibility obtains, I shall speak, for short, of the concept *F* being *equinumerous*[27] to the concept *G*, but I must ask that this word be regarded as an arbitrarily

---

[27] The German term is 'gleichzahlig', which Austin misleadingly translated as 'equal'. Since the German word was itself an invented one, 'equinumerous' seems an appropriate translation.

chosen form of expression, whose meaning is to be gleaned not from its linguistic construction but from this stipulation.

I therefore offer the definition:

80   the Number that belongs to the concept F is | the extension[s] of the concept 'equinumerous to the concept F'.

§69. That this definition is correct will hardly, perhaps, be clear at first. For is an extension of a concept not thought to be something different [from a number]? What it is thought to be is evident from the basic assertions that can be made about extensions of concepts. They are the following:

(1)   [that] equality [holds between them],
(2)   that one is more inclusive [*umfassender*] than another.

Now the proposition

'The extension of the concept "equinumerous to the concept F" is equal to the extension of the concept "equinumerous to the concept G"'

is true if and only if the proposition

'The same number belongs to the concept F as to the concept G'

is also true. Here there is thus complete agreement.

Certainly, we do not say that one number is more inclusive than another, in the sense in which the extension of a concept may be more inclusive than that of another; but the case in which

the extension of the concept 'equinumerous to the concept F'

is more inclusive than |

81   the extension of the concept 'equinumerous to the concept G'

---

[s] I believe that for 'extension of the concept', simply 'concept' could be said. But two different objections would arise:

1.   [that] this contradicts my earlier claim that the individual numbers are objects, as indicated by the definite article in such expressions as 'the number two' and by the impossibility of speaking of ones, twos, etc. in the plural, as well as by the fact that the number constitutes only a part of the predicate of a number statement;

2.   that concepts can be of equal extension, without coinciding.

Now I am actually of the opinion that both objections can be met; but that would lead us too far away here. I assume that it is known what the extension of a concept is.

cannot occur either; but rather, if all concepts that are equinumerous to G are also equinumerous to F, then conversely, all concepts that are equinumerous to F are also equinumerous to G. This 'more inclusive' should not, of course, be confused with 'greater', which occurs amongst numbers.

Admittedly, the case can still be imagined in which the extension of the concept 'equinumerous to the concept F' is more inclusive or less inclusive than the extension of another concept, which, according to our definition, could not then be a Number; and it is not usual to call a Number more inclusive or less inclusive than the extension of a concept; but there is also nothing to stop us adopting such a form of speech, should such a case occur.

[The rest of Part IV (§§70–86; *GL*, pp. 81–99), in which Frege provides a sketch of his logicist reduction of arithmetic, is omitted here; but a summary of the argument, with some clarificatory interpolations (in square brackets), is offered below.

Completion of our definition and proof of its worth (§§70–83)

Definitions, Frege writes, prove themselves by their fruitfulness; and his definition of number is to be justified by showing how the well-known properties of numbers can be derived from it (§70). [Although Frege does not himself expressly do so, it is worth noting that from Frege's explicit definition (as given at the end of §68) we can now *derive* the proposition (Nb) that, according to Frege, had been inadequately defined contextually by means of (Na):[28]

(Na)   The concept F is equinumerous to the concept G. (There are as many objects falling under concept F as under concept G, i.e. there are just as many F's as G's.)

(Nb)   The number of F's is equal to the number of G's. (The number that belongs to the concept F is the same as the number that belongs to the concept G.)

For what we have are the following two explicit definitions:

(Ne)   The Number that belongs to the concept F is the extension of the concept 'equinumerous to the concept F'.

(Nε)   The Number that belongs to the concept G is the extension of the concept 'equinumerous to the concept G'.

---

[28] The labelling that follows – (Na), (Nb), etc. – has been added for ease of presentation. For further discussion of (Na) and (Nb), see the Introduction, pp. 15ff. above.

Furthermore, according to Frege (cf. §68), from (Na) we can infer (Nd):

(Nd)   The extension of the concept 'equinumerous to the concept *F*' is equal to the extension of the concept 'equinumerous to the concept *G*'.

(Nb) clearly then follows from (Nd), (Ne) and (Nε). What we have thus done is derive (Nb) not *directly* from (Na), but *indirectly* via (Nd) and the explicit definitions. So if – *pace* Frege himself – we felt unhappy about the explicit definitions, but found the contextual method legitimate, we could still accept Frege's starting-point, the move from (Na) to (Nb).[29]]

The first step is to provide a more exact definition of 'equinumerosity' [involved in both (Na) and (Ne)]. Frege has already indicated that this is to be defined in terms of one-one correlation (cf. §§63, 68), and the key point here is that this can itself be characterized independently of number (despite the phrase '*one-one* correlation'). Frege gives an example to illustrate the idea: 'If a waiter wants to be sure of laying just as many knives as plates on a table, he does not need to count either of them, if he simply lays a knife right next to each plate, so that every knife on the table is located right next to a plate. The plates and knives are thus correlated one-one, by means of the same spatial relationship.' (§70.) Generalizing, then, two concepts *F* and *G* are equinumerous if there is a relation *R* that correlates one-one the objects falling under *F* with the objects falling under *G*, and this, as Frege had already shown in the *Begriffsschrift*, can be characterized purely logically. [In modern notation, '*Rxy*' symbolizing that *x* stands in relation *R* to *y*, this can be formalized as follows:

(Na*) $(\forall x)(Fx \rightarrow (\exists y)[Gy \ \& \ (\forall z)(Rxz \leftrightarrow z = y)])$
        $\& \ (\forall y)(Gy \rightarrow (\exists x)[Fx \ \& \ (\forall w)(Rwy \leftrightarrow w = x)])$.

The first conjunct says that for any *F* (i.e. anything that is an *F*), there is one and only one *G* to which it is *R*-related, and the second conjunct adds that for any *G*, there is one and only one *F* to which it is *R*-related. (The first clause, in other words, states the condition for the relation between the *F*'s and the *G*'s to be *many-one*, and the second clause the condition for the relation to be *one-many*, the two clauses providing the combined condition for the relation to be *one-one* – cf. (OO)

---

[29] This is one of the central insights that motivates Wright (1983), in his reconstruction of Frege's arguments. As Dummett (1991a: p. 123) notes, Frege does, in fact, himself derive all his theorems from the original contextual equivalence without further appeal to his explicit definition.

on p. 77 above.)] As Frege remarks in §72, in offering the same analysis there, this 'reduces one-one correlation to purely logical relationships'.

Returning to the problem that Frege felt had been unresolved in §56, we do now have a way of determining whether the number that belongs to the concept *F* is the same as the number that belongs to the concept *G*. [Frege's definitions of propositions of the form 'The number *n* belongs to the concept *F*' ('There are *n* *F*'s') were regarded by him as unsatisfactory (§56), because they did not adequately determine the relevant objects. But propositions of this form, according to Frege (cf. §57), are reducible to propositions that have the preferred form of an equation (identity statement):

(NF) The number *n* is the Number that belongs to the concept *F*.]

The expression '*n* is a Number' is taken as equivalent [*gleichbedeutend*] to the expression 'there is a concept such that *n* is the Number that belongs to it'; and this is now seen as acceptable with Frege's explicit definition [(Ne)] in place. 'Thus the concept of Number is defined, admittedly, it seems, in terms of itself, but nevertheless without error, since "the Number that belongs to the concept *F*" is already defined [as "the extension of the concept 'equinumerous to the concept *F*'"].' (§72.)

All that is then needed to provide definitions of the individual numbers is to find appropriate concepts [to substitute in (NF)]. In the case of the number 0, Frege utilizes the concept *not identical with itself*, yielding the following definition (cf. §74):

[(N0)] The number 0 is the Number which belongs to the concept *not identical with itself* [*sich selbst ungleich*].

In offering this, Frege remarks that there is no objection to taking a concept that contains a contradiction, so long as we do not assume that something falls under it: 'All that can be demanded of a concept on the part of logic and for rigour of proof is its sharp boundary, that for every object it is determined whether it falls under the concept or not. Now this demand is completely satisfied by a concept containing a contradiction such as "not identical with itself"; since of every object it is known that it does not fall under such a concept.' (§74.) Furthermore, the crucial point about Frege's chosen concept is that it can be specified purely logically ('$x \neq x$'), utilizing the Leibnizian definition of identity given in §65. [From (Ne) and (N0) we can then formulate an explicit definition that satisfies Frege's requirements:

(E0) The number 0 is the extension of the concept 'equinumerous to the concept *not identical with itself*'.

Assuming, with Frege, that the notion of an extension is unproblematically a logical notion,[30] we have indeed then managed to characterize the number 0 in purely logical terms.]

The next step in the project is to define the successor relation, relating any two adjacent members of the natural number series. Frege offers this definition of '*n* follows in the natural number series immediately after *m*' (§76):

> [(SR)] There is a concept *F*, and an object *x* falling under it, such that the Number that belongs to the concept *F* is *n* and the Number that belongs to the concept *falling under F but not identical with x* is *m*.

Intuitively, this clearly gives the desired result: there is one less object falling under the latter concept than under the former, and the relationship between the two concepts can be characterized purely logically [cf. (F_{n+1}) in fn. 20, p. 105 above].

Frege goes on to show how the definition yields 1 as the successor of 0 (§77). Take the concept *identical with 0*. Since one and only one object falls under this concept, namely, the number 0, the Number that belongs to this concept is the number 1. The Number that belongs to the concept *falling under the concept 'identical with 0' but not identical with 0*, on the other hand, is clearly 0, since nothing can fall under this concept. So the condition stated in (SR) is satisfied (taking '*F*' as 'identical with 0', giving $x = 0$, $n = 1$ and $m = 0$), and we can conclude that 1 is the successor of 0. What Frege has done here, in other words, is provide a suitable concept to substitute in (NF) to generate a definition of the number 1:

> [(N1)] The number 1 is the Number that belongs to the concept *identical with 0*.

Since 0 has already been defined purely logically, and in fact is the only object that has been so defined up to this point, the concept *identical with 0* is obviously the ideal concept for Frege to take in order to define the number 1 logically. What the argument just given then shows is that this is indeed the number that follows in the natural number series immediately after 0. (Cf. §77.)

[From (Ne) and (N1), the following explicit definition can then be offered:

> (E1) The number 1 is the extension of the concept 'equinumerous to the concept *identical with 0*'.

---

[30] Cf. §68, fn. S (p. 115 above), and §107 (p. 128 below).

With the numbers 0 and 1 now defined, the number 2 can then be generated in a similar way:

(N2)   The number 2 is the Number that belongs to the concept *identical with 0 or 1*.

(E2)   The number 2 is the extension of the concept 'equinumerous to the concept *identical with 0 or 1*'.

The pattern that emerges is clear: each number can be defined in terms of its predecessor(s), since the natural number series up to a given number n has itself $n + 1$ members (since it starts from 0). This suggests the following general definition (cf. §79):

(Nn+1)   The number $n + 1$ is the Number which belongs to the concept *member of the natural number series ending with n*.

Of course, the concept *member of the natural number series ending with n* itself needs to be defined, but once again, the materials for doing so had already been supplied in the *Begriffsschrift* (§§26–9; see pp. 75–6 above), where a logical characterization had been offered, through the notion of an hereditary property, of 'b follows a in the f-series' (cf. *GL*, §79), from which 'b is a member of the f-series beginning with a' could then be defined. Since this is equivalent to 'a is a member of the f-series ending with b', the required logical definition can be provided (cf. *GL*, §81). (SR) can then be used to show that (Nn+1) yields $n + 1$ as the successor of n – substituting 'member of the natural number series ending with n' for 'F', 'n' for 'x', '$n + 1$' for 'n', and 'n' for 'm' (cf. *GL*, §§82–3).[31]]

With Frege's definitions in place, it becomes possible to derive the familiar properties of the natural numbers. For example, [(Nn+1)] implies that every natural number has a successor, i.e. that no member of the natural number series follows after itself, as Frege puts it in §83. In the *Grundlagen* Frege merely states a handful of theorems (§78); the full task was to be undertaken in the *Grundgesetze*.[32]

Infinite Numbers (§§84–86)

In the final subdivision of Part IV, Frege makes some brief remarks about infinite (transfinite) Numbers, the existence of which is unproblematic

---

[31] Frege provides only a sketch here; a fuller proof is given in *GG*, I, §§114–19.

[32] The formal proofs are presented in Part II of *GG* (Vol. I, §§53–179; Vol. II, §§1–54), which has not as yet been translated into English (not that there is much to translate: the vast majority of it is written in Frege's symbolic notation). A useful summary of the main theorems derived in Part II, however, is provided in Currie, 1982: pp. 55–7.

on his account of number. For the Number that belongs to the concept *finite Number*, defined as the concept *member of the natural number series beginning with 0* (§83) is clearly an infinite Number, which Frege symbolizes by '∞_1' ('$\aleph_0$', as it is now written). 'There is nothing at all weird or wonderful about the infinite Number ∞_1 so defined. "The Number that belongs to the concept F is ∞_1," means [*heisst*] no more nor less than: there is a relation that correlates one-one the objects falling under the concept F with the finite Numbers. According to our definitions, this has a perfectly clear and unambiguous sense; and that is sufficient to justify the use of the symbol ∞_1 and secure it a meaning [*Bedeutung*]. That we can form no idea of an infinite Number is quite irrelevant and applies just as much to finite Numbers. Our Number ∞_1 is in this way just as definite as any finite Number: it can without doubt be recognized as the same again and be distinguished from another.' (§84.) Frege goes on to express his agreement with Cantor that infinite Numbers are as legitimate as finite Numbers (§85), though he does suggest that his own method of introducing infinite Numbers, through logical definition, is superior to Cantor's appeal to 'inner intuition' (§86). Furthermore, Frege notes, since on his account numbers are characterized right from the start as belonging to concepts, there is no extension of the meaning of 'Number' when infinite numbers are introduced (since they too are attached to concepts), so that worries about invalidating any fundamental laws are minimized (§85).

The translation resumes at the beginning of the concluding part.]

99

V. Conclusion

§87. I hope in this work to have made it probable that arithmetical laws are analytic judgements and therefore *a priori*. Accordingly, arithmetic would be simply a further developed logic, every arithmetical theorem a logical law, albeit a derivative one. Applications of arithmetic in natural science would be logical processing of observed facts;[T] calculation would be inference. The laws of number will not need, as Baumann[U] thinks, to prove their worth in practice in order to be applicable to the external world; for in the external world, in the totality of the spatial, there are no concepts, no properties of concepts, no numbers. The laws of number are thus not really applicable to external things: they are not laws of nature. But they are certainly applicable to judgements that are made about things in the external world: they are laws of the laws of nature.

[T] Observation itself already involves logical activity.

[U] Op. cit., Vol. II, p. 670.

They do not assert a connection between natural phenomena, but a connection between judgements; and the latter include the laws of nature.

§88.   Kant[V] obviously underestimated the value of analytic judgements – no doubt as a result of defining the concept too narrowly, although 100   the broader concept used here | does appear to have been in his mind.[W] On the basis of his definition, the division into analytic and synthetic judgements is not exhaustive. He is thinking of the case of the universal affirmative judgement. Here one can speak of a subject-concept and ask – according to the definition – whether the predicate-concept is contained in it. But what if the subject is an individual object? What if the question concerns an existential judgement? Here there can be no talk at all of a subject-concept in Kant's sense. Kant seems to think of a concept as defined by a conjunction of marks;[33] but this is one of the least fruitful ways of forming concepts. Looking back over the definitions given above, there is scarcely one of this kind to be found. The same holds too of the really fruitful definitions in mathematics, for example, of the continuity of a function. We do not have here a series of conjunctions of marks, but rather a more intimate, I would say more organic, connection of defining elements. The distinction can be clarified by means of a geometrical analogy. If the concepts (or their extensions) are represented by areas on a plane, then the concept defined by a conjunction of marks corresponds to the area that is common to all the areas representing the marks; it is enclosed by sections of their boundaries. With such a definition it is thus a matter – in terms of the analogy – of using the lines already given to demarcate an area in a new way.[X] But nothing essentially new comes out of this. The more fruitful definitions of concepts draw boundary lines that were not there at all. 101   What can be inferred from them cannot be seen from the start; | what was put into the box is not simply being taken out again. These inferences extend our knowledge, and should therefore be taken as synthetic, according to Kant; yet they can be proved purely logically and are thus analytic. They are, in fact, contained in the definitions, but like a plant in a seed, not like a beam in a house. Often several definitions are needed for the proof of a proposition, which is not therefore contained in any single one and yet does follow purely logically from all of them together.

[V] Op. cit., Vol. III, pp. 39ff. [Cf. Kant, *Critique of Pure Reason*, A6ff./B10ff.]
[W] On p. 43 [B14] he says that a synthetic proposition can only be recognized by the law of contradiction, if another synthetic proposition is presupposed. [Cf. Frege's fn. E to §3, p. 92 above.]
[X] Similarly, if the marks are connected by 'or'.

---

[33] E.g. defining 'horse' as 'four-footed, solid-hoofed and herbivorous mammal'. For the notion of a 'mark' ('Merkmal'), see §53 (pp. 102–3 above); *CO*, pp. 189–90 below.

§89. I must also contradict the generality of Kant's[Y] claim that without sensibility no object would be given to us. Zero and one are objects that cannot be given to us through the senses. Even those who regard the smaller numbers as intuitable will surely have to concede that none of the numbers greater than $1000^{1000^{1000}}$ can be given to them in intuition, and yet we know various things about them. Perhaps Kant used the word 'object' in some other sense; but then zero, one and our ∞_1 entirely drop out of his account; for they are not concepts either, and even of concepts Kant[Y] requires that objects be associated with them in intuition.

In order not to lay myself open to the charge of simply picking holes in the work of a genius to whom we can only look up with grateful admiration, I think I should also emphasize the agreement that by far prevails. To touch only on what is salient here, I see Kant as having performed a great service in drawing the distinction between synthetic and analytic judgements. In calling geometrical truths synthetic and *a priori*, he revealed their true | nature. And this is still worth repeating now, since it is still not often recognized. If Kant was wrong about arithmetic, then that does not, I believe, detract fundamentally from the service he performed. What mattered to him was the existence of synthetic *a priori* judgements; whether they occur only in geometry or also in arithmetic is of less significance [*Bedeutung*].

§90. I do not claim to have made the analytic nature of arithmetical propositions more than probable, since it can still always be doubted whether their proof can be completely constructed from purely logical laws, or whether an assumption of another kind has not intruded somewhere unnoticed. Nor will this doubt be fully allayed by the indications I have given of the proof of some propositions; it can only be removed by a chain of inference free of gaps, with no step taken that is not in accord with one of a few modes of inference recognized as purely logical. Until now hardly a proof has been constructed like this, since the mathematician is content if every transition to a new judgement is self-evidently correct, without enquiring into the nature of this self-evidence, whether it is logical or intuitive. Such a transition is often very complex and equivalent to several simple inferences, alongside which something from intuition can still enter. Progress is by leaps, and from this arises the apparently abundant variety of modes of inference in mathematics; for the bigger the leaps, the more complex the combinations of simple inferences and intuitive axioms they can represent. Nevertheless, such a transition is often immediately self-evident to us, without our being aware of the intermediate steps, and since it does not present

[Y] Op. cit., Vol. III, p. 82 [*Critique of Pure Reason*, A51/B75].

103 itself as one of the recognized logical modes of inference, we are all too ready to take this self-evidence as intuitive and the inferred truth as synthetic, even | when its domain of validity obviously extends beyond the intuitable.

It is not possible this way to separate cleanly the synthetic that is based on intuition from the analytic. Nor is it possible to draw up with certainty a complete list of axioms of intuition, from which every mathematical proof can be constructed according to logical laws.

§91. The requirement that all leaps in an argument be avoided cannot therefore be repudiated. That it is so hard to satisfy lies in the prolixity of a step by step approach. Every proof that is only slightly complicated threatens to become monstrously long. In addition, the enormous variety of logical forms revealed in ordinary language makes it difficult to delimit a set of modes of inference that covers all cases and is easy to survey.

To reduce these deficiencies, I devised my *Begriffsschrift*. It is intended to achieve greater economy and surveyability of expression and to be used in a few fixed forms in the manner of a calculus, so that no transition is permitted that is not in accord with the rules that are laid down once and for all.[Z] No assumption can then slip in unnoticed. In this way I have proved, without borrowing an axiom from intuition, a theorem[AA] that might at first sight be taken as synthetic, which I shall here formulate thus:

If the relation of every member of a series to its successor is many-one [*eindeutig*], and if m and y follow x in this series, then either y precedes m in this series or coincides with m or follows m. |

104   From this proof it can be seen that propositions that extend our knowledge can contain analytic judgements.[BB]

[The remaining sections of the book fall under the heading 'Other numbers', and the first twelve sections (§§92–103; *GL*, pp. 104–13), in which Frege is mainly concerned to refute what he calls the formalist

[Z] It is intended, however, to provide a means of expressing not only logical form, like Boolean symbolism, but also content.
[AA] *Begriffsschrift*, p. 86, formula 133.
[BB] This proof will still be found far too lengthy, a disadvantage that might seem to more than outweigh the near absolute certainty of a mistake or a gap [in a shorter proof]. My aim at the time was to reduce everything to the smallest possible number of the simplest possible logical laws. As a result, I used only a single mode of inference. But even then I pointed out in the Preface, p. vii [p. 51 above], that for further applications more modes of inference would be recommended. This can be done without affecting the validity of the chain of inference, and thus significant [*bedeutende*] abbreviation can be achieved.

theory [*formale Theorie*], are here omitted. The formalist is understood as someone who imagines that one need only postulate that, say, the laws of addition and multiplication, as defined over the natural numbers, hold for any extension of the number system, in order to investigate coherently the properties of that extended system (cf. §96).[34] But, Frege argues, it is quite wrong to suppose that a concept has instances if no contradiction has yet revealed itself – not only are self-contradictory concepts admissible, but even if a concept contains no contradiction, that is still no guarantee that anything falls under it (cf. §§94, 96): 'even the mathematician cannot create whatever he likes, any more than the geographer; he too can only discover what is there and name it' (§96). Frege remarks that 'It is common to act as if mere postulation [*Forderung*] were already its own fulfilment' (§102).[35] Yet 'postulating', say, that through any three points a straight line can be drawn is simply incoherent; and we first have to prove that our postulates contain no contradiction (cf. §102). With the introduction of new numbers, Frege writes, 'the meaning [*Bedeutung*] of the words "sum" and "product" is extended' (§100), and we cannot automatically assume that initial definitions of basic concepts remain valid in any enlarged system (cf. §102).[36] But if we cannot just define new numbers into existence by specifying a list of properties that characterize them, nor arrive at them by simply extending an existing number system taking its axioms for granted, how are they then to be apprehended? Frege takes up this question in §104.]

114 §104.   How, then, are fractions, irrational numbers and complex numbers to be given to us? If we turn for help to intuition, then we introduce something foreign into arithmetic; but if we only define the concept of such a number by its marks, if we only require that the number have certain properties, then nothing guarantees that anything falls under the concept and corresponds to our demands, and yet it is precisely on this that proofs must rest.

Now how is it in the case of the [natural] Numbers? Should we really not talk of $1000^{1000^{1000}}$ before that many objects have been given to us in intuition? Is it until then an empty symbol? No! It has a quite definite sense, even though it is psychologically impossible, in view of the

---

[34] The formalism here is what Dummett (1991a: p. 178) has suggested should be better called 'postulationism', to distinguish it from more sophisticated forms, both those that Frege later attacks in *GG*, II, §§86–137, and those that have subsequently been developed.
[35] Cf. Russell's famous comment that 'The method of "postulating" what we want has many advantages; they are the same as the advantages of theft over honest toil' (*IMP*, p. 71).
[36] Cf. *GG*, II, §§56–65 (pp. 259–68 below), where Frege objects very strongly to what he calls in §57 'the mathematicians' favourite procedure, piecemeal definition'.

brevity of our life, for us to apprehend so many objects;[CC] but nevertheless $1000^{1000^{1000}}$ is an object, whose properties we can recognize, even though it is not intuitable. We can convince ourselves of this by showing that one and only one positive whole number is always expressed by a^n, the symbol introduced for the nth power of a, where a and n are positive whole numbers. To explain this in detail here would lead us too far away. The general strategy will be clear from the way we defined zero in §74, one in §77, and the infinite Number ∞_1 in §84, and from the sketch of the proof that every finite Number in the natural number series has a successor (§§82–83).

So too in the case of the definitions of fractions, complex numbers, etc., everything will depend in the end on finding a judgeable content that can be transformed into an equation whose sides are precisely the 115 new | numbers. In other words, we must fix the sense of a recognition judgement [*Wiedererkennungsurteil*] for such numbers. In doing so, we must heed the doubts that we discussed, in §§63–68, concerning such a transformation. If we proceed in the same way as we did there, then the new numbers will be given to us as extensions of concepts.

§105. On this conception of numbers,[DD] it seems to me, the attraction that work on arithmetic and analysis holds is easily explained. Adapting the familiar words, it might well be said: the real object of reason is reason itself.[37] We are concerned in arithmetic not with objects that become known to us through the medium of the senses as something foreign from outside, but with objects that are immediately given to reason, which can fully comprehend them, as its own.[EE]

And yet, or rather precisely because of this, these objects are not subjective fantasies. There is nothing more objective than arithmetical laws.

[CC] A rough estimate shows that millions of years would not suffice for this.

[DD] If too might be called formalist [*formal*]. Yet it is quite different from what was criticized above under this name.

[EE] By this I do not in the least want to deny that without sense impressions we are as thick as a plank and know nothing of numbers or of anything else; but this psychological proposition does not concern us here at all. I emphasize this again because of the constant danger of confusing two fundamentally different questions.

---

[37] 'der eigentliche Gegenstand der Vernunft ist die Vernunft'. This is presumably an allusion to a remark in Ottilie's Journal in Goethe's novel *Die Wahlverwandtschaften* (Part Two, Chapter Seven): 'das eigentliche Studium der Menschheit ist der Mensch' ('the proper study of mankind is man'); though this remark too has historical predecessors, for example, in Pierre Charron's *De la sagesse* (Bordeaux, 1601, Book I, chapter I, p. 1): 'La vraye science & le vray estude de l'homme, c'est l'homme' – cf. Thiel, 1986: p. 172 – and in Pope's *Essay on Man* (Epistle II, lines 1–2): 'Know then thyself, presume not God to scan, | The proper study of mankind is man'. Cf. also Kant, *Critique of Pure Reason*, preface to the first edition, where Kant writes that 'I have to deal simply with reason itself and its pure thinking' ('daß . . . ich es lediglich mit der Vernunft selbst und ihrem reinen Denken zu tun habe'; Axiv).

§106. Let us now cast a brief glance back over the course of our investigation. After establishing that number is neither a collection of things nor a property of such, nor a subjective product of mental processes, but rather, that a statement of number asserts something objective about a concept, we first attempted to define the individual numbers 0, 1, etc., and the relation of succession in the number series. The first attempt failed, because we had only defined each assertion about | concepts, but not 0, 1 separately, which are only parts of [the predicate involved in] the assertion. This had the result that we were unable to prove the equality of numbers. It showed that the numbers with which arithmetic is concerned must be grasped not as dependent attributes but substantively.[FF] Numbers thus appeared as reidentifiable objects, though not as physical or even merely spatial ones, nor as ones which we can picture through the power of imagination. We then laid down the principle that the meaning of a word is to be defined not in isolation, but in the context of a proposition; only by adhering to this, I believe, can the physical conception of number be avoided, without falling into a psychological one. Now there is one kind of proposition that, for every object, must have a sense, that is, recognition statements, called equations in the case of numbers. As we saw, statements of number too are to be construed as equations. It thus came down to fixing the sense of a numerical equation, expressing it without making use of number words or the word 'number'. The possibility of correlating one-one the objects falling under concept F with those falling under concept G we recognized as the content of a recognition judgement concerning numbers. Our definition thus had to lay it down that this possibility means the same as a numerical equation. We recalled similar cases: the definition of direction in terms of parallelism, shape in terms of similarity, etc.

§107. The question then arose: when is it justified to construe a content as that of a recognition judgement? For this the condition must be fulfilled | that in every judgement the left-hand side of the putative equation can be substituted by the right-hand side without altering its truth. Now, without adding further definitions, we do not initially know anything about the left- or right-hand sides of such an equation than just that they are equal. So all that needed to be demonstrated was substitutability in an equation.

But there still remained one doubt. A recognition statement must always have a sense. If we now construe the possibility of correlating one-one the objects falling under concept F with those falling under concept G as an equation, by saying: 'the Number that belongs to the concept F is equal to the Number that belongs to the concept G',

116

117

[FF] The distinction corresponds to that between 'blue' and 'the colour of the sky'.

hereby introducing the expression 'the Number that belongs to the concept *F*', then the equation only has a sense if both sides have this same form. According to such a definition, we could not judge whether an equation is true or false, if only one side has this form. This led us to the definition:

> The Number that belongs to the concept *F* is the extension of the concept 'concept equinumerous to the concept *F*', where a concept *F* is called equinumerous to a concept *G* if the possibility exists of one-one correlation.

We assumed here that the sense of the expression 'extension of a concept' was known. This way of overcoming the difficulty may well not meet with universal approval, and many will prefer removing the doubt in another way. I too attach no great importance to the introduction of extensions of concepts.

§108.   It now still remained to define one-one correlation; we reduced 118 this to purely | logical relations. After we had then indicated the proof of the proposition 'The number that belongs to the concept *F* is equal to the number that belongs to the concept *G*, if the concept *F* is equinumerous to the concept *G*', we defined 0, the expression '*n* directly follows *m* in the natural number series', and the number 1, and showed that 1 directly follows 0 in the natural number series. We cited a few theorems, which can easily be proved at this point, and then went a little more deeply into the following proposition, which reveals the infinity of the number series:

> 'Every number in the natural number series has a successor'.

We were thus led to the concept 'member of the natural number series ending with *n*', from which we could show that the Number belonging to this directly follows *n* in the natural number series. We first defined it by means of the general relation of the following in a ϕ-series of an object *x* by an object *y*. The sense of this expression too was reduced to purely logical relations. And this enabled us to prove that the inference from *n* to ($n + 1$), which is usually regarded as specifically mathematical, is based on general logical modes of inference.

To prove the infinity of the number series, we then needed the theorem that no finite number follows in the natural number series after itself. We thus arrived at the concepts of finite and infinite number. We showed that the latter is fundamentally no less logically justified than the former. By way of comparison, Cantor's infinite Numbers and his 'following in a succession' were considered, and the difference in formulation pointed out.

§109. From all that has gone before, the analytic and *a priori* nature of arithmetical truths has thus emerged as highly probable; and we achieved | an improvement on Kant's view. We further saw what is still missing in order to raise this probability to certainty, and indicated the path that must lead to this.

119

Finally, we used our results in a critique of a formalist theory of negative, fractional, irrational and complex numbers, which showed up its inadequacies. We recognized its error in assuming as proved that a concept is free from contradiction if no contradiction has revealed itself, and in taking freedom from contradiction as sufficient guarantee that something falls under the concept. This theory imagines that it need only formulate postulates, whose fulfilment then takes care of itself. It behaves like a god, who can create by his mere word whatever he needs. It must also be reprimanded for passing off as a definition what is only a set of instructions, the following of which would introduce something foreign into arithmetic; even though in its formulation it might be regarded as innocent, this is only because it remains a mere set of instructions.

This formalist theory is thus in danger of lapsing back into an *a posteriori* or at least synthetic theory, however much it may give the appearance of soaring on the heights of abstraction.

Now our earlier account of the positive whole numbers shows us the possibility of avoiding the confusion with external things and geometrical intuitions, yet without making the mistake of the formalist theory. As there, it depends on fixing the content of a recognition judgement. If we think of this as everywhere achieved, then negative, fractional, irrational and complex numbers appear as no more mysterious than the positive whole numbers, which are no more real, actual or tangible than they.

Function and Concept[1]

[This lecture was given to the *Jenaische Gesellschaft für Medicin und Natur-wissenschaft* on 9 January 1891, and subsequently published by Frege as a separate work (Jena: Hermann Pohle, 1891). Besides providing Frege's fullest account of his notion of a function, it also marks the first appearance of his distinction between *Sinn* and *Bedeutung*.]

Preface

i I publish this lecture separately in the hope of finding readers who are unfamiliar with the Proceedings of the Jena Society for Medicine and Science. It is my intention, in the near future, as I have indicated elsewhere, to explain how I express the fundamental definitions of arithmetic in my *Begriffsschrift*, and how I construct proofs from these solely by means of my symbols. For this purpose it will be useful to be able to refer [*berufen*] to this lecture so as not to be drawn then into discussions which many might condemn as not directly relevant, but which others might welcome. As befitting the occasion, my lecture was not addressed only to mathematicians; and I sought to express myself in as accessible a way as the time available and the subject allowed. May it then arouse interest in the matter in wider learned circles, particularly amongst logicians.

*   *   *

1 Rather a long time ago[A] I had the honour of addressing this Society about the symbolic system that I entitled *Begriffsschrift*. Today I should

---

[A] On 10 January 1879 and 27 January 1882. [The reference here is to *APCN* and *ACN*, respectively.]

---

[1] Translated by Peter Geach (*TPW*, pp. 21–41/*CP*, pp. 137–56; Preface translated by Michael Beaney from *KS*, p. 125). Page numbers in the margin are from the original publication. The translated text here is from the third edition of *TPW*, with minor revisions made in accordance with the policy adopted in the present volume – in particular, 'Bedeutung' (and cognates such as 'bedeutungslos') being left untranslated, and 'bedeuten' being rendered as 'stand for' as in the second edition (but with the German always in square brackets following it), unless otherwise indicated. For discussion of this policy, and the problems involved in translating 'Bedeutung' and its cognates, see the Introduction, §4 above.

like to throw light upon the subject from another side, and tell you about some supplementations and new conceptions, whose necessity has occurred to me since then. There can here be no question of setting forth my *Begriffsschrift* in its entirety, but only of elucidating some fundamental ideas.

My starting-point is what is called a function in mathematics. The original *Bedeutung* of this word was not so wide as that which it has since obtained; it will be well to begin by dealing with this first usage, and only then consider the later extensions. I shall for the moment be speaking only of functions of a single argument. The first place where a scientific expression appears with a clear-cut *Bedeutung* is where it is required for the statement of a law. This case arose as regards | functions upon the discovery of higher Analysis. Here for the first time it was a matter of setting forth laws holding for functions in general. So we must go back to the time when higher Analysis was discovered, if we want to know how the word 'function' was originally understood. The answer that we are likely to get to this question is: 'A function of x was taken to be a mathematical expression containing x, a formula containing the letter x.'

Thus, e.g., the expression

$$2x^3 + x$$

would be a function of x, and

$$2.2^3 + 2$$

would be a function of 2. This answer cannot satisfy us, for here no distinction is made between form and content, sign and thing signified [*Bezeichnetes*]; a mistake, admittedly, that is very often met with in mathematical works, even those of celebrated authors. I have already pointed out on a previous occasion[B] the defects of the current formal theories in arithmetic. We there have talk about signs that neither have nor are meant to have any content, but nevertheless properties are ascribed to them which are unintelligible except as belonging to the content of a sign. So also here; a mere expression, the form for a content, | cannot be the heart of the matter; only the content itself can be that. Now what is the content, the *Bedeutung* of '$2.2^3 + 2$'? The same as of '18' or '3.6'. What is expressed in the equation '$2.2^3 + 2 = 18$' is that the right-hand complex of signs has the same *Bedeutung* as the left-hand one. I must here combat the view that, e.g., 2 + 5 and 3 + 4 are equal but not the same. This view is grounded in the same confusion of form and content, sign and thing signified. It is as though one wanted to regard the sweet-smelling violet as differing from *Viola odorata* because the names

[B] *Die Grundlagen der Arithmetik* (1884), §§92ff. [cf. pp. 124–5 above]; 'On Formal Theories of Arithmetic' (1885) [*FTA*].

sound different. Difference of sign cannot by itself be a sufficient ground for difference of the thing signified. The only reason why in our case the matter is less obvious is that the *Bedeutung* of the numeral 17 is not anything perceptible to the senses. There is at present a very widespread tendency not to recognize as an object anything that cannot be perceived by means of the senses; this leads here to numerals' being taken to be numbers, the proper objects of our discussion;[C] and then, I admit, 7 and 2 + 5 would indeed be different. But such a conception

4   is untenable, for we | cannot speak of any arithmetical properties of numbers whatsoever without going back to the *Bedeutung* of the signs. For example, the property belonging to 1, of being the result of multiplying itself by itself, would be a mere myth; for no microscopical or chemical investigation, however far it was carried, could ever detect this property in the possession of the innocent character that we call a figure one. Perhaps there is talk of a definition; but no definition is creative in the sense of being able to endow a thing with properties that it has not already got – apart from the one property of expressing and signifying something in virtue of the definition.[D] The characters we call numerals have, on the other hand, physical and chemical properties depending on the writing material. One could imagine the introduction some day of quite new numerals, just as, e.g., the Arabic numerals superseded the Roman. Nobody is seriously going to suppose that in this way we should get quite new numbers, quite new arithmetical objects, with properties still to be investigated. Thus we must distinguish between numerals and their *Bedeutungen*; and if so, we shall have to recognize

5   that the expressions '2', '1 + 1', '3 − 1', '6:3' all | have the same *Bedeutung*, for it is quite inconceivable where the difference between them could lie. Perhaps you say: 1 + 1 is a sum, but 6:3 is a quotient. But what is 6:3? The number that when multiplied by 3 gives the result 6. We say '*the* number', not 'a number'; by using the definite article, we indicate that there is only a single number. Now we have:

$$(1 + 1) + (1 + 1) + (1 + 1) = 6,$$

and thus (1 + 1) is the very number that was designated as (6:3). The different expressions correspond to different conceptions and aspects, but nevertheless always to the same thing. Otherwise the equation $x^2 = 4$

[C] Cf. the essays: H. von Helmholtz, 'Zählen und Messen erkenntnistheoretisch betrachtet' ['Numbering and Measuring from an Epistemological Viewpoint', in *Epistemological Writings* (Dordrecht and Boston, 1977), p. 72], and Leopold Kronecker, 'Über den Zahlbegriff' ['On the Concept of Number'], in *Philosophische Aufsätze: Eduard Zeller zu seinem fünfzigjährigen Doctorjubiläum gewidmet* (Leipzig, 1887).

[D] In definition it is always a matter of associating with a sign a sense or a *Bedeutung*. Where sense and *Bedeutung* are missing, we cannot properly speak either of a sign or of a definition.

would not just have the roots 2 and −2, but also the root (1 + 1) and countless others, all of them different, even if they resembled one another in a certain respect. By recognizing only two real roots, we are rejecting the view that the sign of equality does not stand for [*bedeute*] complete coincidence but only partial agreement. If we adhere to this truth, we see that the expressions:

$$'2.1^3 + 1',$$
$$'2.2^3 + 2',$$
$$'2.4^3 + 4',$$

stand for [*bedeuten*] numbers, viz. 3, 18, 132. So if a function were really the *Bedeutung* of a mathematical expression, it would be just be a number; and nothing new would have been gained for arithmetic [by speaking of functions]. Admittedly, people who use the word 'function' ordinarily

6 have in mind expressions | in which a number is just indicated indefinitely by the letter *x*, e.g.

$$'2.x^3 + x';$$

but that makes no difference; for this expression likewise just indefinitely indicates a *number*, and it makes no essential difference whether I write it down or just write down '*x*'.

All the same, it is precisely by the notation that uses '*x*' to indicate [a number] indefinitely that we are led to the right conception. People call *x* the argument, and recognize the same function again in

$$'2.1^3 + 1',$$
$$'2.4^3 + 4',$$
$$'2.5^3 + 5',$$

only with different arguments, viz. 1, 4, and 5. From this we may discern that it is the common element of these expressions that contains the essential peculiarity of a function; i.e. what is present in

$$'2.x^3 + x'$$

over and above the letter '*x*'. We could write this somewhat as follows:

$$'2.(\ )^3 + (\ )'.$$

I am concerned to show that the argument does not belong with a function, but goes together with the function to make up a complete whole; for a function by itself must be called incomplete, in need of supplementation, or unsaturated [*ungesättigt*]. And in this respect functions differ fundamentally from numbers. Since such is the essence of

7 functions, we can explain | why, on the one hand, we recognize the same function in '$2.1^3 + 1$' and '$2.2^3 + 2$', even though these expressions stand for [*bedeuten*] different numbers, whereas, on the other hand, we

do not find one and the same function in '$2.1^3 + 1$' and '$4 - 1$' in spite of their equal numerical values. Moreover, we now see how people are easily led to regard the form of an expression as what is essential to a function. We recognize the function in the expression by imagining the latter as split up, and the possibility of thus splitting it up is suggested by its structure.

The two parts into which a mathematical expression is thus split up, the sign of the argument and the expression of the function, are dissimilar; for the argument is a number, a whole complete in itself, as the function is not. (We may compare this with the division of a line by a point. One is inclined in that case to count the dividing-point along with both segments; but if we want to make a clean division, i.e. so as not to count anything twice over or leave anything out, then we may only count the dividing-point along with one segment. This segment thus becomes fully complete in itself, and may be compared to the argument; whereas the other is lacking in something – viz. the dividing-point, which one may call its endpoint, does not belong to it. Only by completing it with this endpoint, or with a line that has two endpoints, do we get from it something entire.) For instance, if I say 'the function $2.x^3 + x$',

8   x must not be considered as | belonging to the function; this letter only serves to indicate the kind of supplementation that is needed; it enables one to recognize the places where the sign for the argument must go in.

We give the name 'the value of a function for an argument' to the result of completing the function with the argument. Thus, e.g., 3 is the value of the function $2.x^3 + x$ for the argument 1, since we have: $2.1^3 + 1 = 3$.

There are functions, such as $2 + x - x$ or $2 + 0.x$, whose value is always the same, whatever the argument; we have $2 = 2 + x - x$ and $2 = 2 + 0.x$. Now if we counted the argument as belonging with the function, we should hold that the number 2 is this function. But this is wrong. Even though here the value of the function is always 2, the function itself must nevertheless be distinguished from 2; for the expression for a function must always show one or more places that are intended to be filled up with the sign of the argument.

The method of analytic geometry supplies us with a means of intuitively representing the values of a function for different arguments. If we regard the argument as the numerical value of an abscissa, and the corresponding value of the function as the numerical value of the ordinate of a point, we obtain a set of points that presents itself to intuition (in ordinary cases) as a curve. Any point on the curve corresponds to an argument together with the associated value of the function. |

9   Thus, e.g.,

$$y = x^2 - 4x$$

yields a parabola; here 'y' indicates the value of the function and the numerical value of the ordinate, and 'x' similarly indicates the argument and the numerical value of the abscissa. If we compare with this the function

$$x(x - 4),$$

we find that they have always the same value for the same argument. We have generally:

$$x^2 - 4x = x(x - 4),$$

whatever number we take for x. Thus the curve we get from

$$y = x^2 - 4x$$

is the same as the one that arises out of

$$y = x(x - 4).$$

I express this as follows: the function $x(x - 4)$ has the same value-range[2] as the function $x^2 - 4x$.

If we write

$$x^2 - 4x = x(x - 4),$$

we have not put one function equal to the other, but only the values of one equal to those of the other. And if we so understand this equation that it is to hold whatever argument may be substituted for x, then we have thus expressed that an equality holds generally. But we can also say: 'the value-range of the function $x(x - 4)$ is equal to that of | the function $x^2 - 4x$', and here we have an equality between value-ranges. The possibility of regarding the equality holding generally between values of functions as a [particular] equality, viz. an equality between value-ranges is, I think, indemonstrable; it must be taken to be a fundamental law of logic.[E3]

10

[E] In many phrases of ordinary mathematical terminology, the word 'function' certainly corresponds to what I have here called the value-range of a function. But function, in the sense of the word employed here, is the logically prior [notion].

[2] Frege's term 'Wertverlauf' is here translated as 'value-range'. Alternative translations are 'course-of-values' (Furth, in *BLA*) and 'graph' (Geach, in the third edition of *TPW*). Despite Frege's initial explanation of the term in a geometrical context, 'graph' is inappropriate, since the notion of a function has been generalized, and Frege was insistent that our logical and arithmetical knowledge outstrips our powers of geometrical intuition. But both alternative renderings do have the virtue of indicating that Frege has in mind a set of *pairings* of arguments with values, and not just the range of values themselves. So although 'value-range' is perhaps the simplest and most literal translation, and seems to have become the most widely adopted, it must be remembered, as Frege makes clear here, that it refers to a set of pairings.

[3] This is the first formulation in Frege's work of Axiom V of the *Grundgesetze*, the Axiom that Frege admitted he had never been utterly convinced was a law of logic and that he

We may further introduce a brief notation for the value-range of a function. To this end I replace the sign of the argument in the expression for the function by a Greek vowel, enclose the whole in brackets, and prefix to it the same Greek letter with a smooth breathing. Accordingly, e.g.,

$$\grave{\epsilon}(\epsilon^2 - 4\epsilon)$$

is the value-range of the function $x^2 - 4x$ and

$$\grave{\alpha}(\alpha.(\alpha - 4))$$

is the value-range of the function $x(x - 4)$, so that in

$$`\grave{\epsilon}(\epsilon^2 - 4\epsilon) = \grave{\alpha}(\alpha.(\alpha - 4))`$$

we have the expression for: the first value-range is the same as the second. A different choice of Greek letters is made on purpose, in order to indicate that there is nothing that obliges us to take the same one. |

11                     $`x^2 - 4x = x(x - 4)`,$

understood as above, expresses the same sense, but in a different way.[4] It presents the sense as an equality holding generally; whereas the newly-introduced expression is simply an equation, whose right side, as well its left, has a *Bedeutung* that is complete in itself. In

$$`x^2 - 4x = x(x - 4)`$$

the left side considered in isolation indicates a number only indefinitely, and the same is true of the right side. If we just had '$x^2 - 4x$' we could write instead '$y^2 - 4y$' without altering the sense; for 'y' like 'x' indicates a number only indefinitely. But if we combine the two sides to form an equation, we must choose the same letter for both sides, and we thus express something that is not contained in the left side by itself, nor in the right side, nor in the 'equals' sign; viz. generality. Admittedly, what we express is the generality of an equality; but primarily it is a generality.

Just as we indicate a number indefinitely by a letter, in order to express generality, we also need letters to indicate a function indefinitely. To this end people ordinarily use the letters f and F, thus: '$f(x)$', '$F(x)$', where 'x' replaces the argument. Here the need of a function for sup-

---

himself held responsible for the contradiction that Russell discovered in his system. See pp. 195, 253–4, 279ff. below. For discussion of Axiom V, see the Introduction, pp. 7–8, 18–20 above.

[4] This remark has been the subject of much controversy. What Frege is saying here is that the statement that the two functions $x^2 - 4x$ and $x(x - 4)$ have the same value for each argument 'expresses the same sense, but in a different way' as the statement that the value-range of the one function is equal to that of the other. Since what we have here is an instance of what becomes Axiom V of the *Grundgesetze*, the implication is that Axiom V too embodies sameness of *sense* and not just sameness of *Bedeutung*. Cf. fn. 26 on p. 213 below.

12 plementation is expressed by the fact that the letter f or F | carries along with it a pair of brackets; the space between these is meant to receive the sign for the argument. Thus

$$\grave{\varepsilon}f(\varepsilon)$$

indicates the value-range of a function that is left undetermined.

Now how has the *Bedeutung* of the word 'function' been extended by the progress of science? We can distinguish two directions in which this has happened.

In the first place, the field of mathematical operations that serve for constructing functions has been extended. Besides addition, multiplication, exponentiation, and their converses, the various means of transition to the limit have been introduced – to be sure, people have not always been clearly aware that they were thus adopting something essentially new. People have gone further still, and have actually been obliged to resort to ordinary language, because the symbolic language of Analysis failed; e.g. when they were speaking of a function whose value is 1 for rational and 0 for irrational arguments.

Secondly, the field of possible arguments and values for functions has been extended by the admission of complex numbers. In conjunction with this, the sense of the expressions 'sum', 'product', etc., had to be defined more widely.

In both directions I go still further. I begin by adding to the signs +,
13 –, etc., which serve for constructing a functional expression, | also signs such as =, >, <, so that I can speak, e.g., of the function $x^2 = 1$, where x takes the place of the argument as before. The first question that arises here is what the values of this function are for different arguments. Now if we replace x successively by −1, 0, 1, 2, we get:

$$(-1)^2 = 1,$$
$$0^2 = 1,$$
$$1^2 = 1,$$
$$2^2 = 1.$$

Of these equations the first and third are true, the others false. I now say: 'the value of our function is a truth-value', and distinguish between the truth-values of what is true and what is false. I call the first, for short, the True; and the second, the False. Consequently, e.g., what '$2^2 = 4$' stands for [*bedeutet*] is the True just as, say, '2^2' stands for [*bedeutet*] 4. And '$2^2 = 1$' stands for [*bedeutet*] the False. Accordingly,

$$\text{'}2^2 = 4\text{', '}2 > 1\text{', '}2^4 = 4^2\text{',}$$

all stand for the same thing [*bedeuten dasselbe*], viz. the True, so that in

$$(2^2 = 4) = (2 > 1)$$

we have a correct equation.

The objection here suggests itself that '$2^2 = 4$' and '$2 > 1$' nevertheless tell us quite different things, express quite different thoughts; but likewise '$2^4 = 4^2$' and '$4.4 = 4^2$' express different thoughts; and yet we can replace '2^4' by '4.4', since both signs have the same *Bedeutung*. Consequently, '$2^4 = 4^2$' and '$4.4 = 4^2$' likewise have the same *Bedeutung*.

14   We see | from this that from identity [*Gleichheit*] of *Bedeutung* there does not follow identity of the thought [expressed]. If we say 'The Evening Star is a planet with a shorter period of revolution than the Earth', the thought we express is other than in the sentence 'The Morning Star is a planet with a shorter period of revolution than the Earth'; for somebody who does not know that the Morning Star is the Evening Star might regard one as true and the other as false. And yet the *Bedeutung* of both sentences must be the same; for it is just a matter of interchange of the words 'Evening Star' and 'Morning Star', which have the same *Bedeutung*, i.e. are proper names of the same heavenly body. We must distinguish between sense and *Bedeutung*. '2^4' and '4.4' certainly have the same *Bedeutung*, i.e. are proper names of the same number; but they have not the same sense; consequently, '$2^4 = 4^2$' and '$4.4 = 4^2$' have the same *Bedeutung*, but not the same sense (i.e., in this case: they do not contain the same thought).[F]

Thus, just as we write:

$$'2^4 = 4.4'$$

we may also write with equal justification

$$'(2^4 = 4^2) = (4.4 = 4^2)'$$

and

$$'(2^2 = 4) = (2 > 1)'. \mid$$

15   It might further be asked: What, then, is the point of admitting the signs $=, >, <$, into the field of those that help to build up a functional expression? Nowadays, it seems, more and more supporters are being won by the view that arithmetic is a further development of logic; that a more rigorous establishment of arithmetical laws reduces them to purely logical laws and to such laws alone. I too am of this opinion, and I base upon it the requirement that the symbolic language of arithmetic must be expanded into a logical symbolism. I shall now have to indicate how this is done in our present case.

We saw that the value of our function $x^2 = 1$ is always one of the two truth-values. Now if for a definite argument, e.g. -1, the value of the function is the True, we can express this as follows: 'the number -1 has

---

[F] I do not fail to see that this way of putting it may at first seem arbitrary and artificial, and that it would be desirable to establish my view by going further into the matter. Cf. my forthcoming essay 'Über Sinn und Bedeutung' [pp. 151–71 below].

the property that its square is 1'; or, more briefly, '−1 is a square root of 1'; or '−1 falls under the concept: square root of 1'. If the value of the function $x^2 = 1$ for an argument, e.g. for 2, is the False, we can express this as follows: '2 is not a square root of 1' or '2 does not fall under the concept: square root of 1'. We thus see how closely that which is called a concept in logic is connected with what we call a function. Indeed, we may say at once: a concept is a function whose value is always a truth-value. Again, the value of the function

$$(x + 1)^2 = 2(x + 1) \mid$$

16 is always a truth-value. We get the True as its value, e.g., for the argument −1, and this can also be expressed thus: −1 is a number less by 1 than a number whose square is equal to its double. This expresses the fact that −1 falls under a concept. Now the functions

$$x^2 = 1 \quad \text{and} \quad (x + 1)^2 = 2(x + 1)$$

always have the same value for the same argument, viz. the True for the arguments −1 and +1, and the False for all other arguments. According to our previous conventions we shall also say that these functions have the same value-range, and express this in symbols as follows:

$$\grave{\epsilon}(\epsilon^2 = 1) = \grave{\alpha}((\alpha + 1)^2 = 2(\alpha + 1)).$$

In logic this is called identity [*Gleichheit*] of the extension of concepts. Hence we can designate as an extension the value-range of a function whose value for every argument is a truth-value.

We shall not stop at equations [*Gleichungen*] and inequalities [*Ungleichungen*]. The linguistic form of equations is a statement. A statement contains (or at least purports to contain) a thought as its sense; and this thought is in general true or false; i.e. it has in general a truth-value, which must be regarded as the *Bedeutung* of the sentence, just as, say, the number 4 is the *Bedeutung* of the expression '2 + 2' or London the *Bedeutung* of the expression 'the capital of England'. |

17 Statements in general, just like equations or inequalities or expressions in Analysis, can be imagined to be split up into two parts; one complete in itself, and the other in need of supplementation, or unsaturated. Thus, e.g., we split up the sentence

'Caesar conquered Gaul'

into 'Caesar' and 'conquered Gaul'. The second part is unsaturated – it contains an empty place; only when this place is filled up with a proper name, or with an expression that replaces a proper name, does a complete sense appear. Here too I give the name 'function' to the *Bedeutung* of this unsaturated part. In this case the argument is Caesar.

We see that here we have undertaken to extend [the application of the term] in the other direction, viz. as regards what can occur as an argument. Not merely numbers, but objects in general, are now admissible; and here persons must assuredly be counted as objects. The two truth-values have already been introduced as possible values of a function; we must go further and admit objects without restriction as values of functions. To get an example of this, let us start, e.g., with the expression

'the capital of the German Empire'.

This obviously takes the place of a proper name, and stands for [*bedeutet*] an object. If we now split it up into the parts |

18   'the capital of'

and 'the German Empire', where I count the [German] genitive form as going with the first part, then this part is unsaturated, whereas the other is complete in itself. So in accordance with what I said before, I call

'the capital of x'

the expression of a function. If we take the German Empire as the argument, we get Berlin as the value of the function.

When we have thus admitted objects without restriction as arguments and values of functions, the question arises what it is that we are here calling an object. I regard a regular definition as impossible, since we have here something too simple to admit of logical analysis. It is only possible to indicate what is meant [*gemeint*]. Here I can only say briefly: an object is anything that is not a function, so that an expression for it does not contain any empty place.

A statement contains no empty place, and therefore we must take its *Bedeutung* as an object. But this *Bedeutung* is a truth-value. Thus the two truth-values are objects.

Earlier on we presented equations between value-ranges, e.g.:

$$`\grave\epsilon(\epsilon^2 - 4\epsilon) = \grave\alpha(\alpha(\alpha - 4))`.$$

We can split this up into '$\grave\epsilon(\epsilon^2 - 4\epsilon)$' and '$(\ ) = \grave\alpha(\alpha(\alpha - 4))$'.

This latter part needs supplementation, since on the left of the 'equals'
19 sign it contains an empty | place. The first part, '$\grave\epsilon(\epsilon^2 - 4\epsilon)$', is fully complete in itself and thus stands for [*bedeutet*] an object. Value-ranges of functions are objects, whereas functions themselves are not. We gave the name 'value-range' also to $\grave\epsilon(\epsilon^2 = 1)$, but we could also have termed

it the extension of the concept: square root of 1. Extensions of concepts
likewise are objects, although concepts themselves are not.

After thus extending the field of things that may be taken as arguments, we must get more exact specifications as to the *Bedeutungen*
of the signs already in use. So long as the only objects dealt with in
arithmetic are the integers, the letters *a* and *b* in '*a* + *b*' indicate only
integers; the plus sign need be defined only between integers. Every
widening of the field to which the objects indicated by *a* and *b* belong
obliges us to give a new definition of the plus sign. It seems to be
demanded by scientific rigour that we ensure that an expression never
becomes *bedeutungslos*; we must see to it that we never perform calculations with empty signs in the belief that we are dealing with objects.
People have in the past carried out invalid procedures with divergent
infinite series. It is thus necessary to lay down rules from which it follows, e.g., what

$$\text{'}\odot + 1\text{'}$$

stands for [*bedeutet*], if '$\odot$' stands for [*bedeutet*] the Sun. What rules we
20 lay down is a matter of comparative | indifference; but it is essential
that we should do so – that '*a* + *b*' should always have a *Bedeutung*,
whatever signs for definite objects may be inserted in place of '*a*' and
'*b*'. This involves the requirement as regards concepts, that, for any
argument, they shall have a truth-value as their value; that it shall be
determinate, for any object, whether it falls under the concept or not.
In other words: as regards concepts we have a requirement of sharp
delimitation; if this were not satisfied it would be impossible to set forth
logical laws about them. For any argument x for which '$x + 1$' were
bedeutungslos, the function $x + 1 = 10$ would likewise have no value, and
thus no truth-value either, so that the concept:

'what gives the result 10 when increased by 1'

would have no sharp boundaries. The requirement of the sharp delimitation of concepts thus carries along with it this requirement for functions in general that they must have a value for every argument.

We have so far considered truth-values only as values of functions,
not as arguments. By what I have just said, we must get a value of a
function when we take a truth-value as the argument; but as regards
the signs already in common use, the only point, in most cases, of a
rule to this effect is that there should *be* a rule; it does not much matter what is determined upon. But now we must deal with certain functions that are of importance to us precisely when their argument is a
truth-value. |

21 I introduce the following as such a function:

$$\text{———} x.$$

I lay down the rule that the value of this function shall be the True
if the True is taken as argument, and that contrariwise, in all other cases
the value of this function is the False – i.e. both when the argument is
the False and when it is not a truth-value at all. Accordingly, e.g.

$$\text{———} 1 + 3 = 4$$

is the True, whereas both

$$\text{———} 1 + 3 = 5$$

and also

$$\text{———} 4$$

are the False. Thus this function has as its value the argument itself,
when that is a truth-value. I used to call this horizontal stroke the content stroke – a name that no longer seems to me appropriate.[5] I now
wish to call it simply the horizontal.

If we write down an equation or inequality, e.g. $5 > 4$, we ordinarily
wish at the same time to express a judgement; in our example, we want
to assert that 5 is greater than 4. According to the view I am here presenting, '$5 > 4$' and '$1 + 3 = 5$' just give us expressions for truth-values,
without making any assertion. This separation of the act from the subject matter of judgement seems to be indispensable; for otherwise we
could not express a mere supposition – the putting of a case without a
22 simultaneous | judgement as to its arising or not. We thus need a special
sign in order to be able to assert something. To this end I make use of
a vertical stroke at the left end of the horizontal, so that, e.g., by writing

$$\vdash\text{———} 2 + 3 = 5$$

we assert that $2 + 3$ equals 5. Thus here we are not just writing down
a truth-value, as in

$$2 + 3 = 5,$$

but also at the same time saying that it is the True.[G]

[G] The judgement stroke [*Urteilsstrich*] cannot be used to construct a functional expression;
for it does not serve, in conjunction with other signs, to designate an object. '$\vdash$———
$2 + 3 = 5$' does not designate [*bezeichnet*] anything; it asserts something.

[5] For Frege's earlier account, see *BS*, §2 (pp. 52–3 above). Given the bifurcation of 'content' into 'Sinn' and 'Bedeutung', the term 'content stroke' is indeed now inappropriate.
But even though Frege is concerned here with the level of *Bedeutung* rather than sense,
'*Bedeutung* stroke' would also be inappropriate, since, as Frege has just explained, the
expression that results from inserting a name into the argument-place of the functional
expression '——— x' only stands for [*bedeutet*] the argument itself when that argument
is a truth-value; in all other cases, the *Bedeutung* of the completed expression is the False.

The next simplest function, we may say, is the one whose value is the False for just those arguments for which the value of ——— x is the True, and, conversely, is the True for the arguments for which the value of ——— x is the False. I symbolize it thus:

$$\ \rule[0.35em]{0.6em}{0.4pt}\!\!\top\!\rule[0.35em]{0.6em}{0.4pt}\ x,$$

and here I call the little vertical stroke the negation stroke. I conceive of this as a function with the argument ——— x:

$$(\ \top\!\!-\ x) = (\ \top\!\!-\ (\ \text{---}\ x)),$$

where I imagine the two horizontal strokes to be fused together. But we also have:

$$(\ \text{---}\ (\ \top\!\!-\ x)) = (\ \top\!\!-\ x),\ |$$

23   since the value of $\ \top\!\!-\ x$ is always a truth-value. I thus regard the parts of the stroke in '$\top\!\!-\ x$' to the right and to the left of the negation stroke as horizontals, in the sense of the word that I defined previously. Accordingly, e.g.:

$$\ \top\!\!-\ 2^2 = 5$$

stands for [*bedeutet*] the True, and we may add the judgement stroke:

$$\vdash\!\!\top\!\!-\ 2^2 = 5;$$

and in this we assert that $2^2 = 5$ is not the True, or that 2^2 is not 5. But moreover

$$\ \top\!\!-\ 2$$

is the True, since ——— 2 is the False:

$$\vdash\!\!\top\!\!-\ 2;$$

i.e. 2 is not the True.

My way of presenting generality can best be seen in an example. Suppose what we have to express is that every object is equal to itself. In

$$x = x$$

we have a function, whose argument is indicated by 'x'. We now have to say that the value of this function is always the True, whatever we take as argument. By the sign

$$\ \text{---}\!\cup\!\!\!\!\!\underset{\mathfrak{a}}{\ }\!\!\!\!\!\text{---}\ f(\mathfrak{a})$$

I now understand the True when the function $f(x)$ always has the True as its value, whatever the argument may be; in all other cases $|$

24   $$\ \text{---}\!\cup\!\!\!\!\!\underset{\mathfrak{a}}{\ }\!\!\!\!\!\text{---}\ f(\mathfrak{a})$$

is to stand for [*bedeuten*] the False. For our function $x = x$ we get the first case. Thus

$$\underline{\qquad\curvearrowright\!\alpha\!\curvearrowleft\qquad} f(\alpha)$$

is the True; and we write this as follows:

$$\vdash\!\!\underline{\qquad\curvearrowright\!\alpha\!\curvearrowleft\qquad} \alpha = \alpha.$$

The horizontal stroke to the right and to the left of the concavity are to be regarded as horizontals in our sense. Instead of 'α', any other Gothic letter could be chosen; except those which are to serve as letters for a function, like $\mathfrak{f}$ and $\mathfrak{F}$.

This notation affords the possibility of negating generality, as in

$$\underline{\qquad\top\!\curvearrowright\!\alpha\!\curvearrowleft\qquad} \alpha^2 = 1.$$

That is to say,

$$\underline{\qquad\curvearrowright\!\alpha\!\curvearrowleft\qquad} \alpha^2 = 1$$

is the False, since not every argument makes the value of the function $x^2 = 1$ to be the True. (Thus, e.g., we get $2^2 = 1$ for the argument 2, and this is the False.) Now if

$$\underline{\qquad\curvearrowright\!\alpha\!\curvearrowleft\qquad} \alpha^2 = 1$$

is the False, then

$$\underline{\qquad\top\!\curvearrowright\!\alpha\!\curvearrowleft\qquad} \alpha^2 = 1$$

is the True, according to the rule that we laid down previously for the negation stroke. Thus we have

$$\vdash\!\!\underline{\qquad\top\!\curvearrowright\!\alpha\!\curvearrowleft\qquad} \alpha^2 = 1;$$

i.e. 'not every object is a square root of 1', or 'there are objects that are not square roots of 1'.

25   Can we also express: there are square | roots of 1? Certainly: we need only take, instead of the function $x^2 = 1$, the function

$$\underline{\qquad\top\qquad} x^2 = 1.$$

By fusing together the horizontals in

$$\underline{\qquad\curvearrowright\!\alpha\!\curvearrowleft\qquad}\quad\underline{\qquad\top\qquad} \alpha^2 = 1$$

we get

$$\underline{\qquad\curvearrowright\!\alpha\!\curvearrowleft\!\top\qquad} \alpha^2 = 1.$$

This refers to [*bedeutet*] the False, since not every argument makes the value of the function

$$\underline{\qquad\top\qquad} x^2 = 1$$

to be the True. E.g.:

$$\vdash 1^2 = 1$$

is the False, for $1^2 = 1$ is the True. Now since

$$— \mathfrak{a} \frown \mathfrak{a}^2 = 1$$

is thus the False,

$$\top \mathfrak{a} \frown \mathfrak{a}^2 = 1$$

is the True:

$$\vdash \mathfrak{a} \frown \mathfrak{a}^2 = 1;$$

i.e. 'not every argument makes the value of the function

$$\top x^2 = 1$$

to be the True', or: 'not every argument makes the value of the function $x^2 = 1$ to be the False', or: 'there is at least one square root of 1'.

At this point there may follow a few examples in symbols and words.

$$\vdash \mathfrak{a} \frown \mathfrak{a} \geqq 0,$$

there is at least one positive number; |

26

$$\vdash \mathfrak{a} \frown \mathfrak{a} < 0,$$

there is at least one negative number;

$$\vdash \mathfrak{a} \frown \mathfrak{a}^3 - 3\mathfrak{a}^2 + 2\mathfrak{a} = 0,$$

there is at least one root of the equation

$$x^3 - 3x^2 + 2x = 0.$$

From this we may see how to express existential sentences, which are so important. If we use the functional letter f as an indefinite indication of a concept, then

$$\top \mathfrak{a} \frown f(\mathfrak{a})$$

gives us the form that includes the last examples (if we abstract from the judgement stroke). The expressions

$$\top \mathfrak{a} \frown \mathfrak{a}^2 = 1, \qquad \top \mathfrak{a} \frown \mathfrak{a} \geqq 0,$$

$$\top \mathfrak{a} \frown \mathfrak{a} < 0, \qquad \top \mathfrak{a} \frown \mathfrak{a}^3 - 3\mathfrak{a}^2 + 2\mathfrak{a} = 0,$$

arise from this form in a manner analogous to that in which x^2 gives rise to '1^2', '2^2', '3^2'. Now just as in x^2 we have a function whose argument is indicated by 'x', I also conceive of

$$\top \mathfrak{a} \frown f(\mathfrak{a})$$

as the expression of a function whose argument is indicated by '*f*'. Such a function is obviously a fundamentally different one from those we have dealt with so far; for only a function can occur as its argument. Now just as functions are fundamentally different from objects, so also functions whose arguments are and must be functions are fundamentally different

27   from functions whose arguments are objects and cannot be | anything else. I call the latter first-level, the former second-level, functions. In the same way, I distinguish between first-level and second-level concepts.[H] Second-level functions have actually long been used in Analysis; e.g. definite integrals (if we regard the function to be integrated as the argument).

I will now add something about functions with two arguments. We get the expression for a function by splitting up the complex sign for an object into a saturated and an unsaturated part. Thus, we split up this sign for the True,

$$\text{`3} > \text{2'},$$

into '3' and '*x* > 2'. We can further split up the 'unsaturated' part '*x* > 2' in the same way, into '2' and

$$\text{`}x > y\text{'},$$

where '*y*' enables us to recognize the empty place previously filled up by '2'. In

$$x > y$$

we have a function with two arguments, one indicated by '*x*' and the other by '*y*'; and in

$$3 > 2$$

28   we have the value of this function for the | arguments 3 and 2. We have here a function whose value is always a truth-value. We called such functions of one argument concepts; we call such functions of two arguments relations. Thus we have relations also, e.g., in

$$x^2 + y^2 = 9$$

and in

$$x^2 + y^2 > 9,$$

whereas the function

$$x^2 + y^2$$

has numbers as values. We shall therefore not call this a relation.

[H] Cf. my *Grundlagen der Arithmetik*. I there used the term 'second-order' instead of 'second-level'. The ontological proof of God's existence suffers from the fallacy of treating existence as a first-level concept. [See *GL*, §53 (pp. 102–3 above).]

At this point I may introduce a function not peculiar to arithmetic. The value of the function

is to be the False if we take the True as the *y*-argument and at the same time take some object that is not the True as the *x*-argument; in all other cases the value of this function is to be the True. The lower horizontal stroke, and the two parts that the upper one is split into by the vertical, are to be regarded as horizontals [in our sense]. Consequently, we can always regard as the arguments of our function —— *x* and —— *y*, i.e. truth-values.

Among functions of one argument we distinguished first-level and second-level ones. Here, a greater multiplicity is possible. A function of
29 two arguments may be | of the same level in relation to them, or of different levels; there are equal-levelled and unequal-levelled functions. Those we have dealt with up to now were equal-levelled. An example of an unequal-levelled function is the differential quotient, if we take the arguments to be the function that is to be differentiated and the argument for which it is differentiated; or the definite integral, so long as we take as arguments the function to be integrated and the upper limit. Equal-levelled functions can again be divided into first-level and second-level ones. An example of a second-level one is

$$F(f(1)),$$

where '*F*' and '*f*' indicate the arguments.

In regard to second-level functions with one argument, we must make a distinction, according as the role of this argument can be played by a function of one or of two arguments; for a function of one argument is essentially so different from one with two arguments that the one function cannot occur as an argument in the same place as the other. Some second-level functions of one argument require that this should be a function with one argument; others, that it should be a function with two arguments; and these two classes are sharply divided.

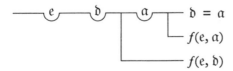

30 is an example of a second-level function with | one argument, which requires that this should be a function of two arguments. The letter *f* here indicates the argument, and the two places, separated by a comma,

within the brackets that follow '*f*' bring it to our notice that *f* represents a function with two arguments.[6]

For functions of two arguments there arises a still greater multiplicity.

If we look back from here over the development of arithmetic, we discern an advance from level to level. At first people did calculations with individual numbers, 1, 3, etc.

$$2 + 3 = 5, \quad 2.3 = 6$$

are theorems of this sort. Then they went on to more general laws that hold good for all numbers. What corresponds to this in symbolism is the transition to algebra. A theorem of this sort is

$$(a + b).c = a.c + b.c.$$

At this stage they had got to the point of dealing with individual functions; but were not yet using the word, in its mathematical sense, and had not yet grasped its *Bedeutung*. The next higher level was the recognition of general laws about functions, accompanied by the coinage of the technical term 'function'. What corresponds to this in symbolism is the introduction of letters like *f*, *F*, to indicate functions indefinitely. A theorem of this sort is

$$\frac{df(x).F(x)}{dx} = F(x).\frac{df(x)}{dx} + f(x).\frac{dF(x)}{dx}.$$

31 Now at this point people had | particular second-level functions, but lacked the conception of what we have called second-level functions. By forming that, we make the next step forward. One might think that this would go on. But probably this last step is already not so rich in consequences as the earlier ones; for instead of second-level functions one can deal, in further advances, with first-level functions – as shall be shown elsewhere.[7] But this does not banish from the world the difference between first-level and second-level functions; for it is not made arbitrarily, but founded deep in the nature of things.

Again, instead of functions of two arguments we can deal with functions of a single but complex argument; but the distinction between functions of one and of two arguments still holds in all its sharpness.

---

[6] The second-level function defined here is that of a *many-one* relation. Cf. *BS*, §31, formula 115 (see p. 77 above); *GG*, I, §23.
[7] Cf. *GG*, I, §§25, 34–7.

Letter to Husserl, 24.5.1891[1]

[Edmund Husserl (1859–1938) first wrote to Frege in 1891, enclosing a copy of his *Philosophie der Arithmetik*, which Frege was later to review, and two other pieces.[2] In his reply, after briefly commenting on one of these pieces, Frege distinguishes his own view of the relationship between concept words and objects from that of Husserl, encapsulating his position very clearly in a diagram.]

Jena
24 May 1891

Dear Doctor,

. . .

96

I thank you especially for your *Philosophy of Arithmetic*, in which you take notice of my own similar endeavours, perhaps more thoroughly than has been done up to now. I hope to find some time soon to reply to your objections.[3] All I should like to say about it now is that there seems to be a difference of opinion between us on how a concept word (common name) is related to objects. The following schema should make my view clear:[4]

proposition	proper name	concept word	
↓	↓	↓	
sense of the proposition (thought)	sense of the proper name	sense of the concept word	
↓	↓	↓	
Bedeutung of the proposition (truth-value)	*Bedeutung* of the proper name (object)	(*Bedeutung* of the concept word (concept)) →	object falling under the concept

---

[1] Translated by Hans Kaal (*PMC*, pp. 63–4; from *WB*, pp. 96–8; page numbers from the latter in the margin).

[2] For details of the Frege/Husserl correspondence, see *PMC*, pp. 60–1/*WB*, pp. 91–3.

[3] Frege's review of Husserl's book finally appeared in 1894; see p. 224 below.

[4] On p. 97 of *WB* there is a facsimile of the page of Frege's letter that includes this schema.

With a concept word it takes one more step to reach the object than with a proper name, and the last step may be missing – i.e., the concept may be empty – without the concept word's ceasing to be scientifically useful. I have drawn the last step from concept to object horizontally in order to indicate that it takes place on the same level, that objects and concepts have the same objectivity (see my *Foundations*, §47).[5] In literary use it is sufficient if everything has a sense; in scientific use there must also be *Bedeutungen*. In the *Foundations* I did not yet draw the distinction between sense and *Bedeutung*. In §97 I should now prefer to speak of 'having a *Bedeutung*' ['*bedeutungsvoll*'] instead of 'having a sense' ['*sinnvoll*']. Elsewhere, too, e.g. in §§100, 101, 102, I would now often replace 'sense' by '*Bedeutung*'.[6] What I used to call judgeable content is now divided into thought and truth-value.[7] Judgement in the narrower sense could be characterized as a transition from a thought to a truth-value. |

98   Now it seems to me that for you the schema would look like this:

concept word

↓

sense of the concept word

(sense)

↓

object falling under the concept

so that for you it would take the same number of steps to get from proper names to objects as from concept words. The only difference between proper names and concept words would then be that the former could refer to[8] only one object and the latter to more than one. A concept word whose concept was empty would then have to be excluded from science just like a proper name without a corresponding object.

. . .

Yours sincerely,

Dr G. Frege

---

[5] See pp. 99–100 above.

[6] It is worth noting that in these sections Frege is criticizing formalism (cf. pp. 124–5 above), where it might seem especially important to draw some kind of distinction between 'Sinn' and 'Bedeutung'.

[7] See *BS*, §2 (pp. 52–3 above), for the early notion of 'judgeable content'; and cf. *CO*, p. 186 below, on the later bifurcation of this notion.

[8] The German construction here is 'sich beziehen auf'.

On Sinn *and* Bedeutung[1]

[This paper was first published in 1892 in the *Zeitschrift für Philosophie und philosophische Kritik*, 100, pp. 25–50. It is Frege's most influential and best known work, containing his fullest account of his distinction between *Sinn* and *Bedeutung*.]

25 Equality[A] gives rise to challenging questions which are not altogether easy to answer. Is it a relation? A relation between objects, or between names or signs of objects? In my *Begriffsschrift* I assumed the latter.[2] The reasons which seem to favour this are the following: $a = a$ and $a = b$ are obviously statements of differing cognitive value [*Erkenntniswert*]; $a = a$ holds *a priori* and, according to Kant, is to be labelled analytic, while statements of the form $a = b$ often contain very valuable extensions of our knowledge and cannot always be established *a priori*. The discovery that the rising sun is not new every morning, but always the same, was one of the most fertile astronomical discoveries. Even today 26 the reidentification of a small planet or a comet is not always a | matter of course. Now if we were to regard equality as a relation between that which the names '*a*' and '*b*' designate [*bedeuten*], it would seem that $a = b$ could not differ from $a = a$, i.e. provided $a = b$ is true. A relation would thereby be expressed of a thing to itself, and indeed one in which each thing stands to itself but to no other thing. What we apparently want to state by $a = b$ is that the signs or names '*a*' and '*b*' designate [*bedeuten*] the same thing, so that those signs themselves would be under discussion; a relation between them would be asserted. But this

---

A I use this word in the sense of identity [*Identität*] and understand '$a = b$' to have the sense of '*a* is the same as *b*' or '*a* and *b* coincide'.

[1] Translated by Max Black (*TPW*, pp. 56–78/*CP*, pp. 157–77). Page numbers in the margin are from the original journal. The translated text here is from the third edition of *TPW*, with minor revisions made in accordance with the policy adopted in the present volume – in particular, 'Bedeutung' (and cognates such as 'bedeutungslos') being left untranslated, and 'bedeuten' being rendered as 'stand for' (or occasionally as 'designate') as in the second edition (but with the German always in square brackets following it), unless otherwise indicated. For discussion of this policy, and the problems involved in translating 'Bedeutung' and its cognates, see the Introduction, §4 above.

[2] See esp. *BS*, §8 (pp. 64–5 above).

relation would hold between the names or signs only in so far as they named or designated something. It would be mediated by the connection of each of the two signs with the same designated thing. But this is arbitrary. Nobody can be forbidden to use any arbitrarily producible event or object as a sign for something. In that case the sentence $a = b$ would no longer be concerned with the subject matter, but only with its mode of designation; we would express no proper knowledge by its means. But in many cases this is just what we want to do. If the sign 'a' is distinguished from the sign 'b' only as an object (here, by means of its shape), not as a sign (i.e. not by the manner in which it designates something), the cognitive value of $a = a$ becomes essentially equal to that of $a = b$, provided $a = b$ is true. A difference can arise only if the difference between the signs corresponds to a difference in the mode of presentation [*Art des Gegebenseins*] of the thing designated. Let a, b, c be the lines connecting the vertices of a triangle with the midpoints of the opposite sides. The point of intersection of a and b is then the same as the point of intersection of b and c. So we have different designations for the same point, and these names ('point of intersection of a and b', 'point of intersection of b and c') likewise indicate the mode of presentation; and hence the statement contains actual knowledge.[3]

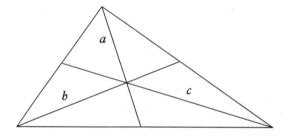

It is natural, now, to think of there being connected with a sign (name, combination of words, written mark), besides that which the sign designates, which may be called the *Bedeutung* of the sign, also what I should like to call the *sense* of the sign, wherein the mode of presentation is contained. In our example, accordingly, the | *Bedeutung* of the expressions 'the point of intersection of a and b' and 'the point of intersection of b and c' would be the same, but not their sense. The *Bedeutung* of 'Evening Star' would be the same as that of 'Morning Star', but not the sense.

[3] A diagram is added here to illustrate Frege's example. Compare this (rather simpler example) with the geometrical example Frege gave in *BS* in motivating his earlier distinction between 'content' and 'mode of determination of content' (see pp. 64–5 above). On the relationship between Frege's earlier and later views, see the Introduction, pp. 21–2 above.

It is clear from the context that by sign and name I have here understood any designation figuring as a proper name, which thus has as its *Bedeutung* a definite object (this word taken in the widest range), but not a concept or a relation, which shall be discussed further in another article.[4] The designation of a single object can also consist of several words or other signs. For brevity, let every such designation be called a proper name.

The sense of a proper name is grasped by everybody who is sufficiently familiar with the language or totality of designations to which it belongs;[B] but this serves to illuminate only a single aspect of the *Bedeutung*, supposing it to have one. Comprehensive knowledge of the *Bedeutung* would require us to be able to say immediately whether any given sense attaches to it. To such knowledge we never attain.

The regular connection between a sign, its sense and its *Bedeutung* is of such a kind that to the sign there corresponds a definite sense and to that in turn a definite *Bedeutung*, while to a given *Bedeutung* (an object) there does not belong only a single sign. The same sense has different expressions in different languages or even in the same language. To be sure, exceptions to this regular behaviour occur. To every expression belonging to a complete totality of signs, there should certainly correspond a definite sense; but natural languages | often do not satisfy this condition, and one must be content if the same word has the same sense in the same context. It may perhaps be granted that every grammatically well-formed expression figuring as a proper name always has a sense. But this is not to say that to the sense there also corresponds a *Bedeutung*. The words 'the celestial body most distant from the Earth' have a sense, but it is very doubtful if they also have a *Bedeutung*. The expression 'the least rapidly convergent series' has a sense, but demonstrably there is no *Bedeutung*, since for every given convergent series, another convergent, but less rapidly convergent, series can be found. In grasping a sense, one is not thereby assured of a *Bedeutung*.

If words are used in the ordinary way, what one intends to speak of is their *Bedeutung*. It can also happen, however, that one wishes to talk about the words themselves or their sense. This happens, for instance, when the words of another are quoted. One's own words then first

[B] In the case of an actual proper name such as 'Aristotle' opinions as to the sense may differ. It might, for instance, be taken to be the following: the pupil of Plato and teacher of Alexander the Great. Anybody who does this will attach another sense to the sentence 'Aristotle was born in Stagira' than will someone who takes as the sense of the name: the teacher of Alexander the Great who was born in Stagira. So long as the *Bedeutung* remains the same, such variations of sense may be tolerated, although they are to be avoided in the theoretical structure of a demonstrative science and ought not to occur in a perfect language.

[4] See 'On Concept and Object', pp. 181–93 below.

designate [*bedeuten*] words of the other speaker, and only the latter have their usual *Bedeutung*. We then have signs of signs. In writing, the words are in this case enclosed in quotation marks. Accordingly, a word standing between quotation marks must not be taken as having its ordinary *Bedeutung*.

In order to speak of the sense of an expression '*A*' one may simply use the phrase 'the sense of the expression "*A*"'. In indirect speech one talks about the sense, e.g., of another person's remarks. It is quite clear that in this way of speaking words do not have their customary *Bedeutung* but designate [*bedeuten*] what is usually their sense. In order to have a short expression, we will say: in indirect speech, words are used *indirectly* or have their *indirect Bedeutung*. We distinguish accordingly the *customary* from the *indirect Bedeutung* of a word; and its *customary* sense from its *indirect* sense. The indirect *Bedeutung* of a word is accordingly its customary sense. Such exceptions must always be borne in mind if the mode of connection between sign, sense and *Bedeutung* in particular cases is to be correctly understood. |

29   The *Bedeutung* and sense of a sign are to be distinguished from the associated idea [*Vorstellung*]. If the *Bedeutung* of a sign is an object perceivable by the senses, my idea of it is an internal image, arising from memories of sense impressions which I have had and acts, both internal and external, which I have performed.[C] Such an idea is often imbued with feeling; the clarity of its separate parts varies and oscillates. The same sense is not always connected, even in the same man, with the same idea. The idea is subjective: one man's idea is not that of another. There result, as a matter of course, a variety of differences in the ideas associated with the same sense. A painter, a horseman, and a zoologist will probably connect different ideas with the name 'Bucephalus'. This constitutes an essential distinction between the idea and the sign's sense, which may be the common property of many people, and so is not a part or a mode of the individual mind. For one can hardly deny that mankind has a common store of thoughts which is transmitted from one generation to another.[D]

In the light of this, one need have no scruples in speaking simply of *the* sense, whereas in the case of an idea one must, strictly speaking, add whom it belongs to and at what time. It might perhaps be said: just as one man connects this idea, and another that idea, with the same

---

[C] We may include with ideas intuitions [*Anschauungen*]: here, sense impressions and acts themselves take the place of the traces which they have left in the mind. The distinction is unimportant for our purpose, especially since memories of sense impressions and acts always go along with such impressions and acts themselves to complete the perceptual image [*Anschauungsbild*]. One may on the other hand understand intuition as including any object in so far as it is sensibly perceptible or spatial.

[D] Hence it is inadvisable to use the word 'idea' to designate something so basically different.

word, so also one man can associate this sense and another that sense. But there still remains a difference in the mode of connection. They are not prevented from grasping the same sense; | but they cannot have the same idea. *Si duo idem faciunt, non est idem.* If two persons picture the same thing, each still has his own idea. It is indeed sometimes possible to establish differences in the ideas, or even in the sensations, of different men; but an exact comparison is not possible, because we cannot have both ideas together in the same consciousness.

The *Bedeutung* of a proper name is the object itself which we designate by using it; the idea which we have in that case is wholly subjective; in between lies the sense, which is indeed no longer subjective like the idea, but is yet not the object itself. The following analogy will perhaps clarify these relationships. Somebody observes the Moon through a telescope. I compare the Moon itself to the *Bedeutung*; it is the object of the observation, mediated by the real image projected by the object glass in the interior of the telescope, and by the retinal image of the observer. The former I compare to the sense, the latter is like the idea or intuition [*Anschauung*]. The optical image in the telescope is indeed one-sided and dependent upon the standpoint of observation; but it is still objective, inasmuch as it can be used by several observers. At any rate it could be arranged for several to use it simultaneously. But each one would have his own retinal image. On account of the diverse shapes of the observers' eyes, even a geometrical congruence could hardly be achieved, and an actual coincidence would be out of the question. This analogy might be developed still further, by assuming A's retinal image made visible to B; or A might also see his own retinal image in a mirror. In this way we might perhaps show how an idea can itself be taken as an object, but as such is not for the observer what it directly is for the person having the idea. But to pursue this would take us too far afield.

We can now recognize three levels of difference between words, expressions, or whole sentences. The difference may concern at most the ideas, or the sense but not the *Bedeutung*, or, finally, the *Bedeutung* as well. With respect to | the first level, it is to be noted that, on account of the uncertain connection of ideas with words, a difference may hold for one person, which another does not find. The difference between a translation and the original text should properly not overstep the first level. To the possible differences here belong also the colouring and shading which poetic eloquence seeks to give to the sense. Such colouring and shading are not objective, and must be evoked by each hearer or reader according to the hints of the poet or the speaker. Without some affinity in human ideas art would certainly be impossible; but it can never be exactly determined how far the intentions of the poet are realized.

In what follows there will be no further discussion of ideas and intuitions; they have been mentioned here only to ensure that the idea aroused in the hearer by a word shall not be confused with its sense or its *Bedeutung.*

To make short and exact expressions possible, let the following phraseology be established:

A proper name (word, sign, combination of signs, expression) *expresses* its sense, *stands for* [*bedeutet*] or *designates* [*bezeichnet*] its *Bedeutung.* By employing a sign we express its sense and designate its *Bedeutung.*

Idealists or sceptics will perhaps long since have objected: 'You talk, without further ado, of the Moon as an object; but how do you know that the name "the Moon" has any *Bedeutung?* How do you know that anything whatsoever has a *Bedeutung?*' I reply that when we say 'the Moon', we do not intend to speak of our idea of the Moon, nor are we satisfied with the sense alone, but we presuppose a *Bedeutung.* To assume that in the sentence 'The Moon is smaller than the Earth' the idea of the Moon is in question, would be flatly to misunderstand the sense. If this is what the speaker wanted, he would use the phrase 'my idea of the Moon'. Now we can of course be mistaken in the presupposition, and such mistakes have indeed occurred. But the question whether the presupposition is perhaps always mistaken need | not be answered here; in order to justify speaking of the *Bedeutung* of a sign, it is enough, at first, to point out our intention in speaking or thinking. (We must then add the reservation: provided such a *Bedeutung* exists.)

So far we have considered the sense and *Bedeutung* only of such expressions, words, or signs as we have called proper names. We now inquire concerning the sense and *Bedeutung* of an entire assertoric sentence. Such a sentence contains a thought.[E] Is this thought, now, to be regarded as its sense or its *Bedeutung?* Let us assume for the time being that the sentence has a *Bedeutung.* If we now replace one word of the sentence by another having the same *Bedeutung,* but a different sense, this can have no effect upon the *Bedeutung* of the sentence. Yet we can see that in such a case the thought changes; since, e.g., the thought in the sentence 'The Morning Star is a body illuminated by the Sun' differs from that in the sentence 'The Evening Star is a body illuminated by the Sun'. Anybody who did not know that the Evening Star is the Morning Star might hold the one thought to be true, the other false. The thought, accordingly, cannot be the *Bedeutung* of the sentence, but must rather be considered as its sense. What is the position now with regard to the *Bedeutung?* Have we a right even to inquire about it? Is it possible that a sentence as a whole has only a sense, but no *Bedeutung?*

[E] By a thought I understand not the subjective performance of thinking but its objective content, which is capable of being the common property of several thinkers.

At any rate, one might expect that such sentences occur, just as there are parts of sentences having sense but no *Bedeutung*. And sentences which contain proper names without *Bedeutung* will be of this kind. The sentence 'Odysseus was set ashore at Ithaca while sound asleep' obviously has a sense. But since it is doubtful whether the name 'Odysseus', occurring therein, has a *Bedeutung*, it is also doubtful whether the whole sentence does. Yet it is certain, nevertheless, that anyone who seriously took the sentence to be true or false would ascribe to the name 'Odysseus' a *Bedeutung*, not merely a sense; for it is of the *Bedeutung* of the | name that the predicate is affirmed or denied. Whoever does not admit the name has a *Bedeutung* can neither apply nor withhold the predicate. But in that case it would be superfluous to advance to the *Bedeutung* of the name; one could be satisfied with the sense, if one wanted to go no further than the thought. If it were a question only of the sense of the sentence, the thought, it would be needless to bother with the *Bedeutung* of a part of the sentence; only the sense, not the *Bedeutung*, of the part is relevant to the sense of the whole sentence. The thought remains the same whether 'Odysseus' has a *Bedeutung* or not. The fact that we concern ourselves at all about the *Bedeutung* of a part of the sentence indicates that we generally recognize and expect a *Bedeutung* for the sentence itself. The thought loses value for us as soon as we recognize that the *Bedeutung* of one of its parts is missing. We are therefore justified in not being satisfied with the sense of a sentence, and in inquiring also as to its *Bedeutung*. But now why do we want every proper name to have not only a sense, but also a *Bedeutung*? Why is the thought not enough for us? Because, and to the extent that, we are concerned with its truth-value. This is not always the case. In hearing an epic poem, for instance, apart from the euphony of the language we are interested only in the sense of the sentences and the images and feelings thereby aroused. The question of truth would cause us to abandon aesthetic delight for an attitude of scientific investigation. Hence it is a matter of no concern to us whether the name 'Odysseus', for instance, has a *Bedeutung*, so long as we accept the poem as a work of art.[F] It is the striving for truth that drives us always to advance from the sense to the *Bedeutung*.

We have seen that the *Bedeutung* of a sentence may always be sought, whenever the *Bedeutung* of its components is involved; and that this is the case when and only when we are inquiring after the truth-value. |

We are therefore driven into accepting the *truth-value* of a sentence as constituting its *Bedeutung*. By the truth-value of a sentence I understand the circumstance that it is true or false. There are no further

---

[F] It would be desirable to have a special term for signs intended to have only sense. If we name them say, representations [*Bilder*], the words of the actors on the stage would be representations; indeed the actor himself would be a representation.

truth-values. For brevity I call the one the True, the other the False. Every assertoric sentence concerned with the *Bedeutung* of its words is therefore to be regarded as a proper name, and its *Bedeutung*, if it has one, is either the True or the False. These two objects are recognized, if only implicitly, by everybody who judges something to be true – and so even by a sceptic. The designation of the truth-values as objects may appear to be an arbitrary fancy or perhaps a mere play upon words, from which no profound consequences could be drawn. What I am calling an object can be more exactly discussed only in connection with concept and relation. I will reserve this for another article.[5] But so much should already be clear, that in every judgement,[G] no matter how trivial, the step from the level of thoughts to the level of *Bedeutung* (the objective) has already been taken.

One might be tempted to regard the relation of the thought to the True not as that of sense to *Bedeutung*, but rather as that of subject to predicate. One can, indeed, say: 'The thought that 5 is a prime number is true'. But closer examination shows that nothing more has been said than in the simple sentence '5 is a prime number'. The truth claim arises in each case from the form of the assertoric sentence, and when the latter lacks its usual force, e.g., in the mouth of an actor upon the stage, even the sentence 'The thought that 5 is a prime number is true' contains only a thought, and indeed the same thought as the simple '5 is a prime number'. It follows that the relation of the thought to the True 35   may not be compared with that of subject to predicate. | Subject and predicate (understood in the logical sense) are just elements of thought; they stand on the same level for knowledge. By combining subject and predicate, one reaches only a thought, never passes from a sense to its *Bedeutung*, never from a thought to its truth-value. One moves at the same level but never advances from one level to the next. A truth-value cannot be a part of a thought, any more than, say, the Sun can, for it is not a sense but an object.

If our supposition that the *Bedeutung* of a sentence is its truth-value is correct, the latter must remain unchanged when a part of the sentence is replaced by an expression with the same *Bedeutung*. And this is in fact the case. Leibniz gives the definition: '*Eadem sunt, quae sibi mutuo substitui possunt, salva veritate*'.[6] If we are dealing with sentences for which the *Bedeutung* of their component parts is at all relevant, then what feature except the truth-value can be found that belongs to such

---

[G] A judgement for me is not the mere grasping of a thought, but the admission [*Anerkennung*] of its truth.

[5] See 'On Concept and Object', pp. 181–93 below.

[6] 'Those things are the same which can be substituted for one another without loss of truth.' This is just the same Leibnizian principle that Frege took as his definition of identity in §65 of the *Foundations* (the difference in formulation is trivial); see p. 112 above.

sentences quite generally and remains unchanged by substitutions of the kind just mentioned?

If now the truth-value of a sentence is its *Bedeutung*, then on the one hand all true sentences have the same *Bedeutung* and so, on the other hand, do all false sentences. From this we see that in the *Bedeutung* of the sentence all that is specific is obliterated. We can never be concerned only with the *Bedeutung* of a sentence; but again the mere thought alone yields no knowledge, but only the thought together with its *Bedeutung*, i.e. its truth-value. Judgements can be regarded as advances from a thought to a truth-value. Naturally this cannot be a definition. Judgement is something quite peculiar and incomparable. One might also say that judgements are distinctions of parts within truth-values. Such distinction occurs by a return to the thought. To every sense attaching to a truth-value would correspond its own manner of analysis. However, I have here used the word 'part' in a special sense. I have in fact transferred the relation between the parts and the whole of the sentence to its *Bedeutung*, by calling the *Bedeutung* of a word part of the *Bedeutung* of the sentence, if the word itself | is a part of the sentence. This way of speaking can certainly be attacked, because the whole *Bedeutung* and one part of it do not suffice to determine the remainder, and because the word 'part' is already used of bodies in another sense. A special term would need to be invented.

The supposition that the truth-value of a sentence is its *Bedeutung* shall now be put to further test. We have found that the truth-value of a sentence remains unchanged when an expression in it is replaced by another with the same *Bedeutung*:[7] but we have not yet considered the case in which the expression to be replaced is itself a sentence. Now if our view is correct, the truth-value of a sentence containing another as part must remain unchanged when the part is replaced by another sentence having the same truth-value. Exceptions are to be expected when the whole sentence or its part is direct or indirect quotation; for in such cases, as we have seen, the words do not have their customary *Bedeutung*. In direct quotation, a sentence designates [*bedeutet*] another sentence, and in indirect speech a thought.

We are thus led to consider subordinate sentences or clauses. These occur as parts of a sentence complex, which is, from the logical standpoint, likewise a sentence – a main sentence. But here we meet the question whether it is also true of the subordinate sentence that its *Bedeutung* is a truth-value. Of indirect speech we already know the opposite. Grammarians view subordinate clauses as representatives of parts of sentences and divide them accordingly into noun clauses, adjective clauses, adverbial clauses. This might generate the supposition that the *Bedeutung* of

[7] 'wenn wir darin einen Ausdruck durch einen gleichbedeutenden ersetzen'.

36

a subordinate clause was not a truth-value but rather of the same kind as the *Bedeutung* of a noun or adjective or adverb – in short, of a part of a sentence, whose sense was not a thought but only a part of a thought. Only a more thorough investigation can clarify the issue. In so doing, we shall not follow the grammatical categories strictly, but rather group together what is logically of the same kind. Let us first search for cases in which the sense of the subordinate clause, as we have just supposed, is not an independent thought. |

37   The case of an abstract noun clause,[8] introduced by 'that', includes the case of indirect speech, in which we have seen the words to have their indirect *Bedeutung*, coincident with what is customarily their sense. In this case, then, the subordinate clause has for its *Bedeutung* a thought, not a truth-value, and for its sense not a thought, but the sense of the words 'the thought that . . .', which is only a part of the thought in the entire complex sentence. This happens after 'say', 'hear', 'be of the opinion', 'be convinced', 'conclude', and similar words.[H] There is a different, and indeed somewhat complicated, situation after words like 'recognize', 'know', 'fancy',[9] which are to be considered later.

That in the cases of the first kind the *Bedeutung* of the subordinate clause is in fact the thought can also be recognized by seeing that it is indifferent to the truth of the whole whether the subordinate clause is true or false. Let us compare, for instance, the two sentences 'Copernicus believed that the planetary orbits are circles' and 'Copernicus believed that the apparent motion of the Sun is produced by the real motion of the Earth'. One subordinate clause can be substituted for the other without harm to the truth. The main clause and the subordinate clause together have as their sense only a single thought, and the truth of the whole includes neither the truth nor the untruth of the subordinate clause. In such cases it is not permissible to replace one expression in the subordinate clause by another having the same customary *Bedeutung*, but only by one having the same indirect *Bedeutung*, i.e. the same customary sense. Somebody might conclude: the *Bedeutung* of a sentence is not its truth-value, for in that case it could always be replaced by another sentence of the same truth-value. But this proves too much; one might just as well claim that the *Bedeutung* of 'Morning Star' is not

---

[H] In 'A lied that he had seen B', the subordinate clause designates [*bedeutet*] a thought, of which it is being said, firstly, that A asserted it as true, and secondly, that A was convinced of its falsity.

---

[8] Frege probably means clauses grammatically replaceable by an abstract noun-phrase; e.g. 'Smith denies *that dragons exist*' = 'Smith denies *the existence of dragons*'; or again, in this context after 'denies', 'that Brown is wise' is replaceable by 'the wisdom of Brown'. (*Tr.*)

[9] The German words here are 'erkennen', 'wissen' and 'wähnen'. The last means 'to imagine', but with the implication of doing so *wrongly*.

Venus, since one may not always say 'Venus' in place of 'Morning Star'. One has the right to conclude only that the *Bedeutung* of a sentence is
38   not *always* its truth-value, and that 'Morning Star' does not | always stand for [*bedeutet*] the planet Venus, viz. when the word has its indirect *Bedeutung*. An exception of such a kind occurs in the subordinate clause just considered, which has a thought as its *Bedeutung*.

If one says 'It seems that . . .' one means [*meint*] 'It seems to me that . . .' or 'I think that . . .'. We therefore have the same case again. The situation is similar in the case of expressions such as 'to be pleased', 'to regret', 'to approve', 'to blame', 'to hope', 'to fear'. If, toward the end of the battle of Waterloo,[10] Wellington was glad that the Prussians were coming, the basis for his joy was a conviction. Had he been deceived, he would have been no less pleased so long as his illusion lasted; and before he became so convinced he could not have been pleased that the Prussians were coming – even though in fact they might have been already approaching.

Just as a conviction or a belief is the ground of a feeling, it can, as in inference, also be the ground of a conviction. In the sentence 'Columbus inferred from the roundness of the Earth that he could reach India by travelling towards the west', we have as the *Bedeutungen* of the parts two thoughts, that the Earth is round, and that Columbus by travelling to the west could reach India. All that is relevant here is that Columbus was convinced of both, and that the one conviction was a ground for the other. Whether the Earth is really round and Columbus could really reach India by travelling west, as he thought, is immaterial to the truth of our sentence; but it is not immaterial whether we replace 'the Earth' by 'the planet which is accompanied by a moon whose diameter is greater than the fourth part of its own'. Here also we have the indirect *Bedeutung* of the words.

Adverbial final clauses beginning 'in order that' also belong here; for obviously the purpose is a thought; therefore: indirect *Bedeutung* for the words, subjunctive mood.

A subordinate clause with 'that' after 'command', 'ask', 'forbid', would appear in direct speech as an imperative. Such a sentence has no *Bedeutung* but only a sense. A command, a request, are indeed not thoughts, but they stand on the same level as thoughts. Hence in sub-
39   ordinate clauses depending upon 'command', | 'ask', etc., words have their indirect *Bedeutung*. The *Bedeutung* of such a clause is therefore not a truth-value but a command, a request, and so forth.

The case is similar for the dependent question in phrases such as 'doubt whether', 'not to know what'. It is easy to see that here also the words are to be taken to have their indirect *Bedeutung*. Dependent clauses

---

[10] Frege uses the Prussian name for the battle – 'Belle-Alliance'. (*Tr.*)

expressing questions beginning with 'who', 'what', 'where', 'when', 'how', 'by what means', etc., seem at times to approximate very closely to adverbial clauses in which words have their customary *Bedeutung*. These cases are distinguished linguistically [in German] by the mood of the verb. With the subjunctive, we have a dependent question and the words have their indirect *Bedeutung*, so that a proper name cannot in general be replaced by another name of the same object.

In the cases so far considered the words of the subordinate clauses had their indirect *Bedeutung*, and this made it clear that the *Bedeutung* of the subordinate clause itself was indirect, i.e. not a truth-value but a thought, a command, a request, a question. The subordinate clause could be regarded as a noun, indeed one could say: as a proper name of that thought, that command, etc., which it represented in the context of the sentence structure.

We now come to other subordinate clauses, in which the words do have their customary *Bedeutung* without however a thought occurring as sense and a truth-value as *Bedeutung*. How this is possible is best made clear by examples.

'Whoever discovered the elliptic form of the planetary orbits died in misery.'

If the sense of the subordinate clause were here a thought, it would have to be possible to express it also in a separate sentence. But it does not work, because the grammatical subject 'whoever' has no independent sense and only mediates the relation with the consequent clause 'died in misery'. For this reason the sense of the subordinate clause is not a complete thought, and its *Bedeutung* is Kepler, not a truth-value. One might object that the sense of the whole does contain a thought as part, viz. that there was somebody who first discovered the elliptic form of the planetary orbits; for whoever takes the whole to be true | cannot deny this part. This is undoubtedly so; but only because otherwise the dependent clause 'whoever discovered the elliptic form of the planetary orbits' would have no *Bedeutung*. If anything is asserted there is always an obvious presupposition that the simple or compound proper names used have a *Bedeutung*. If therefore one asserts 'Kepler died in misery', there is a presupposition that the name 'Kepler' designates something; but it does not follow that the sense of the sentence 'Kepler died in misery' contains the thought that the name 'Kepler' designates something. If this were the case the negation would have to run not

'Kepler did not die in misery',

but

'Kepler did not die in misery, or the name "Kepler" is *bedeutungslos*'.

That the name 'Kepler' designates something is just as much a presupposition for the assertion

'Kepler died in misery'

as for the contrary assertion. Now languages have the fault of containing expressions which fail to designate an object (although their grammatical form seems to qualify them for that purpose) because the truth of some sentence is a prerequisite. Thus it depends on the truth of the sentence

'There was someone who discovered the elliptic form of the planetary orbits'

whether the subordinate clause

'whoever discovered the elliptic form of the planetary orbits'

really designates an object, or only seems to do so while in fact is *bedeutungslos*. And thus it may appear as if our subordinate clause contained as a part of its sense the thought that there was somebody who discovered the elliptic form of the planetary orbits. If this were right, the negation would run:

'Either whoever discovered the elliptic form of the planetary orbits did not die in misery or there was nobody who discovered the elliptic form of the planetary orbits'. |

41　This arises from an imperfection of language, from which even the symbolic language of mathematical analysis is not altogether free; even there combinations of symbols can occur that seem to stand for [*bedeuten*] something but (at least so far) are *bedeutungslos*, e.g. divergent infinite series. This can be avoided, e.g., by means of the special stipulation that divergent infinite series shall stand for [*bedeuten*] the number 0.[11] A logically perfect language (*Begriffsschrift*) should satisfy the conditions, that every expression grammatically well constructed as a proper name out of signs already introduced shall in fact designate an object, and that no new sign shall be introduced as a proper name without being secured a *Bedeutung*. The logic looks contain warnings against logical mistakes arising from the ambiguity of expressions. I regard as no less pertinent a warning against apparent proper names that have no *Bedeutung*. The

---

[11] Cf. *GG*, I, §11; see Appendix 2 below.

history of mathematics supplies errors which have arisen in this way. This lends itself to demagogic abuse as easily as ambiguity – perhaps more easily. 'The will of the people' can serve as an example; for it is easy to establish that there is at any rate no generally accepted *Bedeutung* for this expression. It is therefore by no means unimportant to eliminate the source of these mistakes, at least in science, once and for all. Then such objections as the one discussed above would become impossible, because it could never depend upon the truth of a thought whether a proper name had a *Bedeutung*.

With the consideration of these noun clauses may be coupled that of types of adjective and adverbial clauses which are logically in close relation to them.

Adjective clauses also serve to construct compound proper names, though, unlike noun clauses, they are not sufficient by themselves for this purpose. These adjective clauses are to be regarded as equivalent to adjectives. Instead of 'the square root of 4 which is smaller than 0', one can also say 'the negative square root of 4'. We have here the case of a compound proper name constructed from the expression for a concept with the help of the singular definite article. This is at any rate permis-
42   sible if the concept applies to one | and only one single object.[1] Expressions for concepts can be so constructed that marks[12] of a concept are given by adjective clauses as, in our example, by the clause 'which is smaller than 0'. It is evident that such an adjective clause cannot have a thought as sense or a truth-value as *Bedeutung*, any more than the noun clause could. Its sense, which can also in many cases be expressed by a single adjective, is only a part of a thought. Here, as in the case of the noun clause, there is no independent subject and therefore no possibility of reproducing the sense of the subordinate clause in an independent sentence.

Places, instants, stretches of time, logically considered, are objects; hence the linguistic designation of a definite place, a definite instant, or a stretch of time is to be regarded as a proper name. Now adverbial clauses of place and time can be used to construct such a proper name in much the same way as we have seen noun and adjective clauses can. In the same way, expressions for concepts that apply to places, etc., can be constructed. It is to be noted here also that the sense of these subordinate clauses cannot be reproduced in an independent sentence, since

---

[1] In accordance with what was said above, an expression of the kind in question must actually always be assured of a *Bedeutung*, by means of a special stipulation, e.g. by the convention that 0 shall count as its *Bedeutung* when the concept applies to no object or to more than one. [See fn. 11 above.]

[12] For the notion of a 'mark' ('Merkmal'), see *GL*, §53 (pp. 102–3 above); *CO*, pp. 189–90 below.

an essential component, viz. the determination of place or time, is missing and is just indicated by a relative pronoun or a conjunction.[J]

43   In conditional clauses, also, there most often | recognizably occurs an indefinite indicator, with a correlative indicator in the dependent clause. (We have already seen this occur in noun, adjective, and adverbial clauses.) In so far as each indicator relates to the other, both clauses together form a connected whole, which as a rule expresses only a single thought. In the sentence

> 'If a number is less than 1 and greater than 0, its square is less than 1 and greater than 0'

the component in question is 'a number' in the antecedent clause and 'its' in the consequent clause. It is by means of this very indefiniteness that the sense acquires the generality expected of a law. It is this which is responsible for the fact that the antecedent clause alone has no complete thought as its sense and in combination with the consequent clause expresses one and only one thought, whose parts are no longer thoughts. It is, in general, incorrect to say that in the hypothetical judgement two judgements are put in reciprocal relationship. If this or something similar is said, the word 'judgement' is used in the same sense as I have connected with the word 'thought', so that I would use the formulation: 'A hypothetical thought establishes a reciprocal relationship between two thoughts'. This could be true only if an indefinite indicator is absent;[K] but in such a case there would also be no generality.

If an instant of time is to be indefinitely indicated in both the antecedent and the consequent clause, this is often achieved merely by using

---

[J] In the case of these sentences, various interpretations are easily possible. The sense of the sentence 'After Schleswig-Holstein was separated from Denmark, Prussia and Austria quarrelled' can also be rendered in the form 'After the separation of Schleswig-Holstein from Denmark, Prussia and Austria quarrelled'. In this version, it is surely sufficiently clear that the sense is not to be taken as having as a part the thought that Schleswig-Holstein was once separated from Denmark, but that this is the necessary presupposition in order for the expression 'after the separation of Schleswig-Holstein from Denmark' to have a *Bedeutung* at all. To be sure, our sentence can also be interpreted as saying that Schleswig-Holstein was once separated from Denmark. We then have a case which is to be considered later. In order to understand the difference more clearly, let us project ourselves into the mind of a Chinese who, having little knowledge of European history, believes it to be false that Schleswig-Holstein was ever separated from Denmark. He will take our sentence, in the first version, to be neither true nor false but will deny it to have any *Bedeutung*, on the ground that its subordinate clause lacks a *Bedeutung*. This clause would only apparently determine a time. If he interpreted our sentence in the second way, however, he would find a thought expressed in it which he would take to be false, beside a part which would be *bedeutungslos* for him.

[K] At times there is no linguistically explicit indicator and one must be read off from the entire context.

the present tense of the verb, which in such a case however does not indicate the temporal present. This grammatical form is then the indefinite indicator in the main and subordinate clauses. An example of this is: 'When | the Sun is in the tropic of Cancer, the longest day in the northern hemisphere occurs'. Here, also, it is impossible to express the sense of the subordinate clause in a full sentence, because this sense is not a complete thought. If we say 'The Sun is in the tropic of Cancer', this would refer to our present time[13] and thereby change the sense. Neither is the sense of the main clause a thought; only the whole, composed of main and subordinate clauses, has such a sense. It may be added that several common components may be indefinitely indicated in the antecedent and consequent clauses.

It is clear that noun clauses with 'who' or 'what' and adverbial clauses with 'where', 'when', 'wherever', 'whenever' are often to be interpreted as having the sense of antecedent clauses, e.g. 'Who touches pitch, defiles himself'.

Adjective clauses can also take the place of conditional clauses. Thus the sense of the sentence previously used can be given in the form 'The square of a number which is less than 1 and greater than 0 is less than 1 and greater than 0'.

The situation is quite different if the common component of the two clauses is designated by a proper name. In the sentence:

'Napoleon, who recognized the danger to his right flank, himself led his guards against the enemy position'

two thoughts are expressed:

(1) Napoleon recognized the danger to his right flank;
(2) Napoleon himself led his guards against the enemy position.

When and where this happened is to be fixed only by the context, but is nevertheless to be taken as definitely determined thereby. If the entire sentence is uttered as an assertion, we thereby simultaneously assert both component sentences. If one of the parts is false, the whole is false. Here we have the case that the subordinate clause by itself has a complete thought as sense (if we complete it by indication of place and time). The *Bedeutung* of the subordinate clause is accordingly a truth-value. We can therefore expect that it may be replaced, without harm to the truth-value of the whole, by a sentence having the | same truth-value. This is indeed the case; but it is to be noted that for purely grammatical reasons, its subject must be 'Napoleon', for only then can it be brought into the form of an adjective clause attaching to 'Napoleon'. But if the

---

[13] 'auf unsere Gegenwart beziehen'.

demand that it be expressed in this form is waived, and the connection shown by 'and', this restriction disappears.

Subsidiary clauses beginning with 'although' also express complete thoughts. This conjunction actually has no sense and does not change the sense of the clause but only illuminates it in a peculiar fashion.[L] We could indeed replace the concessive clause without harm to the truth of the whole by another of the same truth-value; but the light in which the clause is placed by the conjunction might then easily appear unsuitable, as if a song with a sad subject were to be sung in a lively fashion.

In the last cases the truth of the whole included the truth of the component clauses. The case is different if an antecedent clause expresses a complete thought by containing, in place of an indefinite indicator, a proper name or something which is to be regarded as equivalent. In the sentence

'If the Sun has already risen, the sky is very cloudy'

the time is the present, that is to say, definite. And the place is also to be thought of as definite. Here it can be said that a relation between the truth-values of antecedent and consequent clauses has been asserted, viz. that the case does not occur in which the antecedent stands for [*bedeute*] the True and the consequent for the False. Accordingly, our sentence is true if the Sun has not yet risen, whether the sky is very cloudy or not, and also if the Sun has risen and the sky is very cloudy. Since only truth-values are here in question, each component clause can be replaced by another of the same truth-value without changing the truth-value of the whole. To be sure, the light in which the subject then appears would usually be unsuitable; the thought might easily seem distorted; | but this has nothing to do with its truth-value. One must always observe that there are overtones of subsidiary thoughts, which are however not explicitly expressed and therefore should not be reckoned in the sense. Hence, also, no account need be taken of their truth-values.[M]

The simplest cases have now been discussed. Let us review what we have learned.

The subordinate clause usually has for its sense not a thought, but only a part of one, and consequently no truth-value as *Bedeutung*. The reason for this is either that the words in the subordinate clause have their indirect *Bedeutung*, so that the *Bedeutung*, not the sense, of the subordinate clause is a thought; or else that, on account of the presence of an indefinite indicator, the subordinate clause is incomplete and expresses

[L] Similarly in the case of 'but', 'yet'.

[M] The thought of our sentence might also be expressed thus: 'Either the Sun has not risen yet or the sky is very cloudy' – which shows how this kind of sentence connection is to be understood.

a thought only when combined with the main clause. It may happen, however, that the sense of the subsidiary clause is a complete thought, in which case it can be replaced by another of the same truth-value without harm to the truth of the whole – provided there are no grammatical obstacles.

An examination of all the subordinate clauses which one may encounter will soon provide some which do not fit well into these categories. The reason, so far as I can see, is that these subordinate clauses have no such simple sense. Almost always, it seems, we connect with the main thoughts expressed by us subsidiary thoughts which, although not expressed, are associated with our words, in accordance with psychological laws, by the hearer. And since the subsidiary thought appears to be connected with our words on its own account, almost like the main thought itself, we want it also to be expressed. The sense of the sentence is thereby enriched, and it may well happen that we have more simple thoughts than clauses. In many cases the sentence must be understood in this way, in others it may be doubtful whether the subsidiary thought belongs to the sense of the sentence or | only accompanies it.[N] One might perhaps find that the sentence

47

'Napoleon, who recognized the danger to his right flank, himself led his guards against the enemy position'

expresses not only the two thoughts shown above, but also the thought that the knowledge of the danger was the reason why he led the guards against the enemy position. One may in fact doubt whether this thought is just slightly suggested or really expressed. Let the question be considered whether our sentence is false if Napoleon's decision had already been made before he recognized the danger. If our sentence could be true in spite of this, the subsidiary thought should not be understood as part of the sense. One would probably decide in favour of this. The alternative would make for a quite complicated situation: we should have more simple thoughts than clauses. If the sentence

'Napoleon recognized the danger to his right flank'

were now to be replaced by another having the same truth-value, e.g.

'Napoleon was already more than 45 years old',

not only would our first thought be changed, but also our third one. Hence the truth-value of the latter might change – viz. if his age was not

[N] This may be important for the question whether an assertion is a lie, or an oath a perjury.

the reason for the decision to lead the guards against the enemy. This shows why clauses of equal truth-value cannot always be substituted for one another in such cases. The clause expresses more through its connection with another than it does in isolation.

Let us now consider cases where this regularly happens. In the sentence

'Bebel fancies [*wähnt*][14] that the return of Alsace-Lorraine would appease France's desire for revenge'

two thoughts are expressed, which are not however shown by means of antecedent and consequent clauses, viz.

(1)   Bebel believes that the return of Alsace-Lorraine would appease France's desire for revenge; |

48   (2)   the return of Alsace-Lorraine would not appease France's desire for revenge.

In the expression of the first thought, the words of the subordinate clause have their indirect *Bedeutung*, while the same words have their customary *Bedeutung* in the expression of the second thought. This shows that the subordinate clause in our original complex sentence is to be taken twice over, with different *Bedeutungen*, of which one is a thought, the other a truth-value. Since the truth-value is not the whole *Bedeutung* of the subordinate clause, we cannot simply replace the latter by another of equal truth-value. Similar considerations apply to expressions such as 'know', 'recognize', 'it is well known'.[15]

By means of a subordinate causal clause and the associated main clause we express several thoughts, which however do not correspond separately to the original clauses. In the sentence 'Because ice is less dense than water, it floats on water' we have

(1)   Ice is less dense than water;
(2)   If anything is less dense than water, it floats on water;
(3)   Ice floats on water.

The third thought, however, need not be explicitly introduced, since it is contained in the remaining two. On the other hand, neither the first and third nor the second and third combined would furnish the sense of our sentence. It can now be seen that our subordinate clause

'because ice is less dense than water'

---

[14] See fn. 9 above.
[15] 'wissen', 'erkennen', 'es ist bekannt'.

expresses our first thought, as well as a part of our second. This is how it comes to pass that our subsidiary clause cannot be simply replaced by another of equal truth-value; for this would alter our second thought and thereby might well alter its truth-value.

The situation is similar in the sentence

'If iron were less dense than water, it would float on water'. |

49 Here we have the two thoughts that iron is not less dense than water, and that something floats on water if it is less dense than water. The subsidiary clause again expresses one thought and a part of the other.

If we interpret the sentence already considered,

'After Schleswig-Holstein was separated from Denmark, Prussia and Austria quarrelled',

in such a way that it expresses the thought that Schleswig-Holstein was once separated from Denmark, we have first this thought, and secondly the thought that, at a time more closely determined by the subordinate clause, Prussia and Austria quarrelled. Here also the subordinate clause expresses not only one thought but also a part of another. Therefore it may not in general be replaced by another of the same truth-value.

It is hard to exhaust all the possibilities given by language; but I hope to have brought to light at least the essential reasons why a subordinate clause may not always be replaced by another of equal truth-value without harm to the truth of the whole sentence structure. These reasons arise:

(1) when the subordinate clause does not stand for [*bedeutet*] a truth-value, inasmuch as it expresses only a part of a thought;
(2) when the subordinate clause does stand for [*bedeutet*] a truth-value, but is not restricted to so doing, inasmuch as its sense includes one thought and part of another.

The first case arises:

(a) for words having indirect *Bedeutung*,
(b) if a part of the sentence is only an indefinite indicator instead of a proper name.

In the second case, the subsidiary clause may have to be taken twice over, viz. once in its customary *Bedeutung*, and the other time in its indirect *Bedeutung*; or the sense of a part of the subordinate clause may likewise be a component of another thought, which, taken together with

the thought directly expressed by the subordinate clause, makes up the
sense of the whole sentence.

It follows with sufficient probability from the foregoing that the cases
where a subordinate clause is not replaceable by another of the same
value cannot be brought in disproof of our view | that a truth-value is
the *Bedeutung* of a sentence that has a thought as its sense.

Let us return to our starting-point.

If we found '$a = a$' and '$a = b$' to have different cognitive values, the
explanation is that for the purpose of acquiring knowledge, the sense of
the sentence, viz., the thought expressed by it, is no less relevant than
its *Bedeutung*, i.e. its truth-value. If now $a = b$, then indeed the *Bedeutung*
of 'b' is the same as that of 'a', and hence the truth-value of '$a = b$' is
the same as that of '$a = a$'. In spite of this, the sense of 'b' may differ
from the sense of 'a', and thereby the thought expressed by '$a = b$' will
differ from that expressed by '$a = a$'. In that case the two sentences do
not have the same cognitive value. If we understand by 'judgement' the
advance from the thought to its truth-value, as in the present paper, we
can also say that the judgements are different.

[*Comments on* Sinn *and* Bedeutung]¹

[This piece was probably written in late 1891/early 1892,[2] and certainly before 1895, when Frege published a critique of a book by Schröder.[3] A draft of the latter formed the first part (now lost) of a bundle of papers of which the second part was the present piece, published post-humously in 1969, and given its title by the editors.[4] In 'Über Sinn und Bedeutung',[5] to which the present piece can be regarded as a sequel, Frege only discussed the *Sinn* and *Bedeutung* of proper names and sentences (the latter seen as themselves proper names – names of the True or the False); and in the early years of Frege scholarship (prior to 1969), there was controversy over whether Frege intended to extend the distinction to concept words and other functional expressions.[6] This piece makes Frege's position quite clear, and throws light on his understanding of concepts.[7]]

128 | In an article ('Über Sinn und Bedeutung') I distinguished between sense and *Bedeutung* in the first instance only for the case of proper names (or, if one prefers, singular terms). The same distinction can also be drawn for concept words. Now it is easy to become unclear about this by confounding the division into concepts and objects with the distinction between sense and *Bedeutung*, so that we run together sense and concept on the one hand and *Bedeutung* and object on the

---

[1] Translated by Peter Long and Roger White (*PW*, pp. 118–25; from *NS* pp. 128–36; page numbers from the latter in the margin).
[2] Cf. fn. C below.
[3] Frege, 'A Critical Elucidation of some Points in E. Schröder, *Vorlesungen über die Algebra der Logik* [*Lectures on the Algebra of Logic*]', in *CP*, pp. 210–28.
[4] Frege, *Nachgelassene Schriften*, ed. H. Hermes, F. Kambartel and F. Kaulbach (Hamburg: Felix Meiner, 1969), pp. 128–36. (The book was translated into English as *PW*, published in 1979.)
[5] This was announced as forthcoming in *FC* in 1891, and published in early 1892, and hence was presumably written in 1890–1.
[6] Both Marshall (1953, 1956) and Grossmann (1961), for example, denied that Frege applied the distinction to functional expressions; Dummett (1955) and Jackson (1962) suggested that it did apply.
[7] See also 'Letter to Husserl, 24.5.1891' (itself not published until 1976, in *WB*), pp. 149–50 above; *IL*, pp. 294–6 below.

other. To every concept word or proper name, there corresponds as a
rule a sense and a *Bedeutung,* as I use these words. Of course in fiction
words only have a sense, but in science and wherever we are concerned
about truth, we are not prepared to rest content with the sense, we also
attach a *Bedeutung* to proper names and concept words; and if through
some oversight, say, we fail to do this, then we are making a mistake
that can easily vitiate our thinking. The *Bedeutung* of a proper name is
the object it designates or names. A concept word stands for [*bedeutet*][8]
a concept, if the word is used as is appropriate for logic. I may clarify
this by drawing attention to a fact that seems to weigh heavily on the
side of extensionalist as against intensionalist logicians: namely, that in
any sentence we can substitute *salva veritate* one concept word for
another if they have the same extension, so that it is also the case that
in relation to inference, and where the laws of logic are concerned, concepts differ only in so far as their extensions are different. The fundamental logical relation is that of an object's falling under a concept: all
relations between concepts can be reduced to this. If an object falls
under a concept, it falls under all concepts with the same extension,
and this implies what we said above. Therefore just as proper names
can replace one another *salva veritate,* so too can concept words, if their
extension is the same. Of course the thought will alter when such re-
placements are made, | but this is the sense of the sentence, not its
Bedeutung.[A] The *Bedeutung,* which is the truth-value, remains the same.
For this reason we might easily come to propose the extension of a
concept as the *Bedeutung* of a concept word; to do this, however, would
be to overlook the fact that the extensions of concepts are objects and
not concepts (cf. my essay 'Function and Concept'). Nevertheless there
is a kernel of truth in this position. In order to bring it out more clearly,
I need to advert to what I said in my work on 'Function and Concept'.
On the view expressed there a concept is a function of one argument,
whose value is always a truth-value.[9] Here I am borrowing the term
'function' from Analysis and, whilst retaining what is essential to it,
using it in a somewhat extended meaning [*Bedeutung*], a procedure for
which the history of Analysis itself affords a precedent. The name of
a function is accompanied by empty places (at least one) where the
argument is to go; in Analysis this is usually indicated by the letter '*x*'

129

[A] Cf. my article 'Über Sinn und Bedeutung' [pp. 151–71 above].

[8] Throughout *PW*, the translators render the verb 'bedeuten' as 'mean'. But in this piece,
given Frege's view, as just stated, that the *Bedeutung* of a proper name is the object it
designates [*bezeichnet*] or names [*benennt*], 'stand for' or 'refer to' seems the more appropriate translation. For discussion of the problems involved in translating 'Bedeutung' and
its cognates, and for the policy adopted in the present volume, see the Introduction, §4
above.

[9] See p. 139 above.

which fills the empty places in question. But the argument is not to be counted as belonging to the function, and so the letter '*x*' is not to be counted as belonging to the name of the function either. Consequently one can always speak of the name of a function as having empty places, since what fills them does not, strictly speaking, belong to them. Accordingly I call the function itself unsaturated, or in need of supplementation, because its name has first to be completed with the sign of an argument if we are to obtain a *Bedeutung* that is complete in itself. I call such a *Bedeutung* an object and, in this case, the value of the function for the argument that effects the supplementing or saturating. In the cases we first encounter the argument is itself an object, and it is to these that we shall mainly confine ourselves here. Now with a concept we have the special case that the value is always a truth-value. That is to say, if we complete the name of a concept with a proper name, we obtain a sentence whose sense is a thought; and this sentence has a truth-value as its *Bedeutung*. To acknowledge this *Bedeutung* as that of the True (as the True) is to judge that the object which is taken as the argument falls under the concept. What in the case of a function is called unsaturatedness, we may, in the case of a concept, call its predicative nature.[B] This | comes out even in the cases in which we speak of a subject-concept ('All equilateral triangles are equiangular' means [*das heißt*] 'If anything is an equilateral triangle, then it is an equiangular triangle').[10]

130

    Such being the essence of a concept, there is now a great obstacle in the way of expressing ourselves correctly and making ourselves understood. If I want to speak of a concept, language, with an almost irresistible force, compels me to use an inappropriate expression which obscures – I might almost say falsifies – the thought. One would assume, on the basis of its analogy with other expressions, that if I say 'the concept *equilateral triangle*' I am designating a concept, just as I am of course naming a planet if I say 'the planet Neptune'. But this is not the case; for we do not have anything with a predicative nature. Hence the *Bedeutung* of the expression 'the concept *equilateral triangle*' (if there is one in this case) is an object. We cannot avoid words like 'the concept', but where we use them we must always bear their inappropriateness in mind.[C] From what we have said it follows that objects and concepts are

---

[B] The words 'unsaturated' and 'predicative' seem more suited to the sense than the *Bedeutung*; still there must be something on the part of the *Bedeutung* which corresponds to this, and I know of no better words. Cf. Wundt's *Logik* [possibly a reference to Vol. I, p. 141 (Stuttgart, 1st edn. 1880); cf. *NS*, p. 129, editors' fn. 2].

[C] I shall deal with this difficulty. [Frege is presumably referring to *CO*; see esp. pp. 184–5, 192–3 below. If this is right, then this would make late 1891/early 1892 the most likely date of composition of this piece, since *CO* was itself published in 1892.]

[10] Cf. *CO*, p. 186 below.

fundamentally different and cannot stand in for one another. And the same goes for the corresponding words or signs. Proper names cannot really be used as predicates. Where they might seem to be, we find on looking more closely that the sense is such that they only form part of the predicate: concepts cannot stand in the same relations as objects. It would not be false, but impossible to think of them as doing so. Hence, the words 'relation of a subject to a predicate' designate two quite different relations, according as the subject is an object or is itself a concept. Therefore it would be best to banish the words 'subject' and 'predicate' from logic entirely, since they lead us again and again to confound two quite different relations: that of an object's falling under a concept [subsumption] and that of one concept being subordinated to another [subordination]. The words 'all' and 'some', which go with the grammatical subject, belong in sense with the grammatical predicate, as we see if we go over to the negative (not all, *nonnulli*).[11] From this alone it immediately follows that the predicate in these cases is different from that which is asserted of an object. And in the same way

131   the relation | of equality [*Gleichheit*], by which I understand complete coincidence, identity,[12] can only be thought of as holding for objects, not concepts. If we say 'The *Bedeutung* of the word "conic section" is the same as that of the concept word "curve of the second degree"' or 'The concept *conic section* coincides with the concept *curve of the second degree*', the words '*Bedeutung* of the concept word "conic section"' are the name of an object, not of a concept; for their nature is not predicative, they are not unsaturated, they cannot be used with the indefinite article. The same goes for the words 'the concept *conic section*'. But although the relation of equality can only be thought of as holding for objects, there is an analogous relation for concepts. Since this is a relation between concepts I call it a second-level relation, whereas the former relation I call a first-level relation. We say that an object *a* is equal to an object *b* (in the sense of completely coinciding with it) if *a* falls under every concept under which *b* falls, and conversely.[13] We obtain something corresponding to this for concepts if we switch the roles of concept and object. We could then say that the relation we had in mind

[11] Compare e.g. 'Frege is a philosopher' ('The object Frege falls under the concept *philosopher*') and 'All logicians are philosophers' ('The concept *logician* is subordinate to the concept *philosopher*'). The negation of the former is 'Frege is not a philosopher', but the negation of the latter is not 'All logicians are not philosophers' ('The concept *logician* is subordinate to the concept *non-philosopher*'), but 'Not all logicians are philosophers' ('The concept *logician* is not subordinate to the concept *philosopher*'); which shows that 'all' and 'not all' 'belong in sense with the grammatical predicate'. Cf. *CO*, p. 187 below. (Cf. *NS*, p. 130, editors' fn. 2.)

[12] Cf. p. 151 above, fn. A.

[13] Frege is again appealing here to the Leibnizian principle that he took as his definition of identity in *GL*, §65 (see p. 112 above). Cf. p. 158 above.

above holds between the concept Φ and the concept X, if every object that falls under Φ also falls under X, and conversely. Of course in saying this we have again been unable to avoid using the expressions 'the concept Φ', 'the concept X', which again obscures the real sense. So for the reader who is not frightened of the *Begriffsschrift* I will add the following: the unsaturatedness of a concept (of first level) is represented in the *Begriffsschrift* by leaving at least one empty place in its designation where the name of the object which we are saying falls under the concept is to go. This place or places always has to be filled in some way or other. Besides being filled by a proper name it can also be filled by a sign which only indicates an object. We can see from this that the sign of equality, or one analogous to it, can never be flanked by the designation of a concept alone, but in addition to the concept an object must also be designated or indicated as well. Even if we only indicate concepts schematically by a function-letter, we must see to it that we give expression to their unsaturatedness by an accompanying empty place as in $\Phi(\ )$ and $X(\ )$. In other words, we may only use the letters (Φ, X), which are meant to indicate or designate concepts, as function-letters, i.e. in such a way that they are accompanied by a place for the argument (the space between the following brackets). This being so, we may not write $\Phi = X$, because here the letters Φ and X do not
132   occur as function-letters. But nor may we | write $\Phi(\ ) = X(\ )$, because the argument-places have to be filled. But when they are filled, it is not the functions (concepts) themselves that are put equal to one another: in addition to the function-letter there will be something else on either side of the equality sign, something not belonging to the function.

These letters cannot be replaced by letters that are not used as function-letters: there must always be an argument-place to receive the 'α'. The idea might occur to one simply to write $\Phi = X$. This may seem all right so long as we are indicating concepts schematically, but a mode of designation that is really adequate must provide for all cases. Let us take an example which I have already used in my paper on 'Function and Concept'.[14]

For every argument the function $x^2 = 1$ has the same (truth-)value as the function $(x + 1)^2 = 2(x + 1)$; i.e. every object falling under the concept *less by 1 than a number whose square is equal to its double* falls under the concept *square root of 1*, and conversely. If we expressed this thought in the way that we gave above,[15] we should have

---

[14] See pp. 138–9 above. Early work on the original manuscript, now lost, suggested that Frege may have intended to delete or bracket this paragraph, which does contain some repetition; cf. *NS*, p. 132, fn. 1.

[15] Frege may have explained the notation used in the following formula in the lost first part of the bundle of papers of which this piece formed the second part (cf. *NS*, p. 132, editors' fn. 3).

$$(\alpha^2 = 1) \overset{\alpha}{\underset{\wedge}{\vee}} ((\alpha + 1)^2 = 2(\alpha + 1))$$

What we have here is that second-level relation which corresponds to, but should not be confused with, equality (complete coincidence) between objects. If we write it

$$—\!\underset{\smile}{\alpha}\!—\quad (\alpha^2 = 1) = ((\alpha + 1)^2 = 2(\alpha + 1)),$$

we have expressed what is essentially the same thought, construed as an equation between values of functions that holds generally. We have here the same second-level relation; we have in addition the sign of equality, but this does not suffice on its own to designate this relation: it has to be used in combination with the sign for generality: in the first line we have a general statement but not an equation. In

$$\grave{\epsilon}(\epsilon^2 = 1) = \grave{\alpha}((\alpha + 1)^2 = 2(\alpha + 1))$$

we do have an equation, but not between concepts (which is impossible) but between objects, namely extensions of concepts.[16]

Now we have seen that the relation of equality between objects cannot be conceived as holding between concepts too, but that there is a corresponding relation for concepts. It follows that the word 'the same' that is used to designate the former relation between objects cannot properly be used to designate the latter relation as well. If we try to use it to do this, the only recourse we really have is to say 'the concept Φ is the same as | the concept X' and in saying this we have of course named a relation between objects,[D] where what is intended is a relation between concepts. We have the same case if we say 'the *Bedeutung* of the concept word A is the same as that of the concept word B'. Indeed we should really outlaw the expression 'the *Bedeutung* of the concept word A', because the definite article before '*Bedeutung*' points to an object and belies the predicative nature of a concept. It would be better to confine ourselves to saying 'what the concept word A stands for [*bedeutet*]', for this at any rate is to be used predicatively: 'Jesus is, what the concept word "man" stands for [*bedeutet*]' in the sense of 'Jesus is a man'.

Now if we bear all this in mind, we shall be well able to assert 'what two concept words stand for [*bedeuten*] is the same if and only if the extensions of the corresponding concepts coincide' without being led astray by the improper use of the word 'the same'. And with this statement we have, I believe, made an important concession to the extensionalist logicians. They are right when they show by their preference for the extension, as against the intension, of a concept that they

[D] These objects have the names 'the concept Φ' and 'the concept X'.

[16] For an explanation of Frege's notation in the last two formulae, see Appendix 2 below.

regard the *Bedeutung* and not the sense of the words as the essential thing for logic. The intensionalist logicians are only too happy not to go beyond the sense; for what they call the intension, if it is not an idea, is nothing other than the sense. They forget that logic is not concerned with how thoughts, regardless of truth-value, follow from thoughts, that the step from thought to truth-value – more generally, the step from sense to *Bedeutung* – has to be taken. They forget that the laws of logic are first and foremost laws in the realm of *Bedeutungen* and only relate indirectly to sense. If it is a question of the truth of something – and truth is the goal of logic – we also have to inquire after *Bedeutungen*; we have to throw aside proper names that do not designate or name an object, though they may have a sense; we have to throw aside concept words that do not have a *Bedeutung*. These are not such as, say, contain a contradiction – for there is nothing at all wrong in a concept's being empty – but such as have vague boundaries. It must be determinate for every object whether it falls under a concept or not; a concept word which does not meet this requirement on its *Bedeutung* is *bedeutungslos*. E.g. the word 'μῶλυ' (Homer, *Odyssey* X, 305) belongs to this class, although it is true that certain marks are supplied.[17] For this reason the context cited need not lack a sense, any more than other contexts in which the name 'Nausicaa',[18] which probably does not stand for [*bedeutet*] or name anything, occurs. But it behaves as if it names a girl, and it is thus assured of a sense. And for fiction the sense is enough. | The thought, though it is devoid of *Bedeutung*, of truth-value, is enough, but not for science.

134

In my *Grundlagen* and the paper 'On Formal Theories of Arithmetic'[19] I showed that for certain proofs it is far from being a matter of indifference whether a combination of signs – e.g. $\sqrt{-1}$ – has a *Bedeutung*[E] or not, that, on the contrary, the whole cogency of the proof stands or falls with this. The *Bedeutung* is thus shown at every point to be the essential thing for science. Therefore even if we concede to the intensionalist logicians that it is the concept as opposed to the extension that is the fundamental thing, this does not mean that it is to be taken

---

[E] It is true that I had not then settled upon my present use of the words 'sense' and 'Bedeutung', so that sometimes I said 'sense' where I should now say 'Bedeutung'. [Cf. p. 150 above.]

---

[17] In Homer's epic, 'μῶλυ' ('mōly') is the name of a magic plant which Hermes gave Odysseus to protect him from the goddess Circe's potions. It is described as having a black root and a milk-white flower: these are the 'marks' ('Merkmale') of which Frege speaks. For the notion of a 'mark', see *GL*, §53 (pp. 102–3 above), and *CO*, pp. 189–90 below.

[18] 'Nausicaa' was the name, in Homer's epic, of the beautiful daughter of the Phaiacian king Alcinoos who brought Odysseus to her father's house after a meeting arranged by Athena (*Odyssey* VI).

[19] *FTA*, in *CP*, pp. 112–21.

as the sense of a concept word: it is its *Bedeutung,* and the extensionalist logicians come closer to the truth in so far as they are presenting
– in the extension – a *Bedeutung* as the essential thing. Though this
Bedeutung is certainly not the concept itself, it is still very closely connected with it.

Husserl takes Schröder[20] to task for the unclarity in his discussion of
the words '*unsinnig*' [without sense], '*einsinnig*' [having one sense], and
'*mehrsinnig*' [having more than one sense], '*undeutig*' [without mean-
ing], '*eindeutig*' [having one meaning], '*mehrdeutig*' [having more than
one meaning] (pp. 48ff. and 69),[21] and unclarity indeed there is, but
even the distinctions Husserl draws are inadequate. It was hardly to be
expected that Schröder's use of the particles '*sinnig*' and '*deutig*' would
not differ from my own; still less can I take issue with him over this,
since when his work appeared nothing had been published by me in
this connection. For him this distinction is connected with that between
common names and proper names, and the unclarity springs from a
faulty conception of the distinction between concept and object. According to him there is nothing amiss with common names that are *mehrdeutig,*
135   they are this when | more than one object falls under the corresponding
concept.[F] On this view it would be possible for a common name to be
undeutig too, like 'round square', without its being defective. Schröder,
however, calls it *unsinnig* as well and is thus untrue to his own way of
speaking; for according to this the 'round square' would have to be
called *einsinnig,* and Husserl was right when he called it a univocal
common name; for 'univocal' and 'equivocal' correspond to Schröder's

---

[F] If, as Husserl says in the first footnote to p. 252, a distributive name is one 'whose
Bedeutung is such that it designates any one of a plurality of things', then a concept word
(common name) is at any rate not a distributive name. [The original editors note that
it is not entirely clear where this footnote was intended to go; *NS,* p. 135, fn. 2.]

[20] The reference is to Husserl's review of Schröder's *Vorlesungen über die Algebra der Logik
(Exakte Logik) I* (Leipzig, 1890), which appeared in the *Göttingischen gelehrte Anzeigen* in
April 1891, pp. 243–78. It is one of the pieces Husserl sent to Frege that occasioned their
first correspondence (see p. 149 above). For discussion of the relationship between
Frege, Husserl and Schröder here, see Simons, 1992.

[21] In the place referred to by Frege Schröder fixes on the adjectives ending in '*deutig*' as
terms for the sizes of extensions of concepts. Schröder speaks generally of names and
calls proper names '*eindeutig*', common names like 'my hand' '*zweideutig*' [having two
meanings], common names in general '*mehrdeutig*' or '*vieldeutig*' [having many meanings]
and names like 'nothing' or 'round square' '*undeutig*'. The corresponding formations with
'*sinnig*' are employed by Schröder to distinguish terms whose use is precisely fixed
('*einsinnig*' or 'univocal'), from terms with multiple meanings ('*doppelsinnig*' [having a
double sense], '*mehrsinnig*' or 'equivocal') and from formations without sense ('*unsinnig*';
'round square' in Schröder's example). With Husserl, Frege chiefly criticizes Schröder for
calling a name like 'round square' '*undeutig*' when for this label to apply the name is
surely already presupposed as being significant as such, so that it cannot at the same time
be designated as '*unsinnig*'. [Translation of original editors' footnote (*NS,* p. 134, fn. 3).]

'*einsinnig*' and '*mehrsinnig*'. Husserl says (p. 250): 'Obviously he confuses two quite different questions here, namely (1) whether a name has a *Bedeutung* (a '*Sinn*'); and (2) whether there does or does not exist an object corresponding to the name'. This distinction is inadequate. The word 'common name' leads to the mistaken assumption that a common name is related to objects in essentially the same way as is a proper name, the difference being only that the latter names just one thing whilst the former is usually applicable to more than one. But this is false, and that is why I prefer 'concept word' to 'common name'.[22] A proper name must at least have a sense (as I use the word); otherwise it would be an empty sequence of sounds and it would be wrong to call it a name. But if it is to have a use in science we must require that it have a *Bedeutung* too, that it designates or names an object. Thus it is via a sense, and only via a sense, that a proper name is related to an object.[23]

A concept word must have a sense too and if it is to have a use in science, a *Bedeutung*; but this consists neither of one object nor of a plurality of objects: it is a concept. Now in the case of a concept it can of course again be asked whether one object falls under it, or more than one or none. But this relates directly to the concept and nothing else. So a concept word can be absolutely impeccable, logically speaking, without there being an object to which it is related through its sense and *Bedeutung* (the concept itself). As we see, this relation to an object is more indirect and inessential, so that there seems little point in dividing concept words up according as no object falls under the corresponding concepts or one object or more than one. Logic must demand not only of proper names but of concept words as well that the step from the word to the sense and from the sense to the *Bedeutung* be determinate beyond any doubt. Otherwise we should not be entitled to speak of a *Bedeutung* at all. Of course this holds for all signs and combinations of signs with the same function as proper names or concept words.

[22] Cf. Frege's 'Letter to Husserl, 24.5.1891', pp. 149–50 above.
[23] Since Schröder and Husserl did not distinguish, in the way Frege did, between the *Sinn* and *Bedeutung* of an expression, we have thought it best in this paragraph to preserve the actual German where these terms or (more commonly) their cognates with '*sinnig*' and '*deutig*' occur in quotation from these authors, or where Frege himself uses the latter in alluding to their views. We have given what help we could to the reader by providing renderings in square brackets . . . (*Trs.*) [Frege's own use of 'Bedeutung' also remains untranslated.]

On Concept and Object[1]

[This paper was first published in 1892 in the *Vierteljahrsschrift für wissenschaftliche Philosophie*, 16, pp. 192–205. As the opening paragraph indicates, it was written in response to Benno Kerry's eight articles 'On Intuition and its Psychical Elaboration', which appeared in the journal from 1885 to 1891, the second and fourth articles, in particular, criticizing Frege's views. Kerry was *Privatdozent* in philosophy at the University of Strasburg until his death in 1889.[2]]

192 In a series of articles in this Quarterly on intuition and its psychical elaboration, Benno Kerry has several times referred to my *Grundlagen der Arithmetik* and other works of mine, sometimes agreeing and sometimes disagreeing with me. I cannot but be pleased at this, and I think the best way I can show my appreciation is to take up the discussion of the points he contests. This seems to me all the more necessary, because his opposition is at least partly based on a misunderstanding, which might be shared by others, of what I say about concepts, and because, even apart from this particular reason, the matter is important and difficult enough for a more thorough treatment than seemed to me suitable in my *Grundlagen*.

The word 'concept' is used in various ways; its sense is sometimes psychological, sometimes logical, and sometimes perhaps a confused mixture of both. Since this licence exists, it is natural to restrict it by requiring that when once a usage is adopted it shall be maintained. What I decided was to keep strictly to a purely logical use. The question whether this or that use is more appropriate is one that I should like to leave

---

[1] Translated by Peter Geach (*TPW*, pp. 42–55/*CP*, pp. 182–94). Page numbers in the margin are from the original journal. The translated text here is from the third edition of *TPW*, with minor revisions made in accordance with the policy adopted in the present volume – in particular, 'Bedeutung' (and cognates such as 'bedeutungslos') being left untranslated, and 'bedeuten' being rendered as 'stand for' as in the second edition (but with the German always in square brackets following it), unless otherwise indicated. For discussion of this policy, and the problems involved in translating 'Bedeutung' and its cognates, see the Introduction, §4 above.
[2] Cf. *PW*, p. 87/*NS*, p. 96, editors' fn.

on one side, as of minor importance. Agreement about the mode of expression will easily be reached when once it is recognized that there is something that deserves a special term.

It seems to me that Kerry's misunderstanding results from his unintentionally confusing his own usage of the word 'concept' with mine. This readily gives rise to contradictions, for which my usage is not to blame. |

193   Kerry contests what he calls my definition of 'concept'. I would remark, in the first place, that my explanation is not meant as a proper definition. One cannot require that everything be defined, any more than one can require that a chemist decompose every substance. What is simple cannot be decomposed, and what is logically simple cannot have a proper definition. Now something logically simple is no more given us at the outset than most of the chemical elements are; it is reached only by means of scientific work. If something has been discovered that is simple, or at least must count as simple for the time being, we shall have to coin a term for it, since language will not originally contain an expression that exactly answers. On the introduction of a name for something logically simple, a definition is not possible. There is nothing for it but to lead the reader or hearer, by means of hints, to understand the words as is intended.

Kerry wants to make out that the distinction between concept and object is not absolute. He says: 'In a previous passage I have myself expressed the opinion that the relation between the content of the concept [*Begriffsinhalt*] and the concept-object [*Begriffsgegenstand*] is, in a certain respect, a peculiar and irreducible one; but this was in no way bound up with the view that the properties of being a concept and of being an object are mutually exclusive; the latter view no more follows from the former than it would follow, if, e.g., the relation of father and son were one that could not be further reduced, that a man could not be at once a father and a son (though of course not, e.g., father of the man whose son he was)'.

Let us fasten on this simile. If there were, or had been, beings that were fathers but could not be sons, such beings would obviously be quite different in kind from all men who are sons. Now it is something like this that happens here. A concept – as I understand the word – is predicative.[A] On the other hand, a name of an object, a proper name, is quite incapable of being used as a grammatical predicate. This admittedly needs elucidation, otherwise it might appear false. Surely one can just as well assert of a thing that it is Alexander the Great, or is the number four, or is the planet Venus, as that it is green or is a mammal? |

194   If anybody thinks this, he is not distinguishing the uses of the word 'is'. In the last two examples it serves as a copula, as a mere verbal sign of predication. As such it can sometimes be replaced by the mere personal

---

[A] It is, in fact, the *Bedeutung* of a grammatical predicate.

suffix. Compare, e.g., 'Dieses Blatt ist grün' and 'Dieses Blatt grünt'.[3]
We are here saying that something falls under a concept, and the grammatical predicate stands for [*bedeutet*] this concept. In the first three
examples, on the other hand, 'is' is used like the 'equals' sign in arithmetic, to express an equation.[B] In the sentence 'The Morning Star is
Venus', we have two proper names, 'Morning Star' and 'Venus', for the
same object. In the sentence 'The Morning Star is a planet' we have
a proper name, 'the Morning Star', and a concept word, 'planet'. So
far as language goes, no more has happened than that 'Venus' has been
replaced by 'a planet'; but really the relation has become wholly different. An equation is reversible; an object's falling under a concept is an
irreversible relation. In the sentence 'The Morning Star is Venus', 'is'
is obviously not the mere copula; its content is an essential part of the
predicate, so that the word 'Venus' does not constitute the whole of the
predicate.[C] One might say instead: 'The Morning Star is no other than
Venus'; what was previously implicit in the single word 'is' is here set
forth in four separate words, and in 'is no other than' the word 'is' now
really is the mere copula. What is predicated here is thus not *Venus* but
no other than Venus. These words stand for [*bedeuten*] a concept; admittedly only one object falls under this, but such a concept must still
always be distinguished from the object.[D] We have here a word 'Venus'
that can never be a proper predicate, although it can form | part of a
predicate. The *Bedeutung*[E] of this word is thus something that can never
occur as a concept, but only as an object. Kerry, too, would probably
not wish to dispute that there is something of this kind. But this involves
admitting a distinction, which it is very important to recognize, between
what can occur only as an object, and everything else. And this distinction would not be effaced even if it were true, as Kerry thinks it is, that
there are concepts that can also be objects. There are, indeed, cases that
seem to support his view. I myself have indicated (in *Grundlagen*, §53)
that a concept may fall under a higher concept – which, however, must
not be confused with one concept's being subordinate to another.[4] Kerry

195

[B] I use the word 'equal' ['*gleich*'] and the symbol '=' in the sense of 'the same as', 'no
other than', 'identical with'. Cf. E. Schröder, *Vorlesungen über die Algebra der Logik* (Leipzig,
1890), Vol. 1, §1. Schröder must however be criticized for not distinguishing two fundamentally different relations: the relation of an object to a concept it falls under [subsump-
tion], and the subordination of one concept to another. His remarks on the *Vollwurzel* are
likewise open to objection. Schröder's symbol €does not simply take the place of the copula.
[C] Cf. my *Grundlagen*, §66, fn. [fn. R, p. 113 above].
[D] Cf. my *Grundlagen*, §51 [p. 102 above].
[E] Cf. my paper, 'Über Sinn und Bedeutung', shortly to appear in the *Zeitschrift für Phil.
und phil. Kritik* [pp. 151–71 above].

---

[3] The difference here cannot really be captured in English (literally, 'This leaf is green'
and 'This leaf greens'). A better example in English would be the pair of sentences 'This
person is walking' and 'This person walks'.
[4] See p. 103 above.

does not appeal to this; instead, he gives the following example: 'The concept "horse" is a concept easily attained', and thinks that the concept 'horse' is an object, in fact one of the objects that fall under the concept 'concept easily attained'. Quite so; the three words 'the concept "horse"' do designate an object, but on that very account they do not designate a concept, as I am using the word. This is in full accord with the criterion I gave[F] – that the singular definite article always indicates an object, whereas the indefinite article accompanies a concept word. Kerry holds that no logical rules can be based on linguistic distinctions; but my own way of doing this is something that nobody can avoid who lays down such rules at all, for we cannot understand one another without language, and so in the end we must always rely on other people's understanding words, inflexions, and sentence-construction in essentially the same way as ourselves. As I said before, I was not trying to give a definition, but only hints, and to this end I appealed to the general feeling for the German language. It is here very much to my advantage that there is such good accord between the linguistic distinction and the real one. As regards the indefinite article there are probably no exceptions to our rule at all for us to remark, apart from obsolete formulas like 'Ein edler Rat' ['Councillor']. The matter is not so simple for the definite article, especially in the plural; but | then my criterion does not relate to this case. In the singular, so far as I can see, the matter is doubtful only when a singular takes the place of a plural, as in the sentences 'The Turk besieged Vienna', 'The horse is a four-legged animal'. These cases are so easily recognizable as special ones that the value of our rule is hardly impaired by their occurrence. It is clear that in the first sentence 'the Turk' is the proper name of a people. The second sentence is probably best regarded as expressing a universal judgement, say 'All horses are four-legged animals' or 'All properly constituted horses are four-legged animals'; these will be discussed later.[G] Kerry calls my criterion unsuitable, for surely, he says, in the sentence 'The concept that I am now talking about is an individual concept', the name

196

[F] *Grundlagen*, §51; §66, fn.; §68, fn. on p. 80 [see pp. 102, 113, 115 above].

[G] Nowadays people seem inclined to exaggerate the scope of the statement that different linguistic expressions are never completely equivalent, that a word can never be exactly translated into another language. One might perhaps go even further, and say that the same word is never taken in quite the same way even by men who share a language. I will not enquire as to the measure of truth in these statements; I would only emphasize that nevertheless different expressions quite often have something in common, which I call the sense, or, in the special case of sentences, the thought. In other words, we must not fail to recognize that the same sense, the same thought, may be variously expressed; thus the difference does not here concern the sense, but only the apprehension [*Auffassung*], shading [*Beleuchtung*], or colouring [*Färbung*] of the thought, and is irrelevant for logic. It is possible for one sentence to give no more and no less information than another; and, for all the multiplicity of languages, mankind has a common stock of thoughts. If all composed of the first eight words stands for [*bedeute*] a concept; but he is not taking the word 'concept' in my sense, and it is not in what I have laid down that the contradiction lies. But nobody can require that my mode of expression shall agree with Kerry's.

It must indeed be recognized that here we are confronted by an awkwardness of language, which I admit cannot be avoided, if we say that the concept *horse* is not a concept,[H] whereas, e.g., the | city of Berlin is a city, and the volcano Vesuvius is a volcano. Language is here in a predicament that justifies the departure from custom. The peculiarity of our case is indicated by Kerry himself, by means of the quotation-marks around 'horse'; I use italics to the same end. There was no reason to mark out the words 'Berlin' and 'Vesuvius' in a similar way. In logical discussions one quite often needs to say something about a concept, and to express this in the form usual for such predications – viz. to make what is said about the concept into the content of the grammatical predicate. Consequently, one would expect that the *Bedeutung* of the grammatical subject would be the concept; but the concept as such cannot play this part, in view of its predicative nature; it must first be converted into an object,[I] or, more precisely, an object must go proxy for it. We designate this object by prefixing the words 'the concept', e.g.:

'The concept *man* is not empty'.

Here the first three words are to be regarded as a proper name,[J] which can no more be used predicatively than 'Berlin' or 'Vesuvius'. When we say 'Jesus falls under the concept *man*', then, setting aside the copula, the predicate is:

'someone falling under the concept *man*',

and this means [*bedeutet*] the same as:[5]

transformation of the expression were forbidden on the plea that this would alter the content as well, logic would simply be crippled; for the task of logic can hardly be performed without trying to recognize the thought in its manifold guises. Moreover, all definitions would then have to be rejected as false. [Cf. *PWLB*, pp. 239ff. below.]

[H] A similar thing happens when we say as regards the sentence 'This rose is red': the grammatical predicate 'is red' belongs to the subject 'this rose'. Here the words 'the grammatical predicate "is red"' are not a grammatical predicate but a subject. By the very act of explicitly calling it a predicate, we deprive it of this property.

[I] Cf. my *Grundlagen*, p. X [p. 90 above].

[J] I call anything a proper name if it is a sign for an object.

[5] Here is one occasion on which Frege's use of the German word 'bedeutet' is most naturally translated as 'means' – in the horizontal sense distinguished in the Introduction (see §4). But given Frege's conception that the *Bedeutung* of a concept word is the

197

'a man'.

But the phrase

'the concept *man*'

is only part of this predicate.

Somebody might urge, as against the predicative nature of concepts, that nevertheless we speak of a subject-concept. But even in such cases, e.g. in the sentence

'All mammals have red blood'

we cannot fail to recognize the predicative nature[K] of the concept; for we could say instead: |

198   'Whatever is a mammal has red blood',

or:

'If anything is a mammal, then it has red blood'.

When I wrote my *Grundlagen der Arithmetik*, I had not yet made the distinction between sense and *Bedeutung*,[L] and so, under the expression 'judgeable content', I was combining what I now designate by the distinctive words 'thought' and 'truth-value'. Consequently, I no longer entirely approve of the explanation I gave on p. 77 of that book,[6] as regards its wording; my view is, however, still essentially the same. We may say in brief, taking 'subject' and 'predicate' in the linguistic sense:

[K] What I call here the predicative nature of concepts is just a special case of the need of supplementation, the unsaturatedness, that I gave as the essential feature of a function in my work 'Function and Concept' [see pp. 130–48 above]. It was there scarcely possible to avoid the expression 'the function $f(x)$', although there too the difficulty arose that the *Bedeutung* of this expression is not a function.

[L] Cf. my essay, 'Über Sinn und Bedeutung' in the *Zeitschrift für Phil. und phil. Kritik* [pp. 151–71 above].

concept itself, then since Frege's point is that the two phrases 'someone falling under the concept *man*' and 'a man' are expressions for the same concept, it would not be wrong to use a term such as 'refers to' here, reflecting the vertical sense; though one may well suspect that 'bedeutet' is being used in both senses here, which would certainly make 'means' the more appropriate translation, being equally ambiguous in English. The two phrases that are being said to 'mean' the same have in common not merely sameness of 'reference' (compare e.g. 'a man' – 'ein Mensch' – and, say, 'a rational animal'), but some other element of 'meaning' as well.

[6] See *GL*, §66, fn. (fn. R, p. 113 above).

a concept is the *Bedeutung* of a predicate; an object is something that can never be the whole *Bedeutung* of a predicate, but can be the *Bedeutung* of a subject. It must here be remarked that the words 'all', 'any', 'no', 'some', are prefixed to concept words. In universal and particular affirmative and negative sentences, we are expressing relations between concepts; we use these words to indicate the special kind of relation. They are thus, logically speaking, not to be more closely associated with the concept words that follow them, but are to be related to the sentence as a whole. It is easy to see this in the case of negation. If in the sentence

'All mammals are land-dwellers'

the phrase 'all mammals' expressed the logical subject of the predicate *are land-dwellers*, then in order to negate the whole sentence we should have to negate the predicate: 'are not land-dwellers'. Instead, we must put the 'not' in front of 'all', from which it follows that 'all' logically belongs with the predicate. On the other hand, we do negate the sentence 'The concept *mammal* is subordinate to the concept *land-dweller*' by negating the predicate: 'is not subordinate to the concept *land-dweller*'.[7]

    If we keep it in mind that in my way of speaking expressions like 'the concept *F*' designate not concepts but objects, most of Kerry's objections already | collapse. If he thinks (p. 281) that I have identified concept and extension of concept, he is mistaken. I merely expressed my view that in the expression 'the number that belongs to the concept *F* is the extension of the concept *equinumerous to the concept F*' the words 'extension of the concept' could be replaced by 'concept'.[8] Notice carefully that here the word 'concept' is combined with the definite article. Besides, this was only an incidental remark; I did not base anything upon it.

    Thus Kerry does not succeed in filling the gap between concept and object. Someone might attempt, however, to make use of my own statements in this sense. I have said that to assign a number involves saying something about a concept;[M] I speak of properties ascribed to a concept, and I allow that a concept may fall under a higher one.[N] I have called existence a property of a concept.[9] How I mean this to be taken is best made clear by an example. In the sentence 'There is at least one square root of 4', we are saying something, not about (say) the definite

199

[M] *Grundlagen*, §46 [pp. 98–9 above].
[N] *Grundlagen*, §53 [pp. 102–3 above].

[7] Cf. *CSB*, p. 175 above.
[8] Cf. *GL*, §68, fn. on p. 80 (fn. S, p. 115 above).
[9] On the looseness of this formulation, see fn. 16 on p. 103 above.

number 2, nor about −2, but about a concept, *square root of 4*; viz. that it is not empty. But if I express the same thought thus: 'The concept *square root of 4* is realized', then the first six words form the proper name of an object, and it is about this object that something is being said. But notice carefully that what is being said here is not the same thing as was being said about the concept. This will be surprising only to somebody who fails to see that a thought can be split up in many ways, so that now one thing, now another, appears as subject or predicate. The thought itself does not yet determine what is to be regarded as the subject. If we say 'the subject of this judgement', we do not designate anything definite unless at the same time we indicate a definite kind of analysis; as a rule, we do this in connection with a definite wording. But we must never forget that different sentences may express the same thought. For example, the thought we are considering could also be taken as saying something about the number 4:

'The number 4 has the property that there is something of which it is the square'.

Language has means of presenting now one, now another, part of the | thought as the subject; one of the most familiar is the distinction of active and passive forms.[10] It is thus not impossible that one way of analysing a given thought should make it appear as a singular judgement; another, as a particular judgement; and a third, as a universal judgement.[11] It need not then surprise us that the same sentence may be conceived as saying something about a concept and also as saying something about an object; only we must observe that *what* is being said is different. In the sentence 'There is at least one square root of 4' it is impossible to replace the words 'square root of 4' by 'the concept *square root of 4*'; i.e. what is suitably said of the concept does not suit the object. Although our sentence does not present the concept as a subject, it says something about it; it can be regarded as expressing that a concept falls under a higher one.[°] But this does not in any way efface the distinction between object and concept. We see to begin with that in the sentence 'There is at least one square root of 4' the predicative nature of the concept is not belied; we could say 'There is something that has the property of giving the result 4 when multiplied by itself'. Hence what is said here concerning a concept can never be said concerning an object;

200

[°] In my *Grundlagen* I called such a concept a second-order concept [see p. 103 above]; in my work 'Function and Concept' I called it a second-level concept [see p. 146 above], as I shall do here.

[10] Cf. *BS*, §3 (pp. 53–4 above); §9, last para. (p. 68 above).
[11] On the possibility of alternative analyses, cf. *BS*, §9 (pp. 65–8 above).

for a proper name can never be a predicative expression, though it can be part of one. I do not want to say it is false to say concerning an object what is said here concerning a concept; I want to say it is impossible, senseless, to do so. The sentence 'There is Julius Caesar' is neither true nor false but senseless; the sentence 'There is a man whose name is Julius Caesar' has a sense, but here again we have a concept, as the indefinite article shows. We get the same thing in the sentence 'There is only one Vienna'. We must not let ourselves be deceived because language often uses the same word now as a proper name, now as a concept word; in our example, the numeral indicates that we have the latter; 'Vienna' is here a concept word, like 'metropolis'. Using it in this sense, we may say: 'Trieste is no Vienna'. If, on the other hand, we |
201 substitute 'Julius Caesar' for the proper name formed by the first six words of the sentence 'The concept *square root of 4* is realized', we get a sentence that has a sense but is false; for that so-and-so is realized (as the word is being taken here) is something that can be truly said only concerning a quite special kind of objects, viz. such as can be designated by proper names of the form 'the concept *F*'. Thus the words 'the concept *square root of 4*' have an essentially different behaviour, as regards possible substitutions, from the words 'square root of 4' in our original sentence; i.e. the *Bedeutungen* of the two phrases are essentially different.

What has been shown here in one example holds good generally; the behaviour of the concept is essentially predicative, even where something is being said about it; consequently it can be replaced there only by another concept, never by an object. Thus what is being said concerning a concept does not suit an object. Second-level concepts, which concepts fall under, are essentially different from first-level concepts, which objects fall under. The relation of an object to a first-level concept that it falls under is different from the (admittedly similar) relation of a first-level to a second-level concept. To do justice at once to the distinction and to the similarity, we might perhaps say: an object falls *under* a first-level concept; a concept falls *within* a second-level concept. The distinction of concept and object thus still holds, with all its sharpness.

With this there hangs together what I have said (*Grundlagen*, §53) about my usage of the words 'property' and 'mark';[12] Kerry's discussion gives me occasion to revert once more to this. The words serve to signify relations, in sentences like 'Φ is a property of Γ' and 'Φ is a mark of Ω'. In my way of speaking, a thing can be at once a property and a mark, but not of the same thing. I call the concepts under which an object falls its properties; thus

---

[12] See pp. 102–3 above. The German word translated here as 'mark' is 'Merkmal'.

'to be Φ is a property of Γ'

is just another way of saying:

'Γ falls under the concept of a Φ'.

If the object Γ has the properties Φ, X and Ψ, I may combine them into Ω; so that it is the same thing if I say that Γ has the property Ω, or, that Γ | has the properties Φ, X and Ψ. I then call Φ, X and Ψ marks of the concept Ω, and, at the same time, properties of Γ. It is clear that the relations of Φ to Γ and to Ω are quite different, and that consequently different terms are required. Γ falls under the concept Φ; but Ω, which is itself a concept, cannot fall under the first-level concept Φ; only to a second-level concept could it stand in a similar relation. Ω is, on the other hand, subordinate to Φ.

Let us consider an example. Instead of saying:

'2 is a positive number' and
'2 is a whole number' and
'2 is less than 10'

we may also say

'2 is a positive whole number less than 10'.

Here

to be a positive number,
to be a whole number,
to be less than 10,

appear as properties of the object 2, and also as marks of the concept

positive whole number less than 10.

This is neither positive, nor a whole number, nor less than 10. It is indeed subordinate to the concept *whole number*, but does not fall under it.

Let us now compare with this what Kerry says in his second article (p. 424).[13] 'By the number 4 we understand the result of additively combining 3 and 1. The concept-object here occurring is the numerical individual 4; a quite definite number in the natural number series. This object obviously bears just the marks that are named in its concept, and

---

[13] Frege's original text mistakenly referred to p. 224.

no others besides – provided we refrain, as we surely must, from counting as *propria* of the object its infinitely numerous relations to all other individual numbers; "the" number 4 is likewise the result of additively combining 3 and 1.'

We see at once that my distinction between property and mark is here quite slurred over. Kerry distinguishes here between the number 4 and 'the' number 4. I must confess that this distinction is incomprehensible to me. The number 4 is to be a concept; 'the' number 4 is to be a concept-object, and none other than the numerical individual 4. It needs no proof that what we have here is not my distinction between concept and | object. It almost looks as though what was floating – though very obscurely – before Kerry's mind were my distinction between the sense and the *Bedeutung* of the words 'the number 4'.[P] But it is only of the *Bedeutung* that we can say: this is the result of additively combining 3 and 1.

Again, how are we to take the word 'is' in the sentences 'The number 4 is the result of additively combining 3 and 1' and '"The" number 4 is the result of additively combining 3 and 1'? Is it a mere copula, or does it help to express a logical equation? In the first case, 'the' would have to be left out before 'result', and the sentences would go like this:

'The number 4 is a result of additively combining 3 and 1';
'"The" number 4 is a result of additively combining 3 and 1'.

In that case, the objects that Kerry designates by

'the number 4' and '"the" number 4'

would both fall under the concept

result of additively combining 3 and 1.

And then the only question would be what difference there was between these objects. I am here using the words 'object' and 'concept' in my accustomed way. I should express as follows what Kerry is apparently trying to say:

'The number 4 has those properties, and those alone, which are marks of the concept *result of additively combining 3 and 1*'.

I should then express as follows the sense of the first of our two sentences:

'To be a number 4 is the same as being a result of additive combination of 3 and 1'.

[P] Cf. my essay 'Über Sinn und Bedeutung' cited above.

In that case, what I conjectured just now to have been Kerry's intention could also be put thus:

'The number 4 has those properties, and those alone, which are marks of the concept *a number* 4'.

We need not here decide whether this is true. The inverted commas around the definite article in the | words '"the" number 4' could in that case be omitted.

But in these attempted interpretations we have assumed that in at least one of the two sentences the definite articles in front of 'result' and 'number 4' were inserted only by an oversight. If we take the words as they stand, we can only regard them as having the sense of a logical equation, like:

'The number 4 is none other than the result of additively combining 3 and 1'.

The definite article in front of 'result' is here logically justified only if it is known (1) that there is such a result; (2) that there is not more than one. In that case, the phrase designates an object, and is to be regarded as a proper name. If both of our sentences were to be regarded as logical equations, then, since their right sides are identical, it would follow from them that the number 4 is 'the' number 4, or, if you prefer, that the number 4 is no other than 'the' number 4; and so Kerry's distinction would have been proved untenable. However, it is not my present task to point out contradictions in his exposition; his way of taking the words 'object' and 'concept' is not properly my concern here. I am only trying to set my own usage of these words in a clearer light, and incidentally show that in any case it differs from his, whether that is consistent or not.

I do not at all dispute Kerry's right to use the words 'concept' and 'object' in his own way, if only he would respect my equal right, and admit that with my use of terms I have got hold of a distinction of the highest importance. I admit that there is a quite peculiar obstacle in the way of an understanding with my reader. By a kind of necessity of language, my expressions, taken literally, sometimes miss my thought; I mention an object, when what I intend is a concept. I fully realize that in such cases I was relying upon a reader who would be ready to meet me halfway – who does not begrudge a pinch of salt.

Somebody may think that this is an artificially created difficulty; that there is no need at all to take account of such an unmanageable thing as what I call a concept; that one might, like Kerry, regard an object's falling under a concept as a relation, in which the same thing could occur

205 now as object, now as concept. | The words 'object' and 'concept' would then serve only to indicate the different positions in the relation. This may be done; but anybody who thinks the difficulty is avoided this way is very much mistaken; it is only shifted. For not all the parts of a thought can be complete; at least one must be unsaturated or predicative; otherwise they would not hold together. For example, the sense of the phrase 'the number 2' does not hold together with that of the expression 'the concept *prime number*' without a link. We apply such a link in the sentence 'The number 2 falls under the concept *prime number*'; it is contained in the words 'falls under', which need to be completed in two ways – by a subject and an accusative; and only because their sense is thus unsaturated are they capable of serving as a link. Only when they have been supplemented in this twofold respect do we get a complete sense, a thought. I say that what such words or phrases stand for [*bedeuten*] is a relation. We now get the same difficulty for the relation that we were trying to avoid for the concept. For the words 'the relation of an object to the concept it falls under' designate not a relation but an object; and the three proper names 'the number 2', 'the concept *prime number*', 'the relation of an object to a concept it falls under', hold aloof from one another just as much as the first two do by themselves; however we put them together, we get no sentence. It is thus easy for us to see that the difficulty arising from the unsaturatedness of one part of the thought can indeed be shifted, but not avoided. 'Complete' and 'unsaturated' are of course only figures of speech; but all that I wish or am able to do here is to give hints.

It may make it easier to come to an understanding if the reader compares my work 'Function and Concept'.[14] For over the question what it is that is called a function in Analysis, we come up against the same obstacle; and on thorough investigation it will be found that the obstacle is essential, and founded on the nature of our language; that we cannot avoid a certain inappropriateness of linguistic expression; and that there is nothing for it but to realize this and always take it into account.

[14] Cf. pp. 139–40 above.

Grundgesetze der Arithmetik, *Volume I*[1]

[Volume I of the *Grundgesetze der Arithmetik*, Frege's *magnum opus*, was published in 1893. In this book he sets out to demonstrate formally what was merely sketched informally in the *Grundlagen* – his proposed derivation of arithmetic from logic. In Part I he provides an exposition of his 'Begriffsschrift', his logical system; and in Part II he uses that system to prove the laws of natural numbers. What follows here is most of the Preface and the Introduction, which reveal Frege's motivation and many of his philosophical assumptions, and §§1–7, 26–29 and 32–33 of Part I, explaining some of his symbolism and his general conception of names and definitions.]

Preface

VI   . . .[2] The ideal of a strictly scientific method in mathematics, which I have here sought to realize, and which might well be named after Euclid, I should like to describe as follows. It cannot be required that everything be proved, because that is impossible; but we can demand that all propositions used without proof be expressly declared as such, so that we can clearly see upon what the whole construction is based. We must then strive to reduce the Number[3] of these primitive laws to a minimum, by proving everything that can be proved. Furthermore, and in this I go beyond Euclid, I demand that all modes of inference used be specified in advance. Otherwise we cannot be sure of satisfying the first demand. This ideal I believe I have now essentially achieved. Only on a few points could even stricter demands be made. In order to secure more flexibility and not to sink into excessive prolixity, I have allowed

[1] Translated by Michael Beaney. Page numbers in the margin are from the original edition. In accordance with the policy adopted in the present volume, 'Bedeutung' and cognates such as 'gleichbedeutend' and 'bedeutungsvoll' have been left untranslated, and the verb 'bedeuten' translated as 'refer to' (but with the German always in square brackets following it), unless otherwise indicated. For discussion of this policy, and the problems involved in translating these terms, see the Introduction, §4 above.
[2] Omitted here are the first three paragraphs (pp. V–VI), which contain brief remarks on the formal derivations in the book.
[3] On the translation of 'Anzahl' as 'Number' (with a capital 'N'), see fn. 6 on p. 91 above.

myself to make tacit use of the interchangeability of subcomponents (conditions)[4] and of the possibility of amalgamating identical subcomponents,[5] and have not reduced the modes of inference to the smallest possible number. Anyone who knows my book *Begriffsschrift* will be able to gather from it how the strictest demands could be satisfied here too, but likewise that this would result in a considerable increase in volume.

VII   Apart from this, I believe, the only things that could justly | be made an issue of in this book concern not the rigour but the choice of course of proof and the intermediate steps. There are often several possible paths that a proof can take; I have not tried to traverse them all, and so it is possible, even probable, that I have not always chosen the shortest. Let anyone who finds fault in this respect do better. Other matters will be debatable. Some might perhaps have preferred to circumscribe more widely the permissible modes of inference and thereby to achieve greater flexibility and brevity. But a halt must be called to this somewhere, if my declared ideal is endorsed at all; and wherever a halt is called, people can always say: it would have been better to permit still more modes of inference.

The completeness in the chains of inference ensures that each axiom, each assumption, each hypothesis, or whatever one wants to call it, upon which a proof is based, is brought to light; and so a basis is gained for judging the epistemological nature of the law that is proved. It is frequently said that arithmetic is only a more highly developed logic; but that remains disputable so long as transitions occur in the proofs that do not take place in accordance with recognized logical laws, but appear to rest on intuitive knowledge. Only if these transitions are analysed into simple logical steps can one be convinced that nothing but logic lies at the base. I have put together everything that can make it easier to judge whether the chains of inference are conclusive and the underpinning firm. If anyone should find anything defective, he must be able to state exactly where the defect, according to him, is located: in the fundamental laws, in the definitions, in the rules or in their application at a certain point. If everything is found in order, then the grounds on which every single theorem rests are precisely known. A dispute can break out here, so far as I can see, only with regard to my fundamental law concerning value-ranges (V), which has not yet perhaps been expressly formulated by logicians, although one has it in mind, for example, when speaking of extensions of concepts.[6] I hold it to be purely logical. At any rate the place is hereby indicated where the decision must be made.

---

[4] E.g. transforming 'If A, then if B, then C' into 'If B, then if A, then C'.

[5] E.g. transforming 'If A, then A, then B' into 'If A, then B'.

[6] For discussion of Axiom V, see the Introduction, pp. 7–8, 18–20 above. Axiom V did indeed turn out to be disputable: Frege himself later held it responsible for the contradiction that Russell discovered in his system. See pp. 253–4, 279–89 below.

My aims require many deviations from what is usual in mathematics. The requirements on the rigour of proofs inevitably result in greater length. Anyone who does not bear this in mind will indeed be surprised at how long-winded the proof often is here of a proposition that he believes can be immediately grasped in a single act of understanding. This will be particularly striking if we compare Dedekind's work *Was sind und was sollen die Zahlen?*,[7] the most thorough work on the foundation of arithmetic that has come to my attention in the last few years.
VIII In much less space it pursues | the laws of arithmetic much further than is done here. This brevity is admittedly only achieved by not really proving much at all. Dedekind often says only that the proof follows from such and such propositions; he uses dots, as in '$\mathfrak{M}(A, B, C . . .)$'; nowhere is there to be found a list of the logical or other laws that are taken by him as basic, and even if there were, we could not possibly check whether no others were actually used, since for that to happen the proofs would have to be not merely indicated but carried out in full. Dedekind too is of the opinion that the theory of numbers is a part of logic; but his work hardly helps to confirm this opinion, since the expressions 'system' and 'a thing belongs to a thing' employed by him are not usual in logic and are not reduced to what is recognized as logical. I do not say this as a reproach; for his way of proceeding may have been the most suitable for his purpose; I say it only to set my own aims in a clearer light by contrast. The length of a proof is not to be measured with a ruler. One can easily make a proof look short on paper by missing out many intermediate links in the chain of inference and letting much be merely indicated. One is generally satisfied if every step in the proof is obviously correct, and this is fine if one merely wants to be convinced of the truth of the proposition to be proved. If it is a question, however, of gaining an insight into the nature of this obviousness, this way of proceeding is not enough, but one must write down all intermediate steps, to let the full light of consciousness fall upon them. Mathematicians are normally only concerned with the content of a proposition and with the fact that it is proved. What is new here is not the content of the proposition, but how the proof is carried out – on what foundations it rests. That this essentially different standpoint requires another method of treatment should not be surprising. If one of our propositions is derived in the usual way, it will be easy to overlook a proposition that does not seem necessary to the proof. By properly thinking through the proof, I believe, the indispensability of the proposition will be seen, unless quite a different path is to be taken. One may thus occasionally find in our propositions conditions that at first sight seem unnecessary, but that

---

[7] Originally published in 1888; translated in R. Dedekind, *Essays on the Theory of Numbers*, ed. and tr. W. Beman (New York: Dover, 1963).

nevertheless turn out to be necessary, or at least to be dispensable only by means of a proposition that is specially proved.

With this book I carry out a project that I already had in mind at the time of my *Begriffsschrift* of 1879 and announced in my *Foundations* IX *of Arithmetic* of 1884.[A] My aim here is | to justify in detail the view of Number that I explained in the latter book. The most fundamental of my results I expressed there in §46 by saying that a statement of number contains an assertion about a concept;[8] and the account here rests upon this. If anyone takes a different view, let him try to base upon it a consistent and useful symbolic system, and he will see that it does not work. In language the situation is admittedly not so clear; but if one looks carefully one finds that here too a statement of number always involves mention of a concept, not a group, an aggregate or suchlike, and that where these do in fact occur, the group or the aggregate is always determined by a concept, that is, by the properties that an object must have to belong to the group, whilst what makes the group a group, the system a system – the relations of members to one another – is completely irrelevant to the Number.

The reason why the implementation appears so long after the announcement lies in part in internal changes in my *Begriffsschrift*, which forced me to discard an almost completed manuscript. These improvements may be briefly mentioned here. The primitive signs used in my *Begriffsschrift* are to be found again here with one exception. Instead of the three parallel lines I have preferred the ordinary sign of equality [*Gleichheit*], since I have convinced myself that it has in arithmetic precisely the *Bedeutung* that I wish to designate [*bezeichnen*]. I use, that is, the word 'equal' ['*gleich*'] with the same *Bedeutung* as 'coincident with' ['*zusammenfallend mit*'] or 'identical with' ['*identisch mit*'], and this is also how the sign of equality is actually used in arithmetic. The objection that might be raised to this will probably rest on an inadequate distinction between sign [*Zeichen*] and what is designated [*Bezeichnetem*]. Admittedly, in the equation '$2^2 = 2 + 2$' the left-hand sign is different from the right-hand sign; but both designate [*bezeichnen*] or refer to [*bedeuten*] the same number.[B] To the old primitive signs two more have now been added: the smooth breathing [*Spiritus lenis*] for designating the value-range of a function and a sign to represent the definite article of ordinary language.[9] The introduction of value-ranges of functions is

[A] Cf. the Introduction and §§90 and 91 of my *Foundations of Arithmetic* [see pp. 84–91, 123–4 above].

[B] I admittedly also say: the sense of the right-hand sign is different from that of the left-hand sign; but the *Bedeutung* is the same. Cf. my essay on *Sinn* and *Bedeutung* [pp. 151–71 above].

[8] See pp. 98–9 above.

[9] *GG*, I, §§9–11; see Appendix 2 below.

an essential advance, to which a far greater flexibility is owed. The earlier derivative signs can now be replaced by other, rather simpler ones, although the definitions of a many-one relation, of following in a series, and of a mapping are essentially the same as those I gave partly in my

X   *Begriffsschrift* and partly in my *Foundations of Arithmetic*.[10] | But value-ranges also have a quite fundamental importance; I even define Number itself as an extension of a concept, and extensions of concepts count for me as value-ranges. So we simply could not manage without them. The old primitive signs that appear again outwardly unchanged, whose algorithm has also hardly changed, are nevertheless provided with different explanations. The earlier content stroke [*Inhaltsstrich*] reappears as the horizontal [*Wagerechter*].[11] These are consequences of a comprehensive development of my logical views. I had earlier distinguished two elements in that whose external form is an assertoric sentence: (1) the recognition of truth, (2) the content that is recognized as true. The content I called judgeable content. I have now split this up into what I call thought and truth-value. This is the result of the distinction between the sense and *Bedeutung* of a sign. In this case the sense of the sentence is the thought and its *Bedeutung* the truth-value. In addition to this there is the recognition that the truth-value is the True. I distinguish, that is, two truth-values: the True and the False. I have justified this in detail in my above-mentioned essay on sense and *Bedeutung*. Here it may simply be noted that only thus can indirect discourse be correctly construed. The thought, that is, which is normally the sense of a sentence, becomes in indirect discourse its *Bedeutung*. How much simpler and sharper everything becomes through the introduction of truth-values only a detailed study of this book can show. These advantages alone provide strong support for my view, which admittedly may seem strange at first sight. In addition, the essence of a function as distinguished from an object is characterized more sharply than in my *Begriffsschrift*. From this results further the distinction between first- and second-level functions. As I explained in my lecture on 'Function and Concept', concepts and relations are functions as I have extended the *Bedeutung* of this word, and so we also have to distinguish first- and second-level concepts, equal-levelled and unequal-levelled relations.[12]

As one sees, the years have not passed in vain since the appearance

---

[10] Frege's definitions of a relation being many-one (*eindeutig*) and of following in a series are first given in *BS*, Part III (see pp. 75–7 above); cf. *GL*, §§72 and 79 (see pp. 117–20 above). A relation is one-one (*beiderseits eindeutig*, as Frege calls it) if it is both many-one and one-many. Frege's notion of a mapping (*Abbildung*) is only made explicit in *GG*, I, §38. A many-one relation *maps* the concept whose extension is Γ onto the concept whose extension is Δ if it correlates each member of Γ with one member or another of Δ.

[11] Compare *BS*, §2 (pp. 52–3 above) with *GG*, I, §5 (pp. 215–16 below).

[12] See *FC*, pp. 146–8 above.

of my *Begriffsschrift* and my *Foundations*: they have brought the work to maturity. But as I have to admit, precisely that which I recognize as an essential advance stands as a great obstacle in the way of the circulation and influence of my book. And that in which I see not the least part of its value, the rigorous completeness of the chains of inference, will earn it little thanks, I fear. I have moved further away from traditional

XI   conceptions | and in doing so have imposed on my views a paradoxical character. An expression that crops up here or there on briefly flicking through may easily appear strange and produce an unfavourable prejudice. I myself can certainly appreciate to some extent the resistance which my reforms will meet, since to make them I had first to overcome something similar in myself. For I did not achieve them by chance or from any desire for reform, but was forced by the things themselves.

With this I come to the second reason for the delay: the discouragement that occasionally overcame me in the face of the cool reception – or more precisely, the lack of reception – of my above-mentioned works by mathematicians[C] and the adverse currents in scientific thought against which my book would have to struggle. First impressions alone must frighten people off: unfamiliar signs, pages of nothing but strange formulae. So at times I turned to other things. But I could not lock away in my desk the results of my thinking, which seemed valuable to me, for any length of time, and the labour expended required yet more labour so as not to be in vain. So the subject did not let go of me. In a case such as this, where the value of a book cannot be recognized by skimming through, criticism ought to come to my help. But criticism is in general too badly paid. A critic can never hope to be remunerated for the trouble that a thorough study of this book is likely to cause. It only remains to me to hope that someone may have built up enough confidence in the matter beforehand to expect sufficient reward in the mental profit, and that he will then publish the results of his careful examination. Not that only a glowing review could satisfy me; on the contrary! I would far rather have an attack based on a thorough knowledge of my work than praise in general terms that fails to touch the heart of the matter . . .[13]

XII   Otherwise the prospects of my book are admittedly slight. At any rate I must give up on all mathematicians who, on coming across logical expressions such as 'concept', 'relation', 'judgement', think: *metaphysica*

[C] One seeks in vain for [a review of] my *Grundlagen der Arithmetik* in the *Jahrbuch über die Fortschritte der Mathematik*. Researchers in the same area – Dedekind, Otto Stolz, von Helmholtz – seem not to know my works. Nor does Kronecker mention them in his essay on the concept of number.

---

[13] The next sentence and the following paragraph are omitted. Frege offers some tips on how to approach his book – which sections to skip on a first reading, etc.

sunt, non leguntur! – and equally on philosophers who, on catching sight of a formula, cry: *mathematica sunt, non leguntur!* – and there are more than a few such people. Perhaps the number of mathematicians who trouble themselves over the foundation of their science is not at all great, and even these often seem to be in a great hurry to put the basic elements behind them. And I hardly dare hope that my reasons for the meticulous rigour and associated prolixity will convince many of them.

XIII   What is once established, after all, has | great power over the mind. If I compare arithmetic with a tree that opens out above into a multitude of methods and theorems, whilst the root pushes into the depths, then it seems to me that the growth of the root, at least in Germany, is weak. Even in a work that might be included in this movement, E. Schröder's *Algebra der Logik*, growth at the top soon regains the upper hand, before any greater depth is reached, causing a bending upwards and an opening out into methods and theorems.

The widespread tendency to recognize as existing only what can be perceived by the senses is also prejudicial to my book. What cannot be so perceived one tries to deny or else to ignore. Now the objects of arithmetic, the numbers, are of a non-sensible kind; how is one to account for them? Very simply! The numerical signs are declared to be the numbers. In the signs one then has something perceptible, and that is, of course, the main thing. Admittedly the signs have quite different properties from the numbers themselves; but what does that matter? One simply imputes to them the desired properties by so-called definitions. How there can be a definition where no question at all arises as to the connection between sign and what is designated is admittedly a puzzle. As far as possible, sign and what is designated are merged indistinguishably together; depending on what is required, one can then make assertions of existence by pointing to tangibility,[D] or else bring out the real properties of numbers. Sometimes, it seems, the numerical signs are regarded as chess pieces and the so-called definitions as rules of the game. The sign then designates nothing, but is the object itself. One little thing is admittedly overlooked, namely, that we express a thought by '$3^2 + 4^2 = 5^2$', whilst a position of chess pieces states nothing. Where one is satisfied with such superficialities, there is admittedly no basis for a deeper understanding.

It is important to make clear here what definition is and what can be achieved by means of it. It is, it seems, frequently imbued with creative power, whereas nothing more is actually involved than that something is sharply delimited and designated by a name. Just as the geographer

---

[D] Cf. E. Heine, 'Die Elemente der Funktionslehre', in Crelle's *Journal* [*für die reine und angewandte Mathematik*], Vol. 74, p. 173: 'As regards definition I adopt the purely formalist position, by calling *numbers* certain tangible signs, so that the existence of these numbers is not therefore placed in question'.

does not create a sea when he draws boundary lines and says: I shall call the part of the expanse of water bounded by these lines the Yellow Sea, so too the mathematician cannot really create anything by his act of definition. Nor can we by mere definition conjure into a thing a property it does not have in the first place, except for that of now being called by whatever name it may have been given. But that an | oval figure drawn in ink on paper should acquire by a definition the property of yielding one when added to one, I can only regard as a scientific superstition. We could just as well make a lazy pupil diligent by mere definition. Confusion easily arises here by failing to distinguish between concept and object. If we say: 'A square is a rectangle in which the adjacent sides are equal', we define the concept *square* by specifying what properties something must have in order to fall under this concept. These properties I call marks [*Merkmale*] of the concept. But, it should be noted, these marks of the concept are not its properties.[14] The concept *square* is not a rectangle, only such objects as may fall under this concept are rectangles, just as the concept *black cloth* is neither black nor a cloth. Whether there are such objects is not immediately known from the definition. Now suppose one defines, for example, the number zero by saying: it is something that yields one when added to one. With that one has defined a concept, by specifying what property an object must have in order to fall under the concept. But this property is not a property of the defined concept. It is frequently imagined, it seems, that by the definition something has been created that yields one when added to one. A great delusion! Neither has the defined concept this property nor does the definition guarantee that the concept is realized. That first requires an investigation. Only when it has been proved that there is one and only one object with the required property is one in the position to give this object the proper name 'zero'. To create zero is therefore impossible. I have explained this repeatedly, but, it seems, without success.[E]

Within the prevailing logic too there is no hope of understanding the distinction that I draw between the mark of a concept and the property of an object;[F] for it seems to be infected through and through by psychology. If one considers, instead of things themselves, only their subjective representations [*Abbilder*], the ideas [*Vorstellungen*], then naturally all the finer objective distinctions are lost, and others appear instead that are logically completely worthless. And this brings me to speak of what stands in the way of the influence of my book on logicians. It is

XIV

[E] Mathematicians who venture reluctantly into the labyrinths of philosophy are requested to break off reading the Preface at this point.
[F] In B. Erdmann's *Logik* I find no trace of this important distinction.

14 Cf. *GL*, §53 (pp. 102–3 above); *CO*, pp. 189–90 above.

the corrupting intrusion of psychology into logic. What is crucial to the treatment of the science of logic is the conception of logical laws, and XV   this in turn is connected with how | the word 'true' is understood. That the logical laws should be guiding principles for thought in the attainment of truth is generally admitted at the outset; but it is only too easily forgotten. The ambiguity [*Doppelsinn*] of the word 'law' is fatal here. In one sense it states what is, in the other it prescribes what should be. Only in the latter sense can the logical laws be called laws of thought, in laying down how one should think. Any law that states what is can be conceived as prescribing that one should think in accordance with it, and is therefore in that sense a law of thought. This holds for geometrical and physical laws no less than for logical laws. The latter then only deserve the name 'law of thought' with more right if it should be meant by this that they are the most general laws, which prescribe universally how one should think if one is to think at all. But the expression 'law of thought' tempts us into viewing these laws as governing thinking in the same way as the laws of nature govern events in the external world. They can then be nothing other than psychological laws, since thinking is a mental process. And if logic were concerned with these psychological laws, then it would be a part of psychology. And so it is in fact conceived. These laws of thought can then be conceived as guiding principles in so far as they indicate a mean, just as we can say what counts as normal human digestion, grammatical speech, or fashionable dress. We can then only say: the *holding as true* [*Fürwahrgehalten*] of things by people conforms on average with these laws, at present and to the best of our knowledge; if one therefore wants to remain in accordance with this mean, one will conform with them. But just as what is fashionable today ceases to be fashionable after a while and is not at present fashionable amongst the Chinese, so too the psychological laws of thought can only be laid down as authoritative with qualifications. This is certainly so if logic is concerned with things *being held as true* [*Fürwahrgehaltenwerden*] rather than with their *being true* [*Wahrsein*]! And these are what the psychological logicians confuse. Thus B. Erdmann in the first volume of his *Logik*[G] (pp. 272–5) equates truth with general validity and bases this on the general certainty regarding the object of judgement, and this in turn on the general agreement amongst those who judge. So in the end truth is reduced to the *holding as true* of individuals. In response I can only say: *being true* is quite different from *being held as true*, whether by one, or by many, or by all, and is in no way to be reduced to it. There XVI   is no contradiction in something | being true which is held by everyone as false. I understand by logical laws not psychological laws of *holding*

[G] Halle a. S.: Max Niemeyer, 1892.

as true, but laws of *being true*.[15] If it is true that I am writing this in my room on 13 July 1893, whilst the wind howls outside, then it remains true even if everyone should later hold it as false. If being true is thus independent of being recognized as true by anyone, then the laws of truth are not psychological laws, but boundary stones set in an eternal foundation, which our thought can overflow but not dislodge. And because of this they are authoritative for our thought if it wants to attain truth. They do not stand in the relation to thought that the laws of grammar stand to language so that they express the essence of our human thought and change as it changes. Of course, Erdmann's conception of logical laws is quite different. He doubts their absolute, eternal validity and wants to restrict them to our thought as it is at present (pp. 375ff.). 'Our thought' can indeed only mean human thought as it is known to date. Accordingly, the possibility remains open of discovering humans or other beings could make judgements that contradict our logical laws. What if this were to happen? Erdmann would say: here we see that these principles are not universally valid. Certainly! – if these are supposed to be psychological laws, then their linguistic expression must make known the kind of being whose thought is empirically governed by them. I would say: there are thus beings who do not as we do immediately recognize certain truths, but have to rely perhaps on the longer path of induction. But what if beings were even found whose laws of thought directly contradicted our own and therefore frequently led to contrary results in practice as well? The psychological logician could only simply acknowledge this and say: those laws are valid for them, these for us. I would say: here we have a hitherto unknown kind of madness. Anyone who understands logical laws as prescribing how one should think, as laws of *being true*, not as natural laws of human beings' *holding as true*, will ask: who is right? Whose laws of *holding as true* are in accord with the laws of *being true*? The psychological logician cannot ask this, since he would thereby be recognizing laws of *being true*, which would not be psychological. The sense of the word 'true' could not be more wickedly falsified than by incorporating a relation to those who judge! But surely, it will be objected, the sentence 'I am hungry' can be true for one person and false for another. The sentence certainly, but not the thought, since the word 'I' XVII   in the mouth of the other refers to [*bedeutet*] a different person, | and hence the sentence uttered by the other expresses a different thought. All specifications of place, time, and so on, belong to the thought whose truth is at issue; *being true* itself is placeless and timeless. How does the

[15] Here, and in similar contexts in what follows, 'Gesetze des Wahrseins' is translated as 'laws of *being true*', to capture better Frege's contrast between these laws and psychological laws of *holding as true* [*psychologische Gesetze des Fürwahrhaltens*]. Elsewhere, as in the next but one sentence, the phrase is translated more simply as 'laws of truth'.

Principle of Identity now really read? Like this, for example: 'It is impossible for people in the year 1893 to recognize an object as different from itself'? Or like this: 'Every object is identical with itself'? The former law concerns human beings and contains a specification of time; in the latter there is no talk either of human beings or of a time. The latter is a law of *being true*, the former a law of human beings' *holding as true*. Their content is quite different, and they are independent of one another, so that neither can be inferred from the other. That is why it is very confusing to call both by the same name, 'the Principle of Identity'. Such mixing of fundamentally different things is to blame for the murky unclarity that we find amongst the psychological logicians.

Now the question why and with what right we recognize a logical law as true, logic can only answer by reducing it to another logical law. Where that is not possible, logic can give no answer. Leaving aside logic, one can say: we are forced to make judgements by our nature and external circumstances, and if we make judgements, we cannot reject this law – of identity, for example; we must recognize it if we are not to throw our thought into confusion and in the end renounce judgement altogether. I do not wish to either dispute or endorse this view and only remark that what we have here is not a logical implication. What is given is not a ground of *being true*, but of our *holding as true*. And furthermore, this impossibility of our rejecting the law does not prevent us from supposing that there are beings who do reject it; but it does prevent us from supposing that these beings are right in doing so; it also prevents us from doubting whether we or they are right. At least this goes for me. If others dare to recognize and doubt a law in the same breath, then it seems to me like trying to jump out of one's own skin, against which I can only urgently warn. Anyone who has once recognized a law of truth has thereby also recognized a law that prescribes how judgements should be made, wherever, whenever and by whomever they may be made.

Surveying it all, it seems to me that different conceptions of truth lie at the source of the dispute. For me truth is something objective and independent of those who judge; for psychological logicians it is not. What B. Erdmann calls 'objective certainty' | is only a general recognition by those who judge, which is therefore not independent of them but can change with their mental constitution.

We can generalize this still further: I recognize a domain of the objective but non-actual,[16] whereas the psychological logicians automatically

XVIII

---

[16] Furth translates 'ein Gebiet des Objectiven, Nichtwirklichen' as 'a domain of what is objective, which is distinct from that of what is actual' (*BLA*, pp. 15–16), which gives a misleading impression of Frege's conception. For Frege, the realm of the objective includes *both* the whole realm of the actual *and* part of the realm of the non-actual (the non-subjective part), the essential point being that non-actuality does not imply non-objectivity. Cf. *GL*, §26 (see p. 96 above).

assume that the non-actual is subjective. And yet it is not at all obvious why what persists independently of anyone's making judgements is actual [*wirklich*], that is, must clearly be capable of acting [*wirken*] directly or indirectly on the senses. Such a connection between the concepts [of objectivity and actuality] is not to be found. Examples can even be cited that show the opposite. The number one, for example, is not readily taken as actual, except by followers of J. S. Mill. On the other hand, it is impossible to assign to every person his own number one, since it would first have to be investigated how far the properties of these ones coincided. And if one person said 'Once one is one' and another 'Once one is two', then each could only register the difference and say: your one has that property, mine this. There could be no question of a dispute as to who was right, or of an attempt at explanation; for there would be no common object of understanding. Obviously this is quite contrary to the sense of the word 'one' and the sense of the sentence 'Once one is one'. Since the number one, being the same for everyone, confronts everyone in the same way, it can just as little be investigated by psychological observation as the Moon. Whatever ideas [*Vorstellungen*] of the number one there may be in individual minds, these are still to be distinguished from the number one itself, just as ideas of the Moon are to be distinguished from the Moon itself. Because the psychological logicians fail to recognize the possibility of the objective non-actual, they take concepts as ideas and thereby consign them to psychology. But the true situation asserts itself too powerfully for this to be easily carried through. And thus a vacillation arises in the use of the word 'idea' ['*Vorstellung*'], appearing at one moment to refer to [*bedeuten*] something that belongs to the mental life of an individual and that combines with other ideas with which it is associated, according to psychological laws, and at the next to something that confronts everyone in the same way, an owner of the idea being neither mentioned nor even merely presupposed. These two uses are incompatible; for those associations and combinations only happen in individual minds and only happen to something that is quite as private to the individual as his pleasure or pain. One should never forget that the ideas of different people, however similar they may be – something which cannot, incidentally, be exactly determined – do not coincide but are to be distinguished. Each has his own ideas, which are not those of another. Here, of course, I understand XIX 'idea' in the psychological sense. The | vacillating use of this word causes confusion and helps the psychological logicans to conceal their failings. When will an end be put to this once and for all! Everything is eventually dragged into the realm of psychology; the boundary between the objective and the subjective disappears more and more, and even actual objects are treated psychologically as ideas. For what is *actual* other than a predicate? And what are logical predicates other than ideas?

Thus everything leads into idealism and with perfect logical consistency into solipsism.[17] If everyone designated something different by the name 'Moon', namely, one of his ideas, just as he might express his pain by the cry 'Ow!', then admittedly the psychological way of looking at things would be justified; but a dispute about the properties of the Moon would be pointless: one person could quite well assert of his Moon the opposite of what another person, with equal right, said of his. If we could grasp nothing but what is in ourselves, then a [genuine] conflict of opinions, a reciprocity of understanding, would be impossible, since there would be no common ground, and no idea in the psychological sense can be such a ground. There would be no logic that could be appealed to as arbiter in the conflict of opinions . . .[18]

XXIV   . . . If we want to emerge from the subjective at all, then we must conceive of knowledge [*Erkennen*] as an activity that does not create what is known but grasps what already exists. The metaphor of grasping is ideally suited to elucidate the matter. If I grasp a pencil, then various things take place in my body: stimulation of nerves, changes in the tension and pressure of muscles, tendons and bones, changes in the circulation of blood. But the totality of these events neither is the pencil nor creates it. The pencil exists independently of these events. And it is essential to grasping that something is there to be grasped; inner changes alone are not the grasping. So too what we mentally grasp exists independently of this activity, of the ideas and their changes that belong to or accompany this grasping, and is neither the totality of these changes nor created by it as a part of our mental life.

Let us now see how the finer objective distinctions become blurred for the psychological logicians. This has already been mentioned in the case of mark and property. With this is connected the distinction between object and concept, which I have stressed, as well as that between first- and second-level concepts. These distinctions are not, of course, recognizable by the psychological logicians; for them everything is just idea.

XXV   They thus also lack | a correct conception of judgements that we express in language by 'there is'. This existence Erdmann (*Logik* I, p. 311) confuses with actuality, which, as we saw, is also not clearly distinguished from objectivity. Of what thing are we really asserting that it is actual when we say that there are square roots of four? Is it the number two or -2? But neither the one nor the other is named here in any way. And if I were to say that the number two acts or is active or is actual, then

---

[17] Cf. *PWLB*, pp. 244ff. below; *T*, pp. 336ff. below.

[18] The next five pages (pp. XIX–XXIV) are omitted here. To illustrate the points he has been making in criticizing psychological logic, Frege takes the specific example of Erdmann's *Logik*. He quotes a number of passages to show, in particular, that Erdmann has an inadequate conception of objectivity and of the distinction between an idea and the object of which it is an idea.

this would be false and quite different from what I mean [*sagen will*] by the sentence 'There are square roots of four'. The confusion at issue here is almost the grossest that there could possibly be; for it does not involve concepts of the same level, but rather a first-level concept is confused with a second-level concept.[19] This is typical of the obtuseness of psychological logic. Once a somewhat clearer viewpoint has become established, it may seem surprising that such a mistake could be made by a professional logician; but, of course, the distinction between first- and second-level concepts must first have been grasped before the magnitude of this mistake can be gauged, and psychological logic will certainly be incapable of this. What stands most in the way here is that its advocates place such extraordinary value on psychological depth, which is really nothing but psychological falsification of logic. And that is how our thick logic books come into being, swollen with unhealthy psychological fat, which covers all finer forms. Thus a fruitful collaboration between mathematicians and logicians is made impossible. Whilst the mathematician defines objects, concepts and relations, the psychological logician observes the coming and going of ideas, and basically, to him, the mathematician's definitions can only appear foolish, since they do not convey the essence of ideation [*Vorstellung*]. He looks into his psychological peepshow and says to the mathematician: I see nothing at all of what you are defining. And he can only answer: No wonder! For it is not where you are looking.

This may be enough to set my logical viewpoint in a clearer light by contrast. There appears such a world of difference between me and psychological logicians that there is no prospect of influencing them through my book at present. It seems to me as if the tree planted by me would have to raise an enormous weight of stone to make space and light for itself. And yet I do not want to give up all hope that my book might later help to overthrow psychological logic. There is surely bound to be some recognition of my book by mathematicians, which will force psychological logic to come to terms with it. And I believe I can expect XVI some support from this quarter; | mathematicians, after all, are basically engaged on a common crusade against the psychological logicians. The moment the latter just condescend to deal seriously with my book, if only to refute it, I believe I have won. For the whole of Part II is really a test of my logical convictions. It is unlikely from the outset that such a structure could be built on an insecure, defective foundation. Anyone who has different convictions can just try to erect a similar structure upon them, and he will, I believe, come to realize that it does not work, or at least that it does not work so well. And I will only be able to

---

[19] On the distinction between first- and second-level concepts, see *GL*, §53 (pp. 102–3 above); *FC*, p. 146 above; *CO*, pp. 189–90 above.

accept a refutation if someone shows, by actually doing it, that a better, more durable edifice can be erected on different fundamental convictions, or if someone proves to me that my principles lead to obviously false conclusions. But no one will succeed in this. And so may this book, then, even if belatedly, contribute to a renewal of logic.

Jena, July 1893

1   **Introduction**

In my *Foundations of Arithmetic*[H] I sought to make it probable that arithmetic is a branch of logic and need take no ground of proof from either experience or intuition. In this book this will now be demonstrated by deriving the simplest laws of Numbers by logical means alone. But for this to be convincing, much greater demands must be placed on proof than is usual in arithmetic.[I] A limited set of rules and modes of inference must be laid down beforehand, and no step should be taken that is not in accord with one of these. One should thus not be satisfied, as mathematicians have almost always been up to now, that a transition to a new judgement is self-evidently correct, but one must analyse it into the simple logical steps that compose it, and there are often more than a few of these. This way no presupposition can remain unnoticed; every axiom that is needed must be revealed. It is precisely the presuppositions that are tacitly made without clear awareness that obscure insight into the epistemological nature of a law.

For such an undertaking to succeed, the concepts that are needed must, of course, be clearly grasped. This holds especially of what mathematicians like to call a 'set'. Dedekind[J] uses the word 'system' with much the same intention. But despite the explanation that appeared in my *Foundations* four years earlier, he lacks any clear insight into the heart of the matter, though he sometimes comes close to it, as when he says (p. 2): 'Such a system S . . . is completely determined if, for every thing, it is determined whether it is an element of S or not. The system S is therefore the same as the system T, in symbols $S = T$, if every ele-
2   ment of S is also an | element of T, and every element of T is also an element of S.' In other passages, however, he goes astray, e.g. in the following (pp. 1–2): 'It very often happens that different things a, b, c . . . regarded for some reason from a common point of view, are put together in the mind, and it is then said that they form a *system S*'. A hint of the truth is indeed contained in talk of the 'common point of

---

[H] Breslau, 1884 [see pp. 84–129 above].
[I] Cf. my *Foundations*, §90 [pp. 123–4 above].
[J] *Was sind und was sollen die Zahlen?* (Braunschweig, 1888) [tr. in Dedekind, *ETN*].

view'; but 'regarding', 'putting together in the mind' is no objective characteristic. I ask: in whose mind? If they are put together in one mind, but not in another, do they then form a system? What may be put together in my mind must certainly be in my mind. Do things outside me, then, not form systems? Is a system a subjective construction in the individual mind? Is the constellation Orion therefore a system? And what are its elements? The stars, the molecules or the atoms? The following passage is worth noting (p. 2): 'For uniformity of expression it helps if we also allow the special case in which a system *S* consists of a *single* (one and only one) element *a*, i.e. in which the thing *a* is an element of *S*, but every thing different from *a* is not an element of *S*'. It transpires (p. 3) that this is to be understood as implying that every element *s* of a system *S* can itself be regarded as a system. Since in this case element and system coincide, it is here especially clear that according to Dedekind, the elements actually constitute the system. E. Schröder, in his *Vorlesungen über die Algebra der Logik*,[K] advances a step further than Dedekind, in drawing attention to the connection between these systems and concepts, which Dedekind seems to have overlooked. In fact, what Dedekind really means [*meint*] when he calls a system part of a system (p. 2) is either the subordination of a concept to a concept or the falling of an object under a concept, cases which neither he nor Schröder distinguish, due to a shared misconception; for Schröder, too, basically sees the elements as what constitute his *classes*. An empty class should not really occur, on his view, any more than an empty system should, on Dedekind's view; yet the need for it that arises from the nature of things makes itself felt on the two writers in different ways. After the passage just quoted, Dedekind goes on: 'On the other hand, for certain reasons, we shall totally exclude here the empty system, which contains no element at all, although for other investigations it may be convenient to invent it'. According to this, then, such an invention is allowed; only for certain reasons do we refrain from it. Schröder dares to invent | an empty class. Both are thus in agreement, it seems, with many mathematicians, that one is free to invent something that is not there, even something that is unthinkable; for if the elements form the system, then the system is destroyed at the same time as the elements. As to where the limits of such free invention lie, or whether there are any limits at all, there is little clarity and agreement to be found; and yet the correctness of a proof may depend on it. I believe that these questions have been settled, for all reasonable people, in my *Foundations of Arithmetic* (§§92ff.)[20] and in

3

[K] Leipzig, 1890, p. 253. [The reference here seems wrong; p. 100 is a more likely source. Frege later published a critique of Schröder's book: *CES*.]

[20] Frege is referring to his critique of formalism; a summary is provided on pp. 124–5 above.

my paper 'On Formal Theories of Arithmetic'.[21] Schröder invents his null class and thereby becomes entangled in great difficulties.[L] Thus whilst both Schröder and Dedekind lack any clear insight, the true situation nevertheless makes itself felt wherever a system is to be determined. Dedekind then cites properties that a thing must have in order to belong to a system, i.e. he defines a concept by its marks.[M] Now if a concept is constituted by its marks, not by the objects that fall under it, then there are no difficulties or doubts at all concerning an empty concept. Admittedly, then, an object can never at the same time be a concept; and a concept under which only one object falls should not be confused with this object. In the end, it thus remains the case that a statement of number contains an assertion about a concept.[N] I have reduced Number to the relation of equinumerosity [*Gleichzahligkeit*] and the latter to many-one correlation [*eindeutige Zuordnung*].[22] The same holds for the word 'correlation' as for the word 'set'. Both are now widely used in mathematics, yet a deeper insight into what they are really intended to designate is largely absent. If I am right in thinking that arithmetic is a branch of pure logic, then a purely logical expression must be chosen for 'correlation'. I take the word 'relation' ['*Beziehung*']. Concept and relation are the foundation stones upon which I erect my structure.

But even when the concepts have been clearly grasped, it would be hard, indeed almost impossible, without special notation [*Hilfsmittel*],[23] to satisfy the demands that we must here place on proof. My *Begriffsschrift* is just such a notation, and my first task will be to explain it. The following preliminary remarks may be made. It | is not always possible to define everything properly, since it is precisely our concern to go back to what is logically simple, which as such is not really definable. I must then be satisfied with indicating what I mean [*meine*] by hints. I must above all strive to be understood, and I shall therefore try to develop things gradually, without going for full generality and definitive formulation right from the beginning. One may well be surprised at the frequent use of inverted commas; I use them to distinguish the cases where I am speaking of a sign itself from the cases where I am speaking of its *Bedeutung*. However pedantic this may appear, I do regard it as necessary. It is strange how an imprecise spoken or written form of expression,

---

[L] Cf. E. G. Husserl, *Göttingischen gelehrte Anzeigen*, 1891, No. 7, p. 272, where, however, the problems are not solved. [Cf. fn. 20 on p. 179 above.]

[M] On *concept, object, property, mark* [*Merkmal*], cf. my *Foundations*, §§38, 47, 53 [pp. 97, 99–100, 102–3 above] and my essay 'On Concept and Object' [pp. 181–93 above].

[N] §46 of my *Foundations* [pp. 98–9 above].

[21] *FTA*, which also contains a critique of formalism.

[22] On this, see pp. 109–18 above.

[23] 'Hilfsmittel' would literally be rendered as 'means of help' or 'aid', but in this context Frege clearly has in mind the help that is provided by an adequate symbolism.

which may originally only have been used for reasons of convenience and brevity, yet with full awareness of its imprecision, can eventually confuse thought, when that awareness has faded. Numerals end up being taken for numbers, names for what is named, mere notation [*Hilfsmittel*] for the real object of arithmetic. Such experiences teach us how necessary it is to place the strictest demands on precision of spoken and written forms of expression. And I have taken the trouble to respect these demands, at least wherever it seemed to me to matter. |

5   I. EXPLANATION OF THE *BEGRIFFSSCHRIFT*

1. The Primitive Signs

Introduction: function, concept, relation[o]

§1. If asked to state the original *Bedeutung* of the word 'function' in its mathematical use, it is easy to resort to calling a function of x an expression formed from 'x' and particular numbers by means of the symbols for sum, product, power, difference, etc. This is incorrect, because a function is here taken as an *expression*, as a combination of signs, not as what is thereby designated. It is tempting to say '*Bedeutung* of an expression' instead of 'expression'. But the letter 'x' that occurs in the expression does not, like, say, the sign '2', refer to [*bedeutet*] a number, but only indefinitely indicates [*andeutet*] one. In general we obtain different *Bedeutungen* for different numerals substituted for 'x'. For example, in the expression '$(2 + 3.x^2).x$', substituting in turn for 'x' the numerals '0', '1', '2', '3', we obtain as corresponding *Bedeutungen* the numbers 0, 5, 28, 87. None of these *Bedeutungen* can claim to be our function. The essence of a function is revealed rather in the connection established between the numbers whose signs replace 'x', and the numbers that then appear as *Bedeutungen* of our expression – a connection that is represented intuitively in the graph of the curve whose equation in coordinate geometry is

$$\text{'}y = (2 + 3.x^2).x\text{'}.$$

The essence of a *function* thus lies in that part of the expression without the 'x'. The expression of a *function* is *in need of completion* [*ergänzungs-*
6   *bedürftig*], *unsaturated* [*ungesättigt*]. The | letter 'x' merely serves as a place-holder for a numeral to complete the expression, and so makes clear the particular kind of incompleteness that constitutes the peculiar

---

[o] Cf. my lecture on 'Function and Concept' [pp. 130–48 above] and my essay 'On Concept and Object' [pp. 181–93 above]. My *Begriffsschrift* [pp. 47–78 above] no longer entirely corresponds to my current point of view, and is thus only to be consulted with care for elucidation of the exposition here.

essence of the function just designated. In what follows, the letter 'ξ' will be used instead of 'x' for this purpose.[P] This place-holding is to be understood as requiring that all places where 'ξ' stands should only ever be filled by the same sign, never by different signs. I call these places *argument-places*, and that whose sign (name) occupies this place in a given case, I call the *argument* of the function for this case. The function is completed by the argument; what it becomes when completed I call the *value* of the function for the argument. We thus obtain a name of the value of a function for an argument when we fill the argument-places in the name of the function with the name of the argument. So, for example, '$(2 + 3.1^2).1$' is a name of the number 5, composed of the function name '$(2 + 3.\xi^2).\xi$' and '1'. The argument, then, is not to be included with the function, but only serves to complete the function that in itself is *unsaturated*. If, in what follows, an expression such as 'the function $\Phi(\xi)$' is used, then it should always be observed that the role of 'ξ' in the designation of the function is only to make clear the argument-places, and is not such that the essence of the function changes if some other sign replaces 'ξ'.

§2.   To the basic arithmetical operations have been added, in the construction of functions, transition to a limit in its various forms – as infinite series, differential quotients, integrals; and the word 'function' has finally come to be understood in such a general way that, in certain circumstances, the connection between argument and value of a function can no longer be designated at all by the symbols of Analysis but only by words. Another extension has consisted in admitting complex numbers as arguments and hence also as values of functions. In both directions I have gone further.[24] Whilst up to now the symbols of Analysis have not always been sufficient, at the same time not all of them have been used in the construction of function names – '$\xi^2 = 4$' and '$\xi > 2$', for example, have not been allowed as names of functions, as I allow. But this is also to say that the domain of values of functions cannot remain restricted to numbers; for if I take as argument of the function $\xi^2 = 4$ the numbers 0, 1, 2, 3 in turn, then I do not obtain numbers [as values of the function].

$$\text{'}0^2 = 4\text{'}, \quad \text{'}1^2 = 4\text{'}, \quad \text{'}2^2 = 4\text{'}, \quad \text{'}3^2 = 4\text{'}$$

7   are expressions some of true, some of false thoughts. I put | this as follows: the value of the function $\xi^2 = 4$ is a *truth-value*, either the True

---

[P] Nothing, however, is here laid down for the *Begriffsschrift*. 'ξ' will never occur in the development of the *Begriffsschrift* itself; I shall only use it in the explanation of the *Begriffsschrift* and in elucidations.

[24] Cf. *FC*, pp. 137ff. above.

or the False.^Q From this it can be seen that I am not asserting anything when I merely write down an equation, but only *designating* a truth value, just as I am not asserting anything when I merely write down '2²', but only *designating* a number. I say: the *names* '2² = 4' and '3 > 2' *refer to* [*bedeuten*] the same truth-value, which I call for short *the True*. Similarly, for me, '3² = 4' and '1 > 2' *refer to* [*bedeuten*] the same truth-value, which I call for short *the False*, just as the name '2²' *refers to* [*bedeutet*] the number four. Accordingly, I call the number four the *Bedeutung* of '4' and of '2²', and I call the True the *Bedeutung* of '3 > 2'. But I distinguish from the *Bedeutung* of a name its *sense*. '2²' and '2 + 2' do not have the same *sense*, nor do '2² = 4' and '2 + 2 = 4' have the same *sense*. The sense of a name of a truth-value I call a *thought*. I say too that a name *expresses* its sense and *refers to* [*bedeute*] its *Bedeutung*. I *designate* by a name that which it refers to [*bedeutet*].

The function $\xi^2 = 4$ can thus have only two values, namely, the True for the arguments 2 and −2 and the False for all other arguments.

The domain of admissible arguments must also be extended to include all objects whatever. *Objects* are opposed to functions. Accordingly, I count as *objects* everything that is not a function, e.g. numbers, truth-values and the value-ranges to be introduced below. The names of objects, *proper names*, thus carry no argument-places with them, they are saturated, like the objects themselves.

§3.   I use the words

'the function $\Phi(\xi)$ has the same *value-range*[25] as the function $\Psi(\xi)$'

throughout as *gleichbedeutend*[26] with the words

---

^Q I have justified this at greater length in my essay 'Über Sinn und Bedeutung' [pp. 151–71 above].

---

[25] On the translation of Frege's term 'Wertverlauf', see fn. 2 on p. 135 above.

[26] Given that Frege has by this point drawn the distinction between *Sinn* and *Bedeutung*, it would be natural to render 'gleichbedeutend mit' as 'having the same *Bedeutung* as'. But arguably, what Frege intends here is that the two expressions have the same *Sinn* as well as the same *Bedeutung*. There are two pieces of textual evidence, and one fundamental consideration which relates to them, in favour of this. Firstly, in *FC*, in talking of the relationship between two instances of the expressions, he writes that they 'express the same sense, but in a different way', and this is clearly intended to have general significance (see pp. 135–6 above). Secondly, later on in *GG*, when using the same word 'gleichbedeutend' in discussing definitions, Frege specifically states that the *definiendum* is to be taken as having the same sense as well as the same *Bedeutung* as the *definiens* (*GG*, I, §27; see p. 220 below). Furthermore, since what we have here is a formulation of Axiom V of the *Grundgesetze* – stating that the two expressions are equivalent – it should in any case be expected that, as an axiom, it is to be regarded as embodying sameness of sense as well as sameness of *Bedeutung*. For discussion of Axiom V, see the Introduction, pp. 7–8, 18–20 above.

'the functions $\Phi(\xi)$ and $\Psi(\xi)$ always have the same value for the same argument'.

We have this in the case of the functions $\xi^2 = 4$ and $3.\xi^2 = 12$, at least if numbers are taken as arguments. But we can also think of the signs for squaring and multiplication as defined in such a way that the function

$$(\xi^2 = 4) = (3.\xi^2 = 12)$$

has the True as value for any argument whatever. This may also be expressed in logical terms: 'the concept *square | root of 4* has the same extension as the concept *something whose trebled square is 12*'. In the case of such functions, whose value is always a truth-value, one may therefore say 'extension of the concept' instead of 'value-range of the function', and it seems appropriate precisely to call a *concept* a function whose value is always a truth-value.[27]

§4. Up to now the concern has only been with functions of a single argument; but we can easily extrapolate to *functions with two arguments*. These are *doubly in need of completion* in that a function with one argument is obtained when a completion by one argument is effected. Only by a further completion do we reach an object, and this is then called the *value* of the function for the two arguments. Just as the letter 'ξ' served us for functions with one argument, so we use here the letters 'ξ' and 'ζ' to indicate the double unsaturatedness of functions with two arguments, as in

$$\text{'}(\xi + \zeta)^2 + \zeta\text{'}.$$

By replacing 'ζ' by '1', for example, we saturate the function in such a way that we have, in $(\xi + 1)^2 + 1$, a function with only one argument. This use of the letters 'ξ' and 'ζ' must always be kept in mind when an expression such as 'the function $\Psi(\xi, \zeta)$' occurs (cf. §1, fn. P). I call the places at which 'ξ' stands ξ-*argument-places*, and those at which 'ζ' stands ζ-*argument-places*. I say that the ξ-argument-places are *related* [*verwandt*] to one another, just as the ζ-argument-places are to one another, whilst an ξ-argument-place is *not related* to a ζ-argument-place.

The functions with two arguments $\xi = \zeta$ and $\xi > \zeta$ always have a truth-value as value (at least if the signs '=' and '>' are defined in an appropriate way). Such functions we will aptly call relations. In the first relation, for example, 1 stands to 1, and in general every object to itself; in the second, for example, 2 stands to 1. We say that the object Γ *stands in the relation* $\Psi(\xi, \zeta)$ to the object Δ if $\Psi(\Gamma, \Delta)$ is the True;[28] just

---

[27] Cf. *FC*, p. 139 above.

[28] This accords with how modern logicians understand relational expressions of the form '*Rab*' – that *a* stands in the relation *R* to *b*. But cf. *BS*, §10 (p. 69 above), where Frege understood such expressions the opposite way round.

as we say that the object Δ *falls under* the concept $\Phi(\xi)$ if $\Phi(\Delta)$ is the True. It is presupposed here, of course, that the function $\Phi(\xi)$, just like $\Psi(\xi, \zeta)$, always has a truth-value as value.[R] |

9   Signs for functions

§5. We have already said above that nothing at all is asserted in a mere equation; '2 + 3 = 5' simply designates a truth-value, without saying which of the two it is. Even if I wrote '(2 + 3 = 5) = (2 = 2)' and presupposed that it was known that 2 = 2 is the True, I have not thereby asserted that the sum of 2 and 3 is 5, but have merely designated the truth-value of: '2 + 3 = 5' refers to [*bedeute*] the same thing as '2 = 2'. We therefore need another special sign to be able to assert something as true. For this purpose I place before the name of the truth-value the sign '$\vdash$', so that, for example, in

$$\vdash 2^2 = 4\text{'}^\text{S}$$

it is asserted that the square of 2 is 4. I distinguish *judgement* from *thought* in such a way that by *judgement* I understand the acknowledgement of the truth of a *thought*. The representation of a judgement in *Begriffsschrift* by means of the sign '$\vdash$' I call a *Begriffsschrift proposition* or *proposition* [*Satz*] for short.[29] I see this sign as composed of the vertical stroke, which I call the *judgement stroke*, and the horizontal stroke, which I intend now simply to call the *horizontal*.[T] The horizontal mostly occurs in combination with other signs, as here with the judgement stroke, which thus prevents confusion with the minus sign. Where it occurs by itself, it must be made somewhat longer than the *minus sign* to distinguish it. I regard it as a function name in the following way:

$$-\!\Delta$$

[R] There is a difficulty here that can easily obscure the real situation and thereby raise doubts as to the correctness of my view. If we compare the expression 'the truth-value of: Δ falls under the concept $\Phi(\xi)$' with '$\Phi(\Delta)$', then we see that what really corresponds to '$\Phi(\ )$' is 'the truth-value of: ( ) falls under the concept $\Phi(\xi)$' and not 'the concept $\Phi(\xi)$'. The last words thus do not really designate a concept (in our sense), although it appears that they do from their linguistic form. On the predicament in which ordinary language finds itself here, cf. my essay 'On Concept and Object' [pp. 181–93 above].

[S] I frequently make use here, provisionally, of the symbols for sum, product, power, even though they have not yet been defined, to enable easier examples to be formed and to facilitate understanding by means of hints. But it must be kept in mind that nothing is based on the *Bedeutungen* of these symbols.

[T] I used to call it the *content stroke* [see esp. *BS*, §2 (pp. 52–3 above)], when I still combined under the expression 'judgeable content' what I have now learnt to distinguish as truth-value and thought. Cf. my essay 'Über Sinn und Bedeutung' [pp. 151–71 above].

[29] On the translation of 'Satz' here, cf. fn. 34 on p. 220 below.

is the True if Δ is the True, and is otherwise the False, if Δ is not the True.[U] Accordingly,

$$—\xi$$

10   is a function whose value is always a truth-value, or in | our terminology, a concept. Under this concept falls the True and only the True.

$$‘—2^2 = 4’$$

thus refers to [*bedeutet*] the same thing as ‘$2^2 = 4$’, namely, the True. To dispense with brackets, I stipulate that everything to the right of the horizontal is to be regarded as a whole, occupying the argument-place of the function $—\xi$, unless *brackets* forbid this.

$$‘—2^2 = 5’$$

refers to [*bedeutet*] the False, and hence to the same thing as ‘$2^2 = 5$’, whereas

$$‘—2’$$

refers to [*bedeutet*] the False, and hence to something different from the number 2. If Δ is a truth-value, then $—\Delta$ is the same truth-value and consequently

$$\Delta = (—\Delta)$$

is the True. But this is the False if Δ is not a truth-value. We can thus say that

$$\Delta = (—\Delta)$$

is the truth-value of: Δ is a truth-value.

The function $—\Phi(\xi)$ is therefore a concept, and the function $—\Psi(\xi, \zeta)$ is a relation, regardless of whether $\Phi(\xi)$ is a concept and $\Psi(\xi, \zeta)$ a relation.

Of the two signs of which ‘$\vdash$’ is composed, only the judgement stroke contains the assertion.

§6.   We need no special sign to declare that a truth-value is the False, so long as we have a sign by means of which either truth-value is trans-

---

[U] Obviously, the sign ‘Δ’ should not be without *Bedeutung* [*bedeutungslos*], but must refer to [*bedeuten*] an object. Names without *Bedeutung* [*Bedeutungslose Namen*] should not occur in the *Begriffsschrift*. The stipulation is made in such a way that ‘$—\Delta$’ refers to [*bedeutet*] something under all circumstances, so long as ‘Δ’ refers to [*bedeutet*] something. Otherwise $—\xi$ would not be a concept with sharp boundaries, and hence in our sense not a concept at all. I use *capital Greek letters* here as if they were names that referred to [*bedeuteten*] something, without my having specified a *Bedeutung*. In the development of the *Begriffsschrift* itself they will not occur any more than ‘ξ’ and ‘ζ’.

formed into its opposite. Such a sign is also indispensable in other ways. I now stipulate:

The value of the function

$$\top\!\!-\xi$$

shall be the False for every argument for which the value of the function

$$-\!\!\!-\xi$$

is the True, and shall be the True for all other arguments.

We therefore have in

$$\top\!\!-\xi$$

a function whose value is always a truth-value; it is a concept under which all objects fall with the sole exception of the True. From this it follows that '$\top\!\!- \Delta$' always refers to [*bedeutet*] the same thing as '$\top\!\!-$ ($-\!\!\!-\Delta$)' and '$-\!\!\!-\ \top\!\!-\Delta$ and '$-\!\!\!-\ \top\!\!-$ ($-\!\!\!-\Delta$)'. We thus see '$\top\!\!-$' as composed of the small vertical stroke, the *negation stroke*, and the two parts of the horizontal stroke, each of which may be regarded as a *horizontal* in our sense. The transition from '$\top\!\!-$($-\!\!\!-\Delta$)' or '$-\!\!\!-\ \top\!\!-\Delta$' to '$\top\!\!-\Delta$' just as from '$-\!\!\!-\ -\!\!\!-\Delta$' to '$-\!\!\!-\Delta$' I call the *amalgamation* [*Verschmelzung*] of horizontals. |

11   According to our stipulation, $\top\!\!- 2^2 = 5$ is the True; hence

$$\vdash\!\!\top\!\!- 2^2 = 5,$$

in words: $2^2 = 5$ is not the True; or: the square of 2 is not 5.

So too: $\vdash\!\!\top\!\!- 2$.

§7. We have already used the equality sign along the way, in providing examples; but it is necessary to specify it more precisely.

$$'\Gamma = \Delta'$$

refers to [*bedeute*] the True if Γ is the same as Δ; in all other cases it refers to [*bedeute*] the False.

To dispense with brackets, I stipulate that everything to the left of the equality sign, up to the nearest horizontal, as a whole refers to [*bedeute*] the ξ-argument of the function $\xi = \zeta$, unless *brackets* forbid it; and everything to the right of the equality sign, up to the next equality sign, as a whole refers to [*bedeute*] the ζ-argument of the function, unless *brackets* forbid it (cf. §5).

[The rest of the first of the three divisions (entitled 'The Primitive Signs') of Part I of the *Grundgesetze* ('Explanation of the *Begriffsschrift*') is here omitted. In §8, Frege explains how he represents generality (cf. *BS*, §11; pp. 69–72 above); and he introduces, in §§9–10, his symbolism for *value-ranges* (cf. *FC*, pp. 135–7), and in §11, his substitute for the definite article, the function \ξ. He explains, in §12, his *conditional stroke* (cf. *BS*, §5; pp. 55–8 above), and in §13, his formalization of universal and particular propositions (cf. *BS*, §12; pp. 72–4 above). In §§14–18, under the heading 'Inferences and consequences', he formulates his rules of inference and Axioms I, IV and VI of his logical system; and in §§19–25, under the heading 'Extension of the symbolism for generality', he explains his conception of the *level* of a function (cf. esp. *FC*, pp. 146–8 above), and formulates Axioms II, III and V of his logical system. (For further details of all this, and a note on the changes to his earlier system that the *Grundgesetze* introduced, see Appendix 2 below.) An edited selection from the second division of Part I now follows.]

43   **2. Definitions**

                            General remarks

§26. The signs explained above will now be used to introduce new names. Before I go on to the rules to be followed here, however, it will facilitate understanding to divide the signs and combinations of signs into types and give them names.

The Gothic, Roman and Greek letters in the *Begriffsschrift* I shall not call *names*, since they are not intended to refer to [*bedeuten*] anything. On the other hand, I call, for example,

$$\text{`} \underbrace{\qquad}_{\mathfrak{a}} \mathfrak{a} = \mathfrak{a} \text{'}$$

a *name*, since it refers to [*bedeutet*] the True; it is a *proper name*. I thus call a *proper name*, or *name* of an object, a sign, whether simple or complex, that is intended to refer to [*bedeuten*] an object, but not a sign that merely indicates an object.

If, from a proper name, we remove a proper name that forms a part of it or coincides with it, at some or all of the places where it occurs, but in such a way that it remains clear that these places (as *argument-places of the first type*)[30] are filled by one and the same arbitrary proper name, then I call what we thereby obtain a *name* of a first-level function with one argument. Such a name, together with a proper name that fills the argument-places, forms a proper name. We thus also have in 'ξ' itself a function name, if the letter 'ξ' is intended only to make clear the argument-place. The function named by it has the property that its value for every argument coincides with the argument itself.

If, from a name of a first-level function with one argument, we remove a proper name that forms part of it, at all or some of the places where

---

[30] An *argument-place of the first type* is one that admits proper names (cf. *GG*, I, §23).

it occurs, but in such a way that it remains clear that these places (as argument-places of the first type) are filled by one and the same arbitrary proper name, then I call what we thereby obtain a *name* of a first-level function with two arguments.

If, from a proper name, we remove a name of a first-level function that forms part of it, at all or some of the places where it occurs, but in such a way that it remains clear that these places (as argument-places of the second or third type)[31] are filled by one and the same arbitrary name of a first-level function, then I call what we thereby obtain a *name* of a second-level function | with one argument – an argument of the second or third type[32] according to whether the argument-places are of the second or third type.

Names of functions I call for short *function names*.

It is not necessary to continue further with these explanations of the types of names.

If, in a proper name, we replace proper names that form part of it or coincide with it by object-letters, and function names by function-letters, then I call what we thereby obtain an *object-Marke* or *Marke* of an object.[33] If this replacement is only by Roman letters, then I call the *Marke* obtained a *Roman object-Marke*. Object-letters are thus also object-*Marken* and Roman object-letters are Roman object-*Marken*.

A sign (proper name or object-*Marke*) that consists only of the function name '$\xi = \zeta$' and proper names or object-*Marken* standing in the two argument-places, I call an *equation* [*Gleichung*].

If, in a function name, we replace proper names by object-letters, and function names by function-letters, then I call what we thereby obtain a *function-Marke* – a *Marke* of a function of the same kind as that from whose name it was derived. If this replacement is only by Roman letters, then I call the *Marke* obtained a *Roman Marke* of a function. Function-letters are also function-*Marken* and Roman function-letters are Roman function-*Marken*.

The judgement stroke I include neither amongst *names* nor amongst *Marken*; it is a sign of its own special kind. A sign that consists of a judgement stroke and a name of a truth-value prefixed by a horizontal, I call a *Begriffsschrift proposition* or, where there is no danger of confusion,

---

[31] An *argument-place of the second type* is one that admits names of first-level functions with one argument; an *argument-place of the third type* is one that admits names of first-level functions with two arguments (cf. *GG*, I, §23).

[32] *Arguments of the first type* are objects; *arguments of the second type* are first-level functions with one argument; *arguments of the third type* are first-level functions with two arguments (cf. *GG*, I, §23).

[33] The term 'Marke' here has been left untranslated. Furth translates it simply as 'mark', but this might lead to confusion with 'mark' as the translation of 'Merkmal'. In this context, 'Marke' means something like 'schematic expression', of which what are now called 'schematic letters' would just be the simplest type.

a *proposition* [*Satz*].[34] Equally, I call *Begriffsschrift proposition* (or *proposition*) a sign that consists of a judgement stroke and a Roman *Marke* of a truth-value prefixed by a horizontal.[35]

. . .

§27.   In order now to introduce new signs by means of signs already known, we require the *double-stroke of definition*, which appears as a double judgement stroke combined with a horizontal:

$$‘\Vdash’,$$

and is used instead of the judgement stroke where something is to be defined rather than judged. By means of a *definition* we introduce a | new name by stipulating that it is to have the same sense and the same *Bedeutung* as a name composed of already known signs. The new sign thereby becomes *gleichbedeutend*[36] with the *definiens*; the definition is thus immediately transformed into a proposition. We may therefore cite a definition just like a proposition, replacing the definition stroke by the judgement stroke.

A definition will always be presented here in the form of an equation prefixed by ‘$\Vdash$’. We will always write the *definiens* on the left-hand side of the equality sign, and the *definiendum* on the right-hand side. The former will be composed of already known signs.

§28.   For definitions I now lay down the following cardinal principle:

Legitimately formed names must always refer to [*bedeuten*] something.

I call a name *legitimately* formed if it consists only of signs that are introduced as primitive or through definition, and if these signs are used only as they were intended to be used in introducing them, i.e. proper names as proper names, names of first-level functions with one argument as names of such functions, and so on, so that the argument-places are always filled by appropriate names or *Marken* . . .[37]

§29.   We now answer the question: when does a name refer to [*bedeutet*] something? We will confine ourselves to the following cases.

[34] ‘Satz’ can also mean ‘theorem’ (though ‘Lehrsatz’ is more specifically used for this). ‘Theorem’ would be appropriate in the present context, except that the remark ‘where there is no danger of confusion’ would then look odd.
[35] The next paragraph is omitted: Frege notes, finally, that he will call certain signs that indicate how one proposition is derived from another (in his *Begriffsschrift*) *transition-signs* [*Zwischenzeichen*].
[36] Given what Frege has just said in the previous sentence, the use of ‘gleichbedeutend’ here is clearly not intended to suggest that the *definiens* and *definiendum* are merely to be seen as having the same *Bedeutung*. Cf. fn. 26 on p. 213 above.
[37] In the rest of the section, omitted here, Frege notes certain formation rules governing his use of Gothic letters (as bound variables) and lower-case Greek letters (in representing value-ranges). Cf. Appendix 2 below.

46   A name of a first-level function with one argument has | a *Bedeutung* (*refers to* [*bedeutet*] something, is *bedeutungsvoll*) if the proper name that results from this function name by filling its argument-places with a proper name, which itself refers to [*bedeutet*] something, always has a *Bedeutung*.

A proper name has a *Bedeutung* if the proper name that results from inserting it into the argument-places of a *bedeutungsvoll*[38] name of a first-level function with one argument always has a *Bedeutung*, and if the name of a first-level function with one argument that results from inserting the proper name in question into the ξ-argument-places of a *bedeutungsvoll* name of a first-level function with two arguments always has a *Bedeutung*, and if the same holds too for the ζ-argument-places.

A name of a first-level function with two arguments has a *Bedeutung* if the proper name that results from this function name when its ξ-argument-places are filled by a *bedeutungsvoll* proper name, as also when its ζ-argument-places are filled by a *bedeutungsvoll* proper name, always has a *Bedeutung* . . .[39]

[The next two sections are omitted here. In §30 Frege notes that the preceding specifications presuppose that the primitive names have a *Bedeutung*; and in §31 he attempts to show that his primitive names do indeed all have a *Bedeutung*.[40]]

50   **§32.** Thus it is shown that our eight primitive names have a *Bedeutung*, and hence that the same holds too for all names legitimately constructed from them. However, not only a *Bedeutung*, but also a sense belongs to all names legitimately formed from our signs. Every such name of a truth-value *expresses* a sense, a *thought*. That is, by our stipulations, it is determined under what conditions the name refers to [*bedeute*] the True. The sense of this name, the *thought*, is the thought that these conditions are fulfilled. Now a *Begriffsschrift* proposition consists of the judgement stroke and a name or Roman *Marke* of a truth-value. (Such a *Marke*, however, is transformed into a name of a truth-value by the introduction of Gothic letters instead of Roman ones and the prefixing of concavities,

---

[38] In this and the following sections, the term 'bedeutungsvoll', like 'Bedeutung', is left untranslated (it occurs as 'bedeutungsvollen' in the German, since it is used in the genitive).

[39] Frege goes on to make corresponding specifications in the cases of second- and third-level functions, omitted here.

[40] The eight primitive names Frege considers are three names of first-level functions with one argument – involving the horizontal, the negation stroke, and the description stroke; two names of first-level functions with two arguments – involving the conditional stroke, and the equality sign; two names of second-level functions with one argument of the second type – involving his symbol for the universal quantifier, and his notation for the value-range of a function; and one name of a third-level function – involving second-order quantification. Frege's purported proof that these primitive names all have a *Bedeutung* is highly problematic. For discussion, see Resnik, 1986; Dummett, 1991a: ch. 17.

as specified in §17.[41] If we assume this is done, then we only have the case in which the proposition is composed of the judgement stroke and a name of a truth-value.) By means of such a proposition, then, it is asserted that this name refers to [*bedeute*] the True. Since at the same time the name expresses a thought, then we have in every legitimately formed *Begriffsschrift* proposition a judgement that a thought is true; and | there is no possibility at all that a thought is lacking. It will be up to the reader to make clear to himself the thought expressed by each *Begriffsschrift* proposition that occurs, and I will do my best to facilitate this as much as possible at the outset.

51

The names, either simple or themselves already complex, of which the name of a truth-value consists, contribute to the expression of the thought, and the contribution that an individual name makes is its *sense*. If a name is part of the name of a truth-value, then the sense of the former is part of the thought expressed by the latter.

§33. The following are the principles that govern definitions:

1.   Every name legitimately formed from defined names must have a *Bedeutung*. It must thus always be possible to provide a name, constructed from our eight primitive names, that is *gleichbedeutend*[42] with it, and this name must be unambiguously determined by the definitions, aside from the inessential choice of Gothic and Greek letters.

2.   It follows from this that the same thing should never be defined twice, since it would then remain in doubt whether these definitions were in accord with one another.

3.   The defined name must be simple; i.e. it should not be composed of already known or yet to be defined names; since it would otherwise remain in doubt whether the definitions of the names were in accord with one another.

4.   If, in a definition, we have on the left-hand side of the equation a proper name that is legitimately formed from our primitive names or defined names, then this always has a *Bedeutung*, and we can place on the right-hand side a simple sign that has not yet been used, which is now introduced by the definition as a *gleichbedeutender* proper name, so that in future we may replace this sign, wherever it occurs, by the name standing on the left-hand side. Obviously, it should never be used as a function name, since the route back to the primitive names would then be cut off.

---

[41] Frege is referring here to the transition from schematic expressions to propositions involving bound variables. For an explanation of Frege's notation for generality, involving a concavity in the horizontal stroke, cf. *BS*, §11 (pp. 69ff. above), where the symbolism was first introduced, and Appendix 2 below.

[42] On Frege's use of this term throughout this section, cf. §27 and fn. 36 on p. 220 above, and fn. 26 on p. 213 above.

5. A name introduced for a first-level function with one argument should only contain a single argument-place. With more argument-places it would be possible to fill them with different names, and then the defined name would be used as the name of a function with more arguments, without having been defined as such. If a name of a first-level function with one argument is defined, the argument-places on the left-hand side of the equation must be filled with one Roman object-letter, which also makes clear the argument-place of the new function name on the right-hand side. The definition then says that the proper name that results on the right-hand side by | inserting a *bedeutungsvoll* proper name in the argument-place is always to be *gleichbedeutend* with that that results on the left-hand side by inserting the same proper name in all argument-places. The one argument-place of the name defined thus represents all those of the *definiens*. Wherever the defined function name may subsequently occur, its argument-place must always be filled by a proper name or an object-*Marke*.

6. A name introduced for a first-level function with two arguments must contain two and no more than two argument-places. The linked argument-places on the left-hand side must be occupied by one and the same Roman object-letter, which also makes clear one of the two argument-places on the right-hand side; the other argument-places must contain a different Roman letter. The definition then says that the proper name that results on the right-hand side by inserting *bedeutungsvoll* proper names in the argument-places is always to be *gleichbedeutend* with that that results on the left-hand side by inserting the same proper names in the corresponding argument-places. One of the argument-places on the right-hand side thus represents all ξ-argument-places on the left-hand side, and the other all ζ-argument-places.

7. There should thus never occur on one side of the equation in a definition a Roman letter that does not also stand on the other side. If the object-*Marke* on the left-hand side is transformed into a legitimately formed proper name, by replacing the Roman letters by proper names, then by our stipulations the function name defined always has a *Bedeutung*.

Cases other than those just discussed will not occur in what follows.

[The rest of Volume I of the *Grundgesetze* is here omitted. In the remainder of the second division of Part I, Frege offers some particular definitions (§§34–46); and then, in the third division (entitled 'Derived laws'), provides a summary of his axioms and rules, and derives certain theorems (§§47–52). In Part II, entitled 'Proof of the Basic Laws of Number', which, in Volume I, runs from §53 to §179 (it continues into Volume II), he turns to the formal demonstration of the laws of arithmetic.]

Review of E. G. Husserl, Philosophie der Arithmetik *I*[1]

[Husserl's *Philosophie der Arithmetik* was published in 1891, and contained some criticism of Frege's *Grundlagen*. Husserl sent a copy of his book to Frege, occasioning their first correspondence,[2] and Frege published a detailed review of Husserl's book in 1894, in the *Zeitschrift für Philosophie und philosophische Kritik* 103, pp. 313–32. Frege criticizes, amongst other things, Husserl's understanding of concepts,[3] his view that 0 and 1 are not numbers, and his appeal to abstraction in his account of number;[4] and Frege's critique was instrumental in converting Husserl away from the psychologism that had characterized his *Philosophie der Arithmetik*.[5] All that is extracted here is Frege's response to Husserl's criticisms of his definitions in the central sections of the *Grundlagen*, which provides a clear statement of what has come to be known as the paradox of analysis, and the response that Frege offered to it utilizing his distinction between *Sinn* and *Bedeutung*.]

318   Given the partly psychological, partly logical way of thinking we have just characterized, it is easy to understand the author's verdict on definition. An example from elementary geometry may illustrate this. The usual definition given there is: 'A right angle is an angle equal to its adjacent angle'. The author's comment on this would probably be: 'The idea of rectangularity is a simple one; so it is a wholly misguided undertaking to want to give a definition of it. Our idea of rectangularity contains nothing of its relation to another, adjacent angle. It is indeed correct to

---

[1] Translated by Hans Kaal (*CP*, pp. 199–201; from *KS*, pp. 182–4). Page numbers in the margin are from the original journal.

[2] See pp. 149–50 above.

[3] Cf. pp. 149–50 above.

[4] Frege's arguments against a position such as Husserl's had already been provided in *GL* (see esp. pp. 94–8 above). For discussion of Frege's critique of Husserl, see Bell, 1990a: ch. 1; Dummett, 1991a: chs. 8, 12.

[5] For Husserl's later anti-psychologism, see especially the *Prolegomena* to his *Logische Untersuchungen* (Halle, 1900).

say that the concepts "right angle" and "angle equal to its adjacent angle" have the same extension, but it is not correct to say that they have the same content. So what is being defined is not the content, but the extension of the concept. If this definition were correct, then any assertion of rectangularity, instead of being as such about the concrete pair of sides before us, would always be about its relation to another pair. All I can admit (cf. p. 114) is that equality with an adjacent angle gives us a necessary and sufficient criterion of rectangularity.' It is in a similar way that the author judges the definition of numerical equality by means of

319 the concept of a one-one | correlation. 'The simplest criterion of equality of number is just that the *same* number results in counting the sets to be compared' (p. 115). Naturally; the simplest way of testing rectangularity is by applying a protractor! The author forgets that this counting rests itself on a one-one correlation, namely of the numerals 1 to n and the objects of the set. Each of the two sets needs to be counted. This makes the matter less simple than it is if we consider a relation that correlates the objects of the two sets without numerals as intermediaries.

If words and combinations of words refer to [*bedeuten*] ideas, then for any two of them there are only two possibilities: either they designate the same idea or they designate different ideas. In the former case it is pointless to equate them by means of a definition: this is 'an obvious circle'; in the latter case it is wrong. These are also the objections the author raises, one of them regularly. A definition is also incapable of analysing the sense, for the analysed sense just is not the original one. In using the word to be explained, I either think clearly everything I think when I use the defining expression: we then have the 'obvious circle'; or the defining expression has a more richly articulated sense, in which case I do not think the same thing in using it as I do in using the word to be explained: the definition is then wrong. One would think that a definition was unobjectionable in the case where the word to be explained had as yet no sense at all, or where we were asked explicitly to regard its sense as non-existent so that it was first given a sense by the definition. But in the last case too, the author refutes the definition by reminding us of the difference between the ideas (p. 107). To evade all objections, one would accordingly have to create a new verbal root and form a word out of it. This reveals a split between psychological logicians and mathematicians. What matters to the former is the sense of the words, as well as the ideas which they fail to distinguish from the sense; whereas what matters to the latter is the thing itself: the |

320 *Bedeutung* of the words.[A] The reproach that what is defined is not the concept but its extension actually affects all mathematical definitions.

[A] On this point the reader is asked to compare my essay on *Sinn* and *Bedeutung* [pp. 151–71 above; originally published in the same journal as this review].

For the mathematician, it is no more right and no more wrong to define a conic as the line of intersection of a plane with the surface of a circular cone than to define it as a plane curve with an equation of the second degree in parallel coordinates. His choice of one or the other of these expressions or of some other one is guided solely by reasons of convenience and is made irrespective of the fact that the expressions have neither the same sense nor evoke the same ideas. I do not intend by this that a concept and its extension are one and the same, but that coincidence in extension is a necessary and sufficient criterion for the occurrence between concepts of the relation that corresponds to identity [*Gleichheit*] between objects.[B] It should be noted in this connection that I am using the word 'equal' ['*gleich*'] without further addition in the sense of 'not different', 'coinciding', 'identical'.[6] As psychological logicians lack any understanding of definition, they also lack any understanding of identity. This relation cannot but remain perfectly mysterious to them; for if words designated ideas throughout, one could never say '*a* is the same as *b*'; for to be able to say this, one would first have to distinguish *a* from *b*, and they would then just be different ideas. All the same, I agree with the author that Leibniz's explanation that '*Eadem sunt, quorum unum potest substitui alteri salva veritate*'[7] does not deserve to be called a definition, even if my reasons are different from his. Since any definition is an equation [*Gleichung*], identity [*Gleichheit*] itself cannot be defined. Leibniz's explanation could be called a principle that brings out the nature of the relation of identity, and as such it is of fundamental importance. The author's explanation, 'We simply say of any two contents that they are identical [*einander gleich*] | if there is an identity between . . . the characteristic marks [*Merkmalen*] which happen to be at the centre of our interest' (p. 108) is not at all to my taste.

321

[B] For identity in the proper sense of the word does not occur between concepts. Cf. my essay on concept and object [pp. 181–93 above].

[6] Cf. *SB*, fn. A (p. 151 above); *CO*, fn. B (p. 183 above); *GG*, I, p. IX (p. 197 above).
[7] 'Those things are the same of which one can be substituted for the other without loss of truth.' Cf. *GL*, §65 (pp. 111–12 above), where Frege does, in fact, regard it as a definition; and *SB*, p. 158 above.

Logic[1]

[What follows here is the first two sections of a work simply called 'Logic', dating from 1897, which was only published in Frege's *Posthumous Writings*.[2] Frege made various attempts during his life to write a textbook on logic: all that in the end was published by him was the series of three papers that appeared under the title of 'Logical Investigations'.[3] In the first section of 'Logic', Frege explains his conception of truth and thought, and in the second section, entitled 'Separating a thought from its trappings', he discusses the importance of isolating thoughts from their linguistic expression, and the nature of logic.[4]]

Introduction

The predicate *true*, thoughts, consequences for the treatment of logic

When entering upon the study of a science, we need to have some idea, if only a provisional one, of its nature. We want to have in sight a goal to strive towards; we want some point to aim at that will guide our steps in the right direction. The word 'true' can be used to indicate such a goal for logic, just as can 'good' for ethics and 'beautiful' for aesthetics. Of course all the sciences have truth as their goal, but logic

---

[1] Translated by Peter Long and Roger White (*PW*, pp. 128–49; from *NS*, pp. 139–61; page numbers from the latter in the margin). In accordance with the policy adopted in this volume (see the Introduction, §4 above), 'Bedeutung' and cognates such as 'bedeutungslos' have been here left untranslated, and 'bedeuten' rendered as 'stand for' (but with the German in square brackets following it). Unless otherwise indicated, where the verb 'mean' appears in this translation, it has been used in rendering certain German constructions involving 'sollen' or 'wollen'.

[2] *PW*, pp. 126–51/*NS*, pp. 137–63. For the dating of this work, see fn. 19 below.

[3] See pp. 325ff. below. There is a certain degree of overlap between the first two sections of 'Logic' and Frege's later essay on 'Thought' (pp. 325–45 below): they can thus be regarded as an early draft.

[4] The third and fourth (i.e. final two) sections, just two pages long, are entitled 'Negation' and 'Compound Thoughts' (*PW*, pp. 149–51/*NS*, pp. 161–3): they were later to be worked up into the second and third parts of 'Logical Investigations'. Also omitted here is the (incomplete) list of contents that precedes the first section of 'Logic' (*PW*, pp. 126–8/*NS*, pp. 137–9).

is concerned with the predicate 'true' in a quite special way, namely in a way analogous to that in which physics has to do with the predicates 'heavy' and 'warm' or chemistry with the predicates 'acid' and 'alkaline'. There is, however, the difference that these sciences have to take into account other properties besides these we have mentioned, and that there is no one property by which their nature is so completely characterized as logic is by the word 'true'.[5]

Like ethics, logic can also be called a normative science. How must I think in order to reach the goal, truth? We expect logic to give us the answer to this question, but we do not demand of it that it should go into what is peculiar to each branch of knowledge and its subject matter. On the contrary, the task we assign logic is only that of saying what holds with the utmost generality for all thinking, whatever its subject matter. We must assume that the rules for our thinking and for our holding something to be true are prescribed by the laws of truth. The former are given along with the latter. Consequently we can also say: logic is the science of the most general laws of truth. The reader may find that he can form no very precise conception from this description. The author's inadequacy and the awkwardness of language are probably to blame for this. But it is only a question of giving a rough indication of the goal of logic. What is still lacking in the account will have to be made good as we go on.

Now it would be futile to employ a definition in order to make it clearer what is to be understood by 'true'. If, for example, we wished to say 'an idea is true if it agrees with reality' nothing would have been 140 achieved, | since in order to apply this definition we should have to decide whether some idea or other did agree with reality. Thus we should have to presuppose the very thing that is being defined. The same would hold of any definition of the form '*A* is true if and only if it has such-and-such properties or stands in such-and-such a relation to such-and-such a thing'. In each case in hand it would always come back to the question whether it is true that *A* has such-and-such properties, or stands in such-and-such a relation to such-and-such a thing. Truth is obviously something so primitive and simple that it is not possible to reduce it to anything still simpler. Consequently we have no alternative but to bring out the peculiarity of our predicate by comparing it with others. What, in the first place, distinguishes it from all other predicates is that predicating it is always included in predicating anything whatever.[6]

If I assert that the sum of 2 and 3 is 5, then I thereby assert that it is true that 2 and 3 make 5. So I assert that it is true that my idea of

[5] Cf. *T*, pp. 325–6 below.
[6] Cf. *T*, pp. 326–7 below.

Cologne Cathedral agrees with reality, if I assert that it agrees with reality. Therefore it is really by using the form of an assertoric sentence that we assert truth, and to do this we do not need the word 'true'. Indeed we can say that even where we use the form of expression 'it is true that . . .' the essential thing is really the assertoric form of the sentence.

We now ask: what can the predicate 'true' be applied to? The issue here is to delimit the range of application of the word. Whatever else may be the case, the word cannot be applied to anything that is material. If there is any doubt about this, it could arise only for works of art. But if we speak of truth in connection with these, then we are surely using the word with a different *Bedeutung* from the one that is meant [*gemeint*] here. In any case it is only as a work of art that a thing is called true. If a thing had come into existence through the blind play of natural forces, our predicate would be clearly inappropriate. For the same reason we are excluding from consideration the use that is made by, say, an art critic when he calls feelings and experiences true.

No one would deny that our predicate is, for the most part, ascribed to sentences. We are not, however, concerned with sentences expressing wishes, questions, requests and commands, but only with assertoric sentences, sentences that is to say, in which we communicate facts and propound mathematical laws or laws of nature.

Further, it is clear that we do not, properly speaking, ascribe truth to 141 the series of sounds which constitute a sentence, but to its sense; | for, on the one hand, the truth of a sentence is preserved when it is correctly translated into another language, and, on the other hand, it is at least conceivable that the same series of sounds should have a true sense in one language and a false sense in another.

We are here including under the word 'sentence' the main clause of a sentence and clauses that are subordinate to it.

In the cases which alone concern logic the sense of an assertoric sentence is either true or false, and then we have what we call a thought proper. But there remains a third case of which at least some mention must be made here.

The sentence 'Scylla has six heads' is not true, but the sentence 'Scylla does not have six heads' is not true either; for it to be true the proper name 'Scylla' would have to designate something. Perhaps we think that the name 'Scylla' does designate something, namely an idea. In that case the first question to ask is 'Whose idea?' We often speak as if one and the same idea occurred to different people, but that is false, at least if the word 'idea' is used in the psychological sense: each person has his own idea. But then an idea does not have heads, and so one cannot cut heads off an idea either. The name 'Scylla' does not therefore designate an idea. Names that fail to fulfil the usual role of a proper name, which is to name something, may be called mock proper names [*Scheineigennamen*]. Although the tale of William Tell is a legend and not history and the name 'William Tell' is a mock proper name, we cannot deny it a sense. But the sense of the sentence 'William Tell shot an apple off his son's head' is no more true than is that of the sentence 'William Tell did not shoot an apple off his son's head'. I do not say, however, that this sense is false either, but I characterize it as fictitious.[7] This may elucidate the sense in which I am using the word 'false', which is as little susceptible of a definition proper as is the word 'true'.

If the idealist theory of knowledge is correct then all the sciences would belong to the realm of fiction [*Dichtung*]. Indeed one might try to reinterpret all sentences in such a way that they were about ideas. By doing this, however, their sense would be completely changed and we should obtain quite a different science; this new science would be a branch of psychology.

Instead of speaking of 'fiction', we could speak of 'mock thoughts' ['*Scheingedanke*']. Thus if the sense of an assertoric sentence is not true, it is either false or fictitious, and it will generally be the latter if it contains a | mock proper name.[A] The writer, in common with, for example, the painter, has his eye on appearances. Assertions in fiction are not to be taken seriously: they are only mock assertions. Even the thoughts are not to be taken seriously as in the sciences: they are only mock thoughts. If Schiller's *Don Carlos* were to be regarded as a piece of history, then to a large extent the drama would be false. But a work of fiction is not meant to be taken seriously in this way at all: it is all play. Even the proper names in the drama, though they correspond to names of historical persons, are mock proper names; they are not meant to be taken seriously in the work. We have a similar thing in the case of an historical painting. As a work of art it simply does not claim to give a visual representation of things that actually happened. A picture that was intended to portray some significant moment in history with photographic accuracy would not be a work of art in the higher sense of the word, but would be comparable rather to an anatomical drawing in a scientific work.

The logician does not have to bother with mock thoughts, just as a physicist, who sets out to investigate thunder, will not pay any attention to stage-thunder. When we speak of thoughts in what follows we shall understand thoughts proper, thoughts that are either true or false.

The sense of an assertoric sentence I call a thought. Examples of

---

[A] We have an exception where a mock proper name occurs within a clause in indirect speech.

---

[7] Cf. *SB*, p. 157 above.

thoughts are laws of nature, mathematical laws, historical facts: all these find expression in assertoric sentences. I can now be more precise and say: The predicate 'true' applies to thoughts.

Of course we speak of true ideas[8] as well. By an idea we understand a picture that is called up by the imagination: unlike a perception it does not consist of present impressions, but of the reactivated traces of past impressions or actions. Like any other picture, an idea is not true in itself, but only in relation to something to which it is meant to correspond. If it is said that a picture is meant to represent Cologne Cathedral, fair enough; it can then be asked whether this intention is realized; if there is no reference [*Hinblick*] to an intention to depict something, there can be no question of the truth of a picture. It can be seen from this that the predicate *true* is not really conferred on the idea itself, but on the thought that the idea depicts a certain object. And this thought is not an idea, nor is it made up of ideas in any way. Thoughts are fundamentally different from ideas (in the psychological sense). The idea of a red rose is something different from the thought that this rose is red. Associate ideas or run them together as we may, we shall finish up with an idea and never with something that could be true. This difference also comes out in the modes we have of communicating. The | proper means of expression for a thought is a sentence. But a sentence is hardly an appropriate vehicle for conveying an idea. I have only to remind you how inadequate any description is by comparison with a pictorial representation. Things are not so bad where it is a matter of representing sounds, since we have the resources of onomatopoeia; but onomatopoeia has nothing whatever to do with the expression of thoughts, and whilst in translation the play of sounds is easily lost, the thought must be preserved if we are to speak of a translation at all. Conversely, pictures and musical compositions without accompanying words are hardly suited for expressing thoughts. It is true that we may associate all kinds of thoughts with some work of art or other but there is no necessary connection between the two, and we are not surprised when someone else associates different thoughts with it.[9]

In order to shed a clearer light on the peculiarity of the predicate *true*, let us compare it with the predicate *beautiful*. We can see, to begin with, that what is beautiful admits of degrees, but what is true does not. We can think two objects beautiful, and yet think one more beautiful than the other. On the other hand, if two thoughts are true, one is not

143

---

[8] In the German, '*Vorstellungen*'. Throughout this essay the difficult word '*Vorstellung*' has been generally rendered by 'idea'. Admittedly this makes certain passages read unnaturally, but the gist of what Frege is saying should be clear if the reader bears in mind the explanation he gives here of how the term '*Vorstellung*' is being used. (*Trs.*)

[9] According to the first editors of Frege's *Nachlaß* (the original manuscripts are now lost), the next two paragraphs were crossed through by Frege. (Cf. *NS*, p. 143, fn. 1.)

more true than the other. And here there emerges the essential difference that what is true is true independently of our recognizing it as such, but what is beautiful is beautiful only for him who experiences it as such. What is beautiful for one person is not necessarily beautiful for another. There is no disputing tastes. Where truth is concerned, there is the possibility of error, but not where beauty is concerned. By the very fact that I consider something beautiful it is beautiful for me. But something does not have to be true because I consider it to be true, and if it is not true in itself, it is not true for me either. Nothing is beautiful in itself: it is only beautiful for some being experiencing it and this is necessarily implicit in any aesthetic judgement. Now it is true that we also make judgements of this kind which seem to lay claim to being objective. Whether we are aware of it or not the assumption of a normal human being always underlies such judgements, and each one of us cannot help but think that he himself is so close to the normal human being that he believes he can speak in his name. What, then, we mean by 'This rose is beautiful' is 'This rose is beautiful for a normal human being'. But what is normal? That depends on the circle of human beings one has in mind. If there is some remote mountain valley where nearly all the people have goitres, then having a goitre will be looked on as normal there, and those who lack such an adornment will be considered ugly. How is a negro from the heart of Africa to be weaned from the view that the narrow nose of the European is ugly, whereas the broad nose of the negro is beautiful? And cannot a negro *qua* negro be just as normal as a white man *qua* white man? Cannot a child be just as normal as a grown-up? The ideas that are awakened in us by the power of association have a great influence on the judgements a man forms of what is beautiful, and these ideas depend upon what he has absorbed in earlier life. But this | varies from person to person. And even if we managed to define a normal human being and so 'beautiful' in an objective sense, it would still be only possible to do this on the basis of the subjective sense. Far from having rid ourselves of this, we would have recognized it as the root sense. We could not alter the situation by trying to substitute an ideal human being for a normal one. In the absence of experiences and ideas there would be no instance of anything subjectively beautiful and therefore no instance of anything objectively beautiful either. There is therefore much to be said for the view that the real work of art is a structure of ideas within us and that the external thing – the painting, the statue – is only a means for producing the real work of art in us. On this view, anyone who enjoys a work of art has his own work of art, with the consequence that there is no contradiction whatever between varying aesthetic judgements. Hence: *de gustibus non disputandum.*

144

If anyone tried to contradict the statement that what is true is true independently of our recognizing it as such, he would by his very assertion contradict what he had asserted; he would be in a similar position to the Cretan who said that all Cretans are liars.

To elaborate: if something were true only for him who held it to be true, there would be no contradiction between the opinions of different people. So to be consistent, any person holding this view would have no right whatever to contradict the opposite view; he would have to espouse the principle: *non disputandum est*. He would not be able to assert anything at all in the normal sense, and even if his utterances had the form of assertions, they would only have the status of interjections – of expressions of mental states or processes, between which and such states or processes in another person there could be no contradiction. And in that case his assertion that something was true only for us and through being recognized by us as such would have this status too. If this view were true, it would be impossible to claim that any of his own opinions was more justified in the eyes of others than the opposite opinion. A view that made such a claim would be unjustified; this would mean [*das hiesse*], however, that every opinion would be unjustified in the usual sense of the word, and so also those opinions to which we were opposed. There would be no science, no error and no correction of error; properly speaking, there would be nothing true in the normal sense of the word. For this is so closely bound up with that independence of being recognized as true, which we are emphasizing here, that it cannot be separated from it. If anyone seriously and sincerely defended the view we are here attacking, we should have no recourse but to assume that he was attaching a different sense to the word 'true'.

We can go a step further. In order to be true, thoughts – e.g. laws of nature – not only do not need to be recognized by us as true: they do not have to have been thought by us at all. A law of nature is not invented by us, but discovered, and just as a desolate island in the Arctic Ocean was there long before anyone had set eyes on it, so the laws of nature, and likewise those of mathematics, have held good at all times and not just since they were discovered. This shows us that these thoughts, if true, | are not only true independently of our recognizing them to be so, but that they are independent of our thinking as such. A thought does not belong specially to the person who thinks it, as does an idea to the person who has it: everyone who grasps it encounters it in the same way, as the same thought. Otherwise two people would never attach the same thought to the same sentence, but each would have his own thought; and if, say, one person put $2 \cdot 2 = 4$ forward as true whilst another denied it, there would be no contradiction, because what was asserted by one would be different from what was rejected by the other. It would be quite impossible for the assertions of different people to contradict one another, for a contradiction occurs only when it is the very same thought that one person is asserting to be true and another to be false. So a dispute about the truth of something would be futile. There would simply be no common ground to fight on; each thought would be enclosed in its own private world and a contradiction between the thoughts of different people would be like a war between ourselves and the inhabitants of Mars. Nor must we say that one person might communicate his thought to another and a conflict would then flare up in the latter's private world. It would be quite impossible for a thought to be so communicated that it should pass out of the private world of one person into that of another. The thought that entered the latter's mind as a result of the communication would be different from the thought in the former's mind; and the slightest alteration can transform a truth into a falsehood. If we wanted to regard a thought as something psychological, as a structure of ideas, without, however, adopting a wholly subjective standpoint, we should have to explain the assertion that $2 + 3 = 5$ on something like the following lines: 'It has been observed that with many people certain ideas form themselves in association with the sentence "$2 + 3 = 5$". We call a formation of this kind the sense of the sentence "$2 + 3 = 5$". So far as we have observed hitherto these formations are always true; we may therefore make the provisional statement "Going by the observations made hitherto, the sense of the sentence '$2 + 3 = 5$' is true".' But it is obvious that this explanation would not work at all. And it would leave us where we were, for the sense of the sentence 'It has been observed that with many people certain ideas form themselves etc.' would of course be a formation of ideas too and the whole thing would begin over again. A soup that tastes pleasant to one person, may be nauseous to another. In such a case each person is really making a judgement about his own sensation of taste, and this is different from the other's. The same would hold for thoughts if a thought were related to a sentence in the same kind of way as sensations of taste are related to the chemical stimuli that excite them.

If a thought, like an idea, were something private and mental, then the truth of a thought could surely only consist in a relation to something that was not private or mental. So if we wanted to know whether a
146   thought | was true, we should have to ask whether the relation in question obtained and thus whether the thought that this relation obtained was true. And so we should be in the position of a man on a treadmill who makes a step forwards and upwards, but the step he treads on keeps giving way and he falls back to where he was before.

A thought is something impersonal. If we see the sentence '$2 + 3 = 5$' written on a wall, we have no difficulty at all in recognizing the thought expressed by it, and we do not need to know who has written it there in order to understand it.

A sentence like 'I am cold' may seem to be a counter-example to our thesis that a thought is independent of the person thinking it, in so far as it can be true for one person and false for another, and thus not true in itself. The reason for this is that the sentence expresses a different thought in the mouth of one person from what it expresses in the mouth of another. In this case the mere words do not contain the entire sense: we have in addition to take into account who utters it. There are many cases like this in which the spoken word has to be supplemented by the speaker's gesture and expression, and the accompanying circumstances. The word 'I' simply designates a different person in the mouths of different people. It is not necessary that the person who feels cold should himself give utterance to the thought that he feels cold. Another person can do this by using a name to designate the one who feels cold.

In this way a thought can be clothed in a sentence that is more in keeping with its being independent of the person thinking it. The possibility of doing this distinguishes it from a mental state expressed by an interjection. Words like 'here' and 'now' only acquire their full sense through the circumstances in which they are used. If someone says 'It is raining', the time and place of utterance have to be supplied. If such a sentence is written down, it often no longer has a complete sense, because there is nothing to indicate who uttered it, and where and when. As regards a sentence containing a judgement of taste like 'This rose is beautiful', the identity of the speaker is essential to the sense, even though the word 'I' does not occur in it. So the explanation for all these apparent exceptions is that the same sentence does not always express the same thought, because the words need to be supplemented in order to get a complete sense, and how this is done can vary according to the circumstances.[10]

Whereas ideas (in the psychological sense of the word) have no fixed boundaries, but are constantly changing and, Proteus-like, assume different forms, thoughts always remain the same. It is of the essence of a thought to be non-temporal and non-spatial. In the case of the thought that $3 + 4 = 7$ and the laws of nature there is hardly any need to support this statement. If it should turn out that the law of gravitation ceased to be true from a certain moment onwards, we should conclude that it was not true at all, and put ourselves out to discover a new law: the new one would differ in containing a condition which would be satisfied at one time but not at another. It is the same with place. If it should transpire that the law of gravitation was not valid in the neighbourhood 147 of Sirius, | we should search for another law which contained a condition

---

[10] Cf. *T*, pp. 331–3 below. For discussion of some of the problems that indexicality raises for Frege's conception of thought, which surface in the last two paragraphs, see the Introduction, pp. 31–5 above.

that was satisfied in our solar system but not in the neighbourhood of Sirius. If someone wished to cite, say, 'The total number of inhabitants of the German Empire is 52,000,000', as a counter-example to the timelessness of thoughts, I should reply: This sentence is not a complete expression of a thought at all, since it lacks a time-determination. If we add such a determination, for example, 'at noon on 1 January 1897 by central European time', then the thought is either true, in which case it is always, or better, timelessly, true, or it is false and in that case it is false without qualification.[11] This holds of any particular historical fact: if it is true, it is true independently of the time at which it is judged to be true. It is no objection that a sentence may acquire a different sense in the course of time; for what changes in such a case is of course the language, not the thought. In another language this shift need not take place. It is true of course that we speak of men's thoughts as being liable to change. However it is not the thoughts which are true at one time and false at another: it is only that they are held to be true at one time and false at another.

What if it is objected that I am attaching to the word 'thought' a sense that it does not ordinarily have, and that other people understand by it an act of thinking, which is obviously private and mental? Well, the important thing is that I remain true to my way of using it; whether this agrees with the ordinary use is of less importance. It may well be the case that people sometimes understand by the word 'thought' an act of thinking – in any case this is not always so[B] – and such an act cannot be true. |

[B] Dedekind, in proposition 66 of his work *Was sind und was sollen die Zahlen?*, uses this word as I do. For he is attempting there to prove that the totality of things that can be objects of his thinking is infinite. Let s be such an object; then Dedekind calls $\phi(s)$ the thought that s can be an object of his thinking. And this thought can now itself be an object of his thinking. Thus $\phi(\phi(s))$ is the thought that the thought that s can be an object of his thinking can be an object of his thinking. We can see from this what '$\phi(\phi(\phi(s)))$', '$\phi(\phi(\phi(\phi(s))))$' and so on, are supposed to stand for [*bedeuten*]. It is essential to the proof that the sentence 's can be an object of Dedekind's thinking' always expresses a thought when the letter 's' designates such an | object. Now if, as Dedekind wishes to prove, there are infinitely many such objects s, there must also be infinitely many such thoughts $\phi(s)$. Now presumably we shall not hurt Dedekind's feelings if we assume that he has not thought infinitely many thoughts. Equally he should not assume that others have already thought infinitely many thoughts which could be the objects of his thinking; for this would be to assume what was to be proved. Now if infinitely many thoughts have not yet been thought, the infinitely many thoughts $\phi(s)$ must comprise infinitely many thoughts that are not thought, in which case it cannot be essential to a thought that it should be thought. And this is precisely what I am maintaining. If there were only thoughts that are thought, the sign '$\phi(s)$' would not always have a *Bedeutung*; to ensure that it did have, it is not sufficient for 's' to stand for [*bedeutete*] something that could be an object of Dedekind's thinking: it would also have to have been thought by someone in order to be

---

[11] Cf. *GL*, §46 (p. 99 above), where the same example was used in discussing concepts.

148   In logic, as in other sciences, it is open to us to coin technical terms, regardless of whether the words are always used in precisely that way in everyday life. It does not matter if the *Bedeutung* we fix on is not altogether in line with everyday use or does not accord with the word's etymology; what does matter is to make it as appropriate a vehicle as possible for use in expressing laws. Provided there is no loss of rigour, the more compendious the formulation of the complete system of laws, the more felicitous is the apparatus of technical terms.

   Now we cannot regard thinking as a process which generates thoughts. It would be just as wrong to identify a thought with an act of thinking, so that a thought is related to thinking as a leap is to leaping. This view

149 is | in harmony with many of our ways of talking. For do we not say that the same thought is grasped by this person and by that person? And that each person has the same thought over and over again? Now if thoughts only came into existence as a result of thinking or if they were constituted by thinking, then the same thought could come into existence, cease to exist, and then come into existence again, which is absurd. As I do not create a tree by looking at it or cause a pencil to come into existence by taking hold of it, neither do I generate a thought by thinking. And still less does the brain secrete thoughts, as the liver does gall.

   The metaphors that underlie the expressions we use when we speak of grasping a thought, of conceiving, laying hold of, seizing, understanding, of *capere, percipere, comprehendere, intelligere,* put the matter in essentially the right perspective. What is grasped, taken hold of, is already there and all we do is take possession of it. Likewise, what we see into or single out from amongst other things is already there and does not come into existence as a result of these activities. Of course all metaphors go lame at some point. We are inclined to regard what is independent of our mental processes as something spatial or material,

---

a possible object of Dedekind's thinking. If this were not the case, then the sign '$\phi(s)$' would have no *Bedeutung* for the given s. The sun ($\odot$) can be an object of Dedekind's thinking; hence the first two members and perhaps a few successive members of the series '$\odot$', '$\phi(\odot)$', '$\phi(\phi(\odot))$' ... have a *Bedeutung*. But as we progressed along the series we would be bound eventually to reach a member that was *bedeutungslos*, because the thought which it was meant to designate had not been thought, and so was not to hand. In that case '$\phi(s)$' would resemble a power series which did not converge for every value of the argument. The fact that the series diverged would correspond to the sign '$\phi(s)$' becoming *bedeutungslos* [*dem Bedeutungsloswerden des Zeichens* '$\phi(s)$']. If we assume a power series with radius of convergence 4 and if we assume, further, that the series has the value 2 for 1 as argument and the value 5 for 2 as argument, then the corresponding series of numbers 1, 2, 5 comes to an end at this point and does not go on to infinity. In the same way the series $\odot$, $\phi(\odot)$, $\phi(\phi(\odot))$, does not go on to infinity if there are only thoughts that are thought. So the validity of Dedekind's proofs rests on the assumption that thoughts obtain independently of our thinking. We can see how this use is one to which the word 'thought' naturally lends itself.

and the words that we have just listed make it look as if this is what a thought actually is. But this is not where the point of the comparison lies. What is independent of our mental processes, what is objective, does not *have* to be spatial or material or actual. If we were to disregard this we should easily slip into a kind of mythology. To say 'The laws of gravitation, of inertia, of the parallelogram of forces cause the Earth to move as it does move', might make it look as if these laws, so to speak, took the Earth by the ears and kept it on the path they prescribe. Such a use of the words 'affect', 'cause', would be misleading. On the other hand, it is all right to say that the Sun and planets act on one another in accordance with the laws of gravitation.

So even if physical bodies and thoughts resemble one another in being independent of my inner life, we are not entitled to conclude from this that thoughts can be moved as bodies can, or can be smelled or tasted, and it would be invalid to seek somehow to draw from the absurdity of such inference an objection to our views. Although a law of nature obtains quite independently of whether we think of it or not, it does not emit light or sound waves by which our visual or auditory nerves could be affected. But do I not then see that this flower has five petals? We can say this, but if we do, the word 'see' is not being used in the sense of having a mere visual experience: what we mean [*meinen*] by it is bound up with thinking and judging. Newton did not discover the law of gravitation because his senses were especially acute.

If we wish to speak of a thought as being actual, we can do so only in the sense that the knowledge that someone has of e.g. a law of nature has an influence on the decisions he makes, which in their turn may affect the course of history. We should then be thinking of the recog-
150 nition of a | law as a case of a law's acting upon us, and it is perhaps possible to do this, just as we can regard, say, the seeing of a flower as the flower's indirectly acting on us.

We can disregard thoughts and we can take possession of them. We might conceive of the latter as a case of our acting on thoughts, which seems to speak against their being timeless. But the thought is not changed in itself by being thus acted on, just as the Moon is apparently unaffected whether we take any notice of it or not. So even though it may be possible to speak of thoughts as acting on us, we cannot speak of ourselves as acting on thoughts. We might cite, as an instance of thoughts being subject to change, the fact that they are not always immediately clear. But what is called the clarity of a thought in our sense of this word is really a matter of how thoroughly it has been assimilated or grasped, and is not a property of a thought.

It would be wrong to think that it is only true thoughts that obtained independently of our mental life, and that false ones, on the other hand, belonged, as ideas do, to our inner life. Almost everything that we have said about the predicate *true* holds for the predicate *false* as well. In the strict sense it applies only to thoughts. Where it looks to be predicated of sentences or ideas, still at bottom it is being predicated of thoughts. What is false is false in itself and independently of our opinions. A dispute over the falsity of something is at the same time a dispute over the truth of something. Therefore the thing whose falsity can be a matter for dispute does not belong to some mind or other.

Separating a thought from its trappings

In an assertoric sentence two different kinds of thing are usually intimately bound up with one another: the thought expressed and the assertion of its truth. And this is why these are often not clearly distinguished. However, one can express a thought without at the same time putting it forward as true. A scientist who makes a scientific discovery usually begins by grasping just a thought, and then he asks himself whether it is to be recognized as true; it is not until his investigation has turned out in favour of the hypothesis, that he ventures to put it forward as true. We express the same thought in the question 'Is oxygen condensable?' and in the sentence 'Oxygen is condensable', joining it in the one case with a request and in the other with an assertion.

When we inwardly recognize that a thought is true, we are making a judgement: when we communicate this recognition, we are making an assertion.

We can think without making a judgement.

We have seen that the series of sounds that compose a sentence is often not sufficient for the complete expression of a thought. If we wish

151   to bring the essence of a thought | into as sharp a focus as possible, we ought not to overlook the fact that the converse case is not uncommon, the case where a sentence does more than express a thought and assert its truth. In many cases a sentence is meant to have an effect on the ideas and feelings of the hearer as well; and the more closely it approximates to the language of poetry, the greater this effect is meant to be. We have indeed stressed the fact that language is but poorly suited for calling up at will an idea in the mind of a hearer with any precision. Who would ever rely on words to evoke as precise a mental picture of an Apollo as can be produced without difficulty by looking at a piece of sculpture? Even so, we do say that the poet paints things. And in fact it cannot be denied that the spoken word affects the ideas we have just because it enters consciousness as a complex of auditory sensations. Right from the start we experience the series of sounds themselves, the tone of the voice, the intonation and rhythm with feelings of pleasure or displeasure. These sensations of sound are linked to auditory ideas that resemble them and these latter are linked in turn

with further ideas reactivated by them. This is the domain of onomato-poeia. Here we may cite the Homeric verse (*Odyssey* IX, 71): τριχθά τε καὶ τετραχθὰ διέσχισεν ἲς ἀνέμοιο.[12]

This is quite independent of the aim of words to express thoughts. Here the sounds are acting only as a sensory stimulus. But because sequences of such sounds are meant to have a sense they act upon the imagination in yet a different way. Anyone who hears the word 'horse' and understands it will probably have straightaway a picture of a horse in his mind. This picture, however, is not to be confused with the sense of the word 'horse'; for the word 'horse' gives no clue to the colour of the horse, or to its carriage when standing still or in motion, or to the side from which it is seen and the like. If different people were able, say, immediately to project onto a canvas the ideas that sprung up in their minds on hearing the word 'horse', then we should be presented with quite different pictures. And even with the same person the word 'horse' does not always conjure up the same idea. Here a great deal depends on the context. We may compare e.g. the sentences 'With what joy he rides his gallant horse' and 'I just saw a horse stumble on the wet asphalt'.

So there can be no question of the same idea always being associated with the word 'horse'. Thus in virtue of its sense such a word will excite a certain idea in us, but by itself it is far from determining this idea completely. Generally speaking the most we are entitled to assume is that the ideas of the speaker and hearer are very roughly in agreement. If several artists produce, independently of one another, illustrations of the same poem, they will diverge considerably from one another in the portrayal they give. Thus the poet does not really paint anything: he only provides the impetus for others to do so, furnishing hints to this end, and leaving it to the hearer to give his words body and shape. And in this connection it is useful to the poet to have at his disposal a num-ber of different words that can be substituted for one another without 152 altering the thought, | but which can act in different ways on the feelings and imagination of the hearer. We may think e.g. of the words 'walk', 'stroll', 'saunter'. These means are also used to the same end in everyday language. If we compare the sentences 'This dog howled the whole night' and 'This cur howled the whole night', we find that the thought is the same. The first sentence tells us neither more nor less than does the second. But whilst the word 'dog' is neutral as between having pleasant or unpleasant associations, the word 'cur' certainly has unpleasant rather than pleasant associations and puts us rather in mind

---

[12] Transliterated, the whole clause reads (*Odyssey*, IX, lines 70–1): . . . *histia de sphin/ trichtha te kai tetrachtha dieschisen is anemoio* ('the sails were torn into three or four parts by the violence of the wind').

of a dog with a somewhat unkempt appearance. Even if it is grossly unfair to the dog to think of it in this way, we cannot say that this makes the second sentence false. True, anyone who utters this sentence speaks pejoratively, but this is not part of the thought expressed. What distinguishes the second sentence from the first is of the nature of an interjection. It might be thought that the second sentence does nevertheless tell us more than the first, namely that the speaker has a poor opinion of the dog. In that case, the word 'cur' would contain an entire thought. We can put this to the test in the following way.[13]

We assume that the first sentence is true and the second sentence is spoken by someone who does not actually feel the contempt which the word 'cur' seems to imply. If the objection were correct, the second sentence would now contain two thoughts, one of which was false; so it would assert something false as a whole, whilst the first sentence would be true. We shall hardly go along with this; rather the use of the word 'cur' does not prevent us from holding that the second sentence is true as well. For we have to make a distinction between the thoughts that are expressed and those which the speaker leads others to take as true although he does not express them. If a commander conceals his weakness from the enemy by making his troops keep changing their uniforms, he is not telling a lie; for he is not expressing any thoughts, although his actions are calculated to induce thoughts in others. And we find the same thing in the case of speech itself, as when one gives a special tone to the voice or chooses special words. If someone announces the news of a death in a sad tone of voice without actually being sad, the thought expressed is still true even if the sad tone is assumed in order to create a false impression. And we can substitute words like 'ah' and 'unfortunately' for such a tone of voice without altering the thought. Naturally things are different if certain actions are specifically agreed on as a means of communicating something. In language common usage takes the place of such agreements. Of course borderline cases can arise because language changes. Something that was not originally employed as a means of expressing a thought may eventually come to do this because it has constantly been used in cases of the same kind. A thought which to begin with was only suggested by an 153 expression | may come to be explicitly asserted by it. And in the period in between different interpretations will be possible. But the distinction itself is not obliterated by such fluctuations in language. In the present context the only essential thing for us is that a different thought does not correspond to every difference in the words used, and that we have a means of deciding what is and what is not part of the thought, even

---

[13] For more explicit formulations of a criterion of identity for thoughts, cf. pp. 299–300 and 305–6 below.

though, with language constantly developing, it may at times be difficult to apply.

The distinction between the active and passive voice belongs here too. The sentences 'M gave document A to N', 'Document A was given to N by M', 'N received document A from M' express exactly the same thought; we learn not a whit more or less from any one of these sentences than we do from the others. Hence it is impossible that one of them should be true whilst another is false. It is the very same thing that is here capable of being true or false. For all this we are not in a position to say that it is a matter of complete indifference which of these sentences we use. As a rule stylistic and aesthetic reasons will give the preference to one of them. If someone asks 'Why has A been arrested?' it would be unnatural to reply 'B has been murdered by him', because it would require a needless switch of the attention from A to B. Although in actual speech it can certainly be very important where the attention is directed and where the stress falls, it is of no concern to logic.

In translating from one language to another it is sometimes necessary to dispense with the original grammatical construction altogether. Nevertheless, this need not affect the thought and it must not do so, if the translation is to be correct. But it is sometimes necessary to sacrifice the feeling and colour of the original.

Again in the two sentences 'Frederick the Great won the battle of Rossbach' and 'It is true that Frederick the Great won the battle of Rossbach', we have, as we said earlier, the same thought in a different verbal form. In affirming the thought in the first sentence we thereby affirm the thought in the second, and conversely. There are not two different acts of judgement, but only one.

(From all this we can see that the grammatical categories of subject and predicate can have no significance for logic.)

The distinction between what is part of the thought expressed in a sentence and what only gets attached to the thought is of the greatest importance for logic.[14] The purity of the object of one's investigation is not of importance only to the chemist. How would the chemist be able to recognize, beyond any doubt, that he has arrived at the same results by different means, if the apparent difference of means could be traced back to impurities in the substances used? There is no doubt that the first and most important discoveries in a science are often a matter of recognizing something as the same again. However self-evident it may seem to us that it is the same sun which went down yesterday and rose today, and however insignificant therefore this discovery | may seem to us, it has certainly been one of the most important in astronomy and

154

---

[14] Cf. fn. G of *CO*, pp. 184–5 above; *T*, pp. 330–1 below.

perhaps the one that really laid the foundations of the science. It was also important to recognize that the Morning Star is the same as the Evening Star, that three times five is the same as five times three. It is just as important not to distinguish what is the same as it is to be alive to differences when they don't hit one in the eye. So it is quite wrong to think that one can never make too many distinctions. It does nothing but harm to insist on distinctions where they are not relevant. Thus in general mechanics we shall take care not to speak of the chemical differences between substances and not to state the law of inertia in a special form for, say, each chemical element. We shall only take those differences into account that are essential to the formulation of the laws with which we are actually concerned. Above all, we must not let ourselves be seduced by the presence of extraneous factors into seeing distinctions where there are none.

In logic we must reject all distinctions that are made from a purely psychological point of view. What is referred to as a deepening of logic by psychology is nothing but a falsification of it by psychology.

In human beings it is natural for thinking to be intermingled with having images and feeling. Logic has the task of isolating what is logical, not, to be sure, so that we should think without having images, which is no doubt impossible, but so that we should consciously distinguish the logical from what is attached to it in the way of ideas and feelings. There is a difficulty here in that we think in some language or other and that grammar, which has a significance for language analogous to that which logic has for judgement, is a mixture of the logical and the psychological. If this were not so, all languages would necessarily have the same grammar. It is true that we can express the same thought in different languages; but the psychological trappings, the clothing of the thought, will often be different. This is why the learning of foreign languages is useful for one's logical education. Seeing that the same thought can be worded in different ways, we learn better to distinguish the verbal husk from the kernel with which, in any given language, it appears to be organically bound up. This is how the differences between languages can facilitate our grasp of what is logical. But still the difficulties are not wholly removed in this way, and our logic books still keep dragging in a number of things – subject and predicate, for example – which do not, strictly speaking, belong to logic. For this reason it is useful to be acquainted also with a means of expressing thoughts that is of a radically different nature, such as we have in the formula language of arithmetic or in my *Begriffsschrift*.

The first and most important task is to set out clearly what the objects to be investigated are. Only if we do this shall we be able to recognize the same as the same: in logic too, such acts of recognition probably constitute the fundamental discoveries. Therefore let us never forget that two different sentences can express the same thought, that we are concerned with only that part of a sentence's content which can be true or false. |

155   Even if there were only a jot more to the thought contained in the passive form than in the active, it would be conceivable that this jot should be false whilst the thought contained in the active form was true, and that we should not be entitled without more ado to go over from the active to the passive form. Likewise if there were only a jot more to the thought contained in the active form than in the passive, we should not be able to go over from the passive form to the active without examining the particular case in hand. But if both transitions can always be made *salva veritate*, then this confirms that what is true here, namely the thought, is not affected by this change of form. This serves as a warning not to attach too much weight to linguistic distinctions, as logicians are prone to: a case in point being the assumption that every thought – or judgement as it is usually called – has a subject and a predicate, so that the subject and predicate of a thought are determined by the thought, as the subject and predicate of a sentence are unambiguously given along with the sentence. If we make this assumption, we only get involved in quite unnecessary difficulties, and, grappling with them to no effect, we only strengthen the impression that the science of logic is really quite superfluous.

We shall have no truck with the expressions 'subject' and 'predicate', of which logicians are so fond, especially since they not only make it more difficult for us to recognize the same as the same, but also conceal distinctions that are there. Instead of following grammar blindly, the logician ought rather to see his task as that of freeing us from the fetters of language. For however true it is that thinking, at least in its higher forms, was only made possible by means of language, we have nevertheless to take great care not to become dependent on language; for very many of the mistakes that occur in reasoning have their source in the logical imperfections of language. Of course if we see the task of logic to be that of describing how people actually think, then we shall naturally have to accord great importance to language. But then the name logic is being used for what is really only a branch of psychology. This is as if one imagined that one was doing astronomy when one was developing a psychophysical theory of how one sees through a telescope. In the former case the things that are the proper concern of logic do not come into view any more than in the latter case do the problems of astronomy. Psychological treatments of logic arise from the mistaken belief that a thought (a judgement as it is usually called) is something psychological like an idea. This view leads necessarily to an idealist theory of knowledge; for if it is correct, then the parts that we distinguish in a thought, such as subject and predicate, must belong as much to psychology as do thoughts themselves. Now since every act of cognition is realized in judgements, this means the breakdown of every bridge leading to what is objective. And all our striving to attain to this can be no more than an attempt to draw ourselves up by our own bootstraps. The most we can do is to try to explain how it comes to seem that there is such a thing as what is objective, how we come to assume the existence of something that is not part of our mind | without, however, our thereby having any justification for this assumption. Physiological psychology[15] provides us with the most striking case of this slide into idealism because its realistic point of departure stands in such sharp contrast to it.[16] We start out with nerve fibres and ganglion cells and make assumptions about impulses and how they are transmitted, and we seek in this way to make ideation more intelligible, since we can't help regarding processes in the ganglion cells and nerve fibres as more intelligible than the process of ideation. As befits a science worthy of the name, we do not hesitate to take it for granted, when we proceed like this, that ganglion cells and nerve fibres are objective and real. This will probably work perfectly well so long as we confine ourselves to ideation. But we do not stop there: we move on to thinking and judgement as well, and at this point what began as realism suddenly turns into an extreme form of idealism; in this way realism itself cuts off the branch on which it is sitting. Now everything is dissolved into ideas and as a result the earlier explanations themselves become illusory. Anatomy and physiology turn into fictions. The whole physio-anatomical foundation of nerve fibres, ganglion cells, stimuli, impulses and transmission of impulses disintegrates. And what are we left with? Ideas of nerve fibres, ideas of ganglion cells, ideas of stimuli and so on. And what did we start off with the intention of explaining! The having of ideas! Well, can one say of these explanations that there is any truth or reason in them at all? Standing by a river one often sees eddies in the water. Now would it not be absurd to claim that such an eddy of water was sound or true? And even if the dance of the atoms and molecules in my brain was a thousand times more spirited and frenzied than the dance of gnats on a summer evening, would it not be just as absurd to assert that it was sound or true? And if the explanations above were gyrations of this sort, could we ever say they were true? And is it any different in the end if these explanations are congeries of ideas? And the phantasms that pass before the mind of the typhus victim in a constant procession, as one picture gives way to another, are they true? They are no more true than they are false; they are simply processes, as an eddy in water

---

[15] Frege almost certainly has in mind here the work of Wilhelm Wundt, whose *Grundzüge der physiologischen Psychologie* first appeared, in two volumes, in 1873–4, and in many editions thereafter (cf. *NS*, p. 156, editors' fn. 1).

[16] Cf. *T*, pp. 338–9 below.

is a process. And if we are to speak of a right, it can only be the right of things to happen as they do happen. One phantasm contradicts another no more than one eddy in water contradicts another.

If the visual idea of a rose is associated with the idea of a delicate scent and to these are added the auditory ideas of the words 'rose' and 'scent', as well as the motor ideas associated with uttering these words, and if we go on and on heaping associations upon associations until the most complex and elaborate idea is formed, what purpose does it serve? Do we really think we should have a thought as a result? The result would no more be a thought than an automaton, however cunningly contrived, is a living being. | Put something together out of parts that are inanimate and you still have something inanimate. Combine ideas and you still have an idea and the most varied and elaborate associations can make no difference. Even if, on top of these, the whole is imbued with feelings and moods, it is all to no avail. The law of gravitation can never come into existence in this way, for this law is quite independent of everything that goes on in my mind and of how my ideas change and fluctuate. But still the grasping of this law is a mental process! Yes, indeed, but it is a process which takes place on the very confines of the mental and which for that reason cannot be completely understood from a purely psychological standpoint. For in grasping the law something comes into view whose nature is no longer mental in the proper sense, namely the thought; and this process is perhaps the most mysterious of all. But just because it is mental in character we do not need to concern ourselves with it in logic. It is enough for us that we can grasp thoughts and recognize them to be true; how this takes place is a question in its own right.[c] It is surely enough for the chemist too that he can see, smell and taste; it is not his business to investigate how these things take place. It is not immaterial to the success of a scientific investigation that questions which can be treated independently of others are not confounded with them, with the result that we create unnecessary difficulties. That easily leads to our seeing things crossways on. So we shall not trouble ourselves with asking how we actually think or arrive at our convictions. It is not the holding something to be true that concerns us but the laws of truth.[17] We can also think of these as prescriptions for making judgements; we must comply with them in our judgements if we are not to fail of the truth. So if we call them laws of thought or, better, laws of judgement, we must not forget we are concerned here with laws which, like the principles of morals or the laws

[c] I should say that this question is still far from being grasped in all its difficulty. People are usually quite content to smuggle thinking in through a back door in the imagination, so that they don't themselves know how it really got in.

[17] Cf. *GG*, I, Preface, pp. 202–4 above.

of the state, prescribe how we are to act, and do not, like the laws of nature, define the actual course of events. Thinking, as it actually takes place, is not always in agreement with the laws of logic any more than people's actual behaviour is always in agreement with the moral law. I therefore think it better to avoid the expression 'laws of thought' altogether in logic, because it always misleads us into thinking of laws of thought as laws of nature. If that is what they were we should have to assign them to psychology. We could, with equal justice, think of the laws of geometry and the laws of physics as laws of thought or laws of judgement, namely as prescriptions to which our judgements must conform in a different domain if they are to remain in agreement with the truth. Logic, then, is no more the right place for conducting psychological 158 investigations than is geometry or physics. | To explain how thinking and judging take place is certainly a feasible undertaking, but it is not a logical one.

Accordingly, the logician does not have to ask what course thinking naturally takes in the human mind. What is natural to one man may well be unnatural to another. The great difference between grammars itself bears witness to this. The logician need fear nothing less than to be reproached with the fact that his statements do not accord with how we think naturally. The normal person with no training in mathematics would find it highly unnatural if he were to have the rudiments of the subject explained to him in terms of the utmost rigour, and for that very reason. A prudent teacher will therefore tend to let rigour go by the board in introducing the subject and will only seek to awaken the need for it bit by bit. Even in the history of mathematics we find that the highest degree of rigour is achieved only towards the end and that consequently it is at the farthest removed from what is natural.[18] Hence to strive to present the process of thinking in its natural form would lead us directly away from logic. If the logician tried to take account of objections on the score that what he said was unnatural, he would be in danger of involving himself in endless disputes over what is natural – disputes which logic is quite incapable of resolving on its own grounds and which, therefore, do not belong to logic. To resolve them we should presumably have to resort to observing primitive peoples.

But above all we should be wary of the view that it is the business of logic to investigate how we actually think and judge when we are in agreement with the laws of truth. If that were so, we should have constantly to have one eye on the one thing and one eye on the other, and continue paying attention to the latter whilst taking a sidelong glance at the former, and in the process we should easily lose sight of a definite goal altogether. We should be seduced into asking unclear questions

---

[18] Cf. *GL*, Introd., pp. 88–9 above.

and as a result a satisfactory outcome to our investigations would be as good as impossible.

What are often called laws of thought, namely laws in accordance with which judging, at least in normal cases, takes place, can be nothing but laws for holding something to be true, not laws of truth. If a man holds something to be true – and the psychological logicians will surely hold that their own statements at least are true – he thereby acknowledges that there is such a thing as something's being true. But in that case it is surely probable that there will be laws of truth as well, and if there are, these must provide the norm for holding something to be true. And these will be the laws of logic proper. In supplement No. 26 to the 1897 Proceedings of the *Allgemeine Zeitung*, T. Achelis writes in an essay entitled 'Völkerkunde und Philosophie':[19] 'But we are now clear about this, that the norms which hold in general for thinking and acting cannot be arrived at by the one-sided exercise of pure deductive abstraction alone; what is required is an empirico-critical determination of the objective principles of our psychophysical organization which are valid at all times for the great consciousness of mankind.' |

159   It is not quite clear whether this is about laws in accordance with which judgements are made or about laws in accordance with which they should be made. It appears to be about both. That is to say, the laws in accordance with which judgements are made are set up as a norm for how judgements are to be made. But why do we need to do this? Don't we automatically judge in accordance with these laws? No! *Not* automatically; normally, yes, but not always! So these are laws which have exceptions, but the exceptions will themselves be governed by further laws. So the laws that we have set up do not comprise all of them. Now what is our justification for isolating a part of the entire corpus of laws and setting it up as a norm? To do that is like wanting to present Kepler's laws of planetary motion as a norm and then being forced, alas, to recognize that the planets in their wilfulness do not behave in strict conformity with them but, like spoilt children, have disturbing effects on one another. Such behaviour would then have to be severely reprimanded.

On this view we shall have to exercise every care not to stray from the path taken by the solid majority. We shall even mistrust the greatest geniuses; for if they were normal, they would be mediocre.

With the psychological conception of logic we lose the distinction between the grounds that justify a conviction and the causes that actually

---

[19] The essay concerned a review of A. Vierkandt, *Naturvölker und Culturvölker, ein Beitrag zur Sozialphilosophie* (Leipzig, 1896). The supplement appeared on 3 February. (Cf. *NS*, p. 158, editors' fn. 1.) It is the quotation from this essay by Achelis, together with a reference in an example in the first section to 'noon on 1 January 1897' (*PW*, p. 135/ *NS*, p. 147), that makes 1897 the most likely date of composition of the present work.

produce it. This means that a justification in the proper sense is not possible; what we have in its place is an account of how the conviction was arrived at, from which it is to be inferred that everything has been caused by psychological factors. This puts a superstition on the same footing as a scientific discovery.

If we think of the laws of logic as psychological, we shall be inclined to raise the question whether they are somehow subject to change. Are they like the grammar of a language, which may, of course, change with the passage of time? This is a possibility we really have to face up to if we hold that the laws of logic derive their authority from a source similar to that of the laws of grammar, if they are norms only because we seldom deviate from them, if it is normal to judge in accordance with our laws of logic as it normal to walk upright. Just as there may have been a time when it was not normal for our ancestors to talk upright, so many modes of thinking might have been normal in the past which are not so now, and in the future something might be normal that is not so at the present time. In a language whose form is not yet fixed there are always points of grammar on which our sense of idiom is unreliable, and a similar thing would have to hold in respect of the laws of logic whenever we were in a period of transition. We might, for instance, be in two minds whether it is correct to judge that every object is identical with itself. If that were so, we should not really be entitled to speak of logical laws, but only of logical rules that specify what is regarded as normal at a particular time. We should not be entitled to express such a rule in a form like 'Every object is identical with itself' for there is here no mention at all of the class of beings for whose judgements the rule is meant to be valid, but we should have to say something like 'At the present time it is normal for human beings – with the possible exception | of certain primitive peoples for whom the matter has not yet been investigated – to judge that every object is identical with itself'. However, once there are laws, even if they are psychological, then, as we have seen, they must always be true, or better, they must be timelessly true if they are true at all. Therefore if we had observed that from a certain time a law ceased to hold, then we should have to say that it was altogether false. What we could do, however, is to try to find a condition that would have to be added to the law. Let us assume that for a certain period of time people make judgements in accordance with the law that every object is identical with itself, but that after this time they cease to do so. Then the cause of this might be that the phosphorus content in the cerebral cortex had changed, and we should then have to say something like 'If the amount of phosphorus present in any part of man's cerebral cortex does not exceed 4 per cent, his judgement will always be in accordance with the law that every object is identical with itself'.

160

We can at least conceive of psychological laws that refer[20] in this way to the chemical composition of the brain or to its anatomical structure. On the other hand, such a reference would be absurd in the case of logical laws, for these are not concerned with what this or that man holds to be true, but with what is true. Whether a man holds the thought that $2.2 = 4$ to be true or to be false may depend on the chemical composition of his brain, but whether this thought is true cannot depend on that. Whether it is true that Julius Caesar was assassinated by Brutus cannot depend upon the structure of Professor Mommsen's brain.

People sometimes raise the question whether the laws of logic can change with time. The laws of truth, like all thoughts, are always true if they are true at all. Nor can they contain a condition which might be satisfied at certain times but not at others, because they are concerned with the truth of thoughts and if these are true, they are true timelessly. So if at one time the truth of some thought follows from the truth of certain others, then it must always follow.

Let us summarize what we have elicited about thoughts (properly so-called).

Unlike ideas, thoughts do not belong to the individual mind (they are not subjective), but are independent of our thinking and confront each one of us in the same way (objectively). They are not the product of thinking, but are only grasped by thinking. In this respect they are like physical bodies. What distinguishes them from physical bodies is that they are non-spatial, and we could perhaps really go as far as to say that they are essentially timeless – at least inasmuch as they are immune from anything that could effect a change in their intrinsic nature. They are like ideas in being non-spatial.

Since thoughts are not mental in nature, it follows that every psychological treatment of logic can only do harm. It is rather the task of this science to purify logic of all that is alien and hence of all that is psychological, | and to free thinking from the fetters of language by pointing up the logical imperfections of language. Logic is concerned with the laws of truth, not with the laws of holding something to be true, not with the question of how people think, but with the question of how they must think if they are not to miss the truth.

161

---

[20] 'auf . . . Bezug nehmen'.

On Euclidean Geometry[1]

[The following piece is taken from Frege's *Posthumous Writings*, and was probably written between 1899 and 1906, at the time that Frege was engaged in a debate with Hilbert on the foundations of geometry. Frege published two papers on the matter in 1903 and 1906,[2] his main concern being to refute Hilbert's conception of axioms. For Frege, axioms were *true propositions*, and the development of non-Euclidean geometries did not at all show that Euclidean geometry was not a body of (synthetic *a priori*) truths about the world. The remarks that follow reflect Frege's view throughout his career.]

183 No man can serve two masters. One cannot serve both truth and untruth. If Euclidean geometry is true, then non-Euclidean geometry is false, and if non-Euclidean geometry is true, then Euclidean geometry is false.

    If given a point not lying on a line one and only one line can be
184 drawn through that point parallel to that line then, given | any line *l* and point *P* not lying on *l*, a line can be drawn through *P* parallel to *l* and any line that passes through *P* and is parallel to *l* will coincide with it.

    Whoever acknowledges Euclidean geometry to be true must reject non-Euclidean geometry as false, and whoever acknowledges non-Euclidean geometry to be true must reject Euclidean geometry.

    People at one time believed they practised a science, which went by the name of alchemy; but when it was discovered that this supposed science was riddled with error, it was banished from among the sciences. Again, people at one time believed they practised a science, which went by the name of astrology. But this too was banished from among the sciences once men had seen through it and discovered that it was unscientific. The question at the present time is whether Euclidean or non-Euclidean geometry should be struck off the role of the sciences

[1] Translated by Peter Long and Roger White (*PW*, p. 169; from *NS*, pp. 183–4; page numbers from the latter in the margin).

[2] *FGI* and *FGII*. See also the Frege–Hilbert correspondence: *PMC*, pp. 31–52/*WB*, pp. 55–80.

and made to line up as a museum piece alongside alchemy and astrology. If one is content to have only phantoms hovering around one, there is no need to take the matter so seriously; but in science we are subject to the necessity of seeking after truth. There it is a case of in or out! Well, is it Euclidean or non-Euclidean geometry that should get the sack? That is the question. Do we dare to treat Euclid's elements, which have exercised unquestioned sway for 2000 years, as we have treated astrology? It is only if we do not dare to do this that we can put Euclid's axioms forward as propositions that are neither false nor doubtful. In that case non-Euclidean geometry will have to be counted amongst the pseudo-sciences, to the study of which we still attach some slight importance, but only as historical curiosities.

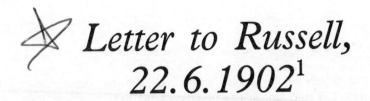

Letter to Russell, 22.6.1902[1]

[Russell first wrote (in German) to Frege on 16 June 1902, informing him of the contradiction that has come to be known as Russell's paradox. His opening paragraph is worth quoting in full:

> I have known your *Grundgesetze der Arithmetik* for a year and a half, but only now have I been able to find the time for the thorough study I intend to devote to your writings. I find myself in full accord with you on all main points, especially in your rejection of any psychological element in logic and in the value you attach to a *Begriffsschrift* for the foundations of mathematics and of formal logic, which, incidentally, can hardly be distinguished. On many questions of detail, I find discussions, distinctions and definitions in your writings for which one looks in vain in other logicians. On functions in particular (§9 of your *Begriffsschrift*) I have been led independently to the same views even in detail. I have encountered a difficulty only on one point. You assert (p. 17)[2] that a function could also constitute the indefinite element. This is what I used to believe, but this view now seems to me dubious because of the following contradiction: Let *w* be the predicate of being a predicate which cannot be predicated of itself. Can *w* be predicated of itself? From either answer follows its contradictory. We must therefore conclude that *w* is not a predicate. Likewise, there is no class (as a whole) of those classes which, as wholes, are not members of themselves. From this I conclude that under certain circumstances a definable set does not form a whole.[3]

Russell goes on to request offprints of Frege's articles, and expresses his hope that the second volume of *Grundgesetze* will soon appear. In his reply, dated just six days later, Frege encloses copies of 'On Concept and Object' and 'On *Sinn* and *Bedeutung*', amongst other things, and then goes on as follows.]

---

[1] Translated by Hans Kaal (*PMC*, pp. 132–3; from *WB*, pp. 213–5, p. 214 containing a facsimile of the second page of Frege's letter; page numbers from the latter in the margin).
[2] See p. 68 above.
[3] *PMC*, pp. 130–1; tr. from *WB*, p. 211.

Jena
22 June 1902

Dear Colleague,

. . .

213   Your discovery of the contradiction has surprised me beyond
words and, I should almost like to say, left me thunderstruck, because it has rocked the ground on which I meant to build arithmetic. It seems accordingly that the transformation of the generality
of an equality [*Gleichheit*] into an equality of value-ranges (§9 of my
Grundgesetze) is not always permissible, that my law V (§20, p. 36)
is false, and that my explanations in §31 do not suffice to secure
a *Bedeutung* for my combinations of signs in all cases. I must give
some further thought to the matter. It is all the more serious as the
collapse of my law V seems to undermine not only the foundations
of my arithmetic but the only possible foundations of arithmetic as
such. And yet, I should think, it must be possible to set up conditions
for the transformation of the generality of an equality into an equality
of value-ranges so as to retain the essentials of my proofs. Your discovery is at any rate a very remarkable one, and it may perhaps lead
to a great advance in logic, undesirable as it may seem at first sight.

Incidentally, the expression 'A predicate is predicated of itself'
does not seem exact to me. A predicate is as a rule a first-level
function which requires an object as argument and which cannot
therefore have itself as argument (subject). Therefore I would rather
say: 'A concept is predicated of its own extension'.[4] If the function
215     $\Phi(\xi)$ is a concept, I designate its extension (or the pertinent | class)
by '$\grave{\epsilon}\Phi(\epsilon)$' (though I now have some doubts about the justification
for this). '$\Phi(\grave{\epsilon}\Phi(\epsilon))$' or '$\grave{\epsilon}\Phi(\epsilon) \cap \grave{\epsilon}\Phi(\epsilon)$' is then the predication of
the concept $\Phi(\xi)$ of its own extension.

The second volume of my *Grundgesetze* is to appear shortly. I
shall have to give it an appendix where I will do justice to your
discovery.[5] If only I could find the right way of looking at it!

Yours sincerely,
G. Frege

---

[4] Given Frege's absolute distinction between concept and object, it is clear that his
system does not fall prey to the contradiction that Russell first formulates ('Can *w* be predicated of itself?'). For a predicate, according to Frege, is a function requiring 'satura-
tion' by an object, and hence cannot have itself as argument, since a 'gap' for an object
would still remain. But Russell's alternative formulation in terms of classes indicates the
general nature of the paradox, and Frege immediately recognized that his own system was
undermined by an analogous contradiction. For whilst, on Frege's view, a predicate
cannot be predicated of itself, a concept can be predicated of its own extension; and it
was from this assumption that the problem arose. For discussion of the paradox, and its
effect on Frege, see the Introduction, pp. 7–8, 18–20 above.

[5] See pp. 279–89 below.

Letter to Russell, 28.12.1902[1]

[Frege and Russell corresponded frequently during the period from June 1902 to the end of 1904, discussing not only possible solutions to Russell's paradox, but also their conceptions of proposition, thought, truth, function, object, value-range, and so on.[2] The following letter contains an explanation of Frege's distinction between *Sinn* and *Bedeutung*.]

234

Jena
28 December 1902

Dear Colleague,

You could not bring yourself to believe that the truth-value is the *Bedeutung* of a proposition. I do not know whether you read my essay on sense and *Bedeutung* in Vol. 100 of the *Zeitschrift für Philosophie und philosophische Kritik*.[3] The distinction between the sense and the *Bedeutung* of a sign is important in our case too. It frequently happens that different signs designate the same object but are not necessarily interchangeable because they determine the same object in different ways. It could be said that they lead to it from different directions. The words 'Morning Star' and 'Evening Star' designate the same planet, Venus; but to recognize this, a special act of recognition [*Erkenntnistat*] is required; it cannot simply be inferred from the principle of identity. Wherever the

235

coincidence of *Bedeutung* is not self-evident, we have | a difference in sense. Thus the sense of '$2^3 + 1$' is also different from the sense of '3^2' even though the *Bedeutung* is the same, because a special act of recognition is required in order to see this. Thus the equations '$3^2 = 3^2$' and '$2^3 + 1 = 3^2$' do not have the same cognitive value[4] even though their truth-value is the same. The difference is one of sense: the thoughts expressed are different. If a thought were the

[1] Translated by Hans Kaal (*PMC*, pp. 152–3; from *WB*, pp. 234–5; page numbers from the latter in the margin).
[2] See *PMC*, pp. 130–70/*WB*, pp. 200–51.
[3] See pp. 151–71 above.
[4] 'sind . . . für die Erkenntnis nicht gleichwertig'.

Bedeutung of a proposition, then it would not change if one of its parts was replaced by another expression with the same *Bedeutung*. I now ask: does the whole proposition only have a sense, or does it also have a *Bedeutung*? What we talk about is the *Bedeutungen* of words. We say something about the *Bedeutung* of the word 'Sirius' when we say: 'Sirius is bigger than the Sun'. This is why in science it is of value to us to know that the words used have a *Bedeutung*. Of course, in poetry and legend it makes no difference to us. When we merely want to enjoy the poetry we do not care whether, e.g., the name 'Odysseus' has a *Bedeutung* (or, as it is usually put, whether Odysseus was an historical person). The question first acquires an interest for us when we take a scientific attitude – the moment we ask, 'Is the story true?', i.e., when we take an interest in the truth-value. In poetry too there are thoughts, but there are only pseudo-assertions. This is also why a poet cannot be accused of lying if he knowingly says something false in his poetry. Now it would be impossible to see why it was of value to us to know whether or not a word had a *Bedeutung* if the whole proposition did not have a *Bedeutung* and if this *Bedeutung* was of no value to us; for whether or not that is so does not affect the thought. Moreover, this *Bedeutung* will be something which will have value for us precisely when we are interested in whether the words are *bedeutungsvoll*, and hence, when we inquire about truth. The *Bedeutung* of the proposition must be something which does not change when one sign is replaced by another with the same *Bedeutung* but a different sense. What does not change in the process is the truth-value. If the sign of identity is used between propositions, then the truth-value must be recognized as the *Bedeutung* of the proposition (indirect speech calls for special consideration). The propositions 'The Morning Star is a planet' and 'The Evening Star is a planet' do not have the same sense; but the latter arises from the former if the proper name 'Morning Star' is replaced by 'Evening Star', a proper name with the same *Bedeutung*.[5] It follows from this that the propositions must agree in their *Bedeutungen*: (The Morning Star is a planet) = (The Evening Star is a planet) according to the law[6]

$$\vdash\!\!\!\begin{array}{c} F(a) = F(b) \\ a = b. \end{array}$$

---

[5] 'der Eigenname "Morgenstern" durch den gleichbedeutenden "Abendstern" ersetzt wird'.

[6] I.e. Leibniz's Principle of the Indiscernibility of Identicals – '$a = b \to (\forall F)(Fa \leftrightarrow Fb)$', in modern notation, making explicit the second-order quantification over properties. Cf. fn. 25 on p. 112 above.

This shows that the thought expressed by the proposition cannot be what is recognized as the same, any more than the sense of 'Morning Star' can be said to coincide with the sense of 'Evening Star' when we write 'Morning Star = Evening Star', or the sense of '$2^3 + 1$' can be said to coincide with the sense of '3^2' in the equation '$2^3 + 1 = 3^2$'.

. . .

Yours sincerely,
G. Frege

Grundgesetze der Arithmetik, *Volume II*[1]

[Volume II of Frege's *Grundgesetze* was published in 1903, ten years after the appearance of Volume I. The first fifty-four sections of Volume II constitute the remainder of Part II ('Proofs of the Basic Laws of Number'), which had begun at §53 of Volume I. Part III, entitled 'The Real Numbers', takes up the rest of Volume II (§§55–245), but remained unfinished. A third volume was clearly planned, but by then Frege had been informed of Russell's paradox, and although Frege made an attempt to resolve it in an appendix to the second volume, added whilst the book was in press, the paradox effectively dealt a death-blow to Frege's logicist project.[2] Frege's account of the real numbers follows the pattern of his earlier account of the natural numbers: a critique of rival views precedes the formal presentation of his own theory.[3] What follows here are §§55–67, on the principles of definition, §§138–47, offering his critique of 'creative definition', and his appendix ('Nachwort') on Russell's paradox.]

---

[1] Translated by Peter Geach (*TPW*, pp. 139–61, 214–24), with additions (§§55, 138, 145) translated by Michael Beaney. Page numbers in the margin are from the original edition. In accordance with the policy adopted in the present volume (see the Introduction, §4 above), 'Bedeutung' and cognates such as 'gleichbedeutend' have been left untranslated, and 'bedeuten' rendered as 'stand for' as in the second edition of *TPW* (but with the German always in square brackets following it), unless otherwise indicated.

[2] See the Introduction, pp. 7–8 above.

[3] This is reflected in the fact that Part III of *GG* is itself divided into two parts, the first entitled 'Critique of Theories of the Irrational Numbers' (§§55–164), and the second 'Theory of Magnitude' (§§165–245). The subdivisions of the former are as follows: (a) 'Principles of Definition' (§§55–67; most of it translated in *TPW*, and here given in full); (b) 'Cantor's Theory of the Irrational Numbers' (§§68–85); (c) 'The Theories of the Irrationals of E. Heine and J. Thomae' (§§86–137, containing his attack on formalism; translated in *TPW*, pp. 162–213); (d) 'The Construction of New Objects, according to R. Dedekind, H. Hankel, O. Stolz' (§§138–47; most of it translated in *TPW*, and here given in full); (e) 'Weierstrass' Theory' (§§148–55); (f) 'Review and Outlook' (§§156–9); (g) 'Magnitude' (§§160–4).

69

III. THE REAL NUMBERS

1. CRITIQUE OF THEORIES OF THE IRRATIONAL NUMBERS

(a) Principles of Definition

§55. Before we examine what prominent mathematicians have said about numbers – in particular, irrational numbers – it will be as well to first lay down and justify a few principles of definition that have been disregarded by almost all writers in this area, so that we do not have to go into it in detail every single time. We have already laid down such principles for the *Begriffsschrift* in Volume I; here we shall mainly be concerned with definitions in ordinary language. The only differences between the two accounts, of course, will be ones that are grounded in the different nature of these means of expression.

1. Principle of Completeness

§56. A definition of a concept (of a possible predicate) must be complete; it must unambiguously determine, as regards any object, whether or not it falls under the concept (whether or not the predicate is truly ascribable to it). Thus there must not be any object as regards which the definition leaves in doubt whether it falls under the concept; though for us human beings, with our defective knowledge, the question may not always be decidable. We may express this metaphorically as follows: the concept must have a sharp boundary. If we represent concepts in extension by areas on a plane, this is admittedly a picture that may be used only with caution, but here it can do us good service. To a concept without sharp boundary there would correspond an area that had not a sharp boundary-line all round, but in places just vaguely faded away into the background. This would not really be an area at all; and likewise a concept that is not sharply defined is wrongly termed a concept. Such quasi-conceptual constructions cannot be recognized as concepts by logic; it is impossible to lay down precise laws for them. The law of excluded middle is really just another form of the requirement that the concept should have a sharp boundary. Any object Δ that you choose to take either falls under the concept Φ or does not fall under it; *tertium non datur*. E.g. would the sentence 'Any square root of 9 is odd' have a comprehensible sense at all if *square root of 9* were not a concept with a sharp boundary? Has the question 'Are we still Chris-

70   tians?' really got a | sense, if it is indeterminate whom the predicate 'Christian' can truly be ascribed to, and who must be refused it?

§57.   Now from this it follows that the mathematicians' favourite procedure, piecemeal definition, is inadmissible. The procedure is this:
first they give the definition for a particular case – e.g. for positive
integers – and make use of it; then, many theorems later, there follows
a second definition for another case – e.g. for negative integers and
zero. Here they often commit the further mistake of making specifications all over again for the case they have already dealt with. Even if in
fact they avoid contradictions, in principle their method does not rule
them out. What is more, as a rule they do not attain to completeness,
but leave over some cases, as to which they make no specification; and
many are naïve enough to employ the word or symbol for these cases
too, as if they had assigned a *Bedeutung* to it. Such piecemeal definition
is a procedure comparable to drawing the boundary of a part of a surface in bits, perhaps without making them join up. But the chief mistake is that they are already using the symbol or word in theorems before
it has been completely defined – often, indeed, with a view to further
development of the definition itself. So long as the *Bedeutung* of a word
or symbol is not completely defined, or known in some other way, the
word or symbol may not be used in an exact science – least of all with
a view to further development of its own definition.

§58.   Now, of course, it must be admitted that scientific progress,
which has been effected by conquering wider and wider domains of
numbers, made such a procedure almost inevitably necessary; and this
necessity might serve as an excuse.[A] It would indeed have been possible
71 | to replace the old symbols and terms by new ones, and logic really

---

[A] Thus, Peano says (*Revue de mathématiques*, VI, pp. 60–1 [quoted by Frege in Italian]):
'Frege requires one definition alone for every sign. And this is my opinion too, if it is a
matter of a sign not containing variable letters (F_2 [Peano's *Formulary of Mathematics*,
Volume II], §1, p. 7). But if the *definiendum* contains variable letters, i.e. is a function
of such letters, then, so far as I can see, it is in general necessary to give conditional or
hypothetical definitions of the expression (ibid., p. 7'), and to give as many definitions
as there are kinds of entities on which we perform this operation. Thus the formula $a + b$
will be first defined when a and b are integers, then a second time when they are fractions, then again when they are irrational or complex. The same sign + is met with
between infinite transfinite numbers (F_1 VI) and then a new definition must be given. It
is met with again between two vectors, and will be defined over again; and so on. With
the progress of science the meaning [*significato*] of this same formula is always being
further extended. The various meanings [*significati*] of the symbol $a + b$ have common
properties; but these are insufficient to determine all the values that this expression can
have.
'The same happens for the formula $a = b$. In some cases its meaning [*significato*] can
be assumed as a primitive idea, in others it is defined; and precisely in arithmetic, given
the equality of whole numbers, equality is defined between rationals, between irrationals,
between imaginary numbers, etc. In geometry it is usual to define equality between two
areas or two volumes, equality between two vectors, etc. With the progress of science, the
need is more and more felt to extend the meaning [*significato*] of the expression $a = b$.

demands this; but that is a hard decision to make. And this horror over the introduction of new symbols or words is the cause of many obscurities in mathematics. The old definitions likewise could have been rejected as unsound, and new ones used, in order to set up the science over again from the beginning; but such a clean cut was never made, because the old definitions were believed indispensable for the beginnings of the science. Didactic requirements may also have made themselves heard in this connection. In this way people have got used to piecemeal definition; and what was originally an awkward makeshift became customary, and was admitted as one of the legitimate methods of science. The result is that nowadays hardly anybody is shocked when a symbol is first defined for a limited domain and then used in order to define the same symbol once more for a wider domain; for general custom has a power of justifying what is done, just as fashion can give the cachet of beauty to the most detestable mode. It is all the more necessary to emphasize that logic cannot recognize as concepts quasi-conceptual constructions that are still fluid and have not yet been given definitive and sharp boundaries, and that therefore logic must reject all

The various meanings [*significati*] | have common properties, but I do not see how they suffice to determine all the possible meanings of equality.

'Moreover, there is a wide diversity of opinion between various authors as regards the concept of equality. A study of this question would be very useful, especially if it were carried out with the aid of symbols as well as words.'

Peano here appeals to a practical need; but this does not upset the reasons I mentioned in my letter to him [see *PMC*, pp. 112–18/*WB*, pp. 181–6]. It may be difficult to satisfy the demands of logic always in giving definitions; but it must be possible.

We may perhaps allow several conditional definitions of the same symbol when it is obvious from their form that they collectively cover all possible cases and do not make multiple specifications for any case, and when none of these partial definitions is used before they are all given – none, therefore, is used in another partial definition. In this case the definitions *formally* admit of being combined into a single definition. But this form of definition is best avoided, if possible.

In regard to the 'equals' sign we shall do well to keep to our convention that equality [*Gleichheit*] is complete coincidence, identity [*Identität*]. Of course bodies equal in volume are not identical, but they have the same volume. The signs on either side of the 'equals' sign must thus in this case be taken as signs not for bodies but for their volumes, or for the numerical values obtained by measuring in terms of the same unit volume. We shall not speak of equal vectors, but rather of a certain attribute of the vectors (let us call it 'directed length') which can be the same in different vectors. On this view, the progress of science will not require us to widen the *Bedeutung* of the formula '$a = b$'; we shall merely take into account new attributes (*modi*) of objects.

In his last sentence Peano coolly makes a momentous assertion. If mathematicians have divergent opinions about equality, this means [*heisst*] nothing less than that mathematicians disagree as to the content of their science; and if we regard science as essentially consisting of thoughts, not of words and symbols, it means [*heisst*] that there is no united science of mathematics at all – that mathematicians just do not understand one another. For almost all arithmetical propositions, and many geometrical ones, depend for their sense, directly or indirectly, upon the sense of the word 'equals'.

72   piecemeal definition. For if the first | definition is already complete and
has drawn sharp boundaries, then either the second definition draws
the same boundaries – and then it must be rejected, because its content
ought to be proved as a theorem – or it draws different ones – and then
it contradicts the first one. For example, we may define a conic section
as the intersection of a plane with a conical surface of rotation. When
once we have done this, we may not define it over again, e.g. as a curve
whose equation in Cartesian coordinates is of the second degree; for
now that has to be proved. Likewise we cannot now define it as a plane,
figure whose equation in linear coordinates is of the second degree; for
that would also include the point-pair, which cannot be regarded as the
intersection of a plane and a conic surface. Here, then, the boundary
of the concept is not drawn in the same way, and it would be a mistake
to use here the same term 'conic section'. If the second definition is not
ruled out by the first one in either of these ways, that is possible only
because the first one is incomplete and has left the concept unfinished,
i.e. in a condition in which it may not be employed at all – in particular,
not for definitions.

§59.   It will be not unprofitable to give an example, so as to counter-
balance the abstractness of these remarks. E. Heine sets up the following definition:[B]

'Number signs are called equal or interchangeable when they belong
to equal series of numbers, and unequal or non-interchangeable when
they belong to unequal series (§1, Def. 3).'

What would people say to the following definition?

'Signs are called white when they belong to white objects.'

Now I may legitimately take, as a sign for the white sheet of paper
that I have before me, a circular black patch, so long as I have not
already employed this sign in some other way. And such a patch would
now be white by definition. As against this, we must say: in using the
expression 'if they belong to white objects', the definition presupposes
that we know the *Bedeutung* of the word 'white'; for otherwise it would
be wholly unspecified what signs belong to white objects. Very well! If
the word 'white' is known, we cannot want to define it over again. We
ought to regard it as quite self-evident that a word may not be defined
by means of itself; for if we do that we are in one breath treating the
word as known and as unknown. If it is known, a definition is at least
superfluous; if it is not known, it cannot serve for the purpose of def-
73   inition. This is so obvious, | and yet people sin against it so often! We
get the same case for Heine's definition. The use of the words 'if they

[B] 'Die Elemente der Funktionslehre', Crelle's *Journal* [*für die reine und angewandte
Mathematik*], Vol. 74, §2, Def. 2. From my here raising only one objection to this definition it must not be inferred that I regard it as otherwise unexceptionable.

belong to equal series of numbers' presupposes that we know what the word 'equal' stands for [*bedeute*], and this is the very word that is to be defined.

§60. Heine would probably remark in answer to this that the *Bedeutung* of the word 'equal' is not presupposed as known in all cases; in his Def. 3 in §1 it is supposed as given only for unbracketed number-series, whereas here he is speaking of bracketed number-series and other symbols. Besides the reasons against this procedure given above, it may be added that double definition of a word is objectionable because then we are left in doubt whether the definitions do not contradict each other. People ought at least to ask for a proof that there is no contradiction; but this duty is regularly evaded, and indeed in Heine there is not to be found a trace of such a proof. In general, we must reject a way of defining that makes the correctness of a definition depend on our having first to carry out a proof; for this makes it extraordinarily difficult to check the rigour of the deduction, since it is necessary to inquire, as regards each definition, whether any propositions have to be proved before laying it down – an inquiry, however, that is almost always left undone. People are hardly ever conscious of this sort of gap, which is therefore specially dangerous as regards rigour. In arithmetic it just will not do to make any assertion you like without proof or with a sham proof, and then wait and see if anybody succeeds in proving its falsity; on the contrary, it must be demanded that every assertion that is not completely self-evident should have a real proof; and this involves that any expressions or symbols used in the proof, unless they may be regarded as generally known, must be introduced in an unexceptionable way.

And moreover it is so easy to avoid a plurality of definitions for one and the same symbol. Instead of first defining a symbol for a limited domain and then using it for the purpose of defining itself in regard to a wider domain, we need only choose different signs, and confine the *Bedeutung* of the first, once for all, to the narrower domain; in this way the first definition is now complete and draws sharp boundary-lines. This in no way prejudges the relation between the *Bedeutungen* of the two signs; we can investigate this, without its being possible that the result of the investigation should make it questionable whether the definitions were justified.

It really is worth the trouble to invent a new symbol if we can thus remove not a few logical difficulties and ensure the rigour of the proofs. But many mathematicians seem to have so little feeling for logical | purity and accuracy that they prefer to use a word with three or four different *Bedeutungen* rather than make the frightful decision to invent a new word.

§61. Piecemeal definition likewise makes the status of theorems uncertain. If, e.g., the words 'square root of 9' have been defined with a restriction to the domain of positive integers, then we can prove, e.g., the proposition that there is only one square root of 9; but this is at once overthrown when we extend our treatment to negative numbers and supplement the definition accordingly. But who can tell if we have now reached a definitive proposition? Who can tell but that we may see ourselves driven to recognize four square roots of 9? How are we really going to tell that there are no more than two square roots of −1? So long as we have no final and complete definitions, it is impossible. It may perhaps be objected that in that case some propositions would no longer hold good. The same reason would go against admitting a second square root of 9. In this way we never have really firm ground underfoot. If we have no final definitions we likewise have no final theorems. We never emerge from incompleteness and vagueness.

§62. We get the same case for a relation as for a concept: logic can recognize a relation only if it is determinate, as regards any one object and any other object, whether or not the one stands to the other in that relation. Here too we have a *tertium non datur*; the case of its being undecided is ruled out. If there were a relation for which this requirement were not fulfilled, then the concepts that we can derive from it by partly filling it up (Vol. I, §30)[4] likewise would not have completely sharp boundaries, and would thus, strictly speaking, not be concepts at all, but inadmissible sham concepts. If, e.g., the relation *greater than* is not completely defined, then it is likewise uncertain whether a quasi-conceptual construction obtained by partly filling it up, e.g. *greater than zero* or *positive*, is a proper concept. For it to be a proper concept, it would have to be determinate whether, e.g., the Moon is greater than zero. We may indeed specify that only numbers can stand in our relation, and infer from this that the Moon, not being a number, is also not greater than zero. But with that there would have to go a complete definition of the word 'number', and that is just what is most lacking.

It is just as regards the relation *greater than* that piecemeal, and therefore incomplete, definition, is, so to say, good form in mathematics. The words 'greater than' are first defined in the domain of positive integers, i.e. incompletely. The pseudo-relation thus obtained, which |
75 it is wrong to use at all, is then used in order to complete the first definition; and here, of course, one cannot always tell when the definition of the relation *greater than* is to count as complete. For the relation of equality the case is quite similar; here too piecemeal definition is

---

[4] See also Vol. I, §4 (pp. 214–15 above).

absolutely a part of good form.[C] Nevertheless we must stick to our point: without complete and final definitions, we have no firm ground underfoot, we are not sure about the validity of our theorems, and we cannot confidently apply the laws of logic, which certainly presuppose that concepts, and relations too, have sharp boundaries.

§63.   At this point it is easy to draw a conclusion in regard to functions that are neither concepts nor relations. Let us take as an example the expression 'the half of something', which purports to be a name of such a function. Here the word 'something' is keeping a place open for the argument; it corresponds to the letter 'ξ' in '$^1/_2\xi$'. Such an expression can become part of a concept name, e.g. 'something the half of which is less than one'.

Now if this last expression is actually to stand for [*bedeuten*] a concept with sharp boundaries, then it must be determinate, e.g. as regards the Moon whether the half of it is less than one. But in order that this should happen, the expression 'the half of the Moon' must have a *Bedeutung*; i.e. there must be one and only one object designated by this. Now according to common usage this is not the case, for nobody knows which half of the Moon is meant [*gemeint*]. So here, too, we must make a more precise specification, so that it is determined, as regards every object, which object is the half of it; otherwise it is wrong to use the expression 'the half of x' with the definite article. Thus a first-level function of one argument must always be such as to yield an object as its value, whatever object we may take as its argument – whatever object we may use to saturate the function.[D]

§64.   We must make the corresponding requirement as regards functions with two arguments. The expression |

76   'the sum of one object and another object'

purports to be the name of such a function. Here too, then, it must be determinate, as regards any one object and any other object, which object is the sum of the one and the other; and there must always be

---

[C] In practice, indeed, when mathematicians give proofs, they do all treat equality as identity; although in theory most of them will not allow that this is true. But nobody is going to say, e.g., that the equation '$4x - 3 = 3$' has the roots 6/4 and 3/2, on the ground that 6/4 is indeed equal to 3/2 but does not coincide with it. If 6/4 and 3/2 do not coincide, then they are different, and our equation has at least two different roots. It is remarkable to see what a frightful conflict there is, for many mathematicians, between their explicit theory and their tacitly adopted practice. But if equality in mathematics is identity, then a plurality of definitions for it is a senseless procedure.

[D] Cf. what was said about functions in Vol. I [§§1–4; see pp. 211–15 above]; and the author's work 'Function and Concept' [pp. 130–48 above].

such an object. If that is not the case, then it is likewise indeterminate which object gives the result one when added to itself. In that case, therefore, the words 'something that gives the result one when added to itself' do not stand for [*bedeuten*] any concept with sharp boundaries, i.e. anything that can be used in logic. And the question how many objects there are that give the result one when added to themselves is unanswerable.

But can we not stipulate that the expression 'the sum of one object and another object' is to have a *Bedeutung* only when both objects are numbers? In that case, you may well think, the concept *something that gives the result one when added to itself* is one with sharp boundaries; for now we know that no object that is not a number falls under it. E.g. the Moon does not fall under it, since the sum of the Moon and the Moon is not one. This is wrong. On the present view, the sentence 'The sum of the Moon and the Moon is one' is neither true nor false; for in either case the words 'the sum of the Moon and the Moon' would have to stand for [*bedeuten*] something, and this was expressly denied by the suggested stipulation. Our sentence would be comparable, say, to the sentence 'Scylla had six dragon necks'. This sentence likewise is neither true nor false, but fiction, for the proper name 'Scylla' designates nothing. Such sentences can indeed be objects for scientific treatment, e.g. of myth; but no scientific investigation can issue in them. If our sentence 'The sum of the Moon and the Moon is not one' were a scientific one, then it would assert that the *Bedeutung* of the words 'the sum of the Moon and the Moon' did not coincide with the *Bedeutung* of the word 'one'; but with the stipulation suggested above, the former words would not have any *Bedeutung*; accordingly, we could not truly assert either that their *Bedeutung* did coincide with the *Bedeutung* of the word 'one' or that it did not coincide with it. Thus it would be impossible to answer the question whether the sum of the Moon and the Moon is one, or whether the Moon falls under the concept *something that gives the result one when added to itself*. In other words, what we have just called a concept would not be a genuine concept at all, since it would lack sharp boundaries. But when once we have introduced the expression '*a* added to *b* gives the result *c*', we can no longer stop the construction of a concept name like 'something that gives the result one when added to itself'. If people would actually try to lay down laws that stopped the formation of such concept names as this, which, though linguistically possible, are inadmissible, they would soon find the task
77   exceedingly difficult and probably impracticable. | The only way left open is to give to the words 'sum', 'addition', etc., if one means to use them at all, such definitions that the concept names constructed out of the words in a linguistically correct manner stand for [*bedeuten*] concepts with sharp boundaries and are thus admissible.

Thus the requirement we have here set up – that every first-level function of two arguments must have an object as its value for any one object as its first argument and any other object as its second – is a consequence of the requirement that concepts must have sharp boundaries and that we may not tolerate expressions which seem by their structure to stand for [*bedeuten*] a concept but only create an illusion of so doing, just as we may not admit proper names that do not actually designate an object.

§65. What has been said about verbal expressions holds good also for arithmetical symbols. If the sign of addition has been completely defined, then

$$`\xi + \xi = \zeta`$$

gives us the name of a relation – the relation of single to double. If that is not the case, then we cannot say whether the equation

$$`x + x = 1`$$

has a unique solution or several solutions. Now anybody will answer: 'I forbid anything but numbers to be taken into account at all'. We dealt above with a similar objection; here we may throw light on the matter from other sides. If anybody wants to exclude from consideration all objects that are not numbers, he must first say what he understands by 'number', and then further extension of the term is inadmissible. Such a restriction would have to be incorporated in the definition, which would thus take some such form as: 'If a and b are numbers, then $a + b$ stands for [*bedeutet*] . . .' We should have a conditional definition.[E] But the sign of addition has not been defined unless the *Bedeutung* of every possible complex symbol of the form '$a + b$' is determined, whatever *bedeutungsvolle* proper names may take the places of 'a' and 'b'. If on the contrary such complex symbols are defined, e.g. only for the case when symbols for real integers are taken instead of 'a' and 'b', then what has really been defined is only the complex symbols, not the sign of addition: an offence against the second principle of definition, which we still have to discuss. And yet people cannot help imagining they know the *Bedeutung* of the sign of addition; and accordingly they employ it also in cases for which no definition has been given.

As soon as people aim at generality in propositions they will need in arithmetical formulae not only symbols for definite objects – e.g. the proper name '2' – but also letters that only indicate and do not designate;[F] and this already leads them, quite unawares, beyond the domain

---

[E] Cf. the author's letter to G. Peano, *Revue de mathématiques*, Vol. VI, pp. 53ff. [see *PMC*, pp. 112–18/*WB*, pp. 181–6].

[F] Cf. [*GG*,] Vol. I, pp. 31–2 [§17].

within which they have defined their symbols. One may try to avoid the dangers thus arising by not making the letters indicate objects in general (as I did), but only those of a domain with fixed boundaries. Let us suppose for once that the concept *number* has been sharply defined; let it be laid down that italic letters are to indicate only numbers; and let the sign of addition be defined only for numbers. Then in the proposition '$a + b = b + a$' we must mentally add the conditions that a and b are numbers; and these conditions, not being expressed, are easily forgotten.[G] But let us deliberately not forget them for once! By a well-known law of logic, the proposition

'If a is a number and b is a number then $a + b = b + a$'

can be transformed into the proposition

'If $a + b$ is not equal to $b + a$, and a is a number, then b is not a number'

and here it is impossible to maintain the restriction to the domain of numbers. The force of the situation works irresistibly towards the breaking down of such restrictions. But in this case our antecedent clause

'if $a + b$ is not equal to $b + a$'

is senseless, assuming that the sign of addition has not been completely defined.

Here again we likewise see that the laws of logic presuppose concepts with sharp boundaries, and therefore also complete definitions for names of functions, like the 'plus' sign.[H] In Vol. I we expressed this as follows: every function name must have a *Bedeutung*. Accordingly all conditional definitions, and any procedure of piecemeal definition, must be rejected. Every symbol must be completely defined at a stroke, so that, as we say, it acquires a *Bedeutung*.

All of this hangs very close together, and may be regarded as derived from the principle of completeness in definitions. |

79   2. Principle of Simplicity in the Expression defined[I]

§66. Given the *Bedeutung* of an expression and of a part of it, obviously the *Bedeutung* of the remaining part is not always determined. So

---

[G] E.g. do people always bear it in mind, when they extend the number-domain, that thereby the sense of the conditions is changed; that all general propositions proved up to that point acquire a new content of thought; and likewise that all the proofs break down?
[H] It is self-evident that certain functions are indefinable, because of their logical simplicity. But these too must have values for all arguments.
[I] Vol. I, §33, 3 [p. 222 above].

we may not define a symbol or word by defining an expression in which it occurs, whose remaining parts are known. For it would first be necessary to investigate whether – to use a readily understandable metaphor from algebra – the equation can be solved for the unknown, and whether the unknown is unambiguously determined. But as I have already said above, it is not feasible to make the correctness of a definition depend on the outcome of such an investigation – one which, moreover, would perhaps be quite impracticable. Rather, the definition must have the character of an equation that is solved for the unknown, and on the other side of which nothing unknown occurs any longer.

Still less will it do to define two things with one definition; any definition must, on the contrary, contain a single sign, and fix the *Bedeutung* of this sign. One equation alone cannot be used to determine two unknowns.

Moreover, we sometimes find a whole system of definitions set up, each one containing several words that need definition, in such a way that each of these words occurs in several of the definitions. This is like a system of equations with several unknowns; and here again it remains completely doubtful whether the equations can be solved and whether the solution is unambiguously determined.

Any symbol or word can indeed be regarded as consisting of parts; but we do not deny its simplicity unless, given the general rules of grammar, or of the symbolism, the *Bedeutung* of the whole would follow from the *Bedeutungen* of the parts, and these parts occur also in other combinations and are treated as independent signs with a *Bedeutung* of their own. In this sense, then, we may say: the word (symbol) that is defined must be simple. Otherwise it might come about that the parts were also defined separately and that these definitions contradicted the definition of the whole.

Of course names of functions, because of their characteristic unsaturatedness, cannot stand alone on one side of a defining equation; their argument-places must always be filled up somehow or other. In the *Begriffsschrift*, as we have seen,[J] this is done by means of italic letters, which must then occur on the other side as well. In language, instead of these, there occur pronouns and particles ('something', 'what', 'it') which indicate indefinitely. This is no | violation of our principle; for these letters, pronouns, particles do not stand for [*bedeuten*] anything, but only indicate [*andeuten*].

§67.   Often there is an offence against both principles of definition at once. E.g. the 'equals' sign is defined along with what stands to the right and left of it. In this case the 'equals' sign has already been defined

80

J Vol. I, §33, 5 [p. 223 above].

previously, but only in an incomplete way. Thus there arises a queer twilight; the 'equals' sign is treated in a half-and-half way, as known and again as unknown. On the one hand, it looks as though we were meant to recall the earlier definition and extract from it something to go towards determining what now appears on the right and left sides of the 'equals' sign. On the other hand, however, this earlier definition will not do for our present case. A similar thing happens over other signs too. This twilight is needed by many mathematicians for the performance of their logical conjuring tricks. The ends that are meant to be achieved in this way are unexceptionally attained through our transformation of an equality that holds generally into an equality between value-ranges, by Axiom V (Vol. I, §3, §9, §20).

It has not been my aim to give here a complete survey of all that has to be observed in giving definitions; I will content myself with stating these two principles, the ones against which mathematicians sin most often.

[The next seventy sections (*GG*, II, pp. 80–140) are omitted here. In §§68–85 Frege discusses Cantor's theory of the irrational numbers,[5] and in §§86–137 he criticizes E. Heine's and J. Thomae's formalist theories of irrational numbers.[6]]

140   **(d) The Construction[7] of New Objects, according to R. Dedekind, H. Hankel, O. Stolz**

§138. We now turn to the account that R. Dedekind has given in his work on continuity and irrational numbers.[K] He says there in §1, p. 6: 'To express the fact that the signs *a* and *b* stand for [*bedeuten*] one and the same rational number, one writes $a = b$ or $b = a$'.

Here the sharpness of the distinction between sign and what it stands for [*bedeutet*] is welcome and noteworthy, as is the conception of the equality sign, which exactly agrees with our own. By contrast, Thomae remarks:[L] 'Now if equality or the equality sign = were only to stand for [*bedeuten*] identity, then we would be left with trivial knowledge, or if one prefers, the conceptual necessity *a* is *a* ($a = a$)'.

[K] *Stetigkeit und irrationale Zahlen* (Braunschweig: Vieweg & Sohn, 1892).

[L] *Elementare Theorie der analytischen Functionen einer complexen Veränderlichen*, 2nd edn. (Halle a. S., 1898).

[5] For an account of Frege's critique of Cantor, see Dummett, 1991a: ch. 21.

[6] Translated in *TPW*, pp. 162–213.

[7] Throughout these sections 'Schaffen' and its cognates have been translated as 'construction' and its cognates. But it should be borne in mind that the more usual rendering of the term is 'creation'.

This is a mistake. The knowledge that the Evening Star is the same as the Morning Star is of far greater value than a mere application of the proposition '$a = a$' – it is no mere result of a conceptual necessity. The explanation lies in the fact that the sense of signs or words (Evening Star, Morning Star) with the same *Bedeutung* can be different, and that it is precisely the sense of the proposition – beside its *Bedeutung*, its truth-value – that determines its cognitive value.

It follows from Dedekind's quoted remark that for him numbers are not signs, but the *Bedeutungen* of signs.

These three points:

(1)   the sharp distinction between sign and its *Bedeutung*,
(2)   the definition of the equality sign as the identity sign,
(3)   the conception of numbers as the *Bedeutungen* of number signs, not as the signs themselves,

hang most closely together and place Dedekind's view in the starkest contrast to every formalist theory, which regards signs or | figures as the real objects of arithmetic. All the more astonishing, then, is the endorsement that Dedekind gives to Heine's conception, in saying with regard to the essay that we discussed above:[8] 'In essentials I do fully agree with the content of this work, as it cannot indeed be otherwise'.

This agreement does not actually exist at all. On the contrary, Dedekind's view is much closer to Cantor's.

§139.   Dedekind gives the name *cut* [*Schnitt*] to a division of the rational number system into two classes such that any number in the first class is smaller than any number in the second; and he shows that every rational number generates a cut, or properly speaking two cuts, but that there are cuts not generated by any rational number. He then goes on to say (§4, p. 14):

'Now whenever we are presented with a cut (A_1, A_2) not generated by any rational number, we construct a new, irrational number a, which we regard as completely defined by this cut; we shall say that the number a corresponds to this cut, or generates this cut.'

It is in this construction that the heart of the matter lies. We must first notice that this procedure is quite different from what is done in formalist arithmetic – the introduction of a new sort of figures and special rules for manipulating them. There the difficulty is how to tell whether these new rules may turn out to conflict with those laid down previously and how to straighten out such a conflict. Here we are concerned with the question whether construction is possible at all;

---

[8] 'Die Elemente der Funktionslehre', Crelle's *Journal für die reine und angewandte Mathematik*, Vol. 74; discussed, in particular, in *GG*, II, §§86–137 (tr. in *TPW*, pp. 162–213).

whether, if it is possible, it is unrestrictedly possible; or whether certain laws must be observed when we are constructing. In the last case it would first have to be proved that the construction was justified in accordance with these laws, before we might perform the act of creation [*Schöpfung*]. These inquiries are here completely lacking, and thus there is lacking the main thing – what the proofs carried out by means of irrational numbers depend upon for their cogency.

The power of construction, if it does exist, cannot in any case be unrestricted; as we see from the fact that no object combining inconsistent properties can be constructed.

§140.   We are led to the same result by the following consideration. In mathematics it is no rare thing for an auxiliary object to be needed in order to prove a proposition; i.e. an object not mentioned in the proposition itself. In geometry we have auxiliary lines and points. In arithmetic, similarly, we have auxiliary numbers. E.g. a square root of -1 is
142 needed in order to prove propositions that | deal only with real numbers. In number theory we prove by means of the indices that the congruences '$x^n \equiv 1$' and '$x^\delta \equiv 1$' on the prime modulus p have the same roots, δ being the greatest common factor of n and $p - 1$; here we require a primitive root, viz. the base of the indices, as an auxiliary number. In our proofs too auxiliary objects have already occurred: cf. Vol. I, §94. We likewise saw there how to get rid of such an object again. For there must be no mention of it in the proposition to be proved, although we need some of its properties in the proof (e.g. we need the property of being a primitive root in relation to the prime number p, in proving the proposition of number theory mentioned above). We must first introduce conditional clauses, expressing the supposition that an object has the said properties. If we know such an object, we can eliminate the conditions. If we cannot mention such an object (as happens in our example, where we are speaking not of this or that definite prime number, but of a prime number in general) then at any rate we must prove that there always is such an object (e.g. a primitive root in relation to the prime number p). How much easier this would be if we could without more ado construct the objects required! If we do not know whether there is a number whose square is -1, then we construct one. If we do not know whether there is a primitive root in relation to a prime number, then we construct one. If we do not know whether there is a straight line passing through certain points, then we construct one. Unfortunately this is too easy to be right. Certain limits on the power of construction would have to be admitted. If an arithmetician admits in general the possibility of construction, his most important task will be a clear exposition of the laws that must be observed, in order that then he may go on to prove, before every single act of creation,

that it is permitted according to these laws. Otherwise everything becomes vague, and proofs degenerate into a mere sham, a comfortable make-believe.

§141. Hankel says at the beginning of section 7 of his *Theorie der complexen Zahlensysteme*:

'In this section we are dealing with numbers α, β, ..., linearly compounded out of the units ι_1, ι_2, ... ι_n, which obey the rules of multiplication expressed in the relations:

$$\iota_1\iota_1 = 0, \quad \iota_2\iota_2 = 0, \quad \ldots \quad \iota_n\iota_n = 0, \quad \iota_k\iota_m = -\iota_m\iota_k.'$$

With these so-called units he then proves, e.g., the multiplication theorem for determinants; or rather, he imagines that he proves it. | Really there is just a stupendous conjuring trick; for nowhere is it proved that there are such units, nowhere is it proved that the properties ascribed to these units are not mutually contradictory. In fact it remains obscure what these properties actually are; for nowhere is it stated what a product must be taken to be in this case. Properly, the propositions given above, '$\iota_1\iota_1 = 0$' and the rest, must be introduced as conditions; and the law of multiplication for determinants must also appear as depending on these conditions. Eliminating the conditions remains an unsolved problem if we use this method of proof. A solution would be possible if 'ι_1', 'ι_2', and so on were proper names of objects satisfying the conditions. We do not know what a product or a sum is for this sort of numbers. But let us just suppose we did know; in that case we should know of ι_1 the property that $\iota_1\iota_1 = 0$ – a property shared with ι_2, ι_3, etc. – and further we should know certain relations in which ι_1 would have to stand to other unknowns, ι_2, ι_3, etc. Clearly ι_1 is not determined by this. We do not know how many such objects there are, nor whether there are any at all. Even the class these objects are supposed to belong to is undetermined. Let us suppose that such a class contains the objects

$$\iota_1, \quad \iota_2, \quad \ldots \quad \iota_9.$$

Then the class containing only the objects

$$\iota_1\iota_2\iota_3, \quad \iota_4\iota_5\iota_6, \quad \iota_7\iota_8\iota_9,$$

has the same general property; so likewise has the class containing only the objects

$$\iota_1\iota_4\iota_7, \quad \iota_2\iota_5\iota_8, \quad \iota_3\iota_6\iota_9;$$

so have many other classes. Consequently, even the class these objects belong to is not determined; still less are they themselves determined; and it is impossible to regard 'ι_1', 'ι_2', etc., as proper names with *Bedeutung* [*bedeutungsvolle Eigennamen*], like '2' and '3'. The only thing left is to regard them as indicating objects, like '*a*', '*b*', '*c*', not as standing for [*bedeutend*] or designating objects. But then the question is whether there are objects satisfying the conditions mentioned above. These conditions are not even complete; for there is missing the condition that the product of an ordinary number and a product of certain ι-numbers is different from the product of another ordinary number and the same product of ι-numbers. Otherwise, given

$$a.\iota_1\iota_2\iota_3 = b.\iota_1\iota_2\iota_3,$$

we could not infer $a = b$.

144　　Now the proof that there are such ι-objects is lacking. Perhaps Hankel believed he was constructing them by the words quoted above; | but he still owes us the proof that he was entitled so to construct them.

§142. If we had tried to carry out in our *Begriffsschrift* Hankel's proof of his proposition about determinants, we should, so to say, have run our noses against this obstacle. The reason why it is so easily overlooked with Hankel's method of proof is that the assumptions are not all written down in Euclid's style and strict precautions taken to use no others. If this were done, assumptions could not so easily be made to vanish by a conjuring trick.

What is more, many proofs carried out by means of the imaginary unit stand on no firmer footing than Hankel's proof, which we have just been talking about. The reason why the mistake hits you in the eye more in the latter case is not that there is any essential logical difference, but that people are already used to the imaginary unit more than they are to alternating numbers. One need only use a word or symbol often enough, and the impression will be produced that this proper name designates something; and this impression will grow so strong in the course of time that in the end hardly anybody has any doubt about the matter.

§143. Creative definitions are a first-rate discovery. Otto Stolz writes thus:[M]

'6. *Definition.* In the case where lim (*f:g*) is a positive number or is +∞, there shall be a thing distinct from the moments, designated by $\mathfrak{u}(f): \mathfrak{u}(g)$, and satisfying the equation $\mathfrak{u}(g).[\mathfrak{u}(f): \mathfrak{u}(g)] = \mathfrak{u}(f).$'

Let us compare this with the following:

'*Definition.* If the points A, B, C, D, E, F are so situated that the lines joining AD, BE, CF pass through the same point, then there shall be

---

[M] *Vorlesungen über allgemeine Arithmetik* (Leipzig: Teubner, 1885), Part I, p. 211.

a thing that is a straight line and passes through the intersections of the straight lines joining AB and DE, BC and EF, CA and FD.'

The cases will be pronounced entirely different; but no essential logical difference will come out on more precise investigation. We do not use the second definition; instead, we enunciate and prove a theorem. But the inestimable advantage of a creative definition is that it saves us a proof. And it is child's play to attain this advantage; we need only choose as a title the word 'definition' instead of | the word 'theorem'. This is certainly an urgent necessity, otherwise the nature of the proposition might be mistaken.

We find another example of a creative definition on p. 34 (op. cit.), where we read:

'1. *Definition.* "If in case (D_1) no magnitude of System (I) satisfies the equation $b \circ x = a$, then it shall be satisfied by *one and only one new thing not found in* (I); this may be symbolized by $a \cup b$, since this symbol has not yet been used. We thus have

$$b \circ (a \cup b) = (a \cup b) \circ a = a."^{N}$$

Since the new objects possess no further properties, we can assign them properties arbitrarily, so long as these are not mutually inconsistent.'

Creation is thus performed in several stages. After the first, the thing is indeed there, but it is, so to say, stark naked, devoid of the most necessary properties; these are assigned to it only in later creative acts, and it will then have to be hailed as the lucky owner of these properties. Admittedly the power of creating is here restricted by the proviso that the properties must not be mutually inconsistent; an obvious restriction, but one very hard to observe. How do we tell that properties are not mutually inconsistent? There seems to be no criterion for this except the occurrence of the properties in question in one and the same object. But the creative power with which many mathematicians credit themselves thus becomes practically worthless. For as it is they must certainly prove, before they perform a creative act, that there is no inconsistency between the properties they want to assign to the object that is to be, or has already been, constructed; and apparently they can do this only by proving that there is an object with all these properties together. But if they can do that, they need not first construct such an object.

§144.   Or is there perhaps still another way of proving consistency? If there were one, it would be of the highest significance [*Bedeutung*] for

---

N As regards o he says (p. 26): 'The combination o is called *thesis*'. We might conclude from the definite article that the symbol o had a definite *Bedeutung*. This, however, is not the case; it is meant just to indicate a combination. But what we are to understand by 'combination' and 'result of a combination' we are not told.

all mathematicians who credit themselves with a power of creating. And yet hardly anybody seems to concern himself with devising such a type of proof. Why not? Probably people think a proof of consistency super-
146 fluous, because | any inconsistency would be noticed at once. What a fine thing if it were so! How simple all proofs would then be in their form! The proof of Pythagoras' theorem would go something like this:

'Suppose that the square on the hypotenuse were not equal in area to the squares on the other two sides taken together. Then there would be a contradiction between this supposition and the known axioms of geometry. Consequently our supposition is false, and the square on the hypotenuse is exactly equal in area to the squares on the other two sides taken together.'

It would be equally easy to prove the law of reciprocity for quadratic residues:

'Let p and q be primes, of which at least one is congruent to 1 modulo 4, and let p be a quadratic residue of q. Now suppose q were not a quadratic residue of p; this would obviously contradict our hypotheses and the known laws of arithmetic (anyone who does not see this does not count). Consequently our supposition is false, and q must be a quadratic residue of p.'

On these patterns it would be easy to carry out any proof. Unfortunately this method is too simple to be acceptable. We see well enough that not every contradiction lies quite open to view. Moreover, we have no reliable criterion for the cases when it is supposed possible to infer the absence of a contradiction from its not being apparent. In these circumstances the mathematicians' alleged power of creation must surely be considered worthless; for just where the exercise of it would be of value, it is tied up with conditions that apparently cannot be fulfilled. Besides, how do we know that avoidance of contradiction is the only thing to be observed in the act of construction?

§145. Like Thomae, Stolz calls his conception formalist. It would not be beside the point, then, to draw attention to the big difference that there nevertheless is between the two theories. Where Stolz constructs a new – at any rate a non-sensible – thing, which he supplies with a sign, Thomae introduces a new sort of figures, with associated rules. Thus Stolz speaks of a thing designated by $\mathfrak{u}(f) : \mathfrak{u}(g)$, just as he speaks of a thing that can be designated by $a \cup b$. We would have enclosed these signs in inverted commas, to make clear that we were just speaking of the signs, not of their *Bedeutung*. Incidentally, Stolz distinguishes between sign and what is designated as sharply as we do; and it does not occur to him at all to treat signs themselves as the real objects of arithmetic. Stolz's arithmetic has content despite his use of the word 'formalist'. One easily sees through the similarity of form to

147   the difference | of subject matter. In fact, Thomae's theory of an arith-
metical game is quite a different science from Stolz's arithmetic. No
proposition, even if it had exactly the same formulation, has the same
sense for both Thomae and Stolz; since the former is concerned with
physical objects – figures – and arbitrarily laid down rules for their
manipulation; the latter is concerned with non-sensible objects. Obviously, these are totally different questions, whether numbers are figures,
for whose manipulation rules are laid down; or whether numbers are
the *Bedeutungen* of number signs and can be constructed. In both cases
we run into difficulties that seem insurmountable. In Thomae's case
they consist in seeing whether the new rules can come into conflict with
the old, and settling such conflict; in Stolz's case they consist in proving
that no contradiction occurs between the properties of the thing to be
constructed, which mostly involves considering the properties of already
existing things. Doubt still arises here as to whether a construction is
anyway possible.

Dedekind agrees with Stolz in his conception of construction; for
him too numbers are not signs, but the *Bedeutungen* of number signs.
G. Cantor too is to be included in this group, although his view is less
sharply expressed.[o]

§146.   It has thus been made probable that a mathematician is denied
the power of actual construction, or at any rate that it is tied up with
conditions that render it worthless. As against this, somebody might
indicate that we ourselves have nevertheless constructed new objects,
viz. value-ranges (Vol. I, §§3, 9, 10). What, then, did we do there? Or
rather, in the first place, what did we not do? We did not enumerate
properties and then say: we construct a thing that is to have these
properties. Rather, we said: if a (first-level) function (of one argument)
and another function are such as always to have the same value for the
same argument, then we may say instead that the value-range of the
first is the same as that of the second. We are then recognizing something common to the two functions, and we call this the value-range of
the first function and also the value-range of the second function. We
must regard it as a fundamental law of logic that we are justified in thus
recognizing something common to both, and that accordingly we may
transform an equality holding generally into an equation (identity). This
transformation must not be regarded as a definition; neither the word
148   'same' or the 'equals' sign, nor | the word 'value-range' or a complex
symbol like '$\acute{\varepsilon}\Phi(\varepsilon)$', nor both together, are being defined by means of
it. For the sentence

[o] As to which standpoint H. Hankel adopts in his *Theorie der complexen Zahlensysteme*
(Leipzig, 1867), it is hard to say, since in his work there are conflicting remarks. Most
likely, he did not properly distinguish between sign and what is designated.

'The value-range of the first function is the same as the value-range of the
second function'

is complex, and contains as a part the word 'same', which must be
regarded as completely known. Similarly the symbol '$\acute{\varepsilon}\Phi(\varepsilon) = \acute{\alpha}\psi(\alpha)$' is
complex and contains as a part the 'equals' sign which is already known.
So if we tried to regard our stipulation in §3 as a definition, this would
certainly be an offence against our second principle of definition.[P]

§147.   People have indeed clearly already made use of the possibility
of transformation that I have mentioned; only they have ascribed coincidence to functions themselves rather than value-ranges. When one
function has in general the same value as another function for the same
argument, it is usual to say: 'the first function is the same as the second'
or 'the two functions coincide'. The expression is different from ours,
but all the same here too we have an equality holding generally transformed into an equation (identity).[Q]

Logicians have long since spoken of the extension of a concept, and
mathematicians have used the terms set, class, manifold; what lies behind
this is a similar transformation; for we may well suppose that what mathematicians call a set (etc.) is nothing other than an extension of a concept, even if they have not always been clearly aware of this.

What we are doing by means of our transformation is thus not really
anything novel; but we do it with full awareness, appealing to a fundamental law of logic. And what we thus do is quite different from the
lawless, arbitrary construction of numbers by many mathematicians. |
149   If there are logical objects at all – and the objects of arithmetic are
such objects – then there must also be a means of apprehending, of
recognizing, them. This service is performed for us by the fundamental

---

[P] In general, we must not regard the stipulations in Vol. I, with regard to the primitive
signs, as definitions. Only what is logically complex can be defined; what is simple can
only be pointed to.

[Q] Likewise, very few mathematicians will take thought over using '$f = g$' to express the
circumstance that $f(\xi)$ always has the same value as the function $g(\xi)$ for the same argument. This certainly involves a mistake, arising from a defective conception of the nature
of a function. An isolated function-letter without a place for an argument is a monstros-
ity, just as an isolated functional symbol like '*sin*' is. For what is distinctive of a function,
as compared with an object, is precisely its unsaturatedness, its needing to be completed
by an argument; and this feature must also come out in the symbolism. Such a symbolism as '$f = g$' is inadmissible, as is brought out by the fact that in particular cases it breaks
down. If you put, e.g., $\xi^2 - 1$ for $f(\xi)$ and $(\xi - 1)(\xi + 1)$ for $g(\xi)$, then it hits you in the
eye that you cannot write down anything corresponding to the equation '$f = g$'. But if
symbolism is in order it must always be possible to make such a transition within the
symbolism from general to particular. Accordingly the symbolism '$f = g$' cannot be recognized as correct; but nevertheless it shows that mathematicians have already made use of
the possibility of our transformation.

law of logic that permits the transformation of an equality holding generally into an equation. Without such a means a scientific foundation for arithmetic would be impossible. For us this serves towards the ends that other mathematicians intend to attain by constructing new numbers. We thus hope to be able to develop the whole wealth of objects and functions treated of in mathematics out of the germ of the eight functions whose names are enumerated in Vol. I, §31. Can our procedure be termed construction? Discussion of this question may easily degenerate to a quarrel over words. In any case our construction (if you like to call it that) is not unrestricted and arbitrary; the mode of performing it, and its legitimacy, are established once for all. And thus here the difficulties and objections vanish that in other cases make it questionable whether the construction is a logical possibility; and we may hope that by means of our value-ranges we shall attain what has been missed by following any other way.

[In the next sections of Part III, Frege discusses Weierstrass' theory (§§148–55), offers a 'Review and Outlook' (§§156–9) and some brief remarks on 'Magnitude' (§§160–4), before turning to the formal development of his theory of real numbers (§§165–245), which remained incomplete at the end of Volume II. What follows here is the appendix ('Nachwort') that Frege wrote whilst the book was in press attempting to deal with the contradiction that Russell had informed him of in June 1902.]

253

Appendix[9]

Hardly anything more unfortunate can befall a scientific writer than to have one of the foundations of his edifice shaken after the work is finished.

This was the position I was placed in by a letter of Mr Bertrand Russell,[10] just when the printing of this volume was nearing its completion. It is a matter of my Axiom (V).[11] I have never disguised from myself its lack of the self-evidence that belongs to the other axioms and

---

[9] The numbered footnotes that follow, except 10, 12, 13, 22 and 27, are supplied by Peter Geach (the translator), with minor revisions by the editor.

[10] See pp. 253–4 above.

[11] See Vol. I, §§3, 20. Cf. also *FC* for an explanation of the ideas used; especially pp. 135–6, 139 above. For any (first-level) function of one argument, there is some object that is its *value-range*; and two such functions by Axiom (V) have the same value-range if and only if their values are always equal for any given argument. Concepts (see p. 139 above) are functions whose values can only be the True or the False. For the value-ranges of concepts, which are called their *extensions*, the principle runs thus: two concepts are equal in extension if and only if whatever falls under either falls under the other.

that must properly be demanded of a logical law. And so in fact I indicated this weak point in the Preface to Vol. I (p. VII).[12] I should gladly have dispensed with this foundation if I had known of any substitute for it. And even now I do not see how arithmetic can be scientifically established; how numbers can be apprehended as logical objects, and brought under review; unless we are permitted – at least conditionally – to pass from a concept to its extension. May I always speak of the extension of a concept – speak of a class? And if not, how are the exceptional cases recognized? Can we always infer from one concept's coinciding in extension with another concept that any object that falls under the one falls under the other likewise? These are the questions raised by Mr Russell's communication.

Solatium [*sic*] *miseris socios habuisse malorum*.[13] I too have this comfort, if comfort it is; for everybody who in his proofs has made use of extensions of concepts, classes, sets,[R] is in the same position as I. What is in question is not just my particular way of establishing arithmetic, but whether arithmetic can possibly be given a logical foundation at all.

But let us come to the point. Mr Russell has discovered a contradiction which may now be stated.

Nobody will wish to assert of the class of men that it is a man. We
254   have here a class that does not belong to itself. | I say that something belongs to a class when it falls under the concept whose extension the class is. Let us now fix our eye on the concept: *class that does not belong to itself*. The extension of this concept (if we may speak of its extension) is thus the class of classes that do not belong to themselves. For short we will call it the class K. Let us now ask whether this class K belongs to itself. First, let us suppose it does. If anything belongs to a class, it falls under the concept whose extension the class is. Thus if our class belongs to itself, it is a class that does not belong to itself. Our first supposition thus leads to self-contradiction. Secondly, let us suppose our class K does not belong to itself; then it falls under the concept whose extension it itself is, and thus does belong to itself. Here once more we likewise get a contradiction!

What attitude must we adopt towards this? Must we suppose that the

---

[R] Mr R. Dedekind's 'systems' also come under this head. [Cf. *GG*, I, Introd., pp. 208–10 above.]

[12] See p. 195 above.

[13] 'It is a comfort to the wretched to have companions in misery' (in the Latin the first word is usually '*Solamen*'). Spinoza quotes it in the Note to Prop. LVII of Part IV of the *Ethics*, where he refers to it as a proverb. In Marlowe's *Doctor Faustus*, Mephistopheles quotes it in reply to Faustus' question as to why Lucifer should want his soul (2.1, line 42). Frege's own use of the proverb thus had greater significance than he realized. Twenty-four years after writing the *Begriffsschrift*, in which Frege first made his pact with Logic to discover the ultimate nature of number, his hubris had finally caught up with him.

law of excluded middle does not hold good for classes? Or must we suppose there are cases where an unexceptionable concept has no class answering to it as its extension? In the first case we should find ourselves obliged to deny that classes are objects in the full sense. For if classes were proper objects, the law of excluded middle would have to hold for them. On the other hand, there is nothing unsaturated or predicative about classes that would characterize them as functions, concepts, or relations. What we usually consider as a name of a class, e.g. 'the class of prime numbers', has rather the nature of a proper name; it cannot occur predicatively, but *can* occur as the grammatical subject of a singular proposition, e.g. 'The class of prime numbers contains infinitely many objects'. If we were going to dispense classes from the law of excluded middle, we might think of regarding them (and in fact value-ranges generally) as improper objects. These could then not be allowed as arguments for all first-level functions. But there would also be functions that could have as arguments both proper and improper objects. At least the relation of equality (identity) would be a function of this sort. (An attempt might be made to escape this by assuming a special sort of equality for improper objects. But that is certainly ruled out. Identity is a relation given to us in such a specific form that it is inconceivable that various kinds of it should occur.) But now we should get a great multiplicity of first-level functions.[14] First, there would be those that could have only proper objects as arguments; secondly, those that could have both proper and improper objects alike as arguments; lastly, those that could have only improper objects as arguments. There would also come about another division of first-level func-
255   tions, on the basis of their values. | Here we should have to distinguish, first, functions that had only proper objects as values; secondly, those that had both proper and improper objects alike as values; lastly, those that had only improper objects as values. First-level functions would be divided in both ways simultaneously; we should thus get a ninefold division of types [*Arten*]. To these again there would correspond nine types of value-ranges – of improper objects – between which we should have to draw logical distinctions. Classes of proper objects would have to be distinguished from classes of classes of proper objects; extensions of relations[15] holding between proper objects would have to be distinguished

---

[14] For the distinction between first-level and second-level functions, see *FC*, p. 146 above; *CO*, pp. 189–90 above.

[15] 'Extension of a relation' answers to the single word '*Relation*', which Frege·uses as short for '*Umfang einer Beziehung*' – *GG*, II, §162. Relations that always hold between the same objects, like concepts under which the same objects fall, are equal in extension; and Frege holds that an extension is always an object (*FC*, pp. 140–1 above), although the concept or relation whose extension it is is not an object but a function taking only the True or the False as its value (*FC*, pp. 139, 146 above).

from classes of proper objects, and from classes of extensions of relations holding between proper objects; and so on. We should thus get an incalculable multiplicity of types; and in general objects belonging to different types could not occur as arguments of the same function. But it appears extraordinarily difficult to set up a complete system of rules for deciding which objects are allowable arguments of which functions. Moreover, it may be doubted whether improper objects can justifiably be introduced.

If these difficulties scare us off from the view that classes (including numbers) are improper objects; and if we are likewise unwilling to recognize them as proper objects, i.e. as possible arguments for any first-level function; then there is nothing for it but to regard class names as sham proper names, which would thus not really have a *Bedeutung*. They would have to be regarded as part of signs that had a *Bedeutung* only as wholes.[5] Now of course one may think it advantageous for some end to form different signs that partly resemble one another, without thereby making them into complex signs. The simplicity of a sign requires only that the parts that may be distinguished within it should have no separate *Bedeutung*. On this view, then, even what we usually regard as a number sign would not really be a sign at all, but only an inseparable part of a sign. A definition of the sign '2' would be impossible; instead we should have to define many signs, which would contain '2' as an inseparable part, but could not be regarded as logically compounded of '2' and another part. It would thus be illicit to replace such an inseparable part by a letter; for as regards the content of the whole sign, there would be no complexity. The generality of arithmetical propositions would thus be lost. Again, it would be incomprehensible how we could speak of a number of classes or a number of numbers.

I think this is enough to show that this way too is barred. There is thus nothing left but to regard extensions of concepts, | or classes, as objects in the full and proper sense of the word. At the same time, however, we must admit that the interpretation we have so far put on the words 'extension of a concept' needs to be corrected.

Before we go into the matter more closely, it will be useful to track down the origin of the contradiction, by means of our symbols.[16] The supposition that Δ is a class not belonging to itself may be expressed as follows:

<Δ is the extension of some concept under which Δ does not fall>.

---

[5] Cf. Vol. I, §29 [pp. 220–1 above].

[16] These are not reproduced here. Passages in angled brackets < > are translated from Frege's symbolic language.

And the class of all classes that do not belong to themselves will be designated thus:

<the extension of the concept *object that is the extension of some concept under which it does not itself fall*>.

I will use the sign '∀' as short for this in the deduction that follows . . . Accordingly I shall use

<'∀ is the extension of some concept under which ∀ does not fall'>

to express the supposition that ∀ does not belong to itself.[17]
Now we have, by (Vb):[18]

<If the concept $f(\xi)$ is equal in extension to the concept *object that is the extension of some concept under which it does not itself fall*, then ∀ falls under $f(\xi)$ if and only if ∀ is the extension of some concept under which ∀ does not itself fall>.

Or, using our abbreviation . . . we get:[19]

(α)   <If ∀ is the extension of some concept under which ∀ itself does not fall, then it follows that, if ∀ is the extension of the concept $f(\xi)$, ∀ falls under $f(\xi)$>.

And now we get [since $f(\xi)$ may be any concept you like]:

(β)   <If ∀ is the extension of some concept under which ∀ does not itself fall, then ∀ falls under every concept whose extension it is>.

I.e. if ∀ does not belong to itself, then ∀ does belong to itself.[20] That is one side.
On the other side we have:

(γ)   <If ∀ falls under every concept whose extension it is, then, if ∀ is the extension of the concept $f(\xi)$, ∀ falls under $f(\xi)$>.

---

[17] By what is clearly a slip, Frege has 'belongs to itself'.
[18] Frege's Axiom (V) is deductively equivalent to the conjunction of his two theorems (Va) and (Vb). (Va) amounts to the assertion: If two functions always have the same value for the same argument, then they have the same value-range; in particular, if whatever falls under either one of two concepts falls under both, then they are equal in extension. (Vb) makes the converse assertion: If functions have the same value-range, then they always have the same value for the same arguments; in particular, if concepts are equal in extension then whatever falls under one falls under the other.
[19] This is a transition from 'If P, then Q if and only if R' to 'If R, then, if P, then Q'.
[20] Frege, by a slip corrected here, switches 'does belong' and 'does not belong'.

If we substitute for '$f(\xi)$'

<'ξ is the extension of some concept under which ξ does not fall'>,

we have:

(δ)   <If ∀ falls under every concept whose extension it is, then it follows that, if ∀ is the extension of the concept ξ *is the extension of some concept under which ξ does not fall*, then ∀ itself is the extension of some concept under which ∀ does not fall>.

Taking into account our abbreviation, we get:

(ε)   <If ∀ falls under every concept whose extension it is, then [if ∀ is ∀, then] ∀ is the extension of some concept under which ∀ does not fall>.

I.e. if ∀ does belong to itself, ∀ does not belong to itself.[21] From (ε) there follows [since $(P \rightarrow \neg P) \rightarrow \neg P$] |

257   (ζ)   <∀ is the extension of some concept under which ∀ does not fall>

and from this together with (β) we get

(η)   <∀ falls under every concept whose extension it is>.

The propositions (ζ) and (η) contradict one another. The only place where the mistake can lie is our law (Vb), which must therefore be false.

. . . Along with (Vb), (V) itself has collapsed but not (Va). There is nothing to stop our transforming an equality that holds generally into an equality of value-ranges [in accordance with (Va)]; all that has been shown is that the converse transformation [in accordance with (Vb)] is not always allowable. Of course this means admitting that the way I introduced value-ranges (Vol. I, §3) is not always legitimate. We cannot in general take the words

'the function $\Phi(\xi)$ has the same value-range as the function $\Psi(\xi)$'

as *gleichbedeutend*[22] with the words

'the functions $\Phi(\xi)$ and $\Psi(\xi)$ always have the same value for the same argument';

[21] The same slip as above is corrected here (see the previous footnote).
[22] On Frege's use of this term, see fn. 26 on p. 213 above.

and we must take into account the possibility that there are concepts with no extension (at any rate, none in the ordinary sense of the word). Thus the justification of our second-level function $\grave{\epsilon}\phi(\epsilon)$[23] becomes shaky. And yet such a function is indispensable for laying the foundation of arithmetic.

We shall now try to complete our inquiry by reaching the falsity of (Vb) as the final result of a deduction, instead of starting from (Vb) and thus running into a contradiction. In order to be independent of the symbolism for value-ranges, which is still suspect, we shall carry out the deduction quite generally, with regard to any second-level function that takes an argument of the second type.[24] ... Our complex symbol <'the extension of the concept *object that is the extension of some concept under which it does not fall*'> | will accordingly be replaced by:

258

<'the *M* of the concept *object that is the M of some concept under which it does not fall*'>.[25]

... This formula contains '*M*' twice over, initially and in the middle ... We at once have the following result:

<If *a* falls under every concept of which it is the *M*, then it follows that, if *a* is the *M* of the concept *object that is the M of some concept under which it does not fall*, then *a* is itself the *M* of some concept under which it does not fall>.

Hence:[26]

(μ)   <If *a* falls under every concept of which it is the *M*, then *a* is not the *M* of the concept *object that is the M of some concept under which it does not fall*>.

Hence:

(v)   <If *a* is the *M* of the concept *object that is the M of some concept under which it does not fall*, then *a* is the *M* of some concept under which *a* does not fall>.

---

[23] This symbol means 'the value-range of the function $\phi(\xi)$'. For a concept as argument, its value will thus be the extension of that concept. On the term 'second-level function', see *FC*, p. 146 above.

[24] An argument of the second type – *GG*, I, §23, p. 40 – is a first-level function of one argument; i.e. a function whose single argument is always an object, like *the square of* ξ or *the capital of* ξ. On Frege's view, a concept like ξ *is a prime number* is a function of this sort; its value is always either the True (e.g. for the argument 3) or the False (e.g. for 4, or the Moon, as argument). Cf. *FC*, p. 139 above.

[25] The reader will probably find it helpful to think of a concrete example – e.g. taking 'the *M* of . . .' to mean 'the number of objects falling under . . .'.

[26] The transition here is from 'If *P*, then, if *Q*, then not *P*' to 'If *P*, then not *Q*'.

If for short we put '$\Phi(\xi)$' instead of

<'ξ is the M of some concept under which ξ itself does not fall'>,

and substitute <'the M of the concept $\Phi(\xi)$'> for 'a', then we have, by
(v),

<The M of the concept $\Phi(\xi)$ falls under $\Phi(\xi)$>;

i.e. the value of our second-level function for the concept $\Phi(\xi)$ as argument falls under this very concept. On the other hand, we also have by
(v):

<The M of the concept $\Phi(\xi)$ is an object that is the M of some concept
it does not fall under>.

I.e. there is a concept which, when taken as argument of our second-
level function, gives the same value as $\Phi(\xi)$ gives, but under which the
value in question does not fall. In other words: for any second-level
function that takes an argument of the second type, there are two concepts yielding the same value when taken as arguments of the function,
259   the first of which has the value in question falling under it, | but the
second of which has not . . . |

260   Our proof has been carried out without the use of propositions or
symbols whose justification is in any way doubtful. Our proposition
then holds good for the function $\dot{\varepsilon}\phi(\varepsilon)$ too, supposing this to be legitimate; it may be stated in words as follows:

If in general, for any first-level concept, we may speak of its extension,
then the case arises of concepts having the same extension, although
not all objects that fall under one fall under the other as well.

This, however, really abolishes the extension of the concept, in the
261   sense we have given the word. We may | not say that in general the
expression 'the extension of one concept coincides with that of another'
is *gleichbedeutend*[27] with the expression 'all objects that fall under the
one concept fall under the other as well, and conversely'. We see from
the result of our deduction that it is quite impossible to give the words
'the extension of the concept $\phi(\xi)$' such a sense that from concepts'
being equal in extension we could always infer that every object falling
under one falls under the other likewise.

Our proposition may also be reached in another way. We have:

<If a is not the M of any concept that a itself falls under, then, if a is the
M of the concept *object that is not the M of any concept that it falls under*,
it follows that a does not fall under this concept>.[28]

---

[27] Again, on the use of this term, see fn. 26 on p. 213 above.
[28] As before, it will be easier to follow this abstract reasoning in a particular case, e.g.
by taking 'the M of . . .' to mean 'the number of objects falling under . . .'.

Hence:[29]

(ψ)   <If *a* is not the *M* of any concept that it falls under, then *a* is not the *M* of the concept *object that is not the M of any concept that it falls under*>.

Hence:

(ω)   <If *a* is the *M* of the concept *object that is not the M of any concept that it falls under*, then *a* falls under some concept of which it is the *M*>.

If for short we put '$\Psi(\xi)$' instead of

<'ξ is not the *M* of any concept that ξ itself falls under'>,

and substitute <'the *M* of the concept $\Psi(\xi)$'> for '*a*', then we have, by (ω),

<The *M* of the concept $\Psi(\xi)$ does not fall under $\Psi(\xi)$>.

I.e. the value of our second-level function for the concept $\Psi(\xi)$ as argument does not fall under the concept $\Psi(\xi)$. On the other hand, we likewise have, by (ω),

<The *M* of the concept $\Psi(\xi)$ falls under some concept of which it is the *M*>.

I.e. there is a concept which, when taken as argument of our second-level function, gives the same value as $\Psi(\xi)$ gives, and which has the value in question falling under it. Thus here likewise we have two concepts yielding the same value when taken as arguments of the second-level function, the second of which has the value in question falling under it and the first of which has not . . . |

262   Let us now try taking the function <*the extension of the concept $\phi(\xi)$*> as the second-level function referred to in our propositions. We then have in <the concept *object that is the extension of some concept under which it does not fall*> a concept under which its own extension falls [by (v)]; but by (v) there is also a concept, coinciding in its extension with the one just mentioned, under which the extension in question does not fall. We should very much like to give an example. How is such a concept to be found? That is not possible without more precise specification as to our function <*the extension of the concept $\phi(\xi)$*>; for our previous

---

[29] This transition is one from 'If *P*, then, if *Q*, then not *P*' to 'If *P*, then not *Q*'.

criterion for coincidence between concepts in their extension here leaves us in the lurch.

On the other hand, we have in <the concept *object that is not the extension of any concept that it falls under*> a concept under which its own extension does not fall [by (ω)]; but by (ω) there is a concept, coinciding in extension with the one just mentioned, under which the extension in question does fall. All this discussion naturally presupposes that '<the extension of the concept $\phi(\xi)$>' is a logically correct name of a function.

In both cases we see that the exceptional case is constituted by the extension itself, in that it falls under only one of two concepts whose extension it is; and we see that the occurrence of this exception can in no way be avoided.[30] Accordingly the following suggests itself as the criterion for equality in extension: The extension of one concept coincides with that of another when every object that falls under the first concept, except the extension of the first concept, falls under the second concept likewise, and when every object that falls under the second concept, except the extension of the second concept, falls under the first concept likewise.

Obviously this cannot be taken as *defining* the extension of a concept, but only as specifying the distinctive property of this second-level function.

By transferring to value-ranges in general what we have said about extensions of concepts, we get the Axiom (V'):

<Two first-level functions of one argument have the same value-range if and only if they always have the same value for any argument that is not the value-range of either>.

This is to replace Axiom (V) (Vol. I, §20, p. 36). From this law there follows (Va).[31] (Vb) on the other hand must give place to one of the laws (V'b) or (V'c) [which may be stated in words as follows]:

<If two functions have the same value-range, then they have equal values for any argument that is not the value-range of one of the functions>.[32]

---

[30] In the actual form here presented, Frege's way out of Russell's paradox only leads to new contradictions: see Quine, 1955; Geach, 1956. The central idea, however, that the extension of the concept should itself be treated as the sole 'exceptional case', admits of certain generalizations, which are not definitely known to regenerate paradox; the investigation of these is of considerable technical difficulty, and seems to go naturally with certain reconstructions of quantification theory. See Hintikka, 1956; 1957. For more recent discussion, see Dummett, 1991a: chs. 17–18, 23–4; 1994; Boolos, 1993; Clark, 1993.

[31] For (Va) and (Vb), see fn. 18 on p. 283 above.

[32] For concepts this means: If two concepts are equal in extension, then any object that is not the extension of one of them falls under one if and only if it falls under the other.

Let us now convince ourselves that the contradiction that arose pre-
263 viously between propositions (β) and (ε) is now | avoided. We proceed
just as we did in deducing (β), making use of (V'c) instead of (Vb). As
before, let '∀' be short for

<'the extension of the concept *object that is the extension of some concept
under which it does not fall*'>.

By (V'c) we have:

<If the concept $f(\xi)$ is equal in extension to the concept *object that is the
extension of some concept under which it does not fall,* then, if ∀ is not the extension of the latter concept, ∀ falls under $f(\xi)$ if and only if ∀ is the extension
of some concept under which it does not fall>.

Using our abbreviation we get:

<If the concept $f(\xi)$ is equal in extension to the concept *object that is the
extension of some concept under which it does not fall,* then, if ∀ is not the same
as ∀, ∀ falls under $f(\xi)$ if and only if ∀ is the extension of some concept
under which it does not fall>.

This is obviously true, because of the sub-clause <'if ∀ is not the same
as ∀'>, and on that very account can never lead to a contradiction . . .[33]
265   It would here take us too far to follow out further the result of
replacing (V) by (V'). We cannot but see that many propositions must
have sub-clauses [conditions] added; but we need scarcely fear that this
will raise essential difficulties for the course of the proofs. Anyhow, all
propositions discovered up to now will need to be checked through.
     The prime problem of arithmetic may be taken to be the problem:
How do we apprehend logical objects, in particular numbers? What justi-
fies us in recognizing numbers as objects? Even if this problem is not
yet solved to the extent that I believed it was when I wrote this volume,
nevertheless I do not doubt that the way to a solution has been found.

                                                 Jena, October 1902

---

[33] The next two pages are omitted here: Frege briefly considers the effect of his modi-
fication of Axiom (V) on some of his earlier stipulations.

Letter to Russell,
13.11.1904[1]

[Despite Frege's attempts to convince Russell in his letters of 28.12.1902[2] and 21.5.1903,[3] Russell wrote back, on 24.5.1903, that 'I still do not quite share your opinion about *Sinn* and *Bedeutung*'.[4] In the following excerpt from Frege's reply, Frege elucidates the distinction further.]

Jena

13 November 1904

Dear Colleague,

. . .

. . . According to my way of speaking, a thought can be designated and it can be expressed. The former happens in indirect speech. 'Copernicus thought that the planetary orbits are circular' is an example of this. The subordinate clause introduced by 'that' designates a thought, while the whole proposition (main clause and subordinate clause) expresses a thought. Copernicus himself was able to express the thought that the planetary orbits are circular. In our whole proposition, the proper name 'Copernicus' designates a man, just as the subordinate clause 'that the planetary orbits are circular' designates a thought; and what is said is that there is a relation between this man and that thought, namely that the man took the thought to be true. Here the man and the thought occupy, so to speak, the same stage. On the other hand, the man and the thought of the whole proposition 'Copernicus thought that the planetary orbits are circular' do not occupy the same stage. If it is said that the name 'Copernicus' here designates a man, then it cannot be said that the whole proposition designates a thought; for the connection between the man and the name is quite different from that between the whole proposition and the thought. The man is designated, the thought is expressed. Moreover, the man

---

[1] Translated by Hans Kaal (*PMC*, pp. 164–5; from *WB*, pp. 246–7; page numbers from the latter in the margin).

[2] See pp. 255–7 above.

[3] *PMC*, pp. 156–8/*WB*, pp. 239–41.

[4] *PMC*, p. 159/*WB*, p. 242.

is not placed in relation to the thought. Compare this with the following example: '7 − 1' designates a number, just as '7' and '1' designate numbers. These numbers occupy, so to speak, the same stage. The kind of connection between the sign '7 − 1' and the number 7 − 1 or 6 is the same as that between the sign '7' and the number 7. Now instead of the sign '7' we can also take the sign '4 + 3', and '4 + 3 − 1' now designates the same number as '7 − 1' because '4 + 3' designates the same number as '7'. We can regard 7 − 1 as a value of the function $\xi − 1$ for the argument 7. And it makes no difference to the value which of the signs '7', '4 + 3', '$4^2 − 3^2$' we use, all of which have the same *Bedeutung*.[5] In this way, we cannot regard the thought that 7 is greater than 6 as a value of the function $\xi > 6$ for the argument 7; for we get another thought if we substitute '4 + 3' for '7', and yet another if we substitute '$4^2 − 3^2$' for it. We thus find that the thought depends on something other than what is designated by the sign; for this is the same for '7' and for '4 + 3'. A sign must therefore be connected with something other than its *Bedeutung*, something that can be different for signs with the same designation. Signs | do not just designate something; they also express something. This is the sense. Indeed, the two propositions '7 = 7' and

$$\frac{5^2.211 − 4}{753} = 7$$

do not have the same cognitive value for us, even though the sign

$$\frac{5^2.211 − 4}{753}$$

has the same designation as '7'. The cognitive value [*Erkenntniswert*] therefore does not depend only on the *Bedeutung*; the sense is just as essential. Without the latter we should have no knowledge at all. When I say '7 − 1 = 6', the number 7 does not occupy the same stage as the sense of '7 − 1', any more than it occupies the same stage as the thought that 7 − 1 = 6. On the other hand, the sense of the sign '7' occupies the same stage as this thought; it can be said to be part of this thought, as well as part of the sense of '7 − 1'. We must therefore conceive of this thought as the sense of this proposition and say accordingly: the proposition expresses the thought. Now, can we not be satisfied with the sense of the proposition and do without a *Bedeutung*? For it does sometimes happen that a sign has a sense but no *Bedeutung*, namely in legend and poetry. Thus the sense is independent of whether there is a *Bedeutung*.

247

---

[5] 'welches der gleichbedeutenden Zeichen "7", "4 + 3", "$4^2 − 3^2$" wir gebrauchen'.

Accordingly, if all that matters to us is the sense of the proposition, the thought, then all we need to worry about is the sense of the signs that constitute the proposition; whether or not they also have a *Bedeutung* does not affect the thought. And this is indeed the case in legend and poetry. Conversely, if it is not immaterial to us whether the signs that constitute the proposition are *bedeutungsvoll*, then it is not just the thought which matters to us, but also the *Bedeutung* of the proposition. And this is the case when and only when we are inquiring into its truth. Then and only then does the *Bedeutung* of the proposition enter into our considerations; it must therefore be most intimately connected with its truth.[6] Indirect speech must here be disregarded; for we have seen that, in it, the thought is designated, not expressed. Disregarding it, we can therefore say that any true proposition can be replaced by any true proposition without detriment to its truth, and likewise any false proposition by any false proposition. And this is to say that all true propositions refer to [*bedeuten*] or designate the same thing, and likewise all false propositions . . .

Yours sincerely,
G. Frege

[6] Cf. *SB*, pp. 156–8 above.

Introduction to Logic[1]

[The piece entitled 'Introduction to Logic', published in Frege's *Post-humous Writings*,[2] is a set of diary notes written by Frege in August 1906, presumably as part of his attempt to write a textbook on logic.[3] What follows here is the final section, entitled 'Sinn und Bedeutung'.[4]]

208   Proper names are meant to designate objects, and we call the object designated by a proper name its *Bedeutung*. On the other hand, a proper name is a constituent of a sentence, which expresses a thought. Now what has the object got to do with the thought? We have seen from the sentence 'Mont Blanc is over 4000 m high' that it is not part of the thought.[5] Is then the object necessary at all for the sentence to express a thought? People certainly say that *Odysseus* is not an historical person, and mean by this contradictory expression that the name 'Odysseus' designates nothing, has no *Bedeutung*. But if we accept this, we do not on that account deny a thought-content to all sentences of the *Odyssey* in which the name 'Odysseus' occurs. Let us just imagine that we have convinced ourselves, contrary to our former opinion, that the name 'Odysseus', as it occurs in the Odyssey, does designate a man after all. Would this mean that the sentences containing the name 'Odysseus' expressed different thoughts? I think not. The thoughts would strictly remain the same; they would only be transposed from the realm of fiction to that of truth. So the object designated by a proper name seems to be quite inessential to the thought-content of a sentence which

---

[1] Translated by Peter Long and Roger White (*PW*, pp. 191–6; from *NS*, pp. 208–12; page numbers from the latter in the margin).

[2] *PW*, pp. 185–96/*NS*, pp. 201–12.

[3] Cf. p. 227 above.

[4] The previous sections are entitled 'Dissociating assertoric force from the predicate' (*PW*, p. 185), 'The hypothetical mode of sentence composition' (*PW*, pp. 185–7) and 'Generality' (*PW*, pp. 187–91).

[5] Cf. the previous section: 'we can't say that an object is part of a thought as a proper name is part of the corresponding sentence. Mont Blanc with its masses of snow and ice is not part of the thought that Mont Blanc is more than 4000 m high; all we can say is that to the object there corresponds, in a certain way that has yet to be considered, a part of the thought' (*PW*, p. 187).

contains it. To the thought-content! For the rest, it goes without saying that it is by no means a matter of indifference to us whether we are operating in the realm of fiction or of truth. But we can immediately infer from what we have just said that something further must be associated with the proper name, something which is different from the object designated and which is essential to the thought of the sentence in which the proper name occurs. I call it the sense of the proper name. As the proper name is part of the sentence, so its sense is part of the thought.

The same point can be approached in other ways. It is not uncommon for the same object to have different proper names; but for all that they are not simply interchangeable. This is only to be explained by the fact that proper names with the same *Bedeutung* can have different senses. The sentence 'Mont Blanc is over 4000 m high' does not express the same thought as the sentence 'The highest mountain in Europe is over 4000 m high', although the proper name 'Mont Blanc' designates the same mountain as the expression 'the highest mountain in Europe'. The two sentences 'The Evening Star is the same as the Evening Star' and 'The Morning Star is the same as the Evening Star' differ only by a proper name with the same *Bedeutung*. Nevertheless they express different thoughts. So the sense of the proper name 'the Evening Star' must
209 be different from that of the proper name 'the Morning Star'. | The upshot is that there is something associated with a proper name, different from its *Bedeutung*, which can be different as between proper names with the same *Bedeutung*, and which is essential to the thought-content of the sentence containing it. A sentence proper, in which a proper name occurs, expresses a singular thought, and in this we distinguished a complete part and an unsaturated one.[6] The former corresponds to the proper name, but it is not the *Bedeutung* of the proper name, but its sense. The unsaturated part of the thought we take to be a sense too: it is the sense of the part of the sentence over and above the proper name. And it is in line with these stipulations to take the thought itself as a sense, namely the sense of the sentence. As the thought is the sense of the whole sentence, so a part of the thought is the sense of part of the sentence. Thus the thought appears the same in kind as the sense of a proper name, but quite different from its *Bedeutung*.

Now the question arises whether to the unsaturated part of the thought, which is to be regarded as the sense of the corresponding part of the sentence, there does not also correspond something which is to be construed as the *Bedeutung* of this part. As far as the mere thought-content is concerned it is indeed a matter of indifference whether a proper

---

[6] See the previous section: *PW*, pp. 187–8. Cf. *FC*, pp. 139–40 above; *CSB*, pp. 173–4 above; *CO*, pp. 192–3 above; *GG*, I, §1 (pp. 211–12 above).

name has a *Bedeutung*, but in any other regard it is of the greatest importance; at least it is so if we are concerned with the acquisition of knowledge. It is this which determines whether we are in the realm of fiction or truth. Now it is surely unlikely that a proper name should behave so differently from the rest of a singular sentence that it is only in its case that the existence of a *Bedeutung* should be of importance. If the thought as a whole is to belong to the realm of truth, we must rather assume that something in the realm of *Bedeutung* must correspond to the rest of the sentence, which has the unsaturated part of the thought for its sense. We may add to this the fact that in this part of the sentence too there may occur proper names, where it does matter that they should have a *Bedeutung*. If several proper names occur in a sentence, the corresponding thought can be analysed into a complete and unsaturated part in different ways. The sense of each of these proper names can be set up as the complete part over against the rest of the thought as the unsaturated part. We know that even in speech the same thought can be expressed in different ways, by making now this proper name, now that one, the grammatical subject. No doubt we shall say that these different phrasings are not equivalent. This is true. But we must not forget that language does not simply express thoughts; it also imparts a certain tone [*Beleuchtung*] or colouring [*Färbung*] to them. And this can be different even where the thought is the same. It is inconceivable that it is only for the proper names that there can be a question of *Bedeutung* and not for the other parts of the sentence which connect them. If we say 'Jupiter is larger than Mars', what are we talking about? About the heavenly bodies themselves, the *Bedeutungen* of the proper names 'Jupiter' and 'Mars'. We are saying that they stand in a certain relation to one another, and this we do by means of the

210 words 'is larger than'. This relation holds between | the *Bedeutungen* of the proper names, and so must itself belong to the realm of *Bedeutungen*. It follows that we have to acknowledge that the part of the sentence 'is larger than Mars' is possessed of a *Bedeutung*, and not merely a sense.[7] If we split up a sentence into a proper name and the remainder, then this remainder has for its sense an unsaturated part of a thought. But we call its *Bedeutung* a concept. In doing so we are of course making a mistake, a mistake which language forces upon us. By the very fact of introducing the word 'concept', we countenance the possibility of sentences of the form '*A* is a concept', where *A* is a proper name. We have thereby stamped as an object what – as being completely different in kind – is the precise opposite of an object. For the same reason the definite article at the beginning of 'the *Bedeutung* of the remaining part of the sentence' is a mistake too. But language forces us into such

---

[7] '. . . als bedeutungsvoll anerkennen müssen, nicht [nur] als sinnvoll'.

inaccuracies, and so nothing remains for us but to bear them constantly in mind, if we are not to fall into error and thus blur the sharp distinction between concept and object.[8] We can, metaphorically speaking, call the concept unsaturated too; alternatively we can say that it is predicative in character.

We have considered the case of a compound sentence consisting of a quasi-antecedent and quasi-consequent, where these quasi-sentences contain a letter ('*a*', say).[9] When the letter is subtracted from each of these quasi-sentences the remainder corresponds to an unsaturated part of a thought, and we may now say that such a part of a thought is the sense of the part of a sentence referred to as the remainder. Now such a part also has a *Bedeutung*, and this we have called a concept. So we have one concept occurring as the *Bedeutung* of what is left over from the quasi-antecedent, and one concept occurring as the *Bedeutung* of what is left over from the quasi-consequent. These concepts are here brought into a special connection with one another (we could also say 'relation') and this we call subordination: that is to say, the concept in the quasi-antecedent is made subordinate to the concept in the quasi-consequent. If we regard a singular sentence as composed of a proper name and the remainder, then to a proper name there corresponds an object as its *Bedeutung* and to the remainder a concept. Here the concept and object present themselves as connected or related in a special way, which we call subsumption. The object is subsumed under the concept. It is clear that subsumption is totally different from subordination.

We have seen that it is true of parts of sentences that they have *Bedeutungen*. What of a whole sentence, does this have a *Bedeutung* too? If we are concerned with truth, if we are aiming at knowledge, then we demand of each proper name occurring in a sentence that it should have a *Bedeutung*. On the other hand, we know that as far as the sense of a sentence, the thought, is concerned, it does not matter whether the

---

[8] On the problem to which Frege is alluding here, see *CO*, pp. 181–93 above.

[9] The notion of a 'quasi-sentence' ('uneigentlicher Satz') was introduced in the previous section of 'Introduction to Logic': something that 'has the grammatical form of a sentence and yet is not an expression of a thought, although it may be part of a sentence that does express a thought, and thus part of a sentence proper' (*PW*, p. 190/*NS*, p. 207). To explain Frege's point in the present paragraph, consider, for example, the proposition 'All whales are mammals' (cf. *FA*, §47; p. 100 above), which Frege construes as 'For all *a*, if *a* is a whale, then *a* is a mammal'. Here '*a* is a whale' counts as the 'quasi-antecedent', and '*a* is a mammal' as the 'quasi-consequent'. Removing the '*a*' yields an 'unsaturated' concept-expression, '( ) is a whale' – or 'ξ is a whale' as Frege tends to write it, 'ξ' being used merely to indicate the argument-place (cf. *GG*, I, §1; pp. 211–12 above). 'All whales are mammals' is then understood as involving *subordination* ('The concept *whale* is subordinate to the concept *mammal*'), whilst, by contrast, 'Willy is a whale', say, involves *subsumption* ('The object Willy is subsumed under the concept *whale*'). Cf. *CSB*, pp. 174–5 above; *CO*, pp. 189–90 above; 'Letters to Husserl, 1906', p. 303 below; *NLD*, p. 363 below.

parts of the sentence have *Bedeutungen* or not. It follows that there must be something associated with a sentence which is different from the thought, something to which it is essential that the parts of the sentence should have *Bedeutungen*. This is to be called the *Bedeutung* of the |

211 sentence. But the only thing to which this is essential is what I call the truth-value – whether the thought is true or false. Thoughts in myth and fiction do not need to have truth-values. A sentence containing a proper name without *Bedeutung* [*bedeutungslosen Eigennamen*] is neither true nor false; if it expresses a thought at all, then that thought belongs to fiction. In that case the sentence has no *Bedeutung*. We have two truth-values, the True and the False. If a sentence has a *Bedeutung* at all, this is either the True or the False. If a sentence can be split up into parts, each of which has *Bedeutung* [*bedeutungsvoll ist*], then the sentence also has a *Bedeutung*. The True and the False are to be regarded as objects, for both the sentence and its sense, the thought, are complete in character, not unsaturated. If, instead of the True and the False, I had discovered two chemical elements, this would have created a greater stir in the academic world. If we say 'the thought is true', we seem to be ascribing truth to the thought as a property. If that were so, we should have a case of subsumption. The thought as an object would be subsumed under the concept of the true. But here we are misled by language. We do not have the relation of an object to a property, but that of the sense of a sign to its *Bedeutung*. In fact at bottom the sentence 'It is true that 2 is prime' says no more than the sentence '2 is prime'. If in the first case we express a judgement, this is not because of the word 'true', but because of the assertoric force we give the word 'is'.[10] But we can do that equally well in the second sentence, and an actor on the stage, for example, would be able to utter the first sentence without assertoric force just as easily as the second.[11]

A sentence proper[12] is a proper name, and its *Bedeutung*, if it has one, is a truth-value: the True or the False. There are many sentences which can be analysed into a complete part, which is in its turn a proper

212 name, | and an unsaturated part, which stands for [*bedeutet*] a concept. In the same way there are many proper names, whose *Bedeutung*[*en*] are not truth-values, which can be analysed into a complete part, which is in its turn a proper name, and an unsaturated part. If this latter is to have *Bedeutung* [*bedeutungsvoll sein soll*], then the result of saturating it with any proper name with *Bedeutung*[13] must once more be a proper

[10] Cf. *MBLI*, pp. 322–4 below.

[11] Frege's footnote at this point, remarking on the use of letters in arithmetic, is here omitted.

[12] 'Ein eigentlicher Satz', i.e. not a 'quasi-sentence' ('ein uneigentlicher Satz').

[13] Throughout this paragraph, the phrase 'proper name with *Bedeutung*' has been used (instead of 'meaningful proper name' as in *PW*) to translate the German phrase 'bedeutungsvoller Eigenname'.

name with *Bedeutung*. When this happens, we call the *Bedeutung* of this unsaturated part a function. At this point, however, we need to make a reservation, similar to that we made earlier when the word 'concept' was introduced, about the unavoidable inaccuracy of language. The unsaturated part of a sentence, whose *Bedeutung* we have called a concept, must have the property of yielding a genuine sentence when saturated by any proper name with *Bedeutung*; this means that it must yield the proper name of a truth-value. This is the requirement that a concept have sharp boundaries. For a given concept, every object must either fall under it or not, *tertium non datur*.[14] From this it follows that a requirement similar to that we have just laid down is to be made of a function. As an example let us start off from the sentence '3 − 2 > 0'. We split this up into the proper name '3 − 2' and the remainder ' > 0'. We may say this unsaturated part stands for [*bedeute*] the concept of a positive number. This concept must have sharp boundaries. Every object must either fall or not fall under this concept. Let us now go further and split the proper name '3 − 2' up into the proper name '2' and the unsaturated part '3 − '. Now we may also split the original sentence '3 − 2 > 0' up into the proper name '2' and the unsaturated part '3 − > 0'. The *Bedeutung* of this is the concept of something that yields a positive remainder when subtracted from 3. This concept must have sharp boundaries too. Now if there were a proper name with *Bedeutung* *a* such that the unsaturated part '3 − ' did not yield a proper name with *Bedeutung* when saturated by it, then the unsaturated part '3 − > 0', when saturated by *a*, would not yield a proper sentence [i.e. itself a proper name with *Bedeutung*] either; that is to say, we should not be able to say whether the object designated by *a* fell under the concept which is the *Bedeutung* of '3 − > 0'. We can see from this that the usual definitions of the arithmetical signs are inadequate.

---

[14] Cf. esp. *GG*, II, §56 (p. 259 above).

A Brief Survey of my Logical Doctrines[1]

[The editors of the *Posthumous Writings*, in which this piece appears, suggested that it constitutes a revision, probably made soon afterwards (since the originals were found together in that order), of part of the August 1906 diary notes, 'Introduction to Logic'.[2] What follows here is just the first section, entitled 'Thought' ('Der Gedanke'), which contains one of only two explicit formulations in Frege's work of a criterion for sameness of thought.[3]]

213   When I use the word 'sentence' ['*Satz*'][4] in what follows I do not mean [*meine*] a sentence that serves to express a wish, a command, or a question, but one that serves to make an assertion. Although a sentence can be perceived by the senses, we use it to communicate a content that cannot be perceived by the senses. We are making a judgement about this content when we accept it as true or reject it as false. When a sentence is uttered the assertion that it is true usually goes hand in hand with the communication of the content. But the hearer does not have to adopt the speaker's stance; not that he has to reject the content either. He can simply refrain from making a judgement. We may now think of the content of a sentence as it is viewed by such a hearer.

     Now two sentences *A* and *B* can stand in such a relation that anyone who recognizes the content of *A* as true must straightaway [*ohne weiteres*] also recognize that of *B* as true, and conversely, that anyone who accepts the content of *B* must immediately [*unmittelbar*] accept that of *A* (*equipollence*). It is here being assumed that there is no difficulty

---

[1] Translated by Peter Long and Roger White (*PW*, pp. 197–8; from *NS*, pp. 213–14; page numbers from the latter in the margin).
[2] Cf. *PW*, p. 197, fn. 1/*NS*, p. 213. fn. 1. Part of the diary notes are reprinted above (pp. 293–8).
[3] The other is contained in a letter Frege wrote to Husserl, also in 1906 (see pp. 305–6 below). Questions are raised, however, as to the compatibility of the two criteria, since on the face of it they do not appear to be consistent with one another (though neither ended up being published by Frege himself). For discussion, see van Heijenoort, 1977; Picardi, 1993; Beaney, 1996: §8.1.
[4] The word 'Satz' has alternatively been translated as 'proposition' in this volume. See the Glossary above.

in grasping the content of *A* and *B*. The sentences need not be equivalent in all respects. For instance, one may have what we may call a poetic aura, and this may be absent from the other. Such a poetic aura will belong to the content of the sentence, but not to that which we accept as true or reject as false. I assume there is nothing in the content of either of the two equipollent sentences *A* and *B* that would have to be immediately accepted as true by anyone who had grasped it properly.[5] The poetic aura then, or whatever else distinguishes the content of *A* from that of *B*, does not belong to what is accepted as true; for if this were the case, then it could not be an immediate consequence of anyone's accepting the content of *B* that he should accept that of *A*. For the assumption is that what distinguishes *A* and *B* is not contained in *B* at all, nor is it something that anyone must recognize as true straight off.

214   So one has to separate off from the content of a sentence the part that alone can be accepted as true or rejected as false. I call this | part the thought expressed by the sentence. It is the same in equipollent sentences of the kind given above. It is only with this part of the content that logic is concerned.[6] I call anything else that goes to make up the content of a sentence the colouring [*Färbung*] of the thought.[7]

Thoughts are not psychological entities and do not consist of ideas in the psychological sense. The thought in Pythagoras' theorem is the same for all men; it confronts everyone in the same way as something objective, whereas each man has his own ideas, sensations, and feelings, which belong only to him. We grasp thoughts but we do not create them.

In myth and fiction thoughts occur that are neither true nor false. Logic has nothing to do with these. In logic it holds good that every thought is either true or false, *tertium non datur*.

---

[5] Without this qualification, all self-evident propositions would be in danger of coming out, on this criterion, as expressing the same thought. Cf. the qualification Frege makes in formulating his other criterion; p. 305 below.

[6] Compare what Frege says here with his earlier explanation of the notion of 'conceptual content' in *BS*, §3 (pp. 53–4 above)

[7] Cf. *PWLB*, pp. 239–44 above.

Letters to Husserl, 1906[1]

[After Frege's and Husserl's initial exchange of letters in 1891,[2] there was a break of some fifteen years, no doubt connected with the critical review that Frege had written of Husserl's *Philosophie der Arithmetik*,[3] before the correspondence was renewed, initiated once again by Husserl's sending Frege some of his work. Husserl's letters are lost; what follows here are Frege's two letters in reply, which centre on the logical importance of distinguishing the objective content or *thought* expressed by a proposition.[4]]

101

Jena
                                  30 October to 1 November 1906

Dear Colleague,

As I thank you very much for kindly sending me your article,[5] may I at the same time pass on to you some observations that occurred to me as I was reading it, since I do not have the time now to go into it thoroughly.

Logicians make many distinctions between judgements which seem to me immaterial, and on the other hand they do not make many distinctions which I regard as important. It seems to me that logicians still cling too much to language and grammar and are too much entangled in psychology. This is apparently what prevents them from studying my *Begriffsschrift*, which could have a liberating effect on them. They find that my *Begriffsschrift* does not correctly represent mental processes; and they are right, for this is not

---

[1] Translated by Hans Kaal (*PMC*, pp. 66–71; from *WB*, pp. 101–6; page numbers from the latter in the margin).

[2] See p. 149 above.

[3] See p. 224 above.

[4] The footnotes that follow, except 6, 9, 10, 16 and 17, are those of the editors of *WB*.

[5] The article in question is the fifth and concluding article in the series *Bericht über deutsche Schriften zur Logik in den Jahren 1895–99*, in *Archiv für systematische Philosophie* X (1904), pp. 101–25. There is no way of telling whether Frege also received the other articles. The fifth article is a critical discussion of Anton Marty, *Über subjektlose Sätze und das Verhältnis der Grammatik zur Logik und Psychologie*, 6th and 7th articles, *Vierteljahrsschrift für wissenschaftliche Philosophie* XIX (1895), pp. 19–87 and 263–334.

its purpose at all. If it occasions entirely new mental processes, this does not frustrate its purpose. Apparently it is still thought to be the task of logic to study certain mental processes. Logic has really no more to do with them than with the movements of celestial bodies. It is in no sense part of psychology. Pythagoras' theorem expresses | the same thought for all men, whereas everyone has his own images, feelings and decisions, different from everyone else's. Thoughts are not mental entities, and thinking is not an inner generation of such entities but the grasping of thoughts which are already present objectively. One should make only those distinctions with which the laws of logic are concerned. In gravitational mechanics no one would want to distinguish bodies according to their optical properties. Object and concept are not distinguished at all or much too little. Of course, if they are both ideas in the psychological sense, the difference is hardly noticeable. This is connected with the distinction between first- and second-level concepts, which is very important, but who among logicians knows anything about it? In logic, one must decide to regard equipollent propositions as differing only according to form. After the assertoric force with which they may have been uttered is subtracted, equipollent propositions have something in common in their content, and this is what I call the thought they express. This alone is of concern to logic. The rest I call the colouring [*Färbung*] and the shading [*Beleuchtung*] of the thought. Once we decide to take this step, we do away at a single stroke with a confused mass of useless distinctions and with the occasion for countless disputes which cannot for the most part be decided objectively. And we are given free rein to pursue proper logical analyses. Judged psychologically, the analysing proposition is of course always different from the analysed one, and all logical analysis can be brought to a halt by the objection that the two propositions are merely equipollent, if this objection is indeed accepted.[6] For it will not be possible to draw a clearly recognizable limit between merely equipollent and congruent propositions. Even propositions which appear congruent when presented in print can be pronounced with a different intonation and are not therefore equivalent in every respect. Only now that logical analysis proper has become possible can the logical elements be recognized, and we can see the clearing in the forest. All that would be needed would be a single standard proposition for each system of equipollent propositions, and any thought could be communicated by such a standard proposition. For given a standard proposition everyone would have the whole system of equipollent

102

---

[6] Cf. Frege's response to Husserl's criticisms of his definitions in *GL*; pp. 224–6 above.

propositions, and he could make the transition to any one of them whose illumination was particularly to his taste. It cannot be the task of logic to investigate language and determine what is contained in a linguistic expression. Someone who wants to learn logic from language is like an adult who wants to learn how to think from a child. When human beings created language, they were at the stage of childish pictorial thinking. Languages are not made so as to match logic's ruler. Even the logical element in language seems hidden behind pictures that are not always accurate. At an early time in the creation of language there occurred, it seems, a tremendous exuberance in the growth of linguistic forms. At a later time much of this had to be got rid of again and simplified. The main task of the logician is | to free himself from language and to simplify it. Logic should be the judge of languages. We should either tidy up logic by throwing out subject and predicate or else restrict these concepts to the relation of an object's falling under a concept (subsumption). The relation of subordination of one concept under another is so different from it that it is not permissible to speak of subject and predicate also in this case.

With regard to propositions combined by 'and' and 'neither . . . nor' (p. 121)[7] I am essentially in agreement with you. I would put it like this: The combination of two propositions by 'and' corresponds to the combination of two thoughts into one thought, which can be negated as a whole and also recognized to be true as a whole.

With regard to the question whether the proposition 'If A then B' is equipollent to the proposition 'It is not the case that A without B', one must say the following.[8] In a hypothetical construction we have as a rule improper propositions [*uneigentliche Sätze*]

---

[7] The page reference is to Husserl's fifth article cited in fn. 5 above. Husserl there criticizes Marty's view that in the case of statements combined by 'and' and 'neither . . . nor' the affirmation or negation does not extend uniformly to the whole statement but is divided up between each of the two partial statements (cf. Marty, op. cit., p. 300).

[8] Husserl (ibid., pp. 121ff.) criticizes Marty's view (ibid., p. 304, fn.) that the two propositions are 'identical in sense'. Besides denying that they have 'congruence', Husserl also denies them 'equivalence (equipollence)'. The latter is present for Husserl if the negation of the two propositions also yields again 'something equivalent'. Now according to Husserl, the negation of 'If A then B' yields 'A can hold without B holding', and the negation of 'It is not the case that A (A does not hold) without B' (as Husserl puts it with reference to Marty) yields 'A holds without B holding'. This is why the two propositions are not equipollent for Husserl. In present-day terms, Husserl's analysis differs from Frege's subsequent analysis in that Frege regards 'if . . . then' as defined as *material* implication, whereas Husserl appears to mean *strict* implication. In terms of strict implication, 'if . . . then' can be explained as 'It is not possible that A holds without B holding'. The negation of this yields 'It is possible that A holds without B holding'. If this is replaced by 'It may be that A holds without B holding', then we can also use instead Husserl's formulation above: 'A may hold without B holding'.

of such a kind that neither the antecedent by itself nor the consequent by itself expresses a thought, but only the whole propositional complex.[9] Each of the [improper] propositions is then only a component part that indicates [*andeutenden Bestandteil*], and each proposition points to the other (*tot . . . quot . . .*). In mathematics, such component parts are often letters (If $a > 1$, then $a^2 > 1$). The whole proposition thereby acquires the character of a law, namely generality of content. But let us first suppose that the letters 'A' and 'B' represent proper propositions. Then there are not just cases in which A is true and cases in which A is false; but | either A is true or A is false; *tertium non datur*. The same holds for B. We then have four combinations:

104

A is true and B is true,
A is true and B is false,
A is false and B is true,
A is false and B is false.

Of these the first, third, and fourth are compatible with the proposition 'If A then B', but not the second.[10] We therefore obtain by negation:[11] A is true and B is false, or: A holds without B holding, just as on the right-hand side.[12]

Let us suppose in the second place that the letters 'A' and 'B' represent improper propositions; then it is better if we replace 'A' and 'B' by '$\Phi(a)$' and '$\Psi(a)$', where 'a' is the component part that indicates. The proposition 'If $\Phi(a)$ then $\Psi(a)$' now has generality of content, and its negation cancels this generality and says that there is an object, say Δ, such that $\Phi(\Delta)$ is true and $\Psi(\Delta)$ is false. This is presumably what you mean [*meinen*] by the words 'A may hold without B holding'.[13] The proposition '$\Phi(a)$ does not hold

[9] Cf. *IL*, p. 296 above, where 'uneigentlicher Satz' is translated as 'quasi-sentence'.
[10] Cf. *BS*, §5 (pp. 55–7 above).
[11] 'Negation' is here applied to 'If A then B'. Thus Frege applies here the procedure, mentioned by Husserl, of comparing the negations of the two propositions.
[12] We must imagine the two propositions 'If A then B' and 'It is not the case that A without B' as combined into an equation, whose left side is (at first) the proposition 'If A then B' and whose right side is (at first) the proposition 'It is not the case that A without B'. This corresponds to the equation used by Husserl (ibid., p. 121). If, like Frege, we interpret the left-hand side as a material implication, then the two sides agree after negation according to Frege's analysis.
[13] This assumption of Frege's is only partly correct, as shown by Husserl's fn. 11, ibid., p. 122. For Husserl there distinguishes the cases in which A and B 'mean' ['*bedeuten*'] propositions and those in which they 'mean' concepts, and hence just those cases that Frege wants to distinguish here. Accordingly, Husserl does not, contrary to Frege's assumption, reserve the form with 'may' for the latter case but also extends it to the former case, which must then be interpreted as strict implication. The latter case is also called 'formal implication' after Russell and Whitehead (*Principia Mathematica* I, pp. 20ff.)

without $\Psi(a)$ holding' is now understood as follows: 'In general, whatever a may be, $\Phi(a)$ does not hold without $\Psi(a)$'. By negation we obtain: 'It is not in general the case that, whatever a may be, $\Phi(a)$ does not hold without $\Psi(a)$'. In other words: 'There is at least one object, say Δ, such that $\Phi(\Delta)$ is true while $\Psi(\Delta)$ is false'. We get the same as on the left-hand side.[14] In each case we therefore have an equipollence. If we consult my *Begriffsschrift*, which is now already twenty-eight years old, we find the answer to such a question without further ado. Now are these propositions also | congruent? This could well be debated for a hundred years or more. At least I do not see what criterion would allow us to decide this question objectively.

105

But I do find that if there is no objective criterion for answering a question, then the question has no place at all in science.

Yours sincerely,
G. Frege

*   *   *

Jena
9 December 1906

Dear Colleague,

Thank you very much for your letter of 16 November,[15] which prompts me to make the following remarks.

It seems to me that an objective criterion is necessary for recognizing a thought again as the same, for without it logical analysis is impossible.[16] Now it seems to me that the only possible means of deciding whether proposition A expresses the same thought as proposition B is the following, and here I assume that neither of the two propositions contains a logically self-evident component part in its sense. If *both* the assumption that the content of A is false and that of B true *and* the assumption that the content of A is true and that of B false lead to a logical contradiction, and if this

---

[14] Cf. fn. 12 above.

[15] Husserl's letter of 16 November is lost, together with another letter of 10 November. These two letters contained Husserl's reply to Frege's letter of 30 October to 1 November. According to Scholz [the original editor of Frege's writings], the first letter dealt with 'equipollent propositions and "colouring"' as well as logic in general, while the second letter dealt with 'the paradoxes', possibly Russell's paradox. On 21 December 1906 to 13 January 1907 Husserl wrote another two-part letter to Frege which is also lost. The first part was a continuation of Husserl's letter of 16 November and contained remarks on 'the paradoxes' and 'hypothetical structures'. The second part was a reply to the present letter.

[16] Compare the criterion Frege formulates in *BSLD*, pp. 299–300 above; and on the compatibility of the two criteria, see the references cited in fn. 3 on p. 299 above.

can be established without knowing whether the content of A or B is true or false, and without requiring other than purely logical laws for this purpose, then nothing can belong to the content of A, as far as it | is capable of being judged true or false, which does not also belong to the content of B; for there would be no basis at all in the content of B for any such surplus,[17] and according to the presupposition above, such a surplus would not be logically self-evident either. In the same way, given our supposition, nothing can belong to the content of B, as far as it is capable of being judged true or false, except what also belongs to the content of A. Thus what is capable of being judged true or false in the contents of A and B is identical, and this alone is of concern to logic, and this is what I call the thought expressed by both A and B. One can indeed count many sorts of things as part of the content of A, e.g. a mood, feelings, ideas; but none of these is judged true or false; at bottom it is of no concern to logic, just as whatever is incapable of being judged morally good or bad is of no concern to ethics. Is there another means of judging what part of the content of a proposition is subject to logic, or when two propositions express the same thought? I do not think so. If we have no such means, we can argue endlessly about logical questions without result.

I have further doubts about the following. You write, 'The form containing "all" is normally so understood that the existence of objects falling under the subject and predicate concepts is part of what is meant [*mitgemeint*] and is presupposed as having been admitted'. It seems to me that you can only give this the sense you want it to have if you strike out the words 'part of what is meant' ['*mitgemeint*']. For if existence was part of what was meant, then the negation of the proposition 'All m are n' would be 'There is an m that is not n, or there is no m'. But it seems to me that this is not what you want. You want existence to be presupposed as having been admitted, but not to be part of what is meant. Now I use the expressions containing 'all' in such a way that existence is neither part of what I mean [*mitmeine*] nor something I presuppose as having been admitted. Linguistic usage cannot be absolutely

---

[17] The German here reads: 'denn für einen solchen Überschuss fehlte es an jeder Begründung im Inhalte von B'. The translation in *PMC* is ambiguous: 'for there would be no reason at all for any such surplus in the content of B'. Frege is not speaking of a surplus in the content of B, but of a surplus in the content of A, for which there would be no *basis* in the content of B given the assumption just stated that, in effect, A and B are logically equivalent. The only possible counterexample would be if A, but not B, contained a 'logically self-evident component part' – e.g. if A were the proposition 'B & $(C \lor \neg C)$'. A would then have a 'surplus', and yet still be logically equivalent to B. But it is precisely this possibility that is ruled out by Frege's additional presupposition, as he immediately goes on to note.

decisive here, since we need not be concerned with what linguistic usage is. Instead, we can lay down our linguistic usage in logic according to our logical needs. The reason for the usage I have laid down is simplicity. If a form of expression, like the one containing 'all', is to be used as a fundamental form in logical considerations, it is not feasible to use it so as to express two distinguishable thoughts at the same time, unless the proposition consists of two propositions combined by 'and'. For one must always strive to go back to the elements, to the simple. It must be possible to express the main thought without incidental thoughts [*Nebengedanken*].[18] This is why I do not want the incidental thought of existence to be part of what I mean when I use an expression containing 'all'.

As always,

Yours sincerely,
G. Frege

---

[18] The term 'Nebengedanken' may have been taken from H. Lotze, *Logik* (Leipzig, 1880), 2nd edn., e.g. §57.

Logic in Mathematics[1]

['Logic in Mathematics' is the longest piece in Frege's *Posthumous Writings*,[2] and according to the original editors,[3] was written in the spring of 1914. This is likely, since Frege gave a course with this title in 1914, a course which Rudolf Carnap attended,[4] and the piece is presumably Frege's lecture notes. What follows here is the first nine pages, in which Frege focuses on the conception of axioms and definitions.]

219 *Mathematics has closer ties with logic than does any other discipline*; for almost the entire activity of the mathematician consists in drawing inferences. In no other discipline does inference play so large a part, although inferences do occur here and there in other disciplines. Part of the mathematician's activity, besides drawing inferences, is to give definitions. Most disciplines are not concerned with the latter at all; only in jurisprudence is it of some importance, for although its subject matter is quite different, it is in several respects close to mathematics. Jurisprudence takes its materials from history and psychology and for this reason these must claim to have some share in it. And there is nothing resembling this with mathematics.

Inferring and defining are subject to logical laws. From this it follows that logic is of greater importance to mathematics than to any other science.

If one counts logic as part of philosophy, there will be a specially close bond between mathematics and philosophy, and this is confirmed by the history of these sciences (Plato, Descartes, Leibniz, Newton, Kant).

But are there perhaps modes of inference peculiar to mathematics which, for that very reason, do not belong to logic? Here one may point to the inference by mathematical induction from n to $n + 1$. Well, even a mode of

---

[1] Translated by Peter Long and Roger White (*PW*, pp. 203–11; from *NS*, pp. 219–29; page numbers in the margin from the latter).

[2] *PW*, pp. 203–50/*NS*, pp. 219–70.

[3] Cf. *NS*, p. 219, fn. 1.

[4] Cf. Bynum, 1972a: p. 52. Frege's course may well have had a major influence on Carnap's notion of 'explication', in particular.

inference peculiar to mathematics must be subject to a law and this law, if it is not logical in nature, will belong to mathematics, and can be ranked with the theorems or axioms of this science. For instance, mathematical induction rests on the law that can be expressed as follows:

If the number 1 has the property Φ and if it holds generally for every positive whole number n that if it has the property Φ then $n + 1$ has the property Φ, then every positive whole number has the property Φ.[5]

If this law can be proved, it will be included amongst the theorems of mathematics; if it cannot, it will be included amongst the axioms. If one draws inferences by mathematical induction, then one is actually making an application of this theorem or axiom; that is, this truth is taken | as a premise of an inference. For example: the proof of the proposition $(a + b) + n = a + (b + n)$.

So likewise in other cases one can reduce a mode of inference that is peculiar to mathematics to a general law, if not a law of logic, then one of mathematics. And from this law one can then draw consequences in accordance with general logical laws.

Now let us examine somewhat more closely what takes place in mathematics, beginning with *inference*.

We may distinguish two kinds of inferences: inferences from two premises and inferences from one premise.

Now we make advances in mathematics by choosing as the premises of an inference one or two propositions that have already been recognized as true. The conclusion obtained from these is a new truth of mathematics. And this can in turn be used, alone or together with another truth, in drawing further conclusions. It would be possible to call each truth thus obtained a theorem. But usually a truth is only called a theorem when it has not merely been obtained as the result of an inference, but is itself in turn used as a premise in the development of the science, and that not just for one but for a number of inferences. In this way chains of inference are formed connecting truths; and the further the science develops the longer and more numerous become the chains of inference and the greater the diversity of the theorems.

But one can also trace the chains of inference backwards by asking from what truths each theorem has been inferred. As the diversity of theorems becomes greater as we go forward along the chains of inference, so, as we step backwards, the circle of theorems closes in more and more. Whereas it appears that there is no limit to the number of steps forward we can take, when we go backwards we must eventually come to an end by arriving at truths which cannot themselves be inferred in turn from other truths. Going backwards we come up against the axioms and postulates. We may come up against definitions as well, but

---

[5] Cf. *BS*, Part III (see pp. 75–6 above).

we shall take a closer look at that later. If we start from a theorem and trace the chains of inference backwards until we arrive at other theorems or axioms, postulates or definitions, we discover chains of inference starting from known theorems, axioms, postulates or definitions and terminating with the theorem in question.

The totality of these inference-chains constitutes the *proof* of the theorem. We may say that a proof starts from propositions that are accepted as true and leads via chains of inferences to the theorem. But it can also happen that a proof consists only of a single chain of inference. In most cases a proof will proceed via truths which are not called theorems for the simple reason that they occur only in this proof, and are not used elsewhere. A proof does not only serve to convince us of the truth of what is proved: it also serves to reveal logical relations between truths. This is why we already find in Euclid proofs of truths that appear to stand in no need of proof because they are obvious without one. |

221   Science demands that we prove whatever is susceptible of proof and that we do not rest until we come up against something unprovable. It must endeavour to make the circle of unprovable *primitive truths* as small as possible, for the whole of mathematics is contained in these primitive truths as in a kernel. Our only concern is to generate the whole of mathematics from this kernel. The essence of mathematics has to be defined by this kernel of truths, and until we have learnt what these primitive truths are, we cannot be clear about the nature of mathematics. If we assume that we have succeeded in discovering these primitive truths, and that mathematics has been developed from them, then it will appear as a system of truths that are connected with one another by logical inference.

Euclid had an inkling of this idea of a *system*; but he failed to realize it and it almost seems as if at the present time we were further from this goal than ever. We see mathematicians each pursuing his own work on some fragment of the subject, but these fragments do not fit together into a system; indeed the idea of a system seems almost to have been lost. And yet the striving after a system is a justified one. We cannot long remain content with the fragmentation that prevails at present. Order can only be created by a system. But in order to construct a system it is necessary that in any step forward we take we should be aware of the logical inferences involved.

When an inference is being drawn, we must know what its premises are. We must not allow the premises to be confused with the laws of inference, which are purely logical; otherwise the logical purity of the inferences will be lost and it would not be possible, in the confusion of premises with laws of inference, clearly to distinguish the former. But if we have no clear recognition of what the premises are, we can have no certainty of arriving at the primitive truths, and failing that we cannot construct a system. For this reason we must avoid such expressions as 'a moment's reflection shows that' or 'as we can easily see'. We must put the moment's reflection into words so that we can easily see what inferences it consists of and what premises it makes use of. In mathematics we must never rest content with the fact that something is obvious or that we are convinced of something, but we must strive to obtain a clear insight into the network of inferences that support our conviction. Only in this way can we discover what the primitive truths are, and only in this way can a system be constructed.

Let us now take a closer look at the axioms, postulates and definitions:

The *axioms* are truths as are the theorems, but they are truths for which no proof is given in our system, and for which no proof is needed. It follows from this that there are no false axioms, and that we cannot accept a thought as an axiom if we are in doubt about its truth; for it is either false and hence not an axiom, or it *is* true but stands in need of proof and hence is not an axiom. Not every truth for which no proof is required is an axiom, for such a truth might still be proved in our system. Whether a truth is an axiom depends therefore on the system, 222 and it is possible for a truth | to be an axiom in one system and not in another. That is to say, it is conceivable that there should be a truth *A* and a truth *B*, each of which can be proved from the other in conjunction with truths *C*, *D*, *E*, *F*, whilst the truths *C*, *D*, *E*, *F* are not sufficient on their own to prove either *A* or *B*. If now *C*, *D*, *E*, *F* may serve as axioms, then we have the choice of regarding *A*, *C*, *D*, *E*, *F* as axioms and *B* as a theorem, or *B*, *C*, *D*, *E*, *F* as axioms, and *A* as a theorem. We can see from this that the possibility of one system does not necessarily rule out the possibility of an alternative system, and that we may have a choice between different systems. So it is really only relative to a particular system that one can speak of something as an axiom.

Here, in passing, I may say something about the expressions '*thought*' and '*sentence*'. I use the word 'sentence' to refer to a sign that is normally complex, whether it is made up of sounds or written signs. Of course this sign must have a sense. Here I am only considering sentences in which we state or assert something. We can translate sentences into another language. The sentence in the other language is different from the original one, for its constituents (component sounds) are different and are put together differently; but if the translation is correct, it will express the same sense and of course it is really the sense that concerns us. The sentence is of value to us because of the sense that we grasp in it, which is recognizably the same in the translation too. I call this sense a thought. What we prove is not a sentence, but a thought. And it is neither here nor there which language is used in giving the 223 proof. It is true that in mathematics we often speak | of proofs of a theorem [*Lehrsatz*], understanding by the word 'sentence' ['*Satz*'] what

I am calling a thought, or perhaps not distinguishing properly between the expression in words or signs and the thought expressed.[6] But for the sake of clarity it is better to draw this distinction. A thought cannot be perceived by the senses, but in the sentence it is represented by what can be heard or seen. For this reason I do not use '*Lehrsatz*' but '*Theorem*', and not '*Grundsatz*' but '*Axiom*', understanding by theorems and axioms true thoughts. This, however, is to imply that a thought is not something subjective, is not the product of any form of mental activity; for the thought that we have in Pythagoras' theorem is the same for everybody, and its truth is quite independent of its being thought by so-and-so or indeed by anyone at all. We are not to regard thinking as the act of producing a thought, but as that of grasping a thought.

Postulates seem at first sight to be essentially different from axioms. In Euclid we have the postulate 'Let it be postulated that a straight line may be drawn from any point to any other'.

This is obviously introduced with a view to making constructions. The postulates, so it seems, present the simplest procedures for making every construction, and postulate their possibility. At first we might perhaps think that none of this is of any help in providing proofs, but only for solving problems. But this would be a mistake, for sometimes an auxiliary line is needed for a proof, and sometimes an auxiliary point, an auxiliary number – an auxiliary object of some kind. In the proof of a theorem an auxiliary object is one of which nothing is said in the theorem, but which is required for the proof, so that this would collapse if there were no such object. And if there is no such object, it seems that we must be able to create one and we need a postulate to ensure that this is possible. But what in actual fact is this drawing a line? It is not, at any rate, a line in the geometrical sense that we are creating when we make a stroke with a pencil. And how in this way are we to connect a point in the interior of Sirius with a point in Rigel? Our postulate cannot refer to any such external procedure.[7] It refers rather to something conceptual. But what is here in question is not a subjective, psychological possibility, but an objective one. Surely the truth of a theorem cannot really depend on something we do, when it holds quite independently of us. So the only way of regarding the matter is that by drawing a straight line we merely become ourselves aware of what obtains independently of us. So the content of our postulate is essentially this, that given any two points there is a straight line connecting them. So a postulate is a truth as is an axiom, its only peculiarity being that it asserts the existence of something with certain properties. From this it

---

[6] The play that Frege is here making on the words '*Lehrsatz*' and '*Satz*' is lost in translation, so we have enclosed them in square brackets after their English equivalents. (*Trs.*)

[7] 'Ein solches äusseres Tun kann nicht gemeint sein in unserem Postulate.'

follows that there is no real need to distinguish axioms and postulates. A postulate can be regarded as a special case of an axiom. |

224   We come to *definitions*. Definitions proper must be distinguished from *elucidations*.[8] In the first stages of any discipline we cannot avoid the use of ordinary words. But these words are, for the most part, not really appropriate for scientific purposes, because they are not precise enough and fluctuate in their use. Science needs technical terms that have precise and fixed *Bedeutungen*, and in order to come to an understanding about these *Bedeutungen* and exclude possible misunderstandings, we provide elucidations. Of course in so doing we have again to use ordinary words, and these may display defects similar to those which the elucidations are intended to remove. So it seems that we shall then have to provide further elucidations. Theoretically one will never really achieve one's goal in this way. In practice, however, we do manage to come to an understanding about the *Bedeutungen* of words. Of course we have to be able to count on a meeting of minds, on others' guessing what we have in mind. But all this precedes the construction of a system and does not belong within a system. In constructing a system it must be assumed that the words have precise *Bedeutungen* and that we know what they are. Hence we can at this point leave elucidations out of account and turn our attention to the construction of a system.

In constructing a system the same group of signs, whether they are sounds or combinations of sounds (spoken signs) or written signs, may occur over and over again. This gives us a reason for introducing a simple sign to replace such a group of signs with the stipulation that this simple sign is always to take the place of that group of signs. As a sentence is generally a complex sign, so the thought expressed by it is complex too: in fact it is put together in such a way that parts of the thought correspond to parts of the sentence. So as a general rule when a group of signs occurs in a sentence it will have a sense which is part of the thought expressed. Now when a simple sign is thus introduced to replace a group of signs, such a stipulation is a definition. The simple sign thereby acquires a sense which is the same as that of the group of signs. Definitions are not absolutely essential to a system. We could make do with the original group of signs. The introduction of a simple sign adds nothing to the content; it only makes for ease and simplicity of expression. So definition is really only concerned with signs. We shall call the simple sign the *definiendum*, and the complex group of signs which it replaces the *definiens*. The *definiendum* acquires its sense only from the *definiens*. This sense is built up out of the senses of the parts of the *definiens*. When we provide an elucidation, we do not build the sense

---

[8] Here, and in what follows, the term 'Erläuterung' has been translated by 'elucidation' rather than 'illustrative example' as originally used by the translators.

of a sign up out of simpler constituents in this way, but treat it as simple. All we do is to guard against misunderstanding where an expression is ambiguous.

A sign has a *Bedeutung* once one has been bestowed upon it by definition, and the definition goes over into a sentence asserting an identity. Of course the sentence is really only a | tautology and does not add to our knowledge. It contains a truth which is so self-evident that it appears devoid of content, and yet in setting up a system it is apparently used as a premise. I say apparently, for what is thus presented in the form of a conclusion makes no addition to our knowledge; all it does in fact is to effect an alteration of expression, and we might dispense with this if the resultant simplification of expression did not strike us as desirable. In fact it is not possible to prove something new from a definition alone that would be unprovable without it. When something that looks like a definition really makes it possible to prove something which could not be proved before, then it is no mere definition but must conceal something which would have either to be proved as a theorem or accepted as an axiom. Of course it may look as if a definition makes it possible to give a new proof. But here we have to distinguish between a sentence and the thought it expresses. If the *definiens* occurs in a sentence and we replace it by the *definiendum*, this does not affect the thought at all. It is true we get a different sentence if we do this, but we do not get a different thought. Of course we need the definition if, in the proof of this thought, we want it to assume the form of the second sentence. But if the thought can be proved at all, it can also be proved in such a way that it assumes the form of the first sentence, and in that case we have no need of the definition. So if we take the sentence as that which is proved, a definition may be essential, but not if we regard the thought as that which is to be proved.

It appears from this that definition is, after all, quite inessential. In fact considered from a logical point of view it stands out as something wholly inessential and dispensable. Now of course I can see that strong exception will be taken to this. We can imagine someone saying: Surely we are undertaking a logical analysis when we give a definition. You might as well say that it doesn't matter whether I carry out a chemical analysis of a body in order to see what elements it is composed of, as say that it is immaterial whether I carry out a logical analysis of a logical structure in order to find out what its constituents are or leave it unanalysed as if it were simple, when it is in fact complex. It is surely impossible to make out that the activity of defining something is without any significance when we think of the considerable intellectual effort required to furnish a good definition. – There is certainly something right about this, but before I go into it more closely, I want to stress the following point. To be without logical significance is still by no means to be without psychological significance. When we examine what actually goes on in our mind when we are doing intellectual work, we find that it is by no means always the case that a thought | is present to our consciousness which is clear in all its parts. For example, when we use the word 'integral', are we always conscious of everything appertaining to its sense? I believe that this is only very seldom the case. Usually just the word is present to our consciousness, allied no doubt with a more or less dim awareness that this word is a sign which has a sense, and that we can, if we wish, call this sense to mind. But we are usually content with the knowledge that we can do this. If we tried to call to mind everything appertaining to the sense of this word, we should make no headway. Our minds are simply not comprehensive enough. We often need to use a sign with which we associate a very complex sense. Such a sign seems, so to speak, a receptacle for the sense, so that we can carry it with us, while being always aware that we can open this receptacle should we have need of what it contains. It follows from this that a thought, as I understand the word, is in no way to be identified with a content of my consciousness. If therefore we need such signs – signs in which, as it were, we conceal a very complex sense as in a receptacle – we also need definitions so that we can cram this sense into the receptacle and also take it out again. So if from a logical point of view definitions are at bottom quite inessential, they are nevertheless of great importance for thinking as this actually takes place in human beings.

An objection was mentioned above which arose from the consideration that it is by means of definitions that we perform logical analyses. In the development of science it can indeed happen that one has used a word, a sign, an expression, over a long period under the impression that its sense is simple until one succeeds in analysing it into simpler logical constituents. By means of such an analysis, we may hope to reduce the number of axioms; for it may not be possible to prove a truth containing a complex constituent so long as that constituent remains unanalysed; but it may be possible, given an analysis, to prove it from truths in which the elements of the analysis occur. This is why it seems that a proof may be possible by means of a definition, if it provides an analysis, which would not be possible without this analysis, and this seems to contradict what we said earlier. Thus what seemed to be an axiom before the analysis can appear as a theorem after the analysis.

But how does one judge whether a logical analysis is correct? We cannot prove it to be so. The most one can be certain of is that as far as the form of words goes we have the same sentence after the analysis as before. But that the thought itself also remains the same is problematic. When we think that we have given a logical analysis of a word or sign that has been in use over a long period, what we have is a complex expression the sense of whose parts is known to us. The sense of the

227 complex expression must be yielded by that of its parts. But does it
coincide with the sense of the word with the long established use? | I
believe that we shall only be able to assert that it does when this is self-
evident. And then what we have is an axiom. But that the simple sign
that has been in use over a long period coincides in sense with that of
the complex expression that we have formed, is just what the definition
was meant to stipulate.

We have therefore to distinguish *two quite different cases*:

1. We construct a sense out of its constituents and introduce an
entirely new sign to express this sense. This may be called a 'constructive definition' ['*aufbauende Definition*'],[9] but we prefer to call it a 'definition' *tout court*.

2. We have a simple sign with a long established use. We believe
that we can give a logical analysis of its sense, obtaining a complex
expression which in our opinion has the same sense. We can only allow
something as a constituent of a complex expression if it has a sense we
recognize. The sense of the complex expression must be yielded by the
way in which it is put together. That it agrees with the sense of the long
established simple sign is not a matter for arbitrary stipluation, but can
only be recognized by an immediate insight. No doubt we speak of a
definition in this case too. It might be called an 'analytic definition'
['*zerlegende Definition*'] to distinguish it from the first case.[10] But it is
better to eschew the word 'definition' altogether in this case, because
what we should here like to call a definition is really to be regarded as
an axiom. In this second case there remains no room for an arbitrary
stipulation, because the simple sign already has a sense. Only a sign
which as yet has no sense can have a sense arbitrarily assigned to it. So
we shall stick to our original way of speaking and call only a constructive definition a definition. According to that a definition is an arbitrary
stipulation which confers a sense on a simple sign which previously had
none. This sense has, of course, to be expressed by a complex sign
whose sense results from the way it is put together.

Now we still have to consider the difficulty we come up against in
giving a logical analysis when it is problematic whether this analysis is
correct.

---

[9] The term is potentially misleading here, since 'constructive definitions' are only constructive in the sense of playing an abbreviatory role in the 'building up' of a system –
they are not 'fruitful' in the sense in which Frege appeared to use this term in relation
to 'splitting up contents in new ways' in *GL*; cf. esp. §§64, 88 (pp. 110–11, 122 above).

[10] The term 'analytic definition' (which might more literally be translated as 'analysing
definition') is also potentially misleading: except where they are more correctly regarded
as 'axioms' (as explained in what follows), 'analytic definitions' are not 'analytic' in the
Kantian sense; or rather, we might say, where a definition *is* 'analytic', then it must
actually be understood as either a 'constructive definition' or an 'axiom'.

Let us assume that A is the long-established sign (expression) whose sense we have attempted to analyse logically by constructing a complex expression that gives the analysis. Since we are not certain whether the analysis is successful, we are not prepared to present the complex expression as one which can be replaced by the simple sign A. | If it is our intention to put forward a definition proper, we are not entitled to choose the sign A, which already has a sense, but we must choose a fresh sign B, say, which has the sense of the complex expression only in virtue of the definition. The question now is whether A and B have the same sense. But we can bypass this question altogether if we are constructing a new system from the bottom up; in that case we shall make no further use of the sign A – we shall only use B. We have introduced the sign B to take the place of the complex expression in question by arbitrary fiat and in this way we have conferred a sense on it. This is a definition in the proper sense, namely a constructive definition.

If we have managed in this way to construct a system for mathematics without any need for the sign A, we can leave the matter there; there is no need at all to answer the question concerning the sense in which – whatever it may be – this sign had been used earlier. In this way we court no objections. However, it may be felt expedient to use sign A instead of sign B. But if we do this, we must treat it as an entirely new sign which had no sense prior to the definition. We must therefore explain that the sense in which this sign was used before the new system was constructed is no longer of any concern to us, that its sense is to be understood purely from the constructive definition that we have given. In constructing the new system we can take no account, logically speaking, of anything in mathematics that existed prior to the new system. Everything has to be made anew from the ground up. Even anything that we may have accomplished by our analytical activities is to be regarded only as preparatory work which does not itself make any appearance in the new system itself.

Perhaps there still remains a certain unclarity. How is it possible, one may ask, that it should be doubtful whether a simple sign has the same sense as a complex expression if we know not only the sense of the simple sign, but can recognize the sense of the complex one from the way it is put together? The fact is that if we really do have a clear grasp of the sense of the simple sign, then it cannot be doubtful whether it agrees with the sense of the complex expression. If this is open to question although we can clearly recognize the sense of the complex expression from the way it is put together, then the reason must lie in the fact that we do not have a clear grasp of the sense of the simple sign, but that its outlines are confused as if we saw it through a mist. The effect of the logical analysis of which we spoke will then be precisely this – to articulate the sense clearly. Work of this kind is very useful; it does not, however, form part of the construction of the system, but must take place beforehand. Before the work of construction is begun, the building stones have to be carefully prepared so as to be usable; i.e. the words, signs, expressions, which are to be used, must have a clear sense, so far as a sense is not to be conferred on them in the system itself by means of a constructive definition.

We stick then to our original conception: *a definition is an arbitrary stipulation* by which a new sign | is introduced to take the place of a complex expression whose sense we know from the way it is put together. A sign which hitherto had no sense acquires the sense of a complex expression by definition.

Letter to Jourdain, Jan. 1914[1]

[Philip Jourdain (1879–1919) first wrote to Frege in 1902, in relation to a history of mathematics that he was then engaged in writing, and they corresponded regularly thereafter.[2] In 1912 Jourdain became a co-editor of the *Monist,* and he wrote to Frege on 15 January 1914 requesting permission to translate part of the *Grundgesetze* for the journal.[3] He also raised three questions, the third of which was 'whether, in view of what seems to be a fact, namely, that Russell has shown that propositions can be analyzed into a form which only assumes that a name has a "Bedeutung", & not a "Sinn", you would hold that "Sinn" was merely a psychological property of a name'.[4] What follows here, in a section from a draft of Frege's reply, is Frege's response.[5]]

Dear Mr Jourdain,

. . .

127   As far as your third question is concerned, I do not believe that we can dispense with the sense of a name in logic; for a proposition must have a sense if it is to be useful. But a proposition consists of parts which must somehow contribute to the expression of the sense of the proposition, so they themselves must somehow have a sense. Take the proposition 'Etna is higher than Vesuvius'. This contains the name 'Etna',

---

[1] Translated by Hans Kaal (*PMC,* pp. 79–80; from *WB,* pp. 127–8; page numbers from the latter in the margin).

[2] See *PMC,* pp. 72–84; *WB,* pp. 109–33.

[3] *PMC,* p. 77/*WB,* p. 125. The translation, undertaken jointly with J. Stachelroth, appeared in the *Monist* in instalments in 1915–17. Part of the Preface, the Introduction and §§1–7 of *GG,* I were reprinted in *TPW.*

[4] *PMC,* p. 78/*WB,* p. 126. The reference is to Russell's theory of descriptions, which was first proposed in 'On Denoting' in *Mind,* 1905.

[5] This particular section was not, in fact, sent. In the letter that *was* sent, on 28 January 1914 (*PMC,* pp. 81–4/*WB,* pp. 129–33), Frege concentrates on the first of Jourdain's questions, concerning the relationship between his theory of first- and second-level functions and Russell's theory of orders in *Principia Mathematica,* 'over almost every sentence' of which 'I stumble', writes Frege (*PMC,* p. 81); and this ended up being a lengthy letter in itself. So it should not be supposed that Frege's not writing up and sending his answer to Jourdain's third question indicates a repudiation of it. Frege's imagined example of 'Afla' and 'Ateb' is one that frequently crops up in the secondary literature on *Sinn* and *Bedeutung.*

which occurs also in other propositions, e.g. in the proposition 'Etna is
in Sicily'. The possibility of our understanding propositions which we
have never heard before rests evidently on this, that we construct the
sense of a proposition out of parts that correspond to the words.[6] If we
find the same word in two propositions, e.g. 'Etna', then we also recognize something common to the corresponding thoughts, something corresponding to this word. Without this, language in the proper sense would
be impossible. We could indeed adopt the convention that certain signs
were to express certain thoughts, like railway signals ('The track is clear');
but in this way we would always be restricted to a very narrow area,
and we could not form a completely new proposition, one which would
be understood by another person even though no special convention
had been adopted beforehand for this case. Now that part of the thought
which corresponds to the name 'Etna' cannot be Mount Etna itself; it
cannot be the *Bedeutung* of this name. For each individual piece of
frozen, solidified lava which is part of Mount Etna would then also be
part of the thought that Etna is higher than Vesuvius. But it seems to
me absurd that pieces of lava, even pieces of which I had no knowledge,
should be parts of my thought. Thus both things seem to me necessary:
128 | (1) the *Bedeutung* of a name, which is that about which something is
being said, and (2) the sense of the name, which is part of the thought.
Without a *Bedeutung*, we could indeed have a thought, but only a mytho-
logical or literary thought, not a thought that could further scientific
knowledge. Without a sense, we would have no thought, and hence also
nothing that we could recognize as true.

To this can be added the following. Let us suppose an explorer travelling in an unexplored country sees a high snow-capped mountain on
the northern horizon. By making inquiries among the natives he learns
that its name is 'Afla'. By sighting it from different points he determines
its position as exactly as possible, enters it in a map, and writes in his
diary: 'Afla is at least 5000 metres high'. Another explorer sees a snow-

---

[6] Cf. the opening passage of *CT* (*CP*, p. 390): 'It is astonishing what language can do.
With a few syllables it can express an incalculable number of thoughts, so that even if
a thought has been grasped by an inhabitant of the Earth for the very first time, a form
of words can be found in which it will be understood by someone else to whom it is
entirely new. This would not be possible, if we could not distinguish parts in the thought
corresponding to the parts of a sentence, so that the structure of the sentence can serve
as a picture of the structure of the thought. To be sure, we really talk figuratively when
we transfer the relation of whole and part to thoughts; yet the analogy is so ready to hand
and so generally appropriate that we are hardly even bothered by the hitches which occur
from time to time.

'If, then, we look upon thoughts as composed of simple parts, and take these, in turn,
to correspond to the simple parts of sentences, we can understand how a few parts of
sentences can go to make up a great multitude of sentences, to which, in turn, there correspond a great multitude of thoughts.' (Cf. *LM*, p. 225.)

capped mountain on the southern horizon and learns that it is called Ateb.[7] He enters it in his map under this name. Later comparison shows that both explorers saw the same mountain. Now the content of the proposition 'Ateb is Afla' is far from being a mere consequence of the principle of identity, but contains a valuable piece of geographical knowledge. What is stated in the proposition 'Ateb is Afla' is certainly not the same thing as the content of the proposition 'Ateb is Ateb'. Now if what corresponded to the name 'Afla' as part of the thought was the *Bedeutung* of the name and hence the mountain itself, then this would be the same in both thoughts. The thought expressed in the proposition 'Ateb is Afla' would have to coincide with the one in 'Ateb is Ateb', which is far from being the case. What corresponds to the name 'Ateb' as part of the thought must therefore be different from what corresponds to the name 'Afla' as part of the thought. This cannot therefore be the *Bedeutung*, which is the same for both names, but must be something which is different in the two cases, and I say accordingly that the sense of the name 'Ateb' is different from the sense of the name 'Afla'. Accordingly, the sense of the proposition 'Ateb is at least 5000 metres high' is also different from the sense of the proposition 'Afla is at least 5000 metres high'. Someone who takes the latter to be true need not therefore take the former to be true. An object can be determined in different ways, and every one of these ways of determining it can give rise to a special name, and these different names then have different senses; for it is not self-evident that it is the same object which is being determined in different ways. We find this in astronomy in the case of planetoids and comets. Now if the sense of a name were something subjective, then the sense of the proposition in which the name occurs, and hence the thought, would also be something subjective, and the thought one person connects with this proposition would be different from the thought another connects with it; a common store of thoughts, a common science would be impossible. It would be impossible for something one person said to contradict what another said, because the two would not express the same thought at all, but each his own.

For these reasons I believe that the sense of a name is not something subjective ['in one's mental life' here crossed out], that it does not therefore belong to psychology, and that it is indispensable.

---

[7] 'Afla' and 'Ateb' are, of course, 'Alfa' and 'Beta' backwards. The German has been preserved here, since translating 'Afla' as 'Aphla' (as in *PMC*) somewhat obscures this, and 'Ahpla' sounds painful.

My Basic Logical Insights[1]

[According to the original German editor of what eventually came to be published as Frege's *Posthumous Writings*, this piece was written around 1915.[2] It provides a clear statement of what would now be called a 'redundancy theory' of truth.]

The following may be of some use as a key
to the understanding of my results.

Whenever anyone recognizes something to be true, he makes a judgement. What he recognizes to be true is a thought. It is impossible to recognize a thought as true before it has been grasped. A true thought was true before it was grasped by anyone. A thought does not have to be owned by anyone. The same thought can be grasped by several people. Making a judgement does not alter the thought that is recognized to be true. When something is judged to be the case, we can always cull out the thought that is recognized as true; the act of judgement forms no part of this. The word 'true' is not an adjective in the ordinary sense. If I attach the word 'salt' to the word 'sea-water' as a predicate, I form a sentence that expresses a thought. To make it clearer that we have only the expression of a thought, but that nothing is meant to be asserted [*behauptet werden solle*], I put the sentence in the dependent form 'that sea-water is salt'. Instead of doing this I could have it spoken by an actor on the stage as part of his role, for we know that in playing a part an actor only seems to speak with assertoric force. Knowledge of the sense of the word 'salt' is required for an understanding of the sentence, since it makes an essential contribution to the thought – in the mere word 'sea-water' we should of course not have a sentence at all, nor an expression for a thought. With the word 'true' the matter is quite different. If I attach this to the words 'that sea-water is salt' as a predicate, I likewise form a sentence that expresses a thought. For the same reason as before

---

[1] Translated by Peter Long and Roger White (*PW*, pp. 251–2; from *NS*, pp. 271–2; page numbers from the latter in the margin).
[2] *PW*, p. 251, fn. 1/*NS*, p. 271, fn. 1.

I put this also in the dependent form 'that it is true that sea-water is salt'. The thought expressed in these words coincides with the sense of the sentence 'that sea-water is salt'. So the sense of the word 'true' is such that it does not make any essential contribution to the thought. If I assert 'It is true that sea-water is salt', I assert the same thing as if I assert 'Sea-water is salt'. This enables us to recognize that the assertion is not to be found in the word 'true', but in the assertoric force with
272 which the sentence is uttered. This may lead | us to think that the word 'true' has no sense at all. But in that case a sentence in which 'true' occurred as a predicate would have no sense either. All one can say is: the word 'true' has a sense that contributes nothing to the sense of the whole sentence in which it occurs as a predicate.

But it is precisely for this reason that this word seems fitted to indicate the essence of logic. Because of the particular sense that it carried any other adjective would be less suitable for this purpose. So the word 'true' seems to make[3] the impossible possible: it allows what corresponds to the assertoric force to assume the form of a contribution to the thought. And although this attempt miscarries, or rather through the very fact that it miscarries, it indicates what is characteristic of logic. And this, from what we have said, seems something essentially different from what is characteristic of aesthetics and ethics. For there is no doubt that the word 'beautiful' actually does indicate the essence of aesthetics, as does 'good' that of ethics, whereas 'true' only makes an abortive attempt to indicate the essence of logic, since what logic is really concerned with is not contained in the word 'true' at all but in the assertoric force with which a sentence is uttered.

Many things that belong with the thought, such as negation or generality, seem to be more closely connected with the assertoric force of the sentence or the truth of the thought.[4] One has only to see that such thoughts occur in *e.g.* conditional sentences or as spoken by an actor as part of his role for this illusion to vanish.

How is it then that this word 'true', though it seems devoid of content, cannot be dispensed with? Would it not be possible, at least in laying the foundations of logic, to avoid this word altogether, when it can only create confusion? That we cannot do so is due to the imperfection of language. If our language were logically more perfect, we would perhaps have no further need of logic, or we might read it off from the language. But we are far from being in such a position. Work in logic just is, to a large extent, a struggle with the logical defects of language,[5] and yet language remains for us an indispensable tool. Only

---

[3] A different version of the manuscript has 'to be trying to make' in place of 'to make'. (*Eds. of NS.*)
[4] This sentence and the one following are crossed out in the manuscript. (*Eds. of NS.*)
[5] Cf. *SKM*, p. 369 below.

after our logical work has been completed shall we possess a more perfect instrument.

Now the thing that indicates most clearly the essence of logic is the assertoric force with which a sentence is uttered. But no word, or part of a sentence, corresponds to this; the same series of words may be uttered with assertoric force at one time, and not at another. In language assertoric force is bound up with the predicate.

Thought[1]

['Der Gedanke' was published in *Beiträge zur Philosophie des deutschen Idealismus* I (1918–19), pp. 58–77, as the first part of a series of three papers entitled 'Logical Investigations'.[2] With 'Über Sinn und Bedeutung', it is one of Frege's two most influential and widely discussed papers.]

58　Just as 'beautiful' points the way for aesthetics and 'good' for ethics, so do words like 'true' for logic. All sciences have truth as their goal; but logic is also concerned with it in a quite different way: logic has much the same relation to truth as physics has to weight or heat. To discover truths is the task of all sciences; it falls to logic to discern the laws of truth. The word 'law' is used in two senses. When we speak of moral or civil laws we mean [*meinen*] prescriptions, which ought to be obeyed but with which actual occurrences are not always in conformity. Laws of nature are general features of what happens in nature, and occurrences in nature are always in accordance with them. It is rather in this sense that I speak of laws of truth. Here of course it is not a matter of what happens but of what is. From the laws of truth there follow prescriptions about asserting, thinking, judging, inferring. And we may very well speak of laws of thought in this way too. But there is at once a danger here of confusing different things. People may very well interpret the expression 'law of thought' by analogy with 'law of nature' and then have in mind general features of thinking as a mental occurrence. A law of thought in this sense would be a psychological law. And so they might come to believe that logic deals with the mental process of thinking and with the psychological laws in accordance with which this takes place. That would be misunderstanding the task of logic, for truth has not here been given its proper place. Error and superstition have

---

[1] Translated by Peter Geach and R. H. Stoothoff (*CP*, pp. 351–72/*KS*, pp. 342–62). Page numbers in the margin refer to the original journal in which the paper was published. Unless otherwise indicated, where the verb 'mean' appears in this translation, it has been used in rendering certain German constructions involving 'sollen' or 'wollen'.
[2] The other two parts are 'Die Verneinung' ('Negation'; see pp. 346–61 below), and 'Gedankengefüge' ('Compound Thoughts'; *CP*, pp. 390–406/*KS*, pp. 378–94).

causes just as much as correct cognition. Whether what you take for
true is false | or true, your so taking it comes about in accordance with
psychological laws. A derivation from these laws, an explanation of a
mental process that ends in taking something to be true, can never take
the place of proving what is taken to be true. But may not logical laws
also have played a part in this mental process? I do not want to dispute
this, but if it is a question of truth this possibility is not enough. For
it is also possible that something non-logical played a part in the process and made it swerve from the truth. We can decide only after we
have come to know the laws of truth; but then we can probably do without the derivation and explanation of the mental process, if our concern
is to decide whether the process terminates in *justifiably* taking something to be true. In order to avoid any misunderstanding and prevent
the blurring of the boundary between psychology and logic, I assign to
logic the task of discovering the laws of truth, not the laws of taking
things to be true or of thinking. The *Bedeutung* of the word 'true' is
spelled out in the laws of truth.

But first I shall attempt to outline roughly how I want to use 'true'
['*wahr*'] in this connection, so as to exclude irrelevant uses of the word.
'True' is not to be used here in the sense of 'genuine' ['*wahrhaftig*'] or
'veracious' ['*wahrheitsliebend*']; nor yet in the way it sometimes occurs
in discussion of artistic questions, when, for example, people speak of
truth in art, when truth is set up as the aim of art, when the truth of a
work of art or true feeling is spoken of. Again, the word 'true' is prefixed to another word in order to show that the word is to be understood in its proper, unadulterated sense. This use too lies off the path
followed here. What I have in mind is that sort of truth which it is the
aim of science to discern.

Grammatically, the word 'true' looks like a word for a property. So
we want to delimit more closely the region within which truth can be
predicated, the region in which there is any question of truth. We find
truth predicated of pictures, ideas, sentences, and thoughts. It is striking that visible and audible things turn up here along with things which
cannot be perceived with the senses. This suggests that alterations in
sense [*Verschiebungen des Sinnes*] have taken place. So indeed they have!
Is a picture considered as a mere visible and tangible thing really true,
and a stone or a leaf not true? Obviously we could not call a picture true
unless there were an intention involved. A picture is meant to represent something. (Even an idea is not called true in itself, but only with
respect to an intention that the idea should correspond to something).
It might be supposed from this that truth consists in a correspondence
of a picture to what it depicts. Now a correspondence is a relation. But
this goes against the use of the word 'true', which is not a relative term
and contains no indication of anything else to which something is to

correspond. If I do not know that a picture is meant to represent Cologne
Cathedral then I do not know | what to compare the picture with in
order to decide on its truth. A correspondence, moreover, can only be
perfect if the corresponding things coincide and so just are not different
things. It is supposed to be possible to test the genuineness of a bank-
note by comparing it stereoscopically with a genuine one. But it would be
ridiculous to try to compare a gold piece stereoscopically with a twenty-
mark note. It would only be possible to compare an idea with a thing
if the thing were an idea too. And then, if the first did correspond perfectly with the second, they would coincide. But this is not at all what
people intend when they define truth as the correspondence of an idea
with something real. For in this case it is essential precisely that the reality shall be distinct from the idea. But then there can be no complete
correspondence, no complete truth. So nothing at all would be true; for
what is only half true is untrue. Truth does not admit of more or less.
– But could we not maintain that there is truth when there is correspondence in a certain respect? But which respect? For in that case
what ought we to do so as to decide whether something is true? We
should have to inquire whether it is *true* that an idea and a reality, say,
correspond in the specified respect. And then we should be confronted
by a question of the same kind, and the game could begin again. So the
attempted explanation of truth as correspondence breaks down. And
any other attempt to define truth also breaks down. For in a definition
certain characteristics would have to be specified. And in application to
any particular case the question would always arise whether it were *true*
that the characteristics were present. So we should be going round in a
circle. So it seems likely that the content of the word 'true' is *sui generis*
and indefinable.

When we ascribe truth to a picture we do not really mean to ascribe
a property which would belong to this picture quite independently of
other things; we always have in mind some totally different object and
we want to say that the picture corresponds in some way to this object.
'My idea corresponds to Cologne Cathedral' is a sentence, and now it
is a matter of the truth of this sentence. So what is improperly called
the truth of pictures and ideas is reduced to the truth of sentences.
What is it that we call a sentence? A series of sounds, but only if it has
a sense (which is not to say that *any* series of sounds that has a sense
is a sentence). And when we call a sentence true we really mean [*meinen*]
that its sense is true. And hence the only thing that raises the question
of truth at all is the sense of sentences. Now is the sense of a sentence
an idea? In any case, truth does not consist in correspondence of the
sense with something else, for otherwise the question of truth would get
reiterated to infinity.

Without offering this as a definition, I call a 'thought' something for

which the question of truth can arise at all. So I count what is false |
among thoughts no less than what is true.[A] So I can say: thoughts are
senses of sentences, without wishing to assert that the sense of every
sentence is a thought. The thought, in itself imperceptible by the senses,
gets clothed in the perceptible garb of a sentence, and thereby we are
enabled to grasp it. We say a sentence *expresses* a thought.

A thought is something imperceptible: anything the senses can perceive is excluded from the realm of things for which the question of
truth arises. Truth is not a quality that answers to a particular kind of
sense impressions. So it is sharply distinguished from the qualities we
call by the names 'red', 'bitter', 'lilac-smelling'. But do we not see that
the Sun has risen? And do we not then also see that this is true? That
the Sun has risen is not an object emitting rays that reach my eyes; it
is not a visible thing like the Sun itself. That the Sun has risen is recognized to be true on the basis of sense impressions. But being true is not
a sensible, perceptible, property. A thing's being magnetic is also recognized on the basis of sense impressions of the thing, although this property does not answer, any more than truth does, to a particular kind
of sense impressions. So far these properties agree. However, we do need
sense impressions in order to recognize a body as magnetic. On the
other hand, when I find it is true that I do not smell anything at this
moment, I do not do so on the basis of sense impressions.

All the same it is something worth thinking about that we cannot
recognize a property of a thing without at the same time finding the
thought *this thing has this property* to be true. So with every property of
a thing there is tied up a property of a thought, namely truth. It is also
worth noticing that the sentence 'I smell the scent of violets' has just
the same content as the sentence 'It is true that I smell the scent of
violets'.[3] So it seems, then, that nothing is added to the thought by my
ascribing to it the property of truth. And yet is it not a great result when
the scientist after much hesitation and laborious researches can finally
say 'My conjecture is true'? The *Bedeutung* of the word 'true' seems to
be altogether *sui generis*. May we not be dealing here with something
which cannot be called a property in the ordinary sense at all? In spite

---

[A] So, similarly, people have said 'a judgement is something which is either true or false'.
In fact I use the word 'thought' more or less in the sense 'judgement' has in the writings
of logicians. I hope it will become clear in what follows why I choose 'thought'. Such an
explanation has been objected to on the ground that it makes a division of judgements
into true and false judgements – perhaps the least significant of all possible divisions
among judgements. But I cannot see that it is a logical fault that a division is given along
with the explanation. As for the division's being significant, we shall perhaps find we
must hold it in no small esteem, if, as I have said, it is the word 'true' that points the
way for logic.

[3] Cf. *IL*, p. 297 above; *MBLI*, p. 323 above.

of this doubt I will begin by expressing myself in accordance with ordinary usage, | as if truth were a property, until some more appropriate way of speaking is found.

In order to bring out more precisely what I want to call 'thought', I shall distinguish various kinds of sentences.[B] We should not wish to deny sense to a command, but this sense is not such that the question of truth could arise for it. Therefore I shall not call the sense of a command a thought. Sentences expressing wishes or requests are ruled out in the same way. Only those sentences in which we communicate or assert something come into the question. But here I do not count exclamations in which one vents one's feelings, groans, sighs, laughs – unless it has been decided by some special convention that they are to communicate something. But how about interrogative sentences? In a word-question[4] we utter an incomplete sentence, which is meant to be given a true sense just by means of the completion for which we are asking. Word-questions are accordingly left out of consideration here. Propositional questions[5] are a different matter. We expect to hear 'yes' or 'no'. The answer 'yes' means [*besagt*] the same as an assertoric sentence, for in saying 'yes' the speaker presents as true the thought that was already completely contained in the interrogative sentence. This is how a propositional question can be formed from any assertoric sentence. And this is why an exclamation cannot be regarded as a communication: no corresponding propositional question can be formed. An interrogative sentence and an assertoric one contain the same thought; but the assertoric sentence contains something else as well, namely assertion. The interrogative sentence contains something more too, namely a request. Therefore two things must be distinguished in an assertoric sentence: the content, which it has in common with the corresponding propositional question; and assertion. The former is the thought or at least contains the thought. So it is possible to express a thought without laying it down as true. The two things are so closely joined in an assertoric sentence that it is easy to overlook their separability. Consequently we distinguish:

(1) the grasp of a thought – thinking,
(2) the acknowledgement of the truth of a thought – the act of judgement,[C]
(3) the manifestation of this judgement – assertion.

[B] I am not using the word 'sentence' ['*Satz*'] here in quite the same sense as grammar does, which also includes subordinate clauses. An isolated subordinate clause does not always have a sense about which the question of truth can arise, whereas the complex sentence to which it belongs has such a sense. [In the present volume, 'Satz' has alternatively been translated as 'proposition'. Cf. Glossary above.]
[C] It seems to me that thought and judgement have not hitherto been adequately distin-

[4] Frege means a question introduced by an interrogative word like 'who?' (*Trs.*)
[5] I.e. yes-no questions: the German is 'Satzfragen'. (*Trs.*)

We have already performed the first act when we form a propositional question. An advance in science usually takes place in this way: first a thought is grasped, and thus may perhaps be expressed in a propositional question; after appropriate investigations, this thought is finally recog- | nized to be true. | We express acknowledgement of truth in the form of an assertoric sentence. We do not need the word 'true' for this. And even when we do use it the properly assertoric force does not lie in it, but in the assertoric sentence-form; and where this form loses its asser- toric force the word 'true' cannot put it back again. This happens when we are not speaking seriously. As stage thunder is only sham thunder and a stage fight only a sham fight, so stage assertion is only sham assertion. It is only acting, only fiction. When playing his part the actor is not asserting anything; nor is he lying, even if he says something of whose falsehood he is convinced. In poetry we have the case of thoughts being expressed without being actually put forward as true, in spite of the assertoric form of the sentence; although the poem may suggest to the hearer that he himself should make an assenting judgement. There- fore the question still arises, even about what is presented in the assertoric sentence-form, whether it really contains an assertion. And this ques- tion must be answered in the negative if the requisite seriousness is lacking. It is unimportant whether the word 'true' is used here. This explains why it is that nothing seems to be added to a thought by attributing to it the property of truth.

An assertoric sentence often contains, over and above a thought and assertion, a third component not covered by the assertion. This is often meant to act on the feelings and mood of the hearer, or to arouse his imagination. Words like 'regrettably' ['*leider*'] and 'fortunately' ['*gottlob*'] belong here. Such constitutents of sentences are more strongly prom- inent in poetry, but are seldom wholly absent from prose. They occur more rarely in mathematical, physical, or chemical expositions than in historical ones. What are called the humanities are closer to poetry, and are therefore less scientific, than the exact sciences, which are drier in proportion to being more exact; for exact science is directed toward truth and truth alone. Therefore all constitutents of sentences not cov- ered by the assertoric force do not belong to scientific exposition; but they are sometimes hard to avoid, even for one who sees the danger connected with them. Where the main thing is to approach by way of

guished. Perhaps language is misleading. For we have no particular bit of assertoric sen- tences which corresponds to assertion; that something is being asserted is implicit rather in the assertoric form. We have the advantage in German that main and subordinate clauses are distinguished by the word-order. However in this connection we must observe that a subordinate clause may also contain an assertion, and that often neither main nor subordinate clause expresses a complete thought by itself but only the complex sentence does.

intimation what cannot be conceptually grasped, these constituents are fully justified. The more rigorously scientific an exposition is, the less the nationality of its author will be discernible and the easier it will be to translate. On the other hand, the constituents of language to which I here want to call attention make the translation of poetry very difficult, indeed make perfect translation almost always impossible, for it is just in what largely makes the poetic value that languages most differ.

It makes no difference to the thought whether I use the word 'horse' or 'steed' or 'nag' or 'prad'.[6] The assertoric force does not cover the ways in which these words differ. What is called mood, atmosphere, illumination in a poem, what is portrayed by intonation and rhythm, does not belong to the thought. |

64   Much in language serves to aid the hearer's understanding, for instance emphasizing part of a sentence by stress or word-order. Here let us bear in mind words like 'still' and 'already'. Somebody using the sentence 'Alfred has still not come' actually says 'Alfred has not come', and at the same time hints – but only hints – that Alfred's arrival is expected. Nobody can say: Since Alfred's arrival is not expected, the sense of the sentence is false. The way that 'but' differs from 'and' is that we use it to intimate that what follows it contrasts with what was to be expected from what preceded it. Such conversational suggestions make no difference to the thought. A sentence can be transformed by changing the verb from active to passive and at the same time making the accusative into the subject. In the same way we may change the dative into the nominative and at the same time replace 'give' by 'receive'. Naturally such transformations are not trivial in every respect; but they do not touch the thought, they do not touch what is true or false. If the inadmissibility of such transformations were recognized as a principle, then any profound logical investigation would be hindered.[7] It is just as important to ignore distinctions that do not touch the heart of the matter, as to make distinctions which concern essentials. But what is essential depends on one's purpose. To a mind concerned with the beauties of language, what is trivial to the logician may seem to be just what is important.

Thus the content of a sentence often goes beyond the thought expressed by it. But the opposite often happens too; the mere wording, which can be made permanent by writing or the gramophone, does not suffice for the expression of the thought. The present tense is used in two ways: first, in order to indicate a time; second, in order to eliminate any temporal restriction, where timelessness or eternity is part of the thought – consider for instance the laws of mathematics. Which of

---

[6] The German words here are 'Pferd', 'Roß', 'Gaul' and 'Mähre'.
[7] Cf. *CO*, fn. G, pp. 184–5 above; *PWLB*, pp. 240–4 above.

the two cases occurs is not expressed but must be divined. If a time-indication is conveyed by the present tense one must know when the sentence was uttered in order to grasp the thought correctly. Therefore the time of utterance is part of the expression of the thought. If someone wants to say today what he expressed yesterday using the word 'today', he will replace this word with 'yesterday'. Although the thought is the same its verbal expression must be different in order that the change of sense which would otherwise be effected by the differing times of utterance may be cancelled out. The case is the same with words like 'here' and 'there'. In all such cases the mere wording, as it can be preserved in writing, is not the complete expression of the thought; the knowledge of certain conditions accompanying the utterance, which are used as means of expressing the thought, is needed for us to grasp the thought correctly. Pointing the finger, hand gestures, glances may belong here too. The same utterance containing the word 'I' in the mouths of different men will express different thoughts of which some may be true, others false.[8] |

65   The occurrence of the word 'I' in a sentence gives rise to some further questions.

Consider the following case. Dr Gustav Lauben says, 'I was wounded'. Leo Peter hears this and remarks some days later, 'Dr Gustav Lauben was wounded'. Does this sentence express the same thought as the one Dr Lauben uttered himself? Suppose that Rudolph Lingens was present when Dr Lauben spoke and now hears what is related by Leo Peter. If the same thought was uttered by Dr Lauben and Leo Peter, then Rudolph Lingens, who is fully master of the language and remembers what Dr Lauben said in his presence, must now know at once from Leo Peter's report that he is speaking of the same thing. But knowledge of the language is a special thing when proper names are involved. It may well be the case that only a few people associate a definite thought with the sentence 'Dr Lauben was wounded'. For complete understanding one needs in this case to know the expression 'Dr Gustav Lauben'. Now if both Leo Peter and Rudolph Lingens understand by 'Dr Gustav Lauben' the doctor who is the only doctor living in a house known to both of them, then they both understand the sentence 'Dr Gustav Lauben was wounded' in the same way; they associate the same thought with it. But it is also possible that Rudolph Lingens does not know Dr Lauben personally and does not know that it was Dr Lauben who recently said 'I was wounded'. In this case Rudolph Lingens cannot know that the same affair is in question. I say, therefore, in this case:

---

[8] This and the following five paragraphs, concerning thoughts expressed with the use of indexicals, have generated much controversy. For discussion of some of the problems raised, see the Introduction, pp. 31–5 above.

the thought which Leo Peter expresses is not the same as that which Dr Lauben uttered.

Suppose further that Herbert Garner knows that Dr Gustav Lauben was born on 13 September 1875 in N.N. and this is not true of anyone else; suppose, however, that he does not know where Dr Lauben now lives nor indeed anything else about him. On the other hand, suppose Leo Peter does not know that Dr Lauben was born on 13 September 1875 in N.N. Then as far as the proper name 'Dr Gustav Lauben' is concerned, Herbert Garner and Leo Peter do not speak the same language, although they do in fact designate the same man with this name; for they do not know that they are doing so. Therefore Herbert Garner does not associate the same thought with the sentence 'Dr Gustav Lauben was wounded' as Leo Peter wants to express with it. To avoid the awkwardness that Herbert Garner and Leo Peter are not speaking the same language, I shall suppose that Leo Peter uses the proper name 'Dr Lauben' and Herbert Garner uses the proper name 'Gustav Lauben'. Then it is possible that Herbert Garner takes the sense of the sentence 'Dr Lauben was wounded' to be true but is misled by false information into taking the sense of the sentence 'Gustav Lauben was wounded' to be false. So given our assumptions these thoughts are different.

Accordingly, with a proper name, it is a matter of the way that the object so designated is presented. This may happen in different ways, and | to every such way there corresponds a special sense of a sentence containing the proper name. The different thoughts thus obtained from the same sentences correspond in truth-value, of course; that is to say, if one is true then all are true, and if one is false then all are false. Nevertheless the difference must be recognized. So we must really stipulate that for every proper name there shall be just one associated manner of presentation of the object so designated. It is often unimportant that this stipulation should be fulfilled, but not always.

Now everyone is presented to himself in a special and primitive way, in which he is presented to no one else. So, when Dr Lauben has the thought that he was wounded, he will probably be basing it on this primitive way in which he is presented to himself. And only Dr Lauben himself can grasp thoughts specified in this way. But now he may want to communicate with others. He cannot communicate a thought he alone can grasp. Therefore, if he now says 'I was wounded', he must use 'I' in a sense which can be grasped by others, perhaps in the sense of 'he who is speaking to you at this moment'; by doing this he makes the conditions accompanying his utterance serve towards the expression of a thought.[D]

[D] I am not here in the happy position of a mineralogist who shows his audience a rock-crystal: I cannot put a thought in the hands of my readers with the request that they

Yet there is a doubt. Is it at all the same thought which first this and then that man expresses?

A man who is still unaffected by philosophy first of all gets to know things he can see and touch, can in short perceive with the senses, such as trees, stones and houses, and he is convinced that someone else can equally see and touch the same tree and the same stone as he himself sees and touches. Obviously a thought does not belong with these things. Now can it, nevertheless, like a tree be presented to people as the same?

Even an unphilosophical man soon finds it necessary to recognize an inner world distinct from the outer world, a world of sense impressions, of creations of his imagination, of sensations, of feelings and moods, a world of inclinations, wishes and decisions. For brevity's sake I want to use the word 'idea' ['*Vorstellung*'] to cover all these occurrences, except decisions.

Now do thoughts belong to this inner world? Are they ideas? They are obviously not decisions. |

67   How are ideas distinct from the things of the outer world?

First: ideas cannot be seen, or touched, or smelled, or tasted, or heard.

I go for a walk with a companion. I see a green field, I thus have a visual impression of the green. I have it, but I do not see it.

Secondly: ideas are something we have. We have sensations, feelings, moods, inclinations, wishes. An idea that someone has belongs to the content of his consciousness.

The field and the frogs in it, the Sun which shines on them, are there no matter whether I look at them or not, but the sense impression I have of green exists only because of me, I am its owner. It seems absurd to us that a pain, a mood, a wish should go around the world without an owner, independently. A sensation is impossible without a sentient being. The inner world presupposes somebody whose inner world it is.

Thridly: ideas need an owner. Things of the outer world are on the contrary independent.

My companion and I are convinced that we both see the same field; but each of us has a particular sense impression of green. I glimpse a strawberry among the green strawberry leaves. My companion cannot find it, he is colour-blind. The colour impression he gets from the strawberry is not noticeably different from the one he gets from the leaf.

---

should examine it from all sides. Something in itself not perceptible by sense, the thought, is presented to the reader – and I must be content with that – wrapped up in a perceptible linguistic form. The pictorial aspect of language presents difficulties. The sensible always breaks in and makes expressions pictorial and so improper. So one fights against language, and I am compelled to occupy myself with language although it is not my proper concern here. I hope I have succeeded in making clear to my readers what I want to call 'thought'.

Now does my companion see the green leaf as red, or does he see the red berry as green, or does he see both with one colour which I am not acquainted with at all? These are unanswerable, indeed really nonsensical, questions. For when the word 'red' is meant not to state a property of things but to characterize sense impressions belonging to my consciousness, it is only applicable within the realm of my consciousness. For it is impossible to compare my sense impression with someone else's. For that, it would be necessary to bring together in one consciousness a sense impression belonging to one consciousness and a sense impression belonging to another consciousness. Now even if it were possible to make an idea disappear from one consciousness and at the same time make an idea appear in another consciousness, the question whether it is the same idea would still remain unanswerable. It is so much of the essence of any one of my ideas to be a content of my consciousness, that any idea someone else has is, just as such, different from mine. But might it not be possible that my ideas, the entire content of my consciousness, might be at the same time the content of a more embracing, perhaps divine consciousness? Only if I were myself part of the divine being. But then would they really be my ideas, would I be their owner? This so far oversteps the limits of human understanding that we must leave this possibility out of account. In any case it is impossible for us men to compare other people's ideas with our own. I pick the strawberry, I hold | it between my fingers. Now my companion sees it too, this same strawberry; but each of us has his own idea. Nobody else has my idea, but many people can see the same thing. Nobody else has my pain. Someone may have sympathy with me, but still my pain belongs to me and his sympathy to him. He has not got my pain, and I have not got his feeling of sympathy.

Fourthly: every idea has only one owner; no two men have the same idea.

For otherwise it would exist independently of this man and independently of that man. Is that lime tree my idea? By using the expression 'that lime tree' in this question I am really already anticipating the answer, for I mean to use this expression to designate what I see and other people too can look at and touch. There are now two possibilities. If my intention is realized, if I do designate something with the expression 'that lime tree', then the thought expressed in the sentence 'That lime tree is my idea' must obviously be denied. But if my intention is not realized, if I only think I see without really seeing, if on that account the designation 'that lime tree' is empty, then I have wandered into the realm of fiction without knowing it or meaning to. In that case neither the content of the sentence 'That lime tree is my idea' nor the content of the sentence 'That lime tree is not my idea' is true, for in both cases I have a predication which lacks an object. So then I can refuse to answer the question, on the ground that the content of the sentence 'That lime tree is my idea' is fictional. I have, of course, got an idea then, but that is not what I am using the words 'that lime tree' to designate. Now someone might really want to designate one of his ideas with the words 'that lime tree'. He would then be the owner of that which he wants to designate with those words, but then he would not see that lime tree and no one else would see it or be its owner.

I now return to the question: is a thought an idea? If other people can assent to the thought I express in the Pythagorean theorem just as I do, then it does not belong to the content of my consciousness, I am not its owner; yet I can, nevertheless, acknowledge it as true. However, if what is taken to be the content of the Pythagorean theorem by me and by somebody else is not the same thought at all, we should not really say '*the* Pythagorean theorem', but '*my* Pythagorean theorem', '*his* Pythagorean theorem', and these would be different, for the sense necessarily goes with the sentence. In that case my thought may be the content of my consciousness and his thought the content of his. Could the sense of my Pythagorean theorem be true and the sense of his false? I said that the word 'red' was applicable only in the sphere of my consciousness if it was not meant to state a property of things but to characterize some of my own sense impressions. Therefore the words 'true' and 'false', as I understand them, might also be applicable only in the 69 realm of my consciousness, if they were not | meant to apply to something of which I was not the owner, but to characterize in some way the content of my consciousness. Truth would then be confined to this content and it would remain doubtful whether anything at all similar occurred in the consciousness of others.

If every thought requires an owner and belongs to the contents of his consciousness, then the thought has this owner alone; and there is no science common to many on which many could work, but perhaps I have my science, a totality of thoughts whose owner I am, and another person has his. Each of us is concerned with contents of his own consciousness. No contradiction between the two sciences would then be possible, and it would really be idle to dispute about truth; as idle, indeed almost as ludicrous, as for two people to dispute whether a hundred-mark note were genuine, where each meant [*meinte*] the one he himself had in his pocket and understood the word 'genuine' in his own particular sense. If someone takes thoughts to be ideas, what he then accepts as true is, on his own view, the content of his consciousness, and does not properly concern other people at all. If he heard from me the opinion that a thought is not an idea he could not dispute it, for, indeed, it would not now concern him.

So the result seems to be: thoughts are neither things in the external world nor ideas.

A third realm must be recognized. Anything belonging to this realm has it in common with ideas that it cannot be perceived by the senses, but has it in common with things that it does not need an owner so as to belong to the contents of his consciousness. Thus for example the thought we have expressed in the Pythagorean theorem is timelessly true, true independently of whether anyone takes it to be true. It needs no owner. It is not true only from the time when it is discovered; just as a planet, even before anyone saw it, was in interaction with other planets.[E]

But I think I hear an odd objection. I have assumed several times that the same thing as I see can also be observed by other people. But what if everything were only a dream? If I only dreamed I was walking in the company of somebody else, if I only dreamed that my companion saw the green field as I did, if it were all only a play performed on the stage of my consciousness, it would be doubtful whether there were things of the external world at all. Perhaps the realm of things is empty and I do not see any things or any men, but only have ideas of which I myself am the owner. An idea, being something which can no more exist independently of me than my feeling of fatigue, cannot be a man, 70 cannot | look at the same field together with me, cannot see the strawberry I am holding. It is quite incredible that I really have only my inner world, instead of the whole environment in which I supposed myself to move and to act. And yet this is an inevitable consequence of the thesis that only what is my idea can be the object of my awareness. What would follow from this thesis if it were true? Would there then be other men? It would be possible, but I should know nothing of them. For a man cannot be my idea; consequently, if our thesis were true, he cannot be an object of my awareness either. And so this would undercut any reflections in which I assumed that something was an object for somebody else as it was for myself, for even if this were to happen I should know nothing of it. It would be impossible for me to distinguish something owned by myself from something I did not own. In judging something not to be my idea I would make it into the object of my thinking and, therefore, into my idea. On this view, is there a green field? Perhaps, but it would not be visible to me. For if a field is not my idea, it cannot, according to our thesis, be an object of my awareness. But if it is my idea it is invisible, for ideas are not visible. I can indeed have the idea of a green field; but this is not green, for there are no green ideas. Does a missile weighing a hundred kilogrammes exist, according to this view? Perhaps, but I could know nothing of it.

[E] A person sees a thing, has an idea, grasps or thinks a thought. When he grasps or thinks a thought he does not create it but only comes to stand in a certain relation to what already existed – a different relation from seeing a thing or having an idea.

If a missile is not my idea, then, according to our thesis, it cannot be an object of my awareness, of my thinking. But if a missile were my idea, it would have no weight. I can have an idea of a heavy missile. This then contains the idea of weight as a constituent idea. But this constituent idea is not a property of the whole idea, any more than Germany is a property of Europe. So the consequence is:

Either the thesis that only what is my idea can be the object of my awareness is false, or all my knowledge and perception is limited to the range of my ideas, to the stage of my consciousness. In this case I should have only an inner world and I should know nothing of other people.

It is strange how, in the course of such reflections, opposites turn topsy-turvy. There is, let us suppose, a physiologist of the senses. As is proper for someone investigating nature scientifically, he is at the outset far from supposing the things that he is convinced he sees and touches to be his own ideas. On the contrary, he believes that in sense impressions he has the most reliable evidence of things wholly independent of his feeling, imagining, thinking, which have no need of his consciousness. So little does he consider nerve fibres and ganglion cells to be the content of his consciousness that he is on the contrary inclined to regard his consciousness as dependent on nerve fibres and ganglion cells. He establishes that light rays, refracted in the eye, strike the visual nerve endings and there bring about a change, a stimulus. From this something is transmitted through nerve fibres to ganglion cells. Further processes in the nervous system perhaps follow upon this, and | colour impressions arise, and these perhaps combine to make up what we call the idea of a tree. Physical, chemical and physiological occurrences get in between the tree and my idea. Only occurrences in my nervous system are immediately connected with my consciousness – or so it seems – and every observer of the tree has his particular occurrences in his particular nervous system. Now light rays, before they enter my eye, may be reflected by a mirror and diverge as if they came from places behind the mirror. The effects on the visual nerves and all that follows will now take place just as they would if the light rays had come from a tree behind the mirror and had been propagated undisturbed to the eye. So an idea of a tree will finally occur even though such a tree does not exist at all. The refraction of light too, with the mediation of the eye and nervous system, may give rise to an idea to which nothing at all corresponds. But the stimulation of the visual nerves need not even happen because of light. If lightning strikes near us, we believe we see flames, even though we cannot see the lightning itself. In this case the visual nerve is perhaps stimulated by electric currents occurring in our body as a result of the flash of lightning. If the visual nerve is stimulated by this means in just the way it would be stimulated by light rays coming from flames, then we believe we see flames. It just depends on the stimulation of the visual nerve, no matter how that itself comes about.

We can go a step further. Properly speaking this stimulation of the visual nerve is not immediately given; it is only an hypothesis. We believe that a thing independent of us stimulates a nerve and by this means produces a sense impression; but strictly speaking we experience only that end of the process which impinges on our consciousness. Might not this sense impression, this sensation, which we attribute to a nerve stimulation, have other causes also, just as the same nerve stimulation may arise in different ways? If we call what happens in our consciousness an idea, then we really experience only ideas, not their causes. And if the scientist wants to avoid all mere hypothesis, then he is left just with ideas; everything dissolves into ideas, even the light rays, nerve fibres and ganglion cells from which he started. So he finally undermines the foundations of his own construction. Is everything an idea? Does everything need an owner without which it could have no existence? I have considered myself as the owner of my ideas, but am I not myself an idea? It seems to me as if I were lying in a deck-chair, as if I could see the toes of a pair of polished boots, the front part of a pair of trousers, a waistcoat, buttons, parts of a jacket, in particular the sleeves, two hands, some hair of a beard, the blurred outline of a nose. Am I myself this entire complex of visual impressions, this aggregate idea? It also seems to me as if I saw a chair over there. That is an idea. I am not actually much different from the chair myself, | for am I not myself just a complex of sense impressions, an idea? But where then is the owner of these ideas? How do I come to pick out one of these ideas and set it up as the owner of the rest? Why need this chosen idea be the idea I like to call 'I'? Could I not just as well choose the one that I am tempted to call a chair? Why, after all, have an owner for ideas at all? An owner would anyhow be something essentially different from ideas that were just owned; something independent, not needing any extraneous owner. If everything is idea, then there is no owner of ideas. And so now once again I experience opposites turning topsy-turvy. If there is no owner of ideas then there are also no ideas, for ideas need an owner and without one they cannot exist. If there is no ruler, there are also no subjects. The dependence which I found myself induced to ascribe to the sensation, as contrasted with the sentient being, disappears if there no longer is any owner. What I called ideas are then independent objects. No reason remains for granting an exceptional position to that object which I call 'I'.

But is that possible? Can there be an experience without someone to experience it? What would this whole play be without a spectator? Can there be a pain without someone who has it? Being felt necessarily goes with pain, and furthermore someone feeling it necessarily goes with its

72

being felt. But then there *is* something which is not my idea and yet can be the object of my awareness, of my thinking; I myself am such a thing. Or can I be one part of the content of my consciousness, while another part is, perhaps, an idea of the Moon? Does this perhaps take place when I judge that *I* am looking at *the Moon*? Then this first part would have a consciousness, and part of the content of this consciousness would be I myself once more. And so on. Yet it is surely inconceivable that I should be inside myself like this in an infinite nest of boxes, for then there would not be just one I but infinitely many. I am not my own idea; and when I assert something about myself, e.g. that I am not feeling any pain at the moment, then my judgement concerns something which is not a content of my consciousness, is not an idea, namely myself. Therefore that about which I state something is not necessarily my idea. But someone perhaps objects: if I think I have no pain at the moment, does not the word 'I' answer to something in the content of my consciousness? And is that not an idea? That may be so. A certain idea in my consciousness may be associated with the idea of the word 'I'. But then this is one idea among other ideas, and I am its owner as I am the owner of the other ideas. I have an idea of myself, but I am not identical with this idea. What is a content of my consciousness, my idea, should be sharply distinguished from what is an object of my thinking. Therefore the thesis that only what belongs to the content of my consciousness can be the object of my awareness, of my thinking, is false. |

73   Now the way is clear for me to acknowledge another man likewise as an independent owner of ideas. I have an idea of him, but I do not confuse it with him himself. And if I state something about my brother, I do not state it about the idea that I have of my brother.

The patient who has a pain is the owner of this pain, but the doctor who is treating him and reflects on the cause of this pain is not the owner of the pain. He does not imagine he can relieve the pain by anaesthetizing himself. There may very well be an idea in the doctor's mind that answers to the patient's pain, but that is not the pain, and is not what the doctor is trying to remove. The doctor might consult another doctor. Then one must distinguish: first, the pain, whose owner is the patient; secondly, the first doctor's idea of this pain; thirdly, the second doctor's idea of this pain. This last idea does indeed belong to the content of the second doctor's consciousness, but it is not the object of his reflection; it is rather an aid to reflection, as a drawing may be. The two doctors have as their common object [of thinking] the patient's pain, which they do not own. It may be seen from this that not only a thing but also an idea may be a common object of thinking for people who do not have the idea.

In this way, it seems to me, the matter becomes intelligible. If man could not think and could not take as the object of his thinking something of which he was not the owner, he would have an inner world but no environment. But may this not be based on a mistake? I am convinced that the idea I associate with the words 'my brother' corresponds to something that is not my idea and about which I can say something. But may I not be making a mistake about this? Such mistakes do happen. We then, against our will, lapse into fiction. Yes, indeed! By the step with which I win an environment for myself I expose myself to the risk of error. And here I come up against a further difference between my inner world and the external world. I cannot doubt that I have a visual impression of green, but it is not so certain that I see a lime leaf. So, contrary to widespread views, we find certainty in the inner world, while doubt never altogether leaves us in our excursions into the external world. But the probability is nevertheless in many cases hard to distinguish from certainty, so we can venture to judge about things in the external world. And we must make this venture even at the risk of error if we do not want to fall into far greater dangers.

As the result of these last considerations I lay down the following: not everything that can be the object of my acquaintance is an idea. I, as owner of ideas, am not myself an idea. Nothing now stops me from acknowledging other men to be owners of ideas, just as I am myself. And, once given the possibility, the probability | is very great, so great that it is in my opinion no longer distinguishable from certainty. Would there be a science of history otherwise? Would not all moral theory, all law, otherwise collapse? What would be left of religion? The natural sciences too could only be assessed as fables like astrology and alchemy. Thus the reflections I have set forth on the assumption that there are other men besides myself, who can make the same thing the object of their consideration, their thinking, remain in force without any essential weakening.

Not everything is an idea. Thus I can also acknowledge thoughts as independent of me; other men can grasp them just as much as I; I can acknowledge a science in which many can be engaged in research. We are not owners of thoughts as we are owners of our ideas. We do not *have* a thought as we have, say, a sense impression, but we also do not *see* a thought as we see, say, a star. So it is advisable to choose a special expression; the word 'grasp' suggests itself for the purpose.[F] To the grasping of thoughts there must then correspond a special mental capacity, the power of thinking. In thinking we do not produce thoughts, we

[F] The expression 'grasp' is as metaphorical as 'content of consciousness'. The nature of language does not permit anything else. What I hold in my hand can certainly be regarded as the content of my hand; but all the same it is the content of my hand in quite another and a more extraneous way than are the bones and muscles of which the hand consists or again the tensions these undergo.

grasp them. For what I have called thoughts stand in the closest connection with truth. What I acknowledge as true, I judge to be true quite apart from my acknowledging its truth or even thinking about it. That someone thinks it has nothing to do with the truth of a thought. 'Facts, facts, facts' cries the scientist if he wants to bring home the necessity of a firm foundation for science. What is a fact? A fact is a thought that is true. But the scientist will surely not acknowledge something to be the firm foundation of science if it depends on men's varying states of consciousness. The work of science does not consist in creation, but in the discovery of true thoughts. The astronomer can apply a mathematical truth in the investigation of long past events which took place when – on Earth at least – no one had yet recognized that truth. He can do this because the truth of a thought is timeless. Therefore that truth cannot have come to be only upon its discovery.

Not everything is an idea. Otherwise psychology would contain all the sciences within it, or at least it would be the supreme judge over all the sciences. Otherwise psychology would rule even over logic and mathematics. But nothing would be a greater misunderstanding of mathematics than making it subordinate to psychology. Neither logic nor mathematics has the task of investigating minds and contents of consciousness owned by individual men. Their task could perhaps be represented rather as the investigation of *the* mind; of *the* mind, not of minds. |

75   The grasp of a thought presupposes someone who grasps it, who thinks. He is the owner of the thinking, not of the thought. Although the thought does not belong with the contents of the thinker's consciousness, there must be something in his consciousness that is aimed at the thought. But this should not be confused with the thought itself. Similarly Algol itself is different from the idea someone has of Algol.

A thought belongs neither to my inner world as an idea, nor yet to the external world, the world of things perceptible by the senses.

This consequence, however cogently it may follow from the exposition, will nevertheless perhaps not be accepted without opposition. It will, I think, seem impossible to some people to obtain information about something not belonging to the inner world except by sense perception. Sense perception indeed is often thought to be the most certain, even the sole, source of knowledge about everything that does not belong to the inner world. But with what right? For sense perception has as necessary constituents our sense impressions and these are a part of the inner world. In any case two men do not have the same sense impressions though they may have similar ones. Sense impressions alone do not reveal the external world to us. Perhaps there is a being that has only sense impressions without seeing or touching things. To have visual impressions is not to see things. How does it happen that I see the tree just there where I do see it? Obviously it depends on the visual impressions I have and on the particular sort which occur because I see with two eyes. On each of the two retinas there arises, physically speaking, a particular image. Someone else sees the tree in the same place. He also has two retinal images but they differ from mine. We must assume that these retinal images determine our impressions. Consequently the visual impressions we have are not only not the same, but markedly different from each other. And yet we move about in the same external world. Having visual impressions is certainly necessary for seeing things, but not sufficient. What must still be added is not anything sensible. And yet this is just what opens up the external world for us; for without this non-sensible something everyone would remain shut up in his inner world. So perhaps, since the decisive factor lies in the non-sensible, something non-sensible, even without the co-operation of sense impressions, could also lead us out of the inner world and enable us to grasp thoughts. Outside our inner world we should have to distinguish the external world proper of sensible, perceptible things and the realm of what is non-sensibly perceptible. We should need something non-sensible for the recognition of both realms; but for the sense perception of things we should need sense impressions as well, and these belong entirely to the inner world. So the distinction between the ways in which a thing and a thought are given mainly consists in something which is assignable, not to either of the two realms, but to the inner world. Thus I cannot find this distinction to be so great as to make impossible the presentation of a thought that does not belong to the inner world. |

76   A thought, admittedly, is not the sort of thing to which it is usual to apply the term 'actual' ['*wirklich*']. The world of actuality is a world in which this acts [*wirkt*] on that and changes it and again undergoes reactions [*Gegenwirkungen*] itself and is changed by them. All this is a process in time. We will hardly admit what is timeless and unchangeable to be actual. Now is a thought changeable or is it timeless? The thought we express by the Pythagorean theorem is surely timeless, eternal, unvarying. But are there not thoughts which are true today but false in six months' time? The thought, for example, that the tree there is covered with green leaves, will surely be false in six months' time. No, for it is not the same thought at all. The words 'This tree is covered with green leaves' are not sufficient by themselves to constitute the expression of thought, for the time of utterance is involved as well. Without the time-specification thus given we have not a complete thought, i.e. we have no thought at all. Only a sentence with the time-specification filled out, a sentence complete in every respect, expresses a thought. But this thought, if it is true, is true not only today or tomorrow but timelessly. Thus the present tense in 'is true' does not refer to [*deutet . . . auf*] the speaker's present; it is, if the expression be permitted, a tense of timelessness. If we merely use the assertoric sentence-form and avoid the word

'true', two things must be distinguished, the expression of the thought and assertion. The time-specification that may be contained in the sentence belongs only to the expression of the thought; the truth, which we acknowledge by using the assertoric sentence-form, is timeless. To be sure the same words, on account of the variability of language with time, may take on another sense, express another thought; this change, however, relates only to the linguistic realm.

And yet what value could there be for us in the eternally unchangeable, which could neither be acted upon nor act on us? Something entirely and in every respect inactive would be quite unactual, and so far as we are concerned it would not be there. Even the timeless, if it is to be anything for us, must somehow be implicated with the temporal. What would a thought be for me if it were never grasped by me? But by grasping a thought I come into a relation to it, and it to me. It is possible that the same thought as is thought by me today was not thought by me yesterday. Of course this does away with strict timelessness. But we may be inclined to distinguish between essential and inessential properties and to regard something as timeless if the changes it undergoes involve only inessential properties. A property of a thought will be called inessential if it consists in, or follows from, the fact that this thought is grasped by a thinker.

How does a thought act? By being grasped and taken to be true. This is a process in the inner world of a thinker which may have further consequences in this inner world, and which may also encroach on the sphere of the will and make itself noticeable in the outer world as well. If, for example, I grasp the thought we express by the theorem of Py-
77 thagoras, the consequence may be that I | recognize it to be true, and further that I apply it in making a decision, which brings about the acceleration of masses. This is how our actions are usually led up to by acts of thinking and judging. And so thoughts may indirectly influence the motion of masses. The influence of man on man is brought about for the most part by thoughts. People communicate thoughts. How do they do this? They bring about changes in the common external world, and these are meant to be perceived by someone else, and so give him a chance to grasp a thought and take it to be true. Could the great events of world history have come about without the communication of thoughts? And yet we are inclined to regard thoughts as unactual, because they appear to do nothing in relation to events, whereas thinking, judging, stating, understanding, in general doing things, are affairs that concern men. How very different the actuality of a hammer appears, compared with that of a thought! How different a process handing over a hammer is from communicating a thought! The hammer passes from one control to another, it is gripped, it undergoes pressure, and thus its density, the disposition of its parts, is locally changed. There is nothing

of all this with a thought. It does not leave the control of the communicator by being communicated, for after all man has no power over it. When a thought is grasped, it at first only brings about changes in the inner world of the one who grasps it; yet it remains untouched in the core of its essence, for the changes it undergoes affect only inessential properties. These is lacking here something we observe everywhere in physical process – reciprocal action. Thoughts are not wholly unactual but their actuality is quite different from the actuality of things. And their action is brought about by a performance of the thinker; without this they would be inactive, at least as far as we can see. And yet the thinker does not create them but must take them as they are. They can be true without being grasped by a thinker; and they are not wholly unactual even then, at least if they *could* be grasped and so brought into action.

Negation[1]

['Die Verneinung' was published in *Beiträge zur Philosophie des deutschen Idealismus* I (1918–19), pp. 143–57, as the second part of the series of three papers entitled 'Logical Investigations', of which 'Der Gedanke' was the first.[2] This paper considers the case of *false thoughts*, in particular.]

143   A propositional question contains a demand that we should either acknowledge the truth of a thought, or reject it as false. In order that we may meet this demand correctly, two things are requisite: first, the wording of the question must enable us to recognize without any doubt the thought that is involved; secondly, this thought must not belong 144   to fiction. I always assume in what follows that these conditions | are fulfilled. The answer to a question[A] is an assertion based upon a judgement; this is so equally whether the answer is affirmative or negative.

Here, however, a difficulty arises. If a thought has being by being true, then the expression 'false thought' is just as self-contradictory as 'thought that has no being'. In that case the expression 'the thought: three is greater than five' is an empty one; and accordingly in science it must not be used at all – except between quotation-marks. In that case we may not say 'that three is greater than five is false'; for the grammatical subject is empty.

But can we not at least ask if something is true? In a question we can distinguish between the demand for a judgement and the special content of the question, the point as to which we must judge. In what follows I shall call this special content simply the content of the question, or the sense of the corresponding interrogative sentence. Now has the interrogative sentence

---

[A] Here and in what follows I always mean [*meine*] a propositional question when I just write 'question'.

---

[1] Translated by Peter Geach (*CP*, pp. 373–89/*KS*, pp. 362–78). Page numbers in the margin refer to the original journal in which the paper was published. Where the verb 'mean' appears in this translation, it has been used in rendering certain German constructions involving 'sollen' or 'wollen'.

[2] See pp. 325–45 above. The third part was 'Gedankengefüge' ('Compound Thoughts'; *CP*, pp. 390–406/*KS*, pp. 378–94).

'Is 3 greater than 5?'

a sense, if the being of a thought consists in its being true? If not, the question cannot have a thought as its content; and one is inclined to say that the interrogative sentence has no sense at all. But this surely comes about because we see the falsity at once. Has the interrogative sentence

'Is $(21/20)^{100}$ greater than $\sqrt[10]{(10^{21})}$?'

got a sense? If we had worked out that the answer must be affirmative, we could accept the interrogative sentence as making sense, for it would have a thought as its sense. But what if the answer had to be negative? In that case, on our supposition, we should have no thought that was the sense of the question. But surely the interrogative sentence must have some sense or other, if it is to contain a question at all. And are we really not asking for something in this sentence? May we not be wanting to get an answer to it? In that case, it depends on the answer whether we are to suppose that the question has a thought as its content. But it must be already possible to grasp the sense of the interrogative sentence before answering the question; for otherwise no answer would be possible at all. So that which we can grasp as the sense of the interrogative sentence before answering the question – and only this can properly be called the sense of the interrogative sentence – cannot be a thought, if the being of a thought consists in being true. 'But is it not a truth that the Sun is bigger than the Moon? And does not the being of a truth just consist in its being true? Must we not therefore recognize after all that the sense of the interrogative sentence:

"Is the Sun bigger than the Moon?"

is a truth, a thought whose being consists in its being true?' No! Truth cannot go along with the sense of an interrogative sentence; that would contradict the very nature of a question. The content of a question is 145 that as to which we must judge. | Consequently truth cannot be counted as going along with the content of the question. When I raise the question whether the Sun is bigger than the Moon, I am recognizing the sense of the interrogative sentence

'Is the Sun bigger than the Moon?'

Now if this sense were a thought whose being consisted in its being true, then I should at the same time see that this sense was true. Grasping the sense would at the same time be an act of judging; and the

utterance of the interrogative sentence would at the same time be an
assertion, and so an answer to the question. But in an interrogative
sentence neither the truth nor the falsity of the sense may be asserted.
Hence an interrogative sentence has not as its sense something whose
being consists in its being true. The very nature of a question demands
a separation between the acts of grasping a sense and of judging. And
since the sense of an interrogative sentence is always also inherent in
the assertoric sentence that gives an answer to the question, this separation must be carried out for assertoric sentences too. It is a matter
of what we understand by the word 'thought'. In any case, we need a
short term for what can be the sense of an interrogative sentence. I call
this a thought. If we use language this way, not all thoughts are true.
The being of a thought thus does not consist in its being true. We must
recognize that there are thoughts in this sense, since we use questions
in scientific work; for the investigator must sometimes content himself
with raising a question, until he is able to answer it. In raising the question he is grasping a thought. Thus I may also say: The investigator
must sometimes content himself with grasping a thought. This is anyhow already a step towards the goal, even if it is not yet a judgement.
There must, then, be thoughts, in the sense I have assigned to the word.
Thoughts that perhaps turn out later on to be false have a justifiable
use in science, and must not be treated as having no being. Consider
indirect proof: here knowledge of the truth is attained precisely through
our grasping a false thought. The teacher says 'Suppose *a* were not equal
to *b*'. A beginner at once thinks 'What nonsense! I can see that *a* *is*
equal to *b*'; he is confusing the senselessness of a sentence with the
falsity of the thought expressed in it.

Of course we cannot infer anything from a false thought; but the false
thought may be part of a true thought, from which something can be
inferred. The thought contained in the sentence:

> 'If the accused was in Rome at the time of the deed, he did not commit
> the murder'[B]

may be acknowledged to be true by someone who does not know if
the accused was in Rome at the time of the deed nor if he committed
the murder. Of the two component thoughts contained in the whole,
neither the antecedent nor the consequent is being uttered assertively
when the | whole is presented as true. We have then only a single act
of judgement, but three thoughts, viz. the whole thought, the antecedent, and the consequent. If one of the clauses were senseless, the whole

146

[B] Here we must suppose that these words by themselves do not contain the thought in
its entirety; that we must gather from the circumstances in which they are uttered how
to supplement them so as to get a complete thought. [Cf. *T*, pp. 331–2 above.]

would be senseless. From this we see what a difference it makes whether a sentence is senseless or on the contrary expresses a false thought. Now for thoughts consisting of an antecedent and a consequent there obtains the law that, without prejudice to the truth, the opposite of the antecedent may become the consequent, and the opposite of the consequent the antecedent. In English this procedure is called *contraposition*.

According to this law, we may pass from the proposition

'If $(21/20)^{100}$ is greater than $\sqrt[10]{(10^{21})}$, then $(21/20)^{1000}$ is greater than 10^{21}'

to the proposition

'If $(21/20)^{1000}$ is not greater than 10^{21}, then $(21/20)^{100}$ is not greater than $\sqrt[10]{(10^{21})}$'.

And such transitions are important for indirect proofs, which would otherwise not be possible.

Now if the first complex thought has a true antecedent, namely, that $(21/20)^{100}$ is greater than $\sqrt[10]{(10^{21})}$, then the second complex thought has a false consequent, namely, that $(21/20)^{100}$ is not greater than $\sqrt[10]{(10^{21})}$. So anybody who admits the legitimacy of our transition from *modus ponens* to *modus tollens* must acknowledge that even a false thought has being; for otherwise either only the consequent would be left in the *modus ponens* or only the antecedent in the *modus tollens*; and one of these would likewise be abolished as a nonentity.

The being of a thought may also be taken to lie in the possibility of different thinkers' grasping the thought as one and the same thought. In that case the fact that a thought had no being would consist in several thinkers' each associating with the sentence a sense of his own; this sense would in that case be a content of his particular consciousness, so that there would be no *common* sense that could be grasped by several people. Now is a false thought a thought that in this sense has no being? In that case investigators who had discussed among themselves whether bovine tuberculosis is communicable to human beings, and had finally agreed that such communicability did not exist, would be in the same position as people who had used in conversation the expression 'this rainbow', and now came to see that they had not been designating anything by these words, since what each of them had had was a phenomenon of which he himself was the owner. The investigators would have to realize that they had been deceived by a false appearance; for the presupposition that could alone have made all their activity and talk reasonable would have turned out not to be fulfilled; they would not have been giving the question that they discussed a sense common to all of them.

But it must be possible to put a question to which the true answer

147 is | negative. The content of such a question is, in my terminology, a thought. It must be possible for several people who hear the same interrogative sentence to grasp the same sense and recognize the falsity of it. Trial by jury would assuredly be a silly arrangement if it could not be assumed that each of the jurors could understand the question at issue in the same sense. So the sense of an interrogative sentence, even when the question has to be answered in the negative, is something that can be grasped by several people.

What else would follow if the truth of a thought consisted in the possibility of its being grasped by several people as one and the same thing, whereas a sentence that expressed something false had no sense common to several people?

If a thought is true and is a complex of thoughts of which one is false, then the whole thought could be grasped by several people as one and the same thing, but the false component thought could not. Such a case may occur. E.g. it may be that the following assertion is justifiably made before a jury: 'If the accused was in Rome at the time of the deed, he did not commit the murder'; and it may be false that the accused was in Rome at the time of the deed. In that case the jurors could grasp the same thought when they heard the sentence 'If the accused was in Rome at the time of the deed, he did not commit the murder', whereas each of them would associate a sense of his own with the *if*-clause. Is this possible? Can a thought that is present to all the jurors as one and the same thing have a part that is not common to all of them? If the whole needs no owner, no part of it needs an owner.

So a false thought is not a thought that has no being – not even if by 'being' we understand 'not needing an owner'. A false thought must be admitted, not indeed as true, but as sometimes indispensable: first, as the sense of an interrogative sentence; secondly, as part of a hypothetical thought-complex; thirdly, in negation. It must be possible to negate a false thought, and for this I need the thought; I cannot negate what is not there. And by negation I cannot transform something that needs me as its owner into something of which I am not the owner, and which can be grasped by several people as one and the same thing.

Now is negation of a thought to be regarded as dissolution of the thought into its component parts? By their negative verdict the jury can in no way alter the make-up of the thought that the question presented to them expresses. The thought is true or false quite independently of their giving a right or a wrong verdict in regard to it. And if it is false it is still a thought. If after the jury's verdict there is no thought at all, but only fragments of thought, then the same was already the case before the verdict; in what looked like a question, the jury were not presented with any thought at all, but only with fragments of thought; they had nothing to pass a verdict on.

Our act of judgement can in no way alter the make-up of a thought.
148 We can only acknowledge what is there. A true thought cannot | be
affected by our act of judgement. In the sentence that expresses the
thought we can insert a 'not'; and the sentence we thus get does not
contain a non-thought (as I have shown) but may be quite justifiably
used as antecedent or consequent in a hypothetical sentence-complex.
Only, since it is false, it may not be uttered assertively. But this procedure does not touch the original thought in any way; it remains true
as before.

Can we affect a false thought somehow by negating it? We cannot do
this either; for a false thought is still a thought and may occur as a
component part of a true thought. The sentence

'3 is greater than 5',

uttered non-assertively, has a false sense; if we insert a 'not', we get

'3 is not greater than 5',

a sentence that may be uttered assertively. There is no trace here of a
dissolution of the thought, a separation of its parts.

How, indeed, could a thought be dissolved? How could the interconnection of its parts be split up? The world of thoughts has a model in
the world of sentences, expressions, words, signs. To the structure of
the thought there corresponds the compounding of words into a sentence; and here the order is in general not indifferent. To the dissolution or destruction of the thought there must accordingly correspond a
tearing apart of the words, such as happens, e.g., if a sentence written on
paper is cut up with scissors, so that on each scrap of paper there stands
the expression for part of a thought. These scraps can then be shuffled
at will or carried away by the wind; the connection is dissolved, the
original order can no longer be recognized. Is this what happens when
we negate a thought? No! The thought would undoubtedly survive even
this execution of it in effigy. What we do is to insert the word 'not', and,
apart from this, leave the word-order unaltered. The original wording can
still be recognized; the order may not be altered at will. Is this dissolution, separation? Quite the reverse! It results in a firmly-built structure.

Consideration of the law *duplex negatio affirmat* makes it specially
plain to see that negation has no separating or dissolving effect. I start
with the sentence

'The Schneekoppe is higher than the Brocken'.

By putting in a 'not' I get:

'The Schneekoppe is not higher than the Brocken'.

(Both sentences are supposed to be uttered non-assertively.) A second negation would produce something like the sentence

'It is not true that the Schneekoppe is not higher than the Brocken'.

We already know that the first negation cannot effect any dissolution of the thought; but all the same let us suppose for once that after the first 149 negation we had only | fragments of a thought. We should then have to suppose that the second negation could put these fragments together again. Negation would thus be like a sword that could heal on again the limbs it had cut off. But there the greatest care would be wanted. The parts of the thought have lost all connection and interrelation on account of its being negated the first time. So by carelessly employing the healing power of negation, we might easily get the sentence:

'The Brocken is higher than the Schneekoppe'.

No non-thought is turned into a thought by negation, just as no thought is turned into a non-thought by negation.

A sentence with the word 'not' in its predicate may, like any other, express a thought that can be made into the content of a question; and this, like any propositional question, leaves open our decision as to the answer.

What then are these objects, which negation is supposed to separate? Not parts of sentences; equally, not parts of a thought. Things in the outside world? They do not bother about our negating. Mental images in the interior world of the person who negates? But then how does the juror know which of his images he ought to separate in given circumstances? The question put before him does not indicate any to him. It may evoke images in him. But the images evoked in the jurors' inner worlds are different; and in that case each juror would perform his own act of separation in his own inner world, and this would not be a verdict.

It thus appears impossible to state what really is dissolved, split up, or separated by the act of negation.

With the belief that negation has a dissolving or separating power there hangs together the view that a negative thought is less useful than an affirmative one. But still it cannot be regarded as wholly useless. Consider the inference:

'If the accused was not in Berlin at the time of the murder, he did not commit the murder; now the accused was not in Berlin at the time of the murder; therefore he did not commit the murder';

and compare it with the inference:

> 'If the accused was in Rome at the time of the murder, he did not commit the murder; now the accused was in Rome at the time of the murder; therefore he did not commit the murder'.

Both inferences proceed in the same form, and there is not the least ground in the nature of the case for our distinguishing between negative and affirmative premises when we are expressing the law of inference here involved. People speak of affirmative and negative judgements; even Kant does so. Translated into my terminology, this would be a distinction between affirmative and negative thoughts. For logic at any rate such a distinction is wholly unnecessary; its ground must be sought outside logic. I know of no logical principle whose verbal expression 150 makes it necessary, or | even preferable, to use these terms.[C] In any science in which it is a question of conformity to laws, the thing that we must always ask is: What technical expressions are necessary, or at least useful, in order to give precise expression to the laws of this science? What does not stand this test cometh of evil.[3]

What is more, it is by no means easy to state what is a negative judgement (thought). Consider the sentences 'Christ is immortal', 'Christ lives for ever', 'Christ is not immortal', 'Christ is mortal', 'Christ does not live for ever'. Now which of the thoughts we have here is affirmative, which negative?

We usually suppose that negation extends to the whole thought when 'not' is attached to the verb of the predicate. But sometimes the negative word grammatically forms part of the subject, as in the sentence 'No person lives to be more than a hundred'. A negation may occur anywhere in a sentence without making the thought indubitably negative. We see what tricky questions the expression 'negative judgement (thought)' may lead to. The result may be endless disputes, carried on with the greatest subtlety, and nevertheless essentially sterile. Accordingly I am in favour of dropping the distinction between negative and affirmative judgements or thoughts until such time as we have a criterion enabling us to distinguish with certainty in any given case between a negative and an affirmative judgement. When we have such a criterion we shall also see what benefit may be expected from this distinction. For the present I still doubt whether this will be achieved. The criterion

---

[C] Accordingly, in my essay 'Thought' [pp. 325–45 above], I likewise made no use of the expression 'negative thought'. The distinction between negative and affirmative thoughts would only have confused the matter. At no point would there have been occasion to assert something about affirmative thoughts, excluding negative ones, or to assert something about negative thoughts, excluding affirmative ones.

[3] An apparent allusion to Matthew 5 v.37! (*Tr.*)

cannot be derived from language; for languages are unreliable on logical questions. It is indeed not the least of the logician's tasks to indicate
the pitfalls laid by language in the way of the thinker.

After refuting errors, it may be useful to trace the sources from which
they have flowed. One source, I think, in this case is the desire to give
definitions of the concepts one means to employ. It is certainly praise-
worthy to try to make clear to oneself as far as possible the sense one
associates with a word. But here we must not forget that not everything
can be defined. If we insist at any price on defining what is essentially
indefinable, we readily fasten upon inessential accessories, and thus start
the inquiry on a wrong track at the very outset. And this is certainly
what has happened to many people who have tried to explain what a
judgement is and so have | hit upon compositeness.[D] The judgement is
composed of parts that have a certain order, an interconnection, stand
in mutual relations; but for what whole do we not get this?

There is another mistake associated with this one: viz. the view that
the judging subject sets up the connection or order of the parts in the
act of judging and thereby brings the judgement into existence. Here
the act of grasping a thought and the acknowledgement of its truth are
not kept separate. In many cases, of course, one of these acts follows
so directly upon the other that they seem to fuse into one act; but not
so in all cases. Years of laborious investigations may come between
grasping a thought and acknowledging its truth. It is obvious that here
the act of judging did not make the thought or set its parts in order;
for the thought was already there. But even the act of grasping a thought
is not a production of the thought, is not an act of setting its parts
in order; for the thought was already true, and so was already there
with its parts in order, before it was grasped. A traveller who crosses a
mountain-range does not thereby make the mountain-range; no more

151

[D] We are probably best in accord with ordinary usage if we take a judgement to be an
act of judging, as a leap is an act of leaping. Of course this leaves the kernel of the difficulty uncracked; it now lies in the word 'judging'. Judging, we may say, is acknowledging the truth of something; what is acknowledged to be true can only be a thought. The
original kernel now seems to have cracked in two; one part of it lies in the word 'thought'
and the other in the word 'true'. Here, for sure, we must stop. The impossibility of an
infinite regress in definition is something we must be prepared for in advance.

If a judgement is an act, it happens at a certain time and thereafter belongs to the past.
With an act there also belongs an agent, and we do not know the act completely if we
do not know the agent. In that case, we cannot speak of a synthetic judgement in the
usual sense. If we call it a synthetic judgement that through two points only one straight
line passes, then we are understanding by 'judgement' not an act performed by a definite
man at a definite time, but something timelessly true, even if its being true is not acknowledged by any human being. If we call this sort of thing a truth, then it may perhaps be
better to say 'synthetic truth' instead of 'synthetic judgement'. If we do nevertheless prefer the expression 'synthetic judgement', we must leave out of consideration the sense of
the verb 'to judge'.

does the judging subject make a thought by acknowledging its truth. If he did, the same thought could not be acknowledged as true by one man yesterday and another man today; indeed, the same man could not recognize the same thought as true at different times – unless we supposed that the existence of the thought was an intermittent one.

If someone thinks it within his power to produce by an act of judgement that which, in judging, he acknowledges to be true, by setting up an interconnection, an order, among its parts, then it is easy for him to credit himself also with the power of destroying it. As destruction is opposed to construction, to setting up order and interconnection, so also negating seems to be opposed to judging; | and people easily come to suppose that the interconnection is broken up by the act of negation just as it is built up by the act of judgement. Thus judging and negating look like a pair of polar opposites, which, being a pair, are coordinate; a pair comparable, e.g., to oxidation and reduction in chemistry. But when once we see that no interconnection is set up by our judging, but that the parts of the thought were already in their order before our judging, then everything appears in a different light. It must be pointed out yet once more that to grasp a thought is not yet to judge; that we may express a thought in a sentence without asserting its truth; that a negative word may be contained in the predicate of a sentence, in which case the sense of this word is part of the sense of the sentence, part of the thought; that by inserting a 'not' in the predicate of a sentence to be uttered non-assertively, we get a sentence that expresses a thought, as the original one did. If we call such a transition, from a thought to its opposite, negating the thought, then negating in this sense is not coordinate with judging, and may not be regarded as the polar opposite of judging; for what matters in judging is always the truth, whereas we may pass from a thought to its opposite without asking which is true. To exclude misunderstanding, let it be further observed that this transition occurs in the consciousness of a thinker, whereas the thoughts from which and to which the transition occurs were already in being before it occurred; so that this mental event makes no difference to the make-up and the mutual relations of the thoughts.

Perhaps the act of negating, which maintains a questionable existence as the polar opposite of judging, is a chimerical construction, formed by a fusion of the act of judging with the negation that I have acknowledged as a possible component of a thought, and to which there corresponds in language the word 'not' as part of the predicate – a chimerical construction, because these parts are quite different in kind. The act of judging is a mental process, and as such it needs a judging subject as its owner; negation on the other hand is part of a thought, and as such, like the thought itself, it needs no owner, must not be regarded as a content of a consciousness. And yet it is not entirely incomprehensible how there can arise at least the illusion of such a chimerical construction. Language has no special word or syllable to express assertion; assertive force is supplied by the form of the assertoric sentence, which is specially well-marked in the predicate. On the other hand the word 'not' stands in intimate connection with the predicate and may be regarded as part of it. Thus a connection may seem to be formed between the word 'not' and the assertoric force in language that answers to the act of judging.

But it is a nuisance to distinguish between the two ways of negating. Really my only aim in introducing the polar opposite of judging was to accommodate myself to a way of thinking that is foreign to me. I now
153   return to my previous | way of speaking. What I have just been designating as the polar opposite of judging I will now regard as a second way of judging – without thereby admitting that there is such a second way. I shall thus be comprising both polar opposites under the common term 'judging'; this may be done, for polar opposites certainly do belong together. The question will then have to be put as follows:

Are there two different ways of judging, of which one is used for the affirmative, and the other for the negative, answer to a question? Or is judging the same act in both cases? Does negating go along with judging? Or is negation part of the thought that underlies the act of judging? Does judging consist, even in the case of a negative answer to a question, in acknowledging the truth of a thought? In that case the thought will not be the one directly contained in the question, but the opposite of this.

Let the question run, e.g., as follows: 'Did the accused intentionally set fire to his house?' How can the answer take the form of an assertoric sentence, if it turns out to be negative? If there is a special way of judging for when we deny, we must correspondingly have a special form of assertion. I may, e.g., say in this case 'it is false that . . .' and lay it down that this must always have assertoric force attached to it. Thus the answer will run something like this: 'It is false that the accused intentionally set fire to his house'. If on the other hand there is only one way of judging, we shall say assertorically: 'The accused did not intentionally set fire to his house'. And here we shall be presenting as something true the opposite thought to the one expressed in the question. The word 'not' here belongs with the expression of this thought. I now return to the two inferences I compared together just now. The second premise of the first inference was the negative answer to the question 'Was the accused in Berlin at the time of the murder?' – in fact, the answer that we fixed upon in case there is only one way of judging. The thought contained in this premise is contained in the *if*-clause of the first premise, but there it is uttered non-assertively. The second premise of the second inference was the affirmative answer to the question 'Was the accused in Rome at the time of the murder?' These inferences proceed on the same principle, which is in good agreement with the view that judging is the same act whether the answer to a question is affirmative or negative. If on the other hand we had to recognize a special way of judging for the negative case – and correspondingly, in the realm of words and sentences, a special form of assertion – the matter would be otherwise. The first premise of the first inference would run as before:

'If the accused was not in Berlin at the time of the murder, he did not commit the murder'.

Here we could not say 'If it is false that the accused was in Berlin at the time of the murder'; for we have laid it down that to the words 'it is false that' assertoric force must always be attached; but in acknow-
154 ledging the truth of this first premise we are not | acknowledging the truth either of its antecedent or of its consequent. The second premise on the other hand must now run: 'It is false that the accused was in Berlin at the time of the murder'; for being a premise it must be uttered assertively. The inference now cannot be performed in the same way as before; for the thought in the second premise no longer coincides with the antecedent of the first premise; it is now the thought that the accused *was* in Berlin at the time of the murder. If nevertheless we want to allow that the inference is valid, we are thereby acknowledging that the second premise contains the thought that the accused was *not* in Berlin at the time of the murder. This involves separating negation from the act of judging, extracting it from the sense of 'it is false that . . .', and uniting negation with the thought.

Thus the assumption of two different ways of judging must be rejected. But what hangs on this decision? It might perhaps be regarded as valueless, if it did not effect an economy of logical primitives and their expressions in language. On the assumption of two ways of judging we need:

(1) assertoric force for affirmatives;
(2) assertoric force for negatives, e.g. inseparably attached to the word 'false';
(3) a negating word like 'not' in sentences uttered non-assertorically.

If on the other hand we assume only a single way of judging, we only need:

(1) assertoric force;
(2) a negating word.

Such economy always shows that analysis has been pushed further, which leads to a clearer insight. There hangs together with this an economy as regards a principle of inference; with our decision we can make do with one where otherwise we need two. If we *can* make do with one way of judging, then we *must*; and in that case we cannot assign to one way of judging the function of setting up order and connection, and to another, the function of dissolving this.

Thus for every thought there is a contradictory[E] thought; we acknowledge the falsity of a thought by admitting the truth of its contradictory. The sentence that expresses the contradictory thought is formed from the expression of the original thought by means of a negative word.

The negative word or syllable often seems to be more closely united to part of the sentence, e.g. the predicate. This may lead us to think that what is negated is the content, not of the whole sentence, but just of this part. We may call a man uncelebrated and thereby indicate the falsity of the thought that he is celebrated. This may be regarded as the

155 negative | answer to the question 'Is the man celebrated?'; and hence we may see that we are not here just negating the sense of a word. It is incorrect to say: 'Because the negative syllable is combined with part of the sentence, the sense of the whole sentence is not negated'. On the contrary: it is by combining the negative syllable with a part of the sentence that we do negate the content of the whole sentence. That is to say: in this way we get a sentence in which there is a thought contradicting the one in the original sentence.

I do not intend by this to dispute that negation is sometimes restricted just to a part of the whole thought.

If one thought contradicts another, then from a sentence whose sense is the one it is easy to construct a sentence expressing the other. Consequently the thought that contradicts another thought appears as made up of that thought and negation. (I do not mean by this the act of denial.) But the words 'made up of', 'consist of', 'component', 'part' may lead to our looking at it in the wrong way. If we choose to speak of parts in this connection, all the same these parts are not mutually independent in the way that we are elsewhere used to find when we have parts of a whole. The thought does not, by its make-up, stand in any need of completion; it is self-sufficient. Negation on the other hand needs to be completed by a thought. The two components, if we choose to employ this expression, are quite different in kind and contribute quite differently towards the formation of the whole. One completes, the other is completed. And it is by this completion that the whole is kept together. To bring out in language the need for completion, we may write 'the negation of . . .', where the blank after 'of' indicates where the completing expression is to be inserted. For the relation of completing, in the realm of thoughts and their parts, has something similar

---

[E] We could also say 'an opposite thought'.

corresponding to it in the realm of sentences and their parts. (The preposition 'of' ['*von*'], followed by a substantive can also be replaced [in German] by the genitive of the substantive; this may as a rule be more idiomatic, but does not lend itself so well to the purpose of expressing the part that needs completion.) An example may make it even clearer what I have here in mind. The thought that contradicts the thought:

$(21/20)^{100}$ is equal to $\sqrt[10]{(10^{21})}$

is the thought:

$(21/20)^{100}$ is not equal to $\sqrt[10]{(10^{21})}$.

We may also put this as follows:
'The thought:

$(21/20)^{100}$ is not equal to $\sqrt[10]{(10^{21})}$

is the negation of the thought:

$(21/20)^{100}$ is equal to $\sqrt[10]{(10^{21})}$'. |

156   In the last expression (after the penultimate 'is') we can see how the thought is made up of a part that needs completion and a part that completes it. From now on I shall use the word 'negation' (except, e.g., within quotation marks) always with the definite article. The definite article '*the*' in the expression

'*the* negation of the thought that 3 is greater than 5'

shows that this expression is meant to designate a definite single thing. This single thing is in our case a thought. The definite article makes the whole expression into a singular name, a proxy for a proper name.

The negation of a thought is itself a thought, and can again be used to complete *the negation*.[4] If I use, in order to complete *the negation*, the negation of the thought that $(21/20)^{100}$ is equal to $\sqrt[10]{(10^{21})}$, what I obtain is:

the negation of the negation of the thought that $(21/20)^{100}$ is equal to $\sqrt[10]{(10^{21})}$.

---

[4] I.e. to complete the thought-component whose verbal expression is '*the negation (of)* . . .', so as to get a complete thought; just as, in the realm of language, we get a complete designation of a thought by inserting a designation of a thought in the blank of 'the negation of . . .'. (The italics in the text are the translator's, not Frege's.) (*Tr.*)

This is again a thought. Designations of thoughts with such a structure are obtained according to the pattern:

'the negation of the negation of A',

where 'A' takes the place of the designation of a thought. Such a designation is to be regarded as directly composed of the parts:

'the negation of . . .' and 'the negation of A'.

But it may also be regarded as made up of the parts:

'the negation of the negation of . . .' and 'A'.

Here I have first combined the middle part with the part that stands to the left of it and then combined the result with the part 'A' that stands to the right of it; whereas originally the middle part was combined with 'A', and the designation so obtained, viz.

'the negation of A',

was combined with what stood to the left of it:

'the negation of . . .'.

The two different ways of regarding the designation have answering to them two ways of regarding the structure of the thought designated.[5]
If we compare the designations:

'the negation of the negation of: $(21/20)^{100}$ is equal to $\sqrt[10]{(10^{21})}$' and 'the negation of the negation of: 5 is greater than 3'

we recognize a common constituent:

'the negation of the negation of . . .': |

157   this designates a part common to the two thoughts – a thought-component that stands in need of completion. In each of our two cases, it is completed by means of a thought: in the first case, the thought that $(21/20)^{100}$ is equal to $\sqrt[10]{(10^{21})}$; in the second case, the thought that 5 is greater than 3. The result of this completion is in either case a thought. This common component, which stands in need of completion, may be

---

[5] '*bezeichnenden*' is here surely a misprint for '*bezeichneten*' or '*zu bezeichnenden*'. (*Tr.*)

called double negation. This example shows how something that needs completion can be amalgamated with something that needs completion to form something that needs completion. Here we are presented with a singular case; we have something – the negation of . . . – amalgamated with itself. Here, of course, metaphors derived from the corporeal realm fail us; for a body cannot be amalgamated with itself so that the result is something different from it. But then neither do bodies need completion, in the sense I intend here. Congruent bodies *can* be put together; and in the realm of designations we have congruence in our present case. Now what corresponds to congruent designations is one and the same thing in the realm of designata.

Metaphorical expressions, if used cautiously, may after all help towards an elucidation. I compare that which needs completion to a wrapping, e.g. a coat, which cannot stand upright by itself; in order to do that, it must be wrapped round somebody. The man whom it is wrapped round may put on another wrapping, e.g. a cloak. The two wrappings unite to form a single wrapping. There are thus two possible ways of looking at the matter; we may say either that a man who already wore a coat was now dressed up in a second wrapping, a cloak, or, that his clothing consists of two wrappings – coat and cloak. These ways of looking at it have absolutely equal justification. The additional wrapping always combines with the one already there to form a new wrapping. Of course we must never forget in this connection that dressing up and putting things together are processes in time, whereas what corresponds to this in the realm of thoughts is timeless.

If A is a thought not belonging to fiction, the negation of A likewise does not belong to fiction. In that case, of the two thoughts, A and the negation of A, there is always one and only one that is true. Likewise, of the two thoughts, the negation of A and the negation of the negation of A, there is always one and only one that is true. Now the negation of A is either true or not true. In the first case, neither A nor the negation of the negation of A is true. In the second case, both A and the negation of the negation of A are true. Thus of the two thoughts, A and the negation of the negation of A, either both are true or neither is. I may express this as follows:

Wrapping up a thought in double negation does not alter its truthvalue.

[*Notes for Ludwig Darmstaedter*][1]

[These notes were composed in July 1919 for the historian of science Ludwig Darmstaedter, for whose archive Frege had agreed to select some of his correspondence.[2] Written seventeen years after the emergence of the contradiction that undermined Frege's logicism, these notes provide a useful summary of the achievements that he nevertheless felt he had made.]

273   I started out from mathematics. The most pressing need, it seemed to me, was to provide this science with a better foundation. I soon realized that number is not a heap, a series of things, nor a property of a heap either, but that in stating a number which we have arrived at as the result of counting we are making a statement about a concept.[3] (Plato, *Hippias Major*.[4])

The logical imperfections of language stood in the way of such investigations. I tried to overcome these obstacles with my *Begriffsschrift*. In this way I was led from mathematics to logic.

What is distinctive about my conception of logic is that I begin by giving pride of place to the content of the word 'true', and then immediately go on to introduce a thought as that to which the question 'Is it true?' is in principle applicable.[5] So I do not begin with concepts and put them together to form a thought or judgement; I come by the parts of a thought by analysing the thought. This marks off my *Begriffsschrift* from the similar inventions of Leibniz and his successors, despite what the name suggests; perhaps it was not a very happy choice on my part.[6]

Truth is not part of a thought. We can grasp a thought without at the same time recognizing it as true – without making a judgement.[7] Both

[1] Translated by Peter Long and Roger White (*PW*, pp. 253–7; from *NS*, pp. 273–7; page numbers from the latter in the margin).

[2] Cf. *PW*, p. ix/*NS*, p. xxxiv; *PMC*, p. xi; *WB*, pp. xx, 27.

[3] Cf. esp. *GL*, §§45–6 (pp. 98–9 above).

[4] Probably a reference to 300e ff.

[5] Cf. *T*, pp. 325–8 above.

[6] I.e. the term 'Begriffsschrift' – literally, 'concept-script' – might misleadingly suggest that Frege regards *concepts* as more primitive than *thoughts*.

[7] Cf. *T*, pp. 329–30 above.

grasping a thought and making a judgement are acts of a knowing subject, and are to be assigned to psychology. But both acts involve something that does not belong to psychology, namely the thought.

False thoughts must be recognized too, not of course as true, but as
indispensable aids to knowledge, for we sometimes arrive at the truth

274 | by way of false thoughts and doubts. There can be no questions if it
is essential to the content of *any* question that that content should be
true.[8]

Negation does not belong to the act of judging, but is a constituent
of a thought. The division of thoughts (judgements) into affirmative
and negative is of no use to logic, and I doubt if it can be carried
through.[9]

Where we have a compound sentence consisting of an antecedent
and a consequent, there are two main cases to distinguish. The antecedent and consequent may each have a complete thought as its sense.
Then, over and above these, we have the thought expressed by the
whole compound sentence. By recognizing this thought as true, we
recognize neither the thought in the antecedent as true, nor that in the
consequent as true. A second case is where neither antecedent nor
consequent has a sense it itself, but where nevertheless the whole compound sentence does express a thought – a thought which is general in
character. In such a case we have a relation, not between judgements
or thoughts, but between concepts, the relation, namely, of subordination.[10] The antecedent and consequent are here sentences only in the
grammatical, not in the logical, sense. The first thing that strikes us
here is that a thought is made up out of parts that are not themselves
thoughts. The simplest case of this kind is where one of the two parts
is in need of completion and is completed by the other part, which is
saturated, i.e. not in need of completion. The former part then corresponds to a concept, the latter to an object (subsumption of an object
under a concept). However, the object and concept are not constituents
of the thought expressed. The constituents of the thought do refer to
the object and concept,[11] but in a special way. There is also the case
where a part doubly in need of completion is completed by two saturated parts. The former part corresponds to a relation. – An object
stands in a relation to an object. – Where logic is concerned, it seems
that every combination of parts results from completing something that
is in need of completion; where logic is concerned, no whole can consist of saturated parts alone. The sharp separation of what is in need of
completion from what is saturated is very important. In mathematics,

---

[8] Cf. *N*, pp. 346–50 above.
[9] Cf. *N*, pp. 353–4 above.
[10] Cf. *CSB*, p. 175 above; *IL*, p. 296 above.
[11] 'weisen . . . auf Gegenstand und Begriff hin'.

people have basically long been familiar with what is in need of completion (+, :, √, sin, =, >). In this connection they speak of functions, and yet it would seem that in most cases they have only a vague notion of what is at stake.[12]

A general statement can be negated. In this way we arrive at what logicians call existential judgements and particular judgements. The existential thoughts I have in mind here are such as are expressed in German by '*es gibt*'.[13] This phrase is never followed immediately by a proper name in the singular, or by a word accompanied by the definite article, but always by a concept word (*nomen appellativum*) without a definite article. In existential sentences of this kind we are making a statement about a concept. Here we have an instance | of how a concept can be related to a *second-level concept* in a way analogous to that in which an object is related to a concept under which it falls.[14] Closely akin to these existential thoughts are particular thoughts; indeed, the latter may be included among the former.[15] But we can also say that what is expressed by a sentence of the particular form is that a concept stands in a certain *second-level relation* to a concept. The distinction between first- and second-level concepts can only be grasped clearly by one who has clearly grasped the distinction between what is in need of completion and what is saturated.[16] A saturated part obtained by analysing a thought can sometimes itself be split up in the same way into a part in need of completion and a saturated part. The sentence 'The capital of Sweden is situated at the mouth of Lake Mälar' can be split up into a part in need of completion and the saturated part 'the capital of Sweden'. This can further be split up into the part 'the capital of', which stands in need of completion, and the saturated part 'Sweden'. Splitting up the thought expressed by a sentence corresponds to such a splitting up of the sentence. The functions of Analysis correspond to parts of thoughts that are thus in need of completion, without however being such.

A distinction has to be drawn between the sense and *Bedeutung* of a sign (word, expression). If an astronomer makes a statement about the Moon, the Moon itself is not part of the thought expressed. The Moon itself is the *Bedeutung* of the expression 'the Moon'. Therefore in addition to its *Bedeutung* this expression must also have a sense, which can be a constituent of a thought. We can regard a sentence as a mapping

275

---

[12] Cf. *FC*, pp. 130ff. above.

[13] I.e. judgements that are expressed in English by 'there is' or 'there are'. (*Trs.*)

[14] Cf. *CO*, pp. 189–90 above.

[15] For Frege, particular propositions, of the form 'Some *A*'s are *B*'s' (unlike universal propositions, of the form 'All *A*'s are *B*'s'), imply that there *are* some *A*'s (cf. *BS*, §12; pp. 72–4 above), and hence count as existential propositions.

[16] Cf. *FC*, p. 146 above.

of a thought: corresponding to the whole-part relation of a thought and its parts we have, by and large, the same relation for the sentence and its parts. Things are different in the realm of *Bedeutung*. We cannot say that Sweden is a part of the capital of Sweden. The same object can be the *Bedeutung* of different expressions, and any one of them can have a sense different from the sense of any other. Coincidence in the realm of *Bedeutung* can go hand in hand with difference in the realm of sense. This is what makes it possible for a sentence of the form '$A = B$' to express a thought with more content than one which merely exemplifies the law of identity. A statement in which something is recognized as the same again can be of far greater cognitive value than a particular case of the law of identity.[17]

Even a part of a thought, or a part of a part of a thought, that is in need of completion, has something corresponding to it in the realm of *Bedeutung*. Yet it is wrong to call this a concept, say, or a relation, or a function, although we can hardly avoid doing so. Grammatically, 'the concept of God' has the form of a saturated expression. Accordingly its sense cannot be anything in need of completion. When we use the words 'concept', 'relation', 'function' (as this is understood in Analysis), our words fail of their intended target.[18] In this case even the expression 'the *Bedeutung*', with the definite article, should really be avoided. |

276   It is not, however, only parts of sentences that have a *Bedeutung*; even a whole sentence, whose sense is a thought, has one. All sentences that express a true thought have the same *Bedeutung*, and all sentences that express a false thought have the same *Bedeutung* (the *True* and the *False*). Sentences and parts of sentences with a different *Bedeutung* also have a different sense. If in a sentence or part of a sentence one constituent is replaced by another with a different *Bedeutung*, the different sentence or part that results does not have to have a different *Bedeutung* from the original; on the other hand, it always has a different sense. If in a sentence or part of a sentence one constituent is replaced by another with the same *Bedeutung* but not with the same sense,[19] the different sentence or part that results has the same *Bedeutung* as the original, but not the same sense. All this holds for direct, not for indirect, speech.[20]

A thought can also be the *Bedeutung* of a sentence (indirect speech, the subjunctive mood).[21] The sentence does not then express this thought, but can be regarded as its proper name. Where we have a clause in indirect speech occurring within direct speech, and we replace a constituent of this clause by another which has the same *Bedeutung* in direct speech,

---

[17] Cf. *SB*, pp. 151ff. above.

[18] Cf. *CO*, pp. 184–5, 192 above.

[19] 'durch einen gleichbedeutenden, aber nicht gleichsinnigen Bestandteil'.

[20] Cf. *SB*, pp. 154, 158–9 above.

[21] In German, clauses in indirect speech are often put into the subjunctive mood. (*Trs.*)

then the whole which results from this transformation does not necessarily have the same *Bedeutung* as the original.[22]

The miracle of number. The adjectival use of number words is misleading.[23] In arithmetic a number word makes its appearance in the
singular as a proper name of an object of this science; it is not accompanied by the indefinite article, but is saturated. Subsumption: 'Two is
a prime', not subordination.[24] The combinations 'each two', 'all twos'
do not occur.

Yet amongst mathematicians we find a great lack of clarity and little
agreement. Is number an object that arithmetic investigates or is it a
counter in a game? Is arithmetic a game or a science? According to one
man, we are to understand by 'number' a series of objects of the same
kind;[25] according to another, a spatial, material structure produced by
writing;[26] a third denies that number is spatial at all. Perhaps there are
times when arithmeticians merely delude themselves into thinking that
they understand by 'number' what they say they do. If this is not so,
then they are attaching different senses to sentences with the same
wording; and if they still believe that they are working within one and
the same discipline, then they are just deluding themselves. A definition
in arithmetic that is never adduced in the course of a proof, fails of its
277   purpose. | With almost every technical term in arithmetic ('infinite
series', 'determinant', 'expression', 'equation') the same questions keep
cropping up: Are the things we see the subject matter of arithmetic? Or
are they only signs for, means by which we may recognize, the objects
to be investigated, not those objects themselves? Is what is designated
a number? And, if it is not, what else is it? Until arithmeticians have
agreed on answers to these questions and in their ways of talking remain in conformity with these answers, there will be no science of
arithmetic in the true sense of the word – or else a science is made up
of series of words where it does not matter what sense they have or
whether they have any sense at all. Since a statement of number based
on counting contains an assertion about a concept, in a logically perfect
language a sentence used to make such a statement must contain two
parts, first a sign for the concept about which the statement is made,
and secondly a sign for a second-level concept. These second-level concepts form a series and there is a rule in accordance with which, if one
of these concepts is given, we can specify the next. But still we do not
have in them the numbers of arithmetic; we do not have objects, but

---

[22] Cf. *SB*, pp. 159ff. above.
[23] Cf. *GL*, §57 (pp. 106–7 above).
[24] Cf. *CSB*, p. 175 above; *IL*, p. 296 above.
[25] E.g. Weierstrass, criticized by Frege in *GG*, II, §§148–55.
[26] I.e. the formalist, criticized by Frege at greatest length in *GG*, II, §§86–137 (in *TPW*,
pp. 162–213).

concepts. How can we get from these concepts to the numbers of arithmetic in a way that cannot be faulted? Or are there simply no numbers in arithmetic? Could the numerals help to form signs for these second-level concepts, and yet not be signs in their own right?

Bad Kleinen, 26 July 1919.   Dr Gottlob Frege,
                                              formerly Professor at Jena.

Sources of Knowledge of Mathematics and the Mathematical Natural Sciences[1]

[In a diary that he kept from 10 March to 9 May 1924, Frege wrote, on 23 March: 'My efforts to become clear about what is meant by number [*was man Zahl nennen will*] have resulted in failure. We are only too easily misled by language and in this particular case the way we are misled is little short of disastrous.'[2] In the last eighteen months of his life, Frege attempted to come to terms with this, and drew the conclusion that arithmetic had therefore to be given a geometrical rather than logical foundation.[3] In a paper that Frege submitted to a journal in the spring of 1924, entitled 'Sources of Knowledge of Mathematics and the Mathematical Natural Sciences', but which was only finally published in his *Posthumous Writings*,[4] Frege distinguishes three sources of knowledge: sense perception, the logical source of knowledge, and the geometrical and temporal sources of knowledge. Frege continues to insist that 'For mathematics on its own, we do not need sense perception as a source of knowledge',[5] but he now also rejects logic as providing the sole source of knowledge of arithmetic. What follows here is the first four paragraphs of the second section of this paper, entitled 'The Logical Source of Knowledge and Language'.]

288   The senses present us with something external and because of this it is easier to comprehend how mistakes can occur than it is in the case of the logical source of knowledge which is wholly inside us and thus appears to be more proof against contamination. But appearances are

---

[1] Translated by Peter Long and Roger White (*PW*, pp. 269–70; from *NS*, pp. 288–9; page numbers from the latter in the margin).

[2] *PW*, p. 263/*NS*, p. 282.

[3] See the piece that follows, pp. 371–3 below.

[4] *PW*, pp. 267–74/*NS*, pp. 286–94.

[5] *PW*, p. 268/*NS*, p. 287.

deceptive. For our thinking is closely bound up with language and thereby with the external world of the senses. Perhaps our thinking is at first a form of speaking which then becomes an imaging of speech. Silent thinking would in that case be speech which has become noiseless, taking place in the imagination. Now we may of course also think in mathematical signs; yet even then thinking is tied up with what is perceptible to the senses. To be sure, we distinguish the sentence as the expression of a thought from the thought itself. We know we can have various expressions for the same thought. The connection of a thought with one particular sentence is not a necessary one; but that a thought of which we are conscious is connected in our mind with some sentence or other is for us men necessary. But that does not lie in the nature of the thought but in our own nature. There is no contradiction in supposing there to exist beings that can grasp the same thought as we do without needing to clad it in a form that can be perceived by the senses. But still, for us men there is this necessity. Language is a human creation; and so man had, it would appear, the capacity to shape it in conformity with the logical disposition alive in him. Certainly the logical disposition of man *was* at work in the formation of language but equally alongside this many other dispositions – such as the poetic disposition. And so language is not constructed from a logical blueprint.

One feature of language that threatens to undermine the reliability of thinking is its tendency to form proper names to which no objects correspond. If this happens in fiction, which everyone understands to be fiction, this has no detrimental effect. It is different if it happens in a statement which makes the claim to be strictly scientific. A particularly noteworthy example of this is the formation of a proper name after the pattern of 'the extension of the concept *a*', e.g. 'the extension of the concept *fixed star*'. Because of the definite article, this expression appears to designate an object; but there is no object for which this phrase |
could be a linguistically appropriate designation. From this have arisen the paradoxes of set theory which have dealt the death blow to set theory itself. I myself was under this illusion when, in attempting to provide a logical foundation for numbers, I tried to construe numbers as sets. It is difficult to avoid an expression that has universal currency, before you learn of the mistakes it can give rise to. It is extremely difficult, perhaps impossible, to test every expression offered us by language to see whether it is logically innocuous. So a great part of the work of a philosopher consists – or at least ought to consist – in a struggle against language. But perhaps only a few people are aware of the need for this. The same expression – 'the extension of the concept *fixed star*' – serves at the same time to illustrate, in yet another way, the fatal tendency of language to form apparent proper names: 'the concept *fixed star*' is, of itself, one such. The definite article creates the impression that this phrase

289

is meant to designate an object,[6] or, what amounts to the same thing, that 'the concept *fixed star*' is a proper name, whereas 'concept *fixed star*' is surely a designation of a concept and thus could not be more different from a proper name. The difficulties which this idiosyncrasy of language entangles us in are incalculable.[7]

But, isn't thinking a kind of speaking? How is it possible for thinking to be engaged in a struggle with speaking? Wouldn't that be a struggle in which thinking was at war with itself? Doesn't this spell the end to the possibility of thinking?

To be sure, if you search for the emergence of thinking in the development of an individual, you may well describe thinking as an inaudible inner speaking; but that does not capture the true nature of thinking. Cannot a mathematician also think in formulae? The formula language of mathematics is as much a human creation as spoken language, but is fundamentally different from it. Here those traits of spoken language which, as we have seen, lead to logical errors, can be avoided. Yet the influence of speech is so great that they are not always avoided. Thus if we disregard how thinking occurs in the consciousness of an individual, and attend instead to the true nature of thinking, we shall not be able to equate it with speaking. In that case we shall not derive thinking from speaking; thinking will then emerge as that which has priority and we shall not be able to blame thinking for the logical defects we have noted in language.

---

[6] 'Durch den bestimmten Artikel entsteht der Schein, es solle hiermit ein Gegenstand bezeichnet werden . . .'
[7] Cf. *CO*, pp. 181–93 above.

Numbers and Arithmetic[1]

[In this piece, dating from the final year of his life, after admitting the failure, as he sees it, of his attempt to derive arithmetic from pure logic, Frege comes to the conclusion that arithmetic must have a geometrical foundation.[2]]

295   When I first set out to answer for myself the question of what is to be understood by numbers and arithmetic, I encountered – in an apparently predominant position – what was called formalist arithmetic [*formale Arithmetik*]. The hallmark of formalist arithmetic was the thesis 'Numbers are numerals'. How did people arrive at such a position? They felt incapable of answering the question on any rational view of what could be meant [*gemeint*] by it, they did not know how they ought to explain what is designated by the numeral '3' or the numeral '4', and then the cunning idea occurred to them of evading this question by saying 'These numerical signs do not really designate anything: they are themselves the things that we are inquiring about'. Quite a dodge, a degree of cunning amounting, one might almost say, to genius; it is only a shame that it makes the numerals, and so the numbers themselves, completely devoid of content, and quite useless. How was it *possible* for people not to see this? Time and again the same cunning idea occurs to people and it is very possible that there are such people to be found even today. They usually begin by assuring us that they do not intend the numerals to designate anything – no, not anything at all. And yet, it seems, in some mysterious way some content or other must manage to insinuate itself into these quite empty signs, for otherwise they would be useless.

---

[1] Translated by Peter Long and Roger White (*PW*, pp. 275–7; from *NS*, pp. 295–7; page numbers from the latter in the margin).

[2] This is the penultimate piece published in Frege's *Posthumous Writings*; in the final piece, 'A New Attempt at a Foundation for Arithmetic' (*PW*, pp. 278–81/*NS*, pp. 298–302), he actually starts to sketch how such a geometrical foundation might be provided, taking the notions of *line* and *point* as primitive, but there is little more than a page to suggest what he had in mind. We can admire his intellectual courage, though; even at the very end of his life, as his health was deteriorating, Frege was still prepared to start all over again.

That, then, is what formalist arithmetic used to be. Is it now dead? Strictly speaking, it was never alive; all the same we cannot rule out attempts to resuscitate it.[3]

I, for my part, never had any doubt that numerals must designate something in arithmetic, if such a discipline exists at all, and that it does is surely hard to deny. We do, after all, make statements of number. In that case, what are they used to make an assertion about? For me there could be no doubt as to the answer: in a statement of number something is asserted about a concept.[4] I was using the word 'concept' here in the sense that I still attach to it even now. To be sure, among philosophical writers this word is used in a deplorably loose way. This may be all very well for such authors, because the word is then always at hand when they need it. But, this aside, I regard the practice as pernicious.

If I say 'The number of beans in this box is six' or 'There are six
296 beans in this box', | what concept am I making an assertion about? Obviously 'bean in this box'.[A]

Now numbers of different kinds have arisen in different ways and must be distinguished accordingly. To begin with, we have what I call the kindergarten-numbers [*Kleinkinder-Zahlen*]. They are, as it were, drilled into children by parents and teachers: here what people have in mind is the child's future occupation. The child is to be prepared for doing business, for buying and selling. Money has to be counted, and wares too. We have the picture of a child sitting in front of a heap of peas, picking them out one by one with his fingers, each time uttering a number word. In this way something like images of numbers are formed in the child's mind. But this is an artificial process which is imposed on the child rather than one which develops naturally within him. But even if it were a natural process, there would be hardly anything to learn about the real nature of the kindergarten-numbers from the way they originate psychologically. All the same, we can go so far as to say that the series of kindergarten-numbers forms a discontinuous series, which because of this discontinuity is essentially different from the series of points on a straight line. There is always a jump from one number to the next, whereas in a series of points there is no such thing as a next point. In this respect nothing is essentially altered when the child becomes acquainted with fractions. For even after the interpolation of the rationals, the series of numbers including the rationals still has gaps in it. Anything resembling a continuum remains as impossible

---

[A] If something is asserted of a first-level concept, what is asserted is a second-level concept. And so in making a statement of number we have a second-level concept.

[3] For Frege's critique of formalism, see especially *GG*, II, §§86–137 (in *TPW*, pp. 162–213). Cf. also *GL*, §§92–103 (summarized on pp. 124–5 above).

[4] Cf. *GL*, §46 (pp. 98–9 above).

as ever. It is true that we can use one length to measure another with all the accuracy we need for practical life, but we can do this only because practical needs will tolerate small inaccuracies. Things are different in the strict sciences. These teach that there are infinitely many lengths that cannot be measured by a given unit of length. This is what makes the kindergarten-numbers extremely limited in their application. The labours of mathematicians have indeed led to other kinds of numbers, to the irrationals, for example; but there is no bridge which leads across from the kindergarten-numbers to the irrationals. I myself at one time held it to be possible to conquer the entire number-domain, continuing along a purely logical path from the kindergarten-numbers; I have seen the mistake in this. I was right in thinking that you cannot do this if you take an empirical route. I may have arrived at this conviction as a result of the following consideration: that the series of whole numbers should eventually come to an end, that there should be a greatest whole number, is manifestly absurd. This shows that arithmetic cannot be based on sense perception; for if it could be so based, we should have to reconcile ourselves to the brute fact of the series of whole numbers coming to an end, as we may one day have to reconcile ourselves to there being
297   no fixed stars above a | certain size. But here surely the position is different: that the series of whole numbers should eventually come to an end is not just false: we find the idea absurd. So an *a priori* mode of cognition must be involved here. But this cognition does not have to flow from purely logical principles, as I originally assumed. There is the further possibility that it has a geometrical source. Now of course the kindergarten-numbers appear to have nothing whatever to do with geometry. But that is just a defect in the kindergarten-numbers. The more I have thought the matter over, the more convinced I have become that arithmetic and geometry have developed on the same basis – a geometrical one in fact – so that mathematics in its entirety is really geometry. Only on this view does mathematics present itself as completely homogeneous in nature. Counting, which arose psychologically out of the demands of practical life, has led the learned astray.

Appendix 1
Chronology of
Frege's Life and
Works

(What little is known of Frege's life is recorded in Bynum, 1972a, on which the present chronology is based. See also the Introduction, §1 above. For a complete list of Frege's works, arranged chronologically, see the Bibliography below.)

1848 Birth of Friedrich Ludwig Gottlob Frege on 8 November in Wismar, on the Baltic Sea. His father, Karl Alexander (b. 1809), was principal of a private girls' school, and his mother, Auguste Bialloblotzky, was a teacher and later principal of the school.

1864 Entered the *Gymnasium* in Wismar.

1866 Death of Frege's father.

1869 Passed his *Abitur* in the spring and immediately entered the University of Jena, where he spent four semesters, taking courses in chemistry, mathematics and philosophy.

1871 Transferred to the University of Göttingen, where he spent five semesters, taking course in physics, mathematics and philosophy of religion.

1873 Awarded his doctorate on 12 December for his dissertation 'On a Geometrical Representation of Imaginary Forms in the Plane' (*GR*).

1874 Appointed to the post of *Privatdozent* (an unsalaried lectureship) in the mathematics faculty at the University of Jena in May, submitting his *Habilitationsschrift* on 'Methods of Calculation based on an Extension of the Concept of Magnitude' (*MC*). Had a heavy teaching load during the first few years of his career.

1878 Death of Frege's mother.

1879 Publication of *Begriffsschrift* (*BS*). Promoted to *ausserordentlicher Professor* (a salaried position), on the recommendation of Ernest Abbe, his mentor at Jena. His book was, however, poorly received.

1884 Publication of *Die Grundlagen der Arithmetik* (*GL*). Again, the reviews were unfavourable.

1892 Publication of 'On Concept and Object' (*CO*) and 'On *Sinn* and

Bedeutung' (*SB*), heralding the central development in Frege's semantic views.

1893 Publication of Volume I of Frege's *magnum opus*, the *Grundgesetze der Arithmetik* (*GG*). Once again, the reviews were unfavourable. One of them, however, was by Peano, which led to an exchange of letters between Frege and Peano, and through Peano, to Russell's reading of Frege's works.

1894 Review of Husserl's *Philosophie der Arithmetik* (*RH*), which helped convert Husserl to anti-psychologism.

1896 Promoted to the post of Honorary Ordinary Professor. The post was unsalaried, but with no administrative duties, and with a stipend arranged by Abbe from the Carl Zeiss *Stiftung* (a foundation that Abbe had helped set up), Frege acquired more time for research.

1902 Letter from Russell to Frege, dated 16 June, informing him of the contradiction in his logical system.

1903 Publication, at Frege's own expense, of Volume II of the *Grundgesetze*, including a hastily written appendix seeking to respond to Russell's paradox.

1905 Death of Frege's wife, Margaret Lieseburg (b. 1856), leaving Frege with their adopted son, Alfred. (Their natural children had died young, and Alfred had been adopted around 1900.)

1910 Carnap attended Frege's course on logic. Carnap also attended later courses, including one given in 1914 on 'Logic in Mathematics' (*LM*).

1911 Wittgenstein visited Frege, who recommended that he study with Russell.

1918 Retired from the University of Jena, and moved to Bad Kleinen, near Wismar. Publication of 'Der Gedanke' (*T*).

1925 Death of Frege on 26 July at the age of 77.

1935 Frege's *Nachlaß* handed over by Alfred Frege to Heinrich Scholz of the University of Münster, who was planning an edition of Frege's works. Copies were made of most of the important pieces. (For details of the history of Frege's *Nachlaß*, see *NS*, pp. xxxiv–xli/*PW*, pp. ix–xiii.)

1943 Frege's *Nachlaß* deposited in the University Library at Münster.

1944 Alfred Frege killed in action in France on 15 June.

1945 Frege's *Nachlaß* destroyed in a bombing raid on Münster on 25 March.

1950 First English translation, by J. L. Austin, of Frege's *Grundlagen* (*FA*).

1952 First English edition, by P. T. Geach and M. Black, of Frege's published philosophical writings (*TPW*).

1969 Frege's *Nachgelassene Schriften* (*NS*), based on the copies Scholz had made, finally published in German (translated into English as *PW* in 1979).

1976 Frege's correspondence (*WB*) published in German (translated into English, in an abridged edition, as *PMC* in 1980).

Appendix 2
Frege's Logical
Notation

Frege called his logical notation 'Begriffsschrift', which literally means 'concept-script' (it has also been translated as 'conceptual notation', but is left untranslated in the present volume), reflecting his avowed aim of providing a means of capturing the 'conceptual content' ('Begriffsinhalt') of propositions – cf. *BS*, Preface (p. 49 above), and §3 (p. 53 above). The name also formed the title of his first book, which introduced his logical system (see pp. 47–78 above). Since his notation was never adopted by subsequent logicians, a brief account of it and its translation into modern notation is provided here, together with an explanation of the revisions made to it in the *Grundgesetze*.

Frege sets out his symbolism in Part I of the *Begriffsschrift*. He starts by introducing the following symbol (§2):

content ——— ⊢ ———— .

This is seen as made up of a *horizontal stroke*, which Frege calls the *content stroke* (*Inhaltsstrich*), which indicates that what follows is a 'content' that can be asserted (i.e. is the 'content' of a proposition that can be judged to be true), and a *vertical stroke*, which Frege calls the *judgement stroke* (*Urteilsstrich*), which indicates that the content is indeed asserted (i.e. that the relevant proposition is judged to be true). The judgement that the proposition *A* is true is thus represented as follows:

judgement

⊢— *A.*

In §5, Frege notes that if *A* and *B* represent judgeable contents (i.e. are propositions), then there are four possibilities to consider (anticipating Wittgenstein's introduction of *truth-tables* in the *Tractatus*, a treatise that was profoundly influenced by Frege's work):

(1) *A* is affirmed, *B* is affirmed (i.e. both are true);
(2) *A* is affirmed, *B* is denied (i.e. *A* is true, *B* is false);
(3) *A* is denied, *B* is affirmed (i.e. *A* is false, *B* is true);
(4) *A* is denied, *B* is denied (i.e. both are false).

The following symbol is then defined as representing the judgement that *the third of these possibilities does not obtain, but one of the other three does*:

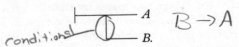

What is represented here is the assertion of the conditional proposition 'If *B*, then *A*', understood as involving the material conditional, i.e. construed as what would be formalized in modern notation as '*B* → *A*', since this is indeed equivalent to '¬(¬*A* & *B*)' (denying the third possibility). The vertical stroke that connects the upper and lower horizontal strokes Frege thus calls the *conditional stroke* (*Bedingungsstrich*). More complex symbols can then be readily constructed, such as the following:

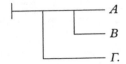

This represents the assertion of the complex conditional proposition '*Γ* → (*B* → *A*)', which is equivalent to '¬(¬*A* & *B* & *Γ*)'. (Cf. *BS*, §5.)

Frege's definition of the conditional thus implies that from the judgements

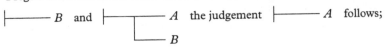

and what is involved here is *modus ponens*, the rule that licenses inferring '*A*' from '*B*' and 'If *B*, then *A*'. 'In logic,' Frege writes, 'following Aristotle, a whole series of modes of inference are enumerated; I use just this one – at least in all cases where a new judgement is derived from more than one single judgement.' If it is possible to manage with a single mode of inference, Frege goes on, 'perspicuity demands that this be done'. (*BS*, §6.)

Frege then defines the *negation stroke* (§7), which he represents by attaching a small vertical stroke to the underside of the content stroke:

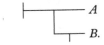

This is understood as *denying* (the content of the proposition) *A*, i.e. as asserting that '¬*A*' is true. Using the conditional and negation strokes, further judgements can then be represented. For example, assertion of the proposition '*A* or *B*', construing 'or' in the inclusive sense, i.e. '*A* ∨ *B*', which is equivalent to '¬*B* → *A*', can be represented as follows:

'*A* & *B*', which is equivalent to '¬(*B* → ¬*A*)', can also be readily represented (note how the *scope* of each negation sign is reflected in Frege's symbolism):

What Frege has thus specified is a system of propositional logic, with negation and the conditional as the primitive connectives, and *modus ponens* as the basic rule of inference. (Frege also makes tacit use of a rule of substitution.) Both conjunction and disjunction can clearly be defined in Frege's system (as Frege himself explains in §7); but it has to be said that, except in the case of conditional propositions, Frege's two-dimensional 'Begriffsschrift' does not render the validity of inferences in propositional logic as perspicuous as modern notation is capable of doing. Of course, it is true that any system that uses some but not all of the propositional connectives either 'deflates' or 'inflates' certain inferences. As an example of each, consider the following 'translations' of one of De Morgan's laws, '$\neg(A \ \& \ B) \leftrightarrow \neg A \lor \neg B$', and one of the distributive laws, '$A \lor (B \ \& \ C) \leftrightarrow (A \lor B) \ \& \ (A \lor C)$', respectively:

(ML)   '$(B \to \neg A) \leftrightarrow (B \to \neg A)$';
(DL)   '$[(C \to \neg B) \to A] \leftrightarrow \neg[(\neg C \to A) \to \neg(\neg B \to A)]$'.

But Frege's notation would certainly add to the 'inflation' of many inferences; and although the possibility of defining '&' and '$\lor$' in terms of '$\to$' and '$\neg$' is instructive (Frege himself frequently emphasizes the value of making do with as few primitives as possible), the lack of simple signs for conjunction and disjunction (even if defined in terms of other connectives) must be regarded as a deficiency of the symbolism.

In §8, Frege defines a symbol for what he calls 'identity of content' ('Inhaltsgleichheit'):

$$\vdash\!\!\!\!\text{——————} (A \equiv B).$$

This is understood as meaning that 'the symbol A and the symbol B have the same conceptual content, so that A can always be replaced by B and vice versa'. The qualifications that are actually needed here, in appealing to intersubstitutability *salva veritate*, were only recognized by Frege later, in his paper 'Über Sinn und Bedeutung' (see esp. p. 159 above). At the time of the *Begriffsschrift*, as §8 reveals, Frege also thought that identity of content was a relation between names rather than contents, a view which he criticizes at the beginning of 'Über Sinn und Bedeutung' (see pp. 151–2 above; cf. the Introduction, pp. 21–2 above).

In the rest of Part I of the *Begriffsschrift* (§§9–12), Frege introduces his notation for what we now know as predicate logic. In §9, he explains his use of function-argument analysis, and in §10 he defines the following symbols as 'A has the property Φ' ('Fa' in modern notation) and 'B stands in the Ψ-relation to A' ('Rba' in modern notation), respectively:

$$\vdash\!\!\!\!\text{——————} \Phi(A),$$

$$\vdash\!\!\!\!\text{——————} \Psi(A, B).$$

In §11, he introduces his key symbol for the universal quantifier, which involves inserting in the content stroke a concavity (*Höhlung*) in which the letter indicating the argument is placed:

$$\vdash\!\!\!\!\text{———}\!\!\smallsmile\!\!\!\!_{\mathfrak{a}}\text{——} \Phi(\mathfrak{a}).$$

This is understood as representing the judgement that 'the function [*Φ*] yields a fact whatever is taken as its argument', i.e. that everything has the property *Φ* (for all *x*, *Fx* – '(∀*x*)*Fx*' as it would be formalized in modern notation).[1] As Frege points out, the concavity with the letter written in it 'delimits the scope [*Gebiet*] of the generality signified by the letter' (§11). As shown in §2 of the Introduction above, appreciation of the *scope* of the quantifier is essential in formalizing statements of multiple generality, where ambiguity may be present.

In §12, Frege considers certain combinations of symbols. Using negation and the universal quantifier, existential judgements such as 'There are some things that do not have the property *X*' (understood as equivalent to 'It is not true that everything is *X*') can be represented:

$$\vdash\!\!\top\frown\!\!\!\alpha\frown\!\!\!\!- X(\alpha).$$

The following symbol, on the other hand, is translated simply as 'There are *Λ*'s' (i.e. 'There is at least one *Λ*'):

$$\vdash\!\!\top\frown\!\!\!\alpha\frown\!\!\!\top\!\!- \Lambda(\alpha).$$

Clearly, what we have here is a definition of the existential quantifier – '(∃*x*)*Fx*', in modern notation, being definable as '¬(∀*x*)¬*Fx*' – although as in the case of conjunction and disjunction, Frege does not introduce a simple sign for the existential quantifier.

Frege also shows how the four types of propositions contained in the Aristotelian square of opposition – traditionally named A, E, I and O propositions – are represented in his system:

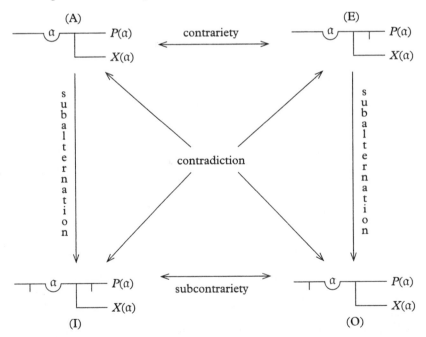

[1] Frege generally uses italicized upper-case Greek letters for function terms, lower-case Gothic (old German) letters for bound variables, and italicized ordinary letters for free

Syllogistic A, E, I and O propositions are thus formalized, in modern notation (substituting '*C*' for '*X*' and '*x*' for '*α*'), as follows:

(A) $(\forall x)(Cx \to Px)$;
(E) $(\forall x)(Cx \to \neg Px)$;
(I) $\neg(\forall x)(Cx \to \neg Px)$, which is equivalent to $(\exists x)(Cx \ \& \ Px)$;
(O) $\neg(\forall x)(Cx \to Px)$, which is equivalent to $(\exists x)(Cx \ \& \ \neg Px)$.

However, although the square of opposition is reproduced in §12 of the *Begriffsschrift*, with the traditional relations marked, Frege does not make clear that contrariety, subcontrariety and subalternation are all invalidated under his formalizations.[2] ((A) and (E) can both be true, if there are no *C*'s; (I) and (O) can both be false, if there are no *C*'s; and (A) does not imply (I), and (E) does not imply (O).) Nevertheless, this aside, it is clear that, in utilizing function-argument analysis and inventing quantifier notation, Frege succeeded in developing the first system of predicate logic.

In Part II of the *Begriffsschrift*, Frege shows how more complex judgements can be represented and derived in his system. All we need note here is the 'kernel' of nine propositions that Frege takes as the axioms of his system (numbered (1), (2), (8), (28), (31), (41), (52), (54) and (58), respectively, in his own account):

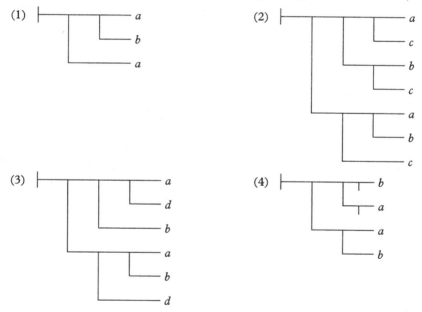

variables. In modern notation, italicized upper-case ordinary letters – such as *F* and *G* – are conventionally used for function terms, italicized lower-case ordinary letters typically from the end of the alphabet – such as *x* and *y* – for bound variables, and italicized lower-case ordinary letters typically from the beginning of the alphabet – such as *a* and *b* – for free variables, as illustrated in the inference schema '$(\forall x)Fx \to Fa$', reflecting the rule of universal elimination.

[2] Two propositions are *contraries* if they cannot both be true but may both be false. Two propositions are *subcontraries* if they cannot both be false but may both be true. One

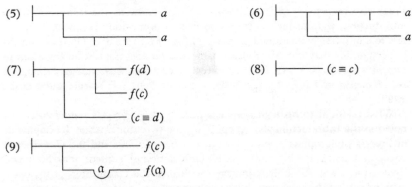

As Łukasiewicz (1934) was later to prove, the first six axioms form a complete set of axioms for propositional logic, though the third axiom can in fact be derived, using just the rules of *modus ponens* and substitution, from the first two (cf. Kneale and Kneale, 1962: pp. 490–1). The other five are independent of one another (cf. Thiel, 1968: p. 21; Bynum, 1972b: p. 73).[3] The axioms can be formulated in modern notation as follows:

(1*) $P \to (Q \to P)$.
(2*) $[R \to (Q \to P)] \to [(R \to Q) \to (R \to P)]$.
(3*) $[S \to (Q \to P)] \to [Q \to (S \to P)]$.
(4*) $(Q \to P) \to (\neg P \to \neg Q)$.
(5*) $\neg \neg P \to P$.
(6*) $P \to \neg \neg P$.

The seventh and eighth formulae involve Frege's symbol for identity of content, and might be re-expressed thus:

(7*) $(a = b) \to (Fa \to Fb)$.
(8*) $a = a$.

(7*) is a version of the Principle of the Indiscernibility of Identicals (cf. fn. 25 on p. 112 above; making explicit the implicit quantification over properties, and replacing the second conditional by the biconditional, gives us '$a = b \to (\forall F)(Fa \leftrightarrow Fb)$'); and (8*), of course, states that everything is identical with itself. The ninth axiom, reflecting what, in a natural deduction system, is the rule of universal elimination, can be formulated as follows:

(9*) $(\forall x)Fx \to Fa$.

proposition is the *subaltern* of another if the second cannot be true without the first being true, but the first may be true without the second being true (i.e. if the second implies the first). For discussion of the relationship between Aristotelian and Fregean logic, see Beaney, 1996: chs. 1–2; app. 1.

[3] It is true that Frege remarks in the Preface to *BS* (see p. 51 above) that he later noticed that the fifth and sixth axioms can be combined into one, but this depended on the introduction of his symbol for identity of content.

Frege also recognizes (*BS*, §11) what we now know as the rule of universal introduction, legitimizing the transition from a proposition involving italic letters to a universally quantified proposition (i.e. 'From *Fa* infer $(\forall x)Fx$' – on the understanding that '*a*' is an arbitrary name and *Fa* does not rest on any assumption in which '*a*' occurs). Here too Frege succeeded in specifying a complete set of axioms and rules for first-order predicate logic (cf. Kneale and Kneale, 1962: p. 489).

What revisions to his logical system were made in Frege's *Grundgesetze*? As noted in the Introduction above (pp. 5–6), the two fundamental developments in Frege's philosophical views between the *Begriffsschrift* and the *Grundgesetze* concerned, firstly, the bifurcation of his early notion of 'content' into 'Sinn' and 'Bedeutung', and secondly, connected with this, the clarification of his ontology, admitting, in particular, both truth-values and extensions of concepts as objects, and hence as legitimate arguments of functions; and these developments did indeed necessitate certain changes in his logical theory. The essential system of 'strokes' remained the same, though Frege talks simply of the 'horizontal' rather than the 'content stroke' (cf. *GG*, I, §5). Taking truth-values as the *Bedeutungen* of sentences involved treating sentences as names, so that what is then seen as following the horizontal stroke is a name of a truth-value (cf. *GG*, I, §§2, 5). The main change – or addition – to the notation itself concerns the introduction of a symbol, '$\acute{\varepsilon}\Phi(\varepsilon)$', with a smooth breathing over the first occurrence of 'ε', for the *value-range* of the function $\Phi(\xi)$; where the function is one that maps objects onto one of the two truth-values, i.e. is a concept, then what we have here is a symbol for the extension of the concept Φ. (Cf. *GG*, I, §9.) In the *Grundlagen*, Frege had defined the natural numbers by identifying them with extensions of logical concepts (see pp. 114–20 above); and by the time of the *Grundgesetze*, he had convinced himself that the appeal to extensions was legitimate (cf. the Introduction, p. 6 above).

As far as the axioms and rules of his logical system were concerned, there was a certain amount of reorganization. Axiom (1) of the *Begriffsschrift* survives unchanged as Axiom I of the *Grundgesetze*, but Axioms (2), (3) and (4) disappear as a result of the specification of a greater number of rules. (Eighteen rules are formulated altogether – see *GG*, I, §48 – but the last six simply concern the use of brackets, Rule 1 is a formation rule for the horizontal stroke, and Rules 9 to 12 are rules of substitution. Rules 2 to 8 are the rules of inference, in propositional and predicate logic.) Axiom (2) becomes provable by means of the rule of *amalgamation of identical subcomponents* (Rule 4; allowing e.g. the transition from 'if *P*, then if *P*, then *Q*' to the simpler 'if *P*, then *Q*'); and Axiom (3) becomes provable by means of the rule of *interchange of subcomponents* (Rule 2; allowing e.g. the transition from 'if *P*, then if *Q*, then *R*' to 'if *Q*, then if *P*, then *R*'). Axiom (4) is made redundant with the introduction of the rule of *contraposition* (Rule 3). Axioms (5) and (6), which, as Frege noted in the Preface to the *Begriffsschrift*, he later realized could be combined using the symbol for identity of content (just as (5*) and (6*) above can be combined as '$\neg\neg P \leftrightarrow P$'), become derivable from Axiom IV of the *Grundgesetze*:

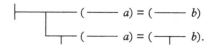

What this says is that either $a = b$ or $a \neq b$. Axiom (7) and (8) of the *Begriffsschrift* are replaced by Axiom III of the *Grundgesetze*:

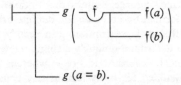

Given that both the expressions contained within the brackets (as governed by 'g') are truth-values, what Axiom III says is that the truth-value named by the expression in the upper brackets falls under every concept under which the truth-value named by '$a = b$' falls (cf. *GG*, I, §20). From this it follows that if $a = b$, than anything that holds of a holds of b, which is Axiom (7) of the *Begriffsschrift*, and that everything is identical to itself, which is Axiom (8). Axiom (9) of the *Begriffsschrift* is retained unchanged as Axiom IIa of the *Grundgesetze*, but a corresponding version, Axiom IIb, is introduced for second-level functions:

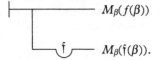

What this says is that whatever holds of all first-level functions of one argument holds of any (cf. *GG*, I, §25). The nine axioms of the *Begriffsschrift* are thus condensed into the first four axioms of the *Grundgesetze*, with some additional rules formulated and with second-order quantification made official.

The most significant development, however, involved the introduction of Axiom V of the *Grundgesetze*, legitimizing value-ranges of functions (extensions of concepts), which Frege formulated as follows:

$$\vdash\ (\acute{\varepsilon}f(\varepsilon) = \acute{\alpha}g(\alpha)) = (\ \neg\!\!\frown\!\!\!\alpha\!\!\!\frown\ f(\alpha) = g(\alpha)).$$

What this asserts is the equivalence between the following two propositions, in effect contextually defining the second by means of the first:[4]

(Vα) The function F has the same value for each argument as the function G.

(Vβ) The value-range of the function F is identical with the value-range of the function G.

In modern notation, adapting Frege's symbol for the value-range of a function, the equivalence can be expressed as follows:

(V*) $\acute{x}Fx = \acute{x}Gx \leftrightarrow (\forall x)(Fx \leftrightarrow Gx).$

It was this axiom that Frege later held responsible for the contradiction that Russell discovered in his system (see pp. 253–4, 279–89 above; cf. the Introduction, pp. 7–8).

---

[4] Cf. the Introduction, pp. 18–19. (Vα) and (Vβ) here are not to be confused with what Frege formulates as (Va) and (Vb) in his appendix to *GG*, II (see p. 283 above), namely, the *conditionals* '(Vα) → (Vβ)' and '(Vβ) → (Vα)', respectively. Cf. fn. 40 on p. 18 above.

Frege's final axiom, Axiom VI, introduces a further new symbol, '\$\backslash\xi$', representing the function that Frege defines to replace the definite article of ordinary language. In ordinary language, definite descriptions, which Frege classifies as proper names, are formed by prefixing the definite article 'the' to a concept expression ('the *F*'). But such descriptions can readily be formed that lack a referent, or that fail to determine uniquely a single referent. Ordinary language is deficient in this respect, according to Frege, whereas in a logical language a referent must be determined for every legitimately constructed proper name. How might this be done in the case of definite descriptions? If we assume that concepts are sharply defined, and that extensions of concepts are objects, then any definite description of the form 'the extension of the concept *F*' is guaranteed a unique referent. So the obvious solution is to admit only definite descriptions of this form into the logical language. But how then do we refer to 'ordinary' objects? Here the strategy is to note that for any given object Δ, there is a concept *is identical with* Δ, which clearly meets the condition of being sharply defined. So the suggestion is to *identify* the object Δ with the extension of this concept (which is itself an object). However, for reasons that Frege spells out in §10 of Volume I of the *Grundgesetze*, there are objections to identifying objects with the corresponding extensions (i.e. with their unit classes).[5] So what Frege does instead is introduce a function that serves the same purpose, *mapping* extensions of concepts under which only one object falls onto that object itself. More precisely, the function $\backslash\xi$ is defined in the following way:

---

[5] The proof may be stated as follows. Using Frege's notation for extensions, '$\acute{\varepsilon}\Phi(\varepsilon)$' representing 'the extension of the concept Φ', Axiom V can be formulated thus:

(V) $(\forall a)[\Phi(a) = \Psi(a)]$
      iff $\acute{\varepsilon}\Phi(\varepsilon) = \acute{\alpha}\Psi(\alpha)$.

The suggestion is to characterize every object Δ as the extension of the concept *is identical with* Δ, i.e. stipulating that $\acute{\varepsilon}(\Delta = \varepsilon)$ be the same as Δ. But now consider the case where Δ is already given as a value-range, say, as $\acute{\alpha}\Phi(\alpha)$. Taking '$\acute{\varepsilon}(\Delta = \varepsilon) = \Delta$', and substituting in, we have:

$$\acute{\varepsilon}(\acute{\alpha}\Phi(\alpha) = \varepsilon) = \acute{\alpha}\Phi(\alpha).$$

By Axiom V, this is equivalent to:

$$(\forall a)[(\acute{\alpha}\Phi(\alpha) = a) = \Phi(a)].$$

However, as Frege then notes, this only refers to the True 'if $\Phi(\xi)$ is a concept under which one and only one object falls, namely $\acute{\alpha}\Phi(\alpha)$'. For in this case, if $a = \acute{\alpha}\Phi(\alpha)$, then both '$\acute{\alpha}\Phi(\alpha) = a$' and '$\Phi(a)$' will refer to the True, so that '$(\acute{\alpha}\Phi(\alpha) = a) = \Phi(a)$' will refer to the True; and if $a \neq \acute{\alpha}\Phi(\alpha)$, then both '$\acute{\alpha}\Phi(\alpha) = a$' and '$\Phi(a)$' will refer to the False, so that '$(\acute{\alpha}\Phi(\alpha) = a) = \Phi(a)$' also refers to the True. But in every other case, there will be some values of a for which '$(\acute{\alpha}\Phi(\alpha) = a) = \Phi(a)$' will refer to the False, i.e. where $a = \acute{\alpha}\Phi(\alpha)$ and does not fall under the concept Φ, or $a \neq \acute{\alpha}\Phi(\alpha)$ and does fall under the concept Φ. So, as Frege concludes, 'our stipulation cannot remain generally valid'. (*GG*, I, §10, p. 18, fn. 1.) Even before the emergence of Russell's paradox, this result should already have alerted Frege to the danger of regarding an extension of a concept as on the same ontological level as the objects that fall under that concept. Cf. the Introduction, pp. 19–20 above.

(1) If the argument is the extension of the concept *is identical with* Δ, i.e. $\grave{\varepsilon}(\Delta = \varepsilon)$, for any given object Δ, then the value of the function is the object Δ itself.

(2) If the argument is not an extension as specified in (1), i.e. is not an extension of a concept under which only one object falls, then the value of the function is the argument itself (i.e. the function maps all other objects onto themselves). (Cf. *GG*, I, §11.)

(2) ensures that the function is defined for all objects; and (1) gives rise to Axiom VI (cf. *GG*, I, §18):

$$\vdash\!\!\!\!\!\!\!\!\!\!\!\!\!\!\!- a = \backslash\grave{\varepsilon}(a = \varepsilon).$$

Frege's strategy might be illustrated by considering the example that Russell used to motivate his theory of descriptions (in 'On Denoting'):

(K) The present King of France is bald.

If there is no King of France (i.e. in Fregean terminology, the definite description lacks a *Bedeutung*), then the proposition as a whole would seem to lack a truth-value (i.e. a *Bedeutung*). Yet (K) remains meaningful, and hence, according to Russell, *must* have a truth-value. To solve the problem, Russell suggests that (K) should be analysed as the following:

(KR) There is one and only one King of France, and whatever is King of France is bald.

The proposition now comes out as *false* because the first conjunct is false (there is no King of France). According to Frege, however, (K) should be rewritten in his ideal logical language thus:

(KF) \ (extension of the concept *present King of France*) is bald.

If there *is* one and only one present King of France, then the value of '\ (extension of the concept *present King of France*)' is that person; if there is not, then the value is the extension itself. If there is no present King of France at all, in other words, then the value is the null set, and it is false that the null set is bald. (If there were somehow more than one King of France, then the value would be the set of such people, and it is equally false that this set is bald; although strictly speaking, of course, the vagueness of ξ *is bald* means that there is no genuine (i.e. logically correct) concept involved here, according to Frege; cf. e.g. pp. 80, 259 above.) So Frege's treatment has the same result as Russell's: propositions involving definite descriptions that fail to refer to a unique entity come out as *false*. The difference is that whilst Russell 'analysed away' the troublesome denoting phrase,[6] Frege ingeniously provided a replacement for it and introduced a technical device to ensure it had a referent (cf. *SB*, p. 163 and p. 164, fn. I above).

---

[6] Cf. fn. 45 on p. 20 above.

Appendix 3
Guide to Further
Reading

The following notes are intended merely to help those new to Frege's philosophy to gain their initial bearings in a secondary literature that has blossomed in the last few years, although it is still relatively manageable in comparison with the secondary literature on some of Frege's contemporaries and successors.[1] Only a selection of the generally more recently published books which focus exclusively on Frege are mentioned here; further works, and in particular, some of the important papers that have been written on Frege, are cited at relevant points in the footnotes to the Introduction and to the translated texts themselves. Publication details of all works referred to in this volume can be found in the Bibliography.

The most elementary introduction to Frege's philosophy is Anthony Kenny's *Frege*, which provides a useful précis of Frege's main works, though with little analysis or assessment. Gregory Currie's *Frege: An Introduction to his Philosophy* offers a more critical introduction, and is especially helpful on Frege's logicism and philosophical logic. For the German reader, Franz von Kutschera's *Gottlob Frege* contains a clear exposition of the main elements of Frege's work. A more substantial introduction, focusing on the development of Frege's conception of sense, but stressing the organic unity of Frege's philosophy, is provided by Michael Beaney in *Frege: Making Sense*.

No one who embarks seriously on a study of Frege can avoid reading and engaging with the work of Michael Dummett, who is by far the single most important and influential commentator (he has written more on Frege than Frege wrote himself). His monumental *Frege: Philosophy of Language*, which appeared in 1973, consisting of a series of essays on topics in Frege's philosophy of lan-

---

[1] The three philosophers who immediately spring to mind here are Nietzsche, who was born just four years before Frege, and Wittgenstein and Heidegger, who were both born forty-one years after Frege. Husserl, born eleven years after Frege, and Russell, born twenty-four years after Frege, are also way ahead of Frege as far as the secondary literature on their work is concerned (they also themselves wrote far more than Frege, though not of the same uniformly high standard).

guage, was the book that assured Frege a central place in contemporary philosophy. To gain a sense of Frege's importance, and the enormous potential of his ideas, one could do no better than to read the first six chapters of this book. Nevertheless, as a pioneering work, the book inevitably had its flaws. Dummett was criticized, in particular, for his lack of historical understanding, being prone to see Frege too much as a modern philosopher of language and not enough as a mathematician, logician and epistemologist responding to developments around him. Dummett sought to respond to various of his critics in *The Interpretation of Frege's Philosophy*, which contains useful further chapters on topics only partially treated in his earlier book. *Frege: Philosophy of Mathematics*, though not published until eighteen years afterwards, is the sequel to his first book. Originally intended to be a series of essays on Frege's philosophy of mathematics modelled on his earlier discussion of Frege's philosophy of language, it ended up as rather a different book (no doubt partly as a result of some of the criticism), providing an account and a critical assessment of the development of Frege's logicist project from the *Grundlagen* to the *Grundgesetze*. It is a masterpiece: lucidly written, historically informed, philosophically penetrating, and essential reading for anyone interested not just in Frege, but in logic and the philosophy of mathematics generally.

Both Hans Sluga's *Gottlob Frege* and Baker and Hacker's *Frege: Logical Excavations* were in many ways written in response to Dummett's first book. Sluga's book aimed to set the historical record straight, and contains a useful account of Frege's German predecessors, although perhaps goes too far in stressing the influence on Frege of philosophers such as Lotze. Baker and Hacker's book, written from a Wittgensteinian standpoint that is sceptical of many of the developments in modern analytic philosophy, is the most critical work on Frege's philosophy that has yet been published. Joan Weiner's *Frege in Perspective* also offers a 'revisionist' reading of Frege that seeks to clarify the differences between Frege's own concerns and those of the contemporary philosopher.

There are several other books which focus on particular aspects of Frege's philosophy that can be recommended for those wishing to explore the relevant topics. David Bell's *Frege's Theory of Judgement* expounds and develops Frege's answer to the so-called problem of the unity of the proposition. Michael Resnik's *Frege and the Philosophy of Mathematics* provides a fine introduction to Frege's philosophy of mathematics. Crispin Wright's *Frege's Conception of Numbers as Objects* offers a sophisticated modern defence of the Platonism and logicism of Frege's *Grundlagen* (which many have felt to be incompatible). Nathan Salmon's *Frege's Puzzle* develops an answer, which owes as much to Russell, to the problem of the informativeness of identity statements. Wolfgang Carl's *Frege's Theory of Sense and Reference* stresses the epistemological dimension of Frege's philosophy.

There are also a number of collections of papers on Frege's work that contain accessible articles. *Studien zu Frege*, in three volumes, edited by Matthias Schirn, *Frege: Tradition and Influence*, edited by Crispin Wright, and *Frege Synthesized*, edited by Leila Haaparanta and Jaakko Hintikka, are the most frequently referred to. *The Philosophy of Frege*, edited in four volumes by Hans Sluga, contains previously published papers, covering all the main aspects of Frege's work. There was also a special edition of *Mind* that came out in October 1992, marking the centenary of Frege's seminal essay 'On *Sinn* and *Bedeutung*'. The large number of articles that are now appearing on Frege's work in all the main philosophical journals are also testament to Frege's continuing, and indeed increasing, importance.

Bibliography

This bibliography contains all works referred to in the editorial text (where full citations have not been provided), by either year of publication or abbreviation, as indicated below in parentheses immediately after the name(s). Included is a full list, arranged chronologically, of all Frege's published works. Unless otherwise indicated, references given in the text are to the relevant publication (edition, collection or translation) *first* named in the bibliography.

Baker, G. P. and Hacker, P. M. S. (1984), *Frege: Logical Excavations* (Blackwell)

Beaney, Michael (1996), *Frege: Making Sense* (Duckworth)

Bell, David (1979), *Frege's Theory of Judgement* (OUP)

—— (1980), 'On the Translation of Frege's *Bedeutung*', *Analysis* 40, pp. 191–5

—— (1984), 'Reference and Sense: An Epitome', in Wright (1984), pp. 184–8

—— (1990a), *Husserl* (Routledge)

—— (1990b), 'How "Russellian" Was Frege?', *Mind* 99, pp. 267–77

Benacerraf, Paul and Putnam, Hilary (1983), eds., *Philosophy of Mathematics: Selected Readings*, 2nd edn. (CUP; 1st edn. Prentice-Hall, Inc., 1964)

Biro, John and Kotatko, Petr (1995), eds., *Frege: Sense and Reference One Hundred Years Later* (Kluwer)

Boole, George (1847), *The Mathematical Analysis of Logic* (Cambridge and London); repr. in *Studies in Logic and Probability*, ed. R. Rhees (London: Watts & Co., 1952)

—— (1854), *The Laws of Thought* (London and Cambridge); repr. as *Collected Logical Works*, Vol. 2 (Chicago and London: Open Court, 1940)

Boolos, George (1993), 'Basic Law (V)', *Proceedings of the Aristotelian Society, Supplementary Volume* 67, pp. 213–33

Burge, Tyler (1979), 'Sinning against Frege', *Philosophical Review* 88, pp. 398–432

—— (1984), 'Frege on Extensions of Concepts, from 1884 to 1903', *Philosophical Review* 93, pp. 3–34

—— (1992), 'Frege on Knowing the Third Realm', *Mind* 101, pp. 633–50

Bynum, Terrell Ward (1972a), 'On the Life and Work of Gottlob Frege', in Frege, *CN*, pp. 1–54

—— (1972b) 'Editor's Introduction', in Frege, *CN*, pp. 55–80

Carl, Wolfgang (1994), *Frege's Theory of Sense and Reference* (CUP)

Carnap, Rudolf (1963), 'Intellectual Autobiography', in Schilpp (1963), pp. 1–84

Clark, Peter (1993), 'Basic Law (V)', *Proceedings of the Aristotelian Society, Supplementary Volume* 67, pp. 235–49

Currie, Gregory (1978), 'Frege's Realism', *Inquiry* 21, pp. 218–21

—— (1981), 'The Origin of Frege's Realism', *Inquiry* 24, pp. 448–54

—— (1982), *Frege: An Introduction to his Philosophy* (Harvester)

—— (1984), 'Frege's Metaphysical Argument', in Wright (1984), pp. 144–57

Davidson, Donald (1967), 'Truth and Meaning', in Davidson (1984), pp. 17–36; orig. in *Synthese* 17, pp. 304–23

—— (1970), 'Semantics for Natural Languages', in Davidson (1984), pp. 55–64

—— (1984), *Inquiries into Truth and Interpretation* (OUP)

Dedekind, R. (1872), *Continuity and Irrational Numbers*, tr. W. Beman, in Dedekind, *ETN*

—— (1888), *Was sind und was sollen die Zahlen?*, tr. W. Beman, in Dedekind, *ETN*

——, (*ETN*) *Essays on the Theory of Numbers*, ed. and tr. W. Beman (New York: Dover, 1963; orig. publ. 1901)

Donnellan, Keith (1966), 'Reference and Definite Descriptions', *Philosophical Review* 75, pp. 281–304

Dudman, Victor H. (1976), 'From Boole to Frege', in Schirn (1976), vol. 1, pp. 109–38

Dummett, Michael (1955), 'Frege on Functions: A Reply', *Philosophical Review* 64, pp. 96–107; repr. in Klemke (1968), pp. 268–83

—— (1967), 'Frege's Philosophy', in Dummett (1978), pp. 87–115; orig. in *The Encylopaedia of Philosophy*, vol. 3, ed. Paul Edwards (New York: MacMillan), pp. 225–37

—— (1975), 'Frege's Distinction between Sense and Reference', in Dummett (1978), pp. 116–43; also in Moore (1992), pp. 228–56

—— (1976), 'Frege as a Realist', in Dummett (1991b), pp. 79–96; orig. in *Inquiry* 19, pp. 455–68

—— (1978), *Truth and Other Enigmas* (Duckworth)

—— (1981a), *Frege: Philosophy of Language*, 2nd edn. (Duckworth; 1st edn. 1973)

—— (1981b), *The Interpretation of Frege's Philosophy* (Duckworth)

—— (1982), 'Objectivity and Reality in Lotze and Frege', in Dummett (1991b), pp. 97–125; orig. in *Inquiry* 25, pp. 95–114

—— (1986), 'Frege's Myth of the Third Realm', in Dummett (1991b), pp. 249–62; orig. in *Untersuchungen zur Logik und zur Methodologie* 3, pp. 24–38

—— (1991a), *Frege: Philosophy of Mathematics* (Duckworth)

—— (1991b), *Frege and Other Philosophers* (OUP)

—— (1994), 'Chairman's Address: Basic Law V', *Proceedings of the Aristotelian Society* 94 (1993–4), pp. 243–51; response to Boolos (1993) and Clark (1993)

—— (1995), 'The Context Principle: Centre of Frege's Philosophy', in Max and Stelzner (1995), pp. 3–19

Evans, Gareth (1981), 'Understanding Demonstratives', in Evans (1985), pp. 291–321; also in Yourgrau (1990), pp. 71–96; orig. in Parret and Bouveresse (1981)

—— (1982), *The Varieties of Reference*, ed. John McDowell (OUP)

—— (1985), *Collected Papers* (OUP)

Forbes, G. (1987), 'Indexicals and Intensionality: A Fregean Perspective', *Philosophical Review* 96, pp. 3–31

Frege, Gottlob, (*GR*) 'On a Geometrical Representation of Imaginary Forms in the Plane' (1873), in *CP*, pp. 1–55

——, (*MC*) 'Methods of Calculation based on an Extension of the Concept of Quantity [Magnitude]' (1874), in *CP*, pp. 56–92

——, (*RS*) 'Review of H. Seeger, *Die Elemente der Arithmetik*' (1874), in *CP*, pp. 93–4

——, (*KSL*) '[17 Key Sentences on Logic]' (1876/77), in *PW*, pp. 174–5

——, (*RGW*), 'Review of A. von Gall and E. Winter, *Die analytische Geometrie des Punktes und der Geraden und ihre Anwendung auf Aufgaben*' (1877), in *CP*, pp. 95–7

——, (*RTSF*), 'Review of J. Thomae, *Sammlung von Formeln, welche bei Anwendung der elliptischen und Rosenhainschen Funktionen gebraucht werden*' (1877), in *CP*, p. 98

——, (*LWCS*), 'Lecture on a Way of Conceiving the Shape of a Triangle as a Complex Quantity' (1878), in *CP*, pp. 99–100

——, (*BS*) *Begriffsschrift, eine der arithmetischen nachgebildete Formelsprache des reinen Denkens* (Halle: L. Nebert, 1879), tr. in *CN*, pp. 101–203; also tr. S. Bauer-Mengelberg, in van Heijenoort (1967), pp. 5–82; most of Part I (§§1–12) also tr. in *TPW*, pp. 1–20, and in *FR*, pp. 47–78

——, (*APCN*) 'Applications of the "Conceptual Notation"' (1879), in *CN*, pp. 204–8

——, (*PWLA*) 'Logic' (between 1879 and 1891), in *PW*, pp. 1–8

——, (*RHLG*), 'Review of Hoppe, *Lehrbuch der analytischen Geometrie* I' (1880), in *CP*, pp. 101–2

——, (*BLC*) 'Boole's Logical Calculus and the Concept-script' (1880/81), in *PW*, pp. 9–46

——, (*LHP*), 'Über den Briefwechsel Leibnizens und Huygens mit Papin' (1881), in *BSA*

——, (*BLF*) 'Boole's Logical Formula-language and my Concept-script' (1882), in *PW*, pp. 47–52

——, (*SJCN*) 'On the Scientific Justification of a Conceptual Notation' (1882), in *CN*, pp. 83–9

——, (*ACN*) 'On the Aim of the "Conceptual Notation"' (1882), in *CN*, pp. 90–100

——, (*DPE*) '[Dialogue with Pünjer on Existence]' (before 1884), in *PW*, pp. 53–67

——, (*LGPP*), 'Lecture on the Geometry of Pairs of Points in the Plane' (1884), in *CP*, pp. 103–7

——, (*GL*) *Die Grundlagen der Arithmetik, eine logisch mathematische Untersuchung über den Begriff der Zahl* (Breslau: W. Koebner, 1884), tr. as (*FA*) *The Foundations of Arithmetic* by J. L. Austin, with German text, 2nd edn. (Blackwell, 1953; 1st edn. 1950); §§55–91, 106–9 also tr. Michael S. Mahoney, in Benacerraf and Putnam (1983), pp. 130–59; selections also tr. in *FR*, pp. 84–129 (for German centenary critical edition, see Frege, *GLT* below)

——, (*RHC*) 'Review of H. Cohen, *Das Prinzip der Infinitesimal-Methode und seine Geschichte*' (1885), in *CP*, pp. 108–11

——, (*FTA*) 'On Formal Theories of Arithmetic' (1885), in *CP*, pp. 112–21

——, (*RCR*), 'Reply to Cantor's Review of *Grundlagen der Arithmetik*' (1885), in *CP*, p. 122

——, (*OLI*) 'On the Law of Inertia' (1891), in *CP*, pp. 123–36

——, (*FC*) 'Function and Concept' (1891), in *TPW*, pp. 21–41; also in *CP*, pp. 137–56; and in *FR*, pp. 130–48

——, (*OCN*) 'On the Concept of Number' (1891/92), in *PW*, pp. 72–86

——, (*SB*) 'On *Sinn* and *Bedeutung*' (1892), in *TPW*, pp. 56–78; also in *CP*, pp. 157–77; and in *FR*, pp. 151–71

——, (*CSB*) '[Comments on *Sinn* and *Bedeutung*]' (1892), in *PW*, pp. 118–25; also in *FR*, pp. 172–80

——, (*CO*) 'On Concept and Object' (1892), in *TPW*, pp. 42–55; also in *PW*, pp. 87–117; in *CP*, pp. 182–94; and in *FR*, pp. 181–93

——, (*DRGC*), '[Draft towards a Review of Cantor's *Gesammelte Abhandlungen zur Lehre vom Transfiniten*]' (1890–2), in *PW*, pp. 68–71

——, (*RGC*) 'Review of Georg Cantor, *Zur Lehre vom Transfiniten*' (1892), in *CP*, pp. 178–81

——, (*GG*) *Grundgesetze der Arithmetik* (Jena: H. Pohle, Band I 1893, Band II 1903; repr. together, Hildesheim: Georg Olms, 1962); Preface, Introd. and §§1–52 of Vol. 1 tr. as (*BLA*) *The Basic Laws of Arithmetic: Exposition of the System*, tr. and ed. with an introd. by Montgomery Furth (University of California Press, 1964); selections from both vols. also tr. in *TPW*; and in *FR*, pp. 194–233, 258–89

——, (*RH*) 'Review of E. G. Husserl, *Philosophie der Arithmetik* I' (1894), in *CP*, pp. 195–209; illustrative extracts in *TPW*, pp. 79–85; extract also in *FR*, pp. 224–6

——, (*CES*) 'A Critical Elucidation of Some Points in E. Schröder, *Vorlesungen über die Algebra der Logik*' (1895), in *CP*, pp. 210–28; also in *TPW*, pp. 86–106

——, (*WN*) 'Whole Numbers' (1895), in *CP*, pp. 229–33

——, (*PWLB*) 'Logic' (1897), in *PW*, pp. 126–51; extract also in *FR*, pp. 227–50

——, (*PCN*) 'On Mr Peano's Conceptual Notation and My Own' (1897), in *CP*, pp. 234–48

——, (*ASCD*) 'The Argument for my Stricter Canons of Definition' (1897/98), in *PW*, pp. 152–6

——, (*LDM*), 'Logical Defects in Mathematics' (1898/9–1903), in *PW*, pp. 157–66

——, (*SN*) 'On Mr H. Schubert's Numbers' (1899), in *CP*, pp. 249–72

——, (*EG*) 'On Euclidean Geometry' (1899–1906?), in *PW*, pp. 167–69; extract in *FR*, pp. 251–2

——, (*FDI*) 'Frege on Definitions – I' (*GG*, II, §§56–67; 1903), in *TPW*, pp. 139–52; also in *FR*, pp. 259–70

——, (*FDII*) 'Frege on Definitions – II' (*GG*, II, §§139–44, 146–7; 1903), in *TPW*, pp. 153–61; also in *FR*, pp. 271–9

——, (*FF*) 'Frege against the Formalists' (*GG*, II, §§86–137; 1903), in *TPW*, pp. 162–213

——, (*FRP*) 'Frege on Russell's Paradox' (*GG*, II, App., pp. 253–65; 1903), in *TPW*, pp. 214–24; also in *FR*, pp. 279–89

——, (*FGI*) 'On the Foundations of Geometry: First Series' (1903), in *CP*, pp. 273–84; also in *FG*, pp. 22–37

——, (*WF*) 'What is a Function?' (1904), in *TPW*, pp. 107–16; also in *CP*, pp. 285–92

——, (*FGII*) 'On the Foundations of Geometry; Second Series' (1906), in *CP*, pp. 293–340; also in *FG*, pp. 49–112

——, (*NHGG*), '[Frege's Notes on Hilbert's *Grundlagen der Geometrie*]' (after 1903), in *PW*, pp. 170–3

——, (*SLPM*) 'On Schoenflies: *Die Logischen Paradoxien der Mengenlehre*' (1906), in *PW*, pp. 176–83

——, (*WRW*) 'What may I Regard as the Result of my Work?' (1906), in *PW*, p. 184

——, (*IL*) 'Introduction to Logic' (1906), in *PW*, pp. 185–96; extract in *FR*, pp. 293–8

——, (*BSLD*) 'A Brief Survey of my Logical Doctrines' (1906), in *PW*, pp. 197–202; also in *FR*, pp. 299–300

——, (*RT*) 'Reply to Mr. Thomae's Holiday *Causerie*' (1906), in *CP*, pp. 341–45

——, (*RPIT*), 'Renewed Proof of the Impossibility of Mr. Thomae's Formal Arithmetic' (1908), in *CP*, pp. 346–50

——, (*LM*) 'Logic in Mathematics' (1914), in *PW*, pp. 203–50; extract in *FR*, pp. 308–18

——, (*BLW*) 'Briefe an Ludwig Wittgenstein aus den Jahren 1914–1920', ed. A. Janik, in McGuinness and Haller (1989), pp. 5–33

——, (*MBLI*) 'My Basic Logical Insights' (1915), in *PW*, pp. 251–2; also in *FR*, pp. 322–4

——, (*T*) 'Thought' (1918), Part I of *LI*, in *CP*, pp. 351–72, and in *FR*, pp. 325–45; also in Salmon and Soames (1988), pp. 33–55; also tr. A. M. and M. Quinton, *Mind* 65 (1956), pp. 289–311, repr. in Strawson (1967), pp. 17–38, and in Klemke (1968), pp. 507–35

——, (*N*) 'Negation' (1918), Part II of *LI*, in *CP*, pp. 373–89; and in *FR*, pp. 346–61

——, (*NLD*) '[Notes for Ludwig Darmstaedter]' (1919), in *PW*, pp. 253–57; also in *FR*, pp. 362–7

——, (*CT*) 'Compound Thoughts' (1923), Part III of *LI*, in *CP*, pp. 390–406

——, (*LG*) 'Logical Generality' (not before 1923), in *PW*, pp. 258–62

——, (*DECN*) '[Diary Entries on the Concept of Number]' (1924), in *PW*, pp. 263–4

——, (*PWN*) 'Number' (1924), in *PW*, pp. 265–6

——, (*SKM*) 'Sources of Knowledge of Mathematics and the Mathematical Natural Sciences' (1924/25), in *PW*, pp. 267–74; extract in *FR*, pp. 368–70

——, (*NA*) 'Numbers and Arithmetic' (1924/25), in *PW*, pp. 275–7; also in *FR*, pp. 371–3

——, (*NAFA*) 'A New Attempt at a Foundation for Arithmetic' (1924/25), in *PW*, pp. 278–81

——, (*TPW*) *Translations from the Philosophical Writings of Gottlob Frege*, ed. Peter Geach and Max Black, 3rd edn. (Blackwell, 1980; 1st edn. 1952)

——, (*BSA*) *Begriffsschrift und andere Aufsätze*, ed. I. Angelelli (Hildesheim: Georg Olms, 1964)

——, (*KS*) *Kleine Schriften*, ed. I. Angelelli (Hildesheim: Georg Olms, 1967), tr. as (*CP*) *Collected Papers on Mathematics, Logic, and Philosophy*, ed. B. McGuinness, tr. M. Black et al. (Blackwell, 1984)

——, (*NS*) *Nachgelassene Schriften*, ed. H. Hermes, F. Kambartel and F. Kaulbach (Hamburg: Felix Meiner, 1969), tr. as (*PW*) *Posthumous Writings* by P. Long and R. White (Blackwell, 1979)

——, (*FG*) *On the Foundations of Geometry and Formal Theories of Arithmetic*, tr. and with an introd. by Eike-Henner W. Kluge (Yale University Press, 1971); letters and papers by Frege now contained in *PMC* and *CP*

——, (*CN*) *Conceptual Notation and related articles*, tr. and ed. with a biog. and introd. by T. W. Bynum (OUP, 1972)

——, (*WB*) *Wissenschaftlicher Briefwechsel*, ed. G. Gabriel, H. Hermes, F. Kambartel, C. Thiel and A. Veraart (Hamburg: Felix Meiner, 1976), abridged for English edition by B. McGuinness and tr. as (*PMC*) *Philosophical and Mathematical Correspondence* by H. Kaal (Blackwell, 1980)

——, (*LI*) *Logical Investigations*, ed. P. T. Geach, tr. P. T. Geach and R. H. Stoothoff (Blackwell, 1977); now contained in *CP*

——, (*GLT*) *Die Grundlagen der Arithmetik*, German centenary critical edition, ed. Christian Thiel (Hamburg: Felix Meiner, 1986)

——, (*FR*) *The Frege Reader*, ed. M. Beaney (Blackwell, 1997)

French, P. A., Uehling, T. E. and Wettstein, H. K. (1981), eds., *Midwest Studies in Philosophy* VI (University of Minnesota Press)

Gabriel, Gottfried (1984), 'Fregean Connection: *Bedeutung*, Value and Truth-Value', in Wright (1984), pp. 188–93

Geach, P. T. (1956), 'On Frege's Way Out', *Mind* 65, pp. 408–9; repr. in Geach (1972), pp. 235–7; also in Klemke (1968), pp. 502–4

—— (1972), *Logic Matters* (Blackwell)

Grossmann, Reinhardt (1961), 'Frege's Ontology', *Philosophical Review* 70, pp. 23–40; repr. in Klemke (1968), pp. 79–98

—— (1969), *Reflections on Frege's Philosophy* (Evanston)

Haaparanta, Leila and Hintikka, Jaakko (1986), eds., *Frege Synthesized* (Dordrecht: D. Reidel)

Hale, Bob (1984), 'Frege's Platonism', in Wright (1984), pp. 40–56

Hintikka, Jaakko (1956), 'Identity, Variables, and Impredicative Definitions', *Journal of Symbolic Logic* 21, pp. 225–45

—— (1957), 'The Vicious Circle Principle and the Paradoxes', *Journal of Symbolic Logic* 22, pp. 245–9

Hume, David (1739–40), *A Treatise of Human Nature*, ed. L. A. Selby-Bigge, 2nd edn. rev. P. H. Nidditch (OUP, 1978)

Husserl, Edmund (1891), *Philosophie der Arithmetik*, in *Gesammelte Werke*, Band 12 (The Hague: Martinus Nijhoff, 1970)

Jackson, Howard (1962), 'Frege on Sense-Functions', *Analysis* 23, pp. 84–7; repr. in Klemke (1968), pp. 376–81

Kant, Immanuel, (*CPR*) *Critique of Pure Reason* (1781 and 1787), tr. Norman Kemp Smith (Macmillan, 1929)

Kenny, Anthony (1995), *Frege* (Penguin)

Klemke, E. D. (1968), ed., *Essays on Frege* (University of Illinois Press)

Kluge, E.-H. W. (1970), 'Reflections on Frege', *Dialogue* IX, pp. 401–9

—— (1980), *The Metaphysics of Gottlob Frege* (The Hague: Martinus Nijhoff)

Kneale, William and Kneale, Martha (1962), *The Development of Logic* (OUP)

Kripke, Saul A. (1980), *Naming and Necessity* (Blackwell, 1980; orig. publ. 1972)

Kusch, Martin (1995), *Psychologism* (Routledge)

Kutschera, Franz von (1989), *Gottlob Frege* (Berlin: Walter de Gruyter)

Leibniz, G. W., (*NE*) *New Essays on Human Understanding*, tr. and ed. P. Remnant and J. Bennett (CUP, 1981)

Long, Peter and White, Roger (1980), 'On the Translation of Frege's *Bedeutung*: A Reply to Dr Bell', *Analysis* 40 pp. 196–202

Lotze, Hermann (1874), *Logik* (Leipzig; 2nd edn. 1880)

Łukasiewicz, Jan (1934), 'On the History of the Logic of Propositions', in McCall (1967), pp. 66–87

Marshall, William (1953), 'Frege's Theory of Functions and Objects', *Philosophical Review* 62, pp. 374–90; repr. in Klemke (1968), pp. 249–67

—— (1956), 'Sense and Reference: A Reply', *Philosophical Review* 65, pp. 342–61; repr. in Klemke (1968), pp. 298–320

Max, Ingolf and Stelzner, Werner (1995), eds., *Logik und Mathematik* (Berlin: de Gruyter)

McCall, Storrs (1967), ed., *Polish Logic, 1920–1930* (OUP)

McDowell, John (1977), 'On the Sense and Reference of a Proper Name', in Platts (1980), pp. 141–66; also in Moore (1992), pp. 111–36; orig. in *Mind* 86, pp. 159–85

—— (1984), '*De Re* Senses', in Wright (1984), pp. 98–109

McGinn, Colin (1983), *The Subjective View* (OUP)

McGuinness, B. and Haller, R. (1989), eds., *Wittgenstein in Focus – Im Brennpunkt: Wittgenstein*, Grazer Philosophische Studien 33/34 (Amsterdam: Rodopi)

Mill, John Stuart (1843) *A System of Logic*, in *Collected Works*, Vol. 7 (University of Toronto Press, 1973)

Moore, A. W. (1992), ed., *Meaning and Reference* (OUP)

Moore, A. W. and Rein, Andrew (1986), '*Grundgesetze*, Section 10', in Haaparanta and Hintikka (1986), pp. 375–84

Noonan, Harold (1984), 'Fregean Thoughts', in Wright (1984), pp. 20–39

Ogden, C. K. and Richards, I. A. (1923), *The Meaning of Meaning* (Routledge, 1st edn. 1923, 10th edn. 1949)

Parret, H. and Bouveresse, J. (1981), eds., *Meaning and Understanding* (Berlin: Walter de Gruyter)

Parsons, Terence (1980), 'Frege's Hierarchies of Indirect Senses and the Paradox of Analysis', in French et al. (1981), pp. 37–57

Penco, Carlo (1994), *Vie della Scrittura: Frege e la svolta Linguistica* (Milano: FrancoAngeli)

Perry, John (1977), 'Frege on Demonstratives', *Philosophical Review* 86, pp. 474–97; also in Yourgrau (1990), pp. 50–70

—— (1979), 'The Problem of the Essential Indexical', *Noûs* 13, pp. 3–21; repr. in Salmon and Soames (1988), pp. 83–101

Picardi, Eva (1993), 'A Note on Dummett and Frege on Sense-Identity', *European Journal of Philosophy* 1, pp. 69–80

Platts, Mark (1980), ed., *Reference, Truth and Reality* (Routledge)

Potts, Timothy C. (1982), 'The Interpretation of Frege', *Theoretical Linguistics* 9, pp. 133–60

Quine, W. V. O. (1955), 'On Frege's Way Out', *Mind* 64, pp. 145–59; repr. in Klemke (1968), pp. 485–501

Resnik, Michael (1980), *Frege and the Philosophy of Mathematics* (Cornell University Press)

——— (1986), 'Frege's Proof of Referentiality', in Haaparanta and Hintikka (1986), pp. 177–95

Ricketts, Thomas G. (1986), 'Objectivity and Objecthood: Frege's Metaphysics of Judgment', in Haaparanta and Hintikka (1986), pp. 65–95

Rorty, R., Schneewind, J. B., and Skinner, Q. (1984), eds., *Philosophy in History* (CUP)

Russell, Bertrand, (*POM*) *The Principles of Mathematics*, 2nd edn. (George Allen & Unwin, 1937; 1st edn. 1903)

———, (*OD*) 'On Denoting', in Russell, *LK*, pp. 41–56, and *EA*, pp. 103–19; orig. in *Mind* 14 (1905)

———, (*IMP*) *Introduction to Mathematical Philosophy* (George Allen & Unwin, 1919)

———, (*LK*) *Logic and Knowledge: Essays 1901–1950*, ed. R. C. Marsh (George Allen & Unwin, 1956)

———, (*MPD*) *My Philosophical Development* (George Allen & Unwin, 1959)

———, (*EA*) *Essays in Analysis*, ed. Douglas Lackey (George Allen & Unwin, 1973)

Russell, B. and Whitehead, A. N., (*PM*) *Principia Mathematica* (CUP, 1910–13; 2nd edn. 1925)

Salmon, Nathan (1986), *Frege's Puzzle* (MIT Press)

Salmon, N. and Soames, S. (1988), eds., *Propositions and Attitudes* (OUP)

Schilpp. P. A. (1963), ed., *The Philosophy of Rudolf Carnap* (Illinois: Open Court)

Schirn, Matthias (1976), ed., *Studien zu Frege* (Stuttgart-Bad Canstatt: Frommann), 3 vols.

Schröder, E. (1880), 'Review of Frege's *Begriffsschrift*', tr. in Frege, *CN*, pp. 218–32

Simons, Peter (1992), 'Why Is There So Little Sense in Grundgesetze?', *Mind* 101, pp. 753–66

——— (1995), 'The Next Best Thing to Sense in *Begriffsschrift*', in Biro and Kotatko (1995), pp. 129–40

Sluga, Hans (1975), 'Frege and the Rise of Analytic Philosophy', *Inquiry* 18, pp. 471–87

——— (1976), 'Frege as a Rationalist', in Schirn (1976), Vol. 1, pp. 27–47

——— (1977), 'Frege's Alleged Realism', *Inquiry* 20, pp. 227–42

——— (1980), *Gottlob Frege* (Routledge)

——— (1984), 'Frege: the Early Years', in Rorty, Schneewind and Skinner (1984), pp. 329–56

——— (1993), ed., *The Philosophy of Frege* (New York and London: Garland Publishing, Inc.), 4 vols.

Spinoza, *Ethics* (1677), ed. with a rev. tr. G. H. R. Parkinson (London: J. M. Dent & Sons Ltd, 1989)

Strawson, P. F. (1950), 'On Referring', in Strawson (1971), pp. 1–27; also in Moore (1992), pp. 56–79; orig. in *Mind* 59, pp. 320–44

—— (1967), ed., *Philosophical Logic* (OUP)

—— (1971), *Logico-Linguistic Papers* (Methuen, London)

Tarski, Alfred (1933), 'The Concept of Truth in Formalized Languages', in *Logic, Semantics, Metamathematics*, tr. J. H. Woodger (OUP, 1956); 2nd edn. ed. J. Corcoran (Hackett, 1983)

Thiel, Christian (1968), *Sense and Reference in Frege's Logic*, tr. T. J. Blakeley (Dordrecht: D. Reidel; first publ. 1965)

—— (1986), 'Anmerkungen des Herausgebers', in Frege, *GLT*, pp. 143–73

Trendelenburg, A. (1867), 'Über Leibnizes Entwurf einer allgemeinen Charakteristik', *Historische Beiträge zur Philosophie*, Vol. 3, pp. 1–47

Tugendhat, Ernst (1970), 'The Meaning of "Bedeutung" in Frege', *Analysis* 30, pp. 177–89; repr. in German in Schirn (1976), Vol. 3, pp. 51–65

Van Heijenoort, J. (1967), ed., *From Frege to Gödel: A Source Book in Mathematical Logic, 1879–1931* (Harvard University Press)

—— (1977), 'Frege on Sense Identity', *Journal of Philosophical Logic* 6, pp. 103–8

Venn, John (1880), 'Review of Frege's *Begriffsschrift*', *Mind* 5, p. 297; repr. in Frege, *CN*, pp. 234–5

Veraart, Albert (1976), 'Geschichte des wissenschaftlichen Nachlasses Gottlob Freges und seiner Edition. Mit einem Katalog des ursprünglichen Bestands der nachgelassenen Schriften Freges', in Schirn (1976), Vol. 1, pp. 49–106

Weiner, Joan (1990), *Frege in Perspective* (Cornell University Press)

Wiggins, David (1975), 'Identity, Designation, Essentialism and Physicalism', *Philosophia* 5, pp. 1–30

—— (1976), 'Frege's Problem of the Morning Star and the Evening Star', in Schirn (1976), Vol. 2, pp. 221–55

Wittgenstein, Ludwig, (*TLP*) *Tractatus Logico-Philosophicus*, tr. D. F. Pears and B. McGuinness (RKP, 1961, 1974); orig. tr. C. K. Ogden (RKP, 1922)

Wright, Crispin (1983), *Frege's Conception of Numbers as Objects* (Aberdeen University Press)

—— (1984), ed., *Frege: Tradition and Influence* (Blackwell, 1984); orig. publ. in *Philosophical Quarterly* 34, No. 136, Special Issue: Frege (July 1984), pp. 183–430

Yourgrau, Palle (1982), 'Frege, Perry, and Demonstratives', in *Canadian Journal of Philosophy* 12, pp. 725–52

—— (1990), ed., *Demonstratives* (OUP)

Index